MACROECONOMIC DECISION MAKING
IN THE WORLD ECONOMY

Text and Cases

Second Edition

MACROECONOMIC DECISION MAKING
IN THE WORLD ECONOMY

Text and Cases

Second Edition

MICHAEL G. RUKSTAD

Graduate School of Business Administration
Harvard University

THE DRYDEN PRESS
Chicago Fort Worth San Francisco Philadelphia
Montreal Toronto London Sydney Tokyo

Acquisitions Editor: Elizabeth Widdicombe
Project Editor: Cathy Crow
Design Director: Alan Wendt
Production Manager: Barb Bahnsen
Director of Editing, Design, and Production: Jane Perkins

Text and Cover Designer: C. J. Petlick, Hunter Graphics
Copy Editor: Mary Englehart
Indexer: Richard Ruane
Compositor: Impressions, Inc.
Text Type: 10/12 Times Roman

Library of Congress Cataloging-in-Publication Data

Rukstad, Michael G.
  Macroeconomic decision making in the world economy : text and cases /
Michael G. Rukstad.—2nd ed.

  p.   cm.
  Bibliography: p.
  Includes index.
  ISBN 0-03-021664-8
  1. Macroeconomics—Case studies. 2. Decision-making—
Case studies. I. Title.
HB172.5.R85   1989   88-31616
339—dc19   CIP

Printed in the United States of America
 90-090-987654

Address orders:
The Dryden Press
Orlando, Florida 32887

Address editorial correspondence:
The Dryden Press
908 N. Elm St.
Hinsdale, IL 60521

The Dryden Press
Holt, Rinehart and Winston
Saunders College Publishing

To my parents
Virgil D. Rukstad and Georgia A. Rukstad
with love

The Dryden Press Series in Economics

PREFACE

Using the Case Method to Teach Macroeconomics

Tens of thousands of students take courses in basic macroeconomics each year. Fewer than 500 of them will ultimately receive Ph.D.'s in economics. Yet most instruction in macroeconomics relies on theoretical texts that lay the groundwork for more advanced study in the field. A perennial question facing instructors in basic macroeconomics courses is, "How is all of this relevant to what's happening in the real world?" This question is particularly appropriate in professional schools of business administration and public policy. For students in such schools, the macroeconomics course they take may well be their first and last academic exposure to macroeconomics. After graduation, they begin professional careers in which they will be expected to analyze and digest macroeconomic events.

Even young Ph.D.'s often have difficulty determining the relative importance of actual economic data, or even locating the sources of such data, since they have not been directly exposed to the practical analysis of macroeconomic events in their graduate work. As any practicing economist will admit, the application of economic theory to the complexities of the real world is a skill that takes much practice. For both types of students, therefore, a persistent problem is to bridge the gap between theoretical rigor and practical applications. The applications required of managers or policy analysts may well call for theoretical refinements that exceed the tools presented in a macroeconomics course.

What is the solution to this problem?

The solution proposed in this book is to offer students an elementary framework of macroeconomic concepts and much practice, with the guidance of an instructor, in analyzing case studies of macroeconomic events. These events have been carefully chosen to resemble those to which students will be exposed in their careers and even in their reading of newspaper accounts of current economic affairs. The framework presented in this book provides a consistent structure on which students may hang the institutional and theoretical detail they will encounter in the analyses of the cases. Each case provides real-world detail comparable to that found in newspaper and magazine articles. But, unlike such articles, it also provides the necessary background material and sufficient information for supporting arguments on both sides of each issue.

The case studies presented here, then, offer an integrated approach to the analysis of macroeconomic events. Each case typically *emphasizes the decision-making process rather than theoretical concepts.* Decisions are not made solely on the basis of economic theory—in fact, political considerations are often dominant factors in explaining particular actions. The cases are designed to facilitate discussion of controversial issues in political economy rather than technical issues of theoretical economics.

For managers and policy analysts, the case studies in this book provide practice in the first stage of a two-stage process of decision making. In this first stage, one must analyze the economic and political trends in the environment, and then, in the second stage, decide how these trends affect the particular action under consideration. For example, one must first understand the dynamics of floating exchange rates in the international economic environment before attempting to make a decision concerning a multinational corporation's allocation of investment capital across countries. Other business casebooks in finance or organizational behavior discuss the second stage, but this book represents, to my knowledge, the first effort to discuss in detail the initial stage in this decision-making process.

Features of This Book

This casebook, therefore, is the first of its kind on the market. Since the standard practice of teaching macroeconomics is theoretical—that is, not based on the case method—a question arises of how one might easily integrate this book into conventional teaching patterns. The answer to that question consists of three parts.

First, the cases themselves are self-contained and thus may be used flexibly to complement any existing textbook. The notes and cases presuppose no previous knowledge of economics other than the basic introductory material contained in Chapter 1. A comprehensive glossary at the end of the book will help students to learn the meaning and application of technical concepts and to recall the more standard ones.

Second, the cases are adaptable to several different levels of instruction. Although both beginning and advanced students will read the same story, they can draw varying theoretical and decision-oriented inferences based on their previous levels of experience with theory and policy analysis.

Third, annotated bibliographies list supplementary references. These references include elementary and intermediate sources from academic and popular journals as well as from three leading macroeconomic textbooks by Robert J. Gordon, Lloyd A. Reynolds, and Rudiger Dornbusch and Stanley Fischer. These guides to other literature make this book adaptable for the assignment of research papers or more detailed empirical studies for class projects.

Uses of This Book

The cases are organized according to three broad topics of macroeconomics: monetary policy, fiscal policy, and international trade and exchange-rate policy. Instructors may choose these cases as supplementary reading in order to illustrate a specific conceptual point; or they may use cases at the completion of a conventional textbook chapter or module in order to allow students to integrate and apply the theoretical material. Alternatively, the cases and their accompanying data can give the students a concise starting point for the testing of empirical hypotheses about significant economic events. This material enables students to minimize the time spent on finding a topic and identifying interesting hypotheses and to maximize the time spent on empirical analysis. (The *Instructor's Manual* makes suggestions for specific applications of the casebook as a supplementary text.)

A second approach is to use the cases as the primary method for teaching the principles and practices of political economy. For professional school students, this is the most appropriate way to use this book. The seventeen chapters can be covered in nine weeks with two one-and-a-half-hour sessions per week and a summary session. Instructors who want to use the book as part of a larger course using case studies exclusively might also consider a complementary paperback book that covers related material for Japan: Bruce R. Scott, John W. Rosenblum, and Audrey T. Sproat, *Cases Studies in Political Economy: Japan 1854–1977* (Boston: Harvard Business School, 1980).

The order in which the cases are taught can be flexible. It need not follow precisely the order of the book's table of contents. A chronological ordering of the cases would be quite valuable, however, to demonstrate to students the evolution of the concepts and practice of political economy. Such an ordering would show, for example, the central concern of political economy swinging from an international focus in the years before the Great Depression to a strong domestic focus in the years afterward, then a third swing of the pendulum during the 1970s and the 1980s back to an emphasis on the interdependence of economic policies among all nations. The sequence below shows the chronological order of the cases in this book.

Chronological Sequence of Cases

The cases (with the chapter numbers listed in parentheses) may be presented in the chronological sequence shown below. The topical themes developed in each section of the table of contents are preserved but the events are now in approximate chronological order. This sequence maximizes the continuity of cases and avoids foreshadowing subsequent events.

	Monetary Policy	Fiscal Policy	International Economy
1920			The United Kingdom and the Gold Standard: 1925 (13)
1930	The U.S. Financial Crisis of 1931 (2)		
		A Keynesian Cure for the Depression (6)	
1960		The Tax Cut of 1964 (7)	
			Kennedy and the Balance of Payments (14)
1970			Nixon's New Economic Policy: 1971 (15)
		The Capital Gains Tax Cut of 1978 (8)	
			The Decline of the Dollar:1978 (16)
1980		The Reagan Plan (9)	
		The Economic Recovery Tax Act of 1981 (10)	
	Paul Volcker and the Federal Reserve 1979–1982 (3)		
			Mexico: Crisis of Confidence (17)
		The Reagan Deficits (11)	
	The United Kingdom under Thatcher (4)		
		Privatization in the United Kingdom (12)	
	Japanese Financial Liberalization (5)		

The Harvard MBA Course: "Business, Government, and the International Economy"

The case method has been the pedagogical lifeblood of the Harvard Business School since 1908, and instruction on macroeconomic topics has been no exception. Macroeconomics is one body of knowledge that has contributed to the interdisciplinary course, "Business, Government, and the International Economy," which is required of all students in the first-year MBA curriculum and the executive programs.

The course was conceived by Professor Bruce R. Scott and nurtured during its formative years by Professors George C. Lodge and John W. Rosenblum (now Dean of the Colgate Darden Graduate School of Business Administration at the University of Virginia). Professor Scott's fundamental insight was that business managers and policy analysts must develop a strategic analysis of countries as business environments. The cases in this book build on that insight by placing macroeconomic events in their proper political and social environments.

Acknowledgments

My greatest debts in the development of this casebook are to my Harvard Business School colleagues in the course, "Business, Government, and the International Economy." Their insights, criticisms, and willingness to teach from early drafts of these cases were invaluable. Over the years, the teaching group offering their enthusiastic assistance has included Professors Norman Berg, Colyer Crum, Robert Cuff, Dennis Encarnation, Adam Klein, Thomas McCraw, David Meerschwam, Alberta Sbragia, Philip Wellons, and especially Richard Vietor and David Yoffie.

Foremost, though, among my colleagues was Professor Thomas McCraw who, as course head during the past four years, carried forward the development of the course in its coherence, intellectual rigor, and teachability. He provided the conceptual impetus for this casebook and remained the major source of encouragement through all of its stages. Without his sharp editorial skills the cases would have lacked their clarity and failed to meet their teaching objectives.

In addition, I am indebted to the following individuals for permission to use their materials in this casebook: Professors Dennis Encarnation (Chapter 1, Note B), George Lodge (Chapter 9, Case), Thomas McCraw (Chapter 6, Case, and Chapter 13, Case), David Meerschwam (Chapter 16, Note), Arthur Schleifer (Chapter 1, Note D), Richard Vietor (Chapter 17, Case), and David Yoffie (Chapter 14, Case and Note).

Professor Daniel Pope of the University of Oregon, who served periodically as a research associate connected with the course, was an ideal collaborator for many of the cases in this book. His extensive historical knowledge and fluid writing style greatly improved the quality of several of them. I also received valuable help from Julia Horn, Nancy Koehn, John O'Reilly, Andrew Regan, Karen Shore, Jeff Singer, and John Wood. They cheerfully suffered through my numerous demands for additional sources, rewrites, and cross references.

Other colleagues and friends read and criticized these cases or experimented with them in their own courses: Michael B. Abrahams (Office of Management and Budget), James Austin (Harvard Business School), Alan Beckenstein (Colgate Darden School, University of Virginia), Gale Blalock (University of Evansville), Joseph Bower (Harvard Business School), Robert Carlson (Babcock School, Wake Forest University), Peter K. Clark (Yale School of Organization and Management), Richard Cooper (Harvard University), Roger Craine (University of California, Berkeley), Mark Eaker (University of North Carolina at Chapel Hill), Dan Fenn (Kennedy Library), Curt Grimm (University of Maryland), Katherine Haltom (Boston University), John Isbister (University of California–Santa Cruz), Peter Jones (University of California, Berkeley), Donald LeCrow (University of Western Ontario), George Lodge (Harvard Business School), Michael Luger (Duke University), Craig MacPhee (University of Nebraska–Lincoln), Kevin Maloney (Amos Tuck School, Dartmouth College), Craig Marcott (College of St. Thomas), Arthur Mead (University of Rhode Island), Hajime Miyazaki (Ohio State University), Frank Nothaft (Board of Governors, Federal Reserve System), Calvin Pava (Harvard Business School), Roy Pearson (College of William and Mary), Bruce Scott (Harvard Business School), Jeffrey Sonnenfeld (Harvard Business School), James Stock (Kennedy School of Government, Harvard), Richard Tedlow (Harvard Business School), Edward Trubac (University of Notre Dame), Laura D'Andrea Tyson (University of California, Berkeley), John Veitch (University of Southern California), Glenn Woroch (University of Rochester), and especially Stephen G. Marks (Boston University), who read the entire manuscript and made many helpful suggestions.

The publication team at The Dryden Press was extremely efficient as well. Special thanks go to Liz Widdicombe and Cathy Crow for their technical assistance and gentle prodding, and to Mary Englehart and Alan Wendt for their help in the preparation of this book. It was a pleasure to work with them. Support for this casebook at the Harvard Business School was generously provided by Dean John H. McArthur, Professors E. Raymond Corey and Michael Yoshino of the Division of Research, Rose Giacobbe and the staff at the Word Processing Center, and a group of helpful secretaries, including Vy Crowe, Susan Griesmer, Cheryl Hines, Peg Nayduch, and Laurie Title.

Finally, the questions and insights of several hundred of my students were indispensable in keeping me pointed in the right direction. To them I owe a humble "thank you" for all they have taught me.

Michael G. Rukstad
Boston, Massachusetts
October 1988

CONTENTS

PART I
INTRODUCTION

CHAPTER 1

The Conceptual Tools
of Political Economy

*The four introductory notes in Chapter 1 describe the conceptual tools
needed to analyze efficiently the case studies in the following chapters.
These same tools will also form the building blocks for the more specific
notes that accompany many of the cases. Even elementary tools can
lead to sophisticated analyses if applied rigorously. The strength of
these concepts is that they impose consistency in the analysis of decision making—consistency with logic, accounting conventions, and observed behavior.*

*The first note, "An Introduction to Economics," presents the two
fundamental concepts of economics, supply and demand. With an understanding of these concepts, one can determine logically the effects of
supply and demand on the price and quantity of oil, steelworkers' labor,
Treasury bills, the Deutschmark, or any other item sold in a market.
The concepts of supply and demand can also be applied to the economy
as a whole. Aggregate supply and aggregate demand represent the total
supply of and demand for all goods and services in the economy and
can be used to summarize the broad forces determining macroeconomic
performance. Governments intervene regularly in the functioning of the
market mechanism of supply and demand. Sometimes the intervention
is focused on a particular market, such as the oil market, but more
often governments attempt to influence aggregate demand and aggregate supply.*

*To measure the aggregate performance of the economy, account-
ing conventions have been developed to show the interrelationships
among the relevant macroeconomic variables. The first note describes
the essentials of the system of national income accounts. The fundamental relationship is that output, or its equivalent, income, can be de-
composed into the expenditures of households, businesses, governments,
and the rest of the world. If we understand what determines those four
expenditures, we shall understand what determines a nation's output
and income.*

*The second note, "An Introduction to Comparative Political Econ-
omy," attempts to broaden our perspective on the determinants of governmental policies and their outcomes. Political institutions play a
large role in shaping economic performance, a role that varies over*

*countries and across time. To ignore the broad trends of growth, consol-
idation, and fragmentation of political institutions is to opt for an analysis based on an ideal world of perfectly functioning markets unfettered
by outside interference, rather than on the real world of imperfect political institutions constraining markets that are sometimes sluggish and
inefficient.*

*The raw material for the analysis of policies and performance usu-
ally comes in the form of quantitative data. Data have become extremely abundant (as a perusal of this book or any business newspaper,
article, or report would indicate) because of the increased sophistication
of the accounting system and the demands for more detailed performance measures by both business and government. The third and
fourth notes in Chapter 1 address the issue of how to use quantitative
data.*

*The third note, "How to Read Data Exhibits," suggests a series of
questions to ask in analyzing data. It classifies each piece of data according to its objective—an indicator of performance, policy, or context.
The plethora of performance measures can be further grouped into measures of output, price, and external balance. Rather than being over-
whelmed by the variety of data, we should recognize the similarities
among the measures.*

*The purpose in analyzing data is to identify patterns of past be-
havior in order to gain insight into future behavior. Simple relationships between two variables may be inferred by "eyeballing" the data.
Do interest rates increase with an increase in fiscal deficits? Does inflation increase when money growth increases? But if we wanted an estimate of how much one variable changes in response to a change in the
other or of what happens to interest rates or inflation when both deficits
and money growth change concurrently, then we must rely on a more
sophisticated eyeballing of the data.*

*The fourth note, "An Introduction to Econometric Models: Data
Resources Inc.," illustrates the workings of a large-scale econometric
model that will produce an answer to the question of how much. Econometric models impose consistency on forecasts by constraining them to
conform to accounting rules and to be consistent with past observed behavior. The forecasts, however, will be no better than the assumptions
fed into the model. Thus an econometric model does not free users from
making judgments. The conceptual tools in the following notes will help
make those judgments as informed as possible.*

Note A
An Introduction to Economics

Economics is a social science that attempts to explain the behavior and interactions of economic actors in terms of the items of value they exchange. Depending on the field within economics, "actors" can mean individuals, households, firms, industries, governments, or entire countries. The "items of value" can be tangible or intangible, monetary or nonmonetary. Most of economics addresses one or more of the following concerns:

1. How should scarce resources be allocated among competing wants? What mix of products should be made, how and for whom?

2. How can sufficient growth be attained so that the well-being of society increases? How can productive capacity be increased?

3. How should productive capacity be utilized so that there will be full employment with stable prices?

Since any allocation of scarce resources must inevitably involve balancing the wants and needs of one group of people against those of another, economics is directly related to politics, ideology, and values. A social convention or rule for the allocation of resources may rely on any one or a combination of four mechanisms: the market system; the authority of a social or governmental institution; the persuasion of ideology, indoctrination, or education; or an individual's moral code.[1] Economics concentrates primarily on the market or exchange mechanism. It leaves to other disciplines (political science, sociology, philosophy) the explanation of alternate mechanisms.

The Economy as a Circular Flow

Even in a simple economy, countless transactions and exchanges occur. Individuals work and consume, firms produce and invest, governments and foreigners purchase goods and services. Millions of decisions are continually made by millions of actors. Money, goods, and other items of value constantly change hands at all levels of the economy. It is obviously impossible to track and study all the individual transactions. It

This note was prepared by Associate Professor Michael G. Rukstad.
Copyright © 1982 by the President and Fellows of Harvard College
Harvard Business School note 9-383-079

[1]These four methods of social control—exchange, authority, persuasion, and moral codes—are set forth in Charles E. Lindblom, *Politics and Markets, The World's Political-Economic Systems* (New York: Basic Books, 1977).

Figure 1

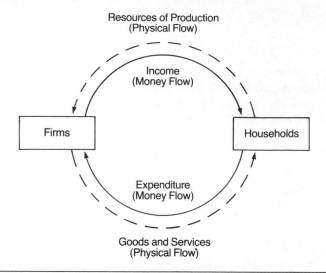

is possible, however, to approximate and classify on an aggregate scale classes of transactions involving goods, services, resources, and their monetary equivalents.

Each actor in an economy is both supplier of some goods or services and a demander of others. In general, households demand manufactured goods and services and supply resources. Firms, on the other hand, demand resources (labor, capital, land, and managerial skills) and supply goods and services. Households and firms must pay the market value for what they use. Similarly, they will be willing to supply the market only if they are compensated appropriately. In a modern nonbarter economy, this compensation is usually in the form of money. Thus, for every transfer of goods or services from seller to purchaser, money representing the market value of the product will flow in the opposite direction. An economy can be depicted as a circular flow composed of households and firms exchanging money for goods and services and for resources of production (see Figure 1).

We can simplify the diagram if we record only the money flows (the solid lines) and leave out the "real" flows of goods, services, and resources (the dotted lines). We should always keep in mind, however, that there are two sides to every transaction. We should also recognize that not all income is spent. Some income is saved and recycled to investment through the financial markets, as in Figure 2. The money flow of savings and borrowing from households to firms is shown in this diagram. (Another side of this transaction is a "real" flow of financial assets from the firms to the households, but this line will be omitted for now, for the sake of simplicity.)

While the basic circular flow diagram provides a useful framework to help us to understand the economy, we have so far neglected two other major actors.

Figure 2

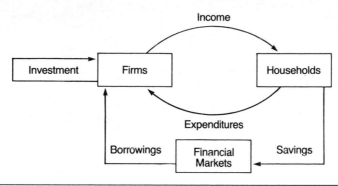

First, the government sector (national, state, and local) is neither a household nor a producer. Yet it affects other actors by its taxation, expenditure, and debt policies.

Second, we cannot consider an economy as isolated from the rest of the world since countries have a great impact on each other owing to transactions such as imports, exports, and foreign borrowing and lending. Therefore we should incorporate both the foreign and government sectors into our flow diagram (see Figure 3). Here, the government sector makes payments to households and firms, collects taxes, borrows savings, and consumes both goods and labor. The foreign sector buys and sells goods and services and borrows and saves in our domestic financial markets.

Notice that this diagram is concerned with final flows, which is to say, expenditures on *final* output. We ignore intermediate flows because including them would involve double counting and exaggeration of the total expenditures we are measuring. Two examples of an intermediate flow are the sale of wheat to the miller to make flour and the sale of flour to a baker to make bread. Only the sale of the bread to the consumer is a final flow or final expenditure. The cost of the flour, and thus the wheat, is included in the price of bread, and should not be double counted.

The Concepts of Supply and Demand

The cornerstones of modern economics are the concepts of supply and demand. The economist's response to our first question on page 5 of how scarce resources are allocated is that the allocation is determined by the market mechanism—by supply and demand. As we will see later, even the answers to the second and third questions about growth and utilization use these same concepts. In a market that consists of a number of buyers and sellers for some particular item, supply-demand analysis determines an "equilibrium" market price and quantity for that item, and describes the conditions under which that equilibrium will change. Accordingly, the next section of this note will focus on three topics: (1)

Figure 3

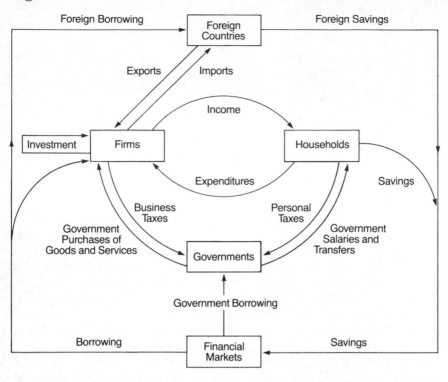

determination of the market price and quantity, (2) changes in the market price and quantity, and (3) market failures and the role of government.

Determination of the Market Price and Quantity

In order to understand the determination of the market price and quantity, we will first examine supply, then demand, then put the concepts together to form a description of a market. The "supply curve" (actually a straight line on a graph) is a schedule of prices and quantities such that for a given price (p_0) the producers would be willing and able to produce a given quantity (q_0). The supply curve slopes upward because higher prices (p_1) are needed in order to compensate a producer for the higher cost of obtaining additional resources needed to produce the larger output (q_1) (see Figure 4). Similarly, the demand curve is a schedule of prices and quantities such that for a given price buyers are willing and able to purchase that quantity of the item. It slopes downward because buyers as a group respond to lower prices by purchasing more. Specifically, the lower prices will induce some buyers to substitute this cheaper product for similar products which are more expensive. For other buyers, the lower price will mean that they can purchase more of everything (including, possibly, more of this particular product) with the income saved

Figure 4

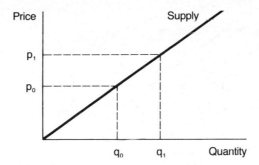

Figure 5

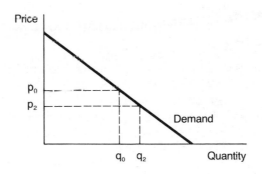

Figure 6

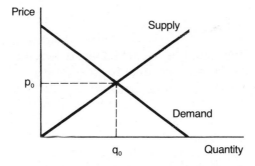

by making the cheaper purchase. Figure 5 shows a typical demand curve. If the price falls to p_2 from the original p_0, then the quantity demanded increases to q_2.

In Figure 6 we bring supply and demand together to form a market for that particular item.

There are three points to keep in mind regarding Figure 6:

Figure 7

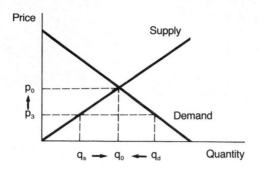

1. In a freely operating market (without external interference such as price controls or quantity rationing), the market price and quantity (p_0 and q_0) are determined simultaneously. One does not "determine" the other.

2. There is only one actual market price (p_0) and one actual quantity transacted (q_0). This means that some buyers and sellers were not able to make a transaction or additional transactions because they could not buy or sell at the going market price. Buyers who were willing and able to pay the market price of p_0 or more, as indicated by the portion of the demand curve to the left of q_0, received the goods produced. Likewise, those suppliers who could produce goods at market price of p_0 or less, as indicated by the portion of the supply curve to the left of q_0, were able to make the sale. This is what economists mean when they say that the market price mechanism allocates scarce resources among competing needs.

3. At any point on the graph other than "equilibrium" (p_0,q_0), both buyers and sellers (in the aggregate) would be dissatisfied and their natural tendency would be to move toward "equilibrium." For example, suppose the price were set too low (at p_3) as in Figure 7. At that price, consumers would demand q_d, which is more than q_s supplied by the producers. When purchasers demand more of a good than is available (i.e., when there is "excess demand"), they will bid up the price.[2] As prices rise, suppliers will have an incentive to produce more of the good and, at the same time, some of the quantity demanded will fall (as indicated by the arrows). This process

---

[2]This assumes there are no price controls. If price controls are set too low as in Figure 7 and prices cannot rise, there will be a permanent state of "excess demand." Since the market cannot allocate resources, some other method will arise or be devised. Most often the rule for allocating the scarce resource is "first come, first served." People wait in lines, such as the gas lines in the United States in the summer of 1979. At other times governments issue rationing coupons such as gasoline coupons during the Second World War in the United States.

Figure 8

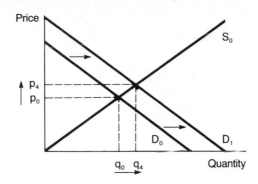

will continue until the market comes to rest at p_0,q_0 once again. The process works in reverse if there is "excess supply" caused by a price which is set too high. The price will start to fall until it reaches p_0 and q_0. Because market forces always push prices and quantity toward one point, that point is called "equilibrium" to connote a combination of price and quantity such that there are no pressures for change. Thus not only do the curves help explain the behavior of consumers and producers, they also show how prices and quantities for a good are determined and remain stable.

Changes in the Market Price and Quantity

Even though market prices and quantities are at equilibrium, new forces can cause either or both the supply and demand curves to shift. Such forces create a new equilibrium point toward which price and quantity will adjust. Consider, first, a shift in demand. The demand for a consumer product such as coffee will shift in response to changes in taste, income, size of the market, price of a substitute product, and other forces. If medical science were to discover that coffee improves one's sex life, the quantity of coffee demanded at all prices would increase. Figure 8 illustrates an increase in demand from D_0 to D_1. The consequence is a movement of the entire demand curve to the right, as shown by the arrows. This is accompanied by a simultaneous increase in the price level to p_4 and an increase in the quantity transacted to q_4.

Imagine, on the other hand, a shift in supply. This might arise if there were a change in the cost of producing coffee, in the number or productivity of coffee producers, or in the technology of harvesting. If, for example, there were a significant coffee crop failure in Brazil, we would expect to see a fall in the quantity supplied at all coffee price levels given in the supply schedule. Figure 9 illustrates a decrease in supply from S_0 to S_1. The result is an increase in the price to p_5 and a fall in the quantity transacted to q_5. A two-day frost in Brazil in 1975 did just that—it triggered events leading to the rise in the world price of coffee by 610 percent

Figure 9

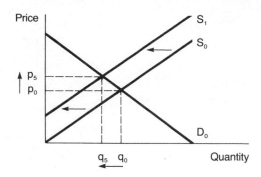

in 21 months.[3] Then as world coffee prices fell in 1976, Brazil tried to raise prices by buying up the crop of Angolan coffee.[4] This type of interference, where successful, could be represented by the process depicted in Figure 8.

One important question we would like to answer is: How much will the quantity demanded or the quantity supplied change when there is a given change in price? In other words, how *responsive* is demand or supply to a given change in price? Certainly responsiveness differs among goods. For example, the price of salt would have to rise significantly before people would cut back on their use of it. On the other hand, if the price of butter rises very much, many people will substitute margarine for butter.

The economic term for the responsiveness of the quantity demanded to a change in price is "elasticity." (Technically, we say "price elasticity" since we may identify other elasticities such as "income elasticity.") Elasticity is defined as the percentage change in quantity divided by the percentage change in price.[5] The convention economists use is

---

[3]Philip A. Wellons, "Brazil in the Mid-1970s: Fast Growth or Slow?" in *World Money and Credit: The Crisis and Its Causes* (Boston: Harvard Business School Division of Research, 1983), 70.

[4]Ibid., 72.

[5]Formally, elasticity $= (\Delta q/q)/ (\Delta p/p)$, where the symbol "$\Delta$," called "delta," means "a change in. . . ." If elasticity is greater than 1, the demand or supply curve is called "elastic," and if elasticity is less than 1, the curve is called "inelastic." There are two points one should keep in mind. First, one should note that elasticity does not mean the slope of the supply or demand curve. Slope is defined as $\Delta p/\Delta q$. Second, elasticity may change over time as people are more able to adjust to the change in prices.

In order to understand the equation for elasticity, we will examine a numerical example involving the demand for oil. In discussions of energy policy, we will be interested in the price elasticity of the demand for oil. In other words, we want to know the percentage decrease in the quantity demanded for a given percentage increase in the price. Assume we currently consume 100 barrels of oil ($q = 100$) and the price is $20 per barrel ($p = 20$). Then imagine that the price increases $2 to $22 per barrel ($\Delta p = 2$). We can easily see that there is a 10 percent change in price ($\Delta p/p = 2/20 = .10$). If the quantity of oil demanded falls by 5 barrels from 100 to 95 barrels as a result of the increase in price, then there is a 5 percent change in quantity ($\Delta q/q = 5/100 = .05$). Thus the elasticity or responsiveness of the demand for oil is 1/2 ($= 5\%/10\%$) and this is called "inelastic."

that if the quantity demanded changes significantly with a given change in price, the demand curve is called "elastic." If the quantity demanded changes very little (is unresponsive to price changes), the curve is "inelastic." The same concept can apply to the supply curve.

Market Failures and the Role of Government

The strength of a market system is that all resources and outputs will efficiently be allocated to their most productive, beneficial uses by the "laws of supply and demand." "Efficiency" to economists means that the economy will get the most output from given resources and this output can be used to improve the well-being of at least some of the members of society, without making anyone worse off. On these grounds, there appears to be no role for government in the economy other than maintaining "the rules of the marketplace," since the market system is performing "optimally."

There are, however, circumstances known as "market failures" which justify government intervention in the economy. We can identify five reasons why markets may fail and the government may have to intervene:

1. Inequity (unfairness).

2. Failure of competition.

3. Underutilized resources.

4. Externalities.

5. Public goods.

Under the first reason, inequity, government intervention is justified even if markets are efficient. Under the second and third reasons, on the other hand, markets may not be efficient owing to underutilized resources or a lack of competition. The last two reasons, externalities and public goods, pose special problems that a market system alone can never handle. Each of these five points is elaborated further in the following paragraphs.

Inequity The distribution of resources and outputs resulting from a perfectly functioning market system will be efficient, but it may not be equitable. If the market's distribution of benefits does not meet society's criterion of equity, government can intervene to redistribute income or wealth. But this raises additional problems. Since government's fiscal tools for redistribution (taxation, expenditures, and transfer payments) may distort incentives for effort and risk-taking, market efficiency may be impaired as a by-product. Hence governments always face trade-offs between equity and efficiency which cannot be resolved by economics alone. Society must make its preferences known through the political process.

Failure of Competition   There are some circumstances which lead to "natural monopolies" and hence, by definition, to a lack of competition. For example, the economics of producing electricity may justify only one large power plant which exploits economies of scale to supply the entire community. To have many smaller, competing power plants would be inefficient (since all would be operating at less than efficient scale). In most countries, governments either regulate or own natural monopolies such as utilities and local telephone systems.

Underutilized Resources   When a national economy exhibits high levels of unemployment, idle factories, huge balance of payments deficits or surpluses, and unanticipated inflation, it is difficult even for economists to argue that all resources are being efficiently utilized by a market system. The question which needs to be answered is: What causes underutilization of resources? John Maynard Keynes believed that underutilized resources were due to a market failure. In "A Keynesian Cure for the Depression" (see Chapter 5), he argued that

our predicament . . . comes from some failure in the immaterial devices of the mind, in the workings of the motives which should lead to the decisions and acts of will, necessary to put in movement the resources and technical means we already have.

Keynes' solution was to increase government expenditures to employ idle labor and unused capital resources and to maintain personal incomes. Other contemporary analysts argued that government was itself part of the problem.[6] The Great Depression, which prompted the Keynes and Douglas articles, was an extreme example of underutilized resources.

Externalities   Externalities are actions of one actor which affect another, but not directly through the market system. The actions of a polluter, for example, affect others by the reduced quality of the air and water they must consume, but the price of the polluter's products does not reflect this cost of pollution. Since the polluter does not have to pay for the deleterious effects of his actions, he has no market incentive to halt such actions. Thus, governments often provide regulatory incentives not to pollute or they introduce market incentives through taxes or subsidies.

Public Goods   Some items have a peculiar characteristic that when one person consumes the benefits, it does not prevent others from also consuming the same benefits. Examples of public goods are national defense and public parks. Their benefits spill over to all, including those "free riders" who have not paid for them or would not choose to. Thus the market system fails to produce an optimal amount and quality of these goods, and government must often intervene.

[6]See excerpts from "There Is One Way Out" by Lewis Douglas, HBS Case 8382061 (Boston: Harvard Business School Division of Research, 1982), 6.

Aggregate Supply and Aggregate Demand

The supply and demand analysis of the previous section describes a single market and the behavior of an individual actor (a household or firm) in that market. Generally, one would expect that market mechanisms will efficiently allocate resources and output throughout the economy, as was described previously. Only under special conditions would another actor (the government) intervene in the operation of a particular market. All of this analysis forms the basis of "microeconomics."

In this book we are more often concerned with analysis of entire economies and the behavior and impact of all actors (households, firms, government, and foreign economies) on national economic performance. This is the purview of "macroeconomics." It will be useful if we develop macroeconomic analogues to the micro concepts of supply and demand and view the economy as one giant market for all goods and services. We will call these broader macro concepts "aggregate demand" and "aggregate supply."

The aggregate demand curve is a schedule relating the total demand for *all* goods and services in an economy to the general price level in that economy. Just as in the case of a micro demand curve, the aggregate demand curve slopes downward, as shown in Figure 10. As the general price level rises, the amount of goods and services that can be purchased with the given stock of money and other financial assets declines. Moreover, a rising price level will make a nation's goods and services less competitive in the international markets; thus there will be less demand for those items by foreigners. The two reasons for the downward slope of the aggregate demand curve, therefore, are the effect of changes in the general price level on a nation's stock of assets and on its international competitiveness.

The aggregate supply curve is a schedule relating the total supply of *all* goods and services in an economy to the general price level. While there is broad agreement among economists about the slope of the aggregate demand curve, considerable controversy attends the shape of the aggregate supply curve. A consensus view is almost impossible to identify.

In any case, the aggregate supply curve tells us how an increase in aggregate demand is divided between an increased price level and increased real output. The range of economic opinion suggests that the aggregate supply curve may be flat, vertical, or upward-sloping. The key element in aggregate supply is how production costs and the price level change with changes in output. For our present purposes we will hypothesize that the aggregate supply curve is relatively flat when we are at low levels of output and becomes steeper as we get closer to the limits of the economy. In other words, there is less inflationary pressure when an economy expands out of deep recession than in the case near full employment. ("Full employment output" or "capacity" or "potential output" is an arbitrary construct. It does not mean that the economy is running full throttle with no possible increase in output. Output can increase, but only at a significant increase in price as bottlenecks begin

Figure 10

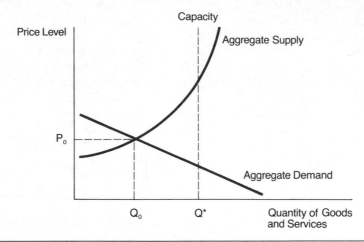

to occur.) We can summarize this relationship by the aggregate supply curve in Figure 10. Notice that the economy is presently operating at less than capacity Q^*. In order to move the economy to Q^*, we need either a rightward shift in aggregate demand or in aggregate supply.

Later in this book we will discuss some of the factors that affect the slope and position of the aggregate supply and demand curves, including the effect of government policy—in other words, which factors are responsible for full-employment output with stable prices. As a preview to that material, Figure 11 schematically organizes some of the components we will be studying. On the right we see that the interaction of aggregate demand and aggregate supply determines the price level and real output. This is the same information which is given by the graph in Figure 10.

Aggregate demand is the result of the interaction of the nonfinancial (or "real") and financial markets. The nonfinancial markets are divided into four types of expenditure, as we will describe in the next section. The financial markets include money and all other financial assets. This will be described in more detail in the note "Money and the Determination of Income" in Chapter 2. As noted earlier, aggregate supply is largely concerned with changes in production costs and profit margins. Production costs include numerous factors including those shown in the lower left corner of Figure 11. It is important to understand that these links are only suggestive of the dominant relationships. There are many links that are not indicated in Figure 11, but that are important nonetheless. In particular, any changes in the price level or real output will "feed back" on all variables listed in the left column.

Introduction to National Income Accounting

In discussing a nation's economy, one quickly comes to questions requiring numerical answers: How large is this country's economy relative to that of others? How has it changed over time? What has caused the

Figure 11

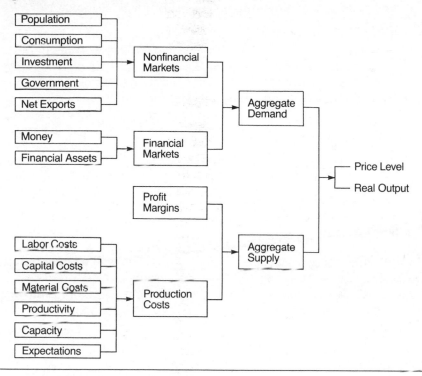

changes? How well has the country done relative to others in satisfying the needs of its population? Just as we need financial statements for a company, we need some sort of accounting system for a country. Not only should this accounting system provide insight into a country's growth, performance, and sectoral behavior, but it should also provide data comparable to similar figures from other countries. Like generally accepted accounting principles, certain conventions are observed in the measurement and analysis of a country's national income.

The broadest measure of the total output of an economy is called the *Gross National Product (GNP)*, which is also sometimes called the Gross National Expenditure (GNE). GNP is defined as *the market value of all final goods and services produced by nationals of a country within a given time period.* A number of points should be kept in mind about this definition:

1. Conceptually it is equivalent to taking the quantities of each final good and service and multiplying them by their current market price: GNP = P × Q, for all goods and services.

2. GNP includes only *final* goods and services—those which are not resold in any form. For example, bread purchased in a supermarket is a final output, but the wheat used to make it is not. The GNP convention avoids counting the price of wheat twice. Thus, GNP

is the sum of the *value added in all transactions.* (Value added is the price of a product minus the cost of material inputs.)

3.   GNP is "produced by nationals of a country" regardless of where they produce it. For example, a Pakistani citizen working in the oil fields of Saudi Arabia or a Swiss banker lending money from a London branch are each producing output and earning income for their home GNPs, assuming that the income is repatriated to the home country. A closely related concept is Gross Domestic Product (GDP), which is identical to GNP except that it is produced by domestic citizens of a country. Thus the Pakistani worker and Swiss banker would not be contributing to their Gross *Domestic* Product since they are not *domestic* residents. To repeat, they do contribute to Gross *National* Product because they are *nationals* of that country. In other words, GNP includes factor income from abroad but GDP does not.

Both of these broad concepts (GNP and GDP), as well as many others which are similar [such as Net National Product (NNP) or National Income (NI)], are attempts to measure the total output and thus the total income of a country. In economics, these numbers are supposed to provide measures of the well-being of the country and its residents.

The next step in the analysis is to break down GNP into useful components so that we can analyze the factors responsible for its growth. Simon Kuznets, a Nobel laureate in economics from Harvard, was originally responsible for developing the National Income Accounts. He and others broke down national output into four basic categories:

- Consumption (C)
- Investment (I)
- Government Spending (G)
- Net Exports $(X-M)$

("X" represents exports and "M" imports, so that net exports is exports minus imports.)

These categories reflect the spending of the four actors in our circular flow diagram of Figure 3: households consume, businesses invest, and government and foreign sectors purchase goods and services. Therefore, we have the *national income accounting identity* given below, in which total output is divided into its four component parts:

$$GNP = C + I + G + (X-M)$$

Since this is the basic identity of the National Income Accounts, a brief definition of each component will help in understanding GNP, its composition, and its importance.

- *Consumption:* Consumer expenditures on final goods and services required for current use. Examples of consumption are: purchases of food, clothing, and cars; payment of rent; and payment for haircuts and cleaning services. Consumption would not include interest payments on consumer debt since it is not for current use nor would it include the purchase of raw materials by businesses since it is not a final purchase.

Investment: Business expenditures made to increase future output of final products. Thus the gasoline engine in a car would not be included but a gas engine used as machinery in producing cars would be included. Examples of investment include: purchase of a new plant or equipment, construction of a building (whether for business or residence), and additions to inventory (whether intentional or not). Investment would not include purchases by "investors" of common stock, bonds, or any other paper financial assets—only physical capital assets are included. (A financial asset is a claim on existing capital assets, not the physical asset itself.) Likewise, investment does not include the purchase of an existing plant or residence.

Government Spending: Government purchases of goods and services. Unlike most countries of the world, the U.S. National Income Accounts do not distinguish between government investment and government consumption. Examples of government spending are: defense expenditures, policemen's salaries, construction of a post office. However, government spending in the GNP accounts does not include Social Security payments or unemployment insurance, since these are transfers of existing income among taxpayers.

Net Exports: Exports increase national income because domestic industry uses capacity and resources to produce them, and because firms are paid for them. Similarly, imports represent income paid to producers in foreign countries and an expenditure of national income that could otherwise have paid for domestically produced goods and services. In calculating GNP, therefore, exports are added to other expenditures, but imports are deducted. (Exports and imports include both goods and services but do not include loans between countries or other exchanges of financial assets.)

This important accounting identity, GNP $= C + I + G + (X - M)$ can be related to the circular flow diagram presented earlier in Figure 3. The flow diagram may be clarified further if we introduce a few assumptions. Assume that (1) only the households pay taxes, (2) the government has a balanced budget (i.e., no government saving or borrowing), and (3) there is a current account balance (i.e., no foreign saving or borrowing). These assumptions, taken together, imply that all domestic savings are available for domestic investment. Figure 3 then will look like Figure 12.

This version of the circular flow diagram defines the flows in terms of the National Income Accounts. Notice that GNP in Figure 12 is equivalent to income in Figure 3. This reiterates our previous point that income and output are two sides of the same coin. The resources which flow in the opposite direction of GNP (but are suppressed in the diagrams) are labor, land, capital, and management skills. The income payments earned

Figure 12

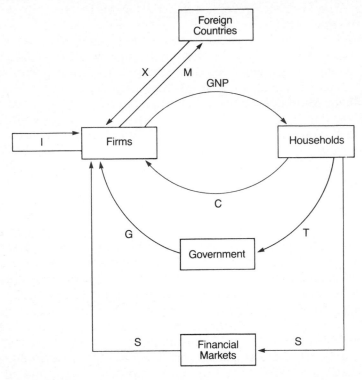

by these resources are wages, rents, interest, and profits, which equal total National Income (NI), as well as GNP in this simple diagram.

In order to visualize the GNP identity, one need only write down the equation for firms, showing all inflows equal to all outflows. The inflows are C, G, I, and X. The outflows are GNP and M. Thus we have

$$C + I + G + X = GNP + M,$$

or

$$C + I + G + X - M = GNP.$$

If we do the same with the household sector, we get another identity— the inflow into the household sector is GNP, the outflows are C, T, and S:

$$GNP = C + T + S.$$

This says that households can dispose of the income they receive in only three ways: they can consume it, they can pay it in taxes, or they can save it. These results for both firms and households are completely general, even when we relax the assumptions we previously made. The more general case will be discussed in the note "Investment and Savings" in Chapter 11.

Note B
An Introduction to Comparative Political Economy

Following World War II (1939–1945) most national economies experienced unprecedented growth. At times a centralization and consolidation of economic and political power accompanied this expansion. Simultaneously, this expansion of economy and polity was also accompanied by a potentially conflicting trend: the growing fragmentation of power and wealth within and between nations. Just as these three trends characterized the evolution of the public and private sectors in the United States,[1] so too expansion, centralization, and fragmentation characterized the evolution of the economy and polity in other industrialized and economically less-developed countries.

From 1950 to 1975, as aggregate world population grew at an annual rate of 1.9 percent, worldwide real gross national product per capita grew annually at an average rate of 3 percent. Certain economies expanded at a phenomenal rate. Industrialized Japan led all countries with 7.9 percent annual growth in per capita income from 1960 to 1975, followed by four newly industrializing economies: Singapore (7.5 percent), South Korea (7.3 percent), Hong Kong (6.5 percent), and Taiwan (6.3 percent). In low-income countries, significant progress could be seen in other basic indicators: literacy doubled and average life expectancy increased by one-fifth. Internationally, foreign trade and investment also grew at unprecedented rates. While the volume of international commerce had grown by only 0.5 percent per year from 1913 to 1948, it leaped to an annual increase of 7 percent from 1948 to 1973. Growth in global trade far outpaced growth of worldwide GNP. Exports and imports now became much more important components of gross national products. Increased economic interdependence also found reflection in direct foreign investment flows, which grew by 13 percent annually from 1960 to 1975.

As national economies expanded and became more interdependent, the size of public sectors was changing as well. In the United States, for example, growth in the federal civil service was twice that of the general population between 1940 and 1970. By 1977 almost one in every five employed Americans worked for some government unit—federal, state, or local. Yet despite such growth, total employment in the U.S. public sector as a percentage of the total labor force remained below average

This note was prepared by Assistant Professor Dennis J. Encarnation, with the assistance of Research Assistant Sigrid Bergenstein.

[1]See Dennis Encarnation, "An Introduction to U.S. Political Economy: Antecedents to the New Deal," HBS Case 0-384-160 (Boston: Harvard Business School Division of Research, 1984).

when compared with other industrial market economies (see Exhibit 1). Few of these public employees in America worked in state-owned enterprises; rather, they, along with their counterparts in other countries, populated agencies that grew up in response to an expansion in the scope of public policy. This was true in all countries—market and nonmarket, industrial and nonindustrial. Much of that policy was directed toward economic activities. Government—whether local, state, or national—began to emerge (1) as a major producer of goods and services, (2) as a principal regulator of otherwise private transactions, (3) as a financier or promoter of economic development, and (4) as an important purchaser or consumer of private production.

Direct government production of goods and services was one indicator of growth in the scope of the public sector. In centrally planned, nonmarket economies (China), state ownership of industry was nearly absolute. Among industrial market economies, Austria operated at one extreme, with extensive state ownership of service providers, distribution channels, natural resource industries, and manufacturers (see Exhibit 2). The United States stood at the opposite extreme: among countries with extensive private sectors, it was the only one with an all-private telecommunications network, one of two with a completely private airline industry, and one of a handful with no public enterprises in oil, gas, or steel. Among less-industrialized economies, especially those with large domestic markets—Brazil, India, Mexico—governments encouraged state ownership in most industries. Furthermore, the trend during the 1960s and 1970s was toward more state ownership.[2] Natural resources were among those industries where government ownership was common. Others included such infrastructure industries as transportation, utilities, and communications. Surprisingly, there was no clear correlation between the scope of government ownership of industry on the one hand and national economic performance on the other. Some economies that grew rapidly over the 1960s and 1970s (Germany, Brazil) had substantial public ownership, while others (Japan, Singapore) relatively little. Some slow performers (Canada, United States) had few state enterprises; others (Britain, India), a great many.

Of course, public ownership of the means of production was only one measure of government involvement in a nation's economy. Even though the United States and Japan, for example, did not encourage state ownership of utilities, active government promotion and regulation of private monopolies expanded the extent of government control in these

---

[2]The pace was often so rapid that Exhibit 2 inevitably understates this trend. The Canada Development Corporation, for example, expanded the equity holdings of the national government in oil, gas, and other natural resource industries (witness the takeover of the Texasgulf Corporation); Alberta and other provincial governments followed a similar pattern of increased government ownership. Yet the chart shows no public ownership of oil and gas in Canada. For additional details, see "Foreign Investment in Canada," HBS Case 4-375-133 (Boston: Harvard Business School Division of Research, 1975).

and related industries. In other words, short of exercising control over a firm's operations as its major shareholder, government served as a principal regulator of private enterprise. Nowhere was this more apparent than in the regulation of direct foreign investment. In market and non-market, industrial and nonindustrial economies alike, national governments nearly always placed significant constraints on decision making by managers of multinational corporations. Limits on ownership in local subsidiaries, rules on how much such companies must export or buy locally, whom they must employ, and how they must finance their operations applied almost everywhere by 1973. The government of Canada, for example, through the Canada Development Corporation Act, the Foreign Investment Review Act, and related legislation, attempted to increase domestic ownership in foreign firms, establish minimum exports, encourage local value-added, and discourage employment of non-Canadians. In virtually all countries, natural resources and service infrastructures were first among those industries where foreign operations were tightly regulated if not excluded altogether. Even the United States, a country that generally did not discriminate between foreign and domestic firms, excluded foreign ownership from coastal trade and a few other vital service industries. Moreover, the trend over the 1960s and 1970s was toward more government regulation of private enterprise generally, and control of foreign investment specifically. Manufacturing operations were subjected to increased scrutiny not only of their "economic" activities, but also of issues involving consumer rights, environmental protection, and employee safety.

Short of assuming a controlling equity position or erecting regulatory constraints, governments also employed a variety of other tools to finance and promote domestic production. Early in the history of most countries, such promotion took the form of tariff protection. For both domestic and foreign investors, barriers to imports served in many industries as the single most important incentive for investments designed to service large domestic markets. As government intervention in commodity markets declined with the General Agreement on Tariffs and Trade, government intervention in capital and other factor markets increased in the 1960s and 1970s. The growth of the Canada Development Corporation and other industrial development banks, along with the proliferation of government export-import banks, was illustrative of this larger trend. Tax concessions, loan guarantees, direct expenditures for debt or equity positions, and cash grants multiplied in their frequency, volume, and scope. For firms that actively competed in international markets, such tax and other concessions often influenced their decisions concerning where to locate their plants. While industrialized market economies reduced import tariffs but raised their interventions in capital and other factor markets, less-industrialized countries, exempt from GATT restrictions, employed both tariff and tax concessions to promote domestic production.

Direct government involvement in national economic development could take yet another form, as when government became a major consumer of private production. Private enterprises in the shipbuilding and aerospace industries in the United States, for example, were very dependent on government procurement, yet there was no government ownership in these industries. Defense contractors were not the only firms affected. In many market-oriented countries—ranging from France to India to Brazil—the central government was the largest single customer for national output. In these countries, access to government procurement was a major investment incentive for both domestic and foreign firms. Worldwide, the size and growth of government spending on consumption, investment, and transfers grew considerably over the 1960s and 1970s. Trends among industrialized market economies reflected this larger pattern (see Exhibit 1). Increased government purchases of privately produced goods and services figured prominently among these increased expenditures.

The Concentration and Centralization of Economic and Political Power

Even as the world economy expanded and became more interdependent, much of the world's wealth remained concentrated in a few countries. By 1970, 65 percent of total world GNP was generated in the industrial market economies, largely unchanged from 1950. Consequently, these countries continued to dominate foreign trade and investment (see Exhibit 3). The United States alone accounted for nearly one-third of world GNP, and remained the largest single source of foreign direct investment. The principal outlet for this investment remained America's northern neighbor, Canada. In Canada and elsewhere, foreign investment was often controlled by a few large multinationals.

Just as foreign trade and investment were correlated with the general level of economic activity across countries, so too types of political regimes were correlated with levels of economic development. In industrial market economies, for example, multiparty democracies dominated, whereas in nonmarket industrial economies (Soviet Union) single-party communist regimes reigned. And in the broad spectrum of economically less-developed countries, a general pattern of authoritarian, often military regimes was discernible: a coup or attempted coup occurred once every 55 days in Africa (1960–1972), once every four months in Latin America (1945–1972), and once every seven months in Asia (1947–1972).[3] Of course, across countries at various levels of economic activity, exceptions to these rules abounded. Among less-industrialized countries, for example, India and Mexico stood out as democracies dominated by a single party.

[3]Computed from Arthur S. Banks, ed., *Political Handbook of the World* (New York: McGraw-Hill, 1979).

Multiparty democracies, limited largely to industrial market countries, were principally of two types: presidential and parliamentary. The American and the British political systems, respectively, were commonly accepted models of each. Many Latin American countries copied in form if not substance the U.S. presidential system, while most former British colonies developed parliamentary governments at some point in their histories. The hallmark of the presidential system was the separation of the executive from the legislature; that of the parliamentary system was the fusion of executive and legislative powers. In a parliamentary democracy, the prime minister (Canada), chancellor (Germany), or premier (Italy) was an elected member of parliament, relying on parliamentary support to remain in power. By contrast, in a presidential system (United States, France), the chief executive was not a member of the legislature and served independent of its term and composition. Both presidential and parliamentary systems could be either unitary or federal in structure. Most were unitary: sovereignty resided with a central government that acted directly on individuals. Some, like Canada, West Germany, and the United States, were federal: sovereignty was divided between a central government and constituent units, each of which had distinct, though sometimes overlapping, areas of jurisdiction.

Similarly, governments in less-industrialized countries could be either unitary (South Korea) or federal (Brazil). With a few notable exceptions (India, Mexico), governments in these countries often combined legislative and judicial functions in one executive body. This executive domination of government was, in general, without effective opposition from political parties, interest groups, or traditional divisions within society. Indeed, political parties rarely operated independently of the government. In many countries, opposition parties were simply outlawed. Legislatures and constitutions were frequently dismissed and dissolved.

Authoritarian governments in less-industrialized countries illustrated the extreme of another worldwide trend: the growing concentration of political power in a very few national institutions. Even in multiparty democracies, the executive branch of government—the central bureaucracy along with the chief executive—was the special beneficiary of centralization. As the size of the bureaucracy and scope of government policy grew, the influence of the Office of the Prime Minister or the Office of the President grew as well. In Britain, for example, the Prime Minister eventually dominated the cabinet and the legislative agenda. Likewise, in the United States, the chief executive increasingly initiated legislation and used personal influence to elicit congressional support. This trend, begun at the turn of the century, accelerated and became institutionalized during the 12–year presidency of Franklin D. Roosevelt (1933–1945).

Economic and Political Fragmentation

When the United Nations Treaty was signed in 1945, immediately after World War II, 47 nations were signators, 28 of which could be classified as economically less-developed. By 1973, 80 new nations would be added to this number, most of which were former Asian or African colonies of European powers. Thirty of these new nations achieved independence and entered the United Nations during 1965–1967 alone. For these new members, a "New International Economic Order," characterized by a greater sharing of the world's wealth, was their rallying cry. The United Nations was their forum.

In 1973, most members of the United Nations could be classified as either "low income" (U.S.$250 per capita or below), or "middle income" (U.S.$250 to $2,500 per capita). Taken together, these economically less-developed nations were often termed *"less-industrialized,"* though this term obscured the fact that the more wealthy middle-income countries were rapidly industrializing. The remaining members of the United Nations, mostly industrialized, were either market oriented or centrally planned. Within each of the categories, nations underwent profound changes. Economic and political centralization appeared almost everywhere, but the results were not shared equally.

In particular, the international political economy remained fragmented, as the gap widened between the industrialized "North"[4] and the poor, largely agrarian economies of the "South." Low-income countries which had accounted for 8.1 percent of the world's GNP in 1955 accounted for only 4.8 percent of world income 20 years later. Yet, their populations had increased from 44.7 percent to 47.1 percent of the world's total during that same period. As a result, several countries, largely in Africa, experienced negative growth rates in GNP per capita. Even among the less-industrialized countries of the "South," a gulf opened up between the vast majority of low- and middle-income countries on the one hand and a few newly industrializing countries (NICs) on the other. The latter included Brazil and Mexico in Latin America and Hong Kong, Singapore, South Korea, and Taiwan in Asia. By 1973 these six countries together accounted for over half of all exports originating in the 120 nations of the less-industrialized "South," and much of the foreign direct investment located outside of the Organization for Economic Cooperation and Development[5] (see Exhibit 3).

National political economies often replicated within their borders the schisms apparent in the international division of labor. Few countries, whether industrialized or less-industrialized, market or nonmarket, were devoid of some type of "dual economy": industrial versus agricultural, high income versus low, rural versus urban, traditional versus modern, small-scale production versus large, monetized versus barter, and educated versus illiterate. Usually these several dimensions were interrelated, so that a "backward" region of a country was often agricultural, rural, traditional, and poor, with minimal linkages to other regions that were

[4]A synonym for industrialized market countries, located largely in the northern hemisphere.

[5]The Organization for Economic Cooperation and Development (OECD) is a Paris-based international organization of the 24 largest noncommunist industrial countries designed to improve economic policies of its signatories.

industrial, urban, and modern. Within most countries, regional differences were quite stark. In Canada, for example, the per capita income in Nova Scotia was one-half that in Ontario. Similar disparities could be found between industrialized and economically "backward" regions in rich and poor countries alike.

Persistent regionalism in economic affairs found reflection in politics. Often during the 1960s and 1970s regional political parties or factions of national parties arose to press regional demands. Responses to these demands were reflected in government policies designed to promote regional development in, for example, Nova Scotia (Canada), Tennessee (United States), Scotland (Britain), Hokkaido (Japan), Bengal (India), or the Amazon (Brazil). One of the objectives of the Canada Development Corporation, for example, was to entice domestic and foreign firms to locate in the less-industrialized Maritime Provinces, and not in industrialized Ontario. Canada and other countries adopted federal structures of government also in response to regional pressures for decentralized policy-making. Even unitary systems were not immune to these pressures. Military coups in Africa, Asia, and Latin America were often the products of fragmented political systems that underlay apparently unitary governments. Nor was militant regionalism limited to less-industrialized countries, as the Parti Quebecois in Canada confirmed.

Another form of political fragmentation appeared in the executive branch of many national governments. The bureaucracies of most nations often included at least three different types of institutions: first, central government departments divided according to functional operations (foreign affairs, treasury) or sectoral interests (agriculture, industry) that were responsible directly to the nation's chief executive; second, central government agencies and state-owned enterprises (the Canada Development Corporation, the Tennessee Valley Authority, the national airlines of many countries) that were more independent of the chief executive; and third, regional administrative units that conducted the affairs of provinces, states, or prefectures. So, for example, a foreign investor in Canada might have to conduct negotiations with a myriad of institutions: the Foreign Investment Review Agency, which reports to the federal cabinet; the Canada Development Corporation, a federal financial institution; agencies of various provincial governments; and numerous other provincial and federal agencies concerned with pollution and other "social" regulations. Should the investment decision have implications for, say, U.S.-Canadian relations, then the foreign ministry might also become involved along with the rest of the federal cabinet.

Conclusion: Political Economy in Comparative Perspective

In the evolution of the public and private spheres of economic life, sharp differences emerged between industrial and nonindustrial, market and nonmarket countries. Similarly, within each of these categories, sharp differences were discernible between, for example, the United States and other industrial market economies; and between older Latin American countries and the newly emerging nations of Africa and Asia.

Despite these inevitable complications, the pattern of differential growth rates between business and government in most countries resembled a two-stage evolution. The rise of big business preceded the rise of big government in the United States, alone of all industrial market economies. In Britain, France, Germany, and Japan, by contrast, a substantial civil bureaucracy was embedded in the society long before the appearance of large-scale industrial enterprise. Not until after World War II did the role of government in the U.S. economy begin to approach levels found in other industrial market economies. Still, the overlap of the public and private sectors remained greater in countries outside the United States than in the United States itself. In Europe and Japan, business-government cooperation sometimes became so close that portions of the public and private sectors could enter relationships of symbiosis or even merger. Such symbiosis was even more pronounced in most economically less-developed countries. Just as colonial regimes blended business and government functions, so too governments in newly independent countries became the principal catalysts of economic development. The symbiosis between business and government approached total convergence in non-market economies (e.g., China), where the role of government as producer, financier, regulator, and consumer was nearly absolute.

Given these differential growth rates of business and government, business executives outside of the United States seldom experienced the autonomy characteristic of their American counterparts. By 1973, few business managers in other industrialized countries, not to mention managers operating in nonmarket or less-industrialized countries, took it for granted that they could make important investment decisions without involving the central government. For them, the government had long been viewed as a principal producer, financier, regulator, and consumer.

An Introduction to Comparative Political Economy

Exhibit 1 Government Spending and Employment in Selected Industrialized Countries

	Government Spending[a]		Government Employment[d]	
Country[b]	As Percent of GDP 1979	Growth 1970–1979[c]	Total Gov't. as Percent of Labor Force 1978[e]	of which: SOEs as Percent of Labor Force 1978[f]
Sweden	59.7%	14.4%	29.6% (2)	8.2% (2)
Netherlands	57.7	10.2	12.8 (11)	7.3 (5)
Denmark	51.1	8.1	18.7 (9)	3.4 (10)
Belgium	49.2	10.5	19.6 (7)	5.2 (9)
Ireland	49.0	9.4	12.8 (13)	7.2 (6)
Austria	49.0	8.7	33.0 (1)	13.7 (1)
West Germany	46.4	7.2	20.6 (5)	7.1 (7)
France	45.0	6.5	21.0 (4)	7.4 (4)
Italy	44.8	6.5	18.5 (10)	6.6 (8)
Britain	43.8	4.1	28.5 (3)	8.1 (3)
Canada	40.3	3.9	20.0 (6)	3.3 (11)
United States	33.4	1.2	18.8 (8)	1.5 (13)
Japan	30.5	9.5	12.9 (12)	2.8 (12)

[a]Includes consumption, investment, and transfer payments recorded as budgetary expenditures.

[b]Rank-ordered according to government spending as percent of GNP.

[c]Increase in government spending as percent of Gross Domestic Product (GDP), 1970–1973 average to 1977–1979 average.

[d]Definitions of the public sector vary across countries, so the figures reported are rough approximations.

[e]Numbers in parentheses refer to rank orders.

[f]For examples of state-owned enterprises (SOEs), see Exhibit 2. Numbers in parentheses refer to rank orders.

Sources: David R. Cameron, "On the Limits of the Public Economy," *Annals of the American Academy of Political and Social Science* (January 1982): 49, derived from OECD publications concerning government spending; *The Economist*, Dec. 30, 1978, derived from OECD publications concerning government employment.

An Introduction to Comparative Political Economy

Exhibit 2   Government Ownership in Selected Industries, 1978

	Posts	Telecommunications	Electricity	Gas	Oil production	Coal	Railways	Airlines	Motor industry	Steel	Shipbuilding
Australia	●	●	●	●	○	○	●	◕	○	○	NA
Austria	●	●	●	●	●	●	●	●	●	●	NA
Belgium	●	●	◕	◕	NA	○	●	●	○	◑	○
Brazil	●	●	●	●	●	●	●	●	◕	○	◕
Britain	●	●	●	●	◕	●	●	◕	◑	◕	●
Canada	●	◕	●	○	○	○	◕	◕	○	○	○
France	●	●	●	●	NA	●	●	◕	◑	◕	○
West Germany	●	●	◕	◑	◕	◑	●	●	◕	○	◕
Holland	●	●	●	◕	NA	NA	●	◕	◑	◕	○
India	●	●	●	●	●	●	●	●	○	◕	●
Italy	●	●	◕	●	NA	NA	●	●	◕	◕	◕
Japan	●	●	○	○	NA	○	◕	◕	○	○	○
Mexico	●	●	●	●	●	●	●	●	◑	◕	●
South Korea	●	●	◕	○	NA	◕	●	○	○	◕	○
Spain	●	◑	○	◑	NA	◑	●	●	○	◑	◕
Sweden	●	●	◑	●	NA	NA	●	◑	○	◕	◕
Switzerland	●	●	●	●	NA	NA	●	◕	○	○	NA
United States	●	○	◕	○	○	○	◕*	○	○	○	○

Privately owned: ○ all or nearly all   Publicly owned: ● all or nearly all   75% ◕   50% ◑   25% ◔

NA – not applicable or negligible production.
*Including Conrail.

Source: Adapted from a chart in *The Economist* (London), Dec. 30, 1978, and reprinted with special permission.

An Introduction to Comparative Political Economy

Exhibit 3 Country Shares of Total World Manufacturing Exports and Total Direct Foreign Investment (DFI) Stock

	Percent of Total World Exports of Manufactures		Percent of Total DFI[a] Stock	
	1963	1973	1967	1973
Industrialized Market Economies	80.5%	82.3%	64.1%	67.9%
Canada	2.6	4.2	17.1	15.9
Britain	11.1	7.0	7.3	8.4
France	7.0	7.3	2.7	2.8
West Germany	15.5	17.0	3.2	6.3
Italy	4.7	5.3	2.3	3.3
Japan	6.0	9.9	0.5	0.6
United States	17.2	12.6	8.8	9.9
Other			22.2	
Low- and Middle-Income Economies	5.3	8.6	29.2	27.6
OPEC[b]	NA[c]	NA	8.1	6.5
Newly Industrializing Countries	2.6	6.3	NA	NA
Brazil	0.1	0.4	3.3	3.4
Mexico	6.2	0.6	1.6	2.0
Hong Kong	0.8	1.1	0.3	0.5
South Korea	0.1	0.8	NA	NA
Singapore	0.4	0.5	0.2	0.5
Taiwan	0.2	1.0	NA	NA
Other	0.8	1.9	NA	NA
Other Less-Developed Economies	2.7	2.3	NA	NA
Of which: India	0.9	0.5	1.2	1.0
Industrialized Nonmarket Economies	13.4	10.0	6.7	4.5
Total[d]	99.2%	100.9%	100.0%	100.0%

[a]Percent of the book value of all direct foreign investment overseas.

[b]Organization for Petroleum Exporting Countries.

[c]Not available.

[d]Errors due to rounding.

Sources: Organization for Economic Cooperation and Development, *The Impact of the Newly Industrializing Countries on Production and Trade in Manufactures* (Paris: OECD, 1979), 19; United Nations Centre on Transnational Corporations, *Salient Features and Trends in Foreign Direct Investment* (New York: UNCTC, 1983), 34, 56, derived from OECD publications; United Nations Centre on Transnational Corporations, *Transnational Corporations in World Development* (New York: UNCTC, 1978), 254, derived from OECD publications.

Note C
How to Read Data Exhibits

Before one turns to data exhibits in the following cases, one should ask, "What information is needed in order to evaluate this case?" This means that one should form hypotheses concerning the problem or likely outcome of the case, then search for supporting or contrary data in the exhibits. As part of this evaluation, one should use the exhibits to verify or refute important assertions made in the text of the case itself. If time permits, one can also peruse other exhibits in order to glean additional information. The first section of this note will proceed through a series of questions one should consider when analyzing data. We will use examples from the data exhibits of Appendix A, "Selected U.S. Statistics (through 1941)." The five questions discussed in this note are:

1. *Which data* should be used?
2. *Which time period* of the data should be used?
3. *Which form* of the data should be used?
4. How does one *evaluate* the data?
5. What are the *limitations* of the data?

Answers to these questions will often form the foundation of discussions, since this is the raw material on which empirical arguments are made.

Which Data?

The many exhibits which often support the text of the following cases can be classified into three categories. Following the country analysis framework,[1] the data may be indicators of performance, policy,[2] or context. Appendix A has 25 exhibits with eleven performance exhibits (1 through 10 and 19), eleven policy exhibits (11 through 18 and 20 through 22), and three contextual exhibits (23 through 25). This decomposition is only suggestive since some data may serve more than one purpose.

This note was prepared by Associate Professor Michael G. Rukstad.
Copyright © 1982 by the President and Fellows of Harvard College
Harvard Business School note 9-383-094

[1]See Bruce Scott, John Rosenblum, and Audrey Sprout, "Country Analysis," *Case Studies in Political Economy: Japan 1854–1977* (Boston: Harvard Business School Division of Research, 1980), 7–17.

[2]Sometimes data will indicate the strategy which a country is pursuing, i.e., both its goals and its policies, but more often this must be derived from the text of the case in combination with the exhibits. Therefore we will speak of data as a "policy indicator" rather than the more comprehensive "strategy indicator."

For example, bank suspensions (Exhibit 15) can be an indicator of monetary policy, but some might want to classify it as an indicator of performance or context as well.

Performance data is often the most abundant since there are so many different aspects of performance one needs to consider. In order to bring structure to an apparent chaos of data, we can use our theory regarding aggregate demand and aggregate supply to organize the data into broad groups. These two aggregate curves together determine output and prices for a particular country. Likewise, we will classify performance data into broad generic categories: output performance and price performance. But a country does not exist in a vacuum since the output and price of one country are affected by the actions of other countries in the international economic environment. Therefore we must consider the external balance between one country and the rest of the international community. These data will be classified as indicators of external performance. The three broad categories for classifying performance data will be:

1.   Output performance.

2.   Price performance.

3.   External performance.

The broadest measure of output performance is real GNP, which we will describe in detail below. This should be the first indicator one examines to assess the general direction of the economy. Exhibits 2 and 4 give GNP in constant prices (real GNP). Other measures are more specific and include the components of real GNP (consumption, investment, government spending, and net exports)[3] and sectoral production (agriculture, mining, manufacturing, and services). One would also include measures such as unemployment and capacity utilization which tend to move with output. Exhibits 2, 3, 4, 6, and 8 largely fall into the "output performance" category.[4]

The broadest measure of price performance is the GNP deflator, which will also be detailed below. The GNP deflator is a price index, as is the consumer price index (CPI).[5] They are measures of the movements

---

[3]Net exports are included here because we are stressing the role net exports have in determining total output. Recall from our earlier discussion that all three performance categories are interrelated.

[4]Exhibits 1 and 5, which only record nominal (current-dollar) data instead of real (constant-dollar) data, will indicate both output and price performance together since the two cannot be distinguished. However, from Exhibits 2 and 4, which have both nominal and real data, we can distinguish both output and price data by using a method we will develop later in this note.

[5]A price index is a weighted average of the individual prices of goods and services. The difference between the GNP deflator and the CPI is the weights that are used. The GNP deflator uses the proportions of goods and services purchased in the current year as the weights assigned to individual prices. The CPI uses the proportions purchased in the base year as the weights. These measures will not give the same answer and neither is "more correct" since they both have a bias away from the "true index," if one could be computed.

Figure 1

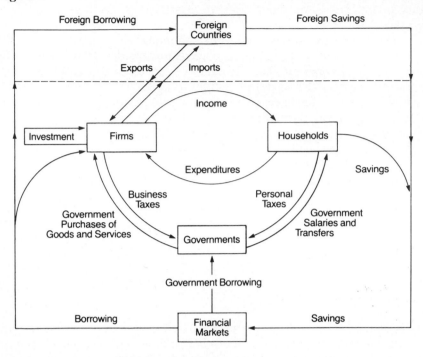

in the general price level for all goods and services. Since production costs tend to move with the price level, we will classify such measures as wage or earnings indexes, wholesale price indexes (WPI), productivity changes, and profit margin data in the "price performance" category. From Exhibits 2, 4, 7, and 9 in Appendix A, we can gather price information.

The external balance is best summarized by the balance of payments (BOP) statement, which is a record of an economy's international economic transactions. Using the circular flow diagram of Figure 1, we can visualize the BOP. Imagine a government accountant standing at the nation's border (the dotted line) who was adding the money inflows (arrows going into the country), and subtracting the money outflows (arrows going out). If the information were recorded as shown on page 35 on lines marked with "*," we would have a balance of payments statement which is the addition of two sections: the current account and the capital account. If the balance of payments is not zero, then official transactions of acceptable financial assets (such as gold reserves in the historical period covered by Appendix A) carried out by the governments of the countries will be used to settle the accounts. These transactions are recorded in the Official Reserve Transaction account. Hence the balance of payments statement will "balance" to zero, except for statistical errors and omissions. Exhibit 19 in Appendix A contains information on the performance of the external balance.[6]

Current	Exports of Goods and Services,	
Account	and Transfer Payment Inflows	*
	− Imports of Goods and Services,	
	and Transfer Payment Outflows	*
	Current Account Balance	

Capital	+ Foreign Savings	*
Account	− Foreign Borrowings	*
	Balance of Payments	
	− Official Reserve Transactions	
	0	

In addition to performance data, cases usually provide *policy data* as well. Policy data are indicators of future performance and are not per se good or bad—it depends on the context, past events, and performance, and especially the goals that a nation is pursuing. This distinguishes these data from performance data or national strategies that can be evaluated on their merits. The usual examples of policy data are money supply figures (Exhibit 11 in Appendix A) or government budget and debt figures (Exhibits 20, 21, and 22). Check these and other policy figures for potential conflicts, which may arise because different decision makers are responsible for different policies.

Further insights can be gained from *contextual data* such as public opinion polls (Exhibits 24 and 25 in Appendix A), demographic data (Exhibit 23), sociological characteristics, and so forth. Often the context will help to explain certain policy decisions or place performance in perspective. For example, policy decisions are affected by contextual factors such as a strong showing in a recent election, a large social group that stands to benefit from the decision, a small collusive group of decision makers, or a strong ideological indoctrination of the masses. In addition, contextual data place performance figures in perspective, such as comparing GNP growth rates to population growth rates in order to determine if the average individual is benefiting from the growth of the economy.

Which Time Period?

Once we decide which data we need to support our hypotheses, we need to determine which time period best supports our intended arguments. One method is to identify key events or policy changes which define the

⁶Notice that this exhibit has all of the elements which comprise the Current Account (Columns 15, 16, and 17), the Capital Account (Columns 18 through 23), and Official Reserve Transaction (Column 24). Column 25 shows that it balances to zero, except for statistical errors and omissions. To verify this, add all the numbers in Columns 15 to 25, which will sum to zero. Notice that Column 15 is a summary of Columns 1 through 14.

end points of the time period. For example, we may be interested in real GNP growth during World War I (1914–1919), which could be compared to the postwar years before the Great Depression started in 1929 (1919–1929). For some purposes this may be useful, but there are problems with defining these periods. In particular, the 1919–1929 period aggregates over an economic depression in 1920 and three sizable booms (see the annual growth rates of real GNP in Exhibit 3 of Appendix A). Notice that real GNP fell significantly in 1920 and 1921. On the other hand, 1922–1923, 1925, and 1929 were boom years. If we just reported the average growth rate of real GNP of this period, it would be 3.4 percent, which smooths over significant business cycles.

This suggests another method for choosing time periods: one could let the peaks and troughs of the data choose the endpoints of the period. Possibly one could divide the period into the postwar recession (1919–1921, during which real GNP declined at approximately 6.5 percent per year) and the subsequent recovery (1921–1929, during which real GNP rose at a 6.0 percent average rate). This division is an improvement over the 1919–1929 period that was initially suggested. However, keep in mind the benefits of suggesting longer time periods, since it concisely summarizes data which would become cumbersome if reported for each individual year.

Finally, one should try to reconstruct the frame of mind with which policy makers and other contemporary observers viewed these data. Policy makers did not have real GNP or unemployment figures during this period, for example, but they did have the consumer price index and industrial production indexes. In addition to asking which data were available to the policy makers, one should consider what horizon they were concerned with when evaluating policy. If we are attempting to explain how policy reacts to sudden poor performance, we should focus on more recent and more highly visible signs of that performance, rather than long time trends.

Which Form of the Data?

If our answer to the first question, "Which data should be used?" is Exhibit 4 in Appendix A, which shows nominal and real GNP, and if the answer to the second question, "Which time period should be used?" is 1929–1930, then we still must determine in what form we will evaluate these data. This section will discuss three important considerations regarding the form of the data. Should we present:

1. Nominal or real data?
2. Levels or growth rates of these data?
3. Ratios of these data and other data?

One crucial distinction is between *nominal* and *real* data. In Column 1 of Exhibit 4 we are given "GNP in current prices," which is nominal GNP. We defined GNP[7] in Note A of this chapter as the *market value of all final goods and services produced by nationals of a country within a given time period*. This was conceptually equivalent to taking the quantity of every good and service produced and multiplying each by its *current* market price. Real GNP, however, is determined by taking the same quantities of every good and service produced and multiplying each by a *base year* (*constant*) price. The constant base year used in Column 3 of Exhibit 4 is 1958. This technique allows us to add quantities of apples and oranges and all other commodities in a consistent manner for comparison over time. One should see that nominal GNP may change due to changes in either the current market price or the quantities produced, whereas real GNP will change only if the quantities produced change.

The general relationship between nominal GNP and real GNP can be expressed in the following form:

$$\text{Nominal GNP} = \text{Implicit Price Deflator} \times \text{Real GNP}$$
$$\text{GNP} = P \times Q.$$

The "Q" used in all notes for this book will indicate real GNP unless specified. Thus the graphs of aggregate supply and aggregate demand in the note "An Introduction to Economics" are determining real GNP. These curves also determine "P," the implicit price deflator, which is an index of the current price level.

If we examine Exhibit 4, we should be able to verify this relationship using actual data. The nominal GNP for 1930 is shown in Column 1 of Exhibit 4 to be $90.4 billion. Column 5 gives us the implicit deflator for 1930 as 49.3, which means that the price level in 1930 was 49.3 percent of the price level of the base year, 1958 (which equals 100). The real GNP for 1930 is shown in the third column to be $183.5 billion. When we multiply the deflator (in its decimal form)[8] and real GNP together, we get:

$$\text{Deflator} \times \text{Real GNP} = \text{Nominal GNP}$$
$$.493 \times 183.5 = 90.4655.$$

The nominal GNP shown in Exhibit 4 is 90.4, which is very close to the nominal GNP we calculated.

This relationship between nominal and real variables is completely general. For example, if we wanted information on the price level of investment goods in 1930 compared to the base year, we could use this same relationship:

$$\frac{\text{Nominal}}{\text{Investment}} = \frac{\text{Investment}}{\text{Deflator}} \times \frac{\text{Real}}{\text{Investment}}.$$

---

[7]Whenever we use the term "GNP" without qualifying it by the word "real," we will be referring to "nominal GNP."

[8]The convention is to express the deflator not as the decimal form that one uses in the equation (.493 in our example), but as the number times 100 (or 49.3). Likewise, the base period is not 1, but 100.

Exhibit 2 gives us nominal investment in 1930 of $10.1 billion and real investment in that year of $27.4 billion. Thus we can rearrange the above equation to get:

$$\text{Investment Deflator} = \frac{\text{Nominal Investment}}{\text{Real Investment}}$$

$$.369 = \frac{10.1}{27.4},$$

which means that the prices of investment goods in 1930 were 36.9 percent of prices in the 1958 base year. Notice that between 1930 and the 1958 base year the investment price index indicates the prices of investment goods inflated more than the general price index during that same period.

A second distinction we must make in deciding what form of the data to use is whether *levels* or *growth rates of the levels* are more helpful. It is difficult to compare, for example, GNPs of different countries measured in different currencies using different base periods. Therefore it will be more useful to examine growth rates of GNP (and growth rates of other variables), since these can be compared across countries. Often we will be interested in more than a static comparison of the levels of variables. We will want a dynamic comparison of how the variables change over time. Growth rates give us some insight into the dynamic process of adjustment, which is a crucial factor in the implementation of policy.

The growth rate (i.e., percentage growth rate or compound growth rate) of a variable over one period of time—for example, real GNP (Q) for the one-year period from 1929 to 1930 in Exhibit 2—is given by the following equivalent expressions:

$$\frac{\Delta \text{Real GNP}}{\text{Real GNP}} = \frac{Q_{1930} - Q_{1929}}{Q_{1929}} = i$$

$$\frac{-20.1}{203.6} = \frac{183.5 - 203.6}{203.6} = -.098 \ (= -9.8\%).$$

Notice that Exhibit 3 gives the computed average annual growth rates of real GNP for all of the years. Now suppose we were examining the five-year period, 1924–1929. One way to describe the period is to say that the annual growth rate or real GNP was 8.4 percent for 1925, 5.9 percent for 1926, 0 percent for 1927, 0.6 percent for 1928, and 6.7 percent for 1929. Or we can ask what the average annual compound growth rate (CGR) was over this five-year period. From Exhibit 3 we can see that it is 4.2 percent, but we will not always have computed tables such as in Exhibit 3. Therefore this can be computed from the following formula[9]

---

[9]Some students may recall another formula for compound growth rates: Future Value = Present Value $\times$ e^{in}, where e = 2.718. . . . The difference between the two formulas is that the formula on page 39 assumes growth is compounded only once per period whereas the formula here assumes continual compounding over the period. The formula on page 39 is the algorithm used by most calculators.

for compound growth rate (i) using the original data from Exhibit 4:

$$\text{Future Value} = \text{Present Value} \times (1 + i)^n$$
$$\text{Real GNP 1929} = \text{Real GNP 1924} \times (1 + i)^5$$
$$203.6 = 165.5 \times (1 + i)^5$$

Most calculators will compute the compound growth rate, i (which equals 4.23 percent in this case), once the future value, the present value, and the number of periods, n, have been entered into the calculator.

We gain intuition for the concept of compound growth if we examine the case of compound interest on savings. Imagine we have $100 of savings which will be "growing" at a 10 percent rate compounded annually (i.c., which earns 10 percent interest compounded annually). After one year we would have $110 using our CGR formula:

$$\text{Future Value} = \text{Present Value} \times (1 + i)^n$$
$$\$110 = 100 \times (1.1)^1 \text{ after 1 ycar}$$
$$\$121 = 100 \times (1.1)^2 \text{ after 2 years}$$

During the second year, the $110 would grow to $121 since we would earn another $10 interest on the principal and $1 interest on last year's interest. It is this last component, earning interest on the past accumulated interest, which makes this "compound interest" or "compound growth." If we just earned $10 of interest on the principal every year and earned no interest on the accumulated interest, then we would have "simple interest" or "simple growth." When we refer to "growth rate" in this book, we will mean "compound growth rate."

One useful approximation to the growth rate of nominal GNP is the *sum* of the growth rates of the price level and of real GNP, even though we *multiply* the price level by real GNP to get nominal GNP. In symbols we have:

$$\text{GNP} = P \times Q$$

$$\frac{\Delta\text{GNP}}{\text{GNP}} \cong \frac{\Delta P}{P} + \frac{\Delta Q}{Q}.$$

For example, if we compute the compound growth rate for nominal GNP, real GNP, and the implicit deflator for the one-year period from 1929 to 1930, we get:

$$\frac{\Delta\text{GNP}}{\text{GNP}} \cong \frac{\Delta P}{P} + \frac{\Delta Q}{Q}$$

$$-12.32 \cong -2.6 + (-9.8).$$

This relationship holds anytime one variable (C) can be expressed as a *product* of other variables (A and B or more):

$$C \cong A \times B.$$

Then we can write the growth rate of C as a *sum* of the growth rates of the other variables:

$$\frac{\Delta C}{C} \cong \frac{\Delta A}{A} + \frac{\Delta B}{B}.$$

This relationship is useful if we want to compute the price inflation of investment goods. We would first construct an investment deflator index for two years, say 1929 and 1930, as we did for 1930 on page 38. Then we would compute the CGR between the two indices. Alternatively, we could compute the CGR for nominal investment and for real investment and then subtract, since the percentage change in the price of investment goods is:

$$\frac{\Delta(\text{P of Investment Goods})}{\text{P of Investment Goods}} = \frac{\Delta(\text{Nominal I})}{\text{Nominal I}} - \frac{\Delta(\text{Real I})}{\text{Real I}}$$

$$-5.4 \quad\quad = \quad\quad -37.6 \quad - (-32.2).$$

The distinctions between real and nominal and between levels and rates of change are useful considerations in determining what form of the data one should use. Another consideration which will be discussed here is the formation of *ratios of two variables* to scale them down for comparison across countries and across time. In fact, our real GNP definition is one example of such a ratio. For example, the real GNP figures (in Column 3 of Exhibit 4) may be growing, but the population (in Column 1 of Exhibit 8) may be growing more rapidly. Thus it is often useful to examine real GNP per capita. Again we could calculate real GNP per person in one year, say 1927, and calculate it in another year, say 1928, and then compute the growth rate. But since we are interested in the growth of GNP per capita over that one-year period, we could subtract the population growth rate from the real GNP growth rate. In this case, the growth rate of real GNP per capita between 1927 and 1928 can be calculated using real GNP data from Exhibit 4 and population data from Exhibit 8.

$$\frac{\Delta(\text{Real GNP/Capita})}{(\text{Real GNP/Capita})} \cong \frac{\Delta\text{Real GNP}}{\text{Real GNP}} - \frac{\Delta\text{Population}}{\text{Population}}$$

$$-0.63 \quad \cong \quad 0.6 \quad - \quad 1.23.$$

Even though real GNP was growing over that year, it was not growing as fast as population. By forming a new variable, real GNP per capita, we have more information on which to evaluate performance. Of course, we could have directly calculated the growth in real GNP per capita (using Column 4 of Exhibit 4), but this data will not always be available.

Another illustration of ratios is the ratio of the component expenditures to GNP, such as:

$$\frac{C}{GNP}, \frac{I}{GNP}, \frac{G}{GNP}, \frac{X}{GNP}, \text{ and } \frac{M}{GNP}.$$

For example, in Exhibit 2 we could calculate the percentage contribution of total investment (Column 6) to real GNP (Column 1) for 1929 and 1932. In 1929, total investment accounted for 19.8 percent of real GNP but this ratio declined to 3.2 percent in 1932. These ratios can be meaningfully compared across countries and over time.

How to Evaluate the Data?

The only way that we can evaluate data is by comparison. In the rest of this section, we will discuss four comparisons which might be made. We could compare the data with:

1.   A government's goals.

2.   The past.

3.   Other countries.

4.   Theory.

The country analysis's framework suggests comparing actual performance to the goals that the policy makers set for themselves. This will give us some perspective on past performance as well as insight into future policy moves. If the U.S. government set a goal of 6 percent real GNP growth over a certain period of time, but achieved only 4 percent growth, we can certainly make the evaluation that actual growth fell significantly short of expectations. Of course, the expectations may have been unjustified. Often, though, goals are more amorphous than this example, and goals are subject to wishful thinking, so we need other benchmarks for comparison.

The most frequent comparison is with the past. If the long-term, say 30-year, trend for real GNP is only 2.5 percent, then the 4 percent growth now is significantly better than in the past. The strength of this evaluation rests on the comparability of the time periods. If the 4 percent was achieved during a period of war, then it should not be evaluated against a period of depression. Sometimes it is difficult to find comparable historical periods for comparison. For example, the world wars or the Great Depression are in a class by themselves, but useful comparisons might be made to the Korean War or the Depression of 1921.

Another form of comparison is with other countries at the same period in time. The cross-national comparison is at the heart of the country analysis. The comparisons are valid only if one understands the role which "special contextual factors" play in determining the data we observe. At other times, the differences in performance will be accounted for by policy differences. As one progresses through this book, one will develop an intuition for evaluating magnitudes of data. The art of country analysis is to assess the relative role of strategy and context in determining performance.

A final method of comparison is to compare actual data to theory. For example, actual real GNP growth of 4 percent may be compared to potential real GNP growth that could be calculated for other observed data such as the growth in the capital stock and the labor force. If we determine that potential real GNP is growing at 5 percent, then we have a theoretical basis for evaluating the actual real GNP growth rate.

What Limitations?

There are limitations to the inferences one can draw from the data presented in the exhibits of Appendix A. However, these limitations also apply, in varying degrees, to the exhibits in all of our cases. We will focus on three considerations: (1) problems with the data itself, (2) problems due to excluded factors, and (3) problems of inference from the data.

All data that we will use are subject to measurement errors and successive revisions—even data from more distant historical periods are still revised today. The older statistics have an additional problem since they are often estimates based on related primary data which were collected for other purposes. Furthermore, since these data are estimates based on modern theory and calculations, these are not the data on which policy makers of the day could base their decisions.

The earliest attempts to measure "national income" date back to a study by Sir William Petty and Gregory King in England in 1665. But by 1919 only 14 countries had attempted such a crude estimate of national income.[10] (In 1843 George Tucker made the first estimates for the United States.) In 1925 Canada and the Soviet Union instituted, for the first time, continuing government estimates of national income, and by 1939 another seven countries followed their example.[11] In 1932 the U.S. Department of Commerce, with the cooperation of Simon Kuznets, began to prepare annual estimates of the national income as part of a congressional investigation into the cause of the Great Depression. John Maynard Keynes, a renowned Cambridge economist, provided the conceptual impetus in the 1930s by specifying his theory in terms of national income and its expenditure components, and this framework was adopted by Kuznets and other early investigators.

Even if the data were completely accurate and readily available, there are other limitations to interpreting the data. There is the problem of excluded and nonquantifiable factors. For example, we use GNP or GNP per capita as a measure of the well-being of the individuals in a society. But GNP excludes many items which do not have a "market value." How do we value the negative aspects of the pollution resulting from the production of that GNP? How do we value the positive aspects of the services of house spouses and leisure labor? So we must use the data as a first guess which must be modified by quantitative approximations or by qualitative judgments accessing the importance of excluded factors. Nonquantifiable factors, such as worker motivation, cultural standards, or innovative ability, should not be excluded or relegated to secondary status in the face of more concrete factors.

Finally, there is a problem common to all inferences drawn from nonexperimental data. We can only observe that two variables appear to

[10]See Paul Studenski, *The Income of Nations* (New York: New York University Press, 1961), Part I, "History."

[11]John Kendrick, *Economic Accounts and Their Uses* (New York: McGraw-Hill, 1972), 16.

be related to each other. We cannot prove that one variable causes the other. There may be some third factor responsible for the relationship we observe. This means that we must hypothesize reasonable explanations for the behavior we observe and then check if these explanations are consistent with the data. Of course, there may be a number of competing explanations which are all *prima facie* reasonable. At this point we must recall other similar cases from different countries or different time periods to determine which explanation has the most universal power to explain and predict.

Note D
An Introduction to Econometric Models: Data Resources Inc.

Econometric forecasts such as those produced by Data Resources Inc. (DRI) provide information on major aspects of the U.S. economy—GNP and its components, inventory levels, price levels, industrial production, financial measures, and the like. Companies seeking to anticipate demand or costs for their own products, or interest rates for specific debt instruments, have much narrower concerns. Because macroeconomic trends clearly have an effect at the company level, however, individual companies often choose to link their demand or cost forecasting with macroeconomic forecasts, either through models developed for them by DRI or other macroeconomic forecasting firms, or through models they develop on their own. In either case, the macromodel drives the company's own forecasting. Figure 1 is a simple diagram showing DRI's conception of this linkage.

Figure 1   The DRI Model of the U.S. Economy

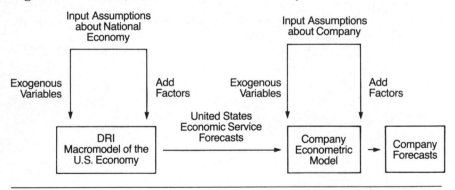

The following discussion summarizes the concept of econometric modeling, the way econometric models are used to forecast, and the necessary judgmental inputs (in the form of assumptions about values

This note was prepared by Alice B. Morgan under the supervision of Professor Arthur Schleifer, Jr.

for exogenous variables and add factors)[1] that keep the forecast from being merely a mechanical output of the model and the data.

Econometric Models

An econometric model is a set of equations relating economic variables to each other, either behaviorally or by definition, so as to approximate the actual economic structure of the real world. Nobel laureate Jan Tinbergen (1903–   ) is generally credited with being the first to employ econometric modeling, and another Nobel laureate, Lawrence Klein, was its major proponent in the United States during the late 1940s and early 1950s. (Klein is largely responsible for the model run by the Wharton Econometric Forecasting Associates.) By the early 1960s, the data base consisting of the National Income and Products Accounts of the U.S. Department of Commerce was sufficiently detailed, accurate, and stable to provide an adequate set of variables for large models, those consisting of 100 to 200 equations. At the same time, the availability of high-speed computers and the development of sophisticated algorithms made it possible to obtain solutions to such models. Model size has continued to increase, in order, as explained by Otto Eckstein, a Harvard economics professor and the founder of DRI, "to model the economic processes more fully as inputs to institutional decision making." More equations permit more variables to be used and economic relationships to be incorporated, and result in more disaggregated analyses and forecasts.

Specification

A model builder makes explicit his assumptions about economic relationships through the mathematical form of the model's equations. For example, an extremely simple model of the U.S. economy might involve just four variables:

- Consumption (C),
- Income (Y),
- Investment (I),
- Government expenditures (G).

In any one period, these variables might be related by means of two equations:

$$C = A + BY + E, \tag{1}$$
$$Y = C + I + G. \tag{2}$$

---

[1]See later sections for discussions of exogenous variables and add factors.

The first equation states that C (consumption) is a linear function of Y (income) plus E, a "disturbance" term. A and B are parameters of the first equation—numbers that represent the true (but unknown)[2] numerical relationship between Y and C. Equation 1 is a *behavioral* equation, in the sense that it describes the way consumption has behaved as a function of income in the past (and presumably will behave in the future); it is also a *stochastic* equation in the sense that even if Y were known with certainty in any one period, the value of C deduced from Equation 1 would be uncertain because of the disturbance E and the fact that the values of A and B are uncertain. Equation 2, on the other hand, is a definition: Y (income) is by definition the sum of C (consumption), I (investment), and G (government spending). Equation 2, having no error term, is nonstochastic. In this two-equation model, I and G must be determined outside the model. They are "exogenous" variables, while the variables C and Y, whose values are determined by the model, are "endogenous."[3]

The model expressed by Equations 1 and 2 is a "static" model: all the relationships bear on a single time period.

The following is an example of a dynamic model:

$$C(t) = A + B^*Y(t - 1) + E(t), \tag{3}$$
$$I(t) = I(t - 1) + H^*[C(t) - C(t - 1)] + E'(t), \tag{4}$$
$$Y(t) = C(t) + I(t) + G(t). \tag{5}$$

The t in parentheses indicates a particular time period, and t − 1 indicates the preceding period. C, Y, I, and G are defined as above, but the equations involve lagged as well as current values of these variables. Both E and E' are disturbance terms.

Equations 3 and 4 are behavioral or stochastic, while Equation 5 is a definition. This model implies that consumption in a given time period varies linearly with income in the preceding period (Equation 3), and that the change in investment from the previous period is proportional to the change in consumption from the previous period (Equation 4).

The endogenous variables (those variables whose values are determined by the model) are C(t), I(t), and Y(t). Variables whose values must be supplied to the model are Y(t − 1), C(t − 1), I(t − 1), and G(t). These variables are called "predetermined" in the econometrics literature, and they in turn can be partitioned into two subgroups: the "lagged endogenous variables" Y(t − 1), C(t − 1), and I(t − 1), whose values are available from data already in hand, and the "exogenous" variable G(t),

---

[2]Although A and B are unknown, the model builder usually assumes that A is close to 0 and B is positive but less than 1: consumption should tend to increase roughly in proportion to increases in income, but consumption will generally not exceed income.

[3]With a little algebraic manipulation, we can express the two endogenous variables in terms of the exogenous variables plus a disturbance term. Assuming B ≠ 1,

$$C = A/(1 - B) + [B/(1 - B)](I + G) + E/(1 - B), \tag{1'}$$
$$Y = A/(1 - B) + (I + G)/(1 - B) + E/(1 - B). \tag{2'}$$

This is called the "reduced form" of the original equations.

whose value must be supplied to the model judgmentally.[4] (In "static" models like the one represented by Equations 1 and 2, the predetermined variables I and G are necessarily exogenous.)

Estimation

Next, the model builder must use data on income and consumption to estimate the parameters A, B, and (in the second model) H through regression analysis. The parameter estimates are denoted with lower-case letters, and whereas Equations 1-5 express structural relationships, Equations 1*-5* express regression estimates of those structural relationships:

$$C = a + b*Y + e, \tag{1*}$$
$$Y = C + I + G, \tag{2*}$$
$$C(t) = a + b*Y(t - 1) + e(t), \tag{3*}$$
$$I(t) = I(t - 1) + h*[C(t) - C(t - 1)] + e'(t), \tag{4*}$$
$$Y(t) = C(t) + I(t) + G(t). \tag{5*}$$

The residual e in Equation 1* represents the difference between the actual value of C and the value estimated by the equation in which the residual appears, and similarly for the other residuals.

Verification and Testing of an Econometric Model

Before a model is used to forecast, it has to prove itself as a set of equations that make economic sense, that behave reasonably when solved using actual data, and that are likely to continue to make sense in the future. DRI accordingly tested its model using several types of simulation. One way was to introduce extreme values for some of the exogenous variables. Intuitively reasonable forecasts generated under these "exogenous shocks" tended to validate the model. Another way was to use the model and past data to "predict" values already in hand. Still another

---

[4]The reduced form, in which each endogenous variable is expressed in terms of predetermined variables only, can be shown to be:

$$C(t) = A + B*Y(t - 1) + E(t), \tag{3'}$$
$$I(t) = A*H + I(t - 1) + B*H*Y(t - 1) - H*C(t - 1) + H*E(t) + E'(t), \tag{4'}$$
$$Y(t) = A*(1 + H) + I(t - 1) + B*(1 + H)*Y(t - 1) - H*C(t - 1) + G(t) \\ + (1 + H)*E(t) + E'(t). \tag{5'}$$

It might at first appear that, because the lags are for one period only, known values of the lagged endogenous variables permit forecasts only one period ahead, but this is not true. If t is the period that is to be forecast, and if we are now in Period $t - 2$, then $C(t)$ can be computed in Equation 3' by using Equation 5' to compute $Y(t - 1)$ and substituting this value into Equation 3'. $C(t)$ will then depend on $I(t - 2)$, $Y(t - 2)$, $C(t - 2)$, and $G(t - 1)$, all of whose values, except for $G(t - 1)$, are known in Period $t - 2$. The values of $I(t)$ and $Y(t)$ can similarly be computed from data available in Period $t - 2$, and this process can be rolled backward to provide forecasts any number of periods ahead based on known values of the lagged endogenous variables. Notice, however, that in all cases the value of the exogenous variable cannot be known at the time of the forecast.

series of tests consisted of running the model out to a distant time horizon. Such simulations permitted assessment of the model's stability. If the model passed these and further validation tests, it could be treated as a reliable first cut at the future.

Exogenous Variables

The exogenous variable G(t) in the dynamic model represented by Equations 3-5 must either be known (the government might have announced its spending plans) or forecasted (on the basis of political, social, and economic conditions). Typical exogenous variables in macroeconomic models include policy variables whose values depend on government monetary and fiscal plans; prices determined outside the United States, such as OPEC's oil price; and others that are treated as exogenous for particular modeling purposes, e.g., the number of car-miles driven in a given year. Many variables can be either exogenous or endogenous, according to the preference of the model builder as reflected in the form and number of equations in a particular model. The policy variables, in particular, pose serious forecasting difficulties because they are eventually determined by political and psychological considerations as well as economic and social ones. In November 1981, for example, the DRI model forecasted a $130 billion budget deficit for 1983. Faced with this prediction, most of DRI's senior forecasting staff felt that some governmental action would be taken to prevent what at that time appeared to be too great a deficit. The staff examined the size, possible variations, and associated effects of many exogenous variables representing tax actions, government spending, government financing, and monetary policy; and individuals offered their views about appropriate and likely changes in some of these variables. Allen Sinai, DRI's Senior Vice President—Financial Sector, recalled:

> When we looked at the deficit forecasts we knew we couldn't go with those numbers. We had to think ourselves into the roles of government policymakers and forecast what they would do. I asked myself, "If I were Paul Volcker, the Chairman of the Federal Reserve, what would I want written on my tombstone?" My answer was, "Here lies the man who ended inflation," and it gave me some idea what kind of decisions Volcker would make.

Once the model is in place, the exogenous variables forecasted, and all relevant data series updated, the forecast can be generated.

Forecasting with the DRI Model of the U.S. Economy

As new data came in, DRI ran its current econometric models, checking forecasts against actuals. Periodically, existing models were refit to include the most recent data; such refitting changed parameter estimates and hence forecasts. In addition to refitting an already specified model with new data, DRI and other econometric modeling firms periodically respecified their models as economic theories were refined and as new data series became available. DRI had incorporated basic Keynesian assumptions—the circular flow of income and expenditure—into the heart of its model, but the model also included a full representation of the economy's financial system. More recently, the company had added equations reflecting supply-side theory, and the model's structure was continually being analyzed and evaluated.

Chris Probyn, one of the model's architects, explained that DRI usually made significant changes in the model twice a year. Wholesale refitting was necessary in July when the Department of Commerce released revised data for the past several years, and some respecification might also occur at that time. More far-reaching respecification was usually accomplished early in the calendar year.

DRI had constructed its very large model so as to facilitate rapid and economical forecast solutions. Exhibit 1 shows, in simplified form, how major parts of DRI's model related to each other. The three-dimensional blocks at the top of the exhibit represent exogenous variables; the arrows from these blocks show where in the model such variables appear. The flat shapes in the lower half of the exhibit represent the model's sectors; the links connecting the sectors are shown as arrows. The model was structured so that at these links the forecasters could break into the interconnected flow of output from one equation to another with minimal disruption. Probyn noted:

We can interrupt the model solution at the links, and by "excluding" or "exogenizing" a few variables (somewhere between four and ten), we can work with just part of the model, temporarily ignoring the rest of it. To do this, we stipulate certain values for the exogenized variables—values that, in the full solution, would come from other parts of the model. Then we "tune" the unlinked sector, based on our exogenized-variable values, so that the equations are giving mutually consistent results. It's the model's capacity to be treated this way that makes rapid forecasting possible.

Exhibits 2 and 3 give some data about DRI's model as of early 1981. Exhibit 2 provides information on the number and types of equations in the model's sectors (the more important sectors appear as the flat shapes in Exhibit 1). This exhibit also indicates the location of the model's 128 exogenous variables. In Exhibit 3, economic categories appear in the first column, and the theory underlying the model's treatment of each appears in the second column. The connections with other elements in the model are indicated in the final column.

Forecasting at DRI was an ongoing process, with those individuals who made exogenous forecasts constantly gathering information that would enable them to do so sensibly. At the same time, data from industry and government sources were accumulated and banked in the computer, and information from DRI staff who worked closely with government and business personnel was also steadily gathered and discussed. There were several subsidiary models run during the month, but the major macroeconomic forecast was produced in a frenzy of activity as soon as the Bureau of Economic Analysis of the U.S. Department of Commerce released the National Income and Product Account data it published every month. (This generally occurred between the nineteenth and twenty-first day of the month.) Banking the data to update DRI's time series required about five to eight hours; it included checking data for consistency and updating those series that DRI tracked which depended on more than one government statistic (e.g., many of the ratio series). The model was then solved for an initial forecast, and critical variables were examined in the light of current data and anticipated trends. Values for certain variables were chosen (i.e., those variables were exogenized) and those individuals responsible for tuning specific sectors of the model—the consumption equations or the investment block—then started work. The necessary comparison and cross-checking took place over the next few days. Outputs were scrutinized by appropriate personnel: for example, Allen Sinai checked all the financial forecasts. Any variable whose forecast appeared unreasonable was analyzed and revised as necessary. Otto Eckstein also reviewed the complete forecast, providing a final opportunity for questioning and revision. The forecast was usually ready for release less than one week after the government had made its data public.

Add Factors

Because each sector of the model used variables that appeared in other sectors, it was necessary to cross-check constantly to be certain that results were internally consistent, and to make adjustments when they were not. Such adjustments were termed "add factors," and they might be required for any one of a large number of reasons.

If an equation were systematically under- or overforecasting, it could be corrected with an add factor. To determine the need for such an add factor, the "null solution" of the equation was run. The null solution can best be explained through an example. First, using data from, say, 1970–1977, the equation's parameters were estimated. Then the equation was solved using later-known values for both endogenous and predetermined variables (e.g., with data from 1978–1981), and also using the coefficients estimated in the aforementioned period of fit (1970–1977). This null solution thus provided a time series of values for the residual term (e in the examples above). DRI ran the null solution for at least 16 quarters of known data. Equations showing biased errors, or correlated errors, could be adjusted through the use of add factors—alterations in the constant term of the equation.[5]

As Otto Eckstein explained:

---

[5]Since the errors were simply the differences between actual and forecast, statistical tests would determine whether they conformed to the standard "ordinary-least-squares" regression assumption that they were independently drawn from identical distributions with zero mean. If the evidence seemed to contradict this assumption, appropriate adjustments in the constant term would be made; these adjustments were called "add factors."

There may be genuine serial correlation, so the add factors simply phase out the error terms according to formula. Policy, such as the legislated paths for the future prices of natural gas, may be a constraining variable, and add factors must therefore override the model solution. Some errors may be explained by nonrecurring events, such as harsh weather, strikes, or supply disruptions. But in the most difficult case, the surprising terms indicate economic change.

Add factors are also the vehicle for introducing the information content of data not built into the model. Survey evidence on business and household plans, leading indicator signals, and even fragmentary evidence from direct field contact with the actors in the economy will add to forecasting performance. The model is an information-processing device, and all usable evidence, including the enormous body of data with positive information content not included in the model structure, should be considered. For example, it has long been known that filtered results from investment surveys beat any equation for the first few quarters. The construction of add factors is a means of giving weight to such evidence.

Consistency within or between blocks of equations, and with other DRI models, might also demand add factors. These would be incorporated as the month's forecast was developed.[6]

---

[6]For an example of add factors used to make macromodel output consistent with that of a separate, more detailed model, see the "Tire Model" discussion in Arthur Schleifer, Jr., *Data Resources, Inc., The Tire-Production Forecast,* Harvard Business School Case Services, Case 9-183-096.

An Introduction to Econometric Models: Data Resources Inc.

Exhibit 1   The DRI Model of the U.S. Economy

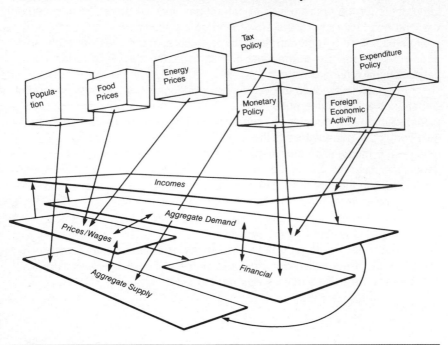

An Introduction to Econometric Models: Data Resources Inc.

Exhibit 2   The DRI Model

	Stochastic Equations	Nonstochastic Equations	Total Equations	Exogenous Variables
Final GNP Demands	64	148	212	83
Consumption	19	30	49	5
Housing	8	12	20	2
Business fixed investment	7	22	29	11
Inventories	6	6	12	4
Government	10	38	48	34
Foreign	14	40	54	27
Incomes	15	37	52	6
Wages, salaries, and supplements	0	6	6	3
Corporate profits	3	6	9	—
Interest	3	1	4	1
Other	9	24	33	2
Financial	112	81	193	46
Monetary and reserve aggregates	8	14	22	8
Interest rates and stock prices	26	1	27	18
Commercial bank loans and investments	6	1	7	2
Flow of funds—households	20	12	32	—
Flow of funds—nonfinancial corporations	25	33	58	10
Flow of funds—mortgage activity	10	12	22	8
Flow of funds—government	3	1	4	—
Flow of funds—commercial banks, savings and loan associations, mutual savings banks, life insurance companies, and others	6	1	7	—
Equity market, inflation expectations, and others	6	3	9	—
Consumer installment credit	2	3	5	—
Supply, capacity, operating rates	6	6	12	5
Prices, wages, and productivity	57	37	94	14
Population Employment, unemployment, and the labor force	9	1	10	14
Industry	112	96	208	6
Production	59	17	76	4
Investment	24	43	67	—
Capital stock	0	32	32	—
Employment	29	4	33	2
Total	375	406	781	174

Source: Data Resources Inc.

An Introduction to Econometric Models: Data Resources Inc.

Exhibit 3   Economic Theory and Specifications in the DRI Model

	Theoretical Foundations	Extensions
Households	Utility maximization	
Consumption	Temporary and permanent income, real and financial assets, relative prices	Variance of income, debt burden, demographic structure, consumer confidence (modeled from macro risks of inflation and unemployment)
Labor supply	Unemployment rate, wages	Demographics composition of the labor force
Wages	Price expectations, unemployment	Temporary and permanent price expectations
Firms	Profit maximization	
Fixed investment	Rental price of capital, stock adjustment	Long- and short-term output expectations, surprises in actual output, cost of capital by financial sources, debt burden, balance sheet optimum, pollution abatement requirements
Inventory investment	Stock adjustment to sales expectations	Errors in sales expectations, capacity utilization, delivery conditions, debt burden
Production	Variable coefficient input-output relations, supply from production functions including energy	Effects of several capacity constraints on output and price
Employment	Output, wage rates, productivity trends	Cyclical productivity swings
Pricing	Material cost, unit labor cost, demand-supply disequilibrium, exchange rate	Vendor performances, stage of processing
Financial institutions	Profit-maximizing portfolio behavior	
Portfolio decisions	Balance sheet, expected own and alternative rates of return and opportunity costs	Modeling of flow of funds of households, corporations, financial institutions
Interest rates	Price expectations, supply and demand of liquidity, sectoral borrowing demands	Segmented short- and long-term markets, competitive equity returns, interrelated portfolio adjustment dynamics
Central bank	Exogenous in policy parameters	
State and local governments	Utility maximization for spending and taxes subject to budget constraint	Optimal revenue combination, demographic structure
Federal government		
Spending	Real full employment values as policy variables	Policy levers for major fiscal instruments
Taxes	Income distribution, activity levels	Rates as policy variables
Rest of world		
Exports	Activity levels and relative prices abroad, exchange rate	World grain reserves, exchange rate response to balance of trade constraint
Imports	Relative prices, exchange rate, input-output relations	Capacity utilization, excess demand, real income

Source: Data Resources Inc.

Bibliography

Note A: An Introduction to Economics

Dornbusch, Rudiger, and Stanley Fischer, *Macroeconomics*, 3rd ed. (New York: McGraw-Hill, 1984). Chapter 2 describes national income accounting in more detail than presented in this note. This is a good reference for the definitions and relationships among the disaggregated components of the national income identity.

Gordon, Robert J., *Macroeconomics,* 3rd ed. (Boston: Little, Brown, 1984). Chapter 2 covers some material that is included in later notes, but pages 46–55 are directly relevant. The list of items included in and excluded from GNP on page 47 is helpful.

Reynolds, Lloyd G., *Macroeconomics: Analysis and Policy*, 5th ed. (Homewood, IL: Irwin, 1985). Chapters 1, 2, and 3 elaborate on the topics contained in this note. Chapter 1 explains economics and the circular flow. Chapter 2 gives a concise discussion of the microeconomic concepts of supply and demand. Chapter 3 defines national output and income and their components. The presentation is elementary and methodical.

Sommers, Albert T., *The U.S. Economy Demystified: What the Major Economic Statistics Mean and Their Significance for Business* (Lexington, MA: Lexington Books, 1985). Chapter 1 has an excellent description of the National Income Accounts with very good graphical presentations of the components of the accounts. It is written by the chief economist for the Conference Board.

Note B: An Introduction to Comparative Political Economy

Bergsten, C. Fred, and Lawrence B. Krause, eds., *World Politics and International Economics* (Washington, DC: Brookings Institution, 1975). Though some of these essays are becoming dated, the introductory framework by Bergsten, Robert Keohane, and Joseph Nye, Jr., is a readable, thoughtful discussion of the interaction of international economics and international politics.

Katzenstein, Peter J., ed., "Between Power and Plenty: Foreign Economic Policies of Advanced Industrial States," *International Organization*, Vol. 31, No. 4, Autumn 1977. This special volume is an excellent collection of scholarly papers specifically on comparative political economy. The introductory and concluding essays by Katzenstein present a useful framework for comparing the other essays on Britain, Japan, West Germany, Italy, and France.

Spero, Joan E., *The Politics of International Economic Relations, 2d ed. (New York: St. Martin's, 1981). The introduction that presents the link between economics and politics and Chapter 1, "The Management of International Economic Relations since World War II," are a valuable survey of international political economy.*

Note C: How to Read Data Exhibits and **Note D: An Introduction to Econometric Models**

Eckstein, Otto, *The DRI Model of the U.S. Economy* (New York: McGraw-Hill, 1983). Most of this book is written for the econometrician concerned with the detailed specification of the model. However, the historical perspective in Chapter 1 and the relationship between theory and econometric models in Chapter 2 are of interest to the general reader.

Intriligator, Michael D., *Econometric Models, Techniques, and Applications* (Englewood Cliffs, NJ: Prentice-Hall, 1978). Brief (two-page) descriptions are given of a number of large econometric models, including DRI (pages 449–451). These models are then compared in a survey on pages 451–459. The remaining parts of the book assume the reader has a good statistical background.

Pindyck, Robert S., and Daniel L. Rubinfeld, *Econometric Models and Economic Forecasts*, 2d ed. (New York: McGraw-Hill, 1981). For those readers who want an introduction to econometrics, this is a good start. The book has many examples and emphasizes forecasting techniques. The mathematics is kept to a minimum, though some calculus is required.

Sommers, Albert T., *The U.S. Economy Demystified: What the Major Economic Statistics Mean and Their Significance for Business* (Lexington, MA: Lexington Books, 1985). For those readers having difficulty interpreting specific data series, this short book provides a wealth of information.

PART II
MANAGING MONETARY POLICY

The three chapters in this section are designed to convey the principles of monetary theory and to clarify the unresolved issues of monetary policy. The principles of monetary theory that describe the supply of and demand for money and their potential effects on the rest of the economy have been known for the half-century spanned by the cases in these chapters. For example, a reduction in the supply of money raises real interest rates, but by how much? During periods of economic stability, the relationships among the variables are fairly predictable.

The difficulty occurs during periods of instability when the traditional patterns are no longer reliable. The U.S. bank failures in the early 1930s, the large-scale export of North Sea oil from the United Kingdom in the late 1970s, and the financial deregulation in the United States in the early 1980s are examples of the economic instability hindering the estimation of traditional monetary relationships. The direction of change suggested by the principles remains the same, but instability in the economic environment adds uncertainty regarding the magnitude of the effect.

The practice of monetary policy changes significantly as policymakers experiment with new methods of monetary control and new objectives. The methods of monetary control change in response to new objectives or a different ideology. The change in the Fed's operating procedure in 1979 to controlling reserves rather than interest rates—an example of the former reason—was driven by the Fed's desire to control inflation. An example of the latter reason was Prime Minister Margaret Thatcher's abandonment of credit controls because they were inconsistent with her free-market ideology. The importance of changing methods is that the outcome is affected not only by the objective, but also by the process; the volatile interest rates following the Fed's change in procedures in 1979 is a clear example.

The greatest changes in monetary policy, however, result from changes in the objectives pursued by the central bank. Initially, the Federal Reserve carved out a narrow task for itself, as described in the case "The U.S. Financial Crisis of 1931." Fifty years later, the Fed was responsible for maintaining the financial health of all U.S. financial institutions, the creditworthiness of Third World debtors, domestic economic growth, price stability, and the competitiveness of American business. Monetary policy is elevated to an objective in itself when countries attempt to hit monetary targets without consideration of the economic consequences.

The four cases chosen for the chapters of this section make no claim to providing a comprehensive overview of monetary policy. The first three cases are representative not of the day-to-day management of monetary policy, but rather of crisis management. They represent three of the most significant changes in the monetary policies of the United States and the United Kingdom. The fourth case on Japanese financial liberalization demonstrates the impact of slow evolutionary changes on the conduct of monetary policy. With these studies one can discuss the political economy questions of how decisions are made, by whom, for whom, for what purpose, and with what consequences.

CHAPTER 2
The Principles of Monetary Policy

The dramatic economic events of the Great Depression provide a clear illustration of basic monetary principles and policy. The case, "The U.S. Financial Crisis of 1931," describes the problems and decisions of the U.S. Federal Reserve Board leading up to the collapse of the international monetary system in September 1931, when the United Kingdom abandoned the gold standard. The monetary causes of the depression and the potential monetary solutions can be analyzed in the context of the constraints imposed by institutions and personalities.

The accompanying note, "Money and the Determination of Income," explains the two basic links of monetary policy known to policymakers of the 1930s. There is, first, the link between the levers of Federal Reserve policy and the stock of money, and, second, the link between the stock of money and the total income generated by the economy. It is important for monetary-policy analysts to realize that the Federal Reserve, like other central banks, could not and cannot completely control the supply of money. Likewise, the relationship between money and income was a matter of dispute then, as it is even today. These two links may be thought of as the supply of and demand for money. The first link, the supply link, is the influence of the Federal Reserve on the "money supply process" as described in the second and third sections of the note. The second link, the demand link, is the "quantity theory of money," since the quantity of money demanded is that which is necessary to support all expenditures in the economy, and hence all income.

The difficult issues for the decision makers on monetary policy were not so much the theoretical issues of how monetary policy worked, but rather the practical issues arising from the conflicts among their objectives and the uncertainty regarding the magnitude of the consequences of their actions. Despite the historical setting, the lessons from this episode of monetary history are still applicable today. For example, central bankers must struggle with the conflicting objectives of tight monetary policy and Third World defaults, accommodating fiscal deficits and renewed inflation, and bailing out poorly managed financial institutions and abandoning their monetary growth targets. Uncertainty always abounds whenever new procedures and objectives are introduced, as we shall see not only in this chapter but also in the next two chapters.

Case
The U.S. Financial Crisis of 1931

On September 21, 1931, Great Britain abandoned the gold standard it had so arduously restored in 1925. The decision capped a long summer of European financial crises. In rapid succession, Austrian, Hungarian, and German banks had lost deposits from foreign and domestic lenders and each nation had resorted to tight controls over foreign exchange and gold movements. During that summer of 1931, British authorities spent $1 billion supporting the value of the pound sterling at the high level it had been given six years earlier. By the end of the summer, it was clear that this effort had failed.

Following Britain's departure from gold, a traumatized world financial community quickly focused its anxieties on the situation in the United States. Foreign holders of dollar deposits in American banks began to doubt that their deposits' value was secure. After all, those who had trusted in the pound sterling as a store of wealth had been dealt a heavy blow on September 21. European investors, businessmen, and central bankers who had dollar deposits in the United States and investments in liquid American assets (mostly short-term bankers' acceptances) sought to convert these assets into gold, anticipating an American crisis. This constituted an "external drain" on the American banking system, since the gold that foreigners obtained had been part of the U.S. banking system's reserves. At the same time, American depositors worried about the status of their bank accounts as well. Bank failures in the first eight months of 1931 had totaled 933; together, these banks had deposits of $640.4 million. In the absence of deposit insurance, bank failures frequently meant devastating losses for depositors. Therefore, as foreigners turned their deposits into gold, Americans who anticipated a possible bank failure converted their own deposits into currency at a rapid pace. This leakage, or "internal drain" from the banking system, also contracted the money supply.

In the weeks following the British abandonment of gold, the internal and external drains became immense. On September 22 alone, $116 million of gold was lost. Between September 21 and October 28, gold outflows amounted to $727 million, over 15 percent of the nation's gold stock. The internal drain resulted in an additional $393 million in currency in circulation during the same period. Banks felt the strain; failures reached 305 in September and rose to 522 in October, an average of about 25

This case was prepared by Daniel Pope, Research Associate, under the direction of Associate Professor Michael G. Rukstad.

each business day. The money supply now shrank more rapidly than in the previous two years of depression. In the second half of 1931, money narrowly defined (demand deposits in commercial banks plus currency in the public's hands) fell by $1.7 billion, compared with a decline of $2.7 billion in the previous two years. The broader money supply measure (including time deposits at commercial banks) fell $4.9 billion (12 percent) in the second half of 1931. Between mid-1929 and mid-1931 it had declined $3.6 billion.

The Federal Reserve System: Structure and History

The U.S. central bank—called the Federal Reserve System—bore the responsibility of responding to the financial crisis of the fall of 1931. The tools at its disposal and the ways in which it employed them had been fashioned by both theory and experience. To understand the Fed's actions in the crisis, we must look at its background.

Establishment of the Federal Reserve System in 1913 ended a period of more than three quarters of a century during which the United States had no central bank. Fear of concentrated power pervaded the new plan as well. The Fed's real business was to be conducted by a dozen Federal Reserve Banks, located in major cities across the country. The Federal Reserve Board in Washington had limited and somewhat unclear powers. The Fed's dispersed power was unique; European central banks concentrated authority in one place. By the time of the Great Depression, the secretary of the treasury and the comptroller of the currency sat on the board ex officio; the president of the United States named six others, one of whom was required to represent the interests of agriculture. No more than one board member could come from any single Federal Reserve District. Even after nearly two decades of operations, the locus of responsibility within the Fed was unclear in 1931, and the Fed's relationship with the president and Treasury Department was also ambiguous.

The uncertain power relationships within the system manifested themselves in each of the ways that the Fed controlled money and credit.[1] Since its inception, the Fed's main tool had been the discount rate it charged for loans to member banks. These loans were secured by short-term commercial loans the member banks had made. Bank assets which could be discounted with the Fed were called "eligible paper." Each Federal Reserve Bank set its own discount rate. Although it had been established that the Federal Reserve Board could overrule a bank's discount rate change and could impose another rate in its place, the board's power

---

[1]One method the Fed uses (infrequently) today to control the money supply was unavailable to it before 1933. Today it can adjust the reserve requirements for member banks, but in its earlier years reserve requirements were set by law and the Fed could not alter them. Indeed, reserve requirements remained constant from 1917 through 1933.

to initiate discount rate changes on its own had not been fully tested and had met with vigorous opposition when the board had ordered a rate change for the Federal Reserve Bank of Chicago in 1927.

In addition to discounting eligible commercial paper, the Federal Reserve Banks also provided funds to commercial banks by purchasing bankers' acceptances. These were types of short-term loans, used primarily in financing international trade, which had been guaranteed by a bank. In practice, the Federal Reserve Bank of New York purchased the vast majority of acceptances. The board could approve or disapprove the New York Fed's proposed minimum acceptance rate (the discount rate it charged banks for buying their acceptances), but New York could charge higher rates than the minimum in their actual purchases. Some board members worried that the New York Fed had gained too much power over credit conditions by its ability to set acceptance rates, but the New York Fed replied that its knowledge of market conditions and the need for rapid responses to new circumstances made it essential that they have this power. Since the 1930s, buying bills of acceptance has ceased to be a significant aspect of Federal Reserve money and credit control.

The final policy instrument of the Fed, open market operations in U.S. government securities, was more controversial than the other two. The 1913 Act had allowed each Reserve Bank to purchase these securities "in accordance with the rules and regulations prescribed by the Federal Reserve Board." This apparently consigned the board to a merely advisory role. These open market operations began haphazardly in 1922 when several Reserve banks purchased substantial quantities of government securities, in large measure as a way to gain interest-earning assets. The next year, the Federal Reserve Board, eager to coordinate these purchases, set up an Open Market Investment Committee (OMIC). The governors of the Federal Reserve Banks of Boston, New York, Philadelphia, Chicago, and Cleveland sat on the OMIC and dealt in securities for a systemwide open market investment account. Benjamin Strong, governor of the New York Fed, dominated the OMIC until his death in 1928. The Federal Reserve Board set guidelines for open market operations and had the right to disapprove of the committee's plans, but the OMIC asserted its rights to buy and sell without detailed interference from the board. In 1930, however, the OMIC's membership was broadened to include the governors of all 12 Reserve banks. It was renamed the Open Market Policy Conference (OMPC).[2] The reorganization diluted the influence of the New York Fed, which had been the most consistent exponent of open market operations.

Of these methods of altering bank reserves, only open market operations in government securities were fully discretionary for the Fed. Member bank borrowing by discounting eligible paper depended on commercial bankers' decisions about their own portfolios. Presumably a lower

[2]Today it is known as the Federal Open Market Committee (FOMC).

discount rate would induce such borrowing and a higher rate would retard it, but the quantity of discounts was up to the member banks who borrowed. The case was much the same for buying bills of acceptance. Normally the New York Fed set acceptance rates and then bought all the bills it was offered at those rates. Rarely did it sell acceptances; it simply let these short-term assets "run off" when they came due. These instruments therefore were passive, as opposed to open market operations in government securities, where the Fed itself decided how much to buy or sell on the open market. Yet, as we shall see, open market operations remained, as it were, under a cloud because of the prevailing banking theory of the era.

Since the structure of the Federal Reserve System was permeated with ambiguity, it is not surprising that leaders of the system sometimes distrusted one another and guarded their authority with great care. For example, Federal Reserve Board member Charles S. Hamlin, a Bostonian whose government service dated back to the Cleveland administration, resented the board's governor, Eugene Meyer, who "seems to regard the board [members] as subordinates and not as equals." Hamlin feared that Meyer was too close to President Hoover and Treasury Secretary Ogden Mills on the one hand, and the New York Fed on the other.[3] Meyer in turn told Hamlin that "He was tired of the constant 'yapping' against the Federal Reserve Bank of New York." However, Meyer too was angered by the New York Fed's independence and by the tight relationship between George S. Harrison, governor of the New York Fed, and leading New York commercial and investment bankers. Moreover, Meyer also distrusted President Hoover's judgment. The president was unwilling "to admit even to himself that there were limits to what he understood and could do."[4] Meyer, whom President Hoover once called "the most valuable man I've got," was intelligent, sophisticated, and dedicated. Given $600 by his wealthy father for not smoking before he reached the age of 21, Meyer cleverly parlayed it into the $50,000 he needed to buy a seat on the New York Stock Exchange. There he became an enormously successful broker and financier. In accordance with plans made in his youth, he withdrew from active business management while still in his forties and entered public service, holding several positions in the agencies responsible for economic mobilization during World War I. In the 1920s he headed the Federal Farm Loan Board and became a recognized expert on agricultural credit. Yet Meyer had no commercial banking experience, and it may even be that his Jewish ancestry further separated him from the banking community with which the Fed had to work.

Divided though they were in role and temperament, Federal Reserve leaders shared a common conception of the purpose of a banking system

---

[3]*Memoranda concerning the Federal Reserve Board taken from the Diaries of Charles S. Hamlin* (Washington, DC: Library of Congress, 1984, microfilm).

[4]Merlo J. Pusey, *Eugene Meyer* (New York: Knopf, 1974), 212.

and of a central bank. With varying degrees of tenacity, they held to the doctrine enunciated in the Fed's Tenth Annual Report (1923):

The Federal Reserve System is a system of productive credit. It is not a system of credit for either investment or speculative purposes. Credit in the service of agriculture, industry and trade may be described comprehensively as credit for productive use. The exclusion of the use of Federal Reserve credit for speculative and investment purposes and its limitation to agricultural, industrial or commercial purposes thus clearly indicates the nature of the tests which are appropriate as guides in the extension of Federal Reserve credit.

The implications of this credo were crucial. The Fed should lend money to member banks for reserves only when those loans (discounts) were collateralized with the right kind of productive credit assets, eligible paper. Open market operations in government securities were, according to the theory, deeply flawed. In the words of Adolf C. Miller,[5] board member from 1914 to 1936, ". . . when the Federal Reserve banks operate as investment banks, by buying investments, they force the member banks of the country also to operate as investment banks by buying investments or loaning against investments or by making loans of the kind here described as loans against real estate."[6] Banks would end up in the precarious position of having long-term illiquid assets to cover their short-term deposit liabilities. Meanwhile, the money the Fed paid for its open market purchases would find its way into inflationary speculation, not increasing output of goods and services.[7] Benjamin Strong and George S. Harrison of the New York Fed dissented from such strong versions of this socalled "real bills" theory of banking, but even they felt that production, not speculation, was the objective of the banking system's activity.

The Fed's adherence to the commercial loans banking theory was reinforced by the legal requirements it faced. Just as other banks had to keep reserves in order to offset their deposit liabilities, so too did the Fed have to hold its own reserves against its own liabilities. The Fed's liabilities were the Federal Reserve notes it issued and the deposits that member banks kept at the Fed; the Fed was required to hold gold equal to at least 40 percent of the value of the notes and 35 percent of the amount of the deposits. At the same time, the Federal Reserve notes also had to be 100 percent collateralized. For this purpose, the Fed had to

[5]Though they shared faith in the commercial loans approach, nevertheless Hamlin considered Miller a mere "time server." (Quoted in Milton Friedman and Anna J. Schwartz, *A Monetary History of the U.S. 1867–1960* (Princeton, NJ: Princeton University Press, 1963), 231.

[6]Lester V. Chandler, *American Monetary Policies* (New York: Harper & Row, 1971), 13.

[7]As Miller put it, "When the reserve system puts money into the market by open market purchases, the money goes eventually to the highest bidder, and inasmuch as the open money market of the country is first and foremost in New York where the great call market is, that is the market to which the Federal Reserve money tends to go. And where it first tends to go it has a tendency to stay." Ibid., 14.

keep either gold or bankers' acceptances or eligible commercial paper equal to the volume of notes it issued. Government securities purchased in the open market could not serve as this collateral. The dual requirement of a 40 percent gold reserve and a 100 percent (gold + acceptance + discounted paper) collateral helped tilt the Fed away from open market securities purchases, since these could not be used as collateral.

Moreover, in crises, the dual requirement for backing Federal Reserve notes might become a real problem. The internal drain from deposits to currency would raise the volume of Federal Reserve notes that needed collateral and the external drain would reduce the Fed's gold reserve. If, in the meantime, the Fed failed to acquire enough commercial paper (either because business conditions had slowed or because it set the acceptance and discount rates too high), it would be forced to use more and more of its gold holdings to collateralize the Federal Reserve notes. The "free gold" in the Fed (gold which was not required as reserves or note collateral) would shrink, and the Fed might face its own liquidity crisis and threaten the United States' ability to maintain the gold standard.

The Fed's Experience during the Prosperous 1920s

The Federal Reserve System therefore was constrained by theory and by law to orient its activities away from open market operations and towards discounting commercial loans made by its member banks. During the 1920s, before the onset of the Great Depression, the wisdom of the Fed's stance seemed validated by its own experience and by the performance of the banking system and of the economy as a whole.

The decade had begun with a severe recession in 1920–1921, and although the Fed's medicine was distasteful, the economy's recovery was swift. Expansive credit policies in 1919 and an external drain of gold had left the Fed's free gold at $131 million in March 1920, down 77 percent from the previous June. The Fed's response had been a sharp rise in discount rates, from 4.5 percent to 6 percent in March and then to 7 percent in June 1920. These rates were not lowered until May 1921. In the meantime, the American economy underwent a severe recession. Industrial production fell by about 33 percent from February 1920 to March 1921; wholesale prices declined by 44 percent between May 1920 and June 1921. In assessing the slump, the Fed maintained that the causes had been largely external (and indeed, the recession *had* been international in character) and that the Fed's own conservative policies had ameliorated the severity of the cycle, avoided financial panic and collapse, and saved the gold value of the dollar. These were seen as the valid and necessary objectives of a central banking system.

The rapid and sustained recovery from the recession of 1920–1921 was perhaps the best advertisement for the Fed's doctrines and practices. The following two-year period was highly expansive; the Fed's index of industrial production soared by 63 percent between the July 1921 trough and the May 1923 peak. Until 1929 the American economy remained generally prosperous. Prices were stable and only two minor recessions (in 1923–1924 and in 1927) interrupted the nation's steady economic growth. This was, as Milton Friedman called it, "The High Tide of the Federal Reserve System."

The Fed's response to the two mild recessions of the mid-1920s was in keeping with its goals and procedures. Convinced that "artificially easy money" during an economic downturn would merely flow into inflationary speculation, the Fed pursued a cautious path. Nevertheless, during each of these downturns the Fed did purchase government securities on the open market, thereby exerting downward pressure on interest rates. Its reasons for open market purchases are instructive, however, and reveal another constraint the system felt. During these recessions, the United States was running a balance of payments surplus and was receiving an inflow of gold. Perhaps the main victim of this imbalance was Great Britain. During the 1923–1924 recession, the pound sterling was still floating. In order to restore the pound to its pre-World War I parity with the dollar (as was eventually done in May 1925), the United States would have to experience higher inflation rates and lower interest rates than Great Britain. This would increase the value of the pound sterling relative to the dollar. In 1927, having restored the gold standard and facing endemic payments deficits, the United Kingdom still needed these conditions in order to stay on gold. Benjamin Strong of the New York Fed was a close friend of Montagu Norman, governor of the Bank of England, and was eager to adjust American policies to ease the problems of the British. Indeed, Governor Strong held one crucial conference with central bankers of major European powers in 1927 without even notifying most Federal Reserve Board members. In short, then, the willingness of the Fed to make open market securities purchases during the recessions of the mid-1920s stemmed from international considerations, not from a desire to stimulate the domestic economy.

Federal Reserve Policies in the Depression: 1929–1931

The onset of the Great Depression in 1929 shifted the constraints facing the Federal Reserve System but did not drastically alter its philosophy. Nevertheless, the Fed responded to circumstances and it can be said that changing circumstances modified some economic policy makers' ideas.

In the early months of the depression, the Fed supplied bank reserves through sizable purchases of government securities on the open market—$341 million between November 12, 1929, and January 28, 1930. Discount rates at the New York Fed dropped from 6 percent to 4.5 percent and bill-buying rates were cut by comparable amounts. At the January 1930 meeting of the Open Market Policy Conference, New York argued for more open market purchases, but the majority of the committee was persuaded that credit was already easy to obtain and that more purchases were therefore undesirable. This division between Harrison at the New York Fed and the governors of most of the other Reserve banks was to continue for most of the next two years. There were few more open market securities purchased, and although discount and bill-buying rates were lowered (with the New York Fed's rate reaching 2 percent in December 1930), member bank borrowing from the Fed shrank by 83 percent between July 1929 and September 1930.

In the fall of 1930, a wave of bank failures indicated growing strains on the financial system. Small banks in farm regions were especially vulnerable when farmers, whose crop prices had plunged, were unable to repay their loans. In December 1930, however, the Bank of the United States, with over $200 million in deposits, failed, the largest bank failure in American history. The Bank of the United States was an ordinary commercial bank but carried a name that made some think it was a government institution. Its collapse further weakened faith in the financial system. The "internal drain" of deposits to currency was underway; the ratio of all commercial bank deposits to currency held by the public slipped from 11.54 to 10.57 between October and December 1930 and continued to slip rather steadily through 1931 and 1932. Largely at the prodding of Harrison, and with general support from Governor Meyer, the OMPC and the board approved of some further open market purchases of government securities which were undertaken in the summer of 1931. Bill-buying and discount rates had been lowered that spring, provoking one economist to write to Harrison: "It is an historic event— the lowest rate [1.5 percent] that has ever been established by a central bank in any country. It signifies, I suppose, that we are experiencing the worst depression that has ever been recorded."[8]

At the August 1931 meeting of the Open Market Policy Committee, Harrison presented the case for authorizing $300 million more in open market purchases to add reserves to the member banks. Reducing the discount and bill-buying rates had done no good; there was adequate free gold in the Fed, and although interest rates on the very highest grade of bonds were low, the bond market in general was depressed. There were few buyers for railroad bonds in particular, and the bonds which sat in the asset portfolios of commercial banks were priced too low. Harrison agreed that immediate large open market purchases would probably not alleviate this condition, but he wanted the Fed to be able to jump into the market if it appeared that purchases "might encourage or facilitate recovery."[9] But the conference authorized only $120 million, and the board approved the lower figure. Notably, however, the previously cautious Adolf Miller joined with Eugene Meyer on the board in advocating

[8]Chandler, op. cit., 156.
[9]Ibid., 157.

"bold, experimental use" of open market purchases, "even though it might only serve to demonstrate the limits . . . of such a policy."[10]

The open market purchases approved in August were not implemented because of the onset of the crisis brought about by Britain's leaving the gold standard. Instead, the crisis provoked the response best explained by Walter Bagehot, the English banking theorist.[11] As Bagehot pointed out, "Periods of internal panic and external demand for bullion [precious metal] commonly occur together. . . . The holders of the reserve have, therefore, to treat two opposite maladies at once—one requiring stringent remedies, and especially a rapid rise in the rate of interest; and the other an alleviative treatment with large and ready loans."[12] Therefore the prescription for "this compound disease" was "very large loans at very high rates." Bagehot added that carrying off this feat required "the greatest delicacy, the finest and best skilled judgment . . . to deal at once with such great and contrary evils." Within days of the British announcement, the Fed acted to stop the external drain of gold. It raised the minimum bill-buying rate from 1 percent to 1.25 percent; by October 16, three further increases had occurred and the rate stood at 3.125 percent. For over two weeks prior to this, however, the discount rate had remained unchanged. The New York Fed's directors and officers had first met on October 1, 1931; rather than increase the discount rate, they decided not to act, fearing that foreigners would interpret a rate increase as a sign of panic. After the meeting, however, Eugene Meyer pointedly told Harrison that he had expected New York to raise the discount rate. A week later, the New York bank did act, setting the rate at 2.5 percent, and the Federal Reserve Board unanimously approved. And on October 16 the New York discount rate was put at 3.5 percent.

The Bank of France played a large role in inducing the Federal Reserve to tighten credit as it did in October 1931. At the onset of the crisis the month before, the Bank of France held dollar deposits of $600 million in the United States. Fiercely committed to the gold standard, the directors of the Bank of France had long doubted the wisdom of holding foreign exchange (i.e., dollars)—subject to devaluation and other disasters—when they could hold gold instead. To induce the French to keep their deposits in the United States and not to export gold, interest rates in the United States had to rise. The French were not subtle about this. Governor Moret of the Bank of France wired to Harrison in September 1930, "I take this opportunity to call your attention to the consequence under present circumstances of the very low level of money [interest] rates."[13] During October, French pressure for higher interest rates and for American monetary conservatism increased. "France evi-

[10]Ibid., 158.
[11]Walter Bagehot, *Lombard Street* (London: Henry S. King, 1873).
[12]Ibid., 56.
[13]Chandler, op. cit., 170.

dently feels," noted Hamlin in late November, "that it put a pistol at Governor Harrison's head and made him promise to be conservative and not to permit inflation."[14] Yet Harrison unequivocally denied that he had made any deal with the Bank of France for it to keep its deposits in New York in exchange for tight money. Nevertheless, it is true that gold exports to France subsided in late 1931 while the Fed kept its interest rates up and then accelerated in early 1932 as American discount and acceptance rates were lowered. In the face of a more expansionary policy during the fall crisis, gold exports to France might have counteracted the Fed's efforts to pump reserves into the system.

French gold withdrawals were only part of the more general, though less immediate, problem of maintaining the gold standard in America. This was an unquestioned goal among American policy makers both at the Fed and in the Hoover administration. Yet, if the external drain were not eventually halted, the Fed would at some point lack the gold needed to cover reserve and collateral requirements. In the long run, the United States might not be able to convert dollars to gold at the fixed rate of $20.67 per fine ounce.

In raising interest rates in the face of the Fall 1931 crisis, the main decision makers at the Fed believed not that they were instituting a reign of tight money but that they were putting an end to a period of abnormal ease. They hoped that raising the discount and acceptance rates would increase open market interest rates for commercial loans. This would have the beneficial effect of increasing commercial banks' cash flow and earnings. If anything, banking experts maintained, the higher rates would induce banks to make more, not less, money available to accommodate business transactions. As believers in the commercial loan theory, they put little faith in the alternative policy of open market purchases of government securities. At best, the central bank would be injecting money that would sit as idle, excess reserves in the nation's commercial banks. At worst, the funds would be used for speculation and would breed inflation, not recovery. Even Harrison and Meyer, the members most sympathetic to open market securities operations, agreed in the fall of 1931 that buying high-priced, low-interest government bonds would do little to help raise the depressed prices of railroad and other corporate bonds that were dragging down the asset portfolios of the nation's banks. Open market operations were, they felt, a shotgun approach where careful aim was required.

The Fed's policy in October of raising discount and acceptance rates and refraining from open market purchases won broad business approval. The *Commercial and Financial Chronicle*, for example, felt that it was high time for such moves: "A valuable lesson has been learned . . . that business revival and confidence in security values cannot be brought about by adventurous methods, that is, extending the volume of banking

---

[14]*Diaries of Charles S. Hamlin*, op. cit., Vol. 19, 16a.

credit and increasing the volume of the currency. Federal Reserve easy money policy involved both . . . when there was not the least justification for it in the needs of trade. It is well that these unpardonably low rates are now to be withdrawn."[15] Even *Business Week*, which generally favored easy money policies, conceded that the danger of a $2 billion gold outflow "undoubtedly justifies the advance in money rates."[16]

By November and December, monetary conditions seemed to be easing. The gold outflow stopped and some was even imported. Although the public did continue to convert deposits into currency, this internal drain on the banking system flowed much less rapidly in November and December 1931 than in the weeks immediately following the British departure from gold. The Fed actually felt confident enough to buy about $230 million of government securities on the open market during December 1931 (largely to supply funds for Christmas shopping and to finance a Treasury deficit), but it quickly sold $200 million by mid-January. Bank failures in the last two months of 1931, though still high, were down 36 percent from the previous two months. The economy was still in the doldrums and the financial system still fragile at best, but it looked to many as if the crisis were over and the worst had passed.

[15]*Commercial and Financial Chronicle*, Oct. 10, 1931, 2305.
[16]*Business Week*, Oct. 28, 1931.

Note
Money and the Determination of Income

Money and Its Significance

The importance of money stems from the relationship that has been observed between changes in the supply of money and changes in key macroeconomic indicators of performance such as nominal GNP, real GNP, unemployment, inflation, interest rates, balance of payments, and exchange rates. The broadest performance indicator on this list is nominal GNP since it includes or is closely related to the other variables. Table 1 gives a cross-national comparison of the relationship between the growth of nominal GNP and the growth of the money supply for a number of

Table 1

| | Country | Years | # | Average Annual Compound Rates | | |
				Nominal GNP Growth (%)	Money Supply Growth (%)	Velocity (%)
1	Japan	1921–28	7	1.4	2.8	−1.4
2		1928–31	3	−6.8	−4.6	−2.2
3		1952–71	19	14.5	16.2	−1.7
4		1971–77	6	15.0	14.0	1.0
5	U.S.	1922–29	7	5.0	3.0	2.0
6		1929–33	4	−14.4	−7.0	−7.4
7		1950–69	19	6.4	3.1	3.3
8		1969–79	10	9.8	6.6	3.2
9	Germany	1949–55	6	14.1	13.7	0.4
10		1955–57	2	9.2	5.6	3.6
11		1960–70	10	9.1	7.8	1.3
12		1970–78	8	8.3	10.3	−2.0
13	France	1950–57	7	11.2	12.4	−1.2
14		1960–69	9	10.2	9.4	0.8
15		1970–78	8	13.3	15.6	−2.3

Source: For Japan, data are collected in Bruce Scott, John Rosenblum, and Audrey Sprout, *Case Studies in Political Economy: Japan 1854–1977* (Boston: Harvard Business School Division of Research, 1980). For the United States, see Appendix A of this book and the *Economic Report of the President, 1981.* For Germany, see Harvard Business School cases: Germany (A) 9380120 and Germany (B) 9383113. For France, refer to Bruce Scott and Audrey Sprout, *National Industrial Planning: France and the EEC* (Boston: Harvard Business School Division of Research, 1983).

This note was prepared by Associate Professor Michael G. Rukstad.
Copyright © 1983 by the President and Fellows of Harvard College
Harvard Business School note 9-384-114

Table 2

Country	Years	Nominal GNP	$\cong$	Real GNP	+	Inflation
Germany	1949–1955	14.1%	$\cong$	12%	+	2.1%
France	1970–1978	13.3	$\cong$	4	+	9.3

Source: Bruce Scott and Audrey Sprout, *National Industrial Planning: France and the EEC* (Boston: Harvard Business School Division of Research, 1983).

historical periods. In this note we will use the narrowest definition of money, M-1, which is defined as currency (coins and notes) plus demand deposits (checking accounts). Other definitions of money are described in the note "Implementing Monetary Policy" in Chapter 3.

There are three general observations one can make regarding the relationship examined in Table 1.

1. *Nominal GNP growth is closely related to money supply growth over long periods of time.* Fluctuations in nominal GNP growth or income growth, which are often referred to as business cycles, are related to (some would say, caused by) fluctuations in the rate of growth of money, though causality has not yet been proven.

If we eliminate the very short time periods shown in Table 1 (Lines 2, 6, and 10), then nominal GNP is within approximately two percentage points of money supply growth—sometimes above it for a particular country (Line 4), sometimes below it (Line 3). A notable exception is the United States, which for 29 years has had nominal GNP growth exceed money supply growth by over three percentage points (Lines 7 and 8). Even if we consider one particular time period such as the 1970s (Lines 4, 8, 12, and 15), nominal GNP growth in some countries is above money supply growth (Japan and the United States) and below it in others (France and Germany). In a later section of this note, The Effect of Money on the Economy, we will have more to say on the difference between these variables, known as the growth rate in velocity (see Table 1). This difference will be crucial to policy makers who are concerned with controlling the economy over time horizons that are shorter than those in Table 1.

2. *The rate of growth of the money supply does not determine how nominal GNP growth is divided between its two components: real output and inflation.* For example, the 14.1 percent nominal GNP growth of Germany after the war (Line 9) consisted of 12 percent output growth and 2.1 percent inflation. Compare that division of nominal GNP with the 13.3 percent nominal GNP growth of France in the 1970s (Line 15), which consisted of 4 percent output growth and 9.3 percent inflation (see Table 2).

As we will find in the section, The Effect of Money on the Economy, we need another tool in order to explain the division of nominal GNP into its components of real output growth and inflation. Does this mean that the growth in the money supply has nothing to do with the rate of inflation? No, since we can see from some extreme examples that the following observation also holds.

Table 3

| Brazil | Average Annual Compound Growth Rates | |
Period	General Price Index	Money Supply
1950–1954	12%	18%
1955–1959	31	32
1960–1964	57	68
1965–1970	20	31

Source: Philip A. Wellons, "Brazil in the Mid-1970's: Fast Growth or Slow?" *World Money and Credits: The Crisis and Its Causes* (Boston: Harvard Business School Division of Research, 1983), 80.

3. *Significant, sustained inflations (or deflations) have occurred only when the money supply is increasing (or decreasing) rapidly.* For example, in the case of Brazil shown in Table 3, we see the relationship between the rate of growth of the money supply and the inflation component of nominal GNP. High money growth and high inflation tend to move hand in hand. In this sense, inflation is a monetary phenomenon, but short-term inflation can occur by other means, as we will see in several cases throughout this book.

The relationship between increases in general price levels and increases in the money supply is even more evident if we examine a country that is suffering from hyperinflation, in which *monthly* price increases proceed at double-digit rates or higher. For example, in Germany between August 1922 and November 1923, prices increased at an average rate of 322 percent per month while the money supply increased 314 percent per month.[1]

Conversely, sharp decreases in the money supply over a period of years are usually associated with sharp decreases in prices. Two examples of deflation are Japan (Line 2 of Table 1) and the United States (Line 6 of Table 1) in the Great Depression. In both cases, the money supply declined.

These observations highlight the apparent links between money and critical macroeconomic variables. The goals of government policy are often stated in terms of the performance of these variables, which are largely outside direct government control. Monetary policy is an attempt to change economic performance by changing the supply of money—a variable which is more directly controllable by government. If there were not a direct, predictable relationship between money supply and performance variables, money would lose its significance.

The remainder of this note will focus on the process of money creation, the institutional setting of monetary policy, and the extent to which money affects the economy. Throughout this note we will describe the current theory and practice of monetary policy in order to facilitate

[1]Phillip Cagan, "The Monetary Dynamics of Hyperinflation," in Milton Friedman, ed., *Studies in the Quantity Theory of Money* (Chicago: University of Chicago Press, 1956), 26.

later discussion. The historical setting of monetary policy during the depression is described in the preceding case, "The U.S. Financial Crisis of 1931." The institutional framework and terminology of the U.S. central bank, the Federal Reserve System, will be used in the later sections of this note, but the general principles described here apply to other central banks as well.

The Money Supply Process

As we noted above, the core elements of all definitions of money are currency and demand deposits. What is the origin of this money? The common conception that the government creates it is not accurate, though the government does have some control. As we will see, the creation of money arises from the interactions of three players: the public, banks,[2] and the government.

Currency is printed by a branch of the national treasury in sufficient quantities to satisfy all the demands by the public for cash withdrawals from banks. In fact, currency does not become part of the money supply (as we measure it) when it is printed, only when it is withdrawn from a bank and held by the nonbank public (i.e., held by anyone except the banks and the government). Even though the government tries to control the total money supply, it does not try to control the proportion which is held in the form of currency or demand deposits.

Demand deposits, however, are not created by the government— they are created by commercial banks, though the central bank will try to influence the quantity of demand deposits created, as we will see in the next section. In order to understand how banks create demand deposits, we will first consider a simple economy that has only one bank. Later we will consider the effect of multiple banks in a banking system.

Imagine, first, that the public is holding a certain quantity of currency, say $113.64, and that there are no demand deposits. Hence the money supply equals the quantity of currency, $113.64. (The choice of $113.64 will simplify the other examples in this section.) Then, imagine that the public decides for convenience to deposit 88 percent of the currency ($100) with the bank and in return the bank issues $100 of demand deposits. The money supply is still $113.64, but now it consists of $100 in demand deposits and $13.64 of currency in the hands of the public. *It is essential to understand that demand deposits are accounting book entries and are not physical objects.* They are promises or legal obligations of the bank to make a payment in the future when the owner of the check instructs the bank to "pay to the order of. . . ." Thus the bank creates money by creating promises.

---

[2]For simplicity, in this section we will consider commercial banks as the only financial intermediary creating money and ignore other financial institutions such as savings and loans, mutual savings banks, and credit unions, although the reasoning can be generalized to include them as well.

Table 4   Simplified Balance Sheet for an Average U.S. Commercial Bank

Assets		Liabilities	
Cash and Reserves	10%	Demand Deposits	25%
Government Securities	20	Time and Savings Deposits	55
Loans	55	Other Liabilities	12
Other Assets	15	Capital Account	8
Total	100%	Total	100%

Source: *Federal Reserve Statistical Release* H.8 (510), Dec. 23, 1982.

At this point, it will be useful to have in mind a simplified balance sheet of a modern commercial bank. Table 4 shows the major categories of assets and liabilities and the approximate percentage distribution of these categories for an average modern bank in the United States. Due to different banking laws in different countries and the rapid innovation which has occurred in banking, this percentage distribution varies across countries and over time.[3]

We can further simplify Table 4 by considering just one bank in our simple economy which has received the $100 of currency from the public in exchange for an equal amount in demand deposits. The balance sheet would be:

Assets		Liabilities	
Cash	$100	Demand Deposit	$100

The $100 of initial demand deposits issued by the bank will start a process of multiple demand deposit creation by the entire banking system so that the money supply will grow larger than the original $113.64. This process is driven by the bank's desire to make loans in order to earn interest. The loan which the bank authorizes to a borrower will not be in cash, but will be a promise by the bank to pay on the demand of the borrower; that is, a demand deposit or checking account in the name of the borrower. If, in our example, the bank wanted to make a $50 loan, then the new balance sheet would look like:

Assets		Liabilities	
Cash	$100	Demand Deposit	$100
Loan	50	Demand Deposit	50
	$150		$150

[3]The trend on the asset side of the balance sheet since the Great Depression is toward smaller percentages of total assets being tied up in nonearning assets such as cash and reserves and a higher percentage invested in high-yielding loans. The trend on the liability side has been a significant reduction in the percentage of liabilities in demand deposits and a significant increase in the percentage of funds in time deposits. In particular, a new era of liability management began with the introduction of the large negotiable time deposits in 1961, called certificates of deposit (CDs), which has allowed banks to compete for market funds instead of passively waiting for customers to deposit their funds in checking or savings accounts.

Notice that the bank did not "lend out its cash" by creating a new asset (a loan) and reducing an old asset (cash). Rather, the bank created a new asset (a loan) and created a new liability (a demand deposit) of the same magnitude merely by the stroke of an accountant's pen. Even though the new demand deposit is no more tangible than a promise or a legal right (which it is), the money supply has increased by that amount and money is created. But if a $50 loan is profitable and easily created, wouldn't a $500 or a $5,000 loan be better? It would be more profitable, but there are limits to the loans a bank may authorize.

In reality, the bank is limited in the quantity of money it can create because assets equal to a certain percentage of its total deposits must be set aside in the form of cash and reserves and cannot be lent out. Thus the total amount of demand deposits is limited by the amount of cash and reserves available to support the demand deposits. A simple rule describing bank lending behavior is that a bank will lend out an amount equal to that which it does not have to keep. A bank must keep sufficient cash and reserves in order to satisfy (1) the government's reserve requirement, and (2) the public's demand for cash withdrawals.

All governments require banks to set aside a certain percentage of their deposits as reserves in an account called *required reserves*. Required reserves may be thought of as vault cash earmarked for a special purpose, though usually they are kept in the form of deposits with a Federal Reserve Bank. The purpose of the required reserve is not to ensure the safety of the demand deposits in the event of a "run on the bank," rather it is to limit the quantity of loans and hence demand deposits that the bank can create. In fact, banks are legally unable to use the required reserves to satisfy demands for cash withdrawals.

In order to understand how required reserves can affect the amount of demand deposits that a bank can create, first consider an extreme example. If banking law required banks to have a 100 percent reserve against demand deposits, banks would be unable to make any loans in the manner described above. Any attempted increase in demand deposits (and hence in money supply) must be accompanied by an equal increase in reserves, but all available assets are earmarked to required reserves. The balance sheet for the bank in our example with a 100 percent reserve requirement would be:

Assets		Liabilities	
Required Reserves	$100	Demand Deposits	$100

since all available cash has been earmarked as required to support demand deposits. However, all banking systems today are "fractional" reserve banking systems, which require less than 100 percent reserves against demand deposits. The maximum required reserve ratio for the largest demand deposit in the United States is 14 percent, but the ratio decreases significantly with smaller sizes of demand deposits as well as for other types of liabilities.[4] In this case, the balance sheet would be:

Assets		Liabilities	
Required Reserves	$14	Demand Deposits	$100
Cash	86		

Now that the government's legal reserve requirement has been provided for, the bank must also consider the public's demand for cash withdrawals. When a depositor writes a check, the bank must provide cash either to the depositor or to another bank where the check is redeposited. If the check is redeposited in the same bank, no cash is lost since only the owner of the demand deposit has changed. Since there will continuously be both deposits into and withdrawals from this bank, demand deposits will randomly fluctuate around $100 in our example. The bank must have sufficient cash on hand in order to cover the possibility that cash withdrawals temporarily exceed cash deposits.

Therefore banks will hold *excess reserves*, which are deposits at the Federal Reserve Bank in excess of the legally required reserves. These funds are held to avoid borrowing or liquidating short-term assets in order to supply the public's demand for currency. Today, excess reserves usually amount to no more than 1 percent of a bank's total reserves. Since vault cash and excess reserves do not earn interest for a bank, the bank must weigh the cost of forgoing interest income on the cash and reserves against the borrowing cost of obtaining additional cash and reserves if it should run short.

In our numerical example, we will now consider other banks in order to trace the process of multiple demand deposit creation by the entire banking system leading to a money supply larger than the original $113.64. The first bank which received the initial $100 in cash and created $100 in demand deposits must set aside $14 for required reserves. In addition, after the bank calculates the probability of cash withdrawals and the relative cost of funds, the bank will set aside, say, an additional $1 for excess reserves. Thus a bank may lend an amount equal to that which it does not have to keep, or in this case $85. The loan and new demand deposits are recorded below:

Assets		Liabilities	
Required Reserves	$14	Demand Deposits	$100
Excess Reserves	1		
Cash	85		
Loan	85	Demand Deposit	85
Total	$185	Total	$185

[4] As of 1980, all depository institutions in the United States are subject to reserve requirements. Prior to that time, it only applied to banks that were members of the Federal Reserve System. However, all states had reserve requirements, though not as strict.

The money supply has now increased by $85 to a total of $198.64 (= $113.64 + $85). The borrower, a farmer, took out the loan in order to purchase $85 of fertilizer with a check drawn on this bank. The bank will reduce its cash (asset) and its demand deposits (liability) by $85, when the cash is transferred to the fertilizer dealer, so the balance sheet now is:

Assets		Liabilities	
Required Reserves	$14	Demand Deposits	$100
Excess Reserves	1		
Loan	85		
Total	$100	Total	$100

Finally, the dealer will deposit 88 percent of the $85 (approximately $75) in a second bank and keep the remaining 12 percent (approximately $10) in cash. (We are assuming a constant currency-to-deposit ratio of 12/88.) The story now starts over. The second bank must keep 15 percent of the $75 of demand deposits as total reserves (14 percent for required and 1 percent for excess reserves) and it can lend out the remaining 85 percent ($63.75) so that the balance sheet for the second bank after the check for the second loan has cleared will be:

Assets		Liabilities	
Required Reserves ($75 × 14%)	$10.50	Demand Deposits	$75
Excess Reserves ($75 × 1%)	0.75		
Loan	63.75		
Total	$75	Total	$75

The total money supply after this second loan is now $262.39 (= $113.64 + $85 + $63.75) compared to the initial $113.64. But this is not the end of the process—more deposits and more loans will be made by other banks, which will further increase the money supply.

This story may be schematically summarized by Table 5. This table illustrates the *relending process* that caused the initial money supply of $113.64 to be expanded fourfold to $454.56. At each stage, some of the initial money "leaked out" of the relending stream. It is these *leakages* into cash in the hands of the public and into reserves in the vaults (and on the books) of the Federal Reserve Banks that limited the amount of money that could be created. The larger the leakages, the smaller the amount of loans and hence new money that can be created, and vice versa.

The money supply process described in this section and schematically illustrated in Table 5 can be presented even more compactly in the *money supply equation*:

Table 5

Bank Number	Money Supply	Demand Deposits	Loans

1 $113.64 —— 88% —→ $100.00 —— 85% —→ $ 85.00

12% Cash Leakage → $13.64   15% Reserve Leakage → $15.00

2 $ 85.00 —— 88% —→ $ 75.00 —— 85% —→ $ 63.75

12% Cash Leakage → $10.00   15% Reserve Leakage → $11.25

3 $ 63.75 —— 88% —→ $ 56.10 —— 85% —→ $ 47.68

12% Cash Leakage → $ 7.65   15% Reserve Leakage → $ 8.42

4 $ 47.68 ————————→ etc.

Totals	$454.56	$54.56	$400.00	$60.00	$340.00
	Total Money Supply	Total Currency	Total Demand Deposits	Total Reserves	Total Loans

$$M = \text{(money multiplier)} \times B$$

$$M = \frac{1}{\text{Total \% of leakages}} \times B,$$

where M is the narrow definition of the money supply[5] (currency plus demand deposits) and B is the *monetary base* or *high-powered money* (currency plus total reserves held at the Federal Reserve Banks). In our example, the monetary base is the $113.64 with which we started.[6]

---

[5]There is a money supply equation for all broader definitions of money, but each has its own money multiplier which is dependent on other factors as well.

[6]This is distributed as $54.56 of currency ($454.56 − $400) and $60 of reserves ($400 − $340) at the end of the process (see the bottom of Table 5). Notice that this totals $114.56 instead of $113.64. The discrepancy is due to an approximation used in calculating the multiplier (i.e., 88% × 15% ≅ 13%).

The *money multiplier* is dependent on the percentage of total leakages at each stage in the relending process. If leakages increase, the multiplier decreases, and vice versa. We examined three sources of leakages: (1) required reserves, (2) excess reserves, and (3) demand deposits being converted into currency. These leakages are sensitive to a number of factors including interest rates. An increase in interest rates should decrease the excess reserves and currency conversion, and vice versa.

In our example, the total percentage of the money supply that "leaked" into cash at each stage was 12 percent (see Table 5). The percentage of the money supply that "leaked" into reserves at each stage was 13 percent (approximately equal to the 88 percent that continued on into demand deposits and the 15 percent of demand deposits that leaked into reserves, or 88% x 15%). Thus the total leakages at each stage were 25 percent, which gives us a money multiplier of 4.

As we mentioned at the outset of this section, the money supply arises from the interaction of the public, banks, and the government in determining the money multiplier and the monetary base. We focused in depth on the role of the banks. In the next section, we will examine the role of the central bank in controlling the money supply.

The Central Bank and Monetary Control

Besides private financial intermediaries such as banks, the other major actor in the financial markets is the central bank, a governmental institution. The primary function of the central bank is to manage the growth of bank reserves and hence money supply in order to allow for a stable expansion of the economy. A related function is to be a lender of last resort in order to prevent bank failures. This means supplying reserves to the banking system when there is a financial panic resulting in a "run on the bank." Finally, the central bank performs a number of administrative services for commercial banks and government such as check clearing, insuring currency, financial regulation, and serving as both the bankers' bank and government's bank.

In order to implement its primary task of controlling the money supply, today there are three tools which a central bank can use to change bank reserves:

1.   A change in the *reserve requirement ratio.*

2.   A change in the *discount rate.*

3.   *Open market operations.*

A change in the reserve ratio is seldom used but potentially very powerful. A decrease in the ratio will increase the money multiplier, and vice versa. The discount rate is the interest rate that the central bank charges banks that need to borrow additional reserves.[7] It is an administered interest rate set by the central bank, not a market rate; therefore much of its importance stems from the signal which the Fed is sending to the financial markets. As a result, short-term market interest rates tend to follow its movements.

The most frequently used tool today is open market operations (OMO), which is the buying and selling of government securities by the Fed. In the simplest story, when the Fed purchases a security from the public and gives money in return, it increases the money supply in the hands of the public. Conversely, the money supply decreases when the Fed sells a security. This is illustrated below:

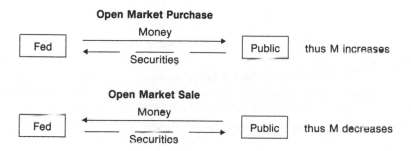

Notice that the terms "purchase" and "sell" refer to actions of the Fed, not the public. For example, an open market purchase means the Fed is buying but the public is selling. More realistically in the case of an open market purchase of securities by the Fed, the seller of the security[8] receives from the Fed a check drawn on the Fed itself. When the seller deposits it in his bank, the bank automatically has an increased reserve balance with the Fed. Thus the new reserves can be used to support additional loans. Through this process, the money supply has increased.

The Federal Reserve and other central banks control the quantity of high-powered money, i.e., currency and total reserves. These are the liabilities of the central bank that are held as assets by the public. Since the central bank is a banker's bank, we would expect to find assets similar to those held by other banks—cash, investments, and loans. The gold stock may be thought of as being roughly analogous to "cash." Its importance has diminished as the international monetary system has moved from a gold standard to a gold-exchange standard to a floating-exchange system established in the 1970s. The other assets are loans to member banks called "discounts" and investments in government securities and other financial instruments.

The balance sheet of the Federal Reserve System has changed sig-

---

[7]In addition to borrowing from the Fed, banks may also borrow from other banks, which is called the *federal funds market*. This is a misnomer since federal funds do not refer to funds of the federal government, rather to funds available for short-term interbank lending.

[8]Actually the Fed carries out its open market operations only with the nation's largest security dealers and banks, and not with the public at large.

Table 6   Federal Reserve Balance Sheet

Assets	Liabilities

Federal Reserve Credit Outstanding
  Bills Discounted
  Bills Bought
  U.S. Government Securities
  Other Credit Outstanding
 	
Gold Stock
 	
Other Assets
	Money in Circulation
	
	Member Bank Reserves
	  Required Reserves
	  Excess Reserves
	
	Other Liabilities

nificantly since its establishment in 1914. As an example, Exhibits 12 and 13 in Appendix A give selected assets and liabilities of the Fed between 1919 and 1941. The categories are summarized in Table 6. This information allows one to assess *how* the Fed was able to increase high-powered money (liabilities) since there must have been an offsetting asset. If the Fed increased bank reserves through open market operations, U.S. government securities would increase, since the Fed would exchange its reserves for a government security held by the public. Alternatively, if the Fed increased bank reserves by loans to member banks, we would notice an increase in Bills Discounted. Notice that reserves may also increase when there is a gold inflow, and vice versa. In fact, if a country were on a rigid gold standard, high-powered money would change only when the gold stock changes.

The Effect of Money on the Economy

Unlike the preceding two sections describing the institutional process of creating money, the effect of money on the economy has been very controversial over the years. The two main schools of thought emerging from the controversy are the Monetarist and the Keynesian approaches, with the former ascribing a larger role to money in determining GNP. The difference between the schools, often exaggerated, are in degree and relative emphasis. Most of their differences can only be resolved empirically—that is, by statistically testing claims of each side against the historical record.

The common feature of both explanations, however, is that money affects the aggregate demand for all goods and services in an economy. Hence money (at least partially) determines nominal income or nominal GNP, but only in conjunction with aggregate supply. Notice in the following graph that an increase in the money supply increases nominal income (from $P_0 \times Q_0$, which is the shaded area, to $P_1 \times Q_1$). However, the division of any increase in nominal income into its price and quantity component is determined by aggregate supply, which neither Monetarist nor Keynesian monetary theories explains since both are theories of aggregate demand. Milton Friedman called this "the central common defect of the two approaches as theories of short-run change in nominal income."[9]

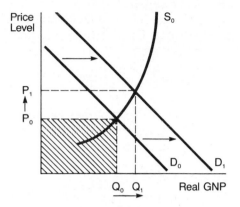

If the aggregate supply curve were vertical at Q_0, then all of the increase in aggregate demand from D_0 to D_1 would be reflected in increased prices to P_2 as in Case A. If the aggregate supply curve were horizontal at P_0, then all of the same increase in aggregate demand would be reflected in increased output to Q_2 as in Case B below.

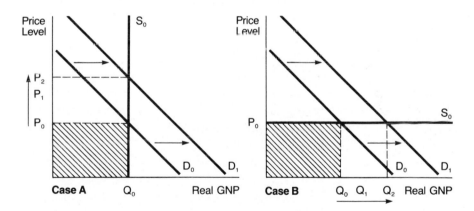

In addition to inflation and real GNP, other key economic variables such as the components of GNP, interest rates, and exchange rates are affected at different speeds through various channels as changes in the supply and demand for money are transmitted to nominal income. Therefore the short-term macroeconomic adjustment to performance problems depends critically on the transmission process.

[9]Milton Friedman, "A Theoretical Framework for Monetary Analysis," *Journal of Political Economy*, (March/April 1970): 222.

Monetarist Approach

One approach to the question of how money affects the economy is the monetarist quantity theory approach, which has a long tradition dating back to the 1600s with Jean Bodin's and later David Hume's explanation of the classical quantity theory. Today Milton Friedman is the patriarchal leader of the monetarist school, which has enjoyed a renaissance since the late 1960s. This note will focus on the monetarist approach since this basic framework was familiar to economists and policy makers during the Great Depression.

The modern "quantity theory of money" asserts that changes in the money supply are the most important causes of changes in nominal GNP. A stronger position held by some monetarists is that the two changes are proportional—that is, a 10 percent increase in the money supply will bring about a 10 percent increase in nominal income. These positions can be summarized by the *quantity theory equation*:

$$M \times V = P \times Q,$$

where M is money, V is velocity, P is the general price level, and Q is real output or real GNP. You will recognize P × Q as being nominal income or nominal GNP. Velocity is defined to be the average number of times in a year that a money stock is spent in purchasing final goods and services (GNP). It can be calculated by dividing (P × Q) by M; therefore the quantity equation in one sense is nothing more than an accounting identity. To breathe life into the equation and transform it into a theory of how nominal income is determined, we must explain velocity.

Monetarists believe that velocity is stable. This does not necessarily mean that they believe velocity is constant—it may change but it changes slowly and predictably, they say, so we need only to understand its long-term trends. Recall from the note "How to Read Data Exhibits" in Chapter 1 that we can take an equation that is the product of levels of variables, such as M × V = P × Q, and approximate it as an equation that is the sum of rates of change of those same variables:

$$\frac{\Delta M}{M} + \frac{\Delta V}{V} \cong \frac{\Delta P}{P} + \frac{\Delta Q}{Q}.$$

Table 1 on page 71 recorded values for $\Delta M/M$ and for $\Delta GNP/GNP$ ($\cong \Delta P/P + \Delta Q/Q$) so we could solve for the percentage annual change in velocity for each example.

The reason for a rising trend of velocity is that individuals and firms are willing and able to economize on money holdings (i.e., to become more efficient at turning over a given inventory of dollars by respending them more quickly), and of course, velocity will decline for the opposite reason. Velocity is closely related to the demand for money holdings. If, for example, there is a greater demand for holding wealth in the form of money, then money is not being spent on goods, services, or other assets. Hence the increased demand for money means a decreased velocity or rate of spending, and vice versa.

Financial innovations and changes in spending and payments patterns have led people to economize on cash balances (to demand less money). A financial innovation such as the introduction of new interest-earning assets—new stocks, bonds, money market funds, savings and time deposits—has encouraged people to keep their wealth in those attractive alternatives since it can be quickly converted back to money. The liquidity of those assets is further enhanced as secondary markets for trading those securities improve, such as well-developed stock, bond, and futures markets. This can be a particularly important structural improvement in less-developed countries, since the risk of holding interest-earning assets is reduced. Moreover, the increased attention devoted to corporate cash management has also served to increase velocity. Likewise, credit cards have allowed consumers to make transactions while keeping smaller cash balances than they previously held. Certain changes in spending and payments habits will also increase velocity. Shorter pay periods for wages and receivables, automatic tellers and longer banking hours, and automatic bank deposit and payments have induced both firms and households to hold less cash.

A second reason people might be willing to economize on cash balances (to demand less money) is high interest rates. An individual holding a lot of money in times of high interest rates suffers a lost opportunity if he does not transfer some of that money to interest-earning assets. Thus the potential for additional interest income serves as a catalyst for economizing on the money balances. Once these economies are learned, they will probably be continued by the new spending habits. For example, the recent period of high interest rates in the 1970s encouraged people to seek out liquid, high-return assets such as money market mutual funds to store their wealth during the month and then transfer funds at the end of the month to a checking account to pay rent, credit card, and other bills. The funds did not rest idly in the checking account (i.e., money holdings or cash balances) during the month, but were quickly "turned over"—i.e., turned over to the managers of the high-yielding money market fund, thus freeing the money to be used in the purchase of goods or services (possibly investment goods in this case).

The conclusion drawn from such observations is that velocity increases with increases in interest rates and vice versa. Both monetarists and Keynesians agree on this principle but disagree on the magnitude of the effect. Monetarists believe that even large changes in the interest rate will change velocity only slightly and Keynesians would argue that the induced change in velocity is significant. Again, the difference is one of degree, so this is an empirical question which can be answered only by analyzing the historical record. The policy prescription one chooses will depend on answers to such empirical questions.

The implication of a stable velocity is far-reaching: a change in nominal income can result only from a change in the money supply which is controlled by the central bank. Thus, say the monetarists, the supply and demand for money is the only market we need to consider when trying to explain business cycles—there is no need to examine consumption, investment, government, or net foreign expenditures, since these are not the sources of variations in nominal income. These components may be changing individually, but movements in the interest rate and relative prices will adjust individual expenditures so that in the aggregate, the total spending is determined by the supply and demand for money. Moreover, a stable velocity also implies that the demand for money will not be changing abruptly, which might also change nominal income. Hence money supply is the only determinant of nominal income. In this case, the business cycles are induced by the errors of policy makers adversely manipulating the money supply.

Monetarists assert that money supply exerts a direct influence on nominal GNP in so many ways that one cannot delineate all of them. They reason that individuals who suddenly have additional money would want to reduce their holdings of money and increase their spending on other financial assets and goods and services. Recall that increased spending on financial assets is just a transfer of wealth from one form (money) to another form (financial assets). But monetarists are concerned only with the total increase in spending on final goods and services (GNP) and not with the particular allocation of the spending among the components of GNP. The allocation of spending among the financial assets and the components of GNP will be determined by the free market mechanism—individuals will simply choose those items with the most attractive relative price. We can summarize the monetarist mechanism for transmitting changes in the money supply in GNP:

$$\left. \begin{array}{l} \text{Money supply} \\ \text{Money demand} \end{array} \right\} \quad \rightarrow \quad \begin{array}{l} \text{Spending on all} \\ \text{goods, services, and assets} \end{array} \quad \rightarrow \quad \text{GNP.}$$

The note in the next chapter will contrast the monetarist transmission mechanism with the Keynesian mechanism, which depends on interest rates as the channels for affecting GNP.

Discussion Questions for Case and Note

1. Evaluate the goals of the Federal Reserve in the 1920s and in the early 1930s. Why might the Fed have pursued these goals? What alternative goals might have been pursued?
2. What factors were responsible for the collapse of the money supply between 1929 and 1933?
3. What actions might you, as a member of the Federal Reserve, have taken in the financial crisis of the early 1930s? When?
4. Did monetary forces "cause" the Great Depression?

Bibliography

Dornbusch, Rudiger, and Stanley Fischer, *Macroeconomics*, 3rd ed. (New York: McGraw-Hill, 1984). Chapters 8 and 9 contain a more detailed discussion of the material in the note to this chapter. Chapter 8, "The Demand for Money," elaborates on the income velocity of money (pages 269–274). Chapter 9, "The Money Supply and the Fed," derives the money multiplier and explains the monetary base (pages 281–300).

Friedman, Milton, and Anna J. Schwartz, *A Monetary History of the United States, 1867–1960* (Princeton, NJ: Princeton University Press, 1963). A scholarly, monetarist interpretation of the "high tide" of the Federal Reserve System in the 1920s and the "great contraction" from 1929–1933 is presented on pages 240–419. A summary of this argument can be found in Milton Friedman, "The Control of Money," in *Capitalism and Freedom* (Chicago: University of Chicago Press, 1962), 45–51.

Gordon, Robert J., *Macroeconomics*, 3rd ed. (Boston: Little, Brown, 1984). The evolution of the quantity theory of money from the classical statement of the theory to the modern monetarist reinterpretation is developed on pages 469–479 of Chapter 15. Chapter 16 explains the money supply process using the "T" accounts as in the note to this chapter. There are also examples of the Fed's control of money from the 1930s to the 1980s.

Reynolds, Lloyd G., *Macroeconomics: Analysis and Policy*, 5th ed. (Homewood, IL: Irwin, 1985). Chapter 6, "The Supply of Money," is an elementary account of the money supply process covering the same topics as this chapter.

Ritter, Lawrence S., and William L. Silber, *Money*, 5th and rev. ed. (New York: Basic Books, 1985). For a brief, lively, elementary introduction to money supply and demand, see Chapters 2 and 3 of this very readable book.

CHAPTER 3
The Era of High, Volatile Interest Rates

There can be little doubt that the financial environment of the early 1980s has undergone a fundamental transformation unparalleled since the Great Depression. Interest rates have been at the highest, most volatile level in history. Failures, mergers, and competition from new entrants have plagued financial institutions. The opportunities and problems of the financial marketplace have become more international than in any previous period.

All of these events coincided with the tenure of Paul Volcker as chairman of the Federal Reserve Board of Governors since 1979. Some of the turbulence may have been inevitable, given the second oil shock and its aftermath. However, one might postulate that the landmark changes in monetary policy and institutional structure undertaken by the Federal Reserve and the Congress in late 1979 and early 1980 were a major contributing factor.

The case in this chapter, "Paul Volcker and the Federal Reserve: 1979–1982," describes the first three years of a monetary policy experiment. The Fed changed the focus of its operating procedure for controlling the money supply from targeting interest rates to targeting reserves. It also intensified its commitment to hitting its preannounced monetary growth targets. At the same time, Congress initiated widespread deregulation of financial institutions. These changes were followed by the worst U.S. postwar recession and a very rapid disinflation. The case encourages discussion on the best strategy and implementation of monetary policy, the effect of deregulation on its conduct, the causes of the recession and disinflation, and the competitive implications of the recent changes in monetary policy for financial institutions.

To aid in understanding the context of the Fed's monetary policy, a note, "Implementing Monetary Policy," is included in this chapter. The note extends the monetary principles discussed in the previous chapter to include the determination and consequences of changes in interest rates. Interest rates are an important mechanism for the transmission of changes in monetary policy to economic performance. The note also presents a taxonomy of alternative monetary strategies. A monetary strategy is a statement of an objective and the operational procedures to achieve that objective. As the note illustrates, a change in the means by which the Fed conducts monetary policy can have as significant an effect on the financial environment as a change in its objectives.

Case
Paul Volcker and the Federal Reserve: 1979–1982

Through the spring of 1979, the U.S. economy was rapidly deteriorating as a result of the second oil shock. Inflation during the first six months of the year exceeded a 13 percent annualized rate, the first time it had surpassed a double-digit rate since the aftermath of the first oil shock of 1974 (see Exhibit 12 at the end of this case). The renewed surge in inflation arising from this "supply-side" shock presented a major problem for G. William Miller, chairman of the Federal Reserve Board. Miller continued to advocate a monetary policy, known as "gradualism," that attempted to reduce inflation by gradually reducing money growth rates, yet trying not to induce a recession by high interest rates. Miller believed that the Fed's interest rate instrument, the federal funds rate,[1] should be "managed" within a narrow range (1/2 of 1 percent) in order to maintain economic stability (see Exhibit 1).

By the summer of 1979, both the economic and political landscape had changed for the Carter administration. The president had to confront severe internal dissension within the White House, which abruptly came to a head during mid-July. In a major reorganization touched off by the resignations of Attorney General Griffin Bell and Energy Secretary James Schlesinger, and the forced resignations of Health, Education and Welfare Secretary Joseph Califano, Transportation Secretary Brock Adams, and Treasury Secretary W. Michael Blumenthal, Miller moved from the Fed to the Treasury post. In his 1½ years as Fed chairman, Miller, the former Textron chairman, had been regarded as soft on inflation. Miller was not the president's first choice for Treasury secretary. It was only after Chase Manhattan Bank Chairman David Rockefeller and General Electric Chairman Reginald Jones turned Carter down that he called on Miller, a recognized Carter team player, to take over Treasury.[2]

Faced with an imminent reelection campaign, Carter saw the perceived failure of his economic policies to reduce inflation as a major impediment to his reelection hopes, and many people felt that his administration was in disarray. To say that the economic situation had deteriorated was an understatement. Facing the second oil crisis, an accelerating inflation rate, continued weakness of the U.S. dollar (see Exhibit 14), soaring gold prices, and a need to restore confidence in the U.S.

This case was prepared by Associate Professor Michael G. Rukstad, with the assistance of Jeff Singer, MBA 1984.
Copyright © 1985 by the President and Fellows of Harvard College
Harvard Business School case 9-386-055
[1]The rate of interest charged by banks for overnight interbank loans.

[2]*Fortune*, Sept. 10, 1979, 62.

economy, President Carter sought a strong Fed chairman who would be tough on inflation and also boost private sector morale. He offered the position to Paul Volcker on July 24, 1979.

Paul Volcker

Volcker came to the chairman's post with a great deal of experience. At the time of his appointment, he was in his fourth year as president of the Federal Reserve Bank of New York, the Fed's largest and most powerful member bank, and a member of the Fed's Open Market Committee (FOMC). From 1969 to 1974, he served as Treasury under-secretary for monetary affairs. While in this post, he was a key architect of the 1971 devaluation of the U.S. dollar and the switch from fixed to floating exchange rates in 1973. Volcker had also been a vice president of the Chase Manhattan Bank from 1965 to 1969 and a Senior Fellow at Princeton University's Woodrow Wilson School of Public and International Affairs in 1974–75.

Volcker's Treasury post, his experience at the New York Fed, and his record in the private sector enabled him to develop an independent reputation and a constituency of his own both in Congress and in the business community that he brought to the chairmanship. He had a wide network of contacts in central banks, finance ministries, and commercial banks throughout the world; President Carter hoped that their confidence in Volcker would lead to a halt of the dollar's decline when he was appointed.

Earlier in 1979, Volcker had challenged the FOMC's gradualist approach to monetary policy and reducing inflation; he argued for tighter monetary policy to fight the rampant inflation plaguing the United States' economy. He advocated allowing the federal funds rate, and interest rates in general, to rise above the Fed's current bounds, but his proposals were defeated by a majority of FOMC members.

Now, as chairman, Volcker would have the opportunity to play a more influential role in molding Fed policies. His first priority in the new job was clear: restore price stability. In a 1978 speech he asserted that "inflation can only persist over a long period of time with excessive monetary growth ... we must control the money supply and reduce its growth."[3] The challenge he faced was to restore economic stability with low inflation while not letting monetary policy be so restrictive that the economy would fall into a deep recession. It was this challenge that led him to leave the New York Fed and his home in New York City, and to take a major salary cut (from $116,000 to $57,500), in order to lead the Federal Reserve Board of Governors in Washington, DC. His recent

[3]*Fortune*, Sept. 10, 1979, 62.

predecessors had been unable to restore economic growth with a sustainably low inflation rate. He knew that all eyes were now on him, both in the United States and abroad.

1979: The Year Things Got Out of Control

The U.S. economy began 1979 on a positive note. The GNP growth rate during 1978 had been stronger than anticipated and unemployment had fallen (see Exhibits 9 and 11), although consumer prices continued to rise (see Exhibit 12). The government had been trying to slow economic growth gradually in order to reduce inflationary pressures; the continued strength of both GNP and inflation in 1978 seemed to indicate that gradualism was not working. The Carter administration imposed voluntary wage and price controls in October 1978 and introduced a "lean and austere"[4] budget for fiscal 1980. The budget was intended to slow economic growth without precipitating a recession.[5]

The principal economic objective for Carter in early 1979 had become the fight against inflation, "the most complicated and intractable and corrosive problem of them all,"[6] according to the president. Carter recognized that reducing inflation would likely require slowing economic growth and would lead to higher unemployment. While the inherent risks and costs of battling inflation were evident, the alternative approaches to implementing a monetary policy consistent with that objective were still being debated in the White House and at the Fed. Several members of the administration argued that gradual reduction of money supply growth was still the best policy; these advisers believed that sharply higher interest rates (which would be necessary if money growth slowed quickly) would lead to even *higher* inflation because higher interest rates would increase business operating costs, which in turn would be passed on to consumers in the form of higher prices. On the other hand, the gradual approach to decreasing money supply growth appeared to have failed in the past and advocates of a much tighter monetary policy argued that such a major policy shift was the only way to break inflationary expectations, despite the risk of triggering a recession. President Carter came down on their side.

Two factors contributed significantly to the surge in inflation and inflationary expectations during 1979. The major cause was a second oil shock. Although 1979 was supposed to be a moderate year on world oil markets—with preannounced OPEC price increases of 14.5 percent over the year—the situation changed rapidly. The Shah of Iran's fall from

---

[4]*New York Times,* Jan. 23, 1979, 1.
[5]Ibid.
[6]*New York Times*, Jan. 7, 1979, Sec. 12, 1.

power in January, followed by the Ayatollah Khomeini's capturing control of Iran, soon brought havoc to the energy markets that was reminiscent of the initial energy crisis of 1973–1974. Oil production in Iran fell from six million bbls./day in 1978 to next to nothing during the months of revolutionary upheaval.[7] The void left by Iran in oil export markets was filled to some degree by Saudi Arabia and other OPEC members' increased production, but a shortfall of two million bbls./day remained. The impact on oil prices was devastating, sending oil from $12.70/bbl., in January, to $18.00/bbl. by midyear.

The second problem was a continued weakness in the U.S. dollar, which, after recovering slightly from its late 1978 low,[8] faced renewed pressure during the summer of 1979 and was falling toward its previous low (see Exhibit 14). Due to the heavy demand for imports in the United States, the weak dollar continued to push U.S. consumer prices higher. Furthermore, its weakness was a reflection of investors' lack of confidence in the U.S. economy and existing policies to combat inflation.

By late summer, the CPI was rising at an underlying rate of over 13 percent per annum; even higher rates of increase in producer prices indicated that further consumer price inflation was forthcoming. Unemployment, too, had taken a turn for the worse, breaking the 6 percent barrier in August.

Volcker Takes Over

Given this performance and continued pessimistic outlook, Volcker believed that the Fed had to take a much more aggressive stand against inflation by putting the brakes on money supply growth. Using traditional tools of monetary policy (open market operations, reserve requirements, and changes in the discount rate), Volcker had to decide whether the Fed should continue to focus on the federal funds rate or to shift its focus to the reserve aggregates in order to meet its M-1 targets.[9] Under Miller's leadership, the Fed had tried to achieve its annual money growth rate targets, announced annually since 1975, while concurrently keeping the federal funds rate within a narrow band. However, in the first four years' experience with money targeting, money growth was outside the target range about half the time, while the federal funds rate seldom went outside its bounds (see Exhibit 1).[10] Miller had feared that allowing interest rates to exceed Fed targets would trigger a recession.

[7]See Richard Vietor, *Carter, OPEC & "Big Oil": 1979*, HBS case 9-382-116.

[8]See the Chapter 16 case, "The Decline of the Dollar: 1978."

[9]For details on the choice of instruments and targets, see the following note, "Implementing Monetary Policy."

[10]Lawrence Roos, "Monetary Targets—Their Contribution to Policy Formation," Federal Reserve Bank of St. Louis, *Review* (May 1979): 13.

Early in his tenure as chairman, Volcker signaled his inclination to increase interest rates in order to meet his money supply goals: "Short-term interest rates are not likely to decline as long as the inflation rate continues high,"[11] he told Congress in late August. Although many people felt Volcker had the power to direct the route the economy would take, others argued that Volcker's power as Fed chairman would be less than publicly perceived. It is the Fed Open Market Committee (FOMC) that sets Fed policy. The FOMC is comprised of the seven governors of the Federal Reserve Board (FRB), appointed for fourteen-year terms by the president, and five of the twelve Federal Reserve Bank presidents. Volcker had only one vote in twelve. As chairman of the FOMC, he "is first among equals in setting the monetary policy of the U.S.," according to one of his colleagues, Monroe Kimbrel, president of the Federal Reserve Bank of Atlanta. "He does not make unilateral decisions affecting credit targets."[12]

Volcker realized that he had been given a mandate from the president and Congress to lead the Fed toward a more restrictive monetary policy. Other countries, among them the United Kingdom, had already adopted a strong monetarist philosophy in order to reduce inflation[13] (see Exhibit 3). After his appointment, it became apparent that the FOMC was willing to risk a "modest recession"[14] to prevent even higher inflation and a lower U.S. dollar. The Fed increased the federal funds rate band that Miller had resisted raising, and increased the discount rate to a record 10.5 percent during Volcker's first month as chairman; these changes in turn put pressure on commercial banks. Chase Manhattan boosted its prime lending rate to a record 13 percent in early September, and other banks followed.

In the first week of October, Volcker went to Belgrade, Yugoslavia, for an IMF meeting. The U.S. commitment to fighting inflation came under fire at the conference because of the continued rapid expansion of money and credit in the United States.[15] The Fed was exceeding its 1979 money growth targets and the economy remained surprisingly strong. His international colleagues emphasized how they too were suffering as a result of weak U.S. economic policies. The West Germans, in particular, presented a stark message to Volcker, Treasury Secretary Miller, and other members of the U.S. contingent. When inflation hit a "resurgent" level of 5 percent during the summer, the West German Bundesbank intervened in the markets and caused short-term interest rates to rise a full point. Bundesbank President Otmar Emminger was determined to get inflation back under 3 percent. One Dusseldorf banker articulated his

[11]Federal Reserve Bank of New York, *Quarterly Review* (Autumn 1979): 44.
[12]*Forbes*, Sept. 17, 1979, 98.
[13]See the Chapter 4 case, "The United Kingdom under Thatcher."
[14]*Forbes*, Sept. 17, 1979, 98.
[15]Federal Reserve Bank of New York, *Quarterly Review* (Summer 1980): 50.

colleagues' concerns to the Americans at the conference: "You must do something about your inflation. You must follow our example and get rid of negative [real] interest rates."[16]

The exchange rate problems of a weak dollar and a strong mark, the Germans felt, were not due to their actions but were a result of weak U.S. anti-inflation policies. "Carter's policy of gradualism simply will not work,"[17] one Frankfurt banker asserted. The managing director of the Bundesbank, Wilfred Guth, left Volcker with the message, "It would help if the United States would take further steps to restrain expansion of money and credit."[18] Earlier in the conference, in reaction to an assertion by Miller during a speech that U.S. inflation would drop to a "single digit" rate by the end of the year, Guth had warned: "If these numbers do not materialize, we will be in deep trouble."[19] Having been "sternly lectured" by his European peers,[20] Volcker returned suddenly to Washington before the Belgrade meeting had ended.

The Shift in Policy: October 6, 1979

On October 6, Volcker called an emergency weekend meeting of the FOMC. The media were reluctant to give up coverage of the Washington visit of Pope John Paul II. The Fed Public Affairs Director Joe Coyne assured the skeptical media, "Long after the Pope is gone, you'll remember this."[21] The press release announced that the Fed would henceforth hit its money growth targets by "placing greater emphasis in day-to-day operations on the supply of bank reserves and less emphasis on confining short-term fluctuations in the Federal-funds rate. To help achieve better control over the reserve base, it will now be necessary—within broad limits—to permit wider fluctuations of that rate if so determined by market forces."[22] Concurrently, the Fed increased the discount rate a full percentage point to 12 percent and introduced a marginal reserve requirement on some managed liabilities. The Fed funds rate, it was agreed, would be permitted to vary within a range of 11.5 percent to 15.5 percent (see Exhibit 1). The discount rate would be managed flexibly to discourage excessive member bank borrowing.[23] All actions were approved unanimously by the FOMC.

[16]*New York Times*, Oct. 7, 1979, Sec. 3, 17.

[17]Ibid.

[18]Ibid.

[19]*New York Times,* Oct. 4, 1979, Sec. 4, 5.

[20]*Fortune*, Nov. 19, 1979, 48.

[21]*Institutional Investor* (May 1984): 140.

[22]Federal Reserve Bank of Atlanta, *Economic Review* (March/April 1980): 9.

[23]Ibid., 7.

The ramifications of this policy change were far-reaching. It was, observers said, the most significant change in the Fed's operating procedures in 50 years; in 1932, in the midst of the Depression, the Fed had abandoned its "real bills" doctrine and started massive open market purchases of government bonds.[24] The substantive procedural issue—changing from a federal funds rate instrument to a nonborrowed reserves instrument—would have a profound impact on financial markets and business operations. The need for action was evident if the Fed were going to achieve its intermediate money target. From April to September, the six-month growth rate (annualized) for M-1 and M-2 had been 10.5 percent and 12 percent, respectively. The respective 1979 target ranges were 3-6 percent and 5-8 percent.

Some observers, however, wondered how significant a policy shift it was. One governor, Henry Wallich, who had been on the board for five years, defended the Fed's record and argued that "the Fed can't take its eye off the interest rate entirely."[25] Volcker, who described himself as a "pragmatic monetarist,"[26] had everyone second-guessing how serious the Fed's intentions were.

But the FOMC was indeed determined to meet its 1979 money growth targets. At the October 6 meeting, the FOMC set its target monetary growth rates for the October-December interval at 4.5 percent for M-1 and 7.5 percent for M-2 (annualized). However, the FOMC was "willing to tolerate somewhat *slower* growth to offset the earlier excesses."[27] With the Trading Desk at the New York Fed operating under its new instructions, the money supply growth was brought under control during the fourth quarter of 1979. M-1 grew at a 3.2 percent annualized rate in the quarter, while M-2 grew at a 6.8 percent rate. For the entire calendar year, the FOMC managed to strike within or close to its targets.

During that same quarter, the prime lending rate was raised from 13.5 percent to a record-high 15.5 percent, and the U.S. dollar rose over 3 percent in value against the German mark, French franc, and Dutch guilder. Critics complained that, despite the Fed's implementation of a tighter monetary policy , neither inflation nor economic growth was slowing down. Defying forecasters' predictions, the U.S. economy remained resilient; initial estimates put real GNP growth over 2 percent for 1979 and inflation was still double-digit. The Fed reminded the critics that the "lagged effect" of monetary policy on inflation would not impact prices until approximately one year later.[28]

Early in the new year, Volcker continued to use every opportunity to reinforce the FOMC's commitment to its objective. Testifying before

[24]See the Chapter 2 case, "The U.S. Financial Crisis of 1931."
[25]*Fortune*, Nov. 19, 1979, 47.
[26]Ibid.
[27]Federal Reserve Bank of New York, *Quarterly Review* (Summer 1980): 50.
[28]Ibid., 15.

the House Banking Committee on February 19, 1980, Volcker reiterated his position: "Let there be no doubt; the Federal Reserve is determined to make every reasonable effort to work toward reducing monetary growth from the levels of recent years, not just in 1980, but in the years ahead."[29] He expressed satisfaction with money and credit growth since October 6, but admitted that "we cannot conclude from those results that our procedures ensure that money growth will always remain tightly on a narrow path over short periods of time, or that that is necessarily wholly desirable."[30] Volcker announced the 1980 target ranges of 4–6.5 percent for M-1 and 6–9 percent for M-2 (see Exhibit 5).

By March 1980, the Fed still appeared to be achieving its money targets, but interest rates rose to unprecedented heights—led by a federal funds rate that soared an additional seven percentage points in the first few months of the year. The question became: How high would Volcker let interest rates go?

Credit Controls Imposed in March 1980

The turmoil evident in the credit markets between October 1979 and March 1980 naturally concerned Volcker. Long-term rates rose to levels that would seem almost prohibitive for bond issues (see Exhibit 2). Investors were suffering large losses from long-term bond holdings; a well-publicized example was a $1 billion IBM bond issue in early October 1979, at a time when rates were beginning to rise. Underwriters' losses on the issue were between $10 million and $15 million, but these losses were relatively small compared to those incurred by the financial institutions that bought the bonds. The market value of the bonds had fallen to about $790 million by late February 1980. Major losses such as this made investors reluctant to finance new long-term bond issues, even if the borrower were willing to pay 15 percent or 18 percent to secure the funding. The household sector was also not inclined to invest in bonds at 14 percent when money market funds were yielding 13 percent and were essentially risk-free.[31]

Commercial banks, like the bond market, also suffered a major shock. The Ayatollah Khomeini's repudiation of Iran's debt jolted the banking system's foreign loan departments, since the deposed shah had borrowed $5 billion for Iran during the final five years of his reign. Conflict between the United States and Iran escalated further on November 4, 1979, when the U.S. Embassy in Iran was taken over by Muslim "students" loyal to the Ayatollah. Concurrently, it was rumored that Iran was

[29]Federal Reserve Bank of Atlanta, *Economic Review* (January/February 1980): 13.
[30]Ibid.
[31]*Fortune*, Mar. 24, 1980, 57–59.

also planning to move its money out of the United States. President Carter, faced with these threats from Iran, froze an estimated $8 billion worth of Iranian assets in the United States on November 14. The freeze, which also applied to overseas subsidiaries of American banks, led to lawsuits as well as grave concerns in the $500 billion Eurodollar market because Eurodollar deposits were assumed to exist independent of national regulations.

As a result of the instability in the bond and Eurodollar markets, borrowers were forced to look to short-term commercial paper and commercial bank loans. Volcker became concerned when he saw commercial loans growing at a 20 percent seasonally adjusted annual rate in January and February, compared to the range of 6-9 percent established by the FOMC for bank credit growth during 1980. This particular range had been determined by estimating the rate of loan expansion that could be accommodated within the money growth targets.

The boom in bank credit, despite the record-high interest rates, led to calls for credit controls in order to bring down interest rates. While Volcker personally did not favor credit controls, he felt the growing pressure from the White House and the financial community to take further action. The prospect of even higher interest rates along with persistent inflation sent both politicians and businesspeople looking for a solution. The financial markets were in a state of panic.

On March 14, 1980, President Carter, in response to worsening inflation scenarios and explosive demands for credit despite high interest rates, announced a five-point proposal to try to control inflation. His proposal included, as one of the planks, instructions to the Fed to regulate credit under the Credit Control Act of 1969. The act allows the president to authorize the Fed's Board of Governors to "regulate and control any and all extensions of credit . . . for the purpose of preventing or controlling inflation generated by the extension of credit in an excessive volume. . . ."[32]

The Board of Governors complied by introducing a voluntary Special Credit Restraint Program, directed toward banks in particular. Banks were asked to stop selling securities in order to raise funds to finance the surge in loan demand. The growth of their loans in 1980 was to be held to 6-9 percent. They were to avoid financing speculative holdings of commodities or precious metals, takeovers or mergers, or backup lines of credit for large borrowers. They were also urged to maintain adequate credit for smaller correspondent banks.

In addition, the Fed imposed a 3 percent surcharge on certain discount window borrowings by large banks as a further disincentive to credit expansion, and a 15 percent special reserve requirement was introduced on increases in assets of money market mutual funds. Finally, the marginal reserve requirement on large certificates of deposit and other

---

[32]Federal Reserve Board of Governors, *The Federal Reserve System* (September 1974): 90.

"managed liabilities" that had been established in October 1979 was raised from 8 percent to 10 percent, and its scope was expanded to include nonmember banks.[33]

The ostensible reason for the controls was that credit demands had continued to grow too quickly and were a cause of inflationary pressures. The program was to complement the Fed's basic monetary tools. By holding loan expansion at a level supported by money supply growth, the Fed's monetary policy tools, it was argued, would be given time to hold down growth in bank reserves and thus money growth.[34]

While the Special Credit Restraint Program was voluntary, the Fed certainly wielded powers of moral suasion over the banks. If the Fed felt its money growth targets were being threatened by overly aggressive bank loan expansion, the FOMC could use a conventional operating tool, such as raising mandatory reserve requirements, to curb the excess growth. This, in turn, could possibly hurt the banks more than compliance with the voluntary program.

Financial Innovation and Deregulation

While the Carter administration and the Fed were imposing additional financial regulations through credit controls, major legislation to deregulate financial institutions, supported by both the White House and the Board of Governors, was being enacted in Congress. Financial deregulation was imperative after a decade of high inflation and high interest rates that had led to changes in spending and savings behavior.

Financial institutions were competing for savers' funds by offering innovative products that circumvented the interest rate ceilings imposed by Regulation Q.[35] These financial innovations included such products as ATS (automatic transfer service), NOW (negotiable order of withdrawal), and MMMF (money market mutual fund). Some of the funds thus acquired were shifted among accounts within financial intermediaries, while the remaining funds left financial intermediaries in search of direct borrowers.[36]

The borrowers were competing directly for savers' funds by offering record-high interest rates. Thrift institutions and savings and loan institutions (S&Ls) were particularly vulnerable to the loss of funds to Trea-

[33]Federal Reserve Bank of Atlanta, *Economic Review* (May/June 1980): 18–19.

[34]Ibid.

[35]Regulation Q established the legal interest rate ceiling that prohibited the payment of interest on checking accounts and imposed 5.25 percent and 5.5 percent limits on savings deposits at commercial banks and savings and loan institutions, respectively.

[36]See Columns 3 and 6 of Exhibit 7 for the growth of ATS, NOW, and MMMF. Notice in Columns 2 and 8 the decline in traditional demand and savings deposits affected by Regulation Q.

sury bills and other direct borrowers, a process known as disintermediation. They were being pinched by the rising cost of their remaining funds
and the lower returns on their (mostly) fixed-rate mortgages. Thus many
financial institutions, facing severe competitive pressures due to a changing economic environment, lobbied Congress to revamp existing regulations so they could compete.

These changes also affected Volcker and the Fed's implementation
of monetary policy. The concern was whether the Fed was targeting the
appropriate monetary aggregate and how that aggregate should be defined.
In February 1980, as a result of the innovations in the financial markets,
the Fed introduced new definitions of the monetary aggregates:

M-1A: Old M-1, less demand deposits held by foreign banks.

M-1B: M-1A + checkable deposits at all financial firms. (Since M-1A
and M-1B were only transition definitions, M-1B was later renamed to be the new M-1, which is currently used.)

M-2: M-1B + shares in money market mutual funds + overnight repurchase agreements + overnight Eurodollar liabilities + savings
and small-time deposits at all depository institutions.

M-3: M-2 + term repurchase agreements + large time deposits (see
Exhibit 7).

The Fed was willing to consider changes toward deregulation. For
years it had been frustrated by an attrition of Federal Reserve bank members, which had limited the Fed's control over the money supply. By
1980, only 5,407 of the 14,395 insured commercial banks in the United
States were Fed member banks. Nonmember banks, which held almost
30 percent of total bank deposits, reported their reserves on a quarterly
basis, requiring the Fed to construct estimates during interim periods.
Also, member banks were upset because nonmember banks were not
required to deposit reserve requirements with the Fed, thereby garnering
competitive advantage.

As a result of this pressure to apply the same rules to all financial
institutions, decrease regulatory power, and introduce free market competition, the Depository Institutions Deregulation and Monetary Control
Act of 1980 (DIDMCA) was signed into law on March 31, 1980. Congressman Reuss called it the most significant financial legislation since
the 1930s; Senator Proxmire went even further, saying it was the most
important piece of legislation since the Federal Reserve Act of 1913.[37]
The legislation represented the outcome of years of effort by Congress,
the regulatory agencies, and the financial industry. It promised to change
dramatically the competitive environment of financial institutions and

---

[37]Federal Reserve Bank of San Francisco, "Money and the Monetary Control Act," *Economic Review* (Winter 1981): 4.

the ability of the Fed to implement monetary control and equalize its costs.

The landmark legislation dictated three broad provisions encompassing all depository institutions (banks, savings and loans, mutual savings banks, and credit unions):

- *Monetary control provisions.* Uniform reserve requirements would be applied to all depository institutions, with an eight-year phase-in for nonmembers. All depository institutions would have the same borrowing privileges at the Fed. The Fed would establish fees for its services. The Fed could impose a 4 percent additional reserve requirement in "extraordinary circumstances."
- *Interest rate deregulation.* Interest rate ceilings on deposits (Regulation Q) would be phased out over six years. State usury ceilings on loans would be raised or eliminated.
- *Competition in financial products across all depository institutions.* All depository institutions could offer interest-paying "checking" accounts (NOW, ATS, and share drafts, for example). Thrift institutions would have broader investment powers.

As significant as these changes were, however, it was credit controls and not deregulation that caused the most severe problems for Volcker during the spring and summer of 1980.

Sharp Recession before the 1980 Election

The imposition of credit controls had a more dramatic impact than either President Carter or the Fed had anticipated. The severity of the economic response to credit controls caused them to be removed almost as soon as they were instituted; by July they had been completely dismantled. Money growth dropped sharply (see Exhibits 5 and 6), and interest rates followed suit. By April the federal funds rate had fallen 10 percentage points from its high of 19.5 percent in mid-March. The monetary policies were already affecting real output. Both real GNP and industrial production plunged during the spring and summer, and unemployment rose 1.5 percentage points (see Exhibits 9, 10, and 11). The prospect of a severe recession encouraged the Fed to accelerate money growth in order to hit its target range for the preferred M-1 aggregate. The drop in interest rates was short-lived since a slowdown in money growth during the last half of 1980 (see Exhibit 6) once again sent interest rates to record highs at year-end (see Exhibits 1 and 2).

As he hit the campaign trail, President Carter was saddled with a dismal economy. Although he was able to fight off Senator Edward Kennedy's challenge for the Democratic Party nomination, both the president and the party were weakened by it. Meanwhile, the Republicans were uniting behind former California Governor Ronald Reagan, who attacked Carter's economic policies by referring to the rise in the "misery index" (the inflation rate plus the unemployment rate). Ironically, this was the same measure Carter had used against President Gerald Ford during the 1976 campaign. Under Carter, the misery index had risen from 13 percent to 19 percent by election time.

Foreign policy problems were also hurting Carter's standing in the polls. The hostages still remained captive in the American Embassy in Iran, and a failed rescue attempt in April had diminished the prospects for an imminent resolution to the embarrassing crisis. The earlier Soviet invasion of Afghanistan in December 1979 also fueled perceptions of American weakness. The combined problems in the economy and in foreign policy contributed greatly to Ronald Reagan's election victory in November.

Monetary Restraint through 1981

Through 1981, Volcker and the FOMC maintained a posture of strict monetary restraint aimed at reducing the double-digit inflation. The new administration of President Reagan encouraged the Fed in these actions.[38] The economy at first staggered and then fell significantly through the second half of the year (see Exhibits 9 and 10). By the end of 1981, the country was in a deep recession, with unemployment approaching its previous postwar high of 9 percent (see Exhibit 11). Even though Reagan could claim success in bringing inflation down from 13.5 percent in 1980 to 10.4 percent in 1981, Volcker and the FOMC realized that much of the reduction was due to favorable declines in commodity and energy prices, particularly at the end of the year.[39]

The deregulations in the financial markets presented many problems for the Fed in implementing its monetary targeting. The growth rates of monetary aggregates diverged more than expected in 1981. The primary target, M-1, remained below the target range through most of the year, while the broader aggregates of M-2 and M-3 were above their target ranges (see Exhibit 5). The growth in NOW, ATS, and other checkable accounts, authorized by the DIDMCA of 1980, amounted to an increase of over $50 billion during the year. Money market mutual funds, also showing phenomenal growth, more than doubled in 1981 to almost $200 billion (see Exhibit 7). Unfortunately for the FOMC, the growth was not smooth and predictable. Technical problems of forecasting and control contributed to surges such as the noticeable April "spike" shown in Exhibits 5 and 6. The FOMC quickly responded to the unintended surge

---

[38]See the Chapter 9 case, "The Reagan Plan."

[39]Reagan's claim to success against inflation is made in his *Economic Report*, February 1982, p. 9. The Fed is more reserved in its assessment in the *Annual Report*, New York Federal Reserve Bank, 1981, p. 18.

in money growth by raising the discount rate and lowering the target path for its nonborrowed reserves instrument.[40]

The monetary restraint was clearly evident in the record-high interest rates persisting throughout the year and even surpassing the previous peak in March 1980. This was unusual given the weak economy. At the beginning of the year, short-term rates were higher than long-term rates, which is typical during periods of restraint (see Exhibit 2). By the end of the year, long-term rates reached their peak and then remained high despite declining economic activity, falling short-term rates, and falling inflation. A final feature of the interest rates during 1981 was their volatility. The rates responded to both money growth and the demands for credit, particularly from the Treasury in order to finance the deficit.[41]

The current deficits were not so major a concern for Volcker as were the expected deficits that would arise because of President Reagan's military buildup and his personal and corporate tax cuts in the Economic Recovery Tax Act (ERTA) passed in August 1981.[42] Deficits typically rise whenever the economy slows down because tax revenues decline and countercyclical spending, such as unemployment compensation, increases. The total increase in the 1981 (calendar year) deficit due to both the personal and corporate tax cuts was only $10.5 billion.[43] However, the cumulative deficit from fiscal year 1982 to fiscal year 1988 due to ERTA would be almost $800 billion.[44] The Fed could either accommodate the increased government spending by abandoning its monetary targets in future years and supplying additional credit, or it could meet its targets and thereby increase interest rates as federal credit demands compete with private demands for credit.

Corporate demand for funds remained high despite the high, volatile interest rates. In part, this may have been due to the accelerated depreciation benefits in Reagan's tax package. One noticeable feature of the corporate credit demand was a shift from long-term to intermediate- and short-term funding for nonfinancial corporations during 1981. About one half of the nonconvertible debt issued in that year was in intermediate-term issues, according to a Salomon Brothers estimate, compared with only one quarter in the late 1970s.[45] Companies were forced to be creative

[40]Federal Reserve Bank of New York, *Quarterly Review* (Spring 1982): 47.

[41]Compare the fluctuations in short-term interest rates in Exhibit 2A and the fluctuations in money growth in Exhibit 6A. The increased growth in April and at year-end correspond to declines in short-term interest rates. Also notice in Exhibit 4 how total credit demand, which is the sum of the domestic nonfinancial and federal credit, fell during 1981. This too is consistent with a fall in short-term rates at year-end.

[42]See Chapters 10 and 11 for a description of the political process leading to the ERTA and the effects of Reagan's fiscal programs on the deficit.

[43]Richard C. Ziemer, *Survey of Current Business* (April 1985): 28.

[44]Congressional Budget Office, *Reducing the Deficit: Spending and Revenue Options* (Washington, DC: U.S. Government Printing Office, 1983), 238.

[45]New York Federal Reserve Bank, *Quarterly Review* (Spring 1982): 39.

in their financing by issuing deep discount debt (often with a zero coupon) to gain tax advantages for themselves and to entice investors who wanted to lock up high yields. Short-term commercial paper was booming to the point where short-term debt comprised almost half of the total corporate debt (compared to only 30 percent in the 1960s).[46]

The deterioration of corporate balance sheets and the prospects of major bankruptcies concerned Volcker, who recalled the financial consequences of the collapse of Penn Central during the credit crunch of 1970. At that time the commercial paper market dried up as investors began to worry about the creditworthiness of the issuers and to turn to commercial banks for liquidity. Even more troubling were the failures of mutual savings banks and savings and loan institutions, which rivaled those of the Great Depression. A widespread panic among the thrifts could spread to other financial institutions. Although not directly the responsibility of the Fed, the consequences of the high interest rates on the thrift institutions were apparent to all regulators. Mergers were the preferred solution, even if it meant combining institutions across state boundaries—a move that would further accelerate financial deregulation. The other solution designed to prevent the loss of deposits to money market funds was the tax-free All-Savers Certificates authorized by the ERTA for only one year starting in October 1981. By year-end, almost $30 billion was deposited in these instruments, all of which would expire in October of the following year.

The high U.S. interest rates created not only domestic problems but also foreign problems. Since U.S. rates were high relative to those of other countries (see Exhibit 3), they contributed to the continual appreciation of the dollar during the first three quarters of 1981. When short-term interest rates fell in the final quarter of the year, so did the exchange rate, though marginally. The strong dollar appeared to be related to the deteriorating U.S. trade balance (see Exhibit 13). Moreover, the high real interest rates and strong dollar made it difficult for the less-developed countries (LDCs) to reduce their current account deficits and thus their dependence on foreign debt. In fact, the total current account deficit of the LDCs increased from $60 billion to $70 billion during the year, while the threat of events such as in Poland contributed to the instability of the international lending market.[47]

The Recession and Financial Strains of 1982

Volcker, still intent on wringing inflationary expectations out of the economy, planned to continue his policy of monetary restraint through 1982. Since the United States, like the rest of the industrial world, was already

[46]*The Economist* (Oct. 16, 1982): 25.

[47]New York Federal Reserve Bank, *Annual Report* (1981): 19.

in a recession, he realized the importance of not pursuing restraint too aggressively. Public opinion, as well as criticism from Treasury Secretary Donald Regan, urged the Fed to ease its monetary grip. Angry farmers surrounded the Federal Reserve building on Constitution Avenue, brandishing signs such as "Help American Agriculture—Eat an Economist." In December 1981, a man was arrested in Washington after threatening to take Fed Board members hostage in protest against high interest rates.[48] On Capitol Hill, congressmen were drafting legislation to curb the Fed's independence. When Volcker was asked what it would take to ease the Fed's tight monetary policy, he replied succinctly, "Impeachment."[49] By August 1982, the recession was deeper than anticipated and signs of stress were showing in the world financial system, characterized by problems in the U.S. government securities market, failures of financial institutions and major corporations at home and abroad, and the potential collapse of the international credit market.

The growth targets for M-1 in 1982 were lowered about three percentage points to the range of 2.5-5.5 percent. The Fed had achieved an actual growth rate for the previous year that was under its target, but early in 1982 the growth of M-1 exceeded its target range due to unanticipated increases in the demand for NOW accounts (see Exhibit 5 and Column 3 of Exhibit 7). By July, the Fed had succeeded in bringing the money growth rate back in line with the target range. In hindsight, the Fed rationalized that people were holding more money as a precaution against the uncertainty of the economic and financial environment.[50] In addition, the decline in short-term interest rates increased the amount of money people were willing to hold, since it was not so costly to hold money instead of an interest-bearing asset. Long-term rates remained high as businesses tried to improve their balance sheets by selling long-term debt and paying down short-term debt.

All measures of output performance indicated that by mid-1982 this was the worst recession for the United States since the Great Depression (see Exhibits 9, 10, and 11). Business failures had reached a rate for the previous two years that was surpassed only by the 1930s. Significant progress against inflation had been made at the end of 1981 and the beginning of 1982. But it was not clear whether this was permanent, since the low level of inflation in 1982 was partially accounted for by falling commodity and energy prices and since the most recent data indicated a rise in the consumer price index (see Exhibit 12).

The relationship between money and GNP, known as velocity, appeared to be breaking down in 1982.[51] Velocity had typically grown at a

[48]*Institutional Investor* (May 1984): 147.

[49]Ibid.

[50]New York Federal Reserve Bank, *Quarterly Review* (Spring 1983): 40.

[51]Velocity is defined as nominal GNP divided by the relevant monetary aggregate. See the Chapter 2 note "Money and the Determination of Income" for a discussion of this concept.

3 percent rate during the postwar years. As the data became available to the Fed, they showed that velocity had declined substantially during the first half of the year (see Exhibit 8). It was not clear to the members of the FOMC whether this was a temporary decline or a more permanent decline. Such a determination was important for conducting monetary policy, since a permanent decline would require the Fed to be more accommodative to GNP growth in the future in order to avoid another severe recession.

The unanticipated depth of the recession contributed to the strains on the financial system. The government securities market was burdened by the record Treasury borrowings brought on by President Reagan's fiscal policies and the low tax receipts due to the recession. For fiscal year 1982, the Treasury accounted for about 35 percent of all funds raised. The number of dealers and the volume of this market had grown tremendously since 1978 because of the large quantity of debt and the interest rate volatility.[52] One of those dealers was Drysdale Government Securities Inc., which failed on May 17 because it was unable to make accrued interest payments on Treasury securities "borrowed" through reverse repurchase agreements.[53] Its failure threatened the entire secondary market in government securities, as well as the financial stability of a number of major banks (primarily Chase Manhattan Bank) since they were involved as intermediaries in purchasing the securities for Drysdale.

The direct pressures on financial institutions were increasing as well. The thrift industry was still being squeezed in early 1982 due to high interest rates. Consolidations were occurring at twice the rate of the previous year. Commercial banks were not hurt as badly as in the 1974–1975 recession, but the failure of Penn Square National Bank of Oklahoma City in July sent another shock wave through the financial community.[54] This was only one of the 42 banks that were closed in the course of the year (compared to 10 the previous year), but it had wider repercussions because of the sale of $2 billion in energy-related loans to other commercial banks. The bust in oil prices, following the boom of the previous three years, hurt the creditworthiness of oil-related assets for both the energy companies and their commercial bankers. The consequences of these failures showed up in the decreased liquidity and higher rates in the certificate of deposit (CD) market.[55]

Before the financial markets could recover from these two shocks,

[52] New York Federal Reserve Bank, *Annual Report* (1982): 7.

[53] A repurchase agreement, known as a "repo" or an "RP," is an agreement in which I sell a security temporarily for a payment of money and agree to repurchase it at a later date at a price that includes an implicit yield. The person who enters into that agreement with me has a reverse repo. See Columns 4 and 11 of Exhibit 7.

[54] For culmination of these events see David Meerschwam, "Continental Illinois and the F.D.I.C.," HBS case #9-385-296.

[55] A CD is a large-denomination (over $100,000), marketable, unsecured time deposit issued by a commercial bank, similar to commercial paper for a nonfinancial corporation.

two more shocks followed in rapid succession in the international credit markets. The first was the default of Banco Ambrosiano Holding Company of Luxembourg, the largest failure in the Euromarket since the collapse of the Herstatt Bank of Austria in 1974. The second, and more significant, was the Mexican debt crisis.[56] On August 12, Mexico suspended interest payments on its foreign debt and sought a rescheduling. This further aggravated the concerns over the quality of bank loans. The high real interest rates in the United States, low energy prices, a lack of growth in the export markets, and the flight of massive amounts of capital out of Mexico helped to precipitate the liquidity crisis. Higher risk premiums were being added to the cost of bank funds, and many banks in the United States and abroad were withdrawing from the international lending market.

In almost three years Paul Volcker had reduced inflation rates by two-thirds. It was unclear how much of this success was due to his new operating procedures and monetary targeting and how much was due to the strength of his leadership as chairman. Some factors, such as the favorable commodity and energy price decreases, contributed to the success, while others, such as the Reagan deficits, made the task more difficult. Some developments—financial deregulation, for example—did both.

It may have been too early to declare victory over inflation in mid-1982, since as recently as 1976 inflation had been at these levels. Yet by August 1982 the severity of the current economic situation and the financial strains on the financial system demanded a reevaluation of the procedures used and objectives sought in the conduct of monetary policy.

---

[56]For a detailed discussion of the Mexican debt crisis, see Mexico: Crisis of Confidence, Chapter 17.

Paul Volcker and the Federal Reserve: 1979–1982

**Exhibit 1   Federal Funds Rate: Actual Path and Federal Open
Market Committee Constraint, Weekly Data Fall 1973
through Summer 1982**

Percent per year   Percent per year

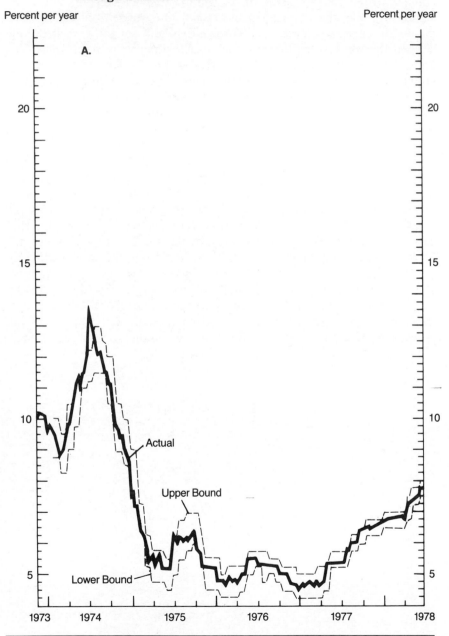

Weekly averages of daily data, not seasonally adjusted.

Source: Ralph C. Bryant, *Controlling Money: The Federal Reserve and Its Critics* (Washington, DC: Brookings Institution, 1983), 96.

Exhibit 1 (Continued)

Percent per year   Percent per year

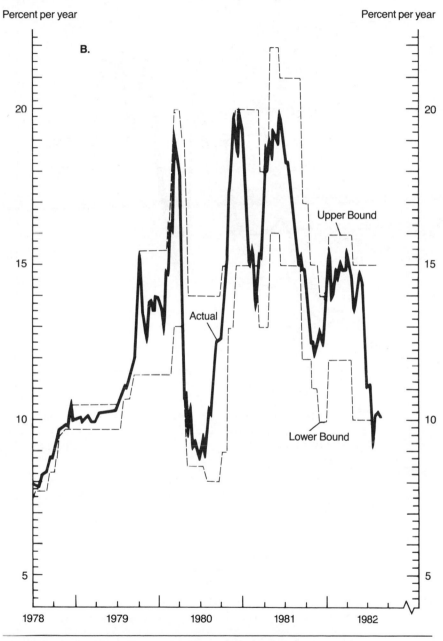

Weekly averages of daily data, not seasonally adjusted.

Paul Volcker and the Federal Reserve: 1979–1982

Exhibit 2   Short-Term and Long-Term Interest Rates: 1977–1982

Monthly averages of daily figures.

Latest data plotted: July.

[a]Data prior to November 1, 1979, are 4- month to 6-month commercial paper rates.

Source: Federal Reserve Bank of St. Louis, *Monetary Trends,* August 25, 1982, 12.

Exhibit 2 (Continued)

Percent   Percent

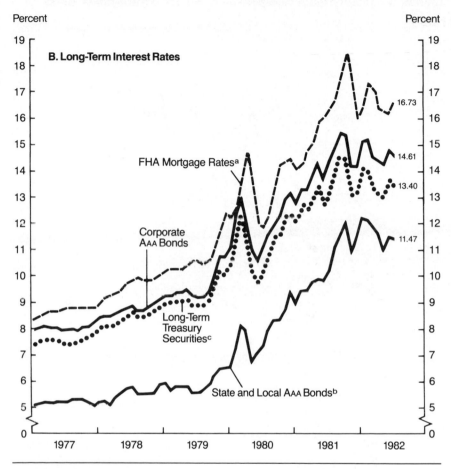

Monthly averages of daily figures.

Latest data plotted: July.

[a]FHA 30-year mortgages.

[b]Monthly averages of Thursday figures.

[c]Average of yields on coupon issues due or callable in ten years or more. Excluding issues with federal estate tax privileges. Yields are computed by this bank.

Paul Volcker and the Federal Reserve: 1979–1982

Exhibit 3   International Comparison of Short-Term Interest Rates

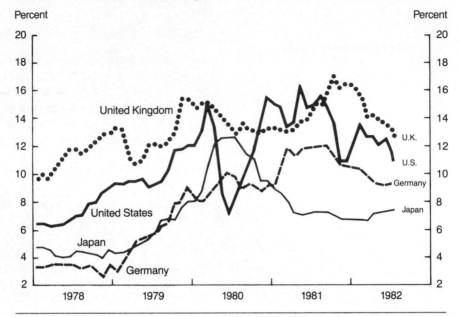

Latest data plotted: July.

Source: Federal Reserve Bank of St. Louis, *International Economic Conditions,* Jan. 24, 1983, 60.

Paul Volcker and the Federal Reserve: 1979–1982

Exhibit 4   Net Funds Raised: Major Nonfinancial Sectors

Billions of dollars   Billions of dollars

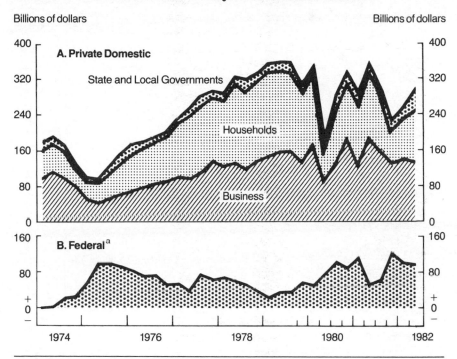

Seasonally adjusted annual rates, quarterly.

[a]Excludes federally sponsored credit agencies.

Source: Board of Governors of the Federal Reserve System, *Federal Reserve Chart Book,* September 1984, 29.

Paul Volcker and the Federal Reserve: 1979–1982

Exhibit 5   Path and Targets of Monetary Aggregates: 1979–1982

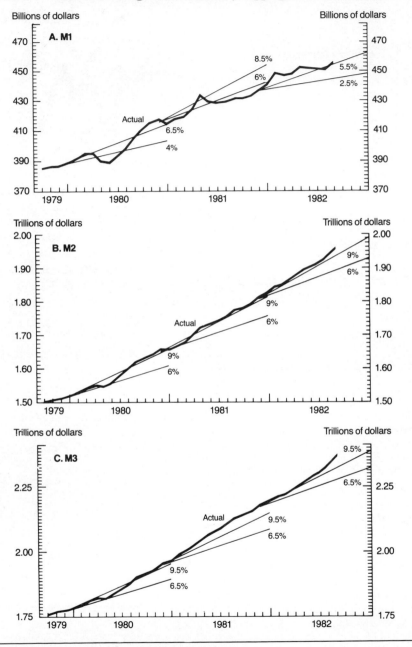

Seasonally adjusted monthly averages of daily data.

Source: Ralph C. Bryant, *Controlling Money: The Federal Reserve and Its Critics* (Washington, DC: Brookings Institution, 1983), 36, 92, 93.

Paul Volcker and the Federal Reserve: 1979–1982

Exhibit 6   Growth of Monetary Aggregates

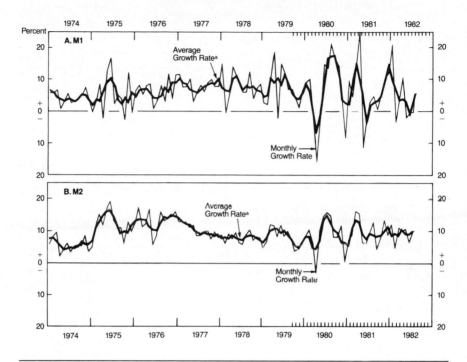

Seasonally adjusted, annual rates, monthly.

Latest month plotted: July 1983.

[a]3-month centered moving average.

Source: Board of Governors of the Federal Reserve System, *Federal Reserve Chart Book*, November 1982.

Paul Volcker and the Federal Reserve 1979–1982

Exhibit 7   Components of the Monetary Aggregates (Billions of Dollars)

Period	M1-A		M1-B	M2		M3			L
						Money Market Mutual Fund (MMMF) Balances			
	Currency	Demand Deposits[a]	Other Checkable Deposits	Overnight Repurchase Agreements (RPs) (Net) NSA	Overnight Eurodollars NSA	General Purpose and Broker/Dealer NSA	Institution Only[b] NSA	Savings Deposits	Small Denomination Time Deposits[c]
	1	2	3	4	5	6	7	8	9
Dec.									
1970	49.1	166.3	.1	1.4	.0	.0	.0	259.3	153.6
1971	52.5	176.8	.2	2.5	.0	.0	.0	290.8	192.0
1972	55.8	193.6	.2	3.1	.0	.0	.0	320.2	233.9
1973	61.5	202.5	.3	6.8	.0	.1	.0	325.9	267.6
1974	67.8	207.4	.4	7.2	.0	2.1	.2	337.6	290.0
1975	73.8	214.1	.9	7.5	.0	3.2	.4	387.7	340.9
1976	80.6	224.4	2.7	13.7	.0	2.8	.6	451.7	396.5
1977	88.6	239.6	4.2	17.8	1.0	2.9	.9	490.4	454.1
1978	97.4	253.9	8.4	22.1	2.0	7.1	3.1	479.9	533.9
1979	106.1	262.2	16.9	22.7	3.6	34.4	9.3	421.7	652.6
1980	116.2	267.2	26.9	30.5	4.5	61.9	13.9	398.9	751.7
1981	123.1	236.4	77.0	31.4	6.7	151.2	33.7	343.6	854.7
1982:									
Jan.	123.8	239.3	81.1	35.7	7.5	154.9	32.5	348.8	852.3
Feb.	124.6	234.5	83.8	35.6	7.3	156.1	30.5	348.6	859.4
Mar.	125.1	233.0	85.8	36.7	6.3	159.4	31.5	350.7	869.9
Apr.	126.3	233.0	88.6	34.6	5.8	162.1	31.5	350.5	881.6
May	127.4	232.7	87.0	35.8	7.0	164.6	32.8	350.9	894.1
June	128.4	231.0	87.5	36.0	7.0	168.9	33.7	349.9	900.9
July	128.8	230.6	87.4	36.4	7.0	171.7	36.7	344.0	919.7

NSA = not seasonally adjusted.

Travelers' checks are a component of money stock but are not shown here.

[a]Demand deposits at all commercial banks other than those due to domestic banks, the U.S. government, and foreign banks and official institutions less cash items in the process of collection and Federal Reserve float.

[b]This component of MMMF is included in M-3, but not M-2.

[c]Small denomination and large denomination deposits are those issued in amounts of less than $100,000 and more than $100,000, respectively.

Source: *Economic Report of the President, 1983* (Washington, DC: U.S. Government Printing Office, 1983), 234.

Exhibit 7 (Continued)

						L
M3						
Large Denomination Time Deposits[c]	Term Repurchase Agreements (RPs) NSA	Term Euro-dollars (Net) NSA	Savings Bonds	Short-Term Treasury Securities	Bankers' Acceptances	Commercial Paper
10	**11**	**12**	**13**	**14**	**15**	**16**
45.0	1.4	2.2	52.0	49.2	3.3	34.5
57.6	2.5	2.7	54.3	36.3	3.5	32.7
73.2	3.3	3.6	57.6	41.1	3.3	35.2
111.2	7.1	5.4	60.4	60.0	4.7	41.9
144.4	8.4	8.0	63.2	53.6	10.6	50.1
129.8	9.0	9.7	67.2	77.1	8.4	48.0
118.2	15.0	13.1	71.7	81.1	8.8	51.7
145.2	21.0	18.7	76.4	89.9	11.8	62.9
194.6	27.5	29.9	80.3	99.3	21.4	79.2
221.8	30.2	42.9	79.6	128.5	26.5	97.0
257.9	37.8	48.4	72.3	156.7	31.8	98.1
300.3	35.4	66.7	67.7	176.5	39.7	104.2
302.6	32.5	69.9	67.8	180.3	40.2	105.5
308.0	32.5	73.8	67.8	186.4	39.1	108.4
312.6	31.5	74.4	67.7	191.0	37.9	110.3
317.2	34.2	78.5	67.7	191.7	38.3	109.7
321.6	32.6	83.3	67.7	191.9	39.9	112.1
328.3	31.2	84.8	67.8	194.8	40.3	115.7
335.8	29.3	84.2	67.7	199.9	40.8	118.7

[c]Small denomination and large denomination deposits are those issued in amounts of less than $100,000 and more than $100,000, respectively.

Paul Volcker and the Federal Reserve: 1979–1982

Exhibit 8   Income Velocity of Money

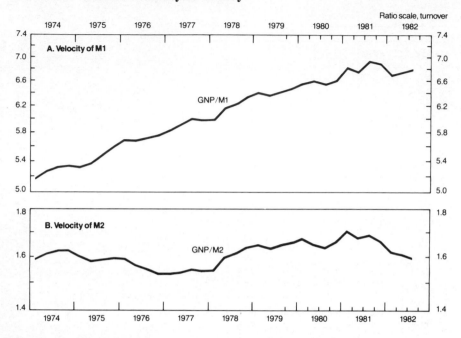

Seasonally adjusted, quarterly.

Source: Board of Governors of the Federal Reserve System, *Federal Reserve Chart Book,* November 1982, 8.

Paul Volcker and the Federal Reserve: 1979–1982

Exhibit 9   Gross National Product

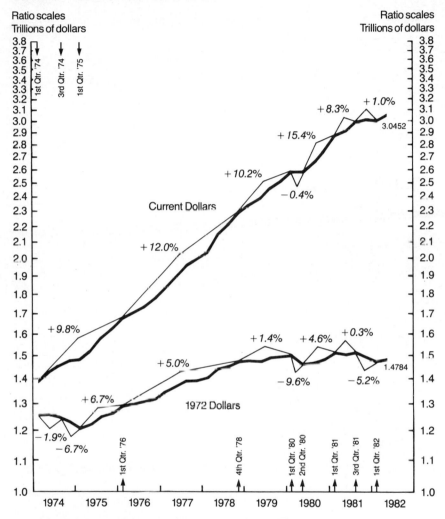

Quarterly totals at annual rates, seasonally adjusted.

Percentages are annual rates of change for periods indicated.

Latest data plotted: second quarter.

Source: Federal Reserve Bank of St. Louis, *National Economic Trends,* Sept. 30, 1982, 13.

Paul Volcker and the Federal Reserve: 1979–1982

Exhibit 10   Industrial Production

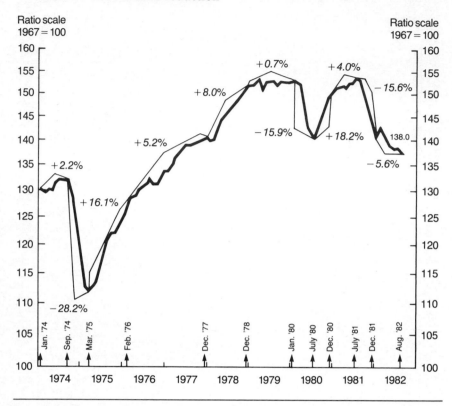

Ratio scale
1967 = 100

Ratio scale
1967 = 100

Seasonally adjusted.

Percentages are annual rates of change for periods indicated.

Latest data plotted: August preliminary.

Source: Federal Reserve Bank of St. Louis, *National Economic Trends,* Sept. 30, 1982, 7.

Paul Volcker and the Federal Reserve: 1979–1982

Exhibit 11 Unemployment Rate

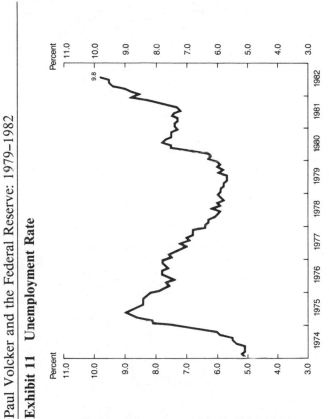

Seasonally adjusted.

Percent of civilian labor force.

Latest data plotted: July.

Source: Federal Reserve Bank of St. Louis, *National Economic Trends*, August 31, 1982, 3.

Paul Volcker and the Federal Reserve: 1979–1982

Exhibit 12 Changes in the Price Indices: 1974–1982

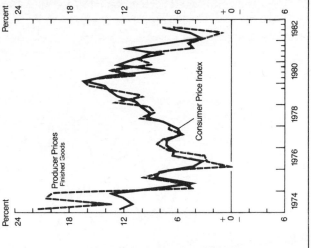

Change at annual rates, seasonally adjusted, quarterly.

Source: Board of Governors of the Federal Reserve System, *Federal Reserve Chart Book*, November 1982, 20.

Paul Volcker and the Federal Reserve: 1979–1982

Exhibit 13   U.S. International Transactions 1974–1982: Current Account and Trade Balance

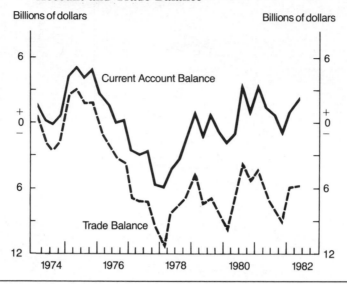

Seasonally adjusted changes, quarterly.

Source: Board of Governors of the Federal Reserve System, *Federal Reserve Chart Book*, September 1982, 74.

Paul Volcker and the Federal Reserve: 1979–1982

Exhibit 14   Movements in the Effective Exchange Rates for the United States: 1974–1982

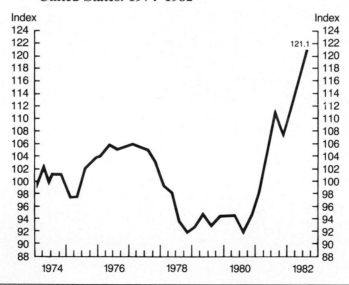

Note: Upward movement indicates an appreciation of the dollar.

Source: Federal Reserve Bank of St. Louis, *International Economic Conditions*, January 24, 1983, 2.

Note
Implementing Monetary Policy

The note "Money and the Determination of Income" in the previous chapter discussed the three tools of monetary policy, how these tools affect the process of money creation, and finally how money affects nominal income. This note will provide the additional details necessary to analyze contemporary debates in monetary policy. One of the fundamental issues in these debates is: What is money and on which of the competing definitions of money should we focus our attention? In the previous note, money was defined as currency and demand deposits, but financial innovations in the past decade have confused this definition. The next section, "The Definition of Money," will lead us through the conceptual problems of appropriately defining a monetary aggregate that is useful for policy-making.

A second fundamental issue is: What is the role of interest rates in the economy and in the conduct of monetary policy? In the previous note, we presented a monetarist transmission mechanism that says that money broadly affects income through numerous channels. In this note, we present a Keynesian transmission mechanism that says that money affects interest rates, which in turn affect income—which mechanism we believe may affect the strategy and implementation of monetary policy. The second section, "The Keynesian Monetary Theory and Interest Rates," explains the role of these financial variables.

The third section, "The Monetarist-Keynesian Debate," tries to highlight areas of disagreement—more often a matter of degree rather than substance. But more important is the common ground to both sides of the debate. The objective is to develop a flexible, eclectic framework that will serve policy analysis.

The final section, "Implementing a Monetary Strategy," presents a broad view of the process by which the central bank achieves its performance goals. There are a number of competing strategies for achieving its objectives: How should a central bank decide which strategy and which operating procedure is most appropriate? Since 1979, this question has been critical for the implementation of monetary policy under Paul Volcker in the United States and under Margaret Thatcher in the United Kingdom.

The Definition of Money

We would all recognize currency (coins and dollar bills) as money, but economists define money not by its physical characteristics, rather by its

This note was prepared by Associate Professor Michael G. Rukstad.
Harvard Business School note 9-386-062

functions. There are three functions of money: (1) medium of exchange, (2) unit of account, and (3) store of wealth.

The primary function of money is to serve as a *medium of exchange* or a means of payment. In this role, money is a social innovation that allows us to make transactions more efficiently than if we had to barter our goods and services for those of others. Currency, for example, serves this purpose by facilitating economic transactions in which some good or service is exchanged for currency that can then be exchanged for some other good or service. The great disadvantage of barter is the high cost in time and money of acquiring information on which transactions can be made. Both parties to the transaction must be willing to accept the other person's good in exchange for their own good; i.e., there must be a double coincidence of wants.

But currency is not the only thing that can be used as a medium of exchange. Checking accounts, credit cards, and wire transfers of funds are also used as a means of payment. In the last few years, financial institutions have been allowed to issue new interest-paying checking accounts such as NOW accounts, money market checking accounts, and credit union share drafts. These are also recognized as acceptable mediums of exchange. Currency is used in almost 90 percent of all transactions, but wire transfers of funds account for approximately three quarters of the dollar value of all transactions. Table 1 gives approximate relative magnitudes for the various methods of payment.

Table 1   Distribution of Methods of Payment

Method of Payment	Percentage of Total Number of All Transactions	Percentage of Total Dollar Value of All Transactions
Cash	88%	0.7%
Checks	10	22.0
Credit cards	2	0.3
Wire transfers	Less than 1/10 of 1%	77.0

Source: Ralph Kimball, "Wire Transfers and the Demand for Money," *New England Economic Review*, Federal Reserve Bank of Boston (March/April 1980): 8.

A second function of money is that it serves as a *unit of account* or a standard of value. We express the value of all other items we exchange in terms of money. For example, we say that a gallon of milk costs 2 dollars, but not 40 cigarettes or .005 ounce of gold. It is our measuring rod for value just as a yardstick is for distance. But inflation diminishes the usefulness of money as a unit of account, since we do not want our measuring rod to change over time. Inflation erodes the value of money because a given amount of money will purchase fewer goods and services. The value of money can be represented as the inverse of the general price level or $1/P$.

A third function of money is that it serves as a *store of wealth*, i.e., one of the many forms of holding wealth. Alternatively, wealth may be held in the form of real assets (such as homes, factories, machines, etc.) and other financial assets (such as stocks, bonds, certificates of deposit, savings accounts, etc., which are financial claims on real assets).

Money is distinguished from other stores of wealth by its liquidity. The liquidity of an asset depends on how costly it is in terms of time and money to buy or sell the asset and how predictable and stable its price is. Currency, for example, is perfectly liquid since there is no transactions cost or price uncertainty in buying or selling a dollar—a dollar may be bought or sold for a dollar at any time with perfect certainty. At the other extreme, real estate is very illiquid since it may be bought or sold only after a large cost in time and brokerage fees. Furthermore, the price of a real estate transaction is very uncertain. All other assets can be ranked on a continuum between these two extremes according to their relative liquidity.

The three functions of money outlined above identify characteristics of money in the abstract, but we need a measurable definition of money that can be tested by economists and implemented by policymakers. There are two approaches to this problem that are not mutually exclusive: the a priori approach and the empirical approach. The a priori approach, which often leads to a narrower measure of the money supply, focuses on the unique characteristic that we know, a priori, money must possess: it must be a medium of exchange. The other two characteristics are not necessarily unique to money. Thus money is anything that is generally accepted as a means of payment. The measure of money favored by supporters of this approach is currency plus checking accounts of all types. Everyone would agree that these two elements should certainly be included in the definition of money, but the disagreement centers on whether other liquid assets should also be included.[1]

The empirical approach to defining money, which often leads to a broader measure of the money supply, emphasizes the importance of money's role in the economy. Money, in this approach, is any liquid asset(s) that is (are) most closely related to nominal GNP and that can best be controlled by the central bank. Those assets that fit this definition can be determined only by empirically testing which group of liquid assets is the most controllable and leads to the most predictable outcomes. Unfortunately, this empirical problem has not yet been solved, and a solution, if found, would undoubtedly change over time.

Supporters of this approach, such as Milton Friedman, a Nobel laureate formerly of the University of Chicago, tend to favor a definition of money that includes currency, demand deposits, and other highly liquid assets such as time and savings deposits, but this approach entertains a wide variety of alternative definitions.

The various measures of the money stock used by economists and

---

[1]There is also the problem of whether to include credit cards, traveler's checks, Eurodollar demand deposits (checking accounts denominated in dollars but held by banks overseas), or any new type of checking account that may be introduced.

bankers, called *monetary aggregates,* differ over countries and over time. However, there are a few generalizations which will serve as a guide to the monetary aggregates that will be introduced in the cases in this book. Most countries have a menu of money stock measures ranging from a narrow definition of money to increasingly broader definitions. In almost all countries, the narrowest definition of the money supply is called M-1, which is essentially currency plus checking accounts of all types. M-1, which receives the most publicity, is a good proxy to the "transactions money" defined by the a priori approach. In the rest of this note, when we use "money" in a general sense, we will mean M-1, since this is the core element in all definitions of money.

The United States also has three broader measures called M-2, M-3, and L (for Liquidity, the broadest measure). The M-2 aggregate for the United States is basically M-1 plus savings and small time deposits,[2] money market mutual funds, and overnight repurchase agreements. [3] It can be thought of as "transactions money" plus "savings money" that is quickly convertible into transactions money. If we add large time deposits to M-2, we will approximately have M-3. Finally, L is M-3 plus other liquid assets such as Treasury bills, commercial paper, Eurodollars, and bankers' acceptances.[4] See Exhibit 7 of the preceding case, "Paul Volcker and the Federal Reserve," for the components of the monetary aggregates for the years 1970 to July 1982.

Since February 1980, the Federal Reserve Board has used the monetary aggregates defined above.[5] This change was necessary since there had been numerous financial innovations, reforms, and changes in the Federal Reserve operating procedures in the late 1970s. Two important definitions of money that were used prior to that time are M_1, and M_2 (note the subscripts). M_1 is currency plus demand deposits at commercial banks (i.e., it does not include other checkable deposits such as NOW accounts). M_2 is currency plus all commercial bank deposits (i.e., demand, savings, and small time deposits). There were also many other aggregates with which we need not be concerned.

Keynesian Monetary Theory and Interest Rates

The Keynesian approach to the determination of GNP was developed by John Maynard Keynes in his classic 1936 treatise, *The General Theory of Employment, Interest and Money.* This work has been described as an

---

[2]Time deposits under $100,000 denominations.

[3]Banks sell Treasury bills to large depositors overnight with the agreement to repurchase them the next day (often called "repos"). The depositors keep the overnight interest on the bills and the banks keep their happy customers.

[4]Commercial paper is a short-term corporate IOU. Eurodollars are the deposits held in foreign banks but denominated in dollars. Bankers' acceptances are trade credits guaranteed by a bank.

[5]In the transition period, there were two definitions of "transactions money": M-1A and M-1B, roughly corresponding respectively to the old and new concepts of "transactions money."

income-expenditure approach since it determines national income by explaining the key components of total expenditure—consumption, investment, government, and net foreign expenditures:

$$GNP = C + I + G + X - M.$$

This approach, discussed in the Chapter 6 case "A Keynesian Cure for the Depression," assigns a smaller role to money in the determination of income than does the monetarist approach. But for comparison with the monetarist approach, we will isolate the Keynesian monetary theory in this section as one factor among the many that determine total expenditures.

Keynes believed that the supply of and demand for money determined short-term interest rates, which can be thought of as the rental price of money.[6] Keynes argued that the alternative to holding money that pays no interest was to hold an asset that does pay interest, such as a government Treasury bill. This was a major innovation that Keynes introduced into the classical monetary theory, which was the forerunner to the modern quantity theory discussed in the previous note. The implication was that short-term interest rates are determined in the money markets. For example, an increase in the money supply would lower interest rates because people would want to shift their wealth from money, which is now in surplus in their portfolios, to short-term assets that pay interest. Therefore the demand for short-term interest-earning assets increases, bidding up the price of those assets, just as the increased demand for any commodity will bid up the price of that commodity.

When the price of an asset changes in one direction, its interest rate always changes in the opposite direction. The fact is always true, regardless whether one is a monetarist or a Keynesian. In the above case of an increased money supply causing asset prices to increase, the interest rate must decline. An asset such as a bond is a claim to a certain or an expected stream of future payments, let's say $80 every year. This financial claim (a piece of paper) may be bought and sold for a price determined by the supply and demand for that asset. If the asset initially sold for $800, the interest rate would be 10 percent (= $80/$800) per year. If, however, an increased demand for that asset pushed up its price to $1,000, then that claim to $80 every year would only have an 8 percent interest rate (= $80/$1,000); hence the price increases and the interest rate decreases. This is the reason we say that the price and the interest rate of an asset are inversely related.

Short-term interest rates are determined in the money market and affected by monetary policy, but we must now explain what determines long-term interest rates on corporate and government bonds as well as

---

[6]This definition captures the two essential characteristics of an interest rate: it has a time dimension and it is a relative price. It makes no sense to say that the interest rate is 2 percent unless we qualify it by saying "per year" or "per month." In this sense, an interest rate is not like a price. The price of an automobile is $10,000—period. However, the rental price of an automobile is $200 per month, or 2 percent per month. The 2 percent, moreover, is a relative price—the $200 price of renting for one month the services of an automobile relative to the $10,000 price of purchasing a new automobile, or $200/$10,000 = 2 percent.

on other long-term financial instruments such as mortgages. One would expect that the price of a bond is determined in the capital market by the supply and demand for that asset. While this is true, it does not give us a relationship between short-term interest rates and long-term interest rates. Such a relationship is called the *term structure of interest rates.*

Since investors have a choice of holding either long-term bonds or short-term bonds, they will increase the demand for those financial assets that they consider cheap and sell those that they consider overpriced in order to earn a capital gain. By this process of arbitrage, investors will drive long-term interest rates to a level that equals the returns they might expect to receive from rolling over a series of short-term assets. (Of course, this must reflect any differences in risk and the cost of making the transactions.)

For example, if the current interest rate on both a one-year and a two-year bond were 10 percent, then an investor would decide which asset to purchase on the basis of his or her expectation of the interest rate that will prevail on a one-year bond purchased next year after the first one-year bond falls due. If the investor expected an interest rate higher than 10 percent, he or she would purchase a one-year bond, which then would be rolled over into a higher expected yield at the end of the first year. Alternatively, if the short-term rate expected to prevail next year were lower than 10 percent, the investor would lock in the two-year 10 percent yield by purchasing the two-year bond. Therefore not only is current monetary policy important in determining long-term interest rates, but expected monetary policy is also important.

One other factor that has been particularly important in recent years in determining the level of interest rates is inflation. One would expect that both borrowers and lenders would take into account the fact that inflation reduces the real cost of borrowing or, equivalently, it increases the real cost of lending. In times of inflation, a borrower can pay back a loan in terms of cheaper (inflated) dollars; thus there is an incentive to borrow more, which drives up the nominal interest rate. Likewise, a lender will want to receive a certain real return (after adjusting for inflation) and will charge a higher nominal interest rate on the credit extended. The relationship between nominal and real interest rates is often called "the Fisher effect," in honor of the Yale economist Irving Fisher, who was a contemporary of Keynes. The *Fisher effect on nominal interest rates* may be summarized as follows:

$$i = r + \Delta P^e/P,$$

where i is the nominal interest rate (which is reported in newspapers), r is the real interest rate (which is unobserved), and $\Delta P^e/P$ is the expected price inflation (which is also unobserved). Even though the real interest rate is unobserved, it is an important variable since economic actors must make their investment decisions on the basis of the real interest rate, i.e, the nominal interest rate adjusted for inflation.

In the Keynesian monetary story, interest rates play a key role in determining the effect of money on the economy. To continue our account of an increase in the money supply driving down real short-term interest

rates, we generally would expect real long-term rates to fall as well. However, expectations of many factors determine how far nominal long-term
rates will fall. In the Keynesian transmission mechanism, the fall in real
long-term rates will generally operate through two major channels:

1.   Stimulate investment as the cost of capital falls.

2.   Stimulate consumption as the value of wealth increases.

Generally, Keynesians assign a larger role to the first factor. A decrease
in real long-term rates will lower the cost of capital, which is the cost of
obtaining funds for business investment. With cheaper funds available,
a firm will be inclined to undertake additional investment projects that
were not profitable at a higher cost of capital; hence investment and GNP
increases. Also, a decrease in interest rates will mean capital gains on
bonds and, generally, a higher value of stocks. The individuals holding
these assets will recognize an increased value of their wealth, which should
stimulate consumption and GNP.
     We can summarize the Keynesian monetary transmission mecha-
nism as follows:

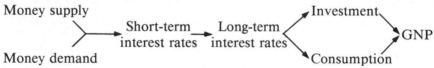

Notice that a change in the money supply first affects the financial markets
by affecting asset prices and interest rates and then through specific channels it affects the real markets, or the markets for goods and services.

The Monetarist-Keynesian Debate

The monetarist and Keynesian approaches described in the previous note
and in the preceding pages of this note are not necessarily inconsistent.
In this section, we will highlight some of the differences and unresolved
empirical issues.
     Monetarists and Keynesians differ on at least four major points,
which may be stated as four monetarist propositions:[7]

1.   Money is the most important cause of changes in nominal GNP
     (*quantity theory*).

2.   Monetary policy is transmitted to nominal GNP broadly and di-
     rectly (*monetarist transmission mechanism*).

3.   Because the private economy, in particular the demand for money,

[7]These and other differences are discussed in Thomas Mayer, et al., *The Structure of Monetarism* (New York: Norton, 1978).

is inherently stable, there is no need for government stabilization policies (*stable velocity*).

4.   Most of the change in nominal income will be reflected in prices and not in output (*flexible prices*).

The Keynesian response would be the negation of the above propositions. Notice that the differences between the two positions are a matter of degree: How important is money, how broadly is it transmitted, how stable is the economy, and how flexible are prices? The answers to these questions are extremely important for policymakers who must decide whether to intervene in the economy and for the timing and methods if it becomes necessary to do so.

Both the monetarist and Keynesian explanations can be used to explain nominal income or nominal GNP, but they highlight different determinants. In the following equation, we can combine the two explanations into one relationship:[8]

$$M \times V = GNP = C + I + G + NX .$$

Both sides of the equation will always be "correct" because they are both identities. A particular change in nominal GNP can be explained by a Keynesian using a monetarist framework, just as the same event can be explained by a monetarist using a Keynesian framework. Both individuals will feel constrained in their explanations since the key determinants, in their eyes, are not given prominence.

The two stylized explanations are not intended to offer mutually exclusive alternatives to the reader; rather they are intended to give some insight into why there is a debate between monetarists and Keynesians and why the policy prescriptions might differ. One should develop his or her own evaluation of the debate based on cases we will be studying. The two frameworks are only tools to express compactly the relationships that one believes to be most important.

Implementing a Monetary Strategy

If the three tools of monetary policy (open market operations, the discount rate, and the reserve requirements) directly affected the goals pursued by the central bankers, there would be no problem of how to implement monetary policy. Policymakers would simply set the levels of their tools to correspond to the desired level of nominal income, unemployment, inflation, or whatever goal they specified. Unfortunately, central bankers can only indirectly influence their ultimate goals, and then only with a lag between the time they change the tools and the time

---

[8]In order to avoid the confusion of M for money supply on the left side of the equation and M for imports on the right side, "net exports" (NX) is written in place of exports (X) minus imports (M) on the right side and the letter "M" is reserved for money supply.

they observe the effect of the change on the economy. In the interim, central bankers must design operating procedures that allow them to make midcourse corrections so they reach their ultimate objectives.

The general strategies available to the central bankers are outlined schematically in Figure 1. The top half shows possible paths linking the tools and the goals; the bottom half lists questions that must be answered at each stage in order to design a monetary strategy. On the far left are the three primary tools of monetary policy—the levers that policymakers can adjust to influence the economy. On the far right are the goals of the central bank's actions. For simplicity, only one very general goal, nominal income, is presented, though the goals may certainly be more complicated combinations of global, national, and sectoral performance objectives measured in terms such as desired levels of inflation or unemployment, growth rates of real output or industrial production, or stability of exchange rates or interest rates. Policymakers must make trade-offs among goals because they do not have sufficient instruments or understanding of the economy to achieve all of their objectives.

When policymakers change the settings of their tools, the variables that are directly affected and controlled by the central bank are called *instruments*. There are two broad categories of instruments: reserve aggregates[9] and short-term interest rates.[10] These instruments may be thought of as "quantity" and "price" instruments, respectively.

The central bank can choose only one instrument. If the central bank sets the amount of, say, total reserves (a quantity), then the federal funds rate (a price) will be determined by the market and cannot be controlled by the central bank, and vice versa. The choice of instruments depends on how well a particular instrument is related to the intermediate targets or ultimate goals, and how well it insulates the economy from unforeseen disturbances.[11]

A decision even more important for policymakers than instrument choice is instrument variation. Central bankers must decide how often the instrument will be adjusted and how new information about the interim progress of the economy will be used. If the instrument is fixed (or pegged) for long periods of time without change, then the central bank is using an instrument *rule*. If changes are made frequently in response to new information, then it is using instrument *discretion*.

The purpose of an instrument is to have a market variable that the central bank can control directly with fast, accurate information on its level. But because reserve aggregates or short-term interest rates are not

[9]These primarily include the monetary base, total reserves, nonborrowed reserves, borrowed reserves, and international reserves.

[10]These primarily include the federal funds rate and the Treasury bill rate, although the exchange rate could also be an instrument.

[11]Economists generally believe that pegging an interest rate will better insulate nominal income from financial shocks and that pegging a reserve aggregate will better insulate nominal income from spending shocks, but no instrument will best insulate the economy from both.

Figure 1   Implementing a Monetary Strategy

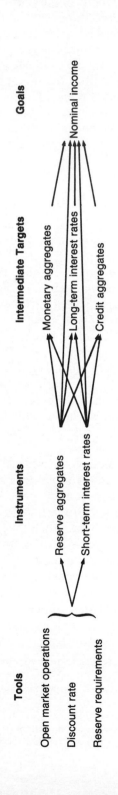

Tools	Instruments	Intermediate Targets	Goals
Open market operations	Reserve aggregates	Monetary aggregates	Nominal income
Discount rate	Short-term interest rates	Long-term interest rates	
Reserve requirements		Credit aggregates	

Questions Relating to Choice of a Monetary Strategy

Which instrument should be chosen?	Should an intermediate target be used?	What is the primary goal?
Should it be adjusted often?	If so, which intermediate target should be chosen?	What are the secondary goals?
	Should it be adjusted often?	What are the possible trade-offs among the goals?

(or pegged) for long periods of time without change, then the central bank is using an instrument *rule*. If changes are made frequently in response to new information, then it is using instrument *discretion*.

The purpose of an instrument is to have a market variable that the central bank can control directly with fast, accurate information on its level. But because reserve aggregates or short-term interest rates are not objectives in themselves, a decision must be made whether to manipulate the instruments in order to achieve the goals or whether to choose an intermediate target. An *intermediate target* should be a variable that has a direct effect on our goal and is controllable by the use of our instruments.

Three often-cited candidates for intermediate targets are (1) a monetary aggregate, (2) long-term interest rates, or (3) a credit aggregate.[12] If an intermediate-target regime is chosen, then the central bankers must decide which target to use and how often to change it. These questions are the same as at the instrument stage of the decision, but they do not necessarily have to be answered in the same way. For example, monetarists usually argue for a rule fixing the growth in the monetary aggregate, but they argue for discretion in the use of the instrument (a reserve aggregate is usually preferred) in order to achieve the monetary target.

Through the 1970s, the industrial countries have gradually altered their operating procedures from an instrument regime[13] to an intermediate-target regime focused on some monetary aggregate. The United States started this change in 1970 and, after 1975, the Federal Reserve was required by Congress to announce annual monetary targets. Germany made the transition starting in 1974, Canada in 1975, and the United Kingdom in 1976.

At the risk of oversimplification, one might characterize U.S. monetary policy in the 1950s and 1960s as a discretionary-instrument regime using short-term interest rates (actually all "money market conditions") to achieve the primary objective of stable interest rates. In the 1970s, the operating procedure was effectively a discretionary-instrument regime using the federal funds rate in order to maintain real growth while paying lip service to the need for targeting monetary aggregates in order to control inflation. After October 6, 1979, the Federal Reserve adopted an intermediate-target regime using nonborrowed reserves as the discretionary instrument in order to achieve stricter adherence to the fixed targets for the monetary aggregate and thus greater control over inflation.

---

[12]Credit aggregates include such variables as bank credit, debt (private domestic nonfinancial), and the broadest category, nonfinancial domestic credit. See Exhibit 4 of the previous case.

[13]Usually the instrument regime was the control of short-term interest rates in order to achieve an ultimate objective without the use of an intermediate target.

Discussion Questions for Case and Note

1. What were the strengths and weaknesses of the Fed's operating procedure that was used after October 6, 1979?
2. What were the consequences of deregulation for the conduct of monetary policy?
3. What alternative monetary strategies could the Fed have pursued? How effective would they have been?
4. To what extent were monetary factors responsible for the recession of 1981 and 1982? Was Volcker responsible for the fall in inflation?
5. What were the implications of the Fed's monetary experiment and financial deregulation for financial institutions?

Bibliography

Friedman, Benjamin M., "Lessons from the 1979–82 Monetary Policy Experiment," *American Economic Review* (May 1984): 382–387. This is an advanced but nontechnical argument against the success of the monetary policy experiment and monetarist propositions.

Friedman, Milton, "Lessons from the 1979–82 Monetary Policy Experiment," *American Economic Review* (May 1984): 397–400. Professor Friedman also criticizes the Fed's conduct during these three years, but he defends monetarism. The Fed's experiment, he argues, was not a "monetarist experiment."

Gordon, Robert J., *Macroeconomics*, 3rd ed. (Boston: Little, Brown, 1984). The relevant sections for this chapter are the more advanced discussions of the choice of instruments (pages 466–468), the changes in money demand (pages 479–484), and the practice and limitations of countercyclical monetary policy in the 1980s (pages 513–525).

Reynolds, Lloyd G., *Macroeconomics: Analysis and Policy*, 5th ed. (Homewood, IL: Irwin, 1985). A brief, elementary description of the conduct of monetary policy is given on pages 263–268.

Ritter, Lawrence S., and William L. Silber, *Money*, 5th and rev. ed. (New York: Basic Books, 1985). This book contains an elementary discussion of the monetarist and Keynesian views (Chapter 4), the consequences of high interest rates (Chapter 7), and a good summary of Federal Reserve policymaking (Chapters 8–11, but especially pages 135–143).

CHAPTER 4
Using Monetary Policy to Induce Structural Change

Monetary policy under Prime Minister Margaret Thatcher has been an integral part of the government's strategy to reduce inflation and induce the structural changes necessary for revitalizing the lagging British economy. The conduct of monetary policy, especially in the United States, is usually left to the discretion of central bankers with occasional meddling and abundant criticism from politicians. The potential exists for conflict between the economic policy of the government and the monetary policy of the central bank, such as with the coexistence of Reagan's expansionary fiscal policy with Volcker's contractionary monetary policy. Since the Bank of England is not independent of the U.K. government, the government is held directly responsible for the bank's actions. Thatcher has been particularly aggressive in managing monetary policy to meet her policy objectives.

There are two methods of controlling the money supply. One method, used by the United States, Germany, and Canada, is the control of bank credit from the supply side by restricting the supply of reserves to the banking system. The other method, used by the United Kingdom, France, Italy, and Japan, controls bank credit from the demand side by restricting the demands for bank credit by the government sector, the private sector, and the foreign sector. Under this latter scheme, fiscal policy, interest rates, and exchange rates are used to reduce the credit demands of government, private, and foreign sectors, respectively. In the United Kingdom, then, other government policies are subordinated to monetary policy if the government is determined to meet its monetary objectives.

This chapter describes Margaret Thatcher's objectives, policies, and performance in her first term as prime minister from 1979 to 1983. There are two issues facing government decision makers: the operational issue of the best method of implementing monetary policy and the strategic issue of how monetary policy can contribute to broad structural change in the economy. The major issue for firms in the United Kingdom is how these policies affect the long-term ability to compete. As in the previous chapter, the government's answer to both the operational and strategic issues has implications for the competitiveness of British firms.

Case
The United Kingdom under Thatcher

Unless we change our ways and our direction, our greatness as a nation will soon be a footnote in the history books, a distant memory of an offshore island lost in the mists of time—like Camelot remembered kindly for its noble past.

—Margaret Thatcher in Bolton
(May 1, 1979)

Two days later Margaret Thatcher led her Conservative Party to victory in what she called "a watershed election. The result was decisive, with a difference of two million votes between the two major parties, the largest difference since 1935."[1] The British electorate, eager for her promise of a dramatic national revival, had embarked on an experiment in economic management, which soon became known as "Thatcherism." When she became prime minister, Mrs. Thatcher committed the nation to a fundamental shift in the British economy by applying the doctrines of monetarism and setting the private sector free of government control.

Four years later, her experiment seemed to have "left Britain in the slow lane," in the words of *The Economist*. Unemployment had more than doubled to a level of 13 percent in March 1983, manufacturing output had fallen to a 15-year low, and Mrs. Thatcher's main target, inflation, was expected to be 7 percent by the end of 1983 compared to the 10 percent rate when she had taken office. Yet Thatcher's popularity was high—fueling speculation that she would call an election before the time mandated in May 1984. Was Britain just emerging from an invigorating economic cold shower as a slimmer and fitter competitor in world markets? Or had the experiment been a disastrous long-term setback to British economic growth?

The Context of Mrs. Thatcher's Election

Some political analysts have seen the election of Mrs. Thatcher as part of a worldwide swing to the right in the late 1970s. The election of Malcolm Fraser in Australia in 1975, the defeat of Olaf Palme in Sweden in the same year, the passage of Proposition 13 in California in 1978, the

This case was prepared by Associate Professor Michael Rukstad, with the assistance of John O'Reilly, MBA 1982.
Copyright © 1982 by the President and Fellows of Harvard College
Harvard Business School case 9-382-125

[1]Quoted in Hugh Stephenson, *Mrs. Thatcher's First Year* (London: J. Norman, 1980). (Stanley Baldwin was elected as Conservative Prime Minister in 1935).

victory of Thatcher in 1979, and the election of Ronald Reagan in the United States in 1980 are all cited as examples. Lord Blake, a conservative historian writing a few months before the election, saw "a wind of change in Britain and much of the democratic world and it comes from the right not the left." This wind of change was fanned by Conservatives to the right of the party like Thatcher's "guru," Sir Keith Joseph. They rediscovered *The Wealth of Nations*, Adam Smith's bible of the free market economy, and preached a return to classical economic liberalism. Exploiting a growing public distaste for the size of the public sector, they built a widespread expectation that a future Tory government would reduce the burden of taxation and increase individual incentives.

Mrs. Thatcher preached this philosophy with a fervor which earned her the description of the "Joan of Archconservatism." Her dogmatism and commitment contrasted strongly with the pragmatism which had marked British governments of both parties since 1951. Their short-term outlook was increasingly seen by the public as connected to Britain's continuing economic decline during the 1970s. "The election of Margaret Thatcher in 1979 owed a great deal to her being perceived as a leader who would not allow political considerations to deflect her from the task of national survival."[2] As a result she gained a much stronger personal identification with a set of policies than any leader since Churchill: hence "Thatcherism."

It was against the background of the declining economic performance of Britain during the 1970s and the policy failures of the 1974–1979 Labour government that the new conservatism of the Tories flourished. The steady deterioration of Britain's economic performance created the conditions for Mrs. Thatcher's election. In terms of Gross Domestic Product (GDP) growth rates and GDP per capita, Britain grew more slowly than its competitors in the OECD. During the years 1973–1978, the average annual growth of real GDP was 1.1 percent for the United Kingdom compared to 2.5 percent for all OECD countries. By 1978 this trend was reflected in a per capita GDP for the United Kingdom of $5,496 compared to $7,683 for all OECD countries. Unemployment in Britain doubled—rising from 2.6 percent in 1973 to 5.7 percent in 1978. However, this slower growth and rising unemployment did not lead to lower inflation. The United Kingdom had an average annual inflation rate of 16.2 percent over this five-year period while the OECD average was 10 percent. There is disagreement about the exact causes of Britain's poor performance in the 1970s, but most analysts seem to agree with the broad conclusion of a recent study by the Brookings Institution that "Britain's economic malaise stems largely from its productivity problem whose origins lie deep in the social system."[3]

---

[2]*The Wall Street Journal*, Jan. 27, 1982, 27.

[3]Richard Caves and Lawrence Krause, eds., *Britain's Economic Performance* (Washington, DC: Brookings Institution, 1980).

This general economic decline was punctuated by a series of damaging failures with the economy recorded by James Callaghan's Labour government. In December 1976 the pound was rescued from outside by the International Monetary Fund (IMF), a scenario usually reserved for struggling third-world nations.[4] Then in 1978–1979 the centerpiece of t] e government's incomes policy, the "special relationship" with the unions over pay policy, faded away. The public sector unions staged a "winter of discontent" which disrupted or halted all the most sensitive public services (see Exhibit 16 at the end of this case).

The repeated attempts of both Labour and Conservative governments of the 1970s to deal with inflation through formal incomes policies was a critical inheritance for Mrs. Thatcher. Edward Heath's Conservative government was elected in 1970 with a platform to stop inflation, which was very similar to Mrs. Thatcher's a decade later. Despite his expansionary 1971 budget, the sharp recession in the spring of 1971 sent unemployment over one million. Heath meanwhile introduced a controversial Industrial Relations Act, attempting to create a set of rules to govern pay bargaining and strike activities. In early 1972 the miners went on strike for a 25 percent raise from the government, disrupted the nation's power supplies, and won their demands after seven weeks. Other unions followed this example and inflation threatened to get out of control. This prompted Mr. Heath to adopt a statutory wages policy. A wage freeze beginning in the autumn of 1972 followed by controlled pay raises succeeded in controlling inflation only until the oil shock at the end of 1973. The miners again went on strike in the winter of 1973–1974, forcing the government to put the country on a three-day work week. Mr. Heath took the issue to an election in 1974 and lost to Harold Wilson of the Labour Party. Mrs. Thatcher, as Education Minister in the Heath government, drew her rejection of pay policy and fear of policy reversals from this experience.

The 1974–1979 Labour government used a Prices Commission (with veto power over price rises) as well as a formal wages policy. After annualized wage inflation hit 32 percent in August 1975, the government dropped its vague "social contract" and introduced a more explicit four-phase policy. The first three phases were largely observed, but with inflation of 8.4 percent in mid-1978 and North Sea oil giving the economy a strong surge of growth, the government was unable to enforce its Phase 4 guideline of 5 percent. The public sector unions forgot their special relationship with Labour as their frustrations were vented in the extensive strikes of the winter of 1978–1979.

[4]See HBS case 9-382-118 by John Rosenblum and Bruce Scott, "The U.K. and the IMF: 1976," for a detailed discussion of these events.

The Monetarist Philosophy

During the years as leader of the Opposition, Mrs. Thatcher became a disciple of two Nobel laureate economists, Milton Friedman and Friedrich von Hayek. Their economic philosophy, Monetarism, was echoed in the Conservative manifesto of 1979: "To master inflation, proper monetary discipline is essential, with publicly stated targets for the growth of the money supply." The major appeal of Monetarism to Mrs. Thatcher and the Conservatives was that it offered a possibility to control wage inflation without resorting to a statutory incomes policy.

Monetarism focuses on the growth of the money supply as the key determinant of the growth in nominal GNP—essentially, this is an affirmation of the Quantity Theory of Money. Monetarists believe that the economy will quickly adjust back to a "natural" unemployment rate on its own accord without the destabilizing influence of government policy interference. Their prescription for reducing the inflation component of nominal GNP is simply a reduction in the growth of the money supply without further government policy manipulations. The problem for Mrs. Thatcher would be exactly how to control the money supply in order to control inflation.

The first step in implementing monetary policy was to choose the appropriate definition of the money supply as the target. There were a number of candidates ranging from the narrowest definition, M1 (currency and demand deposits) to the broadest definition, PSL2 ("Public Sector Liquidity 2"). However, Sterling M3 (£M3) seemed to have the closest correlation with inflation in the early 1970s, so it was chosen in hopes that a reduction in inflation would follow a reduction in Sterling M3. Sterling M3 is defined to be currency plus *all* Sterling deposits held by both the U.K. *public* and *private* sectors. (M1 is only currency plus Sterling *demand* deposits held by the U.K. *private* sector.)

The framework for discussing monetary control in Britain is based on an accounting identity that decomposes Sterling M3 into its components. The identity can be written in two parts:

PSBR − Gilt sales + Increase in bank lending = DCE,

DCE + Net external flows − Nondeposit liabilities = £M3.

Exhibit 8 gives this decomposition for £M3 for the years 1977–1982. These terms are defined below using their more familiar American substitutes:

PSBR = "Public Sector Borrowing Requirement," or the government deficit.

Gilt sales = Sales of "gilt-edged stock" by the Bank of England, which are analogous to sales of long-term government bonds in the United States.

Bank lending = All bank lending (in Sterling) to the U.K. private sector.

DCE = "Domestic Credit Expansion," which is Column 6 of Exhibit 8: $(1 + 2) - (3 + 4) + 5 = 6$.

Net external flows = The official financing of the balance payments
     and all nonofficial bank flows.

Nondeposit liabilities = Mostly bank equity and capital reserves.

£M3 = M1 plus all Sterling deposits, which is Column 9 of Exhibit 8:
     $6 + 7 + 8 = 9$.

Essentially, this identity tells us that Sterling M3 will increase if there is
a government deficit that is not financed by the sale of bonds (PSBR −
Gilt sales), or an increase in bank lending, or a net inflow of Sterling
from abroad. Through this identity, monetary, fiscal, and exchange rate
policy were all intertwined.

The second step in implementing monetary policy was to choose
the appropriate instrument for achieving the monetary target. There are
three generic instruments available for this purpose: (1) direct controls
on the reserve requirements, (2) interest rate controls, or (3) monetary
base controls. Thatcher wanted to reduce the growth of £M3 by reducing
the PSBR and by increasing the interest rates, if necessary, in order to
increase gilt sales and decrease bank lending.

The movement toward stricter monetary policy in the United Kingdom began as part of the IMF stabilization program. The Labour Chancellor of the Exchequer, Denis Healey, began to set targets for the growth
of money supply defined in terms of Sterling M3. Controlling Sterling
M3 required frequent shifts of the government-administered interest rate
known as the Minimum Lending Rate (MLR), and the use of the bank
"corset." The "corset" was a reserve requirement on various sources of
funds for a bank which increased the cost of obtaining these funds. The
Bank of England used it to control the banks' balance sheets, and thereby
their lending capacity. Healey also introduced a system of cash limits on
government spending in order to control the PSBR. Along with open
market operations, these were the tools of monetary control that Mrs.
Thatcher and her Chancellor of the Exchequer, Sir Geoffrey Howe, inherited in May 1979.

Margaret Thatcher: Policies and Personality

The Conservative Party has traditionally regarded itself as the party of
"one nation." Tracing the paternalist lineage of Disraeli, Churchill, and
Macmillan, the Tories see themselves as balancing the interests of all the
institutions, groups, and social classes in British society to maintain social
stability. However, in the bitterness following the defeat of the Heath
government in 1974, the party felt a need to return to its right-wing grass
roots and elected Margaret Thatcher as its new leader. She represented
a clean break from the Conservative tradition. "I'm not a consensus
politician or a pragmatic politician," she said of herself. "I'm a conviction
politician."[5]

[5]*The Observer*, Feb. 25, 1979.

Mrs. Thatcher's convictions were those of the right of the party. Her economic philosophy was three-pronged:

1. Reduce inflation by strict monetary control: Mrs. Thatcher felt that "real economic progress can only come from the breaking of inflationary expectations and from the restoration of confidence in the value of money—until then businessmen will not take the risks which create genuine job opportunities."[6] She proposed to "wring inflation out of the system" by the strict control of monetary policy as described above.

2. Reduce government interference in the economy: Mrs. Thatcher intended to "roll back the frontiers of the public sector." She felt that government intervention stifled economic growth and encroached on individual liberties. She therefore wanted to cut overall government spending, reduce government ownership of industry by selling off some publicly owned companies (like British Airways), halt the trend toward maintaining unprofitable and declining sectors of the economy with government subsidies, and improve the efficiency of the government and civil service.

3. Stimulate productivity by increasing incentives: "To become more prosperous, Britain must become more productive and the British people must be given more incentive," stated the Tory manifesto of 1979. Much of the responsibility for achieving this goal was placed on entrepreneurs who would be encouraged to work harder and take more risks by reducing the high marginal rates of taxation prevalent in Britain and by changing the structure of taxation more toward indirect taxes. She felt that by shifting the balance of industrial power away from the unions, management could be free to increase productivity faster in the workplace.

These latter policies appealed not only to the Conservatives' middle-class constituency but also to the newly affluent self-employed and higher-income blue-collar workers. The percentage of unskilled labor in the work force was falling, and the percentage of self-employed rising. Also, the higher relative wages won by the unions in the 1970s had begun to blur some of the connection between income and social status. Mrs. Thatcher's personal background as the daughter of a Lincolnshire grocer made her sensitive to these changes. The trends helped make her promise of reduced taxation more widely popular and created her large majority.

On entering office, Mrs. Thatcher faced political problems in implementing her policies. Being Britain's first woman prime minister proved no handicap to her, but she was the least experienced prime minister of modern times. The senior party figures from whom she had to select her

[6]*The Wall Street Journal*, Jan. 27, 1982.

Cabinet had been brought up in the consensus politics of the Macmillan era, and had been supporters of Edward Heath. When she took office, therefore, Mrs. Thatcher was determined to make immediate changes to escape the tendency of the British system toward preserving the status quo, and then avoid any policy reversals. She saw her role in Cabinet not as building consensus, but keeping it pointing in its original direction. Her dominating style soon earned her the description, "the only man in the Cabinet," and Denis Healey of the Labour party likened her single-mindedness to a rhinoceros: "She has an impenetrably thick hide, is liable to mount charges in all directions, and is always thinking on the trot." Yet although her close personal identification with her policies initially added to her executive power, it gave her Cabinet appointees the opportunity to distance themselves from the basic policies. When the economy fell into recession, the politically painful tasks, like expenditure cuts, brought conflict within the Cabinet over policy to the surface. Thus the shifting balance between Mrs. Thatcher and senior Conservatives became a critical factor in implementing the government's economic strategy.

The Application of Thatcherism: 1979

In May 1979, Mrs. Thatcher faced a number of problems which complicated her long-term strategy. The second oil shock resulted in a doubling of world oil prices, but this also coincided with Britain's becoming self-sufficient in oil.

A second complication was that Mrs. Thatcher, as part of her election campaign, had pledged to accept the findings of the Clegg Commission. This commission was created by the Labour government to recommend pay raises for several public sector unions, which would be announced in the summer of 1979. These prospective wage settlements were expected to inflate substantially the PSBR which Mrs. Thatcher had hoped to cut. It was an election promise she felt unable to wriggle out of after she honored another promise within a week of taking office by making large awards to the police (20 percent) and the armed services (32 percent). Overall government expenditure had already been thoroughly pruned by Denis Healey in the years following the IMF negotiations—especially in the capital expenditure category. This also increased the difficulty for the Conservatives in making their promised tax cuts. Meanwhile inflation and unemployment were rising, indicators of output growth were falling, and economists were predicting a severe recession.

The first Conservative budget, presented in June 1979 by Sir Geoffrey Howe, Thatcher's Chancellor of the Exchequer, emphasized long-term policy rather than these immediate problems. It cast the mold of macroeconomic management for the next four years, for it was an attempt to implement almost the entire government economic strategy at once. In fiscal terms it was broadly neutral, i.e., would not stimulate GNP, but it contained moves to abandon the public sector as the prime engine of economic growth and to shift the structure of taxation. Below are details:

1. Monetary policy, as promised, was used to counter inflation, and Sterling M3 was chosen as the principal target variable for money supply with a 7-11 percent target range for monetary growth. To reinforce this tight monetary policy, the Bank of England raised the Minimum Lending Rate (MLR) (British equivalent of the U.S. discount rate) from 12 percent to 14 percent in order to increase gilt sales and reduce bank lending. Furthermore, the corset was to remain in effect while exchange controls were relaxed.

2. The government forecast that it would keep the 1979 PSBR at its actual 1974 level of £8.3 billion, which would be equivalent to reducing it by 1 percent of GDP. To meet its PSBR goals, the government planned to cut its expenditure by £3.5 billion: £1 billion from the sale of assets, £1.5 billion of specific cuts, and £1 billion by a stricter application of cash limits. The specific cuts deeply affected public capital spending. The sale of assets would initially be the reduction of the government's share of British Petroleum from 51 percent to 34 percent, with other sales to be investigated.

3. The budget announced a shift in the structure of taxation: a reduction in (direct) income taxes and an offsetting increase in (indirect) value-added taxes (VAT). The basic rate of income tax was cut from 33 percent to 30 percent, the personal income tax brackets were indexed to inflation, and the top marginal tax rate was cut from 83 percent to 60 percent. This last change was designed to bring Britain in line with its competitors in rewarding senior managers. Value-added-tax (VAT) rates rose from 8 percent for most nonfood goods and 12.5 percent for luxury goods to a single rate of 15 percent for all nonfood goods. This increase in VAT balanced the revenue lost from the income tax cut, and directly increased the Retail Price Index by 3.5 percent. To show the neutral effect of these tax changes on consumer purchasing power, the government later created a new Tax and Prices Index (TPI) as a tool against pay demands based on the retail price index increases resulting from the VAT rise.

The reactions to this budget varied widely. Denis Healey condemned it as "punk monetarism," while the *Economist* judged it to be "perverse." The *Financial Times* Index fell 20 points in the following weeks.

Meanwhile the government's ability to implement its budget policies began to look less certain. There were doubts that the £2.5 billion of public expenditure cuts could be achieved. The inflation projections on which spending was based had been outdated by the government's own actions in raising VAT and the cost of its debt service. And the earnings forecasts for government employees became outdated when the

Clegg Commission reported its awards. In August 1979 the commission awarded increases for 1.4 million workers ranging from 2.7 percent to 25.8 percent—in addition to the 9 percent increases they had all received earlier in the year. Selling public companies like British Leyland and British Airways would also have to be deferred while they continued to make large losses. The government, however, continued with its promises to lift controls on the free working of the economy. In the summer of 1979 the government abolished the Prices Commission, removed dividend control restrictions, and further liberalized exchange controls.

Moreover, the ability of the government to control the money supply was also questioned. Accommodating the PSBR overruns described above and the high corporate loan demand to cover increased debt service obligations led to an unexpectedly high growth in the money supply. The situation came to a head when it proved impossible for the government to sell any gilt-edged stock (equivalent to U.S. Treasury securities) at the prevailing 14 percent rate of interest. Since open market operations were central to restraining monetary growth, Sterling M3 spurted ahead of its 7-11 percent growth range. Mrs. Thatcher was unwilling to relax the target and raised the MLR to a record 17 percent as a signal of her determination to get on top of inflation.

In November 1979, Thatcher proposed a mini-budget designed to improve the government's hold on the money supply. In the mini-budget the 7-11 percent range for monetary growth was extended another year. Although the government committed itself to making a further £1 billion of cuts the next year, and £2 billion the following year, it did not specify where they would come from. In the meantime oil companies would have to pay £700 million of taxes in advance.

Industrialists, the traditional allies of the Conservative party, were complaining publicly about the high exchange and interest rates that the government had engineered. Corporate liquidity was under pressure and the rate of bankruptcies was rising. Cabinet ministers became divided between "wets" and "drys." Wets were spending ministers (e.g., Social Services, Education) who resisted cuts, worrying about their effects on unemployment. Drys were Treasury ministers pressing for a stricter application of monetary policy. Trade unions were complaining about lack of consultation from the government, and the whole board of the National Enterprise Board (which manages government-owned companies) had resigned en masse in November 1979. Yet Mrs. Thatcher appeared to be choosing her battles with the unions carefully. The miners had quietly been awarded an inflationary pay claim, and initial proposals for trade union reform were mild in comparison to Mrs. Thatcher's election rhetoric. She remained unruffled by the economic downturn: "I don't think there'll be 3 years of unparalleled austerity. There will be 3 years of realism, and 3 years, 4 years, 5 years, I hope 10 years of opportunity."[7]

[7]Quoted in Stephenson, op. cit.

Management of the Economy: 1980-1981

The recession deepened significantly in 1980, but the inflation rate continued to rise, reaching an 18 percent annual rate. The March 1980 budget for Thatcher's second year underlined Mrs. Thatcher's conviction that she must persevere with restrictive monetary policies, regardless of the recession. "This lady's not for turning," she proclaimed on television. It was a no-change budget: no compensation for the increasing weakness of private demand or for the hard-pressed corporate sector. In order to encourage expectations of declining inflation and to show her resolution in meeting deflationary monetary targets of £M3, Mrs. Thatcher announced a medium-term financial strategy (MTFS), which integrated monetary and fiscal policy. The MTFS set declining targets for the next four years for £M3 and the PSBR (without specifying output targets) so that the government would not have to rely on excessively high interest rates or incomes policies to reduce inflation. (See Exhibits 9 and 10 for the yearly targets as they were updated.) The monetary growth target remained at 7-11 percent, while interest rates were left unchanged. The PSBR was set at £8.5 billion. Fiscally, the budget was again proclaimed to be neutral. Personal income tax thresholds were still indexed to inflation, capital gains exemptions were raised, as were the "sin" taxes on alcohol, tobacco, and petrol.

Although the inflation rate fell in late 1980, the government was unable to meet its own targets. The PSBR rose to £12 billion in calendar year 1980 (see Exhibit 12), or 5.4 percent of GDP. British Steel, which suffered a protracted strike and conceded a 16 percent pay raise, overspent by £600 million. When faced with overspending or adding huge blocs to the rising unemployment, the government felt unable to refuse more aid to nationalized industry. For example, British Leyland was awarded £990 million over two years. In June 1980, Mrs. Thatcher abandoned the ineffective corset. All the money diverted outside the banking system flowed back in and boosted Sterling M3. These problems of implementation caused Sir Keith Joseph, Industry Minister, to say that the government had "lost the first year." And when commenting on why the British monetarist policies had not had the effects he had predicted, Milton Friedman felt that "unfortunately actual practice has not conformed to policy."

To offset these problems, in November the government introduced more expenditure cuts from the capital budget and a reduction in interest rates to 14 percent from 16 percent. Plans for a supplementary oil tax and a 1 percent rise in employees' national insurance contributions (similar to a Social Security tax) were also announced, but the monetary target remained in the 7-11 percent range.

The repeated attempts to cut government spending had deeply divided Mrs. Thatcher's Cabinet. The failing economy dispirited them and made them appear to the *Economist* as "grim-faced men lashed to the mast of a ship outside their control." By early 1981, Howe seemed to be the only Thatcherite left on the team. He ignored calls from industry for an expansionary package and clung to the original strategy. Howe introduced a deflationary budget for Thatcher's third year in office in March 1981 which stunned both parties with its severity.

1.   To "reaffirm the medium-term financial strategy," Howe set targets of 6-10 percent for monetary growth and £10.5 billion for PSBR (see Exhibits 9 and 10). As a gesture to industry, the MLR was cut from 14 percent to 12 percent. Social Security payments were increased only 9 percent and government expenditure in real terms was to remain constant.

2.   Howe estimated that real incomes had risen 2 percent in 1980 (see Exhibit 15), so "to redress the balance between the personal and public sectors" tax thresholds were left unchanged despite the 15 percent inflation of the previous fiscal year. This raised taxes £2.5 billion through fiscal drag. Another £2.5 billion was raised through substantial increases in the "sin" taxes. This lifted the tax and price index 2.5 percent above the retail price index, and the government elected to cut taxes had by now increased taxes' share of GDP from 32 percent to 35 percent.

3.   £1.4 billion extra revenue was to be raised through a windfall profit tax on banks and a supplementary tax on North Sea oil producers.

The president of the Confederation of British Industry, Sir Raymond Pennock, commented that the budget was "at best a brush-off, at worst a kick in the teeth." Industry felt that the private sector had reacted properly to Conservative stimuli: private sector strikes had dropped to their lowest level for 40 years (see Exhibit 16), and private sector inflation had fallen to a 7 percent annual average. It was the government sector which seemed to be out of control. Government expenditure's share of GDP had risen from 41 percent to 44 percent under the Tories and nationalized industry inflation was running at 20 percent.

During 1981 the government made two changes to its monetary policy. First, to give the market freer rein in setting interest rates, the formal MLR was dropped in August. Henceforth the Bank of England would operate in the open market to keep rates within an unpublished band. Second, the difficulty of interpreting Sterling M3 figures caused the government to use the value of the pound as an indicator of the tightness of money supply. The pound fell in 1981 (see Exhibit 7), causing fears of rising import prices, inflation, and money supply growth. Interest rates were henceforth used to prevent excessive fluctuations of the pound, and thus the money supply.

During 1981 the fall in output ended but there seemed to be little hope of a swift recovery. Unemployment was rising towards the 3 million mark. Over 10,000 businesses had now gone bankrupt since Mrs. Thatcher took office. Interest rates were being kept high by U.S. interest rates, and the fall in the pound was expected to rekindle inflation. That the British work force was taking a cut in real income was part of the government strategy to restore British competitiveness. It also meant that consumption would provide no impetus to output growth.

There were other faint signs of encouragement for the government. Manufacturing productivity rose by 7 percent in the second half of 1981, and wage rises in the private sector were down to 4-6 percent. Corporate liquidity and profitability were being restored while the government at last looked like it was hitting its PSBR target.

Political and Social Changes: 1980-1981

The recessionary conditions of 1980-1981 drew comparisons with the depression of the 1930s. One parallel was the widening difference in living standards between employed and unemployed. The increase in real disposable income in 1980 at a time of falling GDP and employment clearly benefited those who remained employed. The geographical pattern of unemployment also resembled the 1930s, reflecting the selective impact of the recession. In 1979-1981, the number of manufacturing jobs fell 16.5 percent while the number of service sector jobs fell only 3 percent. Therefore, by the end of 1981 the South East, where most service sector jobs were concentrated, had an unemployment rate of only 8.7 percent, against a national average of 11.7 percent. Where manufacturing was the main employer, rates were much higher: 14.3 percent in the Midlands, 13.6 percent in Scotland, 14.9 percent in Wales, and 18.1 percent in Northern Ireland. These rates would have been even higher without two government schemes. Subsidies were paid to employers to keep up to 0.5 million workers on short-time work in mid-1981, and the Youth Opportunities Scheme was giving 240,000 school leavers a year's practical training at government expense in late 1981.

The social tensions created by unemployment exploded into street rioting in 1981. After April riots in the immigrant Brixton neighborhood of London, rioting began again in July in many of the areas most severely affected by the recession. Inner city areas of depressed cities like Liverpool and Manchester were the focus of looting and fighting against the police. Although the riots subsided in time for the royal wedding, Mrs. Thatcher announced a £700 million package aimed mostly at youth employment schemes.

The government's political ability to survive the worsening conditions of 1979-1981 was based on several factors. First, the government's majority had provided an initial mandate for its more unpopular measures. Next, the government had been successful during 1980 in drawing public attention away from the economy on to some successes abroad where Mrs. Thatcher reveled in her nickname of "The Iron Lady." Britain's £1 billion net contribution to the European Economic Community, the EEC, (the next largest was West Germany's £0.3 billion) was a major target for Mrs. Thatcher. Renouncing the role of "Sister Bountiful to the community," she negotiated a plan to reduce the contribution by two-thirds. She achieved a similar foreign policy coup with the resolution of the Zimbabwe-Rhodesia civil war. Domestically Mrs. Thatcher was cautious in dealings with the unions. Her first union legislation—financial support for secret ballots and compensation for job loss due to a closed shop—represented only a mild step toward union control. And against her principles she approved more cash for loss-making publicly owned companies: a three-year £1.1 billion package for British Leyland in January 1981 and the bailout of DeLorean Motors in early 1982 were widely publicized examples.

Mrs. Thatcher benefited most, though, from the internal trends of British politics. The Labour party was unable to exploit the government's problems because of its own internal dissension. The center-right of the party represented by leader James Callaghan dominated the parliamentary party; but the left wing, represented by Tony Benn, increasingly controlled the internal structure and constituency organizations of the party. Using this control, the left wing won two major changes. First, future Labour leaders were to be selected by an electoral college made up of Labour MPs, constituency parties, and trade unions. After Callaghan resigned, the new leader was Michael Foot, widely regarded as a compromise candidate, unable to control either section of the party. Second, all Labour MPs had to submit to reselection by their constituencies before each election. Constituency parties used the change to replace sitting center-right MPs with new left-wing candidates.

Labour party membership fell in response to this leftward movement. Meanwhile trade union membership fell (10 percent in 1981) as its members became unemployed. Mrs. Thatcher benefited from this weakness in her party's traditional opponents. However, the unpopularity of Mrs. Thatcher's policies and the turmoil within the Labour party lay behind a major change in the structure of British politics—the emergence of the Social Democratic Party (SDP). Following the changes in Labour party constitution, three senior figures broke away. They were joined by Roy Jenkins, a former Labour deputy leader and president of the EEC. This "Gang of Four" formed the SDP. Center-right Labour MPs began to desert Labour for the SDP, and the SDP concluded an electoral alliance with the Liberal party. Representing the center ground of British politics, this new alliance caught the imagination of a public apparently tired of the extremism of both major parties. The alliance found itself at the top of the opinion polls with the Conservatives third, and began to win by-elections to vacant parliamentary seats (see Exhibit 17).

Being ranked third in the polls was behind many of the Tory calls for expansion in 1981. Opposition to "Thatcherism" grew within the Cabinet. The organizational structure of British government is based on spending money, and a minister's success is measured by the protection of the departmental budget. Mrs. Thatcher's ministers saw no political reward for them in cutting their budgets any more. Internal battles were fought publicly through leaks to the press, causing delays in reducing the

PSBR. At the time of the 1981 budget, Mrs. Thatcher publicly attacked these "wets," saying she "wished they had more guts." To lessen her vulnerability to party intrigue and to improve the implementation of government economic policy, she began to reshuffle her Cabinet. By mid-1981 she had sacked or shifted every economic and industrial minister besides Howe that she had appointed in 1979. The social and political conditions in which the government's economic strategy operated had thus altered considerably by early 1982.

Developments in 1982 and Early 1983

In early 1982, Mrs. Thatcher moved to increase the control of unions more effectively. The high level of unemployment, the muted reaction to the previous bill, and her new more right-wing employment secretary led her to tackle "secondary" actions. This was a tactic much used in the late 1970s to disrupt suppliers or customers of the company in dispute to increase the union's leverage over the company. The new bill removed trade union immunity from civil suits for damages due to secondary picketing and secondary action. Yet whatever the future of this bill, unlike the rest of the world, British union agreements would still not be enforceable as contracts.

In debating what economic strategy the government should follow for the rest of its term, there was much discussion over whether the recession had "bottomed out" and whether the government's policies were at last beginning to take effect. In March 1982, Chancellor Howe announced his fourth budget—"a budget for industry." The main measures were:

1. The target for monetary growth was listed as 8-12 percent. The target for PSBR was cut from £10.5 billion in 1981-1982 to £9.5 billion or 3.5 percent of GDP, in 1982-1983. Index-linked gilt-edged securities (linked to inflation) would be introduced to finance the PSBR. Government spending would increase only 9 percent and nationalized industry borrowing would decrease 16 percent.

2. The main help to industry was a reduction from 3.5 percent to 2.5 percent on employers' national insurance surcharge. The supplementary petroleum tax was removed while petroleum revenue tax rose to 75 percent.

3. Tax allowances and thresholds were raised by 14 percent, 2 percent ahead of inflation. However, employees' national insurance contributions had already been raised 1 percent, taking up part of this gain. The "sin" taxes were also raised but less than inflation. A major change to encourage personal saving was the provision for the indexation of capital gains for tax purposes. The budget was estimated to put £1.3 billion back into the economy. Although this

was only about 1 percent of government revenue and thus hardly made it a reflationary package, it relieved worried Tories.

On April 2, 1982, Argentine troops captured the disputed Falkland Islands and their dependent, the South Georgia Islands. Thatcher's highly regarded Foreign Secretary Lord Carrington, who misjudged the Argentine intentions, resigned his post and was replaced by Mr. Francis Pym. Ten weeks later Argentina surrendered to the British military forces. Thatcher's handling of the Falkland Islands elevated her popularity in the polls—a lead which was narrowed as Britain moved into its fifth and final year (see Exhibit 17).

The anticipation of an election left commentators wondering whether Mrs. Thatcher would engage in electioneering by dispensing fiscal "give aways" or whether she would reaffirm her commitment to stringent monetary targets. A *Financial Times* editorial declared that "it is some years since a budget aroused so much anticipatory excitement as the one Sir Geoffrey Howe will introduce two weeks from now."[8] On March 15, 1983, Sir Geoffrey Howe announced a "budget for the family, a budget for industry and most of all a budget for Britain's continuing recovery." Despite all the anticipation generated by this final budget before the next election, there were only mild surprises in what was widely regarded as a "boring budget."

The PSBR target for 1983-1984 was set at £8 billion, or 2.75 percent of GDP. In the previous budget, the PSBR target for the fiscal year that just ended (1982-1983) was £9.5 billion. It now appears that the actual PSBR for that year will be closer to £7 billion. The monetary targets for £M3, M1, and PSL2 were all achieved in the previous fiscal year, so the new targets were reduced from the 8-12 percent range to 7-11 percent. The targets depend on assumptions of real output growth, unemployment, inflation, interest rates, and the price of oil. For example, a $5 fall in the price of a barrel of oil would increase the PSBR by £1.5 billion.

When Mrs. Thatcher took office, government expenditure as a proportion of GDP was 40 percent. In the fiscal 1982 and 1983 budgets it was approximately 44 percent. Most of the growth was due to Social Security and debt interest. However, public capital expenditures, which have declined from 14 percent to 9.6 percent of the budget, have partially offset this rise in other expenditures.

In a pre-election interview with *Fortune* (May 16, 1983), Mrs. Thatcher responded to questions regarding her economic policies:

Q.   If you are reelected, what are the main items of legislation you plan for your second term of office?

A.   We shall carry on in the direction in which we have been going. We want less nationalization, less public sector . . . [see Exhibit 18]. When it comes to the general economy, as far as government finances are con-

[8]*Financial Times*, Mar. 2, 1983, 12.

cerned we have been firmly for a very disciplined control of public spending and of the public deficit, which is very, very important indeed.

Q. Everyone admires your success in bringing down inflation (to its current 4.5 percent level), but was the price, say in unemployment, higher than you expected?

A. You simply must get rid of the idea—it's a totally false one—that inflation will lead to more jobs. Over a period of 18 months or two years, it might. But after that, inflation will lead to higher unemployment. . . . If you are a short-term politician . . . you'd go two years before an election for a boom-bust, hoping that the boom would come before and the bust would come after. That's been done too often. . . . That is the way I will not go.

Q. Have your views on monetarism changed at all?

A. We've kept the money supply sound. I mean, don't say money supply is monetarism. It's far older than that. Money supply is a perfectly sound policy, which means that you keep the supply of money in tune with the earnings of the country. If you don't do that, you're a thoroughly dishonest politician.

Q. Many assume that, because of the recent weakness of sterling, there will be some rise in inflation later in the year.

A. Just let's get the difference straight between inflation and price increases. Price increases can occur because of a number of things, because you put an extra tax on, because of supply and demand on agricultural things, [because of exchange rate changes]. Inflation is a general increase in prices throughout the economy, partly because of the supply of money. You find prices will go up and down by virtue of supply and demand. . . . I'm afraid we have come to talk about inflation and price increases as if they were the same. They are not.

On June 9, 1983, Mrs. Thatcher won a landslide election. She became "the first incumbent prime minister since Lord Salisbury 83 years ago to win with a large enough margin to guarantee a full five-year second term. And her party became the first in 24 years to win solid majorities in two consecutive general elections."[9] The Thatcher experiment would now be granted almost a decade in which to implement its structural changes.

[9] *New York Times*, June 10, 1983, 1.

The United Kingdom under Thatcher

Exhibit 1   Expenditure on the Gross Domestic Product
(Millions of Pounds; 1980 Prices; Seasonally Adjusted)

	Gross Domestic Product at Factor Cost (Expenditure Based)[a]	Final Expenditure on Goods and Services at 1980 Prices		General Government Consumption							
		Total[a]	Consumers' Expenditure	Total[a]	Central Government	Local Authorities	Gross Fixed Investment	Stock Building	Exports of Goods and Services	Imports of Goods and Services	Adjustment to Factor Cost
	1	2	3	4	5	6	7	8	9	10	11
Annual											
1972	172,199	246,055	121,519	40,885	24,460	16,407	39,508	−22	44,302	47,101	26,464
1973	185,538	266,716	127,734	42,814	25,158	17,610	41,798	5,047	49,451	52,693	28,208
1974	184,279	265,498	125,552	43,465	26,046	17,407	40,639	2,860	53,072	53,350	25,279
1975	182,858	259,499	124,824	45,814	27,473	18,330	40,297	−2,901	51,657	49,576	26,863
1976	189,743	269,425	125,097	46,249	28,048	18,212	40,856	1,081	56,282	51,641	27,783
1977	192,371	272,734	124,646	45,734	27,876	17,879	39,851	2,638	59,913	52,251	27,763
1978	198,000	282,537	131,485	46,728	28,184	18,544	41,210	2,090	61,024	54,267	30,270
1979	201,419	292,819	137,863	47,612	28,560	19,052	41,586	2,490	63,268	59,908	31,492
1980	196,021	284,577	136,890	48,419	29,474	18,945	39,302	−3,236	63,202	57,702	30,854
1981	193,952	280,231	137,063	48,329	29,650	18,679	35,557	−2,655	61,937	56,256	30,023
1982	198,324	287,248	138,865	49,011	29,904	19,107	37,614	−1,031	62,789	57,997	30,927

Exhibit 1 (Continued)

Quarterly

1979 (1)	48,838	70,561	33,646	11,787	7,093	4,694	10,168	852	14,108	13,895	7,828
(2)	51,163	74,643	35,288	11,956	7,177	4,779	10,375	279	16,745	15,345	8,135
(3)	51,021	73,912	34,261	11,939	7,157	4,782	10,508	1,040	16,164	15,261	7,630
(4)	50,397	73,703	34,668	11,930	7,133	4,797	10,535	319	16,251	15,407	7,899
1980 (1)	49,665	73,167	34,786	12,074	7,265	4,809	10,249	−501	16,559	15,538	7,964
(2)	49,132	71,720	34,000	12,006	7,298	4,708	10,016	−135	15,833	14,962	7,626
(3)	48,644	69,952	34,048	12,100	7,406	4,694	9,653	−1,201	15,352	13,764	7,544
(4)	48,580	69,738	34,056	12,239	7,505	4,734	9,384	−1,399	15,458	13,438	7,720
1981 (1)	49,009	69,544	34,319	12,084	7,436	4,648	8,998	−1,010	15,153	12,992	7,543
(2)	47,885	68,867	34,235	11,954	7,327	4,627	8,785	−1,329	15,222	13,552	7,430
(3)	48,105	70,765	34,232	12,245	7,520	4,725	8,815	−182	15,655	15,062	7,598
(4)	48,953	71,055	34,277	12,046	7,367	4,679	8,959	−134	15,907	14,650	7,452
1982 (1)	49,044	71,323	34,102	12,165	7,464	4,701	9,353	27	15,676	14,624	7,655
(2)	49,197	71,791	34,319	12,194	7,484	4,710	9,146	243	15,889	14,892	7,702
(3)	49,423	71,441	34,930	12,261	7,484	4,777	9,573	−621	15,298	14,247	7,771
(4)	50,660	72,693	35,514	12,391	7,472	4,919	9,542	−680	15,926	14,234	7,799
1983 (1)	51,486	74,318	35,406	12,618	7,590	5,028	9,788	612	15,894	14,952	7,880
(2)	50,410	73,424	35,946	12,529	7,493	5,036	9,223	71	15,655	15,122	7,892

(Continued)

Exhibit 1 (Continued)

Final Expenditure on Goods and Services at 1980 Prices

Percentage Change, Quarter on Corresponding Period of Previous Year

| | Gross Domestic Product at Factor Cost (Expenditure Based)ᵃ | Totalᵃ | Consumers' Expenditure | General Government Consumption | | | Gross Fixed Investment | Stock Building | Exports of Goods and Services | Imports of Goods and Services | Adjustment to Factor Cost |
| | | | | Totalᵃ | Central Government | Local Authorities | | | | | |
	1	2	3	4	5	6	7	8	9	10	11
1979 (1)	0.5	1.0	3.3	1.7	1.5	2.2	-2.0	—	-5.7	1.4	3.5
(2)	2.0	5.3	8.2	2.6	1.8	3.8	-1.7	—	9.5	15.7	8.4
(3)	3.2	4.3	3.3	2.4	1.5	3.7	2.5	—	5.2	10.5	-0.2
(4)	1.2	4.0	4.7	0.9	0.6	1.3	5.1	—	5.5	14.2	4.7
1980 (1)	1.7	3.7	3.4	2.4	2.4	2.5	0.8	—	17.4	11.8	1.7
(2)	-4.0	-3.9	-3.7	0.4	1.7	-1.5	-3.5	—	-5.4	-2.5	-6.3
(3)	-4.7	-5.4	-0.6	1.3	3.5	-1.8	-8.1	—	-5.0	-9.8	-1.1
(4)	-3.6	-5.4	-1.8	2.6	5.2	-1.3	-10.9	—	-4.9	-12.8	-2.3
1981 (1)	-1.3	-5.0	-1.3	0.1	2.4	-3.3	-12.2	—	-8.5	-16.4	-5.3
(2)	-2.5	-4.0	0.7	-0.4	0.4	-1.7	-12.3	—	-3.9	-9.4	-2.6
(3)	-1.1	1.2	0.5	1.2	1.5	0.7	-8.7	—	2.0	9.4	0.7
(4)	0.8	1.9	0.6	-1.6	-1.8	-1.2	-4.5	—	2.9	9.0	-3.5
1982 (1)	0.1	2.6	-0.6	0.7	0.4	1.1	3.9	—	3.5	12.6	1.5
(2)	2.7	4.2	0.2	2.0	2.1	1.8	4.1	—	4.4	9.9	3.7
(3)	2.7	1.0	2.0	0.1	-0.5	1.1	8.6	—	-2.3	-5.4	2.3
(4)	3.5	2.3	3.6	2.9	1.4	5.1	6.5	—	0.1	-2.8	4.7
1983 (1)	5.0	4.2	3.8	3.7	1.7	7.0	4.7	—	1.4	2.2	-2.9
(2)	2.5	2.3	4.7	2.7	0.1	6.9	0.8	—	-1.5	1.5	-2.5

ᵃFor years up to and including 1977, totals differ from the sum of the components because of the method used to rebase on 1980 prices.

Source: Central Statistical Office, *Economic Trends* (London: Her Majesty's Stationery Office, November 1983), 8.

The United Kingdom under Thatcher

Exhibit 2   Gross Domestic Fixed Capital Formation

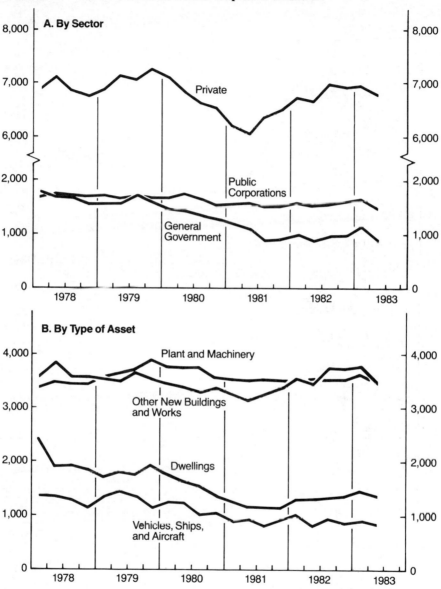

Millions of pounds; 1980 prices; seasonally adjusted.

Source: Central Statistical Office, *Economic Trends* (November 1983), 17.

The United Kingdom under Thatcher

Exhibit 3   Index of Output of the Production Industries

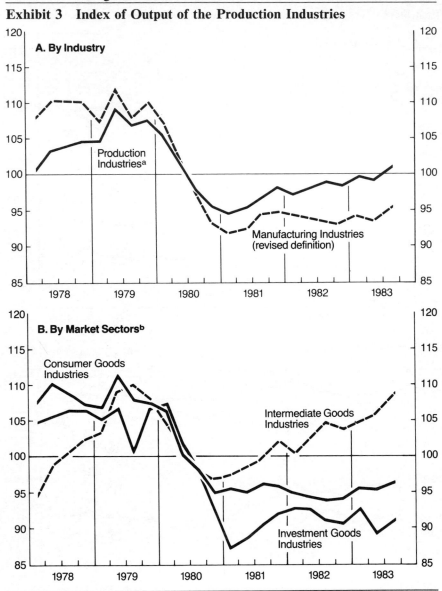

1980 = 100; seasonally adjusted.

ᵃProduction industries are manufacturing industries plus utilities. In 1980 manufacturing accounted for 73.6 percent of output and utilities accounted for the rest.

ᵇIn 1980 intermediate goods industries accounted for 51.3 percent of output, consumer goods for 24.4 percent, and investment goods for 24.3 percent.

Source: Central Statistical Office, *Economic Trends* (November 1983), 27.

The United Kingdom under Thatcher

Exhibit 4   Prices, Wages, Unit Labor Costs, and Unemployment

	Prices		Wages			
	General Index of Retail Prices (All Items) (Unadjusted, 1975 = 100)		Basic Weekly Wage Rates (Manual Workers) (Unadjusted, July 31, 1972 = 100)			
			All Industries and Services		Manufacturing Industry	
	Index	Percentage Increase[a]	Index	Percentage Increase[a]	Index	Percentage Increase[a]
	1	2	3	4	5	6
Annual						
1970	54.2	6.3	78.8	9.9	79.4	10.1
1971	59.3	9.4	89.0	12.9	89.3	12.5
1972	63.6	7.1	101.3	13.8	101.5	13.7
1973	69.4	9.2	115.3	13.8	114.6	12.9
1974	80.5	16.1	138.0	19.7	134.3	17.2
1975	100.0	24.2	178.7	29.5	174.4	29.8
1976	116.5	16.5	213.2	19.3	209.0	19.8
1977	135.0	15.8	227.3	6.7	218.9	4.7
1978	146.2	8.3	259.3	14.0	258.8	18.2
1979	165.8	13.4	298.1	15.0	297.5	14.9
1980	195.6	18.0	351.8	18.0	348.5	17.1
1981	218.9	11.9	387.7	10.2	381.7	9.5
1982	237.7	8.6	414.3	7.0	404.1	5.9
Quarterly						
1979 (1)	155.0	9.6	284.9	19.8	284.5	25.8
(2)	160.7	10.6	292.2	12.1	291.3	10.4
(3)	171.4	16.0	299.9	11.9	296.4	10.6
(4)	176.2	17.3	315.3	13.6	318.0	14.6
1980 (1)	184.6	19.1	334.8	17.5	336.5	18.3
(2)	195.3	21.5	348.3	19.2	345.3	18.5
(3)	199.4	16.4	357.4	19.2	349.9	18.0
(4)	203.2	15.3	366.6	16.3	362.3	13.9
1981 (1)	208.0	12.7	377.0	12.6	372.5	10.7
(2)	218.1	11.7	385.6	10.7	379.4	9.9
(3)	221.9	11.2	391.2	9.5	383.2	9.5
(4)	227.4	11.9	396.8	8.2	391.4	8.0
1982 (1)	231.1	11.1	404.5	7.3	397.6	6.7
(2)	238.5	9.4	413.0	7.1	401.8	5.9
(3)	239.5	8.0	417.3	6.7	404.5	5.6
(4)	241.4	6.2	422.7	6.5	412.3	5.3
1983 (1)	242.6	4.9	429.3	6.1	419.1	5.4
(2)	247.6	3.8	436.0	5.6	421.9	5.0

[a]Percentage increase on year earlier.

Source: Central Statistical Office, *Economic Trends,* Annual Supplement (London: Her Majesty's Stationery Office, 1984), 36, 110, 113, 117.

Exhibit 4 (Continued)

	Unit Labor Costs				Unemployment
	Wages and Salaries per Unit of Output (Seasonally Adjusted, 1980 = 100)				Unemployed Excluding School Leavers (Seasonally Adjusted)
	Whole Economy		Manufacturing Industry		
	Index	Percentage Increase[a]	Index	Percentage Increase[a]	Percentage of Employees
	7	8	9	10	11
Annual					
1970	27.7	9.5	28.4	—[b]	2.6
1971	30.2	9.0	30.9	8.8	3.4
1972	32.5	7.6	32.9	4.3	3.7
1973	35.2	8.3	34.3	4.2	2.6
1974	42.8	21.6	40.8	18.9	2.6
1975	55.7	30.1	52.8	29.4	3.9
1976	61.3	10.0	58.4	10.6	5.2
1977	65.4	6.7	63.4	8.6	5.6
1978	72.5	10.9	71.9	13.4	5.5
1979	82.7	14.1	82.3	14.5	5.1
1980	100.0	20.9	100.0	21.5	6.4
1981	108.7	8.7	109.4	9.4	10.0
1982	114.0	4.9	114.6	4.7	11.7
Quarterly					
1979 (1)	78.9	12.6	78.8	14.9	5.6
(2)	79.6	11.8	79.0	12.9	5.4
(3)	83.9	15.1	82.7	15.7	5.2
(4)	88.0	17.0	87.3	17.2	5.3
1980 (1)	93.0	17.9	90.7	15.1	5.4
(2)	97.3	22.2	97.6	23.5	5.9
(3)	104.0	24.0	104.0	25.8	6.7
(4)	105.7	20.1	107.4	23.0	7.9
1981 (1)	107.0	15.1	109.0	20.2	9.0
(2)	108.6	11.6	108.8	11.5	9.8
(3)	108.9	4.7	109.7	5.5	10.4
(4)	109.5	3.6	111.2	3.5	10.8
1982 (1)	111.3	4.0	113.4	4.0	11.2
(2)	112.3	3.4	115.0	5.7	11.5
(3)	113.2	3.9	115.8	5.6	11.9
(4)	114.5	4.6	118.2	6.3	12.2
1983 (1)	116.0	4.2	116.4	2.6	12.6
(2)	116.6	3.8	118.6	3.1	12.5

[a]Percentage increase on year earlier.

[b]1970 was the first year the index was calculated.

The United Kingdom under Thatcher

Exhibit 5   Productivity (Output per Person Employed)

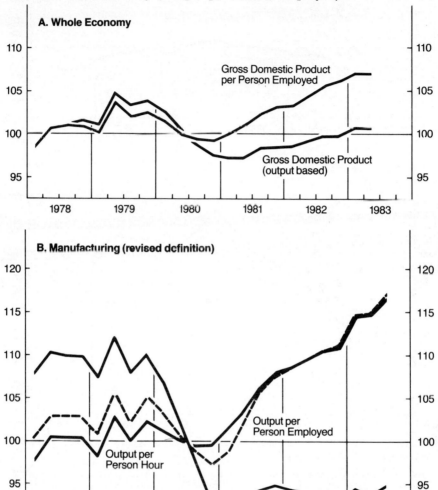

1980 = 100; seasonally adjusted.

Source: Central Statistical Office, *Economic Trends* (November 1983), 35.

The United Kingdom under Thatcher

Exhibit 6   Measures of U.K. Trade Competitiveness

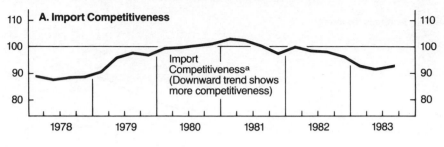

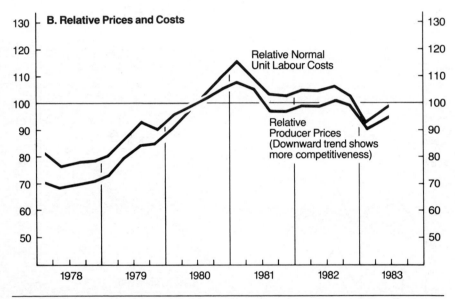

1980 = 100.

aImport competitiveness is defined as the ratio of the wholesale price index for import-competing products relative to the unit value index for imports of finished manufacturers.

Source: Central Statistical Office, *Economic Trends* (November 1983), 47.

Exhibit 6 (Continued)

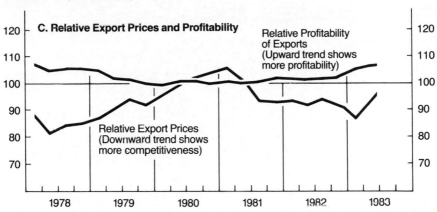

C. Relative Export Prices and Profitability

Relative Profitability
of Exports
(Upward trend shows
more profitability)

Relative Export Prices
(Downward trend shows
more competitiveness)

The United Kingdom under Thatcher

Exhibit 7   Money, GDP, Interest Rates, and Exchange Rates

	Monetary Aggregates				Nominal GDP		Interest Rates		Sterling Exchange Rates	
	Millions of Pounds, Seasonally Adjusted				Billions of Pounds, Based on Expenditure Data		Percentage Rate, Last Friday of Period		Average 1975 = 100	
	M1		£M3							
	Amount[a]	% Change[g]	Amount[a]	% Change[g]	Amount[b]	% Change[g]	Minimum Lending Rate[c]	Treasury Bill Rate[d]	Effective Exchange Rate[e]	% Change[g]
	1	2	3	4	5	6	7	8	9	
Annual										
1970	8,920	7.3	16,460	6.3	51.4	9.8	7.00	6.93	128.1	—
1971	9,900	11.0	18,270	11.0	57.6	24.1	5.00	4.46	127.9	-0.2
1972	11,280[f]	13.9	22,240[f]	21.7	63.8	10.8	9.00	8.48	123.3	-4.0
1973	13,200	12.4	27,870	23.0	73.5	15.2	13.00	12.82	111.8	-9.3
1974	13,240	0.3	32,780	18.0	83.6	13.7	11.50	11.30	108.3	-3.1
1975	15,250	15.2	35,800	9.2	105.4	26.1	11.25	10.93	100.0	-7.7
1976	18,430	15.3	38,710	8.2	125.6	19.2	14.25	13.98	85.7	-14.3
1977	20,430	10.8	41,670	7.6	144.8	15.3	7.00	6.39	81.2	-5.3
1978	24,950	22.1	48,160	15.6	166.5	15.0	12.50	11.91	81.5	0.4
1979	28,030	12.3	54,270	12.7	194.4	16.8	17.00	16.49	87.3	7.1
1980	29,880	6.6	62,840	15.8	226.9	16.7	14.00	13.45	96.1	10.1
1981	32,870	10.0	73,250	16.6	250.0	10.2	—	15.35	95.3	-0.8
1982	35,510	8.0	82,070	12.0	274.2	9.7	—	10.20	90.7	-4.8
1983	42,980	14.3	99,530	11.1	292.0	6.5	—	—	—	—

Exhibit 7 (Continued)

Quarterly

1979 (1)	9.2	27,520	8.8	44.2	6.6	13.00	11.78	82.4	—
(2)	7.2	28,030	13.9	47.7	35.6	14.00	13.79	87.0	24.3
(3)	11.2	28,840	10.5	50.5	25.6	14.00	13.82	91.3	21.3
(4)	7.2	29,360	14.7	52.0	12.4	17.00	16.49	88.5	−11.3
1980 (1)	−2.5	29,260	12.3	54.0	16.3	17.00	16.97	93.0	21.9
(2)	8.2	29,880	20.4	55.9	14.8	17.00	16.32	94.5	6.6
(3)	−3.0	29,660	16.4	57.6	12.7	16.00	14.86	96.7	9.6
(4)	11.7	30,550	19.4	59.4	13.1	14.00	13.58	100.2	15.3
1981 (1)	15.7	31,810	8.8	60.9	10.5	12.00	11.87	101.8	6.5
(2)	12.8	32,870	15.6	61.3	2.7	12.00	12.24	97.8	−14.8
(3)	4.1	33,210	15.4	63.1	12.3	—	15.72	90.6	−26.4
(4)	6.5	33,760	9.1	64.7	10.5	—	15.39	89.7	−3.9
1982 (1)	9.5	36,720	10.7	66.0	8.3	—	12.92	91.2	6.9
(2)	9.2	37,590	7.8	67.7	10.7	—	12.66	90.3	−3.9
(3)	5.7	38,140	5.5	69.1	8.5	—	10.12	91.5	5.4
(4)	20.6	40,220	12.6	71.4	14.0	—	9.96	89.1	−10.1
1983 (1)	14.0	41,690	8.3	73.2	10.5	—	10.23	80.5	−33.4
(2)	12.1	42,980	10.6	72.8	−2.2	—	9.51	84.3	20.3

[a] Annual figures record amount at end of the second quarter (i.e., midyear amounts).

[b] Average over calendar year (1983 is the annualized average for first two quarters).

[c] Previously known as the Bank Rate. From August 20, 1981, the Bank of England has suspended announcement of the Minimum Lending Rate.

[d] Average discount rate on short-term government bills expressed as the yield.

[e] Effective exchange rate is a weighted average of the individual exchange rates of trading partners (increase indicates appreciation).

[f] Line indicates break in series. Growth rates for period after break in series are calculated on basis of consistent estimate (not shown) for previous period.

[g] Percentage change over previous period at annualized rates.

Source: Central Statistical Office, *Economic Trends*, Annual Supplement (London: Her Majesty's Stationery Office, 1984), 4, 6–7, 50, 66, 146–147.

The United Kingdom under Thatcher

Exhibit 8 Counterparts to Changes in Money Stock (Millions of Pounds; Seasonally Adjusted[a,b])

	Domestic Counterparts						External and Foreign Currency Counterparts (7)	Nondeposit Liabilities (Net) (8)	Money Stock Sterling M3 (9)
	Public Sector Borrowing Requirement		Net Acquisition of Public Sector Debt by U.K. Nonbank Private Sector						
	Central Government Borrowing Requirement (1)	Other Public Sector Contribution (2)	Other Public Sector Debt (3)	Central Government Debt (4)	Sterling Lending to U.K. Private Sector[c] (5)	Subtotal of Domestic Counterparts (6)			
Annual									
1977	4,469	1,524	551	7,905	3,188	725	3,847	−442	4,130
1978	8,308	−27	−359	6,359	4,698	6,979	678	−920	6,737
1979	10,375	2,263	1,020	9,895	8,585	10,308	−3,159	−553	6,596
1980	11,096	1,103	261	9,185	10,025	12,778	−454	−1,391	10,933
1981	10,231	399	−901	12,058	11,182	10,878	235	−1,734	9,379
1982	7,785	−2,359	−394	10,833	17,558	12,545	−2,351	−2,159	8,035

Exhibit 8 (Continued)

Quarterly	(1)	(2)	(3)	(4)	(5)	(6)	(7)	(8)	(9)
1979 (1)	1,577	1,255	−164	3,148	2,565	1,781	−585	−67	1,129
(2)	2,828	−179	316	2,907	2,045	2,103	55	−275	1,883
(3)	2,805	925	629	1,701	1,994	3,394	−1,745	−189	1,460
(4)	3,165	262	239	2,139	1,981	3,030	−884	−22	2,124
1980 (1)	296	385	289	1,515	3,424	2,301	135	−595	1,841
(2)	2,968	563	300	1,723	2,278	3,785	−287	−298	3,201
(3)	3,620	412	−31	3,138	2,655	3,580	−561	−332	2,687
(4)	4,212	−257	−297	2,692	1,668	3,228	259	−148	3,339
1981 (1)	2,128	−65	−450	3,902	2,321	932	989	−378	1,543
(2)	5,251	624	−93	3,265	678	3,381	−33	−497	2,851
(3)	2,804	−274	−107	1,726	2,984	3,895	−413	−553	2,929
(4)	48	105	−251	3,225	5,199	2,378	−299	−311	1,768
1982 (1)	−299	474	−65	3,486	6,048	2,802	−163	−295	2,344
(2)	1,206	47	−126	1,146	3,271	3,504	−1,329	−433	1,742
(3)	2,461	−1,038	91	4,034	5,216	2,514	−457	−814	1,243
(4)	4,417	−1,842	−294	2,130	3,246	3,985	−402	−620	2,963
1983 (1)	4,525	−852	−30	1,154	2,086	4,635	−875	−744	3,016
(2)	3,161	−1,178	−221	2,259	3,162	3,107	422	−905	2,624

Note: Relationship among columns: 6 = 1+2−3−4+5; 9 = 6+7+8.

[a]Changes up to and including the fourth quarter of 1981 in the quarterly series have been calculated on the basis of the old banking sector; after that date, changes in each series have been calculated on the basis of the new monetary sector. Figures for the fourth quarter of 1981 are partly estimated.

[b]The seasonally adjusted figures do not always add to the calendar year total, which is the sum of unadjusted quarterly figures.

[c]Banking sector lending *plus* Bank of England Issue Department holdings of commercial bills.

Source: Central Statistical Office, *Economic Trends* (London: Her Majesty's Stationery Office, November 1982 and 1983), 54.

The United Kingdom under Thatcher

Exhibit 9   Money Stock and Liquidity

	180					180
160				12%		160
				8%		

PSL2

£M3

12%
8%

£M3

10%
6%
10%
6%

11%
11%
7%   7%

Upper and Lower Bounds
for Growth Rate

Target Range

12%

8%

12%

8%

M1

Key:
△ Base of the £M3 target range after introduction of
the new monetary sector at mid-November 1981.

PSL2 is Public Sector Liquidity 2, the broadest
monetary aggregate in the United Kingdom.

1979   1980   1981   1982   1983

Billions of pounds; seasonally adjusted; log scale (and successive target ranges: annual growth rates, percent).

Source: Central Statistical Office, *Economic Trends* (July 1983), 53.

The United Kingdom under Thatcher

Exhibit 10   Targets and Performance

	Sterling M3 Percent Change		Public Sector Borrowing Requirement (Billions of Pounds)	
	Target	Actual	Target	Actual
June 1979–Apr. 1980	7-11%	10.3%	8.3	9.9
Feb. 1980–Apr. 1981	7-11	22.2	8.5	13.2
Feb. 1981–Apr. 1982	6-10	13.5	10.5	8.5
Feb. 1982–Apr. 1983	8-12	11.5	9.5	9.0[a]

[a]Treasury projection, November 1982.

Source: Morgan Guaranty, *World Financial Markets*, January 1983, 1.

The United Kingdom under Thatcher

Exhibit 11   General Government Receipts and Expenditure (Millions of Pounds)

| | Receipts[a] | | Goods and Services | | Expenditure Current and Capital Transfers | | | | |
	Taxes, National Insurance, etc., Contributions	Trading Income, Rent, Royalties, Interest, etc.	Final Consump- tion	Gross Domestic Capital Formation	Current Grants and Subsidies	Capital Transfers	Debt Interest	Net Lending, etc.[b]	Total
	1	2	3	4	5	6	7	8	9
Annual									
1970	19,129	2,059	8,991	2,474	5,391	796	2,025	1,219	20,896
1971	20,233	2,341	10,250	2,613	5,924	912	2,089	1,695	23,483
1972	21,461	2,501	11,675	2,777	7,232	820	2,286	1,600	26,390
1973	24,101	2,947	13,372	3,709	8,221	980	2,738	1,526	30,546
1974	30,024	3,790	16,628	4,450	11,200	1,093	3,607	2,240	39,218
1975	38,521	4,486	22,956	5,074	14,332	1,196	4,211	3,755	51,524
1976	44,621	5,354	26,741	5,485	17,044	1,435	5,394	2,365	58,464
1977	50,781	6,187	29,262	4,932	19,515	1,537	6,367	254	61,867
1978	56,425	6,792	33,071	4,717	23,235	2,028	7,207	1,690	71,948
1979	67,437	8,181	38,361	5,213	27,461	1,897	8,961	3,273	85,166
1980	82,144	10,100	48,419	5,742	32,610	2,254	11,363	3,469	103,857
1981	95,382	11,271	54,538	4,612	38,647	2,493	13,218	2,552	116,060
1982	107,088	12,601	60,082	4,594	43,465	2,874	14,265	2,718	127,998

Exhibit 11 (Continued)

Quarterly

1979 (1)	15,919	2,057	8,879	1,503	6,559	500	2,332	554	20,327
(2)	16,046	1,905	9,310	1,018	6,848	456	1,921	672	20,225
(3)	17,225	2,191	9,879	1,337	6,675	448	2,543	1,055	21,937
(4)	18,247	2,028	10,293	1,355	7,379	493	2,165	992	22,677
1980 (1)	20,706	2,439	11,163	1,740	7,833	586	3,155	152	24,629
(2)	18,496	2,420	11,630	1,128	8,144	522	2,344	1,434	25,202
(3)	21,322	2,474	12,526	1,393	8,127	620	3,318	1,159	27,143
(4)	21,620	2,767	13,100	1,481	8,506	526	2,546	724	26,883
1981 (1)	23,409	2,801	13,210	1,709	9,179	671	3,666	339	28,774
(2)	21,063	2,690	13,097	906	9,798	522	2,684	875	27,882
(3)	25,317	2,895	14,068	980	9,835	623	3,958	886	30,350
(4)	25,593	2,885	14,163	1,017	9,835	677	2,910	452	29,054
1982 (1)	28,329	3,137	14,688	1,514	10,288	814	4,265	638	32,207
(2)	24,594	3,083	14,828	719	10,911	534	3,012	195	30,199
(3)	27,287	3,098	15,030	1,133	10,836	629	4,108	1,051	32,787
(4)	26,878	3,283	15,536	1,228	11,430	897	2,880	834	32,805
1983 (1)	30,201	3,272	16,490	1,881	11,701	1,033	4,232	1,020	36,357
(2)	25,324	3,021	15,880	876	11,954	735	2,966	82	32,493

[a]Excluding financial transactions.

[b]Net lending to public corporations, private sector, and overseas; cash expenditure on company securities, etc. (net).

Source: Central Statistical Office, *Economic Trends* (London: Her Majesty's Stationery Office, 1984), 162, 164.

The United Kingdom under Thatcher

Exhibit 12   Financial Transactions of the Public Sector (Millions of Pounds)

	Financial Deficit[a]			Net Lending, etc., to Private Sector and Overseas[b]		Financial Transactions (Net Receipts)	Receipts Public Sector Borrowing Requirement				
	Total	General Government	Public Corporations		Total		Total	Contributions by: Central Government[c]	Local Authorities	Public Corporations	Seasonally Adjusted Total[d]
	1	2	3	4	5	6	7	8	9	10	11
Annual											
1970	−682	−1,511	829	431	−251	−255	4	−664	517	151	4
1971	300	−786	1,086	620	920	−455	1,375	630	676	69	1,375
1972	1,570	828	742	558	2,128	89	2,039	1,585	514	−60	2,039
1973	2,749	1,972	777	880	3,629	−569	4,198	2,320	1,348	530	4,198
1974	4,699	3,164	1,535	1,697	6,396	31	6,365	3,529	2,101	735	6,365
1975	7,560	4,762	2,798	1,833	9,393	−1,084	10,477	8,358	1,634	485	10,477
1976	8,335	6,124	2,211	1,243	9,578	434	9,144	6,791	1,105	1,248	9,144
1977	5,948	4,645	1,303	123	6,071	96	5,975	4,510	180	1,285	5,975
1978	8,009	7,041	968	538	8,547	212	8,335	8,308	662	−635	8,335
1979	8,352	6,275	2,077	475	8,827	−3,811	12,638	10,375	1,761	502	12,638
1980	10,705	8,144	2,561	469	11,174	−993	12,167	11,096	1,785	−714	12,167
1981	8,311	6,855	1,456	881	9,192	−1,566	10,758	10,231	1,116	−589	10,758
1982	7,312	5,591	1,721	801	8,113	2,605	5,508	7,785	−1,605	−672	5,508

Exhibit 12 (Continued)

Quarterly

1979 (1)	2,246	1,797	449	181	2,427	950	1,477	282	1,001	194	3,004
(2)	1,991	1,602	389	237	2,228	-1,173	3,401	3,718	-223	-94	3,128
(3)	2,505	1,466	1,039	115	2,620	-1,175	3,795	2,875	632	288	3,253
(4)	1,610	1,410	200	-58	1,552	-2,413	3,955	3,500	351	114	3,253
1980 (1)	1,791	1,332	459	-103	1,688	2,940	-1,252	-1,882	1,395	-765	1,052
(2)	3,505	2,852	653	426	3,931	-882	4,813	4,542	536	-265	3,909
(3)	3,451	2,188	1,263	183	3,634	-134	3,768	3,295	312	161	3,936
(4)	1,958	1,772	186	-37	1,921	-2,917	4,838	5,141	-458	155	3,270
1981 (1)	2,669	2,225	444	-130	2,539	2,767	-228	-127	576	-677	2,350
(2)	3,612	3,254	358	588	4,200	-3,656	7,856	7,501	313	42	6,272
(3)	2,120	1,252	868	285	2,405	189	2,216	2,240	305	-329	2,710
(4)	-90	124	-214	138	48	-866	914	617	-78	375	-574
1982 (1)	402	103	299	16	418	2,591	-2,173	-2,663	505	-15	486
(2)	2,796	2,327	469	306	3,102	240	2,862	3,098	48	-284	1,651
(3)	2,366	1,351	1,015	265	2,631	950	1,681	2,497	-697	-119	1,774
(4)	1,748	1,810	-62	214	1,962	-1,176	3,138	4,853	-1,461	-254	1,597
1983 (1)	1,959	1,864	95	91	2,050	565	1,485	2,166	-229	-452	4,498
(2)	4,397	4,066	331	-255	4,142	321	3,821	5,456	-915	-720	2,230

aThe excess of current and capital expenditure over receipts; corresponds to a negative figure of Financial surplus/deficit.

bIncluding cash expenditure on company securities (net).

cIncluding borrowing matched by on-lending to local authorities and public corporations.

dCalendar year constrained.

Source: Central Statistical Office, *Economic Trends*, Annual Supplement (London: Her Majesty's Stationery Office, 1984), 165–166.

The United Kingdom under Thatcher

Exhibit 13   Balance of Payments
(Millions of Dollars)
A. Current Account

	Visible Trade			Seasonally Adjusted					Net Seasonal Influences on Current Account	Not Seasonally Adjusted: Current Balance
				Invisibles						
	Exports	Imports	Visible Balance	Credits	Debits	Invisible Balance	Current Balance			
	1	2	3	4	5	6	7	8	9	
Annual									
1977	31,728	34,012	−2,284	16,798	14,536	+2,262	−22	—	−22
1978	35,063	36,605	−1,542	19,130	16,430	+2,700	+1,158	—	+1,158
1979	40,687	44,136	−3,449	23,804	21,008	+2,796	−653	—	−653
1980	47,415	46,182	+1,233	25,943	23,941	+2,002	+3,235	—	+3,235
1981	50,977	47,969	+3,008	29,760	26,221	+3,539	+6,547	—	+6,547
1982	55,546	53,427	+2,119	31,734	28,475	+3,259	+5,378	—	+5,378
Quarterly									
1983 (1)	14,773	14,936	−163	8,290	7,346	+944	+781	+188	+969
(2)	14,677	15,346	−669	8,300	7,802	+498	−171	−575	−746

Exhibit 13 (Continued)   B. Investment and Other Capital Transactions[a] (Not Seasonally Adjusted)

	Overseas Investment in:		U.K. Private Invest- ment Overseas	Official Long- Term Capital	Trade Credit[b]	Foreign Currency Borrowing or Lending Abroad by U.K. Banks[c,d]	Exchange Reserves in Sterling[a]		Other External Banking and Money Market Liabili- ties in Sterling[d]	External Sterling Lending by U.K. Banks[d,f]	Other External Borrow- ing or Lending[g]	Other Trans- actions	Total Invest- ment and Other Capital Trans- actions
	U.K. Public Sector	U.K. Private Sector					British Govern- ment Stocks	Banking and Money Market Liabilities, etc.[d]					
	10	11	12	13	14	15	16	17	18	19	20	21	22
Annual													
1977	+1,432	+2,967	−2,334	−303	−355	+364	+6	−16	+1,481	+58	+813	+56	+4,169
1978	−97	+1,974	−4,604	−336	−630	−433	−113	−	+293	−504	+106	+81	−4,263
1979	+902	+3,434	−6,544	−401	−792	+1,623	+247	+509	+2,580	+205	+449	−66	+2,146
1980	+589	+4,651	−8,146	−91	−1,156	+2,054	+945	+317	+2,558	−2,500	−866	−243	−1,888
1981	+188	+3,174	−10,621	−336	−847	+1,462	+267	−118	+2,607	−2,954	−471	+101	−7,548
1982	+320	+3,174	−10,798	−337	−1,406	+4,173	−31	+438	+4,134	−3,299	+432	+250	−2,950
Quarterly													
1983 (1)	+46	+1,920	−3,167	−229	−445	+529	+78	+451	+1,063	−939	+621	−676	−748
(2)	+379	+1,908	−2,678	−216	−430	+117	+272	−297	+667	+288	+67	+121	+198

[a]Assets: increase−/decrease + Liabilities: increase +/decrease −. Excluding official financing.

[b]Excluding trade credit between related firms (part of United Kingdom and overseas private investment).

[c]Excluding changes in levels resulting from changes in sterling valuation.

[d]Prior to 1982, includes transactions by other financial institutions. For 1982 onwards, these data relate only to transactions reported by U.K. monetary sector institutions. Transactions by other financial institutions are included within Other External Borrowing or Lending.

[e]Sterling reserves of overseas countries and international organizations, other than the IMF, as reported by U.K. banks, etc., in the United Kingdom.

[f]Excluding credit for U.K. exports.

[g]From 1982 onwards, included transactions by other financial institutions (see note d).

(Continued)

Exhibit 13 (Continued)   C. Summary

	Seasonally Adjusted							Not Seasonally Adjusted					
	Visible Trade (Balance)	Invisible (Balance)				Current Balance	Current Balance	Investment and Other Capital Transactions	Allocation of Special Drawing Rights	Official Financing[a]			Balancing Item
		Services	Interest, Profits and Dividends	Transfers	Total					Net Transactions with Overseas Monetary Authorities	Other Foreign Currency Borrowing[b]	Drawings on (+)/Additions to (−) Official Reserves	
	23	24	25	26	27	28	29	30	31	32	33	34	35
Annual													
1977	−2,284	+3,259	+118	−1,115	+2,262	−22	−22	+4,169	—	+1,113	+1,114	−9,588	+3,214
1978	−1,542	+3,816	+661	−1,777	+2,700	+1,158	+1,158	−4,263	—	−1,016	−187	+2,329	+1,979
1979	−3,449	+4,071	+990	−2,265	+2,796	−653	−653	+2,146	+195	−596	−250	−1,059	+217
1980	+1,233	+4,267	−186	−2,079	+2,002	+3,235	+3,235	−1,888	+180	−140	−941	−291	−155
1981	+3,008	+4,249	+1,257	−1,967	+3,539	+6,547	+6,547	−7,548	+158	−145	−1,587	+2,419	+156
1982	+2,119	+3,853	+1,515	−2,109	+3,259	+5,378	+5,378	−2,950	—	−163	+26	+1,421	−3,712
Quarterly													
1983 (1)	−163	+1,120	+356	−532	+944	+781	+969	−748	—	−36	—	+652	−837
(2)	−669	+1,212	−37	−677	+498	−171	−746	+198	—	—	+13	−145	+680

[a] Valued in sterling at market-related rates of exchange.

[b] Includes borrowing by public bodies under the exchange cover scheme, drawings by HM Government on two Eurodollar facilities and a $350 million bond issue in New York.

Source: Central Statistical Office, *Monthly Economic Statistics*, November 1983, 103–104.

Exhibit 14 Value of Exports (F.O.B.) and Imports (C.I.F.): Analysis by Commodity Classes[a]
(Millions of Pounds; Seasonally Adjusted)

| | | | | | | | Manufactures Excluding Erratics | | | | | | |
| | | | | | | | Semimanufactures Excluding Precious Stones | | | Finished Manufactures Excluding Ships, North Sea Installations, and Aircraft | | | | |
Year	Total	Food, Beverages, and Tobacco	Basic Materials	Fuels	Total Manufactures	Total	Total	Chemicals	Other	Total	Passenger Motor Cars	Other Consumer	Intermediate	Capital
	1	2	3	4	5	6	7	8	9	10	11	12	13	14
Exports														
1978	35,380	2,912	1,037	2,375	27,989	26,068	10,117	4,199	5,918	15,951	945	2,918	6,243	5,845
1979	40,637	2,941	1,281	4,324	30,870	28,595	11,562	4,911	6,651	17,033	837	3,102	6,875	6,220
1980	47,357	3,257	1,449	6,429	34,811	31,837	12,602	5,286	7,315	19,236	838	3,388	8,054	6,955
1981	50,698	3,628	1,298	9,616	34,639	32,183	12,240	5,500	6,739	19,944	904	3,407	8,497	7,135
1982	55,538	3,947	1,341	11,193	37,316	34,455	13,086	6,119	6,967	21,369	960	3,529	9,242	7,638
Imports														
1978	39,533	6,141	3,691	4,805	24,351	22,129	9,158	2,757	6,401	12,971	1,774	3,551	3,969	3,677
1979	46,925	6,517	4,180	5,782	29,689	27,364	11,208	3,402	7,806	16,156	2,600	4,480	4,639	4,437
1980	49,773	6,153	4,049	6,875	31,177	28,161	11,937	3,147	8,790	16,225	2,112	4,692	4,759	4,662
1981	51,169	6,537	4,000	7,166	31,993	29,886	11,516	3,597	7,920	18,370	2,221	5,631	5,467	5,051
1982	56,940	7,251	3,930	7,401	37,083	35,098	13,025	4,181	8,844	22,073	2,889	5,972	6,675	6,537

[a]The abbreviation f.o.b. stands for "free on board," and means that costs of insurance and freight (c.i.f.) are excluded.

Source: Central Statistical Office, *Monthly Digest of Statistics*, July 1983, Table 15.1.

The United Kingdom under Thatcher

Exhibit 15   Personal Disposable Income and Savings

	Personal Saving Ratio[a]	1980 Prices	
		Real Personal Disposable Income[b]	
		Millions of Pounds	1980 = 100
Annual			
1970	9.0%	122,123	76.0
1971	7.3	123,687	77.0
1972	9.7	134,511	83.7
1973	11.2	143,870	89.6
1974	12.0	142,713	88.9
1975	12.5	142,629	88.8
1976	11.7	141,639	88.2
1977	10.5	139,318	86.7
1978	12.1	149,602	93.1
1979	12.9	158,295	98.6
1980	14.8	160,620	100.0
1981	12.5	156,630	97.5
1982	10.8	155,627	96.9
Quarterly			
1979 (1)	14.6	38,402	95.6
(2)	12.3	39,190	97.6
(3)	11.9	39,217	97.7
(4)	13.0	41,486	103.3
1980 (1)	15.1	39,959	99.5
(2)	16.5	39,585	98.6
(3)	15.8	40,783	101.6
(4)	11.8	40,293	100.3
1981 (1)	15.9	39,693	98.9
(2)	14.2	38,689	96.4
(3)	12.0	39,206	97.6
(4)	8.2	39,042	97.2
1982 (1)	15.1	39,190	97.6
(2)	13.0	38,199	95.1
(3)	10.1	39,195	97.6
(4)	5.2	39,043	97.2
1983 (1)	11.2	39,005	97.1
(2)	10.0	38,664	96.3

[a]Personal saving as a percentage of personal disposable income.

[b]Personal disposable income revalued by the implied consumers' expenditure deflator (1980 = 100).

Source: Central Statistical Office, *Economic Trends*, Annual Supplement (London: Her Majesty's Stationery Office, 1984), 18, 20.

The United Kingdom under Thatcher

**Exhibit 16   Industrial Stoppages
(In Thousands)**

	Workers Involved[a]	Total Working Days Lost, All Industries and Services
1977	1,155	10,142
1978	1,001	9,405
1979	4,583	29,474
1980	830	11,964
1981	1,499	4,266
1982	2,101	5,313
1983 (1st half)[b]	612	4,486

[a]Where stoppages extend over more than one month, the workers involved are counted in the month in which they first participated.

[b]Annualized amount.

Source: Central Statistical Office, *Monthly Digest of Statistics*, July 1984, 28.

The United Kingdom under Thatcher

Exhibit 17   Public Opinion Polls of Voters' Intentions

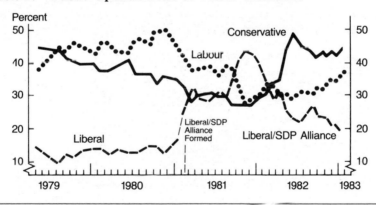

Source: *The Economist*, February 5, 1983.

The United Kingdom under Thatcher

Exhibit 18   Sale of State-Owned Companies

Company (1983 Revenues)	Date of Sale	Amount Raised	Comment
British Petroleum ($41.2 Billion)	1979–1984	$1.04 Billion	Government reduced amount held from 49% to 31.7%
British Aerospace ($2.9 Billion)	1980–1981	$54.6 Million	Government retains 49.3%
British Sugar ($755 Million)	1981	$54 Million	
Cable & Wireless ($825.5 Million)	1981–1983	$55.8 Million	Government retains 23.1%
Britoil ($1.52 Billion)	1981–1983	$796 Million	
Jaguar Cars ($600 Million)	1984	$377 Million	Government limits single shareholders to 15% of shares outstanding
British Telecom ($8.6 Billion)	November 1984	$4-5 Billion (Estimate)	
British Airways ($3.1 Billion)	Spring 1984	N.A.	

These other major nationalized companies also are to be sold, wholly or in part, to the private sector, but dates of sale have not been set: The Post Office, $3.5 billion in 1983 revenue; British Rail, $3.9 billion in 1983 revenue; British Leyland, $4.3 billion; British Shipbuilding, $1.1 billion; British Steel, $4.2 billion; and the National Coal Board, $4.5 billion.

Source: *New York Times*, Oct. 7, 1984.

Discussion Questions for Case

1. Was Margaret Thatcher's strategy successful in her first term as prime minister?
2. How important was monetary policy in the overall success of Thatcher's program?
3. Evaluate the operating procedure for the conduct of monetary policy in the United Kingdom and contrast it with the procedure implemented in the United States by Volcker in 1979.
4. What has been the long-term effect of Thatcher's policies on the competitiveness of British firms?
5. How can government best achieve structural change in an economy?
6. What policies should Thatcher pursue in the future?

Bibliography

Artis, M. J., and M. K. Lewis, *Monetary Control in the United Kingdom* (Oxford: Allan, 1981). This book is institutionally detailed and, in some chapters, technically advanced, but it is helpful for placing Thatcher's monetary policy in historical and theoretical perspective (pages 1–10 and 108–131). The chapter "Controlling the Supply of Money" describes in detail the method of controlling money by controlling counterpart assets.

Riddell, Peter, *The Thatcher Government* (Oxford: Robertson, 1983). In this book the political editor of the *Financial Times* critically surveys the successes and failures in all aspects of government policy during Thatcher's first term as prime minister.

Wood, Geoffrey E., "The Monetary Policy Decision Process in the United Kingdom," in Donald R. Hodgman, ed., *The Political Economy of Monetary Policy: National and International Aspects*, Proceedings of a Conference Held in July 1983, Conference Series No. 26 (Boston: Federal Reserve Bank of Boston, 1983), 93–122. This scholarly paper is a detailed treatment of the institutional structure and decision-making process of monetary policy in the United Kingdom. The author argues that monetary policy had traditionally been focused on achieving stable interest rates and that the Bank of England effectively made the monetary policy decisions. This has changed under Thatcher.

CHAPTER 5

The Consequences of Institutional Change in the Financial System

As in the last chapter, we shall again examine institutional change and its relationship to monetary policy. In the Chapter 4 case, Mrs. Thatcher used monetary policy as a vehicle for driving her broader agenda of changing the institutional structure of labor relations, of government involvement in the economy, and of economic incentives. The case in this chapter considers how institutional change in the Japanese financial sector may affect the conduct of monetary policy, among other issues.

The case, "Japanese Financial Liberalization," spans over two decades of change in the financial system. The changes described are usually small and evolutionary, but in total they represent an economic environment for the 1980s that is dramatically different from that of the 1960s. The scope of financial activity covered by the liberalization extends from domestic to international markets and encompasses all of the nation's financial institutions.

The Japanese government, in particular the Ministry of Finance and the Bank of Japan, relied on the tight direct control of the financial system to accomplish its policy objectives. As direct control was surrendered, the government needed to find other methods of control. The case examines the forces causing the liberalization of financial markets and the implications of these changes for government policy and for the international competitiveness of Japanese financial institutions and corporations.

Case
Japanese Financial Liberalization

Financial liberalization encompasses a broad range of structural changes in the financial system, including the relaxation of international capital controls, the deregulation of domestic interest rates, and the expansion of the scope of competition among financial institutions. Most industrial countries liberalized their financial systems to various degrees during the 1970s and 1980s. Japan was not one of the pioneers in financial liberalization, but considering its rigid financial structure after World War II, it had traveled further along the liberalization path by 1988 than most industrial countries. The consequences of these actions were certain to be significant for Japan as well as the rest of the industrial world.

Japan had been under increasing pressure to liberalize its financial system ever since it joined the Organization for Economic Cooperation and Development (OECD) in 1964. However, not until the 1970s, when Japan became a world economic power, did the pressure for liberalization increase significantly. Although all Japanese government agencies have been concerned with and affected by financial liberalization over the past two decades, none have been more directly involved in managing this process than the Bank of Japan (BOJ)—the nation's central monetary authority—and the Ministry of Finance (MOF)—the powerful, elite financial arm of the Japanese bureaucracy responsible for both monetary and fiscal policies. These two agencies have had to consider the implications of liberalization on their ability to manage the economy while balancing political pressures from Japanese and foreign interest groups.

Japanese Financial Institutions and Markets before the First Oil Shock

The Japanese institutional framework established by the occupation after World War II tightly controlled the country's finances, partly to avert a return to the chaos of the 1920s (when a severe recession caused 36 banks to close their doors) but mainly to assist in Japan's reconstruction and the reduction of the virulent postwar inflation. The postwar financial system was a hybrid of prewar Japanese financial institutions and imported American institutions. The "Dodge Line" of economic reforms (promulgated in 1949 by Joseph Dodge, the American banker and financial adviser to the Supreme Allied Commander, General Douglas

This case was prepared by Associate Professor Michael G. Rukstad with the assistance of Karen Shore and John Wood, MBAs 1988. Copyright © 1988 by the President and Fellows of Harvard College. Harvard Business School case 9-389-035.

MacArthur) checked inflation by 1953 and left a legacy of balanced fiscal budgets and a fixed, undervalued exchange rate. In addition, interest rates were controlled, competition among financial institutions was limited, and international capital controls were maintained. The primary objective was financial stability, which was to become a hallmark of the Japanese financial system before the first oil shock in 1973.

One of the primary functions of the financial system of an economy is to channel funds efficiently from those with a surplus of funds (savers) to those with a deficit of funds (investors). During the 1950s and early 1960s, the abundant savings of households were used to finance the prodigious investment of corporations. Japanese household savings as a percentage of income (near 20 percent) were almost twice the level of most other OECD countries. The net contribution of the government sector to the flow of funds was virtually zero, since government budgets were balanced or in slight surplus during those years. The net flow of funds between Japan and the rest of the world was also small as a percentage of GNP. Exhibit 1 shows the flow of funds among sectors in Japan after 1965.

Japanese corporations generated almost as many funds from the internal sources of depreciation and profits as from the external sources of financial intermediaries and markets. Almost 90 percent of the externally supplied funds were channeled through financial intermediaries (indirect finance) rather than raised in the capital or equity markets through debt or equity securities (direct finance). Because of the rigid capital controls imposed by the MOF, corporate financial liabilities (and financial assets) were yen-denominated. The trends in corporate finance after 1960 are documented in Exhibits 2 and 3.

Before the onset of liberalization in the early 1970s, Japanese financial institutions were highly specialized in order to reduce risk and to control the demand for credit in particular segments during rapid industrialization.[1] Financial institutions specialized along many different dimensions, including by maturity of products (such as short-term or long-term), by types of financial activity (such as lending, underwriting, insurance, or trust), by purpose of finance (such as international trade, home finance, or agriculture), and by size of customer (such as city and regional institutions). See Exhibit 4 for an overview of Japanese financial institutions.

The financial institutions can be segmented into private and public institutions. The most prominent of the private institutions, especially in the early postwar years, were the private commercial banks, which provided short-term credit primarily for industrial customers. The city banks, which were the largest 13 banks, wielded the greatest power among

---

[1]Henry and Mable Wallich, "Banking and Finance," in Hugh Patrick and Henry Rosovsky, eds., *Asia's New Giant: How the Japanese Economy Works* (Washington, DC: Brookings Institution, 1976), 249–315.

financial institutions. They accounted for approximately a quarter of all deposits and lending in the Japanese economy in 1970. The second largest group of deposit-taking institutions consisted of the regional banks, which tended to service smaller customers usually outside the major cities. The regional banks' share of both deposits and lending was approximately 15 percent in 1970.

Apart from the city and regional banks, specialized private financial institutions competed in the long-term credit, trust, insurance, securities, small-business finance, and agricultural finance businesses. The long-term credit banks not only supplied long-term financing to industrial customers, but, in contrast to the city and regional banks, they could raise funds through the issuance of long-term debentures. Trust banks were also engaged in long-term financing in addition to their trust business. Other specialized banks such as the Sogo banks (mutual banks), the Shinkin banks (credit associations), and the various cooperatives were, as a group, a potent force in the financial system. In 1970 they accounted for almost 30 percent of the total banking assets in the economy. The financial activities of banks and securities firms were separated along American lines, under the regulations of Article 65 (comparable to the Glass-Steagall Act in the United States). The restrictive regulations of the MOF prevented financial institutions from competing with one another for customers and market share. The composition of banking assets and banking profitability are shown in Exhibits 5 and 6. The changes in assets and liabilities of all banks between 1960 and 1984 are shown in Exhibit 7.

Public financial institutions, such as the Japan Development Bank, the Export-Import Bank, the Housing Loan Corporation, and the Postal Savings System, supplied funds for specific purposes. The Post Office took deposits from individuals and in turn deposited these funds with the government, which used them primarily to finance public-sector corporations and other government activities through the Trust Fund Bureau of the Fiscal Investment and Loan Program (FILP). The Japanese Postal System, with its more than 20,000 branch offices, was the world's largest deposit-taking institution—a result of the limited investment opportunities available to the frugal Japanese households and the very generous tax benefits afforded to Postal System depositors. In 1970 the Post Office collected 8 percent of all deposits in the financial system, and the Trust Fund Bureau was responsible for 16 percent of all lending and securities held.[2]

The money, capital, and equity markets in Japan were significantly underdeveloped before liberalization. Virtually the only short-term money market that existed in the 1950s and 1960s was the call money market, in which banks could lend and borrow funds among themselves for short

---

[2] By 1985, the Post Office was collecting 15 percent of all deposits and the Trust Fund Bureau was generating 22 percent of credit extended through loans and securities. Total deposits were ¥104 trillion ($670 billion)—a quarter of Japan's national savings.

periods of time (less than 7 days) at market-determined rates. In order to provide this type of funding for securities companies and corporations, these nonbank organizations were permitted to participate in the "gensaki" market in 1967.[3] In the gensaki market, companies would buy and sell authorized bonds (usually government bonds) with a requirement that the bonds be repurchased after a short, specified period (usually less than three months). The bill discount market, established in 1971, was the interbank market in bills of exchange with relatively long maturities (up to four months). A Treasury bill market never developed in Japan because the BOJ underwrote all short-term Treasury issues and held them to maturity. Moreover, no commercial paper market was developed since the gensaki market combined with bank loans appeared to satisfy corporate customers' short-term financing needs. Exhibit 11 shows the changing composition of money market instruments after 1965.

The long-term government bond market, with maturities of seven to ten years, began in 1965. Government bonds were allowed only for the financing of public construction projects. Previously, because the government had balanced budgets or budget surpluses, no bond issues had been needed. The bonds were sold to a syndicate of banks and securities firms at an issue rate determined by the MOF (see Exhibit 10). After one year the bonds could be sold to the BOJ. The trends in the bond market are presented in Exhibit 12.

Japanese Economic Management before the First Oil Shock

During the two decades following the occupation period after World War II (1945–1952), Japan recorded an average real economic growth rate exceeding 10 percent per year—an unprecedented achievement often labeled "the economic miracle."[4] Nonetheless, even this boom period was punctuated by seven recessions—usually quite mild by Western standards until the severe downturn following the first oil shock in 1973. The conduct of monetary and fiscal policy contributed in part to the success of the postwar Japanese economy.[5] Fiscal policy modestly restrained growth during this period because of the persistent government budget surpluses

---

[3]OECD Economic Surveys, *Japan*, July 1984, 49. The market was established in 1949 and then extended in the 1960s and 1970s.

[4]For a detailed discussion of the complex factors contributing to this success, see the case study by Bruce Scott, John Rosenblum, and Audrey Sproat, "A Strategy for Economic Growth," in *Case Studies in Political Economy: Japan, 1854–1977* (Boston: Harvard Business School Press, 1980), 112–149.

[5]See Gardner Ackley and Hiromitsu Ishi, "Fiscal, Monetary, and Related Policies," in Hugh Patrick and Henry Rosovsky, eds., *Asia's New Giant: How the Japanese Economy Works* (Washington, DC: Brookings Institution, 1976), 153–247, for an explanation of the conclusions summarized in the case.

and the small size of government expenditures. However, monetary policy was usually highly stimulative and played a major short-term role in managing the economy, particularly in times of deficits in the balance of payments.

The Bank of Japan (BOJ) had to conform to policy set by the Ministry of Finance (MOF), but in practice it generally exercised independent monetary control.[6] The BOJ had the same tools as other central banks, including the discount window, open-market operations, changes in reserve requirements, and window guidance (often called "moral suasion" in other central banks). During this period of high growth, however, the BOJ tended to control credit predominantly by window guidance—"recommending" quotas on open-market operations, direct limits on discount window borrowings, and quantitative ceilings on banks' lending—all of which effectively resulted in credit rationing.

Institutional rigidities in the other instruments contributed to increased reliance on window guidance.[7] The discount rate, which was an indicator of the BOJ's intentions, varied little (usually within 75 basis points) during the period before the 1970s because most bank lending rates were fixed administratively and thus not tied to the cost of bank borrowing. Open-market operations in government bonds, or even private securities, were greatly hampered by the very thin, virtually nonexistent, markets in these direct securities. The government coerced financial institutions into accepting any open-market sales of securities at unattractive fixed interest rates (see Exhibit 10). Because small changes in the very low reserve requirement produced large changes in banks' abilities to expand credit, precise control of the economy was difficult with this tool.

With credit rationing, interest rates were kept low even during periods of tight money, thus encouraging the strong investment demand that led the economic growth during the two decades of the economic miracle.[8] Also, in order to maintain direct control over interest rates, the MOF and the BOJ set strict relationships among the interest rates available on various instruments, which in turn influenced rates throughout the system (see Exhibit 8). At the same time, a bank cartel called the *kisaikai* (comprised of 22 banks and 7 securities firms) set lending rates under the guidance of the monetary authorities.

The BOJ's power is exemplified by the dependence of the 13 city banks on this institution. From the mid-1950s through the early 1970s, Japanese corporations expanded rapidly and were eager for bank financ-

[6]Bank of Japan, Economic Research Department, *The Bank of Japan: Its Organization and Monetary Policies,* 3rd ed., May 1971, 4.

[7]Ackley and Ishi, "Fiscal, Monetary, and Related Policies," 202–204.

[8]Corporations borrowing from banks were required to keep large compensating balances, which increased the effective loan rate; however, it is generally agreed that interest rates would have been much higher in the absence of controls. See OECD Economic Surveys, *Japan,* July 1984, 43, and OECD, *Monetary Policy in Japan,* December 1972, 37.

ing; so the city banks entered into "overlending." They extended more loans than they could fund in the private markets, with the balance made up by the BOJ—in other words, the banking system borrowed more from the BOJ than it held in cash and deposits with the BOJ (see Exhibit 7). This situation was known as "overloan" when applied to the banking system as a whole. The BOJ gave credit only to the city banks at the official discount rate.[9] Other financial institutions also supplied credit to the city banks, but at the much higher call money rate. As a result, the city banks were heavily dependent on the BOJ and were obliged to follow its suggestions. This loan dependency reinforced the accepted authority of the BOJ.

Japanese monetary policy before the 1973 oil shock was summarized in one account as a unified, highly dependent system:

The tools of monetary policy, the structure of financial markets, and the low interest rate policy . . . are all part of a single system. In this system, monetary policy . . . takes . . . the form of a direct control that involves essentially arbitrary quantitative quotas or ceilings at several points. Instead of allowing impersonal market forces to decide which banks will grow faster or slower, which bank customers will be served or denied, it is all decided (at least in periods of tight money) by various forms of rationing.[10]

The Road to Financial Liberalization in the Domestic Markets

In 1973 the final collapse of the Bretton Woods system of fixed exchange rates and the first oil shock reconfigured the world economic landscape. In Japan these monumental events followed on the heels of double-digit inflation fueled by an easy monetary policy in 1971 and 1972 (see Exhibit 16) and a 25 percent increase in government spending that one observer called "the largest pork-barrel in the history of Japanese public finance."[11] The oil shock in late 1973 further aggravated inflation, pushing annual inflation rates over 20 percent in 1974.

The BOJ instituted a vigorous monetary contraction in 1974 in response to the double-digit inflation. Subsequently the Japanese economic juggernaut slowed to a negative real growth rate in income in 1975 and then continued at a rate half that achieved during the economic miracle. The BOJ announced that it would henceforth focus on monetary control instead of interest rate control as the intermediate target of its monetary policy.[12]

---

[9]OECD Economic Surveys, *Japan,* July 1984, 69.

[10]Ackley and Ishi, "Fiscal, Monetary, and Related Policies," 205.

[11]John Campbell, *Contemporary Japanese Budget Politics* (Berkeley, CA: University of California Press, 1977), 257.

[12]Yoshio Suzuki, *Money, Finance, and Macroeconomic Performance in Japan* (New Haven, CT: Yale University Press, 1986), 184–185.

At the same time that the government was contracting monetary policy, fiscal policy was expanding. The fiscal deficit exploded in 1975 as a result of the recession and the largest tax cut in Japanese history (almost 1 percent of the GNP) in 1974. The MOF was forced to change the law governing fiscal deficits in order to issue government bonds to cover, for the first time, a shortfall in its general account rather than construction spending. The government bond issues for the years 1965 to 1986 are shown in Exhibit 14. In 1977 and early 1978, the MOF sought and received additional changes in the public finance law governing deficits. These changes removed the obligation of the BOJ to accept all government bonds from the bond syndicate after one year, allowed the syndicate to trade the bonds on the secondary market, and allowed the MOF to offer government bonds of shorter maturities. Starting in 1981, the biggest reform in this market was instituted: Banks were allowed to participate in the over-the-counter purchases and sales of government bonds, an activity previously reserved for the securities firms.

Other pressures for change in the financial markets have come from the Post Office, pension funds, and the insurance companies, all of which would like to invest their vast funds in higher-yielding domestic or foreign instruments, but the MOF has closely regulated their investments. These intermediaries were very successful in the late 1970s and early 1980s in gathering deposits. Banks were allowed to issue certificates of deposit in 1979 to compete with the other financial organizations for funds. During the 1980s the Post Office came under attack for its tax-free deposit accounts, known as *maruyu,* which, competitors argued, gave it an unfair advantage in competing for deposits. In 1988, the government abolished *maruyu,* thus paving the way for the deregulation of interest rates on small time deposits. Competition, however, was not confined to the liability side of the balance sheet—institutions were finding new financial instruments that would be attractive to rapidly aging Japanese households with abundant savings. These new instruments included trust accounts, credit card accounts, consumer finance, and the popular zero coupon foreign bond accounts.

The deregulations in the domestic market led to considerable institutional change and growth, but stability had still been preserved. By the 1980s Japanese financial institutions had become major players in the world financial system. Japan claimed nine of the world's ten largest banks (ranked by asset size), and four of the world's ten largest securities firms (ranked by total equity capital), including the top positions in each category held by Dai-Ichi Kangyo Bank and Nomura Securities, respectively. The MOF was pressured by these powerful institutions for additional changes in the domestic market as well as for permission to expand their presence overseas.

The Road to Financial Liberalization in the International Markets

During the 1970s capital controls were used to control the exchange rate.[13] In 1971 and 1972 the Japanese current account surplus put strong upward pressure on the yen (see Exhibit 17). The MOF tightened controls on capital inflows and relaxed capital outflows by residents. When the current account shifted into deficit in 1973 and 1974 as a result of the first oil shock and the yen weakened, the MOF reversed its policies on capital flows. But during the period from 1975 to 1978 when the current account and yen were increasing again, the policy on capital flows shifted once more toward tightening capital inflows and relaxing capital outflows.[14] When the second oil shock occurred in 1979, it was no surprise that the MOF substantially relaxed capital inflows.[15] The pattern of current account balances and yen exchange rate movements is compared in Exhibit 17. The changes in capital outflows and inflows are shown in Exhibit 18.

In December 1980 Japan's Foreign Exchange and Foreign Trade Control Law revealed a fundamental change in the MOF's attitude toward liberalization. Henceforth the operating principle was that external transactions be decontrolled rather than managed as during the 1970s. The first test of this principle came in 1981 and 1982 when the value of the yen fell substantially. Capital controls were not reimposed; rather the BOJ maintained relatively high short-term interest rates to mitigate the decline in the yen, despite the weak demand at home, and the MOF proceeded with further liberalization. Indeed, by May 1984 significant progress came when the joint Ministry of Finance/U.S. Treasury working group issued its report, The Yen/Dollar Exchange Rate Issues. The results are shown in Exhibit 18, which indicates that both outflows and inflows rose to historically high levels. Nonetheless, outflows of capital still surpassed inflows throughout the 1980s.

Despite the progress to date in liberalizing the Japanese financial system, much needs to be done if the yen is to take its place as a major reserve currency in the world economic system. In the 1980s the yen accounted for approximately 4 percent of the world's official reserves. That is much improved in comparison to the mid-1970s when it was less than half a percent. However, the dollar still accounted for over 70 percent of the world's reserves. The challenge for Japanese government officials was how to manage the liberalization of the financial markets and the

[13]OECD Economic Surveys, *Japan,* July 1984, 56.

[14]During this period residents were allowed to hold foreign currency deposits, and in 1977 nonresidents were allowed complete convertibility of their yen deposits—a significant move that opened the doors to the development of the Euro-yen market.

[15]For example, nonresidents were allowed access to the gensaki market, to the newly created yen-denominated CD market, and to another newly created market, unsecured yen-denominated bonds for foreigners (the "Samurai bond" market). Residents were permitted to accept "impact loans," which were foreign currency loans to nonbank residents.

internationalization of the yen in a manner consistent with continued financial stability and economic control.

Japanese Financial Liberalization

Exhibit 1   Sectoral Net Investment (Deficit) and Net Savings (Surplus) as a Percentage of GNP

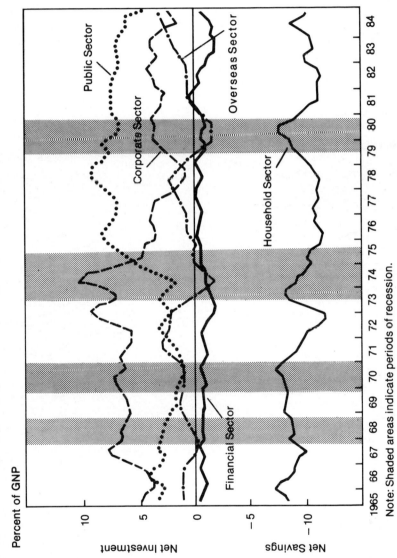

Note: Shaded areas indicate periods of recession.

Source: Yoshio Suzuki, "Financial Innovation in Japan: Its Origins, Diffusion and Impacts," in Marcello DeCecco, ed., *Changing Money: Financial Innovation in Developed Countries* (Oxford: Basil Blackwell, 1987), 230.

Japanese Financial Liberalization

Exhibit 2   Net Supply of Industrial Funds

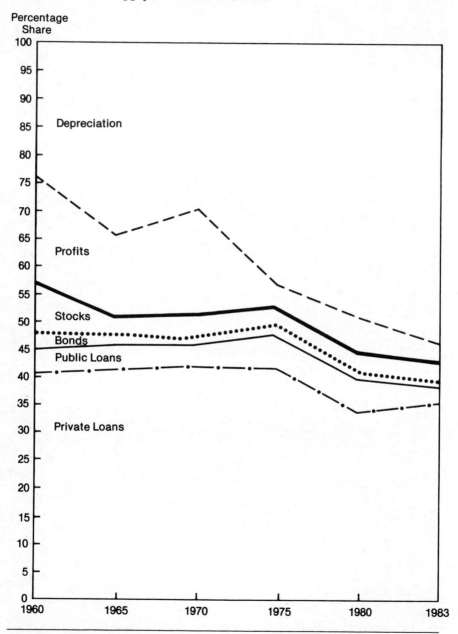

Note: Data are plotted only for the years shown in order to indicate trends.

Source: Bank of Japan, Research and Statistics Department, *Economic Statistics Annual, 1984,* March 1985, 171–174.

Japanese Financial Liberalization

Exhibit 3
A. Increases in Corporate Financial Assets (Average Percent Shares of Total Net Incremental Placements)

	1970–74	1975–79	1980–83
By Instrument			
Deposits	61.2%	40.4%	51.1%
Yen:			
Demand and time	59.0	25.3	7.8
CDs	—	3.9	16.6
Foreign currency	2.2	1.2	26.7
Equity	28.9	29.4	36.5
Other securities	9.9	30.2	12.4
Percent of Total			
In foreign currency	2.8	2.7	34.8
Open-market interest-bearing	8.1	31.3	54.1

Source: *World Financial Markets,* Morgan Guaranty Trust Company of New York, June 1984, 6. Reprinted with permission of J. P. Morgan & Co. Incorporated, whose subsidiary Morgan Guaranty Trust Company publishes *World Financial Markets.*

B. Increases in Corporate Liabilities and Stock Issue (Average Percent Shares of Total Net Incremental Finance)

	1970–74	1978–80	1981–83
By Source			
Loans	83.9	58.1	60.9
Yen	82.5	53.2	47.7
Foreign currency	1.4	4.8	13.2
Bonds	6.0	17.1	14.1
Yen	6.1	13.0	4.6
Foreign currency	0.1	4.1	9.5
Stocks	10.1	24.9	25.0
Domestic issue	10.1	24.1	23.4
Foreign issue	0.0	0.8	1.6
By Currency			
Yen	98.7	90.3	75.8
Foreign currency	1.3	9.7	24.2

Source: *World Financial Markets,* Morgan Guaranty Trust Company of New York, June 1984, 10. Reprinted with permission of J. P. Morgan & Co. Incorporated, whose subsidiary Morgan Guaranty Trust Company publishes *World Financial Markets.*

Japanese Financial Liberalization

Exhibit 4   Financial Institutions in Japan (Numbers in Parentheses: as of End of March 1986[a])

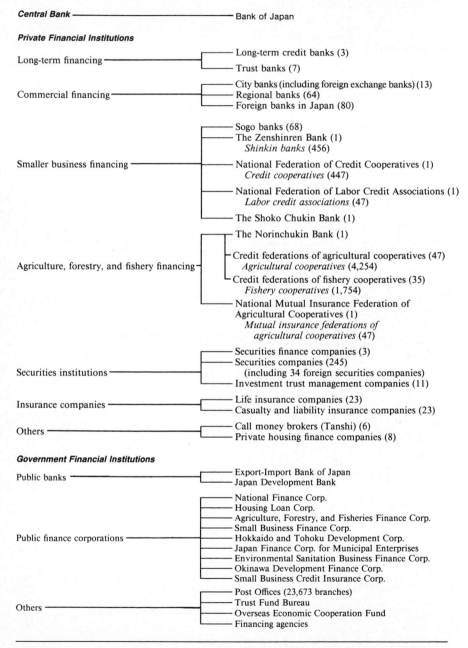

Central Bank ———————————————— Bank of Japan

Private Financial Institutions

Long-term financing
- Long-term credit banks (3)
- Trust banks (7)

Commercial financing
- City banks (including foreign exchange banks) (13)
- Regional banks (64)
- Foreign banks in Japan (80)

Smaller business financing
- Sogo banks (68)
- The Zenshinren Bank (1)
  Shinkin banks (456)
- National Federation of Credit Cooperatives (1)
  Credit cooperatives (447)
- National Federation of Labor Credit Associations (1)
  Labor credit associations (47)
- The Shoko Chukin Bank (1)

Agriculture, forestry, and fishery financing
- The Norinchukin Bank (1)
- Credit federations of agricultural cooperatives (47)
  Agricultural cooperatives (4,254)
- Credit federations of fishery cooperatives (35)
  Fishery cooperatives (1,754)
- National Mutual Insurance Federation of Agricultural Cooperatives (1)
  Mutual insurance federations of agricultural cooperatives (47)

Securities institutions
- Securities finance companies (3)
- Securities companies (245)
  (including 34 foreign securities companies)
- Investment trust management companies (11)

Insurance companies
- Life insurance companies (23)
- Casualty and liability insurance companies (23)

Others
- Call money brokers (Tanshi) (6)
- Private housing finance companies (8)

Government Financial Institutions

Public banks
- Export-Import Bank of Japan
- Japan Development Bank

Public finance corporations
- National Finance Corp.
- Housing Loan Corp.
- Agriculture, Forestry, and Fisheries Finance Corp.
- Small Business Finance Corp.
- Hokkaido and Tohoku Development Corp.
- Japan Finance Corp. for Municipal Enterprises
- Environmental Sanitation Business Finance Corp.
- Okinawa Development Finance Corp.
- Small Business Credit Insurance Corp.

Others
- Post Offices (23,673 branches)
- Trust Fund Bureau
- Overseas Economic Cooperation Fund
- Financing agencies

[a]The number of institutions in 1986 is very similar to the number in 1970. See Bank of Japan, *Money and Banking in Japan* (New York: St. Martin's Press, 1973), 146–147.

Source: *Japan Economic Almanac, 1987,* published by *The Japan Economic Journal.*

Japanese Financial Liberalization

Exhibit 5   Percent Shares of Total Bank Assets, by Type of Financial Institution, 1965–1985

Year	City Banks	Regional Banks	Trust Banks	Long-Term Credit Eanks	Sogo Banks	Shinkin Banks	Credit Co-ops	Labor Credit Co-ops	Agricultural and Fisheries Co-ops
1965	41.1	18.1	10.4	6.5	7.9	8.0	1.8	0.3	5.8
1970	37.9	17.7	10.5	6.7	7.8	9.7	2.2	0.4	7.2
1975	34.7	17.0	12.1	7.2	8.4	10.3	2.3	0.6	7.4
1980	31.4	17.6	14.2	6.9	8.4	10.4	2.4	0.7	7.9
1985	30.9	17.2	18.1	7.1	7.0	9.4	2.2	0.8	7.1

Sources: Bank of Japan, *Economic Statistics Annual, 1985*, 50, 56, 62, 68, 72, 78, 80, 83–84, 86–87, *1977*, 82, 88, 94, 100, 104, 138, 144, 153–154, 158; *1971*, 134–135, 138–139; Edward J. Lincoln, *Japan: Facing Economic Maturity* (Washington, DC: Brookings Institution, 1988), 162.

Japanese Financial Liberalization

Exhibit 6   Banking Industry Return on Net Worth, by Type of Institution, Fiscal Years 1971–1984[a]

Fiscal Year	City Banks	Regional Banks	Long-Term Credit Banks	Trust Banks	Sogo Banks	Shinkin Banks	Securities Firms
1971	30.6	29.0	24.9	34.4	30.4	29.8	30.3
1972	27.3	24.9	26.3	26.7	31.0	28.5	42.6
1973	23.8	25.8	20.1	26.5	32.1	24.1	35.0
1974	24.4	31.3	18.3	24.5	35.2	31.1	9.1
1975	20.3	21.0	19.7	19.7	24.0	27.0	17.1
1976	20.5	18.8	23.5	19.4	21.7	22.4	22.8
1977	16.3	18.7	23.9	15.2	19.9	21.8	31.2
1978	17.4	16.4	19.6	15.8	18.7	19.4	31.1
1979	13.1	14.6	16.4	14.1	17.5	14.3	21.3
1980	16.2	14.7	15.6	12.3	16.4	14.5	19.6
1981	19.7	14.1	11.9	23.2	16.1	14.1	23.2
1982	22.9	17.1	14.7	27.7	20.0	17.7	12.0
1983	24.5	18.3	20.0	16.6	20.0	17.9	27.0
1984	23.8	16.3	18.2	22.6	18.3	15.7	30.0

[a]The profit measure is before-tax profits, including all operating, nonoperating, and extraordinary items. Net worth is based on reported figures for *shihon* (capital) or *jiko shihon* (own capital). For securities firms, the reporting year ends in September rather than December.

Source: Edward J. Lincoln, *Japan: Facing Economic Maturity* (Washington, DC: Brookings Institution, 1988), 167.

Japanese Financial Liberalization

Exhibit 7 Changes in Assets and Liabilities of All Banks in Japan (Percentage of Total Outstanding Assets)

	End of 1960 (%)	1965 (%)	1970 (%)	1975 (%)	1980 (%)	1984 (%)
Liabilities						
Deposits and bank debentures	84.7	83.9	86.0	85.8	83.7	76.8
Demand deposits	28.0	29.5	28.6	28.5	22.7	18.6
Time deposits and bank debentures	56.7	54.4	57.4	57.3	61.0	58.2
Negotiable certificates of deposit (A)	—	—	0.7	—	1.0	2.6
Nonresident yen deposits and foreign currency deposits (B)	—	1.3	1.2	2.4	4.3	5.9
Borrowed money from other financial institutions	1.1	1.9	4.6	0.3	0.2	0.2
Borrowed money from the Bank of Japan	5.6	5.0	4.3	1.5	1.1	1.0
Call money and bills sold (C)	1.8	4.1	5.0	6.1	5.6	7.3
Total (A+B+C)	1.8	5.4	6.9	8.5	10.9	15.8
Assets						
Loans	81.4	80.2	81.8	80.3	74.2	76.3
Less than 1 year[a]	—	79.7	74.9	61.8	58.9	60.1
Over 1 year	—	20.3	25.1	38.2	41.1	39.9
Long-term credit banks	—	10.8	11.2	11.4	10.4	8.9
Negotiable securities	15.3	16.0	14.5	15.5	21.0	17.7
Bonds	12.8	13.4	11.4	12.3	17.2	13.7
Stocks	2.3	2.6	3.1	3.1	3.6	4.0
Call loans and bills purchased	1.1	1.4	1.6	1.5	2.0	3.7
Cash and deposits	2.1	1.7	1.8	2.5	2.5	2.0

[a]Distribution percentage (end of fiscal year).

Source: Bank of Japan, "Application table of flow of funds accounts," etc.; Yoshio Suzuki, "Financial Innovation in Japan: Its Origins, Diffusion, and Impacts," in Marcello DeCecco, ed., *Changing Money: Financial Innovation in Developed Countries* (Oxford: Basil Blackwell, 1987), 250.

Japanese Financial Liberalization

Exhibit 8   Japan's Interest Rate Structure

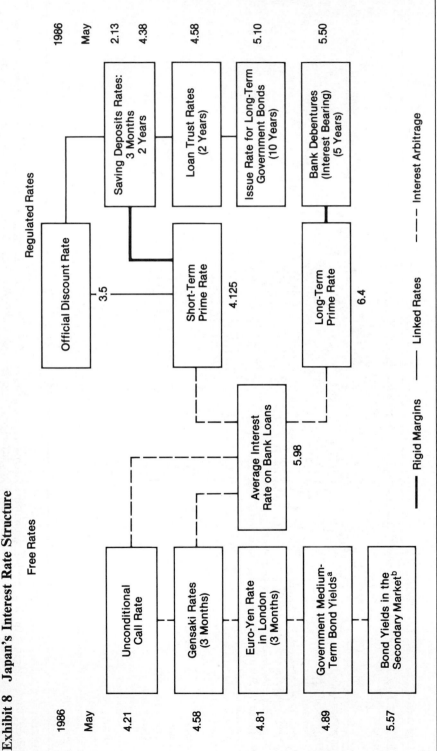

[a]Three-year government bond, yield to subscribers.

[b]Over-the-counter sales yield of public bonds.

Sources: Yoshio Suzuki, *Money, Finance and Macroeconomic Performance in Japan* (New Haven and London: Yale University Press, 1986); and OECD *Economic Surveys, Japan*, November 1986, 26.

Japanese Financial Liberalization

Exhibit 9   Trends in Major Interest Rates

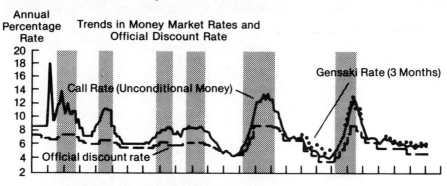

Annual Percentage Rate

Trends in Money Market Rates and Official Discount Rate

Call Rate (Unconditional Money)

Gensaki Rate (3 Months)

Official discount rate

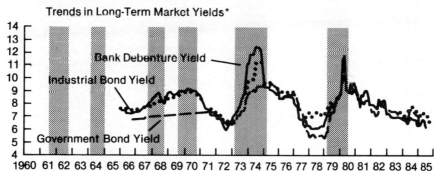

Trends in Long-Term Market Yields*

Bank Debenture Yield

Industrial Bond Yield

Government Bond Yield

1960 61 62 63 64 65 66 67 68 69 70 71 72 73 74 75 76 77 78 79 80 81 82 83 84 85

Note: Shaded areas indicate periods of tight money.

* Average of end of month

Source: Yoshio Suzuki, "Financial Innovation in Japan: Its Origins, Diffusion and Impacts," in Marcello DeCecco, ed., *Changing Money: Financial Innovation in Developed Countries* (Oxford: Basil Blackwell, 1987), 234.

Japanese Financial Liberalization

Exhibit 10   The Issuing Terms of Government Bonds and Secondary Market Rates in Japan

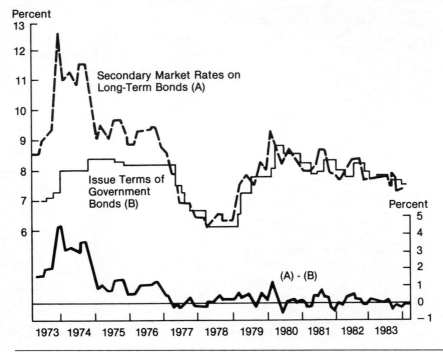

Source: Michael G. Rukstad, "Fiscal Policy and Business–Government Relations,"in Thomas K. McCraw, ed., *America versus Japan* (Boston: Harvard Business School Press, 1986), 317. Reprinted by permission.

Japanese Financial Liberalization

Exhibit 11   Trends in Money Market Transactions

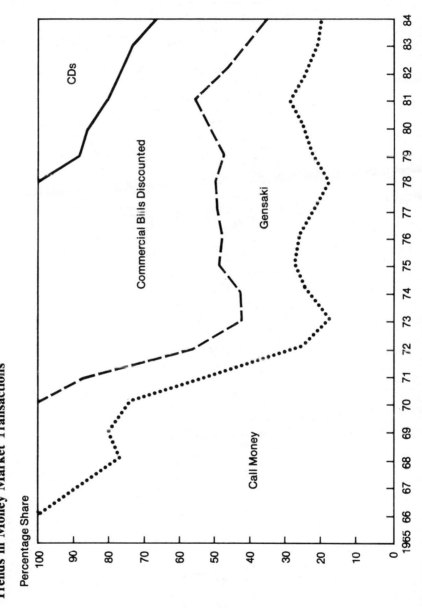

Source: Yoshio Suzuki, "Financial Innovation in Japan: Its Origins, Diffusion and Impacts," in Marcello DeCecco, ed., *Changing Money: Financial Innovation in Developed Countries* (Oxford: Basil Blackwell, 1987), 231.

Japanese Financial Liberalization

Exhibit 12   Trends in Secondary Bond Market Transactions

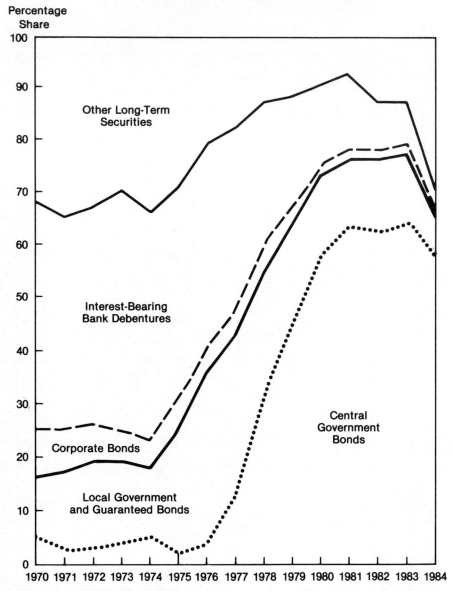

Source: Yoshio Suzuki, "Financial Innovation in Japan: Its Origins, Diffusion and Impacts," in Marcello DeCecco, ed., *Changing Money: Financial Innovation in Developed Countries* (Oxford: Basil Blackwell, 1987), 232.

Japanese Financial Liberalization

Exhibit 13   Short-Term Interest Rates—International

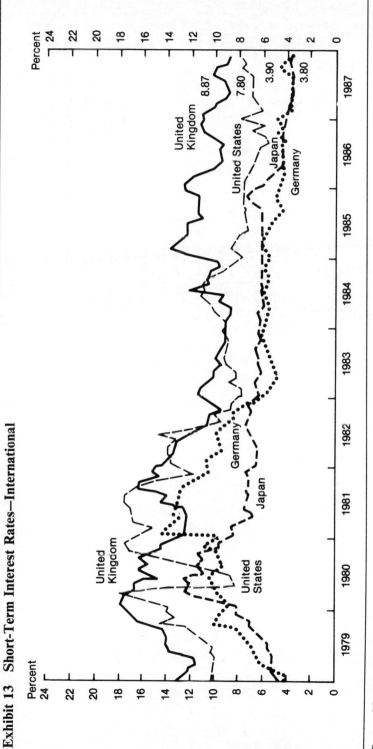

Source: Morgan Guaranty Trusts; Federal Reserve Bank of St. Louis.

Japanese Financial Liberalization

Exhibit 14   Government Securities and Borrowing (Trillion Yen)

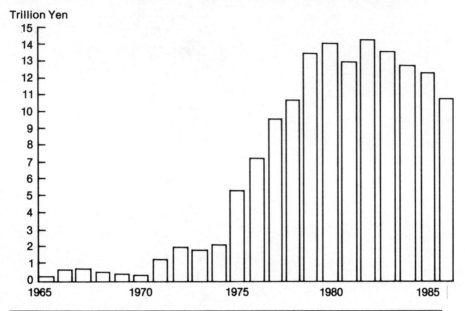

Source: Bank of Japan, Research and Statistics Department, *Economic Statistics Annual,* various issues.

Japanese Financial Liberalization

Exhibit 15 Accounts of the Bank of Japan (Billion Yen)

	1950	1960	1970	1971	1972	1973	1974	1975	1976	1977	1978	1979	1980	1981	1982	1983	1984
Assets																	
Gold and cash	10	27	51	58	44	54	102	115	116	128	228	211	233	245	283	263	330
Bills discounted	48	74	408	39	174	170	131	97	113	161	241	190	226	232	222	207	207
Loans	220	426	1,944	640	1,948	2,099	1,546	1,679	1,342	2,070	2,426	2,251	2,102	1,241	1,879	3,441	3,141
Bills bought	–	–	–	–	715	4,032	4,183	2,323	2,500	3,000	2,850	3,550	3,200	900	1,500	2,500	2,700
Gov't bonds	136	569	2,381	1,543	1,021	2,250	5,250	7,394	8,364	8,091	11,331	13,273	15,835	19,848	19,598	18,039	20,260
Short-term securities	10	378	691	461	671	1,535	2,796	1,405	2,091	4,512	6,609	9,779	11,630	13,876	11,933	10,538	12,815
Foreign assets	–	308	1,123	4,797	4,972	3,725	3,488	3,506	3,688	4,786	3,509	2,409	2,189	2,279	2,539	2,888	3,072
Other	40	29	518	638	164	139	320	504	395	312	304	295	315	315	375	366	378
Total	510	1,435	6,429	7,719	9,042	12,472	15,024	15,623	17,022	18,550	20,892	22,265	24,104	25,064	26,399	27,708	30,091
Liabilities																	
Bank notes issued	422	1,234	5,556	6,407	8,310	10,099	11,667	12,617	14,020	15,438	17,709	19,068	19,347	20,237	21,426	22,466	24,455
Fin. insts. deposits	3	35	298	294	373	1,640	1,994	1,551	1,361	1,279	1,540	1,588	2,644	2,323	2,471	2,625	2,798
Gov't deposits	47	23	42	98	50	72	121	138	153	151	275	137	125	166	287	179	262
Other	30	56	121	456	134	184	391	353	407	447	336	578	669	793	454	591	601
Capital	5	83	408	461	170	474	848	960	1,077	1,239	1,030	891	1,316	1,541	1,759	1,844	1,972
Total	510	1,435	6,429	7,719	9,042	12,472	15,024	15,623	17,022	18,550	20,892	22,265	24,104	25,064	26,399	27,708	30,091

Source: Bank of Japan, Research and Statistics Department, *Economic Statistics Annual, 1984.*

Japanese Financial Liberalization

Exhibit 16   Growth in Real Income and Money Supply (Percentage Change from Previous Year)

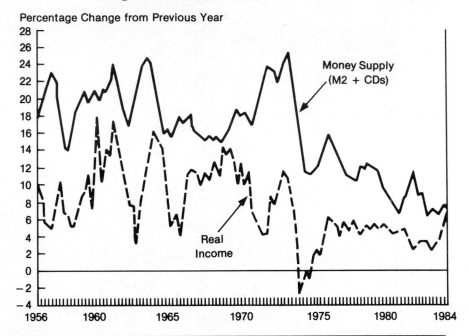

Source: Yoshio Suzuki, *Money, Finance, and Macroeconomic Performance in Japan* (translated by Robert Alan Feldman) (New Haven and London: Yale University Press, 1986), 194.

Japanese Financial Liberalization

Exhibit 17   Current Account and Exchange Rate, 1970–1988

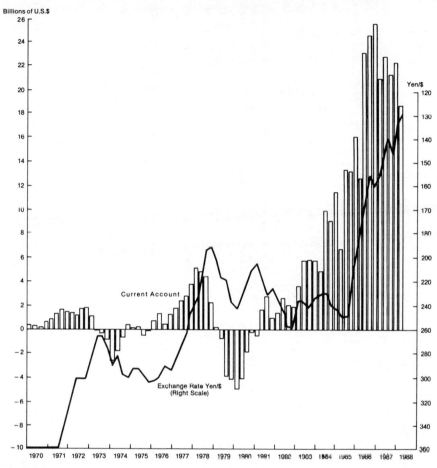

Sources: Bank of Japan, *Balance of Payments Monthly,* various issues; and International Monetary Fund, *International Financial Statistics* (Washington, DC), various issues, as published in Sena Eken, *Integration of Domestic and International Financial Markets: The Japanese Experience,* IMF Staff Papers, September 1984, 514.

Japanese Financial Liberalization

Exhibit 18   Long-Term Capital Movements (Billions of U.S. Dollars)[a]

	1970	1971	1972	1973	1974	1975	1976	1977	1978	1979	1980	1981	1982	1983	1984	1985
Foreign Capital[b]	440	1,149	532	-1,282	182	3,120	3,575	2,063	2,483	3,318	13,141	13,137	12,449	14,759	7,124	17,273
Direct investments	94	210	170	-42	202	226	113	21	8	239	278	189	439	416	-10	642
Portfolio investments[b]	252	940	696	-591	-865	1,518	1,595	1,256	1,654	2,072	11,877	11,852	7,579	8,485	-156	3,851
Import credits	7	8	9	-12	-6	-26	-5	-13	-22	-33	-16	-15	-6	8	3	29
Loans	80	20	-197	-313	-232	166	326	-324	-7	-169	-231	-186	-181	-37	-77	-75
Bonds	44	8	-105	-198	-80	1,235	1,509	1,099	833	2,210	1,236	1,368	4,281	5,663	7,350	12,890
Others	-37	-37	-41	-126	1,003	1	37	24	17	-1,001	-3	-71	337	224	14	-64
Japanese Capital	-2,031	-2,231	-5,004	-8,468	-4,064	-3,392	-4,559	-5,247	-14,872	-16,294	-10,817	-22,809	-27,418	-32,459	-56,775	-81,815
Direct investments	-355	-360	-731	-1,904	-2,012	-1,763	-1,991	-1,645	-2,371	-2,898	-2,385	-4,894	-4,540	-3,612	-5,965	-6,452
Portfolio investments	-62	-195	-1,181	-1,787	-141	-24	-146	-1,718	-5,300	-5,865	-3,753	-8,777	-9,743	-16,024	-30,795	-59,773
Export credits	-787	-863	-308	-1,084	-672	-29	-571	-1,388	-142	1,288	-717	-2,731	-3,239	-2,589	-4,937	-2,817
Loans	-628	-594	-1,683	-3,038	-1,136	-1,295	-1,525	-472	-6,299	-8,102	-2,553	-5,083	-7,902	-8,425	-11,922	-10,427
Others	-199	-219	-1,101	-691	-102	-281	-326	-24	-760	-717	-1,409	-1,324	-1,994	-1,809	-3,156	-2,346
Net[b]	-1,591	-1,082	-4,472	-9,750	-3,881	-272	-984	-3,184	-12,389	-12,976	2,324	-9,672	-14,969	-17,700	-49,651	-64,542
Percent of GNP																
Foreign Capital	0.2	0.5	0.2	-0.3	0	0.6	0.6	0.3	0.3	0.3	1.2	1.1	1.3	1.3	0.6	1.3
Japanese Capital	-1.0	-1.0	-1.6	-2.1	-0.9	-0.7	-0.8	-0.8	-1.5	-1.6	-1.0	-2.0	-2.8	-2.8	-4.5	-6.2
Net	-0.8	-0.5	-1.4	-2.4	-0.9	-0.1	-0.2	-0.5	-1.3	-1.3	0.2	-0.9	-1.5	-1.5	-3.9	-4.9

[a]Minus sign indicates capital outflow.

[b]Excluding foreign investors' gensaki transactions (bond transactions with agreements to repurchase usually within three months). Since the liberalization in 1979 up to the end of 1981, although short-term in nature, those transactions had been classified as long-term capital movements.

Source: Bank of Japan, *Balance of Payments Monthly*; OECD Economic Surveys, *Japan*, 1983–1984 and 1986–1987.

Japanese Financial Liberalization

Exhibit 19   Deviations from Covered Interest Parity[a]

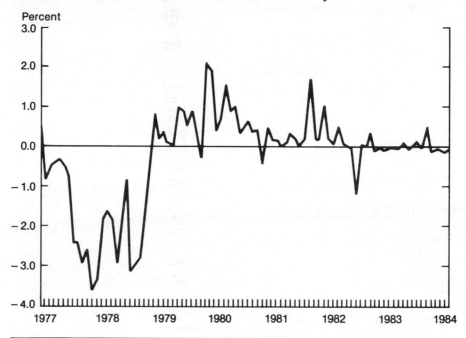

[a]Covered interest parity is the condition in which the foreign interest rate equals the domestic (yen) interest rate plus the expected appreciation of the home currency (yen).

Source: Robert Alan Feldman, *Japanese Financial Markets: Deficits, Dilemmas, and Deregulation* (Cambridge, MA, and London: MIT Press, 1986), 182.

Discussion Questions for Case

1. What are the economic and political forces leading to the liberalization of the Japanese financial system? Which are most important?
2. What additional liberalizations in the Japanese financial system are likely to occur in the future? Why?
3. What are the implications of Japanese financial liberalization for the conduct of Japanese monetary policy? For Japanese financial institutions? For Japanese nonfinancial corporations?

Bibliography

Crum, M. Colyer, and David M. Meerschwam, "From Relationship to Price Banking: The Loss of Regulatory Control," in Thomas K. McCraw, ed., *America versus Japan* (Boston: Harvard Business School Press, 1986). The authors of this chapter compare the Japanese and American financial systems and the unique factors contributing to the separate paths to liberalization in each country.

Feldman, Robert Alan, *Japanese Financial Markets: Deficits, Dilemmas, and Deregulation* (Cambridge, MA: MIT Press, 1986). This scholarly treatise examines the interrelationships among market pressures, innovations, and deregulation. Part of the text will be difficult for those without a background in economics, though Chapters 1, 2, 3, and 10 should be accessible to all readers.

Suzuki, Yoshio, "Financial Innovation in Japan: Its Origins, Diffusion and Impacts," in Marcello DeCecco, ed., *Changing Money: Financial Innovation in Developed Countries* (Oxford: Basil Blackwell, 1987), 229–259. This chapter provides a survey of the causes, channels, and consequences of financial liberalization by one of the leading experts in this field.

Suzuki, Yoshio, *Money, Finance, and Macroeconomic Performance in Japan* (New Haven, CT: Yale University Press, 1986). This is a scholarly treatment of macroeconomic policy in Japan with numerous sections devoted to financial innovation. Part I, on the evolution of the financial system, is particularly relevant to the case in this chapter.

Viner, Aron, *Inside Japanese Financial Markets* (Homewood, IL: Dow Jones–Irwin, 1988). The author provides a current, detailed institutional account of the various financial markets and institutions in Japan.

PART III
MANAGING FISCAL POLICY

At the beginning of the twentieth century, the role of fiscal policy was confined to the fiscal finance of national defense and a few other government activities. Today, fiscal policy has evolved into a powerful tool allowing the government to influence the aggregate expenditures of a nation. The principles of how fiscal policy affects expenditures and income is the subject of the case in Chapter 6, "A Keynesian Cure for the Depression." The basis of the Keynesian analysis is that an additional government expenditure not financed by increased taxes will lead to even more income than that initial expenditure. In times of depression, this prescription offers tremendous opportunities for policymakers.

It was, however, thirty years before the idea became the reality. The opportunity to actively pursue economic growth was not overlooked by the Kennedy political strategists, but it had to be balanced against the detrimental charges that the deficits would damage the economy. The Chapter 7 case, "The Tax Cut of 1964," relates the political and economic considerations leading to the adoption of this aggressive fiscal policy. The government was now using fiscal policy to accomplish its objectives.

Business has always been willing to accept fiscal largess, but traditionally it has not been active in initiating change in fiscal policy. In the mid-1970s, that attitude started to change. One of the first business-initiated fiscal programs is described in the Chapter 8 case, "The Capital Gains Tax Cut of 1978." The tax package was not expected to succeed, but as a result of business's careful attention to the legislative process, it was enacted over the Carter administration's objections. Business, too, was using fiscal policy to accomplish its objectives.

When President Reagan took office in 1981, fiscal policy became the cornerstone of his economic strategy. The underlying objective of Reagan's program is one of the points for discussion in the Chapter 9 case, "The Reagan Plan." The tax proposal was advertised as a supply-side tax cut, since it was supposedly designed to increase the incentives to work, save, and invest. Its political journey from campaign rhetoric to tax law is chronicled in the Chapter 10 case, "The Economic Recovery Tax Act of 1981." The rationale of fiscal policy had apparently changed from managing the aggregate effect on total income to managing the allocative effect on individual incentives.

Since offsetting reductions in government expenditures were not found, the penalty for ignoring the aggregate revenue losses associated with the tax incentives was an ever-increasing deficit. The Chapter 11 case, "The Reagan Deficits," describes the attempts to reduce the deficit after the Reagan plan was instituted in 1981. The consequences of a continued deficit and the strategies for its reduction are the focus of the discussion.

In response to the rising deficits, some countries have sought alternatives to the problematic options of raising taxes or cutting expenditures. In the United Kingdom some observers have argued that Prime Minister Margaret Thatcher had championed privatization as a solution to her fiscal woes. The Chapter 12 case, "Privatization in the United Kingdom," examines the motives and consequences of privatization.

CHAPTER 6
Principles of Keynesian Economics

Most textbook presentations of Keynesian economics are excessively theoretical for business and public policymakers. The reader is asked to manipulate algebraic relationships, but the motivation for doing so has been lost. The case in this chapter, "A Keynesian Cure for the Depression," is based on an article written for the general public in 1933 by the most famous economist of the twentieth century, John Maynard Keynes. Keynes' motivation for constructing a new theory of the determination of income was prompted by years of worldwide economic depression.

The cause of the depression, as Keynes saw it, was inadequate aggregate demand for goods and services. The insight he offers in this article is that a new expenditure by either the public or the private sector on goods or services would lead to a multiplied amount of income— hence the "multiplier" theory of the determination of income. His advice to policymakers was: If the private sector won't spend, the public sector ought to. This article concentrates on the market for goods and services while largely ignoring the market for money and other financial assets. Keynesian monetary theory was outlined in the note to Chapter 3, "Implementing Monetary Policy." The interaction of the monetary sector and the real sector (goods and services) is a more complicated argument that Keynes would develop three years later in The General Theory of Employment, Interest, and Money.

The issues of this chapter's case are the validity of Keynes' diagnosis and the practicality of his prescription. It raises questions of how convincing Keynes' argument was to policymakers and to the general public in the early 1930s. Keynes and Franklin Roosevelt had met in 1934 and occasionally communicated by letter. After their meeting, Roosevelt thought Keynes was more a mathematician than a political economist; Keynes had expected Roosevelt to be more literate in economics. If their meeting had been mutually less disappointing, would a Keynesian solution have returned the United States to prosperity?

Case
A Keynesian Cure for the Depression

Introduction

John Maynard Keynes (1883–1946) was the most influential economist of the
first half of this century. The son of a distinguished logician, Keynes was educated at Eton and studied mathematics at Cambridge. Under the influence
of Alfred Marshall, then the dominant figure in economic thought, Keynes decided to become a professional economist. Although he entered the Civil
Service and was a representative at the Peace Conference following World
War I, he sharply criticized the Treaty of Versailles for its harsh insistence on
reparations from defeated Germany. He left the Treasury. Enormously versa-
tile, he was a successful financier, a Cambridge don, an active editor and
journalist, and a patron of the ballet and theater.

By the mid-1920s, Keynes was convinced that governmental intervention was needed to alleviate unemployment. In 1936, he published *The General Theory of Employment, Interest and Money*, which systematically criticized the economic orthodoxy that market-induced price changes would
automatically return a depressed economy to equilibrium at full employment.
Shortly after the outbreak of World War II, Keynes returned to the Treasury
as an advisor. In the years before his death, he served as Great Britain's
chief negotiator at the Bretton Woods Conference (1944); his plan for a
Clearing Union to create a medium of exchange for international trade was
not adopted, but elements of it are found in the International Monetary Fund
and in the International Bank for Reconstruction and Development (World
Bank), which was devised at Bretton Woods.

Initially considered uncertain, even radical, Keynes' doctrines gained
wide acceptance during and after World War II, as governments in capitalist
democracies tried to use taxation and spending policies to achieve growth,
full employment, and price stability. Keynesian ideas were especially influential in the United Kingdom and the United States. Although Keynes himself
had often been pessimistic about the future performance of market economies, his American interpreters felt his insights would give governments
tools for "fine tuning" and propelling a rapidly growing economy.

The Means to Prosperity was published originally as a series of articles
in March 1933, days after Franklin D. Roosevelt's inauguration and weeks af-

This case was prepared by Research Associate Daniel Pope under the supervision of Pro-
fessor Thomas K. McCraw.
Copyright © 1981 by the President and Fellows of Harvard College
Harvard Business School case 9-382-065

ter Adolf Hitler came to power in Germany. The American edition, excerpted here, speaks directly to the situation in the United Kingdom, but Keynes was also eager to see his advice followed in the United States.

While conditions in 1933 in the two nations were almost equally dire, their paths to the catastrophe had differed. Britain had never recovered from the sharp slump of 1920–1921. Growth in the 1920s had been sluggish, with unemployment running above 10 percent. Heavy industry and exports had been hard hit, especially after the United Kingdom went back on the gold standard in 1925 and overvalued the pound sterling at its prewar level. British gross national product dropped only about 11 percent in current terms and 6 percent in constant prices between 1929 and 1932, but that was sufficient to raise the unemployment rate to 22.5 percent in the latter year. Growth thereafter was steady but unimpressive, spurred on by heavy investments in government-subsidized housing construction.

Excerpts from *The Means to Prosperity* by John Maynard Keynes[1]

I. The Nature of the Problem

If our poverty were due to famine or earthquake or war—if we lacked material things and the resources to produce them, we could not expect to find the means to prosperity except in hard work, abstinence, and invention. In fact, our predicament is notoriously of another kind. It comes from some failure in the immaterial devices of the mind, in the working of the motives which should lead to the decisions and acts of will, necessary to put in movement the resources and technical means we already have. It is as though two motor drivers, meeting in the middle of a highway, were unable to pass one another because neither knows the rule of the road. Their own muscles are no use; a motor engineer cannot help them; a better road would not serve. Nothing is required and nothing will avail, except a little clear thinking.

So, too, our problem is not a human problem of muscles and endurance. It is not an engineering problem or an agricultural problem. It is not even a business problem, if we mean by business those calculations and dispositions and organising acts by which individual entrepreneurs can better themselves. Nor is it a banking problem, if we mean by banking those principles and methods of shrewd judgment by which lasting connections are fostered and unfortunate commitments avoided. On the contrary, it is, in the strictest sense, an economic problem or, to express it better, as suggesting a blend of economic theory with the art of statesmanship, a problem of political economy.

[1]From *The Collected Works of John Maynard Keynes*, Volume IX (London: Macmillan, St. Martin's Press for the Royal Economic Society, 1972). Reprinted with permission of Cambridge University Press.

I call attention to the nature of the problem, because it points us to the nature of the remedy. It is appropriate to the case that the remedy should be found in something which can fairly be called a *device*. Yet there are many who are suspicious of devices, and instinctively doubt their efficacy. There are still people who believe that the way out can only be found by hard work, endurance, frugality, improved business methods, more cautious banking and, above all, the avoidance of devices. But the lorries of these people will never, I fear, get by. They may stay up all night, engage more sober chauffeurs, install new engines, and widen the road; yet they will never get by, unless they stop to think and work out with the driver opposite a small device by which each moves simultaneously a little to his left.

It is the existing situation which we should find paradoxical. There is nothing paradoxical in the suggestion that some immaterial adjustment—some change, so to speak, "on paper"—should be capable of working wonders. The paradox is to be found in 250,000 building operatives out of work in Great Britain, when more houses are our greatest material need. It is the man who tells us that there is no means, consistent with sound finance and political wisdom, of getting the one to work at the other, whose judgment we should instinctively doubt. The calculations which we ought to suspect are those of the statesman who, being already burdened with the support of the unemployed, tells us that it would involve him in heavy liabilities, present and to come, which the country cannot afford, if he were to set the men to build the houses; and the sanity to be questioned is his, who thinks it more economical and better calculated to increase the national wealth to maintain unemployed shipbuilders, than to spend a fraction of what their maintenance is costing him, in setting them to construct one of the greatest works of man.

When, on the contrary, I show, a little elaborately, as in the ensuing chapter, that to create wealth will increase the national income and that a large proportion of any increase in the national income will accrue to an Exchequer, amongst whose largest outgoings is the payment of incomes to those who are unemployed and whose receipts are a proportion of the incomes of those who are occupied, I hope the reader will feel, whether or not he thinks himself competent to criticise the argument in detail, that the answer is just what he would expect—that it agrees with the instinctive promptings of his common sense.

Nor should the argument seem strange that taxation may be so high as to defeat its object, and that, given sufficient time to gather the fruits, a reduction of taxation will run a better chance than an increase of balancing the budget. For to take the opposite view today is to resemble a manufacturer who, running at a loss, decides to raise his price, and when his declining sales increase the loss, wrapping himself in the rectitude of plain arithmetic, decides that prudence requires him to raise the price still more—and who, when at last his account is balanced with nought on both sides, is still found righteously declaring that it would have been the act of a gambler to reduce the price when you were already making a loss.

At any rate, the time seems ripe for reconsidering the possibilities of action. In this belief I here reexamine the advantages of an active policy, beginning with the domestic affairs of Great Britain and proceeding to the opportunities of the World Conference. This Conference may be well timed in spite of its delay. For it will come at a season when bitter experience makes the assembled nations readier to consider a plan. The world is less and less disposed "to wait for the miracle"—to believe that things will right themselves without action on our part.

II. Internal Expansion

[Note: In this section, Keynes demonstrates the workings of the "multiplier." He is advocating additional capital investments, financed not by current revenues but by borrowing. He calls this deficit spending "loan-expenditures." Recipients of these loan-expenditures will themselves spend part of their incomes, which will in turn stimulate further increases in output and employment. "Loan-expenditures" can come from either government or private sources, but Keynes in this section is concerned primarily with the deficit spending by government. He says that the expansionary effects of deficit spending will increase private incomes and therefore raise tax revenues.]

It is often said that in Great Britain it costs £500 capital expenditure on public works to give one man employment for a year. This is based on the amount of labour directly employed on the spot. But it is easy to see that the materials used and the transport required also give employment. If we allow for this as we should, the capital expenditure per man-year of additional employment is usually estimated, in the case of building for example, at £200.[2]

But if the new expenditure is additional and not merely in substitution for other expenditure, the increase of employment does not stop there. The additional wages and other incomes paid out are spent on additional purchases, which in turn lead to further employment. If the resources of the country were already fully employed, these additional purchases would be mainly reflected in higher prices and increased imports. But in present circumstances this would be true of only a small proportion of the additional consumption, since the greater part of it could be provided without much change of price by home resources which are at present unemployed.

Nor have we yet reached the end. The newly employed who supply the increased purchases of those employed on the new capital works will, in their turn, spend more, thus adding to the employment of others; and so on. Some enthusiasts, perceiving the fact of these repercussions, have

[2]Very roughly speaking, a pound sterling of 1933 equals about $25 in 1983 dollars.

greatly exaggerated the total result, and have even supposed that the amount of new employment thus created is only limited by the necessary intervals between the receipt of expenditure of income, in other words by the velocity of circulation of money. Unfortunately it is not quite as good as that. For at each stage there is, so to speak, a certain proportion of leakage.[3] At each stage a certain proportion of the increased income is not passed on in increased employment. Some part will be saved by the recipient; some part raises prices and so diminishes consumption elsewhere, except in so far as producers spend their increased profits; some part will be spent on imports; some part is merely a substitution for expenditure previously made out of the dole or private charity or personal savings; and some part may reach the Exchequer without relieving the taxpayer to an equal extent. Thus in order to sum the net effect on employment of the series of repercussions, it is necessary to make reasonable assumptions as to the proportion lost in each of these ways. . . .

It is obvious that the appropriate assumptions vary greatly according to circumstances. If there were little or no margin of unemployed resources, then, as I have said above, the increased expenditure would largely waste itself in higher prices and increased imports. . . .

Let us call the gross amount of expenditure, provided out of additional borrowing, the *primary expenditure* and the employment directly created by this expenditure the *primary employment*. I have estimated above on the authority of others—and no grounds have been given for questioning the reasonable accuracy of the estimate as a rough guide to the magnitudes involved—that £200 of primary expenditure will provide one man-year of primary employment. It will make no difference to the following argument whether the object of the borrowing is to finance public works or private enterprise or to relieve the taxpayer.[4] This primary expenditure will, in any of these cases, set up a series of repercussions leading to what it is convenient to call *secondary employment*. Our problem is to ascertain the total employment, primary and secondary together, created by a given amount of additional loan-expenditure, i.e., to ascertain the multiplier relating the total employment to the primary employment.

The primary expenditure of an additional £100, provided by borrowing, can be divided into two parts. The first part is the money which, for one reason or another, does not become additional income in the

[3]That is, a leakage from the income-expenditure flow of the circular flow diagram. Of course, this leakage may be reinjected into the income-expenditure flow by expenditures on investment, government, or exports. See Figure 3 of Note A, "An Introduction to Economics," in Chapter 1.

[4]Again, note that this "multiplier" works for both public and private loan-financed expenditure. It also operates when governments reduce taxes without making equivalent reductions in their spending.

hands of an Englishman (or, if we apply the argument to the United States, of an American).

This is mainly made up of (i) the cost of imported materials, (ii) the cost of goods which are not newly produced but merely transferred, such as land, goods taken out of stocks which are not replenished, (iii) the cost of productive resources of men and plant which are not additionally employed but are merely drawn away from other jobs, (iv) the cost of wages which take the place of income previously provided out of funds borrowed for the dole. The second part, which is the money which does become additional income in the hands of an Englishman, has again to be divided into two portions, according as it is saved or spent (spending in this context including all the direct additional expenditure of the recipient, including expenditures on the production of durable objects).

To obtain the multiplier we simply have to estimate these two proportions, namely, what proportion of typical expenditure becomes someone's income and what proportion of this income is spent.[5] For these two proportions, multiplied together, give us the ratio of the first repercussion to the primary effect, since they give us the ratio of the second flow of expenditure to the initial flow of expenditure. We can then sum the whole series of repercussions, since the second repercussion can be expected to bear the same ratio to the first repercussion, as the first bore to the primary effect; and so on.

In existing conditions, I should say that a deduction of 30 percent for expenditure which for one reason or another does not increase incomes, leaving 70 percent accruing to one person or another as current income, would be a reasonable supposition.

What proportion of this additional income will be disbursed as additional expenditure? In so far as it accrues to the wage-earning classes, one can safely assume that most of it will be spent; in so far as it increases profits and salaries and professional earnings, the proportion saved will be larger. We have to strike a rough average. In present circumstances, for example, we might assume that at least 70 percent of the increased income will be spent and not more than 30 percent saved.

On these assumptions the first repercussion will be 49 percent (since $7 \times 7 = 49$) of the primary effect, or (say) one-half; the second repercussion will be one-half of the first repercussion, i.e., one-quarter of the

---

[5]In economics textbooks today, it is generally assumed that all additional expenditures are received as additional income in the hands of the nation's residents, i.e., that the only leakage is the "marginal propensity to save." In this case, the income multiplier depends solely on the proportion of additional income that they choose to spend. This proportion is known as the "marginal propensity to consume," which equals (1 − marginal propensity to save). The standard textbook formula is:

$$\text{Income multiplier} = \frac{1}{\text{Percentage of leakages}} = \frac{1}{\text{Marginal propensity to save}} = \frac{1}{1 - \text{Marginal propensity to consume}}$$

when savings is the only leakage.

primary effect, and so on. Thus the multiplier is 2, since, if I may take the reader back to his schooldays, he will remember that $1 + 1/2 + 1/4 + $ etc. $= 2$. The amount of time which it takes for current income to be spent will separate each repercussion from the next one. But it will be seen that seven-eighths of the total effects come from the primary expenditure and the first two repercussions, so that the time lags involved are not unduly serious.

[Note: We can illustrate the income multiplier process schematically, just as we did with the money multiplier in the note "Money and the Determination of Income" in Chapter 2. Just as the money multiplier led to an increased money supply by a *relending* process, the income multiplier leads to increased income by a *responding* process, illustrated below. Of the £100 of primary expenditure (primary income for those receiving it), there will be some leakages as shown, but approximately half of the initial expenditure will become secondary expenditures for consumption, and so on through successive repercussions.]

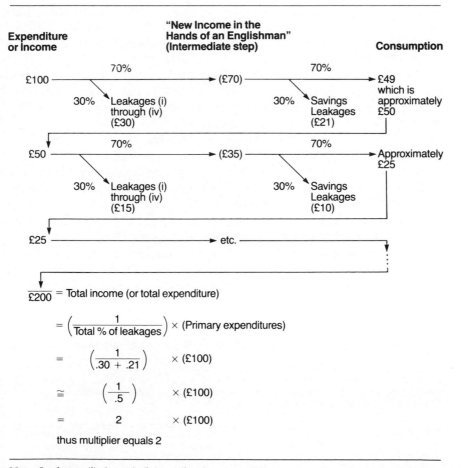

Expenditure or Income   **"New Income in the Hands of an Englishman" (Intermediate step)**   **Consumption**

£100 ——— 70% ———→ (£70) ——— 70% ———→ £49 which is approximately £50

30% Leakages (i) through (iv) (£30)   30% Savings Leakages (£21)

£50 ——— 70% ———→ (£35) ——— 70% ———→ Approximately £25

30% Leakages (i) through (iv) (£15)   30% Savings Leakages (£10)

£25 ———————→ etc. ———————→

$\overline{£200}$ = Total income (or total expenditure)

$= \left(\dfrac{1}{\text{Total \% of leakages}} \right) \times \text{(Primary expenditures)}$

$= \left(\dfrac{1}{.30 + .21} \right) \times (£100)$

$\cong \left(\dfrac{1}{.5} \right) \times (£100)$

$= \quad 2 \quad \times (£100)$

thus multiplier equals 2

Note: Leakages (i) through (iv) are listed on page 219.

It is to be noticed that no additional allowance has to be made for any rise of prices which the increased demand may bring with it. The effect of higher prices will be gradually to diminish the proportion which becomes new income, since it will probably be a symptom that the surplus resources are no longer so adequate in certain directions, with the result that a larger proportion of the new expenditure is merely diverted from other jobs. It is also probable that higher prices will mean higher profits, with the result that, more of the increased income being profit and less of it being wages, more of it will be saved. Thus, as men are gradually brought back into employment and as prices gradually rise, the multiplier will gradually diminish. Moreover, in so far as wages rise it is obvious that the amount of employment corresponding to a given expenditure on wages will also gradually diminish. These modifications, however, would only become relevant as and when our remedy was becoming very successful. A given dose of expenditure at the present stage will, for several reasons, produce a much larger effect on employment than it will be prudent to expect later on when the margin of unused resources is reduced. . . . In what follows I will base my estimates on these figures, which lead to a multiplier of 2. It may interest American readers to consider what assumptions would be most appropriate to present conditions in the United States. Personally I should expect the American multiple to be greater than 2, rather than less.

III. The Relief to the Budget

[Note: In this section, Keynes argues that a £100 primary expenditure will aid the government's budget in two ways. First, it will remove unemployed men and women from the government's dole, decreasing these expenditures. Second, recipients of the additional income generated by loan-expenditures will pay more taxes. He calculates the "benefit to the Exchequer" at £53 for every £100 of loan-expenditure.]

If we apply this reasoning to the projects for loan-expenditure which are receiving support today in responsible quarters, we see that it is a complete mistake to believe that there is a dilemma between schemes for increasing employment and schemes for balancing the budget—that we must go slowly and cautiously with the former for fear of injuring the latter. Quite the contrary. There is no possibility of balancing the budget except by increasing the national income, which is much the same thing as increasing employment.

[Note: Keynes offers suggestions for additional loan-expenditures, including construction of a new ocean liner and an expanded housing program. He computes the additional revenue which the government would gain from each project.]

Substantially the same argument also applies to a relief of taxation. . . . For the increased spending power of the taxpayer will have precisely the same favorable repercussions as increased spending power due to loan-expenditure; and in some ways this method of increasing expenditure is healthier and better spread throughout the community. If the Chancellor of the Exchequer will reduce taxation by £50 million, the half of what he remits will in fact return to him from the saving on the dole and the higher yield of a given level of taxation—though, as I have pointed out above, it will not necessarily return to him in the same budget.

I should add that this particular argument does not apply to a relief of taxation balanced by an equal reduction of government expenditure (by reducing schoolteachers' salaries, for example); for this represents a redistribution, not a net increase, of national spending power. It is applicable to all *additional* expenditure made, not in substitution for other expenditure, but out of savings or out of borrowed money, either by private persons or by public authorities, whether for capital purposes or for consumption made possible by a relief of taxation or in some other way.

If these conclusions cannot be refuted, is it not advisable to act upon them? The contrary policy of endeavouring to balance the budget by impositions, restrictions, and precautions will surely fail, because it must have the effect of diminishing the national spending power, and hence the national income.

The argument applies, of course, both ways equally. Just as the effect of increased primary expenditure on employment, on the national income and on the budget is multiplied in the manner described, so also is the effect of decreased primary expenditure. Indeed, if it were not so it would be difficult to explain the violence of the recession both here and, even more, in the United States. Just as an initial impulse of modest dimensions has been capable of producing such devastating repercussions, so also a moderate impulse in the opposite direction will effect a surprising recovery. There is no magic here, no mystery; but a reliable scientific prediction.

Why should this method of approach appear to so many people to be novel and odd and paradoxical? I can only find the answer in the fact that all our ideas about economics, instilled into us by education and atmosphere and tradition are, whether we are conscious of it or not, soaked with theoretical presuppositions which are only properly applicable to a society which is in equilibrium, with all its productive resources already employed. Many people are trying to solve the problem of unemployment with a theory which is based on the assumption that there is no unemployment. Obviously if the productive resources of the nation were already fully occupied, none of the advantages could be expected which, in present circumstances, I predict from an increase of loan-expenditure. For in that case increased loan-expenditure would merely exhaust itself in raising prices and wages and diverting resources from other jobs. In other words, it would be purely inflationary. But these ideas, perfectly valid in their proper setting, are inapplicable to present circumstances, which can only be handled by the less familiar method which I have endeavoured to explain.

IV. The Raising of Prices

[Note: Between 1929 and 1933, consumer prices in the United Kingdom had declined 14.6 percent; in the United States, 24.4 percent. These price decreases had meant sharp reductions in income for firms and individuals. Thus, odd as it may seem in the 1980s, almost all parties in 1933 wanted to raise price levels. In this section, Keynes argues that demand-expansion, not supply-restriction, is the way to raise prices.]

It is the declared policy of the British government, and also of the representatives of the empire assembled at Ottawa, to raise prices. How are we to do it?

To judge from some utterances of the Chancellor of the Exchequer, he has been attracted to the idea of raising the prices of commodities by restricting their supply. Now, it may well benefit the producers of a particular article to combine to restrict its output. Equally it may benefit a particular country, though at the expense of the rest of the world, to restrict the supply of a commodity which it is in a position to control. It may even, very occasionally, benefit the world as a whole to organise the restriction of output of a particular commodity, the supply of which is seriously out of balance with the supply of other things. But as an all-round remedy, restriction is worse than useless. For the community as a whole it reduces demand, by destroying the income of the retrenched producers, just as much as it reduces supply. So far from being a means to diminish unemployment it is, rather, a method of distributing more evenly what unemployment there is, at the cost of somewhat increasing it.

How, then, are we to raise prices? It may help us to think clearly, if I proceed by means of a series of very simple, but fundamental, propositions.

1. For commodities as a whole there can be no possible means of raising their prices except by increasing expenditure upon them more rapidly than their supply comes upon the market.

2. Expenditure can only be increased if the public spend a larger proportion of the incomes they already have, or if their aggregate spending power is increased in some other way.

3. There are narrow limits to increasing expenditure out of existing incomes—whether by saving less or by increased personal expenditure of a capital nature. Incomes are so curtailed today and taxation so much increased, that many people are already, in the effort to maintain their standard of life, saving less than sound personal habits require. Anyone who can afford to spend more should be encouraged to do so, particularly if he has opportunities to spend on new capital or semi-capital objects. But it is an evasion of the magnitude of the problem to believe that we can solve it in this way. It follows, therefore, that we must aim at increasing aggregate

spending power. If we can achieve this, it will partly serve to raise prices and partly to increase employment.

4.   Putting on one side the special case of people who can earn their incomes by actually producing gold, it is broadly true to say that aggregate spending power within a country can only be raised either (i) by increasing the loan-expenditure of the community; or (ii) by improving the foreign balance so that a larger proportion of current expenditure again becomes income in the hands of home producers. By means of public works the Labour government in Great Britain—though rather half-heartedly and in adverse attendant circumstances—attempted the first. The National government has successfully attempted the second. We have not yet tried both at once.

5.   But there is a great difference between the two methods, inasmuch as only the first is valid for the world as a whole. The second method merely means that one country is withdrawing employment and spending power from the rest of the world. For when one country improves its foreign balance, it follows that the foreign balance of some other country is diminished. Thus we cannot increase total output in this way or raise world prices, unless, as a by-product, it serves to increase loan-expenditure by strengthening confidence in a financial centre such as Great Britain and so making it a more ready lender both at home and abroad.

Currency depreciation and tariffs were weapons which Great Britain had in hand until recently as a means of self-protection. A moment came when we were compelled to use them, and they have served us well. But competitive currency depreciations and competitive tariffs, and more artificial means of improving an individual country's foreign balance such as exchange restrictions, import prohibitions, and quotas, help no one and injure each, if they are applied all round.

We are left, therefore, with the broad conclusion that there is no effective means of raising world prices except by increasing loan-expenditure throughout the world. It was, indeed, the collapse of expenditure financed out of loans advanced by the United States, for use both at home and abroad, which was the chief agency in starting the slump.

A number of popular remedies are rightly popular because they tend to facilitate loan-expenditure. But there are several stages in the task of increasing loan-expenditure; and, if there is a breakdown at any one of them, we shall fail to attain our object. I must ask the reader, therefore, to be patient with a further attempt at orderly analysis.

[Note: Here Keynes discusses how to get private businesses to invest more with borrowed funds. He recommends that central banks try to keep short-term credit "cheap and abundant" and to maintain a low long-term interest rate "for all reasonably sound borrowers." This can be accomplished by the devaluation of national currencies in terms of gold or abandoning rigid gold parities in order to increase reserves of international money. Keynes recognizes that a large government deficit may result in the short run from a program of loan-expenditures; this may actually push interest rates up. Thus, for psychological reasons, it may be necessary to reduce the public loan-expenditure temporarily in order to lower interest rates. However, the reduction should not continue too long, because public loan-expenditures are crucial. Private enterprise is unlikely to invest until *after* sales and profits have begun to rise. In other words, Keynes sees anticipated demand, not the cost of capital, as the main determinant of private investment.]

It is unlikely that private enterprise will, on its own initiative, undertake new loan-expenditure on a sufficient scale. Business enterprise will not seek to expand until *after* profits have begun to recover. Increased working capital will not be required until *after* output is increasing. Moreover, in modern communities a very large proportion of our *normal* programmes of loan-expenditure are undertaken by public and semi-public bodies. The new loan-expenditure which trade and industry require in a year is comparatively small even in good times. Building, transport, and public utilities are responsible at all times for a very large proportion of current loan-expenditure.

Thus the first step has to be taken on the initiative of public authority; and it probably has to be on a large scale and organised with determination, if it is to be sufficient to break the vicious circle and to stem the progressive deterioration, as firm after firm throws up the sponge and ceases to produce at a loss in the seemingly vain hope that perseverance will be rewarded.

Some cynics, who have followed the argument thus far, conclude that nothing except a war can bring a major slump to its conclusion. For hitherto war has been the only object of governmental loan-expenditure on a large scale which governments have considered respectable. In all the issues of peace they are timid, overcautious, half-hearted, without perseverance or determination, thinking of a loan as a liability and not as a link in the transformation of the community's surplus resources, which will otherwise be wasted, into useful capital assets.

I hope that her government will show that Great Britain can be energetic even in the tasks of peace. It should not be difficult to perceive that 100,000 houses are a national asset and 1 million unemployed men a national liability.

*   *   *   *   *

VII. Conclusion

I have endeavoured to cover a wide field in a few words. But my theme has been essentially simple, and I am hopeful, therefore, that I have been able to convey it to the reader.

Many proposals now current are substantially similar in intention to the proposals of this pamphlet. Some deal with one part of the field;

some with another. We shall have need of more than one, if our action is to be adequate to the problem. After making all due allowances for the factors which will cause a larger number of men to appear in the unemployment returns even in good times, Great Britain has the task of putting at least 1 million men back to work. On the figure of £150 primary expenditure to put one man to work for a year, which I have adopted above as my working hypothesis, we should need an increased loan-expenditure *plus* an increased foreign balance amounting altogether to £150 million. We cannot rely on much further assistance towards this total from the foreign balance, until after world recovery has set in. Thus it would be prudent to assume that we have urgent need of the addition of at least £100 million to our annual primary expenditure from increased loan-expenditure at home.

This is a formidable, but not an impossible, figure to attain. At least £50 million might reasonably come from a relief of taxation as a result of suspending the Sinking Fund and borrowing for appropriate purposes; though this would not lead to increased primary expenditure of so much as £50 million. On this basis an additional loan-expenditure of (say) £60 million by private enterprise, assisted and unassisted, local authorities, public boards, and the central government would be a substantial step towards reestablishing employment.

[Note: In this final section, Keynes comments that an improvement in the balance of payments (which will mean more money being spent in the home country) will have the same multiplier effect as an increase in domestic loan-expenditures or a tax cut. His recommendation is to "protect the foreign balance" in conjunction with a deficit spending program.]

I plead, therefore, for a trial of this untried combination in our domestic policy. . . .

For we have reached a critical point. In a sense, it is true that the mists are lifting. We can, at least, see clearly the gulf to which our present path is leading. Few of us doubt that we must, without much more delay, find an effective means to raise world prices; or we must expect the progressive breakdown of the existing structure of contract and instruments of indebtedness, accompanied by the utter discredit of orthodox leadership in finance and government, with what ultimate outcome we cannot predict.

The authorities in power have pronounced in favour of raising world prices. It is, therefore, incumbent upon them to have some positive policy directed to that end. If they have one, we do not know what it is. I have tried to indicate some of the fundamental conditions which their policy must satisfy if it is to be successful, and to suggest the kind of plan which might be capable of realising these conditions.

Discussion Questions for Case

1. Evaluate the Keynesian diagnosis. What were Keynes' assumptions about the functioning of private markets, the nature of unemployment, the role of savings, and the effectiveness of government?
2. What did Keynes mean when he said on page 185 that widespread poverty comes from "some failure in the immaterial devices of the mind . . .?" Do you agree?
3. What are the limitations of the multiplier analysis?
4. How might Roosevelt have gone about implementing a full-scale Keynesian program? How much, roughly, would such a program cost?

Bibliography

Dornbusch, Rudiger, and Stanley Fischer, *Macroeconomics*, 3rd ed. (New York: McGraw-Hill, 1984). The multiplier is derived in Chapter 3, "Aggregate Demand and Equilibrium Income and Output." For the ambitious, an in-depth reading of Chapter 4 will reveal the complete integration of Keynesian monetary theory with the multiplier story.

The Economist (June 4, 11, 18, and 25, 1983). A wide variety of opinions on Keynes and Keynesian economics can be found in the "Keynes Centenary" series written by Nobel laureates Milton Friedman, F. A. Hayek, Sir John Hicks, and Paul Samuelson.

Feldstein, Martin, "The Retreat from Keynesian Economics," *The Public Interest* (Summer 1981), 92–105. Professor Feldstein argues that Keynesian ideas, though they may have been appropriate for another era, are inappropriate today.

Galbraith, John Kenneth, "Keynes, Roosevelt, and the Complementary Revolutions," *Challenge* (January-February 1984), 4–8. The author contrasts the motives and methods of these two contemporaries and arrives at a favorable evaluation of their joint influence on economic affairs.

Gordon, Robert J., *Macroeconomics*, 3rd ed. (Boston: Little, Brown, 1984). This text covers almost identical ground as the Dornbusch-Fischer text. Chapter 3, "Commodity-Market Equilibrium and the Multiplier," gives a refined version of the Keynes' multiplier story presented in this book, and Chapter 4 integrates the financial and nonfinancial sectors.

Keynes, John Maynard, *The General Theory of Employment, Interest, and Money* (London: Macmillan, 1936). Chapters 3 and 10 of this, his most famous work, perfect the principles of effective demand and the multiplier. This book was written for economists and is, consequently, laden with (sometimes archaic) economic terminology. For a summary statement of Keynes' general theory that incorporates both the monetary and real sectors, see Chapter 18.

Leijonhufvud, Axel, *Keynes and the Classics: Two Lectures on Keynes' Contribution to Economic Theory* (London: Institute of Economic Affairs, 1969). This monograph raises interesting issues for the discussion of the case in this chapter, including how Keynes' economics differs from the classical economics that preceded him and how it differs from the Keynesian interpretations that followed him. The discussion of the failure of effective demand in the second lecture gives the intuition for why the multiplier works as it does.

Reynolds, Lloyd G., *Macroeconomics: Analysis and Policy*, 5th ed. (Homewood, IL: Irwin, 1985). In Chapters 4 and 5, the multiplier is developed and related to the equilibrium of the market for goods and services. Equilibrium occurs when demand equals supply. This is one of the most elementary textbook presentations.

Tobin, James, "Keynes' Policies in Theory and Practice," *Challenge* (November/December 1983), 5–11. This sweeping overview of Keynesian economics by an avowed Keynesian argues that, in contrast to Feldstein, Keynes is more relevant today than at any time since the 1930s.

CHAPTER 7
The Zenith of Keynesian Economics

The decade of the 1960s was the golden age of Keynesian economics. In the management of aggregate demand during that era, the perception today generally is that monetary policy played accompaniment while fiscal policy carried the tune. The highly visible reduction in personal and corporate income tax rates in 1964, preceded by tax incentives for investment in 1962, gave the impression of active fiscal management of the economy, sometimes called "fine tuning." The economy rebounded from the stagnant 1950s as predicted by the Keynesian advocates of fiscal activism.

This chapter's case, "The Tax Cut of 1964," describes the process by which the Kennedy administration shaped the landmark tax legislation of 1964. The reduction in taxes, resulting in the intentional increase in the fiscal deficit, was designed to spur economic growth. The note, "Economic Growth and Productivity," distinguishes among the different types and causes of economic growth.

Lessons on three broad issues can be inferred from the case: (1) the efficacy of the fiscal policy process, (2) the management of tax legislation by the president, and (3) the economic consequences of the tax cut. For a balanced discussion of these issues, the case includes political and ideological considerations as well as economic factors. Some would argue that the political considerations were at least as important as the economic factors for the timing and efficacy of the tax cut. The ideological obstacles facing the president when proposing the innovative legislation augmented the typical political difficulties of managing the legislative process. The data on economic performance in Appendix B allow one to speculate on the economic consequences of the tax cut and the contribution of other policies to any apparent success.

Case
The Tax Cut of 1964

Economics has come of age in the 1960s. . . . The paralyzing grip of economic myth and false fears on policy has been loosened, perhaps even broken. We at last accept in fact what was accepted in law 20 years ago in the Employment Act of 1946, namely, that the federal government has an overarching responsibility for the nation's economic stability and growth. And we have at last unleashed fiscal and monetary policy for the aggressive pursuit of those objectives.

These are profound changes. What they have wrought is not the creation of a "new economics," but the completion of the Keynesian Revolution —30 years after John Maynard Keynes fired the opening salvo.[1]

The Evolution of the "New Economics"

In January 1961, the Kennedy administration had begun the New Frontier with a promise to "get the country moving again." For the previous eight years, the Eisenhower administration had argued for a return to economic orthodoxy, which, it believed, would reduce inflation. To Eisenhower, orthodoxy meant minimal government involvement in the economy by reducing government spending, reducing taxes, and balancing the budget. During its two terms of office, the Eisenhower administration was plagued by two major recessions, in 1953–1954 and in 1958. In both cases, Eisenhower resisted attempts to stimulate the economy through fiscal policy. The Eisenhower administration left office with a legacy of unemployment and unused industrial capacity.

The "new economics" of the Kennedy administration, as it was later called by the media, was the product of a complex political evolution involving much infighting and competition for the ear of John F. Kennedy. Walter Heller, Chairman of the Council of Economic Advisers, developed a two-stage economic recovery plan in late 1960 and early 1961. The first stage sought to promote recovery by establishing incentives for business investment and by raising confidence in the dollar. An expansionary monetary policy might have helped investment and growth but fears of inflation and lower interest rates would have weakened the dollar. The Council of Economic Advisers therefore opted for investment

This case was prepared by Associate Professor Michael G. Rukstad.
Copyright © 1982 by the President and Fellows of Harvard College
Harvard Business School case 9-382-078

[1]Walter W. Heller, Chairman of the Council of Economic Advisers under President John F. Kennedy, *New Dimensions of Political Economy* (Cambridge, MA: Harvard University Press, 1966), 1–2.

incentives to improve the business environment without harm to the balance of payments.[2] This first stage terminated with the passage of the Revenue Act of October 1962—a fiscal incentive package including a 7 percent investment tax credit among other reform provisions.

The second stage, which was much more important, was designed to close the "production gap" (the difference between real and potential GNP) and reduce unemployment by means of an aggressive fiscal policy. The administration did not publicly commit itself to such a course until the summer of 1962, though the basic idea had been discussed since before the inauguration. This stage culminated in the passage of the tax cut of February 1964—entitled the Revenue Act of 1964.

Political, Economic, and Foreign Policy Considerations

In the early days of the administration, Kennedy received conflicting advice regarding the probabilities of economic recovery and the need to take drastic action. The assault for a major tax cut was initiated by his pre-inaugural Task Force on Economics. The task force proposal was supported by Walter Heller's Council of Economic Advisers and by Budget Director David Bell. They argued for an immediate cut in order to preempt a recession, lower the current unemployment rate, and close the "production gap."

In the opposing camp were Treasury Secretary Douglas Dillon and Commerce Secretary Luther Hodges, who supported the orthodox budget-balancing philosophy. They urged delay of a major tax cut because of fears over the gold outflow (which would be aggravated if the tax cut ignited domestic inflation) and predictions of recovery which some foresaw on the horizon.

At this time, the attention of the nation and the new administration was focused primarily on foreign policy problems in Berlin, Cuba, Laos, and the Congo. But the economic advice of Kennedy's cabinet officers in Treasury and Commerce, who warned against moving too quickly on a large tax cut, was evident in the president's speeches and news conferences through most of 1961. In fact, the low point in launching the second stage occurred during the Berlin Crisis in the summer of 1961. Despite the sagging economy, President Kennedy considered a $3 billion tax *increase* to offset the increased military expenditures prompted by the U.S.-Soviet confrontation. Even though the tax increase had the support of Kennedy's political advisers and the Treasury, Heller was able to persuade him at the last minute before his televised speech on Berlin to table plans for additional taxes.

Between the summer of 1961 and the summer of 1962, political

---

[2]See the case "Kennedy and the Balance of Payments" in Chapter 14 for a more complete discussion of these events.

Between the summer of 1961 and the summer of 1962, political considerations dominated the discussion of whether and when to announce a second stage program of fiscal stimulus. The key element according to Kennedy's political advisers was the issue of timing of the tax cut. The memoranda by Under Secretary of Treasury Henry Fowler (Exhibit 1 at the end of this case) and Special Counsel Ted Sorensen (Exhibit 2) outline some of these considerations.

At the same time that presidential advisers were debating the timing of a major stimulative tax cut, the Revenue Act of 1962 began its 18-month political odyssey. In an important tax message to Congress on April 20, 1961, Kennedy formally proposed a $1.7 billion investment incentive program. Tax revenues lost as a result of this measure would be offset, as he saw it, by the closing of loopholes on business expense accounts, the creation of withholding tax on dividends and interest, and additional taxes on business overseas. At this time, Kennedy was still concerned with "fiscal responsibility," which meant the avoidance of additional deficits. By October 1962, when the Senate-House Conference Report was issued, all of the original proposals had been scaled down and the withholding tax had been eliminated from the plan. The result was that the $1 billion of tax credits which remained would only be partially offset by the revenue-raising reforms.

Business-Government Relations

In January 1962, the stock market started to decline. Analysts thought this was caused in part by the mediocre performance of the economy and in part by the poor relationship between business and government. That same month, Kennedy had announced wage-price guideposts in order to jawbone labor and business into holding wage-price increases in line with productivity. In April, U.S. Steel raised its prices $6.00 per ton in direct challenge to the president's injunction. In the famous confrontation between Roger Blough of U.S. Steel and Kennedy, Kennedy charged that a $6.00 per ton price hike was socially irresponsible and not consistent with his guideposts.

In the ensuing weeks, business-government relations ebbed to a new low, with fears that mandatory wage-price controls might be instituted in order to combat anticipated inflation caused by the perception of larger deficits. At this point, Treasury Secretary Dillon was still denying any need for an immediate tax cut. Secretary of Commerce Hodges, however, had been won over to the side of the CEA tax-cut advocates.

The headlines were dominated by news of further stock declines. From the record high of 734.91 on December 13, 1961, the Dow-Jones fell 200 points in the next half year. Kennedy was concerned about the lack of confidence in his economic management on the part of business. Heller tried to dismiss the market slide as caused by irrational fears on the part of business, and emphasized the underlying strength of the economy.

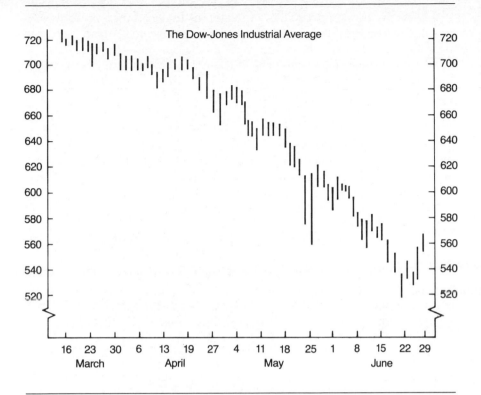

The Dow-Jones Industrial Average

   In subsequent months, Kennedy succeeded in restoring business confidence by initiating three actions favorable to business. The first, in July 1962, was to issue new depreciation schedules which affected 70 percent to 80 percent of all business equipment, resulting in a tax savings of $1.5 billion during the first year it was in effect. The second was the Investment Tax Credit bill (described above) which was passed in October 1962, as was Kennedy's third confidence-winning measure, the Trade Expansion Act of 1962.

Kennedy's Public Commitment to a Tax Cut

In June 1962, the administration had reached a decision to seek large, across-the-board cuts in personal and corporate income taxes to begin sometime in 1963—thereby intentionally running a fiscal deficit. The turning point in Kennedy's mind and in the eyes of commentators occurred in a Yale commencement speech in the same month. Kennedy decided to abandon his attempts to conform to traditional notions of "fiscal responsibility" and instead to attack directly the "persistent, persuasive and unrealistic myths" surrounding deficit spending.

The myths were particularly threatening to the administration's proposal. Former President Eisenhower, for one, objected to the increased deficits and national debt in the pages of the *Saturday Evening Post*:

I say that the time-tested rules of financial policy still apply. Spending for spending's sake is patently a false theory. No family, no business, no nation can spend itself into prosperity. . . . They or their children will pay and pay and pay. In effect, we are stealing from our grandchildren in order to satisfy our desires of today. . . . But all of us would feel more comfortable and secure if our national leadership exercised the foresight and self-discipline to balance its budget and to begin paying back something on the national debt. . . . Imagine how much better the country would feel if it had no debt at all but a healthy surplus![3]

While most of the public and private discussion centered on tax cuts as a means of stimulus, this was hardly the only suggestion in the air as a vehicle for restoring prosperity. Professor John Kenneth Galbraith, then ambassador to India, and Leon Keyserling, former chairman of the Council of Economics Advisers under Truman, both strongly advocated a deficit generated not by tax cuts but by increased public expenditure. Kennedy himself often had the same thought. "You know," he once remarked jokingly, "I like spending money." Political pressures, however, dissuaded him from this course in the 1962–1963 period.

Having decided on a tax cut, Kennedy next struggled with the issue of timing. In a nationwide TV and radio speech on August 13, 1962, he claimed that an immediate cut was unnecessary according to his reading of the current economic statistics, but pledged his commitment to a tax cut package which he would present in detail in January 1963. By December 1962, Kennedy's CEA had prepared extensive briefs on tax cuts, deficits, the debt, the budget, and other economic issues as background for a major speech to the Economic Club of New York. A summary memorandum dated December 16, 1962 (Exhibit 3), outlines the motives and rationale of the administration as well as the wide political support for a tax cut prior to its public presentation.

Kennedy's Case for Tax Reduction

On January 21, 1963, Kennedy presented his Economic Report to Congress. This document elaborated on the reasons for advocating tax cuts and reforms:

Let me make clear why, in today's economy, fiscal prudence and responsibility call for tax reduction even if it temporarily enlarges the federal deficit—why reducing taxes is the best way open to us to increase revenues.

Our choice is not the oversimplified one sometimes posed, between

---

[3]Dwight D. Eisenhower, "Spending into Trouble," *Saturday Evening Post*, May 18, 1963, 15–16.

tax reduction and a deficit on the one hand and a budget easily balanced by prudent management on the other. . . . If we were to try to force budget balance by drastic cuts in expenditures—necessarily at the expense of defense and other vital programs—we would not only endanger the security of the country, we would so depress demand, production, and employment that tax revenues would fall and leave the government budget still in deficit. The attempt would thus be self-defeating.

So until we restore full prosperity and the budget-balancing revenues it generates, our practical choice is not between deficit and surplus but between two kinds of deficits: between deficits born of waste and weakness and deficits incurred as we build our future strength. . . .

I pledged last summer to submit proposals for a top-to-bottom reduction in personal and corporate income taxes in 1963—for reducing the tax burden on private income and the tax deterrents to private initiative that have for too long held economic activity in check. Only when we have removed the heavy drag our fiscal system now exerts on personal and business purchasing power and on the financial incentives for greater risk-taking and personal effort can we expect to restore the high levels of employment and high rate of growth that we took for granted in the first decade after the war.

In order to enlarge markets for consumer goods and services and translate these into new jobs, fuller work schedules, higher profits, and rising farm incomes, I am proposing a major reduction in individual income tax rates. Rates should be cut in three stages, from their present range of 20 to 91 percent to the more reasonable range of 14 to 65 percent. These revisions would directly increase the annual rate of disposable after-tax incomes of American households by some $8 billion when the program is in full effect, with account taken of both tax reductions and tax reform. Taxpayers in all brackets would benefit, with those in the lower brackets getting the largest proportional reductions. American households as a whole regularly spend between 92 and 94 percent of the total after-tax (disposable) incomes they receive. And they generally hold to this range even when income rises and falls; so it follows that they generally spend about the same percentage of dollars of income added or subtracted. If we cut about $8 billion from the consumer tax load, we can reasonably expect a direct addition to consumer goods markets of well over $7 billion. . . .

Even if the tax program had no influence on investment spending—either directly or indirectly—the $8–9 billion added directly to the flow of consumer income would call forth a flow of at least $16 billion of added consumer goods and services. But the program will also generate direct and indirect increases in investment spending. The production of new machines, and the building of new factories, stores, offices, and apartments add to incomes in the same way as does production of consumer goods. This too sets off a derived chain reaction of consumer spending, adding at least another $1 billion of output of consumer goods for every $1 billion of added investment.

To raise the nation's capacity to produce . . . we must invest, and we must grow. . . . As a first step, we have already provided important new tax incentives for productive investment. Last year the Congress enacted a 7 percent tax credit for business expenditures on major kinds of equipment. And the Treasury, at my direction, revised its depreciation rules to reflect today's conditions. Together, these measures are saving business over $2 billion a year in taxes and significantly increasing the net rate of return on capital investment.

The second step in my program to lift investment incentives is to reduce the corporate tax rate from 52 percent to 47 percent, thus restoring the pre-Korean rate. Particularly to aid small businesses, I am recommending that . . . the rate on the first $25,000 of corporate income be dropped from 30 percent to 22 percent. . . . These changes will cut corporate liabilities by over $2.5 billion before structural changes. . . .

The third step toward higher levels of capital spending is a combination of structural changes to remove barriers to the full flow of investment funds, to sharpen the incentives for creative investment, and to remove tax-induced distortions in resource flow. Reduction of top individual income tax rates from 91 percent to 65 percent is a central part of this balanced program.

Fourth, apart from *direct* measures to encourage investment, the tax program will go to the heart of the main deterrent to investment today, namely, inadequate markets. Once the sovereign incentive of high and rising sales is restored, and the businessman is convinced that today's new plant and equipment will find profitable use tomorrow, the effects of the directly stimulative measures will be doubled and redoubled. Thus—and it is no contradiction—the most important single thing we can do to stimulate investment in today's economy is to raise consumption by major reduction of individual income tax rates.

Fifth, side-by-side with tax measures, I am confident that the Federal Reserve and the Treasury will continue to maintain, consistent with their responsibilities for the external defense of the dollar, monetary and credit conditions favorable to the flow of savings into long-term investment in the productive strength of the country.

Congressional Politics

Throughout 1963 the administration was under pressure from both ends of the political spectrum. Liberals wanted more stimulus directed to the lower income levels. Conservatives argued for more tax incentives focused on business investment and for reductions in public expenditures as well. The support of Wilbur Mills (D., Arkansas), who was the powerful chairman of the House Ways and Means Committee, would be essential. Ever since the inauguration Kennedy had actively courted his favor.[4] Kennedy's chief congressional liaison, Larry O'Brien, outlined Mills' po-

[4]Theodore Sorensen, *Kennedy* (New York: Harper & Row, 1965), 432.

sition at the end of 1962 for the president in a memorandum reproduced in Exhibit 4.

In order to facilitate progress of the tax bill through the House Ways and Means Committee, the administration initially emphasized the tax reforms and played down the tax cut. Gradually the emphasis changed as the lackluster performance of the economy continued. One inside observer recounted the Kennedy-Mills courtship:

Initially Mills agreed to a major tax reform bill, with a little tax reduction to help pass it. When presented, it was a tax reform and tax reduction bill. In testimony, it became a tax reduction and tax reform bill. And when it was finally reported by Mills, the president had his major tax cut bill with a little tax reform.[5]

In September 1963, after seven months of hearings and deliberations, the House Ways and Means Committee issued its favorable report on the bill. A week later the House Rules Committee reported the tax bill to the floor for two days of debate. By this point, Mills was an avid supporter of the tax cut, arguing that a temporary deficit now would aid in achieving a balanced budget later. This made the bill more palatable to those who were concerned with fiscal responsibility.

Once the bill had received the approval of Mills and his colleagues in the House, it faced similar challenges from the Senate Finance Committee, which opened hearings on October 15, 1963. The objective of the administration was to appease both the conservative and liberal interests to the extent necessary in order to secure a majority of the political center. The influential chairman of the committee, Senator Harry Byrd (D., Virginia), was expected to oppose the intentional deficits generated by the proposed tax cut and to spearhead the conservative opposition. The liberals still maintained that the proposed fiscal stimulus was inadequate in size and inequitable in distribution. Senator Byrd explained his objections to the administration proposal to Leon Keyserling (the liberal chairman of the Council of Economic Advisers under Truman) during the Senate hearings:

. . . [T]here is not a single president in the history of the United States who has ever deliberately urged a tax reduction on the basis of planned deficits. I think it is even more dangerous to do it at this time because, as you know, Doctor, we have had deficits for three previous years. Now, even the administration admits that, if this bill is passed, there will certainly be deficits for six consecutive years. To my way of thinking, a deficit is bad enough, but when it becomes a habit, when it becomes a custom, it is even worse and may lead to serious consequences. . . . I am anxious to see a tax reduction, but expenditures should be reduced first. I point out repeatedly where these reductions could be made; each year I prepare what I call a Byrd Budget. . . .

Keyserling also wanted to modify the administration proposal with

[5]Ibid.

"a few broad suggestions, keeping within the ambit of the about $11 billion which represented the size of the tax proposal."

First, . . . [a] general corporate tax reduction at this time is unnecessary and wasteful. More than enough was done on this score in 1962. Second, . . . the allocation of about 45 percent of the proposed personal tax cuts to taxpayers with incomes of $10,000 and above, who constitute only about 12½ percent of all taxpayers, is wasteful on economic grounds and indefensible on social grounds. I submit that about half of this amount could most usefully be diverted to tax reduction of a more useful and efficient sort. The two foregoing suggestions come to a total of about $4.2 billion. Third, I respectfully suggest that the exemptions be lifted enough to absorb this $4.2 billion amount. The current customary exemption of $2,400 for a family of four has 67 percent less purchasing power than the 1939 exemption. The families benefiting most by the exemptions are even now hard pressed to make ends meet. Helping them more will help the economy most, and be a most worthy human and social gain.

What I am trying to show and prove, if I can, is that this $11 billion of tax reduction at this time, in its nature, in its composition, is such that a large part of it would be wasted and will do no good, and that part of it is distributed in a way that is socially inequitable and unjust.

Senator Gore (Democrat, Tennessee): What do you mean by wasted?

Mr. Keyserling: I mean that it will not be spent, it will be saved.

Senator Gore: You mean, then, insofar as being stimulative of the economy—is that what you mean by waste?

Mr. Keyserling: That is right. When our large corporations sit around a table to determine their rate of investment, the first thing that they consider is whether investment in plant and equipment will improve their technology and productivity and thus give them a competitive advantage over those who cannot afford to make that investment. The second thing they consider is whether the current and prospective demand for their products justifies the increase in their productive capacity. The argument I am making is that, if our corporations now answer these two questions in the affirmative, there is no problem of a barrier to investment in the form of a lack of funds. Their after-tax profits are very high. Their retained earnings are very high. There is such a prolixity of savings that even the Secretary of the Treasury admits it.

After Keyserling's testimony, the committee heard from Dan Throop Smith, a professor of finance at the Harvard Business School at the time and former Assistant Secretary of the Treasury for Tax Policy under Eisenhower:

The tax bill before you, though it contains several good features, seems on balance to be a bad piece of legislation. [A] deliberate increase of a large existing deficit in relatively good times, with a prospect of continuing deficits for a long period seems foolhardy. The country cannot afford economic experiments which are almost certain at some time or other to weaken confidence in the dollar, both internally and externally. . . . [D]eficit spending . . . was tried and presumably discredited in the 1930s, when after a decade of deficits, we had over 10 million unemployed just before World War II. . . .

Not only is a large tax reduction foolhardy, it is also likely to be futile in dealing with the most serious aspects of our very real problem of unemployment. In recent months there has been increasing recognition of the fact that unemployment is concentrated in particular groups of the population. . . . The distinction between general and structural unemployment has by now become familiar. . . .

Monetary and fiscal measures cannot solve the problems of structural . . . unemployment. Increases in the general availability of credit or artificial increases in general demand will not seek out the pockets of unemployment and unutilized productive equipment. Rather, attempts to reach the pockets of unemployment by artificial increases in total demand will lead to bottlenecks, to shortages, and to increases in costs and prices in areas where there are no significant shortages. . . . Undue reliance on general remedies distracts attention from the need for specific cures and may actually weaken a general system. For example, an attempt to relieve a deficiency of a particular vitamin in a diet simply by eating more will probably continue the deficiency and weaken the patient by obesity. . . .

Our tax structure, however, is very bad. It represses and distorts effort and investment. . . . The discouragement and distortion of taxation arise primarily from excessive tax rates [which occur only in the top income brackets]. . . . Reduction in the bottom bracket rate increases purchasing power and is, of course, welcome on personal grounds. But on economic grounds it is hard to see how it can do anything more than increase purchasing power. . . . The combined effect of rate and structural changes gives a reduction of tax liability of 39 percent in the bottom bracket, decreasing to a reduction of 27 percent for incomes of $3,000 to $5,000, 20 percent for incomes of $5,000 to $10,000, 17 percent for incomes of $10,000 to $20,000, 15 percent for incomes of $20,000 to $50,000, and 13 percent for incomes above $50,000. Thus the relief at the bottom is three times as much as that for the larger incomes. This discrimination makes our tax system commensurately more progressive. . . .

[Finally] the proposed reduction in the corporation income tax is eminently desirable. This tax is coming to be recognized, regardless of its incidence, as a penalty on efficient producers. As international competition becomes more severe, the adverse effects of this penalty on efficiency becomes more serious. The tax rate should be reduced as far as possible in view of revenue requirements.

In response to the testimony of Keyserling and Smith, Secretary of the Treasury Douglas Dillon sent a memorandum to Kennedy on the following day, October 24, 1963. This memorandum is included as Exhibit 5.

After Kennedy's assassination on November 22, 1963, President Lyndon Johnson pushed the compromise tax proposal to a rapid vote in February 1964. There were several explanations for Johnson's ability to overcome the strong ideological debates that entangled Kennedy in 1963. Undoubtedly aided by the sympathy for the slain president, Johnson also relied on his long working relationship with influential senators to expedite the bill. In addition, Johnson's projected 1965 budget spending figure was below the 1964 outlay, which Senator Byrd supported. Finally, the Senate appeared eager to complete action on the tax bill before the upcoming civil rights legislation began in the spring.

The Revenue Act of 1964, signed into law on February 26, 1964, contained the following provisions:[6]

- Individual tax liabilities were cut $6.1 billion in 1964 and $9.1 billion in 1965. Rate reductions and reforms combined were expected to cut tax liabilities an average of 19.4 percent in 1965, with the new rates ranging from 14 percent to 70 percent after 1964, down from the 20 percent to 91 percent range before the act. (For details on the distribution of the tax cut, refer to Exhibit 6.)
- Corporate tax liabilities were cut $1.6 billion in 1964 and $2.4 billion in 1965, representing a 7.7 percent reduction when fully effective. The maximum corporate rate was reduced to 48 percent from 52 percent. The rates also were revised to give special benefit to small businesses.
- A minimum standard deduction aided lower-income families and removed 1.5 million persons from the tax rolls. Broader tax deductions were authorized for medical expenses of persons 65 or older, for dependent care expenses, for the cost of moving to a new job location, and for some types of charitable contributions.
- Various other provisions, including a significant broadening of the value of the 7 percent investment tax credit, which was enacted initially in 1962.

[6]These excerpts may be found in the 1964 *Congressional Quarterly Almanac.*

The Tax Cut of 1964
Exhibit 1

Tuesday, Nov. 13, 1961

Dear Mr. President,
      At the last Cabinet meeting, you suggested that the various de-
partments submit their suggestions on the program promptly for the
coming year.
      This is *not* an official or departmental response. It is a personal
letter written in an unofficial capacity to introduce a memorandum I
hope you will find useful.
      The subject of the memorandum is one to which I have given
considerable attention since the first flowers of recovery bloomed in
the spring. I did so because the history of our business cycle suggested
that the period of early recovery provides the best opportunity to act
so as to sustain an economic advance for a long period and prepare to
meet effectively and overcome rapidly at some future unpredictable
point, the tendency to a recession.
      A concern with the subject—"Sustaining Recovery, Avoiding
Recession, or Minimizing a Decline in the National Economy"—involves both politics and economics.
      The politics are better disposed of in this personal vein in a few
lines; the economics, or some aspects of it, are much more complicated. They are treated in the attached memorandum.
      Your Administration should be inextricably associated with
"good times" in the minds of the people.
      This is a rare political asset.
      Much has been done to capture it by your Administration.
      Ten days after taking office, you announced your program to re-
store momentum to an economy in recession. Shortly thereafter, a recovery was underway. In a few short months, the economy had recovered its losses in gross national product and industrial production
and was breaking new ground.
      Can that rare political asset—Kennedy prosperity—be preserved
until November 1964?
      There is a general consensus that the current economic advance
will continue until at least the latter part of 1962 or early 1963.
      The odds are better than two-to-one in past performance of the
business cycle (as described in the attached memorandum) that there
will be a recession in 1963. They (the odds) lengthen very substantially
that one will occur by sometime in early 1964.
      Playing the averages, the recovery might end in March or April
1963, and the following recession end in June or July 1964. Taking the
last short recovery and recession as a pattern (1958–1961) would show

a new recovery in January 1964. Recoveries similar to the 1945–1948 and 1954–1957 patterns would give rise to recession around the turn of the year 1963–1964, with the likelihood that the election of 1964 would occur in an atmosphere of economic decline.

A forty-four-month recovery would carry through November 1964, putting the election in a frame similar in some ways to the 1936 one, when FDR and the 1933–1937 recovery left the opposition Maine and Vermont.

Sometimes it requires some months to detect and confirm a recovery and memories of recent misery and anxiety do not quickly abate. Therefore, the next best ride on the cycle to a forty-four-month upswing or longer, from a political point of view, would be a healthy recovery of average duration (twenty-five or twenty-six months) followed by a short recession (nine months or less). This would suffuse both the summer and fall months, when most of the voters make up their minds, and November, when they vote, with the glow of a well-confirmed recovery.

Thus, the political implications of the subject of the attached memorandum are self-evident and simple.

The answers to the question raised: how do we keep "good times" or see that they prevail in 1964—are neither self-evident nor simple. They require our best thought in the weeks and months ahead —and a combination of rare economic wisdom and political skill.

I hope you will excuse the handwritten character of this letter, in view of its somewhat delicate nature.

Respectfully,

Henry H. Fowler

P.S.   Secretary Dillon is aware of the general tenor of the enclosed memorandum as we have discussed the problem many times. I am sending him a copy and holding it to that. I did not want to disturb him on his vacation to review the memo in all its detail. HHF

The Tax Cut of 1964

Exhibit 2

The White House
Washington

July 12, 1962

MEMORANDUM FOR THE PRESIDENT

Subject: Tax Cut

A tax cut is a massive economic weapon. It can only be used once. It has not been used in any previous recession in my memory. We have promised a tax cut effective January 1; a bill this year could hardly be effective before October 1—and we may therefore be undertaking a major battle for a 3-month difference. You did not want us to overreact in Berlin with a national emergency—I do not want us to overreact now. I do want us to act when we are certain action is required, even if unprecedented.

Therefore, I am for a tax cut *only when* we can be certain (as certain as such matters can be certain) of the following:

1. That both employment and production are on a decline that will be both substantial and continuing;

2. That a cut in income taxes (which directly helps only those with earned income) will not go largely into savings instead of consumption;

3. That the resultant deficit will not be as large as Eisenhower's $12.4 billion in fiscal 1959;

4. That the tax cut bill we submit will pass both Houses of Congress in the form in which it is submitted, with no danger of a defeat or its being amended so badly it might have to be vetoed;

5. That the economy will not be sufficiently stimulated by the deficit now predicted, by the tax credit, public works, and other spending bills we expect to get, and by existing spending authority (and that we have no chance of getting the stand-by tax authority);

6. That the situation is sufficiently serious to warrant giving up the likelihood of passing our tax reform plans for next year;

7. That the cut we are able to propose, within political and budget-

ary limits, will earn business confidence and not be attacked as the wrong size or in the wrong brackets; and,

8.   That the gains made by a tax cut will not be wiped out by more expensive monetary and debt management policies—but that, on the contrary, everything possible is being done in these two areas to make a tax cut unnecessary (see memo from Senator Douglas, a long-time advocate of tax cuts to fight recessions, who opposes a cut now).

Conclusion: Once you are able to go to the Congress and country with positive answers to these items, such a move will be both right and successful. Until then, it is likely to be neither.

Theodore C. Sorensen

The Tax Cut of 1964
Exhibit 3

The Chairman of the
Council of Economic Advisers
Washington

December 16, 1962

MEMORANDUM FOR THE PRESIDENT

Subject: Recap of Issues on Tax Cuts (and the Galbraithian
Alternative)
A. The Economic Case for Fiscal Action
   1. The cost of a slack economy
      a. The $30–$40 billion loss of potential output in 1962 alone is:
        —8 times our total foreign aid,
        —equals total public and private expenditures on health and
          medical care,
        —well exceeds total expenditures on education,
        —is almost equal to the total GNP of Italy.
      b. Similar losses have occurred in each of the past five years.
        Next year, without a tax cut, we would face a loss of the same
        order:
        —Normal growth of the labor force plus growth in
          productivity add more than $20 billion to our productive
          potential next year.
        —Optimistic forecasts of actual GNP growth for 1963 without
          a tax cut is of roughly this magnitude.
      c. We do not predict a recession in the first half of 1963, but
        there is still one chance in four or five that it will occur. And
        as expansion continues at a slow pace, the chance of a
        recession steadily increases.
      d. These are avoidable losses. Economics is no exact science; but
        economists are almost unanimous in holding that an active
        fiscal policy can prevent this waste. And experience in other
        countries, where popular and parliamentary devotion to
        outworn fiscal doctrine is less rigid, provides impressive
        evidence to support them.
   2. The danger of too little and too late
      a. This is a big country. For example: A budget deficit of $15
        billion:
        —would be about 3 percent of potential GNP in 1963,
        —is equivalent to a deficit of $1.5 billion in 1933 (when GNP
          was 1/10 of its present level),

—is less as a percentage of GNP than Ike's record deficit of $12.5 billion, which translates into $16.5 billion in today's GNP.

Our economy is basically healthy, but one doesn't treat an elephant's earache with an eyedropper. (This metaphor has not been certified by Galbraith.)

b. Fiscal medicine is reasonably sure in its effects, but it takes time to work. Even the Treasury's initial proposal of a two-stage net cut of around $10 billion would probably not achieve 4 percent unemployment (our interim target) until 1965. But we would be well on our way by November 1964— not only to full employment, but to that 4 or 4½ percent growth rate to which we are pledged both at home and in OECD.

B. The Political Case for Fiscal Action
1. Congress may be lukewarm, but powerful groups throughout the country are *ready for action.* When the Chicago Board of Commerce, the AFL-CIO, the CED, and the U.S. Chamber are on the same side—when repeated editorials in *Business Week* are indistinguishable from those appearing in the *Washington Post*—the prospect for action cannot be wholly dim. Can 3,000 members of the N.Y. Economic Club be wrong?
2. To be sure, the supporters of action do not agree on the details. But there seems adequate room for compromise, and the Treasury proposals are superbly conceived to provide something for everyone, and in a way that is solidly defensible on economic grounds.
3. Our world leadership—brilliantly asserted only a few weeks ago in the political field—would be strengthened by vigorous expansion of our economy. Continued economic slack saps our prestige and weakens the dollar. One looks for economic miracles today not to the homeland of revolutionary economic expansion, but to Western Europe and Japan. A booming U.S. economy can do more to cure economic sickness in Latin America—and other primary producing areas—than all our foreign aid.
4. A limping economy in November 1964 would be a greater liability than a near-record deficit.

C. Why Cut Taxes Rather Than Go the Galbraith Way?
The case for bold fiscal action seems inescapable. But why rely primarily on the "conventional wisdom" of tax cuts? The economic effect of a $10 billion tax cut could, after all, be achieved by an extra $9 billion increase in expenditures.
1. But how could we spend an extra $9 billion in a year or two? This would be a *40 percent increase* over FY 1963 Federal nondefense expenditures (excluding interest, agriculture, and

social security). True, our cities need renewal, our colleges and universities have no place for the flood of students about to inundate them, our mass transport system is in a sad state, our mental health facilities a disgrace, our parks and playgrounds inadequate, housing for many groups unsatisfactory. But even if Congress would appropriate the added billions, how could they be spent—in time? Attempts to enlarge spending at the rate required to do the economic job would lead to waste, bottlenecks, profiteering, and scandal.

2. Politically, the case for tax rather than expenditure action is strong:
   —An expansion of spending would bring all of the charges of "fiscal irresponsibility" that attach to tax cuts—after all, deficits would be practically the same either way.
   —But on top of this would be all of the opposition to expansion of government, to over-centralization, to a "power grab" and a "take-over" of the cities, the educational system, the housing market.

3. Tax-cut-induced deficits are also far more acceptable to the world financial community than expenditure-induced deficits, i.e., far less likely to touch off new gold outflows.

4. In the not-too-long run, the tax cut route is likely to bring us closer to our government program goals than an immediate attempt to push the budget up by $10 to $15 billion a year—a vigorous economy, stimulated by tax cuts, will provide a broader economic base and an atmosphere of prosperity and flushness in which government programs can vie much more successfully for their fair share of a bigger pie.

Walter W. Heller

The Tax Cut of 1964
_____

Exhibit 4

The White House
Washington

December 5, 1962

MEMORANDUM FOR THE PRESIDENT

During a telephone conversation with Wilbur Mills, he brought
up the subject of the Tax Bill. He made the following points:

1.   Tax cuts, if any, should not be effective until January, 1964.

2.   Objects strongly to deficit increase and stated initial tax cut dis-
     cussions in August were based on the assumption we would now
     be in economic difficulty. Feels this has not occurred and alters
     the situation.

3.   Tax cut/reform should be a package with proviso that if reform
     delayed in Congress, the cut would be then treated separately. (I
     suggested to him that this might bring about delay in reform if
     the Members would realize the cut was forthcoming in any event.
     He agreed this might cause a procedural problem.)

4.   Feels his Committee is impressed with the need for reform and
     therefore its accomplishment is possible.

5.   Repeatedly emphasized that spending cannot be allowed to rise
     faster than revenue—the reverse must be achieved in the legisla-
     tion to guarantee the claimed ultimate goal of balance.

Concerning your New York speech of next week, he suggested
you hedge on specifics—not get into proposals for the Congress but
rather emphasize economic progress from January, 1961—feels this
real progress has been lost to the public because of the constant tax cut
discussions.

Claims he finds no public interest in a cut and others he has
talked to agree—in his view, little or no political plus and serious possibility of extremely adverse reaction to deficit increase. . . .

Larry O'Brien

The Tax Cut of 1964
Exhibit 5

The Secretary of the Treasury
Washington

October 24, 1963

MEMORANDUM FOR THE PRESIDENT

Testimony completely opposite to that of Leon Keyserling was presented to the Senate Finance Committee yesterday when the bill was attacked by Professor Dan Smith of Harvard, who had been in charge of tax policy during the Eisenhower administration. He vigorously attacked the bill on economic grounds as giving too much relief to consumption, and not enough to investment, and called for sharply lower taxes in the higher brackets.

Similar but less extreme views were also expressed in the testimony of Roswell Magill, who was in charge of tax policy during the second Roosevelt administration, and is now a lawyer in New York. He called for considerably greater reductions in the higher rates of income tax, advocating a 50 percent top rather than the 70 percent in the current bill.

All of this indicates that the bill, as presently drafted, is pretty squarely in the middle and subject to cross fire from extreme elements on both sides. It is for this reason that we feel it is the only type of bill that can be passed, and it is probably about right in its effects. . . .

Douglas Dillon

The Tax Cut of 1964

Exhibit 6   Distribution of Personal Income Tax Changes under the Revenue Act of 1964

Gross Income (Thousands of Dollars)	Number of Taxable Returns (Millions)	Percent	Tax Liability under Existing Law (Millions of Dollars)	Percent	Effect of Revenue Act of 1964 (Millions of Dollars)						Tax Liability under New Law (Millions of Dollars)	Percent
					Rate Change	Percent	Structural Change	Percent	Total	Percent		
	(1)	(2)	(3)	(4)	(5)	(6)	(7)	(8)	(9)	(10)	(11)	(12)
0 to 3	9.7	19.0	1,450	3.1	−400	4.2	−165	−56.9	−565	6.2	885	2.3
3 to 5	10.5	20.6	4,030	8.5	−1,020	10.8	−65	−22.4	−1,085	11.8	2,945	7.7
5 to 10	22.9	44.9	18,300	38.6	−3,905	41.2	+130	+44.8	−3,775	41.1	14,525	38.0
10 to 20	6.7	13.1	12,710	26.8	−2,285	24.1	+125	+43.1	−2,160	23.5	10,550	27.6
20 to 50	1.0	2.0	6,760	14.3	−1,150	12.1	+105	+36.2	−1,045	11.4	5,715	14.9
50 and over	.2	.4	4,170	8.8	−710	7.5	+160	+55.2	−550	6.0	3,620	9.5
Total	51.0	100.0	47,420	100.0	−9,470	100.0	+290	100.0	−9,180	100.0	38,240	100.0

Distribution of Tax Reduction under the Revenue Act of 1964 (Millions of Dollars)

Gross Income (Thousands of Dollars)	Tax Rate Reductions	Percent[a]	Tax Structure Reductions	Percent[a]	Total Reductions	Percent[a]
	(13)	(14)	(15)	(16)	(17)	(18)
0 to 3	−400	−27.6	−165	−11.4	−565	−39.0
3 to 5	−1,020	−25.3	−65	−1.6	−1,085	−26.9
5 to 10	−3,905	−21.3	+130	+.7	−3,775	−20.6
10 to 20	−2,285	−18.0	+125	+1.0	−2,160	−17.0
20 to 50	−1,150	−17.0	+105	+1.6	−1,045	−15.5
50 and over	−710	−17.0	+160	+3.8	−550	−13.2
Total	−9,470	−20.0	+290	+.6	−9,180	−19.4

[a]Change as percent of existing tax liability shown in column (3).

Source: Joint Committee on Internal Revenue Taxation; *1964 Congressional Quarterly Almanac.*

Note
Economic Growth and Productivity

The purposes of this note are (1) to define economic growth, (2) to characterize its types and its determinants, and (3) to relate it to productivity.

"Economic growth" simply means increased output of goods and services. The Great Depression ignited public concern over economic growth, but it was not until after World War II that governments made it an explicit goal of policy. By the 1960s, the world had witnessed very rapid economic growth in the two nations most devastated by the war —Germany and Japan. Now, other countries became eager to imitate that success. After sluggish U.S. growth in GNP during the Eisenhower administration, President Kennedy promised to "get the country moving again." All desks in his Department of Commerce were equipped with the placards: "What have you done for growth today?"[1] But that question was not a well-defined inquiry, since, as we will see, there are different types of growth with different determinants and hence different policy prescriptions.

We can be more specific about the types and determinants of growth if we use the concepts of aggregate supply, aggregate demand, and capacity described in Note A of Chapter 1, "An Introduction to Economics." Since growth is inherently a dynamic process, we must account for that in the graphs of aggregate supply and aggregate demand curves by showing the location of these curves in each of a series of time periods. In Figure 1,

---

Figure 1

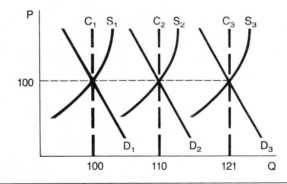

This note was prepared by Associate Professor Michael G. Rukstad.
Copyright © 1984 by the President and Fellows of Harvard College
Harvard Business School note 9-384-138

[1]James Tobin, *The New Economics, One Decade Older* (Princeton, NJ: Princeton University Press, 1974), 13.

Figure 2

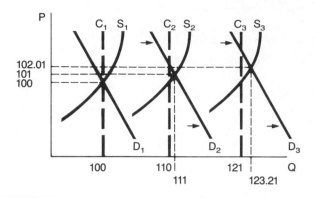

we can represent the aggregate supply, aggregate demand, and capacity curves for Year 1 by S_1, D_1, and C_1 (where the subscript indicates the time period when we observe the curve). For simplicity, the curves for Year 1 are drawn so that the level of prices and the level of output are both 100—indicating a base year for both prices and output. Real output is growing at 10 percent per year between Year 1 and Year 2 (since 110 is 10 percent larger than 100) and between Year 2 and Year 3 (since 121 is 10 percent larger than 110). There is no inflation (since the price index is unchanged) and no unemployment (since, in all three years, we are operating at capacity which is defined to be full employment). Figure 1 shows a special case where growth results from shifting all three curves to the right by the same amount—10 percent per year.

Notice what happens in Figure 2 when the aggregate demand curve shifts to the right by more than 10 percent per year, while capacity and supply grow at the same rate as in Figure 1. In this case we have inflation of 1 percent per year and real economic growth of 11 percent per year.

The same information shown in Figures 1 and 2 can be summarized more concisely in the analogous graphs shown in Figures 3 and 4. Instead of plotting the *level* of prices and the *level* of real output, we are discussing their dynamic counterparts—the *growth* of prices (inflation) and the *growth* of real output. Since Figure 1 indicates no inflation and 10 percent growth in real output, the same information is shown in Figure 3. We did not identify the time periods with subscripts in Figure 3 since the demand, supply, and capacity curves are the same in all three years.

Since the demand curves in Figure 2 were growing faster than the supply and capacity curves in Years 2 and 3, we would have to shift the demand curve in Figure 4 to the right. With capacity and supply unchanged, we would have 1 percent inflation and a real economic growth rate of 11 percent. Of course, if demand were not growing as fast as supply and capacity, we would expect deflation and slower real output growth. In actual experience, we would *never* expect to observe the growth in demand exactly equal to the growth in capacity or supply since these

Figure 3

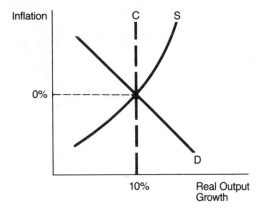

Figure 4

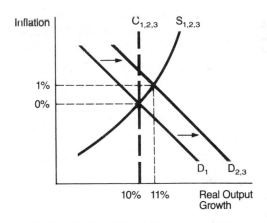

changes are determined by decisions made by different groups of economic actors.

Types of Economic Growth

Such an observation leads us to our first distinction regarding different types of economic growth: *actual* versus *potential*. Actual economic growth is the rate of growth of real output (or GNP) as we observe it in the national income accounts. In terms of the graphs in Figure 1, it is the rate of growth of the actual value of real output from 100 to 110 to 121 determined by the intersection of aggregate demand and aggregate supply. Actual economic growth is not, therefore, determined solely by the growth in aggregate demand, but also by the growth in aggregate supply.

Figure 5

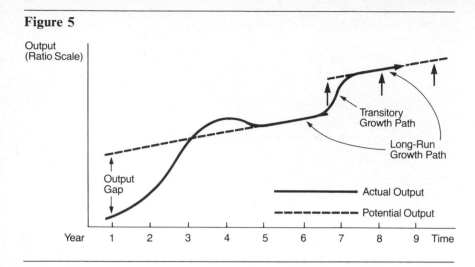

Potential economic growth is the rate of growth of real output or GNP if the economy were at full employment; or, more simply, it is the rate of growth of capacity. Potential growth is not directly observable like actual GNP—instead it is a hypothetical standard for comparing observed values. It must be estimated, based on assumptions regarding what level of capacity constitutes "full employment" of labor and capital resources.

The two types of growth are contrasted in the graph in Figure 5, which plots actual and potential output[2] for each year for a hypothetical economy. The graph shows us that in Year 1 we were not at full employment since our actual level of output was less than our potential level. This is the situation that Walter Heller, economic adviser to President Kennedy, called a "production gap" (see page 231 and Exhibit 3 of the case in Chapter 7, "The Tax Cut of 1964"). The production gap or output gap will be closed if actual output grows faster than potential output, as it does between Years 1 and 3. However, if that more rapid growth rate continues after we have reached our defined level of full employment, actual output will be at a higher level than potential, as in Year 4. (There is nothing inconsistent with this statement since "potential" or "capacity" is not defined as the ultimate limit of production.) However, we cannot continue this rate of actual growth for long without increasing inflation. Therefore, in Years 5 and 6, we attempt to manage the economy so that actual output equals potential output.

Even if we manage the economy so that we operate at our potential, we can further distinguish between two types of growth in potential output: long-run and transitory. Figure 5 also illustrates that distinction. In

---

[2]Technically, it plots the logarithm of actual and potential output for each year. This technique, called a semilogarithmic or ratio scale, is a very common practice in presenting time-series data, since the slope of curve equals the rate of growth of the variable plotted.

Years 5, 6, 8, and 9, we were on a long-run growth path but in Year 7 we had a transitory increase in growth as we shifted from one long-run potential curve to another higher curve. The process of shifting to a higher potential output curve usually relies on "supply-side" management, with emphasis on increased investment. In order to understand these conceptual distinctions between actual and potential growth (both long-run and transitory), it will be necessary to examine the factors thought to contribute to each type of growth. But first, an analogy between the output of an economy and the speed of an automobile will reinforce the distinctions.

If we were driving an automobile in first gear with the accelerator pedal depressed only half way (i.e., not using all of our economic resources), then we would be operating at an actual speed less than our potential speed (as in Year 1 of Figure 5). As we depressed the pedal further, we would eventually be running at potential (where potential is the maximum engine RPMs recommended by the manufacturer)—this would be represented in Year 3. Of course, we could continue to accelerate to an even higher speed and higher RPMs in defiance of the manufacturer's recommendation, as in Year 4 (with the possibility of engine damage, which would be analogous to inflationary damage in an economy); or, we could hold to the long-run potential speed, as in Years 5 and 6.[3] Alternatively, through supply-side management, we could shift from first to second gear in order to achieve a transitory increase in potential speed, as in Year 7. Finally, that transitory increase in speed would peak at the new long-run potential speed, as in Years 8 and 9.

Determinants of Economic Growth

Actual economic growth fluctuates widely over the business cycle; in fact, it is the prime indicator of a business cycle. The factors that determine fluctuations in aggregate demand relative to supply are the same factors that determine actual economic growth. These factors were discussed in Chapter 1 (in particular, see page 17 for a list of the more important elements). Since actual growth is compared to potential growth, we will concentrate on the factors determining potential and then speak of actual output as the degree to which we use our potential.

If we think of an economy as a simple system that transforms factor inputs (capital and labor) into useful outputs of goods and services, then potential output growth will be determined by the growth of capital, the growth of labor, and the growth of productivity (productivity is the efficiency with which an economy transforms inputs into outputs):

---

[3]For this analogy to hold exactly, the potential output curves in Figure 5 should be flat rather than positively sloped. Alternatively, one can retain the positive slope and imagine that the top speed of our automobile drifts upward over time as technological improvements are added to the engine.

$$\text{Potential output growth} = \left(0.3 \times \text{Growth of capital}\right) + \left(0.7 \times \text{Growth of labor}\right) + \left(\text{Growth of productivity}\right)$$

The numbers, 0.3 and 0.7, in the above equation are the relative contributions of capital and labor to the production process in the large industrial countries. In order to simplify the contributions of these three sources to overall growth, we will discuss each in turn, assuming for the moment that the other sources are not growing.

First, consider an increase in the capital stock by 1 percent for only one year, while assuming that there are no changes in labor and productivity. The capital stock is the long-lived assets that enhance the future capacity to produce output. One would expect that potential output would increase by 0.3 percent for the year, since capital only partially contributes to the production of output, and the other part, labor, has not changed. By definition, the ratio of capital to output must increase, since the numerator (capital) changes by a larger percentage than the denominator (output). However, the only way the capital/output ratio can increase is if the proportion of output devoted to investment (I/GNP) and therefore to savings (S/GNP) were to increase permanently.[4] What do we get for our willingness to save and invest permanently a larger proportion of our national output (and therefore to consume less)? We get a *permanent* increase in the level of output or income, but only a *temporary* increase in its rate of growth (0.3 percent for one year).

Now consider what happens if we have a 1 percent increase in the labor force and all other sources of growth are unchanged. In order to keep a close analogy with the example in the previous paragraph, imagine that the increase lasts for only one year (as in the case of a large immigration), and that the workers are fully employed. Output will increase by 0.7 percent for the year. By definition, the output or income per worker must fall if the growth of income (the numerator) is only 0.7 percent, and the growth of labor (the denominator) is 1 percent. Now the country has a dilemma. Either it can maintain its savings rate (S/GNP) and allow its average consumption per person to fall, or it can consume a larger proportion of its income (increased C/GNP) and save less (decreased S/GNP) in order to support the larger population.

A large growth in the labor force, if it is fully utilized, does contribute to a large growth in aggregate output, although GNP *per capita* may actually be declining. It is for this reason that GNP per capita or GNP per worker is often used to measure growth. As in the case of a 1 percent increase in the capital stock, the 1 percent increase in labor force growth for one year will permanently increase the level of output but only tem-

---

[4]Investment, which must be equal to the savings necessary to finance it, is the addition to the capital stock. It will be a permanent increase since a 1 percent increase in capital this year means there will be 1 percent more capital stock to depreciate each year thereafter; and savings and investment are needed for replacement investment. See the Chapter 11 note "Investment and Savings" for additional discussion of this point.

porarily increase the growth of output. This was illustrated graphically in Figure 5 for Year 7 when we temporarily moved from one potential output path to a higher one.

We still need to explain what accounts for the long-run upward trend of potential output, and that answer is found in the third source of economic growth—the growth of productivity.

Determinants of Productivity

Productivity is the efficiency with which an economy transforms inputs into outputs. When we used the term "productivity" on the previous pages, it was a shorthand notation for "total factor productivity," which is the ratio of real output to a weighted average of *all* factor inputs. Total factor productivity must be distinguished from labor productivity or capital productivity, since these partial productivity measures may be changed by factor substitution. For example, as we substitute capital for labor in the production process, labor productivity might increase (and capital productivity might decrease) but that does not necessarily change total factor productivity.

Total factor productivity will change in response to (1) changes in the efficiency of factor inputs and (2) changes in the efficiency of the economic system. Just as output increases when the quantity of capital or labor increases (as we saw in the previous section), it will also increase when the "quality" or efficiency of those factors increases. Tangible investments may affect factor quality by diffusing more quickly the technological improvements embodied in the new capital. But the primary determinant of increased factor efficiency is the degree of intangible investment in research and development, in education and training, and in health and safety. Finally, the quality of labor and capital will be affected by citizens' attitudes and values regarding work, savings, investment, risk, and change.

Changes in the efficiency of the economic system will also affect the growth of productivity. These may arise from economies of scale, improvements in the system of organization and distribution, and improvements in the allocation of resources. This last item includes structural changes in sectors or in the composition of the work force. For example, a movement of resources from lower-productivity farms to higher-productivity manufacturing will improve overall productivity. And a change in the composition of the labor force to include a larger proportion of lower-skilled teenagers will reduce overall productivity.

These are the primary elements in determining the long-term growth in productivity. Exhibit 1 presents estimates by Edward Denison of the Brookings Institution of the magnitudes and relative contributions of factor inputs and productivity in determining economic growth for a number of industrial countries. After reading about various countries, one should be able to discuss in greater detail the underlying reasons for the observed contributions to growth.

Economic Growth and Productivity

Exhibit 1 Sources of Growth of Standardized Growth Rate of National Income, Whole Economy, Various Countries, and Time Periods (Percentage Points)

Item	Japan, 1953–1971	United States, 1948–1969	Canada, 1950–1967[a]	France, 1950–1962	West Germany, 1950–1962	United Kingdom, 1950–1962
Standardized growth rate	**8.81**	**4.00**	**4.95**	**4.70**	**6.27**	**2.38**
Total factor input	**3.95**	**2.09**	**3.02**	**1.24**	**2.78**	**1.11**
Labor	1.85	1.30	1.85	0.45	1.37	0.60
Employment	1.14	1.17	1.82	0.08	1.49	0.50
Hours of work	0.21	−0.21	−0.20	−0.02	−0.27	−0.15
Age-sex composition	0.14	−0.10	−0.13	0.10	0.04	−0.04
Education	0.34	0.41	0.36	0.29	0.11	0.29
Unallocated	0.02	0.03	0.00	0.00	0.00	0.00
Capital	2.10	0.79	1.14	0.79	1.41	0.51
Inventories	0.73	0.12	0.10	0.19	0.33	0.09
Nonresidential structures and equipment	1.07	0.36	0.87	0.56	1.02	0.43
Dwellings	0.30	0.28	0.30	0.02	0.14	0.04
International assets	0.00	0.03	−0.12	0.02	−0.08	−0.05
Output per unit of input, standardized	**4.86**	**1.91**	**1.96**	**3.46**	**3.49**	**1.27**
Advances in knowledge and n.e.c.[b]	1.97	1.19	0.66	1.51	0.87[c]	.079
Improved resource allocation	0.95	0.30	0.64	0.95	1.01	0.12
Contraction of agricultural inputs	0.64	0.23	0.54	0.65	0.77	0.06
Contraction of nonagricultural self-employment	0.30	0.07	0.10	0.23	0.14	0.04
Reduction of international trade barriers	0.01	0.00	0.00	0.07	0.10	0.02
Economies of scale	1.94	0.42	0.66	1.00	1.61	0.36
Measured in U.S. prices	1.06	0.42	0.63	0.51	0.70	0.27
Income elasticities	0.88	—	0.03	0.49	0.91	0.09

[a]Details many not add to totals because of rounding.

[b]Not elsewhere classified.

[c]Estimate for 1955–1962 period.

Source: Edward F. Denison (Brookings Institution) and William K. Chung (U.S. Department of Commerce), "Economic Growth and Its Sources," in Hugh Patrick and Henry Rosovsky, eds., *Asia's New Giant: How the Japanese Economy Works* (Washington, DC: Brookings Institution, 1976), 98.

Discussion Questions for Case and Note

1. Evaluate the objectives of the tax cut proposal. By what criteria should the ultimate success or failure of these objectives be measured?
2. What are the critical issues and assumptions of the tax cut debate? Evaluate the arguments of the supporters of each side of the issue.
3. How well did President Kennedy manage the legislation?
4. What were the estimated economic consequences of the tax cut of 1964? Was this a supply-side or demand-side tax cut?
5. What lessons does this case suggest for the conduct of fiscal policy?

Bibliography

Dornbusch, Rudiger, and Stanley Fischer, *Macroeconomics*, 3rd ed. (New York: McGraw-Hill, 1984). Chapter 10, "Problems of Stabilization Policy," talks about lags, expectations, and uncertainty in general and with some reference to fiscal policy in particular. For additional background information on economic growth and productivity, see Chapter 17.

Gordon, Robert J., *Macroeconomics*, 3rd ed. (Boston: Little, Brown, 1984). A brief discussion of the limitations of fiscal policy is presented in Chapter 17 (pages 547–552). Chapter 18 contains a long discussion of the theory and application of the concepts of economic growth and productivity.

Heller, Walter W., "Kennedy Economics Revisited," in Richard H. Fink, ed., *Supply-Side Economics: A Critical Appraisal* (Frederick, MD: University Publications, 1982), 286–293. Professor Heller takes a brief retrospective view of the supply-side and demand-side components of Kennedy's economic programs.

Okun, Arthur M., "Measuring the Impact of the 1964 Tax Reduction," in Joseph A. Pechman, ed., *Economics for Policymaking: Selected Essays of Arthur M. Okun* (Cambridge, MA: M.I.T. Press, 1983), 405–423. Okun, chairman of the Council of Economic Advisers under President Johnson, estimated the contribution to GNP from the 1964 tax cut using the multiplier framework as described in the Chapter 5 case. Though the article contains a few technical equations, it should be understandable to most readers.

Tufte, Edward R., *Political Control of the Economy* (Princeton, NJ: Princeton University Press, 1978). In this book, a political scientist presents a thorough study of the political business cycle, in which turning points in economic activity are correlated with the timing of elections.

CHAPTER 8
A Business-Initiated Tax Cut

This chapter illustrates the role of business in influencing macroeconomic policy. The emphasis is on the politics, not the economics, of a proposal to cut taxes. The case in Chapter 7, "The Tax Cut of 1964," also described the politics behind the decision but from the point of view of the Kennedy administration rather than of business. The idea for the tax cut of 1964 originated in Kennedy's Council of Economic Advisers. Indeed, business initially opposed the president's proposal because it thought the proposal showed a "lack of fiscal responsibility."

The case in this chapter is a detailed study of the legislative process of the capital gains tax cut of 1978 from its conception to its enactment. A group of businessmen belonging to a small trade association, the American Electronics Association, initiated the proposal to cut the capital gains tax because they felt the tax was hindering their ability to raise additional equity capital. The political environment was not favorable to tax cuts for special interests; in fact, President Carter was advocating an increase in capital gains taxes as part of his package of tax reforms.

There are two broad issues raised by this case that are relevant to business managers and analysts of public policy. The first issue is: What determines the success or failure of a legislative proposal? The strategy for the proposal is set by business managers and their lobbyists. The perception of a need for the legislation, the political constituencies, the prevailing ideologies, and other factors are beyond the direct control of business. Business must decide among alternative tactics for guiding the proposal through the legislative process in order to minimize the damage from factors beyond its direct control.

The second issue is: To what extent do (should) interest groups pursue their private interests rather than the public interest? This question has a long lineage in the political science literature under the topic of "pluralist democracy." Is the notion that "pressure" from rival interest groups determines policy outcomes an accurate description of what transpires in the legislative process? The answer to this question has important implications for political participants who want to influence public policy.

Case
The Capital Gains Tax Cut of 1978

The American Electronics Association (AEA) was anxious to establish contact with the new Carter administration.[1] In February 1977, Kenneth Hagerty, AEA's vice president for governmental affairs, arranged a meeting between Robert Ginsberg of the White House domestic policy staff and Edwin W. Zschau, president of System Industries, to explain the association's opposition to any increase in the effective tax rate on capital gains. Drawing on his own experience and on material compiled by the National Venture Capital Association (NVCA), Zschau prepared for the May 17 meeting. Earlier that month, the Washington representative of the American Electronics Association had learned that tax preferences on capital gains were targeted for elimination in the Carter administration's upcoming tax proposal. The elimination of tax preferences on capital gains would mean that taxpayers holding capital assets would have to pay more taxes since income from capital gains would receive ordinary, rather than preferential, tax treatment.

Zschau filled his allotted 20 minutes with Ginsberg. He introduced himself as the founder of a young, rapidly growing, high-technology firm with 200 employees, typical of other entrepreneurs in the AEA. He went on to say that innovative companies, heavily dependent on equity capital to get started or to grow, faced significant difficulties in raising needed funds in the market. Zschau noted that the number of equity investors in this country had declined consistently since 1969. (Exhibits 1 and 2 reproduce statistics from a NVCA study on the trend in employment growth and public offerings for small firms.) He asserted that "perhaps the single most significant cause of fewer equity investors was the series of increases in capital gains taxes enacted since 1969, which often made high-risk, potentially high-return investment less attractive."[2]

History of Preferential Rates on Capital Gains

Defined by the Internal Revenue Code of 1954 as profits realized on "the sale or exchange of a capital asset," capital gains to individuals and corporations have been taxed at preferential (lower) rates since the Revenue

This case was prepared by Research Assistant Nancy Koehn under the supervision of Associate Professor Michael G. Rukstad.
Copyright © 1985 by the President and Fellows of Harvard College
Harvard Business School case 9–386–060

[1]The events described in this case are presented in detail in Robert Wolcott Johnson, *The Passage of the Investment Incentive Act of 1978: A Case Study of Business Influencing Public Policy* (unpublished doctoral dissertation, Harvard Business School, 1980).

[2]Ibid., 48.

Act of 1921. "The provisions applying to such gains changed frequently during the 1920s and 1930s, but were stabilized beginning in 1942."[3] Only long-term capital gains, held for a time period specified by Congress, were eligible for preferential treatment. The dichotomy between long-term and short-term gains remains in effect today, although Congress has, since 1942, varied the definition of the holding period between six months to one year. (See Exhibit 3 for a summary of the recent capital gains provisions.) Capital gains are taxed by allowing limited deductibility of capital losses and then an exclusion of a percentage of the net capital gain from gross income. The net gain is then taxed at the statutory rate on ordinary income. If, for example, the exclusion were 60 percent, a taxpayer would include 40 percent of the net gain in his or her adjusted gross income, which is then taxed according to the statutory rates. Assuming the taxpayer is in the 50 percent marginal tax bracket, the effective tax rate on the net capital gain would be 20 percent (50 percent tax on 40 percent of the net gain).

The preferential tax treatment of capital gains grew out of a variety of often conflicting economic arguments. Capital gains are taxed only when they are realized (i.e., when the asset is sold). If these gains were taxed at the rates on ordinary income, supporters of preferential rates contend, taxpayers holding appreciated assets would face unusually high tax liabilities in years when gains are realized. Presumably, a capital asset has been appreciating in value over the entire time it has been held. To bunch all the gain in the realization year seems especially burdensome to the taxpayer subject to progressive rates and is at odds with the economic timing of the asset's appreciation. Preferential rates help offset this income-bunching effect.

Proponents also argue that preferential capital gains rates encourage investment because they raise the after-tax return on investments. If capital assets were taxed at ordinary rates, there would be a strong disincentive to sell assets and buy more profitable ones since realization incurs significant tax costs. A new investment would have to carry a promise of especially high returns in order to make the transaction profitable. Investors thus become "locked in" to specific assets, and capital mobility throughout society is reduced. Preferential capital gains rates help economic growth, say the proponents, by stimulating investment, particularly investment in risky assets.[4]

Many supporters of lower capital gains rates cite a reduced cost of capital as a rationale for preferential treatment. For entrepreneurs, preferential rates on capital gains mean they do not need to offer as high a rate of return in the equity market as they would if these assets were taxed at higher rates. Preferential rates supposedly help to encourage venture capital formation in the United States and ameliorate the com-

---

[3]Joseph Pechman, *Federal Tax Policy*, 4th ed. (New York: Norton, 1983), 110.
[4]Ibid., 111.

petitive disadvantage faced by American firms vis-à-vis their industrial trading partners, most of which have much lower capital gains tax rates.[5]

The effect of inflation on capital gains tax liabilities is also used to justify preferential rates. Under an unindexed system, a taxpayer with capital gains pays taxes on the nominal increase of the asset when it is realized. In periods of inflation, a tax on this nominal gain is unfair because the increase does not represent an addition to the taxpayer's real income or wealth. Indeed, a taxpayer could pay capital gains taxes on an asset whose value has declined in real terms but climbed in nominal dollars. Capital gains preferences, supporters argue, help offset the distorting tax effects of inflation.

Finally, proponents maintain, reduced capital gains taxes actually increase Treasury revenues. The additional investment, jobs, economic activity, and corporate and personal income that result from lower capital gains taxes would increase Treasury tax receipts far more than would higher capital gains tax rates. Lower taxes therefore not only encourage desirable enterprise; they also result in larger returns to the government.[6]

For every argument favoring preferential capital gains rates, opponents to taxing capital assets at lower rates have a rebuttal. The problem of income bunching, they argue, could be handled by prorating capital gains over the time that an asset is held or by applying an averaging system to the valuation of the asset. To increase the mobility of capital and avoid the "locked-in" position induced by higher capital gains taxes, opponents of preferential rates like economist Joseph Pechman argue that asset gains should be treated as if they were realized as gifts or at death, with an averaging provision to allow for spreading the gains over several years.[7] This would remove one of the biggest incentives to postponing realization—the current tax-free transferability of capital gains as gifts and at death. Other opponents contend that increased mobility of capital is not necessarily efficient and desirable. When an individual or corporation sells an unproductive asset in order to use those investment funds more effectively, a purchaser must be found for the less promising project. Thus, the argument goes, when capital is highly mobile, resources are not necessarily being released for new, more efficient uses; rather they are being shuffled from one investor to another. This could result in pressures on companies to become short-sighted in order to keep their "impatient capital" from departing for more attractive short-term gains elsewhere.

The cost of capital can be lowered and capital formation encouraged

[5]Norman B. Ture and B. Kenneth Sanders, "Taxation Abroad," in *The Effects of Tax Policy on Capital Formation* (New York: Financial Executives Research Foundation, 1977), 139–178.

[6]Johnson, op. cit., 23.

[7]In fact, the federal tax code already contains provisions for income averaging for individuals receiving income on a sporadic basis.

through more equitable and efficient means, argue opponents of capital gains preferences. Accelerated depreciation plans as well as investment and research and development tax credits stimulate investment without the complexity and paper entrepreneurship of the current tax preferences for capital gains. Taxpayers, lawyers, and accountants spend millions of dollars and hours each year trying to take advantage of the capital gains preferences. Human and financial resources are wasted and misallocated in efforts to reap the highest possible tax savings, instead of increasing efficient individual or business investment. These inefficient tax advantages are inequitable to the extent that they benefit only those with funds to invest in capital assets.

The problem that inflation poses to capital asset valuation, opponents contend, could be solved by indexing the cost basis of the asset (from which gains are calculated) to a price index. If an asset cost $100 when purchased in Year 1 and were sold in Year 2 for $200, and if there were a 10 percent inflation rate, the taxpayer would be taxed not on $100 of gain but on $90 of "real" gain. Opponents of preferential capital gains treatment dispute the supply-side contention that lower taxes will increase government revenues. In 1977, the tax expenditure for capital gains cost the Treasury $16.5 billion in forgone corporate and individual income taxes. Estimates of revenue increases from reduced capital gains taxes are, according to opponents, based on unrealistic assumptions about economic behavior.

Capital Gains Taxation: 1969–1977

Congressional action on capital gains taxes has reflected the conflict between these various arguments. Since 1942, legislators have frequently altered the required holding period, the rate of exclusion, and the additional taxes on capital gains. From 1964 through 1969, a long-term gain was defined by Congress as one that was held more than six months, and these gains were taxed at a maximum rate of 25 percent, even though the maximum statutory rates would have implied a much higher rate. During these years, many of the standard arguments for taxing capital gains at a preferential rate receded in significance. The stock market surged and GNP climbed throughout the 1960s. Investment incentives did not seem a pressing public need. Inflation, which had remained virtually steady at an annual rate of 1.5 percent from 1951 through 1965, expanded somewhat in the late 1960s but was dismissed as only a temporary aberration of an overheated economy. Many saw the low taxation of capital gains as an overgenerous compensation for the relatively small distortions of inflation.

In 1969, tax benefits to higher income groups came under more serious and concentrated attack by the outgoing Secretary of the Treasury, Democrat Joseph W. Barr. Just two days before he relinquished his office to President-Elect Richard Nixon's cabinet choice, David M. Kennedy, Barr released a report criticizing the inequities of the tax system, noting:

We now face the possibility of a taxpayer revolt if we do not soon make major reforms in our income taxes. The revolt will come not from the poor but from the tens of millions of middle-class families and individuals with incomes of $7,000 to $20,000, whose tax payments now generally are based on the full ordinary rates and who pay over half of our individual income taxes.

The middle classes are likely to revolt against income taxes not because of the level or amount of the taxes they must pay but because certain provisions of the tax laws unfairly lighten the burdens of others who can afford to pay. People are concerned and indeed angered about the high-income recipients who pay little or no Federal income taxes. For example, the extreme cases are 155 tax returns in 1967 with adjusted gross incomes above $200,000 on which no Federal income taxes were paid, including 21 with incomes above $1,000,000.[8]

Barr's report produced immediate media interest in capital gains. Voters, angered by inequities in the tax system, bombarded congressional offices with calls and letters. "Tax reform became a major issue almost overnight, and on February 18, 1969, the House Ways and Means Committee opened the most extensive hearings on the subject in a decade."[9] The Senate Finance Committee quickly became involved, and over the next six months Congress debated the issue of tax reform. Although the Nixon administration offered its own tax proposals, Congress adopted only a few outside suggestions and wrote almost the entire bill itself. When the final bill cleared both houses on December 22, 1969, it contained some of the most comprehensive reforms and largest tax cuts since the Revenue Act of 1964. The 1969 Act, reluctantly signed by President Nixon on December 30, repealed the 7 percent investment tax credit, lowered middle-income taxpayers' liabilities through a combination of measures, raised the minimum tax on capital gains from 25 percent in 1969 to 35 percent in 1972, and leveled an additional tax of 10 percent on the excluded half of gains under certain circumstances. Collectively, the capital gains provisions of the 1969 bill raised the effective tax rate on these assets from 25 percent to 32 percent in 1970, to 39 percent in 1971, to 45 percent from 1972 to 1975, and to 49 percent in 1976.

Over the next several years, the economic climate of the nation steadily deteriorated. The stock market slumped, the new-issues market dried up, and inflation fueled by the surges in energy and commodity prices continued to rise. The nation floundered in 1975 in the midst of

---

[8]Statement of Joseph W. Barr, January 17, 1969, in *The Economic Report of the President*, Hearings before the Joint Economic Committee (Washington, DC: U.S. Government Printing Office, 1969), 46.

[9]"Congressionally Initiated Tax Reform Bill Enacted," *Congressional Quarterly Almanac* (Washington, DC: U.S. Government Printing Office, 1969), 589.

the deepest recession since the 1930s. Although the economy showed some signs of recovery in early 1976, many key indicators suggested significant problems. Nevertheless, "despite the weakness indicated by the statistics, many economic analysts, both inside and outside the administration, remained optimistic about the final quarter of 1976 and the prospects for healthy economic growth continuing in 1977."[10]

Within this economic environment, Congress completed action on a broad tax revision bill that continued the personal and corporate tax cuts originally enacted in 1975 while restricting many tax benefits. The bill, signed into law by President Gerald Ford on October 4, 1976, limited capital gains preferences by extending the holding period on assets eligible for preferential rates from six months to nine months. On January 20, 1977, President Jimmy Carter took office. In his campaign he had promised major tax reform, calling the current system a "disgrace to the human race." The Democratic sweep of Congress, begun in the post-Watergate elections of 1974, continued with a veto-proof (two-thirds) party majority in each house. Although many of the arguments for lower capital gains taxes were again relevant to the nation's economy, the prospects in mid-1977 of a major reduction in capital gains preferences had rarely been bleaker.

American Electronics Association's Agenda

On May 18, 1977, the day after the meeting with Ginsberg, the AEA held its Capitol Caucus, the association's annual spring meeting in Washington, DC. Chairman of the House Ways and Means Committee Al Ullman (D-Oregon) spoke to association members about his ideas for integration of the corporate and individual income tax systems. Combining tax systems would, among other things, end double taxation of dividends. The audience was uninterested in Ullman's suggestions. AEA members explained to Ullman their lack of enthusiasm by stating that integration would primarily benefit older, larger companies that paid dividends rather than the faster-growing, smaller, high-technology companies represented in the AEA. The managers of these companies had little interest in making dividends more attractive. Indeed, ending the double taxation of dividends put non-dividend-paying securities at a competitive disadvantage and would increase the pressure on these newer companies to begin paying dividends—funds that could be better used internally to fuel additional growth. Ullman responded by urging the AEA members to try to influence tax policy by organizing themselves, documenting their ideas, and presenting their position to congressional representatives.

AEA Chairman Kenneth Oshman, the president of Rolm Corpo-

---

[10]"Economic Policy," *Congressional Quarterly Almanac* (Washington, DC: U.S. Government Printing Office, 1976), 40.

ration, was the first to act on Ullman's suggestion. At the Capitol Caucus dinner meeting that evening, he announced that the association would be forming a Task Force on Capital Formation and that Zschau would chair the group. Oshman's announcement came as a complete surprise to Zschau and other AEA members. Zschau had not sought this responsibility and had no background in capital formation issues, save for the preparation he had done for the Ginsberg meeting. He was suddenly faced with the somewhat onerous task of organizing a group to fulfill still undetermined goals with unknown resources.

The first thing Zschau did was to organize the task force's membership. He wanted compatible people with broad, diverse views on capital formation who had the time, experience, and motivation to make a significant effort. Zschau, Hagerty, and AEA President E. E. Ferry put the final membership list together, choosing personal friends and business associates. Of the eleven members, six were heads of small and medium-sized electronics firms, two were public affairs directors for high-technology companies, two were venture capitalists, and one was a West Coast investment banker.[11]

Before the task force held its first meeting, Hagerty sought out a lobbyist to represent the group's views in Washington. Charles Gubser, a former congressman who had been the AEA's representative in Washington for tax issues, was retiring, and the association would need a quick replacement. Gubser suggested Mark Bloomfield, a young lawyer and lobbyist with impressive political credentials. In 1977, Bloomfield was with the American Council for Capital Formation (ACCF), a broad-based Washington lobbying group interested in promoting legislation to increase the nation's capital stock. Bloomfield agreed to work with the AEA on a part-time basis (ten hours a month), retaining his full-time position with the ACCF. As soon as he was hired by the AEA, Bloomfield reviewed with Hagerty possible agendas for the task force and agreed that the capital gains issue should be kept under consideration.

At the same time in California, Zschau was busy preparing for the first task force meeting. In early July, he granted a series of interviews to the *Palo Alto Times*, the *San Francisco Chronicle*, and *Business Week*, announcing the formation of the task force and the association's involvement in the capital formation debate. Hagerty meanwhile drafted a letter to President Carter summarizing the central arguments for reducing capital gains taxes or, at the minimum, maintaining current preferences. The letter mentioned the importance of capital gains preferences to young, growing, high-technology companies in staying competitive in the international economy, in generating new jobs, and in continuing rapid technological innovation. The letter also justified preferential capital gains tax rates as compensation for the distorting tax effects of inflation. It stated the importance of preferential rates in encouraging investment.

[11]Johnson, op. cit., 51.

Carter's proposal for the elimination of capital gains preferences, Hagerty wrote, would discourage investment and fail to generate as much revenue as the administration had predicted. Indeed, raising these taxes might yield a net loss to the Treasury, the letter prophesied. The document concluded with the possibility of high-technology firms, starved for domestic funds, being forced to sell their innovations to foreigners. The letter, with Zschau's signature, was sent on July 11, 1977.

While Zschau and Hagerty were writing this letter, task force members received several signals indicating that even maintaining existing capital gains preferences was going to be more difficult than they had originally surmised. In July and August, *The Wall Street Journal* ran two articles on President Carter's strong stand on cutting capital gains preferences.[12] On August 5, five days before the first task force meeting, Barber Conable (R-New York), ranking Republican on the House Ways and Means Committee, dealt another blow to task force members' hopes when he said elimination of capital gains preferences "may be consistent" with a tax package designed to encourage economic growth and "could contribute a great deal" toward simplifying the tax code.[13]

The first meeting of the AEA task force convened on August 10 with Zschau as chairman. Discussion centered around a list, prepared by Zschau and Hagerty, of negative factors contributing to the decline in the nation's capital formation. These factors included climbing capital gains taxes, reduced liquidity of investments caused by security law changes, and increasing government regulations. Group members also focused on positive factors that could "arrest or reverse the decline" in capital formation. Among these were a rollover scheme long favored by one of the task force members, tax credits for research and development, increasing the investment tax credit to 12 percent, and lowering the corporate tax rate. During this meeting, task force members had agreed on two general operating principles. First, the task force should present its own alternative agenda for government action rather than simply reacting to congressional or administration proposals. This agenda should be very specific. Task force members wanted to avoid presenting a general "laundry list" of business objectives that established no priorities between goals. Instead, task force participants sought priorities that were both significant to AEA member companies and important to government decision makers in terms of their macroeconomic benefits (jobs, economic growth, increased investment). Second, whatever issue(s) task force members selected, new, hard data would be used by the task force to support its position and to differentiate the group from the numerous individuals and organizations that present their interests to government officials without substantive qualification. Task force members decided that a survey of AEA companies, assuming managers would release priv-

[12]*The Wall Street Journal*, July 6, 1977, and Aug. 4, 1977.
[13]*The Wall Street Journal*, Aug. 8, 1977.

ileged financial information to the trade association, could be important
and unique documentation to support the group's position.

The second half of the first meeting was devoted to a discussion of
the task force's agenda. High capital gains taxes and a solution to this
problem were the center of discussion. Why did group members so quickly
focus on the issue of high capital gains taxes? A number of personal and
economic factors help explain the almost immediate elimination of other
capital formation issues. Zschau, the task force chairman, and William
Ballhaus, president of Beckman Instruments and one of the group's most
respected members, were already more familiar with capital gains preferences than with other objectives. Since votes were never taken in the
task force meetings, the policies established were largely the result of
Zschau's interpretation of the group's general feelings.[14] Economically,
capital gains taxes were important to virtually every AEA company,
whereas corporate taxes, double taxation of dividends, and other issues
were not so universally significant. Finally, the group already had, at that
first meeting, an agenda or solution for the capital gains tax problem—
Ballhaus's rollover scheme. Indeed, Zschau's summary of the proposals
decided upon in this meeting bears a striking resemblance to those that
Ballhaus had been proposing for several years. Zschau combined the
rollover provisions with a sliding-rate scale to reduce capital gains taxes.
(See Exhibit 5 for a list of the fundamental principles and the draft proposal developed in this first meeting.)

Shortly after this meeting, a survey form was designed for AEA-
member executives to fill out. The objective of the survey was to illustrate
the importance of risk capital to America's economic health. To this end,
the group decided that the survey results would be most effectively expressed in terms of the number of jobs created, new investments made,
exports generated, and taxes paid, rather than in terms of profit margins
and rates of return. Task force members were very interested in illus-
trating the growing difficulty young firms had encountered in raising funds
since the first major changes in the capital gains tax law in 1969. The
survey would thus have to collect data on the companies' financial histories as well as on their current operations.

During the September 7, 1977, task force meeting, discussion centered on Zschau's draft proposal to reduce capital gains taxes. Many
members felt that this plan was too complicated and too concerned with
presenting a fair and balanced plan. Most members thought the group
should avoid presenting any plan in terms of equity. Value judgments
on an issue are too subjective, too difficult to defend effectively, members
argued. Zschau called on each participant for his opinion. Venture capitalist B. Kipling Hagopian, the last person to speak, had throughout the
meeting been uneasy with all the proposals. He insisted that the capital
gains tax really should be zero. When others immediately protested that

---

[14]Johnson, op. cit., 58.

he was being unrealistic, the venture capitalist countered: "The liberals are always making extreme proposals, and pretty soon they're law. We always compromise. If they ask for our arm, we ask if they can't leave just a little above the elbow. Let's play that game, too. If we say the tax should be zero, maybe they'll compromise at 25 percent."[15] The meeting adjourned in disagreement. Many members liked Hagopian's idea, but others thought he was naive. Some men favored the Ballhaus proposal for tax-free rollover of equity investments, while still others liked none of the proposals.

Zschau again summarized the meeting's discussion and prepared a compromise proposal that was sent to group members. He stated that task force members had concluded that the tax rates on capital gains should be reduced to pre-1969 rates or lower. In this document, Zschau outlined the main arguments for this rate reduction (new jobs, productivity increases, additional exports, and innovation), as well as the general strategies the group would use in their efforts to obtain these rate reductions (consult with economists and with other interested organizations, use survey results, form a coalition with other groups, and lobby in Washington, DC).

On September 23, the survey questionnaires were sent to AEA-member companies with a cover letter from AEA Chairman Oshman appealing to managers to reply. While Zschau and others waited for the completed survey, Hagerty wrote the chief counsel of the House Ways and Means Committee to request the opportunity to testify in hearings before the committee. Hagerty never received a reply to his request.

Shortly after Hagerty wrote to the Ways and Means Committee, the office of Senator Gaylord Nelson (D-Wisconsin), chairman of the Senate Select Committee on Small Business, contacted the AEA. Nelson wanted information on the reasons for the rash of foreign investment in America's most advanced technology, an issue that was getting considerable publicity at the time. AEA representatives were eager to respond to Nelson's request. For although the Senate Select Committee had no legislative authority and was not regarded as one of the more important congressional committees, the hearings would provide association members with an opportunity to speak about an issue significant to them. More importantly, testifying would allow AEA members to develop a relationship with Nelson's staff and to establish other congressional connections, connections that might be important to any legislative action the AEA would undertake. The operations and personalities of Capitol Hill are extensively intertwined with the staffs of each committee, representative, and senator. For although they get little publicity, congressional staffers are the principal liaisons between members and the world off the Hill.

Hagerty compiled a list of AEA firms subject to recent acquisition, which Nelson used in preparing for a late October meeting with President

[15]Ibid., 66.

Carter. Shortly after the meeting, Nelson announced committee hearings on the technology-transfer issue. Because AEA members were anxious to testify, they made a bargain with the chief counsel of Nelson's committee. If they were given adequate time and a good time slot (early in the day when the committee meetings are well attended and before the noon deadlines for most reporters), AEA members promised to release the survey data for the first time—data that would document the conditions with which Nelson was concerned. Finally, the committee offered the AEA two hours of testimony in the lead-off slot on February 8, 1978, giving the task force only two weeks to prepare.

The AEA Goes to Washington

As soon as the testimony date was set, a task force meeting was called for January 30. Considerable work remained to be done on the survey, for although the data had been gathered and preliminary results formulated, the information had to be put in a comprehensible and concise form suitable for presentation. In addition, a list of speakers remained to be compiled, speeches needed to be written and rehearsed, and written submissions had to be prepared. During the task force meeting, members went over the draft summary of the survey, the appropriate format for the presentation to the congressional committee, and a list of possible speakers. Robert Noyce, chairman of Intel, was recruited, as was Eugene White, vice-chairman of Amdahl. Task force members Sanford Robertson, an investment banker, volunteered to testify. Frederick Adler, a founder and director of Data General, was asked to speak, and he in turn suggested Craig Berkman, head of Cardiac Resuscitators.

On Wednesday morning, February 8, 1978, Zschau opened the hearing testimony. Zschau and White used their time to discuss foreign acquisitions and to present the AEA survey. Drawing on their own experience, Noyce and Berkman spoke about the difficulty of raising capital, while Robertson and David Morgenthaler, president of NVCA, talked about the problems of supplying risk capital. They said that for individuals the capital gains tax rate in the United States was higher than that in any other industrialized country. "Germany, Japan, and some of America's other more effective international competitors do not normally tax capital gains on personal securities investments within their borders at all. Under existing American laws, foreigners who realize gains on American investments are not subject to any taxes either."[16] Morgenthaler and Robertson closed their testimony with the statement that the most significant cause of the U.S. technology-transfer problem was the shortage of risk capital, and that this shortage was primarily attributable to high capital gains tax rates.

[16]Ibid., 76–77.

At the AEA board meeting in mid-February, Hagerty urged the task force to testify before the Ways and Means Committee and to suggest specific legislation to reduce capital gains taxes. Board members approved the "pre-1969 or lower" plan for cutting the tax rates. Hagerty then contacted Bloomfield at the American Council for Capital Formation in Washington, seeking opportunities for testimony as well as scheduled meetings between AEA witnesses and a few key legislators.

In an effort to get a hearing slot with the Ways and Means Committee, task force members drafted a letter to the chief counsel of the committee. They then sent a personal appeal to Ullman's office, reminding the representative of his advice in 1977 to association members to get involved in government. In late February, task force members were given a testimony date and time—March 7, the second day of public hearings, in the morning.

Meanwhile Hagerty was busy urging Bloomfield to set up meetings with Ways and Means Committee members. Bloomfield, however, was not anxious to bother the people he knew on the Ways and Means Committee with what most congressional experts would have regarded as a very unlikely proposal. After much prodding by Hagerty, Bloomfield set up a meeting between Zschau and Ways and Means Committee member William Steiger, a friend of Bloomfield's from his earlier political work. Through another lobbyist, the AEA approached freshman Congressman Ed Jenkins (D-Georgia), giving him a copy of Zschau's testimony.

At 8:30 on the morning of March 7, prior to his testimony, Zschau met with Steiger. During the 30-minute meeting, Zschau mentioned that the task force's goal was elimination of the capital gains tax. Task force members, Zschau explained, believed that this proposal was in the best interests of the nation. He also said that members had settled upon a compromise position of reducing rates to their pre-1969 levels, when 25 percent was the maximum capital gains tax rate. Steiger said the latter proposal was probably the only realistic one. Zschau asked Steiger if he would be willing to introduce the necessary legislation, and Steiger said he would if Zschau could get a bill drafted.

Before the Ways and Means Committee, Zschau and another task force member each spoke for five minutes. Zschau presented the results of the AEA survey of 325 firms. Other witnesses that morning included the National Food Brokers Association, the National Federation of Independent Businesses, and the National Shoe Retailers Association. Their priorities in tax policy did not coincide with those of the AEA. Indeed, when Ullman asked the panel of witnesses that morning whether, as a group, they had any sort of consensus on what small businesses' tax priorities were, most of the panel said they wanted cuts in the corporate tax rate.

Task force members also listened to testimony given by the next set of witnesses before the Ways and Means Committee that day. One of the witnesses, Robert Baldwin, president of Morgan Stanley and chairman of the Securities Industry Association (SIA), released the results of a Data Resources survey, commissioned by the SIA. According to the survey, reduction of taxes on investment would increase government revenues.[17] After the day's testimony, Zschau, Hagerty, Bloomfield, and Richardson spoke briefly with Representative Jenkins, who agreed to introduce AEA legislation and promised support.

Introduction of the Investment Incentive Act of 1978

A week after the hearings, Chairman Ullman requested that committee members submit descriptions of all their proposed amendments to the omnibus tax bill to the Joint Committee on Taxation staff by March 24. Markup (the debate, discussion, and drafting that determine a bill's content before it comes up for a committee vote) was scheduled for April 10. To Bloomfield, Ullman's request provided an important opportunity to seek out committee interest in the capital gains issue. Ullman himself was unlikely to advocate the administration's position on this issue. In 1977, after several attempts to introduce and support the president's tax reforms promised during the campaign, Ullman found himself without administration backing. The White House had withdrawn its support for specific reforms without advising the Ways and Means chairman. Ullman looked foolish, the White House indecisive.

Bloomfield was no longer representing only the American Electronics Association. In early 1978, the American Council for Capital Formation, the lobbying group for which he worked full time, had become more involved in the capital gains issue. Although the ACCF had always been concerned with capital gains taxation, it had other capital formation issues on its agenda throughout 1977 and had spent the fall of that year narrowing its priorities. Indeed, Richard Rahn, a young economics Ph.D. who served as executive director of the ACCF, had drafted a paper in the early fall of 1977 that outlined the advantages and disadvantages of the president's modified capital gains proposals. He had even gone so far as to have 8,000 "Capital Gains Action Kits" printed up in early October, should the ACCF need to support its position against administration proposals.

Not knowing how much support they would find for capital gains tax reduction, Bloomfield and Rahn together began preparing half a dozen capital gains tax reduction bills for introduction to the Ways and Means Committee. Their proposals ranged from Ballhaus's rollover scheme to eliminating the capital gains tax completely. They knew that without significant committee support their bills would go nowhere. The AEA, and now the ACCF, had Steiger's and Jenkins's pledges to introduce their

[17]Data Resources assumed that the elimination of all taxes on capital gains would result in a 20 percent increase in the Standard & Poor's stock price index. Critics of the survey frequently attacked this assumption.

proposals, but the introduction of a bill was hardly a guarantee of its success. More than 8,000 bills a year are introduced before Congress. Only 2,000 of these have significant support behind them, and only half of these will pass, but most of these legislative measures are small, non-controversial items—a measure allowing a constituent to emigrate, a tax benefit for a ski resort that makes its facilities available to Olympic hopefuls, and the like. It takes considerable legislative (and lobbying) talent, time, and resources to move any major bill through both houses of Congress.

Bloomfield and Rahn worked to have their proposals submitted by as many committee members as possible before Ullman's deadline. Numerous sponsors would give the ACCF more options and show other committee members that these proposals had considerable support. In this way, the ACCF could have some impact in setting the committee's agenda and in setting the terms of the tax debate. Finally, the search for sponsors provided Rahn and Bloomfield the opportunity to make the congressional rounds again, establish contacts, and increase support for the idea of capital gains tax reduction.

Bloomfield and Rahn pursued their campaign, although a capital gains tax cut was still not the first legislative priority of the ACCF. The capital formation lobbying group put corporate rate reduction, increased investment tax credits, and elimination of the double taxation of dividends ahead of capital gains tax relief, not because this last objective was less important to group members, but because they still viewed it as unrealistic. A conversation with Representative James R. Jones (D-Oklahoma) in mid-March gave Rahn and Bloomfield impetus to pursue the capital gains issue further. When the two lobbyists asked Jones for his support in improving the capital gains situation, he said he had already signed onto Steiger's proposal, the AEA bill for a reduction in capital gains taxes to pre-1969 levels. Jones also told them that Jenkins and Representative Bill Frenzel (R-Minnesota) had also signed onto Steiger's bill. Bloomfield and Zschau had left Steiger's office with the understanding that Steiger would look at the bill, although he had promised nothing else in immediate support. It became clear to Bloomfield that Steiger had done some lobbying work on his own, and it began to look as if the Wisconsin representative was taking this initiative much more seriously than either task force or ACCF staffers first assumed.

With the intervention of ACCF staffers Bloomfield and Rahn, task force members had reduced their level of activity. They spent the two weeks following their Ways and Means Committee testimony writing a floor speech for the bill's introduction. Hagerty named the bill the "Investment Incentive Act of 1978." Other task force members tried to increase the press coverage of the capital gains issue, without success. Task force members also spent time debating whether Steiger or Jenkins should introduce their bill. After some deliberation, the ACCF and AEA representatives settled on Steiger. He was better known to both groups and to Congress than the freshman Jenkins. At age 40, Steiger had a reputation for being enthusiastic, very capable, and a man who voted his conscience rather than the party line. Although he was a six-term congressman, he was not widely known outside Congress, making him eager to lead what promised to be a very controversial battle. On March 22, 1978, Steiger introduced H.R. 11773, the Investment Incentive Act of 1978, with cosponsors Jenkins, Jones, and Frenzel.

By this time, the ACCF had decided to commit all of its resources to the battle to reduce capital gains taxes. Bloomfield and Rahn began to believe that although the capital gains issue was still a longshot, it represented an issue wherein the lobbying group, as one of the first interested parties, could enhance its reputation in Washington's legislative community.

Late in March, fueled by ACCF involvement and H.R. 11773's introduction, press interest in the capital gains issue began to increase. On March 16, the *Boston Herald* ran in its finance section a piece, based on AEA testimony, that strongly favored capital gains tax reduction. On March 19, the (Portland) *Oregonian* ran a story on the task force campaign, giving the histories of two member firms and the contributions these companies were making to the local job market. On March 21, the *Washington Post* reprinted a *National Journal* article that outlined the AEA campaign. Late in March, the *New York Times* began covering the issue, and in early April, *Forbes* ran a story on capital gains.[18]

As public interest in H.R. 11773 grew, ACCF and task force members ruled out alternative legislation on capital gains. Most of the bill's supporters were less convinced that reducing capital gains taxes to their pre-1969 rates was an economic panacea to the capital formation problem than they were certain that such an action could be easily communicated and understood. Ballhaus, however, was one of the few task force members who did not throw complete support behind H.R. 11773, believing that his capital gains rollover scheme was far superior. But he was the exception, and most of the bill's backers subordinated their differences to work for a legislation that to them represented a significant improvement over the status quo.

ACCF and task force supporters next faced the task of enlisting more support for the bill from Ways and Means Committee members. Steiger had found votes and would need at least 15 more to carry the bill out of committee. Bill backers decided to use two different tactics to generate committee support for their bill. First, the ACCF and AEA would use their public connections to create public interest in and support for H.R. 11773. Second, the ACCF and AEA planned to use their lobbying resources to speak directly to members of the Ways and Means Committee. Although the bill's supporters did not know exactly which strategies carried the highest probabilities of success, they felt that pursuing

---

[18]See *Boston Herald*, Mar. 16, 1978; *Oregonian*, Mar. 19, 1978; *Washington Post*, Mar. 21, 1978; *New York Times*, Mar. 29, 1978; and *Forbes*, Apr. 3, 1978.

both grassroots and direct persuasion simultaneously was important. Bipartisan support was a top priority in planning the lobbying campaign. Task force members knew that enlisting support in a Democratic-controlled Congress for a Republican-sponsored bill would be difficult, so they devoted much of their initial lobbying efforts to attracting the support of members of the majority party.

In early April, Rahn, Bloomfield, and Richardson began talking to various members of the Ways and Means Committee to drum up broad support for the bill. Although they approached all the committee members initially, the lobbyists focused their efforts on those representatives whose position was not clear. Meanwhile, other ACCF and task force staffers were kept busy supplying information about the bill to congressmen and their interested constituents and to the press.

Zschau realized that one piece of information that H.R. 11773 lacked was econometric estimates of the results of the bill. Although the bill's supporters had presented the AEA survey and used the SIA study to make the economic case for a capital gains cut—a tax reduction that would almost exclusively benefit the upper-income classes, they had not yet gathered specific data on the economic and revenue impacts of H.R. 11773. Zschau took on the task of commissioning these estimates.

While Zschau, Bloomfield, Rahn, and Richardson worked the Hill, other task force members on the West Coast began to orchestrate a strong grassroots campaign. The task force called members of the National Venture Capital Association; Hagerty contacted other industry and trade associations; and Zschau requested prominent AEA members in each of the association's regional districts to talk to their congressmen and to have other members and constituents in their districts do the same. Zschau especially urged association members in districts in which the representatives were "waffling" on H.R. 11773 to phone or write their legislators.

In Washington, the first head count in the Ways and Means Committee yielded few surprises and many noncommitted votes. But by April 5, the total number of supporting votes was 16; 19 yea votes were required to move the bill out of committee. If AEA and ACCF supporters could convince the two remaining Republicans to vote for the bill, proponents would have to find only one more Democratic yes vote. Prospects for H.R. 11773 were beginning to look good. But in the horse trading and arm twisting that goes on committee deliberation, bill supporters knew they faced a difficult job in keeping all their initial commitments to the bill. Opposition to the bill would be strong, especially given the administration's strong stance against lowering capital gains taxes. Only a week later it was necessary to reintroduce H.R. 11773 as H.R. 12111 in order to accommodate eight new cosponsors.

By this point, the ACCF had become the key motivating force behind H.R. 12111. Although Zschau would continue to take charge of econometric documentation for the bill, the central strategic decisions were being made and, to a great extent, implemented by ACCF staffers. As other associations became involved in the fight for H.R. 12111, the task force's role further decreased. AEA task force members prepared to leave Washington for their businesses, where they would continue to stay active in the grassroots campaign for capital gains cuts. AEA members had, to a great extent, accomplished their goal. They had seen a viable plan for capital gains tax reduction placed on the national legislative agenda. Within 18 months of the task force's initial involvement, its members would see the bill that some had called "politically impossible" signed into law.

The Passage of the Investment Incentive Act of 1978: Chronology

1978:

April 20: The House Ways and Means Committee vote on H.R. 12111 is postponed at Ullman's request to give the chairman time to plot a strategy on the bill. Ullman feared he might jeopardize his own committee standing by allowing an initiative opposed by the administration to sail through the Ways and Means Committee.

April 20: President Carter meets with Ullman and opposes capital gains tax cuts.

April 24– 30: House Ways and Means Committee members hear testimony by economists Alan Greenspan, Arthur Okun, and Martin Feldstein on the need for a tax cut. Okun testifies that the revenue impact of a capital gains tax cut would be a wash; Feldstein contends that government revenues would increase.

April 30: In response to the growing publicity surrounding H.R. 12111, a variety of trade associations support the measure, including the U.S. Chamber of Commerce, the National Association of Manufacturers, Merrill Lynch, and the Securities Industry Association.

May 4: Reginald Jones, chairman of General Electric and the Business Roundtable, announces his support of H.R. 12111.

May 11: Senator Hansen introduces S. 3065 with 60 cosponsors in the Senate, killing administration hopes of squelching the initiative in the Senate.

June 6: California's Proposition 13, slashing state and local taxes and services, passes by a large margin. The press labels its passage as the beginning of the "tax revolt."

June 26: President Carter criticizes the Steiger-Hansen bill, saying this measure would provide "huge tax windfalls for millionaires and two bits for the average American."

July 18:   Representative Jones introduces a compromise tax reduction proposal, H.R. 13511, which lowered the rate on capital gains to 35 percent, up from the 25 percent specified in H.R. 12111.

July 27:   The House Ways and Means Committee approves the Jones compromise, H.R. 13511, by a vote of 25 to 12, with 13 committee Democrats supporting the bill.

Aug. 10:   H.R. 13511, in the same form as it emerged from the Ways and Means Committee, passes the House by a vote of 362–49.

Aug. 17:   Secretary of the Treasury Michael Blumenthal testifies before the Senate Finance Committee that the administration might be willing to accept significant cuts in capital gains taxes in exchange for a "better balanced bill" that would provide additional relief to the lower and middle classes.

Sept. 27:   The Senate Finance Committee approves its version of H.R. 13511 by a vote of 15–2. The Finance Committee bill enlarged the House-approved tax cuts for low and middle income taxpayers. Taken together, the Senate provisions to the bill lowered the effective rate on capital gains from the 35 percent as it had been under the House bill to about 28 percent, much closer to the effective rates provided by Steiger's original bill and the AEA's initial proposal.

Oct. 10:   The Senate passes H.R. 13511 by a vote of 86–4.

Oct. 15:   Senate and House conferees complete work on the tax bill and send the measure to President Carter. The effective rate on capital gains becomes 28 percent with the implementation of this bill.

Oct. 15:   The House approves the conference bill 337–38; the Senate passes the measure 72–3.

Nov. 6:   President Carter signs the bill without comment.

The Capital Gains Tax Cut of 1978

Exhibit 1   Average Growth of Sales and Employment: 1969–1974

Type of Company	No. of Companies Sampled	Sales		Jobs	
		1974 (Millions of Dollars)	Increase (%)	1974	Increase (%)
Innovative	5	21,000	13.2	106,000	4.3
Mature	6	36,000	11.4	25,000	0.6
Young high-technology	5	857	42.5	35,000	40.7

Source: Robert Wolcott Johnson, *The Passage of the Investment Incentive Act of 1978: A Case Study of Business Influencing Public Policy* (unpublished doctoral dissertation, Harvard Business School, 1980), 42.

The Capital Gains Tax Cut of 1978

Exhibit 2   Public Underwritings
(Companies with a net worth, prior to the public offering, of
less than $5 million)

Year	Number of Offerings	Total (Millions of Dollars)
1969	548	1,457.7
1970	209	383.7
1971	224	551.5
1972	418	918.2
1973	69	137.5
1974	8	13.1
1975	4	16.2

Source: Robert Wolcott Johnson, *The Passage of the Investment Incentive Act of 1978: A Case Study of Business Influencing Public Policy* (unpublished doctoral dissertation, Harvard Business School, 1980), 43.

The Capital Gains Tax Cut of 1978

Exhibit 3   Recent History of the Capital Gains Provisions of Federal Income Tax

Tax Year or Period	Holding Period	Percent of Gain Taxed as Ordinary Income	Alternative Tax (Highest Rate on Long-Term Gains)
1964–1969	6 months or less	100 (of excess over long-term loss, if any)	None
	Over 6 months	50 (of excess over short-term loss, if any)	25 percent
1970–1976	6 months or less	100 (of excess over long-term loss, if any)	None
	Over 6 months	50 (of excess over short-term loss, if any)	25 percent on first $50,000 of gain only. Additional tax of 10 percent (15 percent in 1976) on excluded half of gain under certain circumstances (highest rate: 0.3221375 in 1970; 0.3875 in 1971; 0.455 in 1972–1975; 0.49125 in 1976)
1977	9 months or less	100 (of excess over long-term loss, if any)	None
	Over 9 months	50 (of excess over short-term loss, if any)	25 percent on first $50,000 of gain only. Additional tax of 15 percent on excluded half of gain under certain circumstances (highest rate: 0.49125)
1978	1 year or less	100 (of excess over long-term loss, if any)	None
	Over 1 year	50 (40 after October 31 only) (of excess over short-term loss, if any)	25 percent on first $50,000 of gain only. Additional tax of 15 percent on excluded half of gain under certain circumstances (highest rate: 0.49125 Jan. 1–Oct. 31; 0.349 Nov. 1–Dec. 31)
1979	1 year or less	100 (of excess over long-term loss, if any)	None
	Over 1 year	40 (of excess over short-term loss, if any)	Graduated additional tax on full amount of gains under certain circumstances (highest rate: 28 percent)

Source: Joseph J. Minarik, "Capital Gains," in Henry Aaron and Joseph Pechman, eds., *How Taxes Affect Economic Behavior* (Washington, DC: Brookings Institution, 1981), 272–273.

Exhibit 3 (Continued)

Treatment of Losses

Net loss (sum of long- and short-term loss, or excess of short-term loss over long-term gain, or excess of long-term loss over short-term gain) deductible from other income up to $1,000; excess short-term losses carried forward indefinitely as short-term loss; excess long-term losses carried forward indefinitely as long-term loss; short-term loss carryovers used first
Net loss (sum of short-term loss and 50 percent of long-term loss, or excess of short-term loss over long-term gain, or 50 percent of excess of long-term loss over short-term gain) deductible from other income up to $1,000; excess short-term losses carried forward indefinitely as short-term loss; excess long-term losses carried forward indefinitely as long-term loss; short-term loss carryovers used first

Net loss (sum of short-term loss and 50 percent of long-term loss, or excess of short-term loss over long-term gain, or 50 percent of excess of long-term loss over short-term gain) deductible from other income up to $2,000; excess short-term losses carried forward indefinitely as short-term loss, excess long-term losses carried forward indefinitely as long-term loss; short-term loss carryovers used first

Net loss (sum of short-term loss and 50 percent of long-term loss, or excess of short-term loss over long-term gain, or 50 percent of excess of long-term loss over short-term gain) deductible from other income up to $3,000; excess short-term losses carried forward indefinitely as short-term loss; excess long-term losses carried forward indefinitely as long-term loss; short-term carryovers used first

Net loss (sum of short-term loss and 50 percent of long-term loss, or excess of short-term loss over long-term gain, or 50 percent of excess of long-term loss over short-term gain) deductible from other income up to $3,000; excess short-term losses carried forward indefinitely as short-term loss; excess long-term losses carried forward indefinitely as long-term loss; short-term loss carryovers used first

The Capital Gains Tax Cut of 1978

Exhibit 4 Realized Net Capital Gains and Net Capital Losses on Individual Income Tax Returns and Selected Economic Indicators: 1954–1977

Year	Net Gains (Thousands of Dollars)	Net Losses (Thousands of Dollars)	Corporate Profits (Billions of Dollars)	Standard and Poor's Index	Percent Change, Gross Domestic Product Deflator	Real Rate of Growth of GNP (Percent)	Baa Corporate Bond Rate (Percent)
1954	3,731,862	379,446	37.8	29.69	1.4	−1.3	3.51
1955	5,126,350	375,213	46.7	40.49	2.2	6.7	3.53
1956	4,991,131	438,465	45.9	46.62	3.2	2.1	3.88
1957	4,128,228	642,695	45.4	44.38	3.4	1.8	4.71
1958	4,879,114	549,110	40.8	46.24	1.6	−0.2	4.73
1959	6,796,602	522,115	51.2	57.38	2.2	6.0	5.05
1960	6,003,859	704,284	48.9	55.85	1.7	2.3	5.19
1961	8,290,879	670,085	48.7	66.27	0.9	2.5	5.08
1962	6,821,421	1,050,393	53.7	62.38	1.8	5.8	5.02
1963	7,468,326	1,019,344	57.6	69.87	1.5	4.0	4.86
1964	8,909,143	969,991	64.2	81.37	1.6	5.3	4.83
1965	11,069,464	888,606	73.3	88.17	2.2	5.9	4.87
1966	10,960,261	1,018,979	78.6	85.26	3.3	5.9	5.67
1967	14,593,683	911,798	75.6	91.93	2.9	2.7	6.23
1968	18,853,870	864,221	82.1	98.70	4.5	4.4	6.94
1969	16,078,215	1,494,887	77.9	97.84	5.0	2.6	7.81
1970	10,655,553	1,648,870	66.4	83.22	5.4	−0.3	9.11
1971	14,558,580	1,403,581	76.9	98.29	5.1	3.0	8.56
1972	18,396,678	1,321,387	89.6	109.20	4.1	5.7	8.16
1973	18,200,682	1,529,396	97.2	107.43	5.8	5.5	8.24
1974	15,377,899	1,907,774	86.5	82.85	9.7	−1.4	9.50
1975	15,799,165	1,727,272	107.9	86.16	9.6	−1.3	10.61
1976	20,207,101	1,645,248	141.4	102.01	5.2	5.7	9.75
1977	23,363,333	2,586,729	159.1	98.20	5.9	4.9	8.97

Source: Joseph J. Minarik, "Capital Gains," in Henry Aaron and Joseph Pechman, eds., *How Taxes Affect Economic Behavior* (Washington, DC: Brookings Institution, 1981), 276.

The Capital Gains Tax Cut of 1978

Exhibit 5   AEA Position: Fundamental Principles and Draft Proposal

Fundamental Principles Underlying the AEA Position

1. An investor should not have to pay taxes on gains from his investment so long as those funds continue to be invested, even though he may have shifted the funds from one investment to another.
2. Losses on investments should offset income for tax purposes without restriction and at least on a basis symmetrical to the way that the gains on those investments would be taxed.
3. Although the gain on a risk investment may be realized in one year, the tax on that gain should take into account the fact that the gain is often the result of several years' investment. . . .
4. The gains subject to the above principles should be limited to those on *risk investments* (equities) in entities that are directly or indirectly job-creating. Investments in assets that are really consumption (e.g., purchasing a car, boat, furniture, real estate, etc.) would not be covered by these principles since the investor receives value through usage from such assets while he owns them, and our arguments on the importance of stimulating investment in order to increase productivity and create jobs do not apply to investments in such assets.
5. If the above principles could be reflected in the new tax policy, then it would not be necessary to have "preferential treatment" for capital gains.

Draft Proposal

1. This proposal is based on the above principles and is designed to fit most closely with the administration's objectives and anticipated recommendations.
2. "Income on risk investments" would be gains (net of losses) on the sale of equity investments in corporations (and, perhaps, broader to include other business structures of similar purpose) adjusted for the holding period and the extent to which the proceeds from the sale are reinvested as described in 3 below.
3. On such equity investments, the net of the gains and losses realized in any one year would be multiplied by a factor between 1.0 for less than one year to 0.5 for greater than ten years. The adjusted net gain (call it "equivalent income on risk investments"), if any, would be further reduced by the increase during the year in the investor's risk investments (at cost).

   Any "equivalent income on risk investments" not covered by the increase in the investor's total portfolio (at cost) would be subject to ordinary income tax.
4. At death, the taxes due on all "equivalent income on risk investments" would be calculated and paid prior to the imposition of regular estate taxes.

Source: Robert Wolcott Johnson, *The Passage of the Investment Incentive Act of 1978: A Case Study of Business Influencing Public Policy* (unpublished doctoral dissertation, Harvard Business School, 1980), 59–60.

The Capital Gains Tax Cuts of 1978

Exhibit 6   Tax Expenditure Estimates for Capital Gains Provisions (Millions of Dollars)

	Corporations							Individuals						
	1978	1979	1980	1981	1982	1983	1984	1978	1979	1980	1981	1982	1983	1984
Before the Investment Incentive Act of 1978														
Capital gains (other than farming, timber, iron ore, and coal)	540	575	635	705	780	865		7,430	7,990	8,585	9,230	9,925	10,665	
Deferral of capital gains on home sales	—	—	—	—	—	—		935	980	1,030	1,080	1,135	1,195	
Capital gains at death	—	—	—	—	—	—		8,120	8,975	9,910	10,945	12,090	13,535	
Capital gains treatment of certain timber income	205	230	250	275	300	335		60	65	70	80	85	95	
Capital gains treatment of iron ore	5	10	10	10	10	10		5	10	10	10	10	10	
Capital gains treatment of certain ordinary income for agriculture	10	10	10	15	15	15		350	365	385	405	425	450	
Exclusion of capital gains on home sales for persons age 65 and over	—	—	—	—	—	—		70	70	70	70	75	75	
Total capital gains tax expenditures	760	825	905	1,005	1,105	1,225		16,970	18,455	20,060	21,820	23,745	26,025	
Total tax expenditures	31,815	34,425	36,356	37,620	37,740	39,820		92,600	101,750	110,215	121,420	133,525	147,690	

Exhibit 6 (Continued)

After the Investment Incentive Act of 1978

Capital gains (other than farming, timber, iron ore, and coal)	555	625	725	785	870	965	7,520	10,150	10,905	11,730	12,615	13,580
Deferral of capital gains on home sales	—	—	—	—	—	—	1,125	1,010	1,115	1,225	1,350	1,485
Capital gains at death	—	—	—	—	—	—	9,015	10,005	11,105	12,275	13,555	14,965
Capital gains treatment of certain timber income	315	355	400	440	485	530	90	100	115	125	140	150
Capital gains treatment of iron ore	10	10	10	10	10	10	10	10	10	10	10	10
Capital gains treatment of certain ordinary income for agriculture	10	10	15	15	15	20	365	385	405	425	445	465
Exclusion of capital gains on home sales for persons age 55 and over	—	—	—	—	—	—	300	535	590	645	710	785
Total capital gains tax expenditures	890	1,000	1,150	1,250	1,380	1,525	18,245	22,195	24,245	26,435	28,825	31,440
Total tax expenditures	38,495	42,760	47,770	52,280	56,180	59,485	112,160	127,560	144,905	163,980	185,755	210,800

Source: Joint Committee on Taxation, *Estimates of Federal Tax Expenditure*, March 14, 1978, and March 15, 1979 (Washington, DC: Government Printing Office, 1978 and 1979).

The Capital Gains Tax Cut of 1978

Exhibit 7 Changes in Tax Liability Resulting from the Capital Gains Tax Reductions of the Investment Incentive Act of 1978, 1973 Income Levels

Adjusted Gross Income (Dollars)	Number of Returns[a] (Thousands)	1973 Tax Liability (Millions of Dollars)	Tax Liability under 1978 Act (Millions of Dollars)	Change in Tax Liability (Millions of Dollars)	Change in Tax Liability (Percent)	Change in Tax Liability (Dollars per Return)
Less than 0	15.1	11.6	1.9	−9.7	−83.9	−645.4
0–2,500	83.3	0.3	0.0	−0.3	−98.0	−3.6
2,500–5,000	98.8	9.5	8.6	−0.9	−9.1	−8.8
5,000–7,500	106.3	33.6	30.8	−2.8	−8.4	−26.5
7,500–10,000	119.8	85.1	83.7	−1.4	−1.7	−12.0
10,000–15,000	244.7	324.0	317.4	−6.6	−2.0	−27.1
15,000–20,000	310.6	666.6	652.4	−14.3	−2.1	−46.0
20,000–25,000	245.0	726.4	708.2	−18.1	−2.5	−74.0
25,000–30,000	171.4	666.6	657.6	−9.0	−1.4	−52.6
30,000–50,000	329.3	2,316.9	2,241.8	−75.2	−3.2	−228.2
50,000–100,000	171.6	2,748.6	2,647.2	−101.5	−3.7	−591.5
100,000–200,000	48.0	1,964.6	1,843.8	−120.8	−6.1	−2,518.8
200,000–500,000	11.6	1,239.7	1,101.5	−138.2	−11.1	−11,880.3
500,000–1,000,000	1.7	495.1	413.6	−81.5	−16.5	−48,030.0
1,000,000 and over	0.6	546.2	434.6	−111.6	−20.4	−181,501.1
Total or average	1,957.6	11,834.9	11,143.0	−691.9	−5.8	−353.4

[a]With dividends of at least $3,000.

Source: Joseph J. Minarik, "Capital Gains," in Henry Aaron and Joseph Pechman, eds., *How Taxes Affect Economic Behavior* (Washington, DC: Brookings Institution, 1981), 266.

288   Part III   Managing Fiscal Policy

Discussion Questions for Case

1. Evaluate the strategy devised by Zschau's task force for cutting capital gains taxes. What were the strengths and weaknesses of the strategy? What were the alternative strategies? How well did the strategy fit with the political environment?
2. How could the task force have improved the implementation of its strategy? What additional preparation would have strengthened its case? To whom should the task force members have talked or with whom should they have aligned their interests? How could the task force have improved its timing?
3. In general, what are the important factors that determine the success or failure of a legislative proposal? Is this case study typical?
4. To what extent should business, or any interest group, be concerned with the public interest? If there are conflicts between the private interest of business and the public interest, how should business argue its case? Is "pressure" a necessary ingredient for influencing policy? If so, what tactics are best?
5. What are the possible effects of the capital gains tax on entrepreneurs? How would you present a case for or against an elimination of the capital gains tax?

Bibliography

Auten, Gerald E., "Capital Gains: An Evaluation of the 1978 and 1981 Tax Cuts," in Charles Walker and Mark Bloomfield, eds., *New Directions in Federal Tax Policy for the 1980s* (Cambridge, MA: Ballinger, 1983), 121–148. This article describes the economic effects of capital gains taxation in nontechnical language and estimates the impact of the 1978 and 1981 tax cuts. There is a good bibliography listing more detailed theoretical and empirical papers on capital gains taxation.

Bauer, Raymond A., Ithiel De Sola Pool, and Lewis A. Dexter, *American Business & Public Policy: The Politics of Foreign Trade*, 2d ed. (New York: Aldine, 1972). This classic, scholarly study of business influence on trade policy disputes the argument that political groups struggle to serve their own well-defined interests and substitutes for that argument an explanation of business-government interaction based on communication among political groups.

Epstein, Edwin M., *The Corporation in American Politics* (Englewood Cliffs, NJ: Prentice-Hall, 1969). This book is one of the first introductions, and still the best, to the issues regarding the political involvement of business.

Fox, J. Ronald, *Managing Business-Government Relations: Cases and Notes on Business-Government Problems* (Homewood, IL: Irwin, 1982). This casebook has many good notes and cases that complement the material in this chapter. In particular, the notes "The Structure of the U.S. Government Decision-Making Process" (pages 133–141) and "Lobbyists and Interest Groups" (pages 307–329) are particularly helpful. The case "Congressman Ned Pattison" (pages 148–165) investigates the powers and concerns of the government's side of the business-government interaction.

CHAPTER 9
The Strategy of Reaganomics

The purpose of this chapter's case, "The Reagan Plan," is not to evaluate how Reaganomics actually worked, but rather to evaluate how it was supposed to work. The case provides a good opportunity to evaluate critically an argument for an innovative program by testing its consistency with logic and observed behavior. In some respects, this was a problem similar to what President Kennedy faced when he announced his tax cut proposal—a similarity not overlooked by the Republican speech writers. The assumptions underlying the new proposal form a sound basis for the analysis. The assumptions on the behavior of expectations are paramount in the analysis of the consequences of the Reagan plan. In addition, one must assess any political, social, or international assumptions that may have affected the success or failure of the plan.

The case consists of two newspaper articles reporting the memorandum to President-Elect Reagan from two Republican strategists, Congressmen David Stockman and Jack Kemp, and Reagan's first State of the Union speech. In addition, economic data that were available at the time have been appended to the case. In the speech, President Reagan outlined the elements of his plan, now generally referred to as "Reaganomics." Both articles are punctuated by references to the expected supply-side consequences of the president's proposal.

Case
The Reagan Plan

A short time after he took office as president of the United States, Ronald Reagan told the American people, "I regret to say that we are in the worst economic mess since the Great Depression."[1] (See Exhibits 1 through 13.)

Several days later, Budget Director David Stockman revealed the administration's remedy: a program of cuts in federal spending accompanied by an across-the-board reduction in income taxes. A vigorous national debate then ensued over what the effects of the administration's policies would be, and whether or not other actions were required to meet the nation's needs.

Peter G. Peterson, chairman of Lehman Brothers Kuhn Loeb, and former adviser to President Nixon, spoke of " a new and remarkable Reagan consensus—a true historic first, the most sweeping reversal in the direction of national economic policy since the New Deal." But he warned: "As broad and deep as this consensus is, and as relieved and enthusiastic as the country is about a more honest sense of its past and a more hopeful sense of its future, one can nonetheless sense an unexpected mix of conflicting emotions. Amidst all the excitement, there are growing signs of disquiet, however respectful and discreet, and growing doubts that somehow the Reagan program really fits the Reagan consensus."[2]

Avoiding an Economic Dunkirk

In November 1980 Ronald Reagan, a one-time movie actor and former Republican governor of California, defeated Jimmy Carter and was elected president of the United States with 51 percent of the popular vote. Along with Reagan, riding the crest of what was perceived as a national wave of "conservatism," came a number of Republican senators and members of Congress. Indeed, for the first time in 26 years the Republican party controlled the U.S. Senate, and the Democratic majority in the House was cut from 117 to 52.

Shortly after the election, two Republican congressmen, David Stockman of Michigan and Jack Kemp of New York, wrote a memorandum giving their advice to the new president. In December President-elect Reagan selected Stockman to head the Office of Management and Budget (OMB). Kemp was elected chairman of the House Republican Conference, which

This case was prepared by Professor George C. Lodge.
Copyright © 1981 by the President and Fellows of Harvard College
Harvard Business School case 9-381-173

[1] *New York Times*, Feb. 6, 1981, A12.

[2] Address to the Women's Economic Roundtable, Mar. 18, 1981.

made him one of his party's leaders in the House. Excerpts follow from the Stockman-Kemp paper, entitled "Avoiding a GOP Economic Dunkirk."[3]

President Reagan will inherit thoroughly disordered credit and capital markets, punishingly high interest rates, and a hair-trigger market psychology poised to respond strongly to early economic policy signals in either favorable or unfavorable ways.

The preeminent danger is that an initial economic policy package that includes the tax cuts but does not contain decisive, credible elements on matters of outlay control, future budget authority reduction, and a believable plan for curtailing the Federal Government's massive direct and indirect credit absorption will generate pervasive expectations of a continuing "Reagan inflation." Such a development would almost ensure that high interest rates would hang over the economy well into the first year, deadening housing and durables markets and thwarting the industrial capital spending boom required to propel sustained economic growth. Thus, "Thatcherization"[4] can only be avoided if the initial economic policy package simultaneously spurs the output side of the economy and also elicits a swift downward revision of inflationary expectations in the financial markets.

A double-dip recession in early 1981 is now at least a 50 percent possibility given emerging conditions in the financial markets and gathering evidence from the output side of the economy. Stagnant or declining real GNP growth in the first two quarters would generate staggering political and policy challenges. These include a further worsening of an already dismal budget posture and a profusion of "quick fix" remedies for various wounded sectors of the economy. The latter would include intense pressure for formal or informal auto import restraints, activation of . . . costly housing bailouts, maintenance of current excessive CETA employment levels, accelerated draw-down of various lending and grant aids under SBA, EDA, and FmHA, a further 13-week extension of federal unemployment benefits, etc.[5]

There is further danger; the federal budget has now become an automatic "coast-to-coast soup line" that dispenses remedial aid with

---

[3] *The Wall Street Journal*, Dec. 12, 1980. Dunkirk is the French coastal town from which the last remnants of the British army escaped the German onslaught in the opening period of World War II.

[4] Thatcherization" refers to the policies of Margaret Thatcher, prime minister of Great Britain, whose attempts to reduce inflation through monetary restraint had increased unemployment and seriously reduced private investment and national growth.

[5] CETA refers to the Comprehensive Employment and Training Act, which provides funds for training unemployed workers and for placing them in jobs in either government or private industry. SBA refers to the Small Business Administration. EDA refers to the Economic Development Administration, which was created in 1965 as part of a Great Society regional development program. Besides providing grants for public works construction, loans for commercial business development, and federal technical assistance to encourage economic growth in rural and urban areas, it supplies financial support for a number of multistate regional commissions. FmHA refers to the Farmer's Home Administration, which administers rural housing rehabilitation loans and disaster loans as voted by Congress.

almost reckless abandon, converting the traditional notion of automatic stabilizers into multitudinous outlay spasms throughout the budget. For instance, the estimates for FY 1981 trade adjustment assistance have exploded from $400 million in the spring to $2.5 billion as of November, and the summer drought will cause SBA emergency farm loan aid to surge by $1.1 billion above planned levels.

For these reasons, the first hard look at the unvarnished FY 1981 and 1982 budget posture by our own OMB people is likely to elicit coronary contractions among some, and produce an intense polarization between supply-side tax cutters and the more fiscally orthodox. An internecine struggle over deferral or temporary abandonment of the tax program could ensue. The result would be severe demoralization and fractionalization of GOP ranks and an erosion of our capacity to govern successfully and revive the economy before November 1982.

President Reagan should declare a national economic emergency soon after inauguration. He should tell the Congress and the nation that the economic, financial, budget, energy, and regulatory conditions he inherited are far worse than anyone had imagined. He should request that Congress organize quickly and clear the decks for exclusive action during the next 100 days on an Emergency Economic Stabilization and Recovery Program he would soon announce.

Five major principles should govern the formulation of the package:

1. A static "waste-cutting" approach to the FY 1981 outlay component of the fiscal hemorrhage will hardly make a dent in the true fiscal problem. Persisting high "misery index" conditions in the economy will drive the soup line mechanisms of the budget faster than short-run, line-item cuts can be made on Capitol Hill. Fiscal stabilization (i.e., elimination of deficits and excessive rates of spending growth) can only be achieved by sharp improvement in the economic indicators over the next 24 months. This means that the policy initiatives designed to spur output growth and to lower inflation expectations and interest rates must carry a large share of the fiscal stabilization burden. Improvement in the "outside" economic forces driving the budget is just as important as success in the "inside" efforts to effect legislative and administrative accounting reductions.

2. For this reason, dilution of the tax-cut program in order to limit short-run static revenue losses during the remainder of FY 1981 and FY 1982 would be counterproductive. Weak real GNP and employment growth over calendar 1981 and 1982 will generate soup line expenditures equal to or greater than any static revenue gains from trimming the tax program.

3. The needed rebound of real GNP growth and especially vigorous expansion in the capital spending sector of the economy cannot be accomplished by tax cuts alone. A dramatic, substantial recision of the regulatory burden is needed both for the short-term cash flow

relief it will provide to business firms and the long-term signal it will provide to corporate investment planners. A major "regulatory ventilation" will do as much to boost business confidence as tax and fiscal measures.

4. High, permanent inflation expectations have killed the long-term bond and equity markets that are required to fuel a capital spending boom and the regeneration of robust economic growth. Moreover, this has caused a compression of the financial liability structure of business into the short-term market for bank loans and commercial paper, and has caused a flight of savings into tangible assets like precious metals, land, etc. The result of this credit market dislocation and inversion is that superheated markets for short-term credits keep interest rates high and volatile and make monetary policy almost impossible to conduct.

The Reagan financial stabilization plan must seek to restore credit and capital market order and equilibrium by supporting monetary policy reform and removing the primary cause of long-term inflation pessimism: the explosive growth of out-year federal liabilities, spending authority, and credit absorption.

This points to the real leverage and locus for budget control: severe recision of entitlement and new obligational authority in the federal spending pipeline, which creates outlay streams and borrowing requirements in FY 1982, FY 1983, and beyond.

Again, the primary aim of the fiscal control component must be to shift long-term inflation expectations downward and restore bond and equity markets. Severe reductions in government spending and federal credit absorption can accomplish this. In turn, robust long-term capital markets would lessen the traffic jam in short-term credit markets by permitting corporate portfolio restructuring and by drawing savings out of unproductive tangible assets. The conditions for reestablishing monetary policy credibility would be achieved and short-term interest rates, demand for money, and inflation expectations would adjust accordingly.

5. Certain preemptive steps must be taken early on to keep control of the agenda and to maintain Capitol Hill focus on the Stabilization and Recovery Program. Foremost, all remaining petroleum product controls and allocations should be cancelled on day one.

Reagan's State of the Union Message

On February 19, 1981, President Reagan presented his "program for economic recovery" to a joint session of Congress and to a national television audience. Herewith are excerpts from his address:[6]

---

[6]*New York Times*, Feb. 19, 1981.

Only a month ago, I was your guest in this historic building and I pledged to you my cooperation in doing what is right for this nation we all love so much.

I am here tonight to reaffirm that pledge and to ask that we share in restoring the promise that is offered to every citizen by this, the last, best hope of man on earth.

All of us are aware of the punishing inflation which has, for the first time in some 60 years, held to double-digit figures for two years in a row. Interest rates have reached absurd levels of more than 20 percent and over 15 percent for those who would borrow to buy a home. All across this land one can see newly built homes standing vacant, unsold because of mortgage interest rates.

Almost eight million Americans are out of work. These are people who want to be productive. But as the months go by despair dominates their lives. The threats of layoff and unemployment hang over other millions, and all who work are frustrated by their inability to keep up with inflation.

One worker in a Midwest city put it to me this way: He said, "I'm bringing home more dollars than I thought I could ever earn, but I seem to be getting worse off." Well, he is. Hourly earnings of the American worker, after adjusting for inflation, have declined 5 percent over the past five years. And furthermore, in the last five years, Federal personal taxes for the average family increased 67 percent.

We can no longer procrastinate and hope things will get better. They will not. If we do not act forcefully, and now, the economy will get worse.

Can we who man the ship of state deny it is out of control? Our national debt is approaching $1 trillion. A few weeks ago I called such a figure—a trillion dollars—incomprehensible. I've been trying to think of a way to illustrate how big it really is. The best I could come up with is to say that a stack of $1,000 bills in your hand only four inches high would make you a millionaire. A trillion dollars would be a stack of $1,000 bills 67 miles high.

Interest on Public Debt

The interest on the public debt this year will be over $90 billion. And unless we change the proposed spending for the fiscal year beginning October 1, we'll add another almost $80 billion to the debt.

Adding to our troubles is a mass of regulations imposed on the shopkeeper, the farmer, the craftsman, professionals and major industry that is estimated to add $100 billion to the price of things we buy and reduces our ability to produce. The rate of increase in American productivity, once one of the highest in the world, is among the lowest of all major industrial nations. Indeed, it has actually declined the last three years.

I have painted a grim picture, but I believe I have painted it accurately. It is within our power to change this picture and we can act in hope. There is nothing wrong with our internal strengths. There has been no breakdown in the human, technological and natural resources upon which the economy is built.

Based on this confidence in a system which has never failed us—but which we have failed through a lack of confidence, and sometimes through a belief that we could fine-tune the economy and get a tune more to our liking—I am proposing a comprehensive four-part program. I will now outline and give in some detail the principal parts of this program, but you will each be provided with a completely detailed copy of the program in its entirety.

This plan is aimed at reducing the growth in government spending and taxing, reforming and eliminating regulations which are unnecessary and counterproductive, and encouraging a consistent monetary policy aimed at maintaining the value of the currency.

If enacted in full, our program can help America create 13 million new jobs, nearly three million more than we would without these measures. It will also help us gain control of inflation.

It is important to note that we are only reducing the rate of increase in taxing and spending. We are not attempting to cut either spending or taxing to a level below that which we presently have. This plan will get our economy moving again, increase productivity growth and thus create the jobs our people must have.

Plans to Reduce Spending

I am asking that you join me in reducing direct Federal spending by $41.4 billion in FY 1982, along with $7.7 billion in user fees and off-budget savings for total savings of $49.1 billion. This will still allow an increase of $40.8 billion over 1981 spending.

I know that exaggerated and inaccurate stories about these cuts have disturbed many people, particularly those dependent on grant and benefit programs for their basic needs. Some of you have heard from constituents afraid that Social Security checks, for example, might be taken from them. I regret the fear these unfounded stories have caused and welcome this opportunity to set things straight.

We will continue to fulfill the obligations that spring from our national conscience. Those who through no fault of their own must depend on the rest of us, the poverty-stricken, the disabled, the elderly, all those with true need, can rest assured that the social safety net of programs they depend on are exempt from any cuts.

The full retirement benefits of the more than 31 million Social Security recipients will be continued along with an annual cost of living increase. Medicare will not be cut, nor will supplemental income for the blind, aged and disabled. Funding will continue for veterans' pensions.

School breakfasts and lunches for the children of low-income families will continue as will nutrition and other special services for the aging. There will be no cut in Project Head Start or summer youth jobs.

All in all, nearly $216 billion providing help for tens of millions of Americans will be fully funded. But government will not continue to subsidize individuals or particular business interests where real need cannot be demonstrated. And while we will reduce some subsidies to regional and local governments, we will at the same time convert a number of categorical grant programs into block grants to reduce wasteful administrative overhead and to give local government entities and states more flexibility and control. We call for an end to duplication in Federal programs and reform of those which are not cost effective.

Already, some have protested there must be no reduction of aid to schools. Let me point out that Federal aid to education amounts to only 8 percent of total educational funding. For this the Federal Government has insisted on a tremendously disproportionate share of control over our schools. Whatever reductions we've proposed in that 8 percent will amount to very little of the total cost of education. It will, however, restore more authority to states and local school districts.

Historically, the American people have supported by voluntary contributions more artistic and cultural activities than all the other countries in the world put together. I wholeheartedly support this approach and believe Americans will continue their generosity. Therefore, I am proposing a savings of $85 million in the Federal subsidies now going to the arts and humanities.

There are a number of subsidies to business and industry I believe are unnecessary. Not because the activities being subsidized aren't of value, but because the marketplace contains incentives enough to warrant continuing these activities without a government subsidy. One such subsidy is the Department of Energy's synthetic fuels program. We will continue support of research leading to development of new technologies and more independence from foreign oil, but we can save at least $3.2 billion by leaving to private industry the building of plants to make liquid or gas fuels from coal.

Export-Import Bank Loans

We are asking that another major business subsidy, the Export-Import Bank loan authority, be reduced by one-third in 1982. We are doing this because the primary beneficiaries of taxpayer funds in this case are the exporting companies themselves—most of them profitable corporations.

And this brings me to a number of other lending programs in which government makes low-interest loans, some of them for an interest rate as low as 2 percent. What has not been very well understood is that the Treasury Department has no money of its own. It has to go into the private capital market and borrow the money to provide those loans. In this time of excessive interest rates the government finds itself paying interest several times as high as it receives from the borrowing agency. The taxpayers—your constituents—of course, are paying that high interest rate and it just makes all other interest rates higher.

By terminating the Economic Development Administration (EDA), we can save hundreds of millions of dollars in 1982 and billions more over the next few years. There is a lack of consistent and convincing evidence that EDA and its regional commissions have been effective in creating new jobs. They have been effective in creating an array of planners, grantsmen and professional middlemen. We believe we can do better just by the expansion of the economy and the job creation which will come from our economic program.

The Food Stamp program will be restored to its original purpose, to assist those without resources to purchase sufficient nutritional food. We will, however, save $1.8 billion in FY 1982 by removing from eligibility those who are not in real need or who are abusing the program. Despite this reduction, the program will be budgeted for more than $10 billion.

We will tighten welfare and give more attention to outside sources of income when determining the amount of welfare an individual is allowed. This plus strong and effective work requirement will save $520 million next year.

I stated a moment ago our intention to keep the school breakfast and lunch programs for those in true need. But by cutting back on meals for children of families who can afford to pay, the savings will be $1.6 billion in FY 1982.

Let me just touch on a few other areas which are typical of the kind of reductions we have included in this economic package. The Trade Adjustment Assistance program provides benefits for workers who are unemployed when foreign imports reduce the market for various American products causing shutdown of plants and layoff of workers. The purpose is to help these workers find jobs in growing sectors of our economy. And yet, because these benefits are paid out on top of normal unemployment benefits, we wind up paying greater benefits to those who lose their jobs because of foreign competition than we do to their friends and neighbors who are laid off due to domestic competition. Anyone must agree that this is unfair. Putting these two programs on the same footing will save $1.15 billion in just one year.

Categorical Grant Programs

Earlier I made mention of changing categorical grants to states and local governments into block grants. We know, of course, that categorical grant programs burden local and state governments with a mass of Federal regulations and Federal paperwork.

Ineffective targeting, wasteful administrative overhead—all can be eliminated by shifting the resources and decision-making authority to local and state government. This will also consolidate programs which are scattered throughout the Federal bureaucracy. It will bring government closer to the people and will save $23.9 billion over the next five years.

Our program for economic renewal deals with a number of programs which at present are not cost-effective. An example is Medicaid. Right now Washington provides the states with unlimited matching payments for their expenditures. At the same time we here in Washington pretty much dictate how the states will manage the program. We want to put a cap on how much the Federal Government will contribute but at the same time allow the states much more flexibility in managing and structuring their programs. I know from our experience in California that such flexibility could have led to far more cost-effective reforms. This will bring a savings of $1 billion next year.

The space program has been and is important to America and we plan to continue it. We believe, however, that a reordering of priorities to focus on the most important and cost-effective NASA programs can result in a savings of a quarter of a billion dollars.

Coming down from space to the mailbox—the Postal Service has been consistently unable to live within its operating budget. It is still dependent on large Federal subsidies. We propose reducing those subsidies by $632 million in 1982 to press the Postal Service into becoming more effective. In subsequent years the savings will continue to add up.

The Economic Regulatory Administration in the Department of Energy has programs to force companies to convert to specific fuels. It has the authority to administer a gas rationing plan, and prior to decontrol it ran the oil price control program. With these and other regulations gone we can save several hundreds of millions of dollars over the next few years.

Now I'm sure there is one department you've been waiting for me to mention. That is the Department of Defense. It is the only department in our entire program that will actually be increased over the present budgeted figure. But even here there was no exemption. The Department of Defense came up with a number of cuts which reduced the budget increase needed to restore our military balance. These measures will save $2.9 billion in 1982 outlays and by 1986 a total of $28.2 billion will have been saved. The aim will be to provide the most effective defense for the lowest possible cost.

I believe my duty as president requires that I recommend increases in defense spending over the coming years.[7] Since 1970 the Soviet Union has invested $300 billion more in its military forces than we have. As a result of its massive military buildup, the Soviets now have a significant numerical advantage in strategic nuclear delivery systems, tactical aircraft, submarines, artillery, and antiaircraft defense. To allow this imbalance to continue is a threat to our national security.

---

[7]The president's budget proposed spending approximately $7 billion more on defense in fiscal year 1982 (beginning October 1, 1981) than had been recommended by President Carter. There would be an increase of $18.5 billion for defense in 1983, rising to an increase of $60 billion in 1986.

Notwithstanding our economic straits, making the financial changes beginning now is far less costly than waiting and attempting a crash program several years from now.

Commitment on Arms Curbs

We remain committed to the goal of arms limitation through negotiation and hope we can persuade our adversaries to come to realistic balanced and verifiable agreements. But, as we negotiate, our security must be fully protected by a balanced and realistic defense program.

Let me say a word here about the general problem of waste and fraud in the Federal Government. One government estimate indicated that fraud alone may account for anywhere from 1 to 10 percent—as much as $25 billion—of Federal expenditures for social programs. If the tax dollars that are wasted or mismanaged are added to this fraud total, the staggering dimensions of this problem begin to emerge.

The Office of Management and Budget is now putting together an interagency task force to attack waste and fraud. We are also planning to appoint as Inspectors General highly trained professionals who will spare no effort to do this job.

No administration can promise to immediately stop a trend that has grown in recent years as quickly as government expenditures themselves. But let me say this: Waste and fraud in the Federal budget is exactly what I have called it before—an unrelenting national scandal—a scandal we are bound and determined to do something about.

Marching in lockstep with the whole program of reductions in spending is the equally important program of reduced tax rates. Both are essential if we are to have economic recovery. It is time to create new jobs, build and rebuild industry, and give the American people room to do what they do best. And that can only be done with a tax program which provides incentive to increase productivity for both workers and industry.

Our proposal is for a 10 percent across-the-board cut every year for three years in the tax rates for all individual income taxpayers, making a total tax cut of 30 percent. This three-year reduction will also apply to the tax on unearned income, leading toward an eventual elimination of the present differential between the tax on earned and unearned income.

The effective starting date for these 10 percent personal income tax rate reductions will be July 1st of this year.

Again, let me remind you this 30 percent reduction in marginal rates, while it will leave the taxpayers with $500 billion more in their pockets over the next five years, is actually only a reduction in the tax increase already built into the system.

Unlike some past tax "reforms," this is not merely a shift of wealth between different sets of taxpayers. This proposal for an equal reduction in everyone's tax rates will expand our national prosperity, enlarge national incomes and increase opportunities for all Americans.

Some will argue, I know, that reducing tax rates now will be inflationary. A solid body of economic experts does not agree. And certainly tax cuts adopted over the past three-fourths of a century indicate these economic experts are right. The advice I have had is that by 1985 our real production of goods and services will grow by 20 percent and will be $300 billion higher than it is today.[8] The average worker's wage will rise (in real purchasing power) by 8 percent and those are after-tax dollars. This, of course, is predicated on our complete program of tax cuts and spending reductions being implemented. (See Exhibit 12 for official and other forecasts.)

The third part of the tax package is aimed directly at providing business and industry with the capital needed to modernize and engage in more research and development. This will involve an increase in depreciation allowances and this part of our tax proposal will be retroactive as of January 1.

Depreciation System

The present depreciation system is obsolete, needlessly complex, and economically counterproductive. Very simply, it bases the depreciation of plant, machinery, vehicles and tools on their original cost with no recognition of how inflation has increased their replacement cost. We are proposing a much shorter write-off time than is presently allowed. We propose a 5-year write-off for machinery; 3 years for vehicles and trucks; and a 10-year write-off for plants.

In fiscal year 1982, under this plan business would acquire nearly $10 billion for investment and by 1985 the figure would be nearly $45 billion. These changes are essential to provide the new investment which is needed to create millions of new jobs between now and 1986 and to make America competitive once again in world markets. These are not make-work jobs, they are productive jobs with a future.

I'm well aware that there are many other desirable tax changes such as indexing the income tax brackets to protect taxpayers against inflation. There is the unjust discrimination against married couples if both are working and earning, tuition tax credits, the unfairness of the inheritance tax especially to the family-owned farm and the family-owned business and a number of others. But our program for economic recovery is so urgently needed to begin to bring down inflation that I would ask you to act on this plan first and with great urgency. Then I pledge to you I will join with you in seeking these additional tax changes at an early date.

American society experienced a virtual explosion in government regulation during the past decades. Between 1970 and 1979, expenditures for the major regulatory agencies quadrupled, the number of pages pub-

---

[8]The preliminary GNP in 1980 was $2,627 billion, expressed in 1980 dollars. President Reagan was using a real 1980 GNP of $1,481 billion, expressed in 1972 dollars.

lished annually in the Federal Register nearly tripled and the number of pages in the Code of Federal Regulations increased by nearly two-thirds.

The result has been higher prices, higher unemployment and lower productivity growth. Overregulation causes small and independent businessmen and women, as well as large businesses, to defer or terminate plans for expansion and, since they are responsible for most of our new jobs, those new jobs aren't created.

We have no intention of dismantling the regulatory agencies—especially those necessary to protect the environment and to assure the public health and safety. However, we must come to grips with inefficient and burdensome regulations—eliminate those we can and reform those we must keep.

I have asked Vice President Bush to head a cabinet-level Task Force on Regulatory Relief. Second, I asked each member of my Cabinet to postpone the effective dates of the hundreds of regulations which have not yet been implemented. Third, in coordination with the Task Force, many of the agency heads have taken prompt action to review and rescind existing burdensome regulations. Finally, just yesterday, I signed an Executive Order that for the first time provides for effective and coordinated management of the regulatory process.

Although much has been accomplished, this is only a beginning. We will eliminate those regulations that are unproductive and unnecessary by Executive Order where possible and cooperate fully with you on those that require legislation.

The final aspect of our plan requires a national monetary policy which does not allow money growth to increase consistently faster than the growth of goods and services. In order to curb inflation, we need to slow the growth in our money supply.[9]

We fully recognize the independence of the Federal Reserve System and will do nothing to undermine that independence. We will consult regularly with the Federal Reserve Board on all aspects of our economic program and will vigorously pursue budget policies that will make their job easier in reducing monetary growth.

A successful program to achieve stable and moderate growth patterns in the money supply will keep both inflation and interest rates down and restore vigor to our financial institutions and markets.

This, then, is our proposal. America's New Beginning: A Program for Economic Recovery. I do not want it to be simply the plan of my Administration—I am here tonight to ask you to join me in making it our plan. Together, we can embark on this road not to make things easy, but to make things better.

Can we do the job? The answer is yes. But we must begin now. Our

---

[9]The White House press release accompanying this speech noted that the president's "economic scenario assumes that the growth of money and credit are steadily reduced from 1980 levels to one-half those levels by 1986."

social, political and cultural, as well as our economic institutions, can no longer absorb the repeated shocks that have been dealt them over the past decades.

We are in control here. There is nothing wrong with America that we can't fix. So I'm full of hope and optimism that we will see this difficult new challenge to its end—that we will find those reservoirs of national will to once again do the right thing. . . .

The people are watching and waiting. They don't demand miracles, but they do expect us to act. Let us act together.

Thank you and good night.

The Reagan Plan

Exhibit 1

A. Federal Revenues and Outlays (Billions of Dollars)

Fiscal Year	Revenues	Outlays	Deficit (−) or Surplus (+)
1981	600.2	654.7	−54.5
1982	650.5	695.5	−45.0
1983	710.1	733.1	−23.0
1984	772.1	771.6	+0.5
1985	851.0	844.0	+7.0
1986	942.1	912.1	+30.0

B. Shift in Budget Priorities

	1962	1981	1984
Dollar Amounts (in Billions)			
DOD—military	46.8	157.9	249.8
Safety net programs	26.2	239.3	313.0
Net interest	6.9	64.3	66.8
All other	26.9	193.2	142.0
Total	106.8	654.7	771.6
Outlay Shares (Percents)			
DOD—military	43.8	24.1	32.4
Safety net programs	24.5	36.6	40.6
Net interest	6.4	9.8	8.6
All other	25.2	29.5	18.4
Total	100.0	100.0	100.0

C. Federal Budget and GNP

Fiscal Year	Outlays as Percent of GNP
1981	23.0
1982	21.8
1983	20.4
1984	19.3
1985	19.2
1986	19.0

Source: A White House report, "America's New Beginning: A Program for Economic Recovery," Feb. 18, 1981 (Washington, DC: U.S. Government Printing Office).

The Reagan Plan

Exhibit 2   Present-Law Depreciation and Accelerated Cost-Recovery System

Item	Present Law on Depreciation	Accelerated Cost-Recovery System
Recovery Periods		
Tangible personal property	Guidelines allow 2½ to 50 years, depending on asset type or activity, with optional 20% variance for each.	3 years (autos, light trucks, and machinery and equipment used for research and development); 5 years (most machinery and equipment); or 10 years (long-lived public utility property).
Real estate	Determined by facts and circumstances or by guidelines ranging from 25 to 60 years, depending on the type of building.	10 years for owner-occupied factories, stores, and warehouses; 15 years for other nonresidential and for low-income housing; 18 years for other residential.
Recovery Method		
Tangible personal property	Straight line; or for new property, taxpayer may elect declining-balance up to 200%, or sum-of-years-digits.	Accelerated write-off built into tables.
Real estate	Same for new residential; up to 150% declining-balance for new, nonresidential; up to 125% declining-balance for used residential; straight-line for used nonresidential.	Same for 10-year property; straight-line for other.
Investment tax credit	3⅓% for machinery and equipment written off or held for 3 to 5 years; 6⅔% for 5 to 7 years; 10% if longer.	6% for 3-year class and 10% for 5-year and 10-year eligible property.
Carryovers	Choice of 20% shorter or longer lives; straight-line or accelerated methods, where allowed. Deductions may add to net operating loss which can be carried over 7 years.	Extends net operating loss and investment credit carryover period from 7 to 10 years.
Timing of eligibility	When placed in service.	When placed in service, or for property with at least a 2-year construction period, as acquired.

Source: A White House report, "America's New Beginning: A Program for Economic Recovery," Feb. 18, 1981 (Washington, DC: U.S. Government Printing Office).

The Reagan Plan

Exhibit 3

A. Direct Revenue Effects of Proposed Tax Reductions (Billions of Dollars)

	Fiscal Years					
	1981	1982	1983	1984	1985	1986
Individual:						
30 percent phased rate reduction	−6.4	−44.2	−81.4	−118.1	−141.5	−162.4
Business:						
Accelerated cost recovery system after interaction with individual tax	−2.5	−9.7	−18.6	30.0	−44.2	−59.3
Total	−8.8	−53.9	−100.0	−148.1	−185.7	−221.7

B. Economic Scenarios

	Calendar Years					
	1981	1982	1983	1984	1985	1986
Nominal gross national product (billions)	$2,920.0	$3,293.0	$3,700.0	$4,098.0	$4,500.0	$4,918.0
Percent change	11.1	12.8	12.4	10.8	9.8	9.3
Real gross national product (billions, 1972 dollars)	1,497.0	1,560.0	1,638.0	1,711.0	1,783.0	1,858.0
Percent change	1.1	4.2	5.0	4.5	4.2	4.2
Implicit price deflator	195.0	211.0	226.0	240.0	252.0	265.0
Percent change	9.9	8.3	7.0	6.0	5.4	4.9
Consumer price index,[a] 1967 = 100	274.0	297.0	315.0	333.0	348.0	363.0
Percent change	11.1	8.3	6.2	5.5	4.7	4.2
Unemployment rate Percent	7.8	7.2	6.6	6.4	6.0	5.6

[a]CPI for urban wage earners and clerical workers (CPI-W).

Source: A White House report, "America's New Beginning: A Program for Economic Recovery," Feb. 18, 1981 (Washington, DC: U.S. Government Printing Office).

The Reagan Plan

Exhibit 4   Growth in Major Components of Real Gross National Product: 1976–1980

Component	1976	1977	1978	1979	1980[a]
Percent Change					
Real gross national product	4.4	5.8	5.3	1.7	−0.3
Personal consumption expenditures	5.7	5.0	4.8	2.0	−0.3
Business fixed investment	7.8	13.5	9.0	2.9	−6.0
Residential fixed investment	19.8	12.5	0	−6.1	−17.6
Government purchases of goods and services	−1.3	3.6	1.6	1.9	1.5
Federal	−0.8	5.0	−1.3	2.1	4.7
State and local	−1.7	2.7	3.3	1.7	−0.3
Real domestic final sales[b]	4.9	5.9	4.4	1.7	−1.3
Change as a Percent of GNP					
Inventory accumulation	0.4	0.4	0.2	−0.8	0
Net exports of goods and services	−0.7	−0.4	0.9	0.8	0.9

Note: Change from fourth quarter to fourth quarter.

[a]Preliminary.

[b]GNP excluding change in business inventories and net exports of goods and services.

Source: *Economic Report of the President, 1981* (Washington, DC: U.S. Government Printing Office), 138.

The Reagan Plan

Exhibit 5   Productivity, Compensation, and Labor Costs

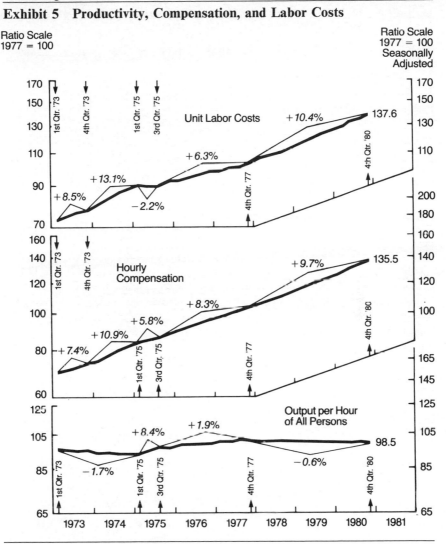

Percentages are annual rates of change for periods indicated.
Latest data plotted: fourth quarter.

Source: U.S. Department of Labor and Federal Reserve Bank of St. Louis.

The Reagan Plan

Exhibit 6   U.S. Price Developments—Measures of Price Change: 1976–1980

Item	1976	1977	1978	1979	1980[a]
Implicit Price Deflators[b]					
Gross national product	4.7	6.1	8.5	8.1	10.0
Personal consumption expenditures	5.0	5.9	7.8	9.5	10.4
Private nonfarm business output	4.9	5.7	8.3	8.3	10.3
Consumer Prices, Total	5.0	6.6	9.0	12.7	12.6[c]
Farm value of food	−12.9	6.4	17.5	7.4	14.5[c]
Energy[d]	6.2	8.2	7.5	36.5	18.9[c]
Home purchase and finance[e]	3.8	8.9	13.4	19.8	17.7[c]
All other	6.3	6.1	7.3	7.9	9.8[c]
Producer Prices of Finished Goods, *Total*	2.7	6.9	8.7	12.6	12.0
Food	−4.4	7.4	11.6	7.8	7.4
Energy	5.0	9.2	6.4	62.0	28.4
All other	5.6	6.4	7.9	9.3	11.1

Note: Percent change from fourth quarter to fourth quarter.

[a]Preliminary.

[b]Seasonally adjusted data.

[c]November 1979 to November 1980.

[d]Includes only prices for direct consumer purchases of energy for the home and for motor vehicles.

[e]"Home purchase and finance" consists of home purchase and financing, taxes, and insurance on owner-occupied homes.

Source: *Economic Report of the President, 1981* (Washington, DC: U.S. Government Printing Office), 149.

The Reagan Plan

Exhibit 7 Change in U.S. Employment, Unemployment, and Participation Rates

Component	1976 IV	1977 IV	1978 IV	1979 IV	1980 IV
	Percent Change from Year Earlier[a]				
Increase in Civilian Employment, Total	3.4	4.4	3.6	2.1	−0.3
Males 20 years and over	2.6	3.3	2.5	1.3	−0.7
Females 20 years and over	4.6	5.2	5.4	3.9	1.5
Both sexes 16–19 years	3.0	8.0	2.6	−0.9	−6.7
White	3.3	4.3	3.2	2.0	−0.2
Black and other	4.2	4.7	7.0	2.9	−0.9
	Percent[b]				
Unemployment rate, total[c]	7.8	6.6	5.9	5.9	7.5
Males 20 years and over	6.0	4.8	4.1	4.4	6.3
Females 20 years and over	7.4	6.7	5.7	5.7	6.7
Both sexes 16–19 years	19.1	16.6	16.3	16.2	18.3
White	7.0	5.7	5.1	5.2	6.6
Black and other	13.3	13.3	11.5	11.3	14.1
Participation rate, total[d]	61.8	62.6	63.5	63.8	63.7
Males 20 years and over	79.9	79.9	79.8	79.6	79.2
Females 20 years and over	47.4	48.6	50.1	51.0	51.4
Both sexes 16–19 years	54.4	56.8	58.4	58.1	56.4
White	62.1	62.9	63.7	64.1	64.1
Black and other	59.6	60.6	61.8	61.7	61.2

[a]Changes for 1978 IV adjusted for the increase of about 250,000 in employment and labor force in January 1978 resulting from changes in the sample and estimation procedures introduced into the household survey.

[b]Seasonally adjusted.

[c]Unemployment as percent of civilian labor force.

[d]Civilian labor force as percent of civilian noninstitutional population.

Source: *Economic Report of the President, 1981* (Washington, DC: U.S. Government Printing Office), 147, 149.

The Reagan Plan

Exhibit 8   Money Stock Measures and Liquid Assets: 1959–1981 (Averages of Daily Figures; Billions of Dollars; Seasonally Adjusted)

Year and Month	M1 Sum of Currency, Demand Deposits, Travelers' Checks, and Other Checkable Deposits (OCD)	M2 M1-B plus Overnight RPs and Eurodollars, MMMF Shares, and Savings and Small Time Deposits	M3 M2 plus Large Time Deposits and Term RPs	L M3 plus Other Liquid Assets	Percent Change from Year or 6 Months Earlier[a]		
					M1	M2	M3
December:							
1959	141.2	297.1	298.3	388.0	—	—	—
1960	142.2	311.7	313.7	402.9	0.7	4.9	5.2
1961	146.7	334.4	338.3	429.5	3.2	7.3	7.8
1962	149.4	361.7	368.7	465.0	1.8	8.2	9.0
1963	154.9	392.0	402.9	502.4	3.7	8.4	9.3
1964	162.0	423.4	438.7	538.9	4.6	8.0	8.9
1965	169.6	457.9	479.1	583.0	4.7	8.1	9.2
1966	173.8	479.2	502.9	614.6	2.5	4.7	5.0
1967	185.2	524.4	556.5	668.0	6.6	9.4	10.7
1968	199.5	567.1	606.2	731.7	7.7	8.1	8.9
1969	205.9	588.6	611.4	762.6	3.2	3.8	.9
1970	216.8	626.4	672.9	814.2	5.3	6.4	10.1
1971	231.0	711.1	771.1	900.7	6.5	13.5	14.6
1972	252.4	803.2	879.5	1,020.3	9.3	13.0	14.1
1973	266.4	859.8	977.9	1,140.3	5.5	7.0	11.2
1974	278.0	908.0	1,060.4	1,246.0	4.4	5.6	8.4
1975	291.8	1,024.4	1,163.0	1,373.5	5.0	12.8	9.7
1976	311.1	1,169.4	1,302.3	1,528.9	6.6	14.2	12.0
1977	336.4	1,296.4	1,462.5	1,722.7	8.1	10.9	12.3
1978	364.2	1,404.2	1,625.9	1,936.8	8.3	8.3	11.2
1979	390.5	1,525.2	1,775.6	2,151.7	7.2	8.6	9.2
1980	415.6	1,669.4	1,965.1	2,378.4	6.4	9.5	10.7
1981	441.9	1,841.2	2,187.2	—	6.3	10.3	11.3
1980:							
Jan.	392.7	1,538.7	1,792.0	2,175.3	5.6	7.7	9.2
Feb.	396.9	1,553.4	1,811.5	2,199.5	6.6	7.9	9.4
Mar.	396.7	1,559.6	1,819.1	2,210.9	5.4	7.1	7.9
Apr.	391.0	1,553.6	1,817.5	2,218.8	2.0	5.7	6.6
May	391.3	1,568.2	1,833.5	2,232.1	1.3	6.8	7.8
June	394.9	1,589.3	1,852.6	2,246.6	2.3	8.6	8.9
July	399.3	1,614.0	1,873.6	2,264.4	3.4	10.0	9.3
Aug.	406.9	1,633.4	1,897.4	2,291.3	5.1	10.6	9.7
Sept.	411.8	1,644.9	1,912.8	2,309.0	7.8	11.2	10.6
Oct.	416.3	1,654.0	1,928.3	2,326.0	13.4	13.3	12.6
Nov.	419.1	1,668.5	1,951.0	2,355.6	14.7	13.2	13.2
Dec.	415.6	1,669.4	1,965.1	2,378.4	10.8	10.3	12.5
1981:							
Jan.	419.2	1,680.8	1,989.3	2,408.7	10.2	8.4	12.7

[a]Monthly percent changes are from 6 months earlier at a compound annual rate.

Source: Board of Governors of the Federal Reserve System.

Exhibit 8 (Continued)

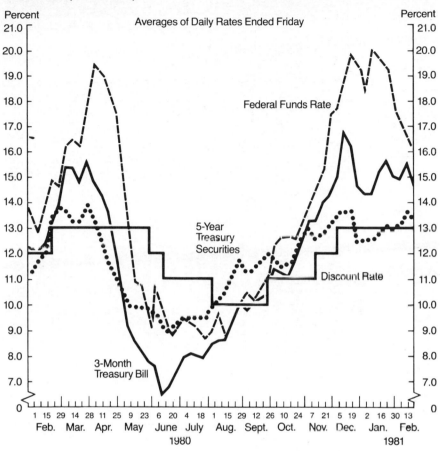

Averages of daily rates ended Friday.

The Reagan Plan

Exhibit 9 Federal Budget Receipts, Outlays, and Debt: Fiscal Years 1977–1982 (Millions of Dollars)

Description	Row Number	Actual				Estimate	
		1977	1978	1979	1980	1981	1982
Budget Receipts and Outlays:							
Total receipts	1	357,762	401,997	465,940	520,050	607,525	711,780
Federal funds	2	241,312	270,484	316,351	350,849	415,239	484,105
Trust funds	3	152,763	168,012	189,641	213,875	242,545	286,113
Interfund transactions	4	−36,313	−36,498	−40,052	−44,674	−50,259	−58,437
Total outlays	5	402,710	450,804	493,635	579,613	662,740	739,296
Federal funds	6	295,756	331,985	362,381	419,214	474,932	530,817
Trust funds	7	143,267	155,318	171,305	205,074	238,068	266,916
Interfund transactions	8	−36,313	−36,498	−40,052	−44,674	−50,259	−58,437
Total surplus or deficit (−)	9	−44,948	−48,807	−27,694	−59,563	−55,215	−27,516
Federal funds	10	−54,444	−61,804	−46,030	−68,364	−59,693	−46,712
Trust funds	11	9,496	12,694	18,335	8,801	4,477	19,196
Outstanding Debt, End of Period							
Gross federal debt	12	709,138	780,425	833,751	914,317	992,398	1,057,664
Held by government agencies	13	157,295	169,477	189,162	199,212	205,293	225,559
Held by the public	14	551,843	610,948	644,589	715,105	787,105	832,105
Federal Reserve System	15	105,004	115,480	115,594	120,846	—	—
Other	16	446,839	495,468	528,996	594,259	—	—

Exhibit 9 (Continued)

Budget Receipts							
Individual income taxes	17	357,762	401,997	465,940	520,050	607,525	711,780
Corporation income taxes	18	157,626	180,988	217,841	244,069	284,013	331,677
Social insurance taxes and contributions	19	54,892	59,952	65,677	64,600	66,009	64,648
	20	108,688	123,410	141,591	160,747	184,824	214,664
Excise taxes	21	17,548	18,376	18,745	24,329	44,393	69,633
Estate and gift taxes	22	7,327	5,285	5,411	6,389	6,909	7,668
Customs duties	23	5,150	6,573	7,439	7,174	7,439	7,800
Miscellaneous receipts:							
Deposits of earnings by Federal Reserve System	24	5,908	6,641	8,327	11,767	13,069	14,710
All other	25	622	772	910	975	899	980
Budget Outlays	26	402,710	450,804	493,635	579,613	662,740	739,296
National defense	27	97,501	105,186	117,681	135,856	161,088	184,399
International affairs	28	4,813	5,922	6,091	10,733	11,314	12,152
General science, space, and technology	29	4,677	4,742	5,041	5,722	6,258	7,590
Energy	30	4,172	5,861	6,856	6,313	8,739	11,973
Natural resources and environment	31	10,000	10,925	12,091	13,812	14,110	14,039
Agriculture	32	5,532	7,731	6,238	4,762	1,112	4,803
Commerce and housing credit	33	98	3,324	2,565	7,782	3,456	8,058
Transportation	34	14,636	15,445	17,459	21,120	24,054	21,551
Community and regional development	35	6,348	11,070	9,542	10,068	11,144	9,084
Education, training, employment, and social services	36	20,985	26,463	29,685	30,767	31,773	34,511
Health	37	38,785	43,676	49,614	58,165	66,032	74,636

(Continued)

Exhibit 9 (Continued)

Description	Row Number	Actual				Estimate	
		1977	1978	1979	1980	1981	1982
Budget Outlays (Continued)							
Income security	38	137,900	146,181	160,159	193,100	231,650	255,006
Veterans' benefits and services	39	18,038	18,974	19,928	21,183	22,591	24,462
Administration of justice	40	3,600	3,802	4,153	4,570	4,786	4,882
General government	41	3,169	3,706	4,093	4,505	5,170	5,246
General purpose fiscal assistance	42	9,499	9,601	8,372	8,584	6,854	6,902
Interest	43	38,009	43,966	52,556	64,504	80,405	89,946
Allowances	44	—	—	—	—	—	1,920
Undistributed offsetting receipts	45	−15,053	−15,772	−18,488	−21,933	−27,796	−31,863
Composition of undistributed offsetting receipts:							
Employer share, employee retirement	46	−4,548	−4,983	−5,271	−5,787	−6,561	−6,798
Interest received by trust funds	47	−8,131	−8,530	−9,950	−12,045	−13,435	−15,165
Rents and royalties on the Outer Continental Shelf	48	−2,374	−2,259	−3,267	−4,101	−7,800	−9,900

Note: Under provisions of the Congressional Budget Act of 1974, the fiscal year for the federal government shifted beginning with fiscal year 1977. Through fiscal year 1976, the fiscal year was on a July 1–June 30 basis. Beginning October 1976 (fiscal year 1977), the fiscal year is on an October 1–September 30 basis. The period July 1, 1976, through September 30, 1976, is a separate fiscal period known as the transition quarter.

Refunds of receipts are excluded from receipts and outlays.

See "Budget of the United States Government, Fiscal Year 1982" for additional information.

Source: *Economic Report of the President, 1981* (Washington, DC: U.S. Government Printing Office), 315.

The Reagan Plan

Exhibit 10 Governmental Surplus or Deficit and Gross National Product: 1958–1980 (Billions of Dollars)

| | Fiscal Years—Unified Budget | | Calendar Years—Government Sector, National Income and Product Accounts | | | |
| | Federal Surplus or Deficit (−)[a] | | Federal Surplus or Deficit (−) | | Federal and State and Local Surplus or Deficit (−) | |
Year	Amount	As Percent of GNP	Amount	As Percent of GNP	Amount	As Percent of GNP
1958	−2.9	−0.7	−10.3	−2.3	−12.6	−2.8
1959	−12.9	−2.7	−1.1	−0.2	−1.6	−0.3
1960	0.3	0.1	3.0	0.6	3.1	0.6
1961	−3.4	−0.7	−3.9	−0.7	−4.3	−0.8
1962	−7.1	−1.3	−4.2	−0.7	−3.8	−0.7
1963	−4.8	−0.8	0.3	0.1	0.7	0.1
1964	−5.9	−1.0	−3.3	−0.5	2.3	−0.4
1965	−1.6	−0.2	0.5	0.1	0.5	0.1
1966	−3.8	−0.5	−1.8	−0.2	−1.3	−0.2
1967	−8.7	−1.1	−13.2	−1.7	−14.2	−1.8
1968[b]	−25.2	−3.0	−6.0	−0.7	−6.0	−0.7
1969[b]	3.2	0.4	8.4	0.9	9.9	1.0
1970	−2.8	−0.3	−12.4	−1.2	−10.6	−1.1
1971	−23.0	−2.2	−22.0	−2.0	−19.4	−1.8
1972	−23.4	−2.1	−16.8	−1.4	−3.3	−0.3
1973	−14.9	−1.2	−5.6	−0.4	7.8	0.6
1974	−6.1	−0.4	−11.5	−0.8	−4.7	−0.3
1975	−53.2	−3.6	−69.3	−4.5	−63.8	−4.1
1976	−73.7	−4.5	−53.1	−3.1	−36.5	−2.1
1977	−53.6	−2.9	−46.4	−2.4	−18.3	−1.0
1978	−59.2	−2.8	−29.2	−1.4	−0.2	0
1979	−40.2	−1.7	14.8	−0.6	−11.9	0.5
1980[c]	−73.8	−2.9	−62.3	−2.4	−34.8	−1.3

[a]Includes off-budget outlays.
[b]A 10 percent income tax surcharge was introduced in July 1968—thus entering calendar year 1968 but fiscal year 1969.
[c]Preliminary.

Source: *Economic Report of the President, 1981* (Washington, DC: U.S. Government Printing Office), 41.

The Reagan Plan

Exhibit 11 Crowding-Out Average Federal and Federally Assisted Borrowing

	Volume ($ Billions)	Absorption Rate[a]	GNP Deflator	3-Month T-bills
1955–1969	$ 9.8	16.6%	2.6%	3.5%
1970–1979	58.1	24.9	6.6	6.3
1980	124.4	35.5	9.0	11.4
1981	154.5[b]	43.0[b]	9.1[b]	NA

[a]Proportion of all capital raised in nonfinancial sector of the U.S. credit markets.
[b]Estimates.

Source: White House fact sheet, Nov. 5, 1981.

The Reagan Plan

Exhibit 12   U.S. Balance of Payments, International Transactions: 1965–1980 (Millions of Dollars)

Year or Quarter	Merchandise[a,b]			Investment Income[c]			Net Military Transactions	Net Travel and Transportation Receipts	Other Services Net[c]	Balance on Goods and Services[c,d]	Remittances, Pensions, and Other Unilateral Transfers[a]	Balance on Current Account[c,d]
	Exports	Imports	Net Balance	Receipts	Payments	Net						
	1	2	3	4	5	6	7	8	9	10	11	12
1965	26,461	−21,510	4,951	7,436	−2,088	5,348	−2,122	−1,280	1,387	8,284	−2,854	5,431
1966	29,310	−25,493	3,817	7,526	−2,481	5,045	−2,935	−1,331	1,365	5,961	−2,932	3,029
1967	30,666	−26,866	3,800	8,021	−2,747	5,274	−3,226	−1,750	1,612	5,709	−3,125	2,584
1968	33,626	−32,991	635	9,368	−3,378	5,990	−3,143	−1,548	1,630	3,563	−2,952	611
1969	36,414	−35,807	607	10,912	−4,869	6,043	−3,328	−1,763	1,833	3,393	−2,994	399
1970	42,469	−39,866	2,603	11,746	−5,516	6,230	−3,354	−2,038	2,180	5,624	−3,294	2,330
1971	43,319	−45,579	−2,260	12,706	−5,436	7,270	−2,893	−2,345	2,495	2,268	−3,701	−1,434
1972	49,381	−55,797	−6,416	14,764	−6,572	8,192	−3,420	−3,063	2,766	−1,941	−3,854	−5,795
1973	71,410	−70,499	911	21,808	−9,655	12,153	−2,070	−3,158	3,184	11,021	−3,881	7,140
1974	98,306	−103,649	−5,343	27,587	−12,084	15,503	−1,653	−3,184	3,986	9,309	−7,186	2,124
1975	107,088	−98,041	9,047	25,351	−12,564	12,787	−746	−2,792	4,598	22,893	−4,613	18,280
1976	114,745	−124,051	−9,306	29,286	−13,311	15,975	559	−2,558	4,711	9,382	−4,998	4,384
1977	120,816	−151,689	−30,873	32,587	−14,598	17,989	1,628	−3,293	5,086	−9,464	−4,605	−14,068
1978	142,054	−175,813	−33,759	42,972	−22,073	20,899	886	−3,188	5,959	−9,204	−5,055	−14,259
1979	182,055	−211,524	−29,469	65,970	−33,460	32,510	−1,275	−2,695	5,806	4,878	−5,666	−788

Exhibit 12 (Continued)

1978:											
I	30,922	−42,063	−11,141	9,607	−4,539	5,068	441	−752	1,415	−4,969	−1,204	−6,173
II	35,404	−43,699	−8,295	9,957	−5,474	4,483	303	−752	1,466	−2,795	−1,307	−4,102
III	36,828	−44,336	−7,508	10,557	−5,717	4,840	139	−910	1,506	−1,933	−1,233	−3,166
IV	38,900	−45,715	−6,815	12,851	−6,343	6,508	3	−774	1,571	493	−1,313	−820
1979:											
I	41,805	−46,919	−5,114	14,263	−7,225	7,038	−29	−611	1,448	2,732	−1,324	1,408
II	42,815	−50,885	−8,070	15,250	−7,980	7,270	−102	−637	1,428	−110	−1,383	−1,493
III	47,198	−54,258	−7,060	18,050	−8,731	9,319	−443	−834	1,524	2,506	−1,407	1,099
IV	50,237	−59,462	−9,225	18,407	−9,524	8,883	−700	−613	1,405	−250	−1,552	−1,802
1980:											
I	54,708	−65,558	−10,850	20,846	−10,752	10,094	−922	−690	1,570	−798	−1,812	−2,610
II	54,710	−62,215	−7,505	16,641	−10,508	6,133	−994	−296	1,557	−1,105	−1,326	−2,431
III[e]	56,288	−59,116	−2,828	19,113	−10,646	8,467	−632	−248	1,618	6,377	−1,477	4,900

[a] Excludes military grants.

[b] Adjusted from census data for differences in valuation, coverage, and timing.

[c] Fees and royalties from U.S. direct investments abroad or from foreign direct investments in the United States are excluded from investment income and included in other services, net.

[d] In concept, balance on goods and services is equal to net exports and imports in the national income and product accounts (and the sum of balance on current account and allocations of special drawing rights is equal to net foreign investment in the accounts), although the series differ because of different handling of certain items (gold, extraordinary military shipments, etc.), revisions, etc.

[e] Preliminary data.

(Continued)

The Reagan Plan

Exhibit 12 (Continued)

Year or Quarter	U.S. Assets Abroad, Net Increase/Capital Outflow (−)				Foreign Assets in the U.S., Net [Increase/Capital Inflow (+)]				Statistical Discrepancy	
	Total	U.S. Official Reserve Assets[a]	Other U.S. Government Assets	U.S. Private Assets	Total	Foreign Official Assets Total	Other Foreign Assets	Allocations of Special Drawing Rights (SDRs)	Total (Sum of the Items with Sign (Reversed))	Of Which: Seasonal Adjustment Discrepancy
	13	14	15	16	17	18	19	20	21	22
1965	−5,715	1,225	−1,605	−5,335	742	134	607	—	−458	—
1966	−7,319	570	−1,543	−6,345	3,661	−672	4,333	—	629	—
1967	−9,758	53	−2,423	−7,387	7,379	3,451	3,928	—	−205	—
1968	−10,977	870	−2,274	−7,833	9,928	−774	10,703	—	438	—
1969	−11,585	−1,179	−2,200	−8,206	12,702	−1,301	14,002	—	−1,516	—
1970	−9,336	2,481	−1,589	−10,228	6,359	6,908	−550	867	−219	—
1971	−12,474	2,349	−1,884	−12,939	22,970	26,879	−3,909	717	−9,779	—
1972	−14,497	−4	−1,568	−12,925	21,461	10,475	10,986	710	−1,879	—
1973	−22,874	158	−2,644	−20,388	18,388	6,026	12,362	—	−2,654	—
1974	−34,745	−1,467	366	−33,643	34,241	10,546	23,696	—	−1,620	—
1975	−39,703	−849	−3,474	−35,380	15,670	7,027	8,643	—	5,753	—
1976	−51,269	−2,558	−4,214	−44,498	36,518	17,693	18,826	—	10,367	—
1977	−35,793	−375	−3,693	−31,725	50,741	36,575	14,167	—	−880	—
1978	−61,191	732	−4,644	−57,279	64,096	33,293	30,804	—	11,354	—
1979	−61,774	−1,133	−3,783	−56,858	37,575	−14,271	51,845	1,139	23,848	—

Exhibit 12 (Continued)

1978:										
I	−15,048	187	−1,009	−14,226	18,204	15,422	2,783	—	3,015	121
II	−5,749	248	−1,257	−4,740	775	−5,273	6,049	—	9,076	732
III	−9,977	115	−1,386	−8,706	17,069	4,777	12,292	—	−3,926	−2,850
IV	−30,418	182	−991	−29,609	28,048	18,368	9,680	—	3,190	1,998
1979:										
I	−7,768	−3,585	−1,102	−3,081	2,201	−8,744	10,945	1,139	3,020	74
II	−15,300	322	−991	−14,631	6,407	−10,095	16,502	—	10,385	1,167
III	−25,215	2,779	−766	−27,228	24,941	5,789	19,152	—	−825	−3,641
IV	−13,492	−649	−925	−11,918	4,025	−1,221	5,246	—	11,269	2,400
1980:										
I	−12,711	−3,268	−1,467	−7,976	7,194	−7,215	14,409	1,152	6,975	−99
II	−25,712	502	−1,191	−25,023	7,949	7,775	174	—	20,194	1,460
III[c]	−20,196	−1,109	−1,320	−17,767	11,003	8,025	2,978	—	4.293	−4,022

Note: Quarterly data for U.S. official reserve assets and foreign assets in the United States are not seasonally adjusted.

[a] Includes extraordinary U.S. government transactions with India.

[b] Consists of gold, special drawing rights, convertible currencies, and the U.S. reserve position in the International Monetary Fund.

[c] Preliminary data.

Source: *Economic Report of the President, 1981* (Washington, DC: U.S. Government Printing Office), 344.

The Reagan Plan

Exhibit 13   Selected International Comparisons, United States and Main Industrial Countries

Real GNP Growth in Major Industrial Countries, 1976–1982 (Percent Change from Previous Period; Seasonally Adjusted Annual Rates)

Country	1976-1979 Annual Average	1980 Year[a]	1980 Second Half[a]	1981 First Half[b]	1981 Second Half[b]	1982 First Half[b]
United States	3.9	− ¾	−1¾	1	2½	3½
Japan	5.9	5	2¾	4	4¼	4¾
Germany	3.8	1¾	−3	½	1½	2
France[c]	3.3	1¾	½	1	2	2¼
United Kingdom[c]	1.5	−2¼	−5¾	½	−2½	0
Italy[c]	3.2	3¾	−3½	−1¼	2¼	2½
Canada	2.9	− ½	− ½	1¾	2	3¼
Total of above countries	3.9	1	−1¼	1¼	2¼	3

[a]OECD estimate.

[b]OECD projection.

[c]Gross domestic product.

Changes in Industrial Production in Major Industrial Countries, 1970–1980 (Percent Change)

Country	To 1980 First Quarter from 1970	To 1980 First Quarter from 1976
Germany	29	15
France	36	10
United Kingdom	15	9
Japan	56	29
United States	41	16

Exhibit 13 (Continued)

Inflation in Major Industrial Countries, 1976–1982 (Percent Change in Prices)

Country	1976-1978 Annual Average	1979	1980	1981	1982 First Half
United States	6.2	8.9	10½	10	9½
Japan	5.5	3.1	6¼	5¼	5
Germany	3.2	3.9	5¼	4	3
France	9.4	10.9	13¾	11¾	9½
United Kingdom	11.7	12.2	15½	12	9
Italy	12.0	14.8	20¾	15¾	13½
Canada	9.8	9.1	9¾	10	9¾
Total of above countries	6.8	8.1	10½	9¼	8¼

Productivity

Country	Real Gross Domestic Product per Employed Person (Average Annual Percent Change)			
	1950–1979	1950–1965	1965–1973	1973–1979
United States	1.8	2.4	1.7	0.5
Canada	2.1	2.7	2.4	.4
France	4.3	4.8	4.5	2.9
Germany	4.8	5.6	4.3	3.1
Japan	6.9	7.2	9.1	3.4
United Kingdom	2.3	2.2	3.4	1.1

Source: *Economic Report of the President, 1981*, 30, 183, 189; U.S. Department of Labor, Bureau of Labor Statistics, *Bulletin 2084*, October 1981 (Washington, DC: U.S. Government Printing Office), 20.

Discussion Questions for Case

1. Evaluate the situation facing President Reagan in February 1981.
2. Does the Reagan strategy address the causes of the U.S. economic problems?
3. How was "Reaganomics" supposed to work in theory?
4. What economic, social, and political assumptions were made in the Stockman-Kemp memorandum and the first State of the Union address? To what extent were they valid?

Bibliography

Evans, Michael K., *The Truth About Supply-Side Economics* (New York: Basic Books, 1983). Evans, an economics forecaster long associated with Chase Econometrics, enumerates the myths and the truths about supply-side economics as he sees them. The reader will find both challenge and support for the various aspects of Reaganomics.

Fink, Richard H., ed., *Supply-Side Economics: A Critical Appraisal* (Frederick, MD: University Publications, 1982). This book of readings contains a number of short, readable articles on the supply side of Reaganomics. Chapter 1 presents the supply-side argument from the point of view of three leading supply-siders, Paul Craig Roberts, George Gilder, and Norman B. Ture. In Chapter 2 the critics speak, including Walter W. Heller, Robert Heilbroner, and Thomas Hazlett.

Tobin, James, "The Reagan Economic Plan: Supply Side, Budget, and Inflation," Federal Reserve Bank of San Francisco, *Economic Review* (April 1981). Professor Tobin, an early critic of Reaganomics, outlines the reasons for his opposition soon after the Reagan plan is announced. Part of this article may be difficult for those without a background in economics.

CHAPTER 10
A Supply-Side Tax Cut

President Reagan's landmark tax legislation, the Economic Recovery Tax Act (ERTA) of 1981, was the largest tax cut in U.S. history. It started as a simple proposal—cut personal income tax rates by 30 percent across the board and cut corporate income taxes by accelerating depreciation write-offs. Six months later, the bill was greatly altered and complicated as a result of the negotiations among the president, Congress, and business interests.

This chapter's case, "The Economic Recovery Tax Act of 1981," offers numerous comparisons with the two previous examples of tax cuts in Chapters 7 and 8. Like the tax cut of 1964, ERTA was initiated by the president to promote economic growth. But the rhetoric was different in 1981, although the impetus and apparent motivations were the same. ERTA was explicitly identified as a supply-side tax cut, untainted by the "failures" of the demand-side policies of the previous decade. As with the tax cut of 1978, business was supportive of the 1981 act, but the role of business had changed. Business interests were aligned with the president in 1981.

The central questions in this case are political and tactical: How well did the president, the Congress, and the business interests manage this legislation? The interests of the participants and their relative sources of power are the keys to understanding the dynamics of this legislation. The opportunities for changing the strategy and the institutional role of business or government in the tax process are also fruitful questions for discussion.

Case
The Economic Recovery Tax Act of 1981

It is time to create new jobs, build and rebuild industry, and give the American people room to do what they do best. And that can only be done with a tax program which provides incentives to increase productivity for both workers and industry.

President Ronald Reagan
State of the Union Address
February 19, 1981

Thus did President Reagan begin the political battle for passage of his controversial tax program. In combination with large reductions in federal spending, this tax plan was designed to spur investment, productivity, and economic growth—the "supply side" of the economy—by returning tax dollars to businesses and workers. Critics of Reagan's untested supply-side economics predicted in early 1981 that the president would never win the $53.9 billion reduction in corporate and individual taxes he sought for 1982, let alone the unprecedented reductions for succeeding years. After almost six months of congressional logrolling, intense pressure from business lobbyists, and frenetic legislative activity, the landmark tax package, known as the Economic Recovery Tax Act (ERTA) of 1981 was signed into law on August 13 by a triumphant President Reagan. Through a combination of rate reductions and new and enlarged tax expenditures,[1] the completed bill was expected to put $759 billion—more money than the federal government would spend in fiscal year 1982—back into the hands of individual and corporate taxpayers over the coming decade.[2]

Origins of the Reagan Tax Cut

The two pillars of ERTA, the accelerated depreciation write-offs for corporations and the across-the-board cuts in personal income tax rates, were present on June 24, 1980, when candidate Ronald Reagan first

This case was prepared by Research Assistant Nancy Koehn under the direction of Associate Professor Michael G. Rukstad.
Copyright © 1985 by the President and Fellows of Harvard College
Harvard Business School case 9–386–038

[1]Defined by the Congressional Budget and Impoundment Control Act of 1974, tax expenditures are those "revenue losses attributable to provisions of the Federal income tax laws that allow a special exclusion or deduction from gross income, or that provide a special credit, preferential tax rate, or deferral of tax liability."

[2]"Congress Enacts President Reagan's Tax Plan," *Congressional Quarterly Almanac* (Washington, DC, 1981): 91.

announced his tax plan to the nation. Reagan's proposals, which incumbent President Jimmy Carter labeled "nonsense," were very similar to tax bills being presented in Congress at that same time. One bill, entitled the "Capital Cost Recovery Act," or "10-5-3," would allow business to depreciate buildings and structural components over ten years, vehicles over five years, and qualified equipment and machinery over three years. Reagan and other proponents of this proposal promised that it would simplify recordkeeping by reducing the assets-depreciation classes, currently numbering 130, to only three and that it would mitigate the effects of inflation on after-tax real profits.[3] The other bill, entitled the "Tax-Reduction Job-Creation Act," promised to cut marginal tax rates—the rates at which an extra dollar of income is taxed—by 10 percent for 1982 only, bringing the 1980 rates ranging from 14 percent to 70 percent to a range of 12 percent to 63 percent for 1981 and beyond. Reagan's announcement of his tax plan brought serious media, legislative, and public attention to these two proposals that had been debated under various guises in Washington policy circles for several years.

Origin of Reagan's Business Tax Cut

Reagan's depreciation scheme, the "10-5-3" proposal, was originally conceived in 1978 by the Carlton group, which was an informal group of about ten business tax lobbyists. Named after the Sheraton-Carlton Hotel near the White House where these lobbyists had held their monthly meetings since 1975, the group represented both the largest, most powerful business lobbies in the nation's capital—the National Association of Manufacturers, the U.S. Chamber of Commerce, the Business Roundtable, and the National Federation of Independent Business—and more specialized business lobbies—the American Council for Capital Formation, the Committee for Effective Capital Recovery, the American Business Conference, the American Retail Federation, and General Electric Corporation.

The Carlton group first gained prominence in 1978 when it led the lobbying fight against Carter's tax reform proposals. With the help of other business-lobbying organizations, Carlton members, especially the American Council for Capital Formation, managed a well-orchestrated, successful effort to increase business tax benefits, most notably a significant reduction in capital gains tax rates. During the legislative battle for passage of the 1978 tax bill, Representative James Jones (D-Oklahoma) and Representative Barber Conable, Jr. (R-New York) of the House Ways and Means Committee approached Carlton group members with the idea

---

[3]After-tax real profits are excessively low during periods of inflation, because inflation increases gross profits but not the depreciation cost write-offs, which are based on historical (noninflated) costs of the assets. Therefore, taxable profits and taxes are larger in real terms than they would be during periods of no inflation.

of overhauling the current depreciation schedule. The congressmen told the group that they would support a new depreciation scheme if the group members could agree on such a schedule. Carlton group members began discussing alternatives to the current system, known as the Accelerated Depreciation Range (ADR). One important criterion guiding the group's debates was the necessity of creating a unified business position, a lesson learned from the 1978 capital gains victory. With a unified business position, "even implausible tax changes could be made politically palatable. When the capital gains reduction first was proposed, it had not been taken seriously; even its original House sponsor thought it would go nowhere. Instead, the capital gains cut not only passed, but the lobbying effort for it helped provide the momentum to defeat the rest of the Carter reform package."[4] With its priorities in mind, Carlton group members went about designing a depreciation scheme that would reduce taxes for almost every business sector and that would be easily communicated and understood.

After several weeks of debate, the Carlton group presented Conable and Jones with the 10–5–3 plan, in much the same form in which it would appear in the 1980 bill. In altering the depreciation rules, Jones, Conable, and Carlton group members responded to the growing public perception that America was facing a capital formation problem. Charls Walker, head of the American Council for Capital Formation and one of the chief authors of 10–5–3, explained the public-policy context of the plan's beginnings:

We saw the beginning of this attitude change (towards a public concern with capital formation) in 1978 with the capital gains legislation. . . . The 1978 capital gains legislation showed that the American middle class has political clout and that these people care about capital formation. They are capitalists. . . . In the late 1970s, Jones and Conable gave us a chance to do something about the capital cost recovery system. This action was indicative of several things: the emergence of the capital formation problem, the belief that the tax system had something to do with it, the international competitiveness aspect of capital formation, the emergence of the middle class as interested in capital formation, and the growing interest of corporate America in tax issues.[5]

Origin of Reagan's Personal Tax Cut

While Carlton group members were debating depreciation schemes, Representative Jack Kemp (R-New York) and Senator William Roth, Jr. (R-Delaware) were calling for a three-year, 30 percent across-the-board cut in rates, based on the Kennedy tax cut of 1964. (See Chapter 6.) An early

---

[4]Robert S. McIntyre and Dean C. Tipps, *Inequity and Decline* (Washington, DC: Center for Budget and Policy Priorities, 1983), 52.

[5]Interview with Charls Walker, May 16, 1984.

public proponent of supply-side economics, Kemp maintained that cutting marginal tax rates would act as a powerful incentive for Americans to work harder and save more, thereby stimulating economic growth. "Generally speaking, if you tax something, you get less of it. If you subsidize something, you get more of it. In America, we tax work, growth, investment, employment, savings and productivity, while subsidizing nonwork, consumption, welfare and debt,"[6] explained Kemp.

The major criticism of the tax cut proposal was that it would exacerbate the country's deficit problems. A faster-growing economy, Kemp and Roth countered, would increase government revenues despite lower tax rates because there would be additional personal and business income to tax. Kemp used the "Laffer curve" to substantiate his claim. The Laffer curve, popularly ascribed to the University of Southern California economist Arthur Laffer, illustrates the relationship between marginal tax rates and total tax revenues. If marginal tax rates are zero, there will be no tax revenue, and if marginal tax rates are 100 percent, there will also be no tax revenue since nobody will attempt to earn income that will be entirely confiscated by the government. At some marginal tax rate between the extremes, the maximum tax revenue will be achieved. At marginal tax rates higher than the maximum revenue point, the "prohibitive range," higher rates result in lower revenues by retarding the tax base. Kemp and Roth placed the 1978 marginal tax rates in the prohibitive range. Therefore cutting tax rates, by their logic, would result in more economic activity and greater revenues.

Kemp was originally converted to tax reduction as a means of stimulating economic activity by *The Wall Street Journal* reporter Jude Wanniski in late 1976. Paul Craig Roberts, a conservative economist on the staff of the House Budget Committee, helped Wanniski, Kemp, and Roth write the tax bill during the following year.[7] Kemp spent much of 1977 and 1978 publicizing the bill to legislators, business groups, even labor audiences. "For the first time in a half century, a Republican had a *positive* response to big-government liberalism. Although Republican politicians tended to doubt the validity of 'supply-side' economics, they recognized its political utility for a party out of power."[8] In late 1977, the Republican National Committee endorsed the Kemp-Roth bill as party policy, and in 1978 Kemp introduced the measure as an amendment to the omnibus tax bill being debated in the House. Although the Kemp-Roth amendment lost on a party-line vote in the House, it received extensive media and legislative attention. Almost overnight, the Kemp-Roth tax cut became one of the parameters of America's ongoing economic debate.

The passage on June 6, 1978, of California's Proposition 13 fed

[6]Quoted in *Fortune*, Apr. 10, 1978, 37.

[7]Source From *The Reagan Revolution* by Rowland Evans and Robert Novak, pp. 64–66. Copyright © 1981 by Rowland Evans, Jr., and Robert Novak. Reprinted by permission of the publisher, E. P. Dutton, a division of NAL Penguin Inc.

public interest in tax reduction. Proposition 13, a state referendum to slash state and local taxes and services, was approved by state voters by an overwhelming margin. Labeling the proposition's passage as the beginning of an American taxpayers' revolt, reporters (and legislators) went looking for reasons for voters' dissatisfaction with taxes. The primary explanation was the rampant inflation of the mid-1970s that pushed the incomes of most taxpayers into higher marginal tax brackets.

Presidential Candidate Reagan's Adoption of a Tax Proposal

In 1978, John Sears also saw the significance of the tax reduction movement. As campaign manager for Ronald Reagan, he perceived the tax-cutting issue as the most important one of the 1980 presidential campaign, an issue that would make Reagan acceptable to the ordinary voter. He went about co-opting the issue for his candidate. Sears contacted Peter Hannaford, a speech writer for Reagan and one of his few aides interested in the appeal of supply-side economics. In May 1978, Hannaford met with Kemp. Kemp said he planned to support Reagan and he expressed interest in having the candidate support the Kemp-Roth tax cut. Reagan himself was initially ambivalent about cutting taxes:

> On the one hand, the Kemp-Roth bill appealed to Reagan's tax-cutting instincts dating back to his early days at Warner Brothers. Unlike many politicians who had spent their entire careers in public service, he understood the incentives and disincentives that affect the private entrepreneur; he knew how the prohibitively high tax rates after World War II deterred him from making more than one or two films a year and how the progressive tax system had ruined the movie industry by discouraging production. He was well aware of the supply-side arguments authored regularly by Bartley and Wanniski on the editorial page of *The Wall Street Journal*, but was probably even more aware of the pleas for Kemp-Roth in the right-wing weekly *Human Events*, perhaps Reagan's favorite periodical.
>
> On the other hand, Reagan could not quite sever his affection for what Laffer called "deep root canal" economics—that is, economics based on the theory that like deep root canal oral surgery, economic austerity *must* be good for you if it is truly painful. For half a century, sadomasochistic Republican orators had promised pain and suffering to voters and, appropriately, had been rewarded with defeat at the polls. After the 1976 election, Reagan's special version of this was to warn that the nation faced a big "bellyache" of unemployment and recession as punishment for its inflationary binge. By 1978, Hannaford was doing his best to remove the "bellyache" from Reagan's repertoire.[9]

[9]Ibid., 69.

Reagan promoted the Kemp-Roth tax cut proposal in late 1978 during the Republican midterm elections and on into 1979. By late 1979, Reagan was not only stressing the importance of tax reduction, he was also talking about the ideas of a "young congressman from New York—Jack Kemp." His speeches sounded more and more like those of the New York representative. Reagan attacked Carter's ephemeral balanced budget, saying " 'anybody can balance the budget by raising taxes, and inflation is a tax.' Tax rates, rising because of inflation, constitute 'a penalty imposed on working men and women.' Tax rate reduction is another way to balance the budget and another way to end inflation. . . ."[10] By the end of the year, Reagan had distanced himself from his Republican rivals who embraced Carter's budget-balancing attempts through higher taxes.

After Reagan lost to George Bush in the Iowa caucuses in early 1980, he fired John Sears, the man who had brought supply-side economics to the campaign. Kemp, Laffer, and other supply-side proponents worried that their theories would atrophy without Sears in the Reagan camp. But two factors kept the doctrine alive and strong in the 1980 campaign. One was the success of a series of Reagan commercials made in January 1980, showing the candidate explaining and endorsing the need for a tax cut. The second factor was the candidate himself. He had, over the last 18 months, become as committed as Jack Kemp to the doctrines of supply-side economics.

One person impressed with his commitment to tax reduction was Washington lobbyist Charls Walker of the Carlton group. Like many of his corporate clients, Walker favored John Connally over Reagan and favored liberalized depreciation for corporations over across-the-board tax cuts for individuals. But always a pragmatist, Walker joined the Reagan camp as an outside adviser in the spring of 1980 after Connally had flopped in the primaries. Walker began reviewing Reagan's tax policies. On June 20, Reagan met in Chicago with big-business supporters and economic advisers, including Walker. Martin Anderson, one of the candidate's key policy aides, did not attend and neither did Jack Kemp. Seizing an important opportunity, Walker warned Reagan that he would have to move quickly on the tax issue before Carter acted to slash individual or corporate taxes. He presented Reagan with a simple tax reduction package: a one-year 10 percent personal income tax cut with liberalized business depreciation schedules attached. Reagan thought Walker's plan was a great one.[11]

On June 23, Kemp and Congressman David Stockman (R-Michigan) were called to a Washington meeting on Republican strategy. There they were given a tax policy statement, written chiefly by Walker, that eliminated the last two years of the Kemp-Roth cuts and included a

[10]Ibid., 71.
[11]Ibid., 79.

lengthy section on liberalized depreciation allowances. To appease Kemp, who was furious about the erasure of the last two years of cuts, Stockman rewrote the tax statement, pledging two more years of tax reduction and making a fuzzy commitment to Walker's depreciation plan. Reagan allowed this bargaining and compromising to proceed, and then the next day he made public his tax plan, which was a product of the latest compromise between the candidate's advisers. Reagan, while clearly committed to the philosophical underpinnings of supply-side economics, was also very vague about the details of implementing this new economic theory.

During the last few months of the campaign, President Carter, who was holed up in the White House trying to solve the hostage crisis in Iran, had little time or opportunity to attack his challenger's tax policies. Carter was kept on the defensive by Reagan's criticisms of his economic and foreign policy initiatives. The issues of inflation and the hostages overrode all else as voters went to the polls November 4 to give Ronald Reagan an undeniable mandate for his fiscal revolution. John Sears' gamble in seizing the tax reduction issue for Ronald Reagan had paid off.

Implementing Reagan's Campaign Promise

In the weeks following the election, Reagan named his cabinet and policy advisers, only a few of whom were ardent supply-siders. "Even if the supply-siders were not totally in control, there was no robust alternative in contention to either their overall philosophical thrust or their tax theory. Ronald Reagan's own determination guaranteed that."[12] Preparation began immediately for the presentation of the president's tax reduction plan to Congress in February. David Stockman, appointed director of the Office of Management and Budget, was worried about the prospect of a $100 billion deficit in fiscal year 1982, so he wanted to move back the effective date of the tax cut from a retroactive date of January 1, 1981, to July 1, 1981. Both Kemp and Stockman recommended that the Kemp-Roth proposal be enhanced by an immediate economic stimulus— the lowering of the 70 percent marginal tax rate on unearned income to 50 percent— since, they argued, the stock and bond markets would benefit enormously. Walker's 10–5–3 depreciation scheme became part of the president's package without any alterations, despite the objections of Kemp and other supply-side purists. Kemp thought 10–5–3 was another tax shelter for large corporations, a benefit that would not really help the nation's entrepreneurs. In the last few days before Reagan's February 18 address to Congress, the president was talked out of the immediate drop in tax rates on unearned income by Martin Anderson, domestic policy adviser. The remainder of Reagan's tax package stayed intact.[13] Almost

[12]Ibid., 104–105.
[13]Ibid., 85.

a month after his inauguration, Reagan presented his tax program to Congress, requesting a cut in individual income tax rates of 10 percent a year for three years and 10–5–3's liberalized depreciation allowances.

The individual rate cuts, once fully enacted, would eliminate the divergence between tax treatment of earned income, taxed under existing law in 1981 at a maximum rate of 50 percent, and unearned income from stocks and bonds, taxed at a top rate of 70 percent. Once the top marginal rate on unearned income dropped to 50 percent following the 30 percent cut in marginal rates, taxpayers would, administration officials maintained, be more likely to save a greater percentage of their income. In fact, Reagan officials believed the tax cuts would lead to a 2 percent increase in the rate of savings, for a total increase of approximately $55 billion. These savings, they claimed, would help finance the deficit without speeding up money supply growth.

If tax cuts were not enacted, "federal taxes would consume a rapidly increasing share of the national income—rising to 23.4 percent of GNP after 1986."[14] According to Treasury officials, tax receipts under the president's program would drop to 20.4 percent of GNP in 1982 and to 19.3 percent in 1985. The estimated cost of the individual cuts was $42 billion in 1982, rising to $215 billion in fiscal 1986. Over the next five years, the tax cuts would cost approximately $626 billion in lost revenue to the Treasury.[15] The president's simplified depreciation plan would, its proponents maintained, "provide the investment needed to create millions of new jobs between now and 1986 and to make America competitive once again in world markets."[16] Once enacted, the business tax breaks under 10–5–3 would be retroactive to January 1, 1981. The new depreciation scheme was expected to cost $188 billion through 1986.[17]

Rostenkowski's Democratic Offensive against Reagan's Tax Cut Proposal

Although most of Congress, as well as the business community, cheered Reagan's call for spending reductions, legislators were less than enthusiastic about the president's request for tax cuts. The reason for congressional skepticism regarding the tax cuts "stemmed partly from Reagan's prosaic rhetoric to describe a radical and exciting new departure [for economic policy]—endorsing 'incentives' to increase productivity for both workers and industry. But it also reflected the decision by the Democrats, and not a few Democrats, to oppose the Reagan Revolution on this

[14]Ibid.

[15]Joint Committee on Taxation, *General Explanation of the Economic Recovery Tax Act of 1981* (Washington, DC: U.S. Government Printing Office, December 1981), 381.

[16]*Congressional Quarterly Almanac,* op. cit.

[17]Joint Committee on Taxation, op. cit.

ground, not on budget cuts."[18] Despite widespread congressional and public mistrust of the efficacy of the Reagan tax proposals, it was, ironically, the personal and party politics in the Democrat-controlled House Ways and Means Committee that would give the president's tax proposal its biggest impetus toward enactment.

Early in 1981, the newly appointed chairman of the House Ways and Means Committee, Dan Rostenkowski (D-Illinois) decided to use the tax bill before Congress to prove his influence over tax policy to the new administration.

The legacy of the Ways and Means chair weighed heavily on the 53-year-old Rostenkowski. For the 17 years since 1958, Wilbur Mills (D-Arkansas) ruled the Ways and Means Committee, setting the standard against which future chairmen would be measured. Mills sought to build a congressional consensus after giving a full hearing to a president's requests and to the views of committee members. When Mills announced a specific plan, he almost always won bipartisan support.[19] Al Ullman (D-Oregon), who succeeded Mills as chairman, had less ability to build viable coalitions. Ullman lost his congressional seat in 1980. Rostenkowski was interested in proving that he was from the Mills school of governance rather than the Ullman school. By creating a tax bill that bore his influence rather than President Reagan's, and by building the House coalitions necessary to assure its passage, Rostenkowski hoped to solidify his own power within Congress and in the eyes of White House officials.

The Ways and Means chairman also had a secondary goal in mind—one that reinforced the first—as he entered the legislative battle for passage of the tax bill: he wanted to "earn" important campaign contributions for Democratic congressional candidates. Toward this end, he met early in 1981 with Richard Kline, a lobbyist for a group of independent oil dealers in Texas, Oklahoma, Kansas, and Colorado, and Representative Tony Coelho (D-California), new chairman of the Democratic Congressional Campaign Committee, to discuss how to attract more independent oil money to Democratic congressional campaigns. (Independent oil money had flowed into congressional campaigns in unprecedented amounts in 1980. More than 95 percent of this money went to Republican candidates.) Kline proposed that the 1981 tax bill include benefits for independent oil dealers. Rostenkowski agreed to support this idea if the votes of enough conservative Democrats who had supported Reagan—mostly from the South and Southwest—could be found to go along with it.

While several Democratic representatives began the process of getting commitments from conservative Democrats on tax benefits for oil and other industries, Rostenkowski set out to draft a Democratic bill that

[18]Evans and Novak, op. cit., 108–109.
[19]John Manley, *The Politics of Finance* (Boston: Little, Brown, 1970), 380.

Reagan could not veto. Rostenkowski knew that his bill would have to contain some tax reduction, but he and other Democratic leaders hoped to craft a bill that avoided the huge revenue losses and the regressivity of across-the-board tax rate cuts.[20] On March 10, Representative William Brodhead (D-Michigan) introduced a bill to end the distinction between earned and unearned income. Brodhead's measure effectively lowered the top rate on unearned income from 70 percent to 50 percent, a proposal Reagan had originally championed but eventually rejected on the advice of his political staff. Rostenkowski supported Brodhead's bill, as did other Democratic leaders.

On March 30, 1981, John Hinckley, Jr., tried to assassinate Ronald Reagan in Washington, DC. The president's popularity soared in the days following the assassination attempt, and by early April it had become clear that any alternative to Reagan's sacrosanct multiyear across-the-board tax cuts would meet stiff opposition in the Republican-controlled Senate and among conservative Democrats. Nevertheless, Rostenkowski was determined to seize the initiative.

On April 9, Rostenkowski announced his own tax reduction plan, one that he said "strikes that essential political and economic balance to pass Congress" while preserving the spirit of the president's plan.[21] The House Ways and Means Committee chairman called for a one-year tax cut of $40 billion, $28 billion of which would go to individuals and $12 billion to businesses. The $40 billion revenue-loss figure was close to the $38 billion target set by the House Budget Committee in drafting the first fiscal 1982 budget resolution. Under Rostenkowski's proposal, all taxpayers' marginal rates would be reduced—not as sharply as the president's 10 percent rate reduction—and income brackets would be widened to retard bracket creep. These reductions were targeted chiefly at taxpayers in the $20,000 to $50,000 income range, although the standard deduction and earned income credit were increased under the Democratic plan to help low-income taxpayers. The chairman's plan also incorporated Brodhead's bill for a reduction in the top rate on unearned income from 70 percent to 50 percent and an easing of the marriage penalty, two proposals with long-standing GOP support. Although Rostenkowski did not present a specific depreciation plan, he promised a liberalization of business depreciation schedules.

Republicans' reaction to Rostenkowski's proposal was generally negative, despite the conservative nature of his plan. Secretary of the Treasury Regan called the tax cuts "puny," while Ways and Means Committee Republican Barber Conable said the proposal was not the consensus bill Rostenkowski maintained it was. Reagan, well aware of his popularity in Congress and among the American people, announced he

---

[20]A regressive tax is one whose burdens fall disproportionately on the lower-income taxpayers; it is the opposite of a progressive tax.

[21]Quoted in *Congressional Quarterly Almanac*, op. cit., 96.

would not retreat from his call for large multiyear individual and business tax cuts.

Despite many business leaders' misgivings about Reagan's individual tax cuts and their revenue effects on the federal deficit, most of the business community supported the administration's tax proposal over that of Rostenkowski. Carlton group members, creators of 10–5–3, were anxious to see their plan enacted into law and thus took the initiative in enlisting and sustaining support for the president's tax package. Throughout the late spring and summer of 1981, the group served as a coordinator of business lobbying support for the tax plan.

In interviews with journalists, Carlton group members took pains to dispel any impression that they made legislative policy, set strategy, or imposed discipline. They preferred to characterize their activities as "information sharing." Nevertheless, the group not only performed that crucial task of shaping a tax plan behind which business could unite, but helped to keep business in line behind that plan. . . . The group "persuaded most of the business lobbying community—often by appealing to the solidarity of their superiors in corporate headquarters—to postpone their more parochial legislative wishes."[22]

The President's Expanded Tax Proposal

In May, as business lobbyists tried to increase support for the president's tax plan, concern in the press and in Congress began to build about the president's business tax cuts. The capital write-offs allowed under the depreciation plan, known as the Accelerated Cost Recovery System (ACRS), were so generous that, in combination with the investment tax credit, "they fully sheltered from taxation the income produced by most types of new investments, and produced an overflow of write-offs that could be used to shelter other income from taxation as well. ACRS was designed to produce, by 1986, an average effective corporate tax rate on profits from new investments of *negative* 63 percent."[23] The press jumped on this aspect of the ACRS depreciation scheme. "The corporate income tax is well on its way to extinction," noted *Business Week*. The "false logic of 10–5–3," which "would give rise to outright tax subsidies," is the "darkest cloud over Washington," *Fortune* said.[24] Both Senate and House members became worried both about the equity of tax subsidies and the total cost of the president's depreciation scheme, estimated at $500 billion over the 1980s. In late May, Treasury Secretary Donald Regan announced that the defects of ACRS would be corrected.

On June 4, the administration presented a revised tax bill, designed

[22]Ian Maitland, "House Divided: Business Lobbying and the 1981 Budget," *Research in Corporate Social Performance and Policy*, volume 5, (1983): 9–10.

[23]Quoted in McIntyre and Tipps, op. cit., 40 and 41.

[24]Ibid., 55.

to deflect the increasingly critical attention focused on ACRS while simultaneously appeasing proponents of the original depreciation scheme by the addition of several new tax "sweeteners." The revised tax plan weakened ACRS by slowing the period over which businesses would be allowed to depreciate buildings. The original bill permitted businesses to write off the cost of commercial buildings over 10 years; the June 4 package changed this allotted period to 15 years. It also reduced the accelerated depreciation that the original plan would have allowed in the early years of an investment's life. All told, the June 4 revision scaled back 10–5–3's benefits by almost a third over the next decade, leaving effective tax rates only "slightly negative."[25]

To appease the business interests upset by the reduction in 10–5–3 benefits, and to attract the support of several conservative Democrats on the House Ways and Means Committee, the administration added 11 additional provisions to the tax bill that Reagan had originally wanted to enact "cleanly." Nearly all of these provisions were designed to appeal to a specific interest or economic group:

- For business leaders, angered by the ACRS scale-backs, the administration offered a reduction in the maximum tax rate levied against unearned income from 70 to 50 percent.
- For high-technology firms, which claimed they would gain little from ACRS in either form, the new package offered a 25 percent tax credit for increases in direct wages attributable to research and development.
- For executives employed by companies doing business abroad, persons working overseas could exclude for U.S. tax purposes the first $50,000 of their income taxable by other nations and half of the next $50,000.
- For farmers and small-business executives who said they could not afford to keep their assets within their families because of high taxes, the ceiling on estate income exempt from taxes was gradually raised from $175,000 to $600,000, and the annual exclusion for gifts was increased from $3,000 to $10,000.
- For the conservative Democrats on the Ways and Means Committee and in the House at large—men who ultimately held the votes that would decide whether the administration or Rostenkowski's bill was enacted—Reagan granted an increased credit to oil-royalty owners against the windfall profits tax on oil revenue. Some 30 Democratic members of the House were from the three big oil-producing states of Texas, Louisiana, and Oklahoma.
- For individual taxpayers, the administration offered an easing of the "marriage penalty" on two-income families, and an increase in

[25]Ibid., 56.

the maximum annual tax-exempt contribution to individual retirement accounts (IRAs).

Finally, the administration revised the timing and amount of the first
individual tax cut from a 10 percent cut scheduled originally for July 1,
1981, to a 5 percent cut scheduled for October 1, 1981, with the two
remaining across-the-board cuts to be effective by July 1, 1983. In sum,
the revisions to the individual and business tax reductions promised to
save the Treasury approximately $29 billion over the cost of the presi-
dent's original bill.[26]

Business's Successful Counterattack

The business community reacted almost instantly to the administration's
revised tax plan, focusing its anger on the reduction in ACRS benefits.
"Business lobbyists had not been party to the negotiations between the
administration and the House Democrats, and when the new plan was
announced it was greeted with the sense of betrayal. The Chamber's chief
economist called it 'a breach of faith with the business community.' "[27]
Washington lobbyists quickly mobilized the CEOs of America's largest
corporations to fly to the capital to protest the scale-back in depreciation
benefits. The Business Roundtable held an emergency meeting the weekend of June 7 and 8. Business lobbyists from various sectors threatened
to withdraw their support of the Reagan program and turn to Rostenkowski, who had indicated his willingness to provide tax benefits to business as generous as those of the original ACRS. During June 7 and 8,
two days nicknamed the "Lear Jet Weekend" for all the corporate planes
that flew into Washington, scores of business leaders arrived in the capital
to lobby Treasury and White House officials to keep all of 10–5–3's original benefits.

On Monday, June 9, the administration announced it was restoring
to ACRS all of its former provisions, keeping the tax sweeteners announced in the June 4 package, *and* adding additional tax benefits to the
proposal, including the "safe-harbor" leasing provision that would allow
profitable corporations to buy tax credits from distressed businesses that
could not otherwise use these tax benefits. Lobbyists for distressed industries like the railroads and airlines had long advocated the refunda-
bility of investment tax credits, but Reagan's February budget failed to
include this provision. In the first week of June, the House Ways and
Means Committee had "approved a proposal to allow companies in six
distressed industries to reclaim unused investment tax credits (ITCs).

---

[26]Richard E. Cohen, "A Reagan Victory on His Tax Package Could Be a Costly One Politically," *The National Journal* (June 13, 1981): 1061.

[27]Maitland, op. cit., 10.

The administration responded by dangling the prospect of liberalized leasing rules before lobbyists for the industries, apparently in a move to head off defections by major money-losing companies tempted by the Ways and Means bill. . . ."[28] The inclusion of safe-harbor leasing in the administration's June 9 package was "one of the key concessions . . . to keep the business community fully behind the Reagan tax plan."[29]

The administration's vacillating posture on ACRS and other tax provisions threatened the Carlton group's strategy of unwavering support for the president's bill. House Ways and Means Committee Democrats contacted Carlton group members and other business lobbyists to solicit support for their own tax plans. But no Carlton group member deviated from the coalition's prearranged strategy to keep business support behind the president. According to the group's de facto chairman, breaking ranks "was an option no one wanted to take; the group believed a 'bidding war' over tax legislation could lessen the chances of winning what it wanted."[30]

A Bidding War

Reagan and his administration had originally wanted a "clean" bill, a tax package free of additional incentives or "sweeteners." The president envisioned the final bill as simply the three-year across-the-board tax cuts and ACRS. But the administration's revised package, announced June 9, with its restoration of 10–5–3 benefits and its additional tax sweeteners for business and individuals, challenged Rostenkowski, who was eager for a political victory over the administration, to devise a tax bill even more attractive to conservative House Democrats. This chaotic competition for a handful of House votes, played out in the tax-writing committees of the Congress, quickly proved irresistible to certain business lobbyists. " 'Reagan's negotiating signaled to some industries and their allies in Congress that it was now acceptable to step up efforts for their provisions.' Although the major business organizations continued to urge restraint, business's united front in support of a clean tax bill was irretrievably breached."[31] Special-interest business lobbyists hurried to make House Democrats, administration officials, and tax-writing committee members aware of what they wanted in the 1981 bill. A political bidding war erupted between the administration and Rostenkowski, with each side trying to promise special-interest groups more in an attempt to win

[28]Ibid., 20.

[29]Thomas Edsall, "How a Lobbyist Group Won a Business Tax Cut," *Washington Post*, Jan. 1, 1982, Sec. G, 1.

[30]Kenneth H. Bacon, "In Tax Cut Fight, 'No-Name' Group Lobbies Hard for Business Viewpoint," *The Wall Street Journal*, June 23, 1981, 23.

[31]Bill Keller, "Democrats and Republicans Try to Outbid Each Other in Cutting Taxes for Business," *Congressional Quarterly Weekly Reports* (June 22, 1981): 406–408.

the swing votes of some 30 House Democrats and a handful of Republican members. The final bill that resulted in August of 1981 resembled a Christmas tree with a tax bauble for every special interest and with little, if any, relation to economic recovery.

Pressuring the House Ways and Means Committee to act quickly on tax legislation, the Senate Finance Committee, under the chairmanship of Senator Robert Dole (R-Kansas), began marking up its own tax bill in mid-June. The Senate Committee attached its tax cut package to a House-passed debt limit measure, a maneuver that made it possible to circumvent the constitutional mandate that revenue-raising bills originate in the House. Dole denied that he was trying to upstage the Ways and Means Committee on its tax-writing privileges, but said he had learned as a Boy Scout "to be prepared."[32] What Dole did not say was that in initiating Senate action on a revenue measure, he was trying to push Rostenkowski into swift action on a House bill. Rostenkowski, intent on gauging the political climate as accurately as possible, had shown no inclination to quickly produce a Democratic tax package. The administration, on the other hand, wanted a speedy enactment of the president's tax proposals so that the individual rate cuts could go into effect October 1, and White House officials had made their wishes known to the Finance Committee chairman. Dole was willing to take technical liberties with the legislative process to ensure speedy passage of the president's tax bill.

The Senate Finance Committee debated just four days on the tax measure, adopting a package very similar to the administration bill proposed June 9. The additions to the Finance Committee bill reflected the input of various business lobbyists. Bowing to the vigorous pressure of the U.S. League of Savings, which represents most of the nation's 4,700 savings and loan institutions (S&Ls), the Finance Committee added a provision to the administration bill on June 22 that allowed mutual banks, credit unions, and savings and loan institutions to issue one-year, tax-exempt certificates, the so-called "all-savers" certificates, which would earn 70 percent of the yield on a one-year Treasury bill. Individuals could exclude up to $1,000 of the certificate interest from their incomes; couples could exclude up to $2,000. The certificates would be issued for one year only, from October 1, 1981, through September 30, 1982. Although the industry's campaign made early headway in Congress, the administration initially refused to consider any form of aid to S&Ls. "Well, the thrifts are losing money. So what?" said Treasury Secretary Regan.[33] But the day after the Senate Finance Committee approval, the administration formally abandoned its opposition to the all-savers certificates. According to estimates by the Joint Committee on Taxation, this provision of the Finance Committee bill was expected to cost the Treasury approximately $4.6 billion in lost government revenue by 1984.

[32]*Congressional Quarterly Almanac* (Washington, DC, 1981), 97–98.
[33]Quoted in Maitland, op. cit., 17.

Pressure from the American Electronics Association (AEA) and the American Business Conference (ABC) resulted in another Finance Committee addition to the administration bill on the following day, June 23. The committee voted, over the opposition of the administration, to liberalize the tax on stock options given employees as part of their work benefits and to increase tax credits for company contributions to employee stock ownership plans (ESOPs). For the previous three years, the AEA had been lobbying for a liberalization of the tax treatment of stock options. Specifically, the organization wanted the taxation of company stock options granted to executives to be deferred until the sale of the stock, rather than be imposed at the time the option was received or exercised, as present law held.[34] Although both the AEA and the ABC initially endorsed Reagan's call for a clean tax bill, by June the letter-writing campaigns and personal visits to Washington of almost 200 executives were bearing fruit.

Some member companies began calling the AEA to ask "What's this grass roots lobbying? I thought we were supporting the president." The association's chief lobbyist explained that the president himself had opened the bidding. The turning point was when the president officially began negotiating. It was obvious that the only things that would have a chance of getting in [the bill] were things that people had an opportunity to hear about.[35]

The representatives of independent oil producers, always eager to be heard, were not to be outdone by the other Washington lobbyists. They too won an important concession in the Finance Committee bill in mid-June. In addition to the $2,500 exclusion granted to oil-royalty owners against the windfall profits tax—a sweetener added to the administration's modified package of June 9 in order to woo oil-state Democrats to the Reagan bill—the Senate Finance Committee approved a gradual decrease in the windfall profits tax on newly discovered oil from the rate of 30 percent in 1981 to 15 percent in 1986. The administration, now paying no more than lip service to the concept of a clean bill, looked the other way. Independent oil dealers, however, were dissatisfied with the Finance Committee concession, calling it a "sop." Dole tried to "cool them off" by arranging a meeting between them and Reagan. Industry lobbyists were not mollified, so they turned their attention to Rostenkowski and the House Ways and Means Committee in an attempt to garner more significant tax benefits.

The Ways and Means Committee, under Rostenkowski's auspices, spent all of June and most of July trying to fashion a tax package that would earn more votes on the floor of the House than would the Republican bill. On July 22, the House committee completed the marking up of its bill. In its final form, the Ways and Means Committee tax package reflected, perhaps even more than did the Finance Committee

[34]Ibid.
[35]Keller, op. cit.

bill, the influence of a barrage of special-interest business lobbyists. In parts, the House bill was so generous that business representatives were suspicious. One chemical company expert was quoted as saying, "People are a little nervous about it [the bill]. It's almost like Greeks bearing gifts."[36] The aggressive bidding for votes in the House committee was best illustrated by the special tax provisions granted to the independent petroleum producers, savings institutions, high-technology firms, and professional commodity traders.

The independent oil producers, who were discontented with the tax benefits provided them by the Finance Committee bill, found relief in the House bill in the waning hours of the debate. At 2 a.m. on July 22, the House committee approved, by a vote of 18 to 17, an exemption of 500 barrels a day from the windfall profits tax. This was expected to cost the Treasury $7 billion through 1986. Trying to hold the votes of conservative House Democrats, Rostenkowski told the more liberal members of his committee who were uneasy supporting such generous tax benefits for oil companies that the choice was "whether you want to lose courageously, or to win. I'd like to win."[37]

Succumbing to pressure from the U.S. League of Savings and anxious not to be outbid by the Senate Finance Committee, the House Ways and Means Committee members adopted a provision similar to that of the Senate bill, allowing thrift institutions to issue all-savers certificates. They also incorporated the administration proposal to raise from $7,500 to $15,000 the deductions for contributions to a Keogh plan (a retirement program established by the self-employed) and to increase deductions for contributions to individual retirement accounts (IRAs).

Although the members of the Ways and Means Committee did not adopt the liberalized tax treatment of stock options approved by the Senate Finance Committee, they did include in their bill another measure championed by the American Electronics Association: a 25 percent tax credit for new expenditures for research and development. The R&D credit was designed to benefit high-technology firms that would not gain nearly as much from ACRS as traditional capital-intensive industries.

The Ways and Means Committee also buckled in to pressure from commodity industry lobbyists and approved an amendment that allowed individuals to continue to defer or reduce tax payments by buying off-setting commodity futures contracts. Under existing law, "at any time one contract reflected a loss and the other a gain, taxes were deferred or minimized by declaring the loss one year and the gain in the next—a technique known as a commodity tax straddle. The Senate Finance Committee bill closed this loophole by requiring that all of a taxpayer's futures contracts be lumped together at year's end, and that the resulting net profit be taxed even though it had yet to be realized. The professional

[36]*Chemical Week* (July 1, 1981).
[37]Maitland, op. cit., 15.

commodity traders initiated an intense lobbying campaign, flying from New York and Chicago to Washington to meet with Ways and Means Committee members and to offer significant campaign contributions for their support of the amendment allowing straddles. Robert Merry of *The Wall Street Journal* called the lobbying effort an "old style, big money approach."[38]

Many of the special tax provisions of the Ways and Means Committee package were similar to those adopted by the Senate committee, since they were designed to appeal to the same interest groups. However, there were significant differences in the basic corporate and personal tax cuts. In place of ACRS, favored by the administration and the Senate Finance Committee, Rostenkowski's committee substituted expensing, a one-year write-off of new-equipment depreciable assets. The House tax plan also gradually lowered the top tax rate on corporate income for companies with annual profits over $100,000, from 46 percent in 1981 to 34 percent in 1986. The Ways and Means Committee business tax proposals were expected to equal the cost of the administration's business package, estimated by the Joint Committee on Taxation at $485 billion through 1990.

In place of the president's three-year, across-the-board tax cuts, the House tax-writing committee adopted a two-year reduction proposal that would slash rates by a total of 15 percent. Essentially, the Democratic plan eliminated the third-year cut in Reagan's modified proposal. It skewed the cuts so that individuals earning under $50,000 would receive more tax benefits than under the administration proposal. Like the administration and the Senate bills, the Ways and Means Committee package included a drop in the rate on investment income from 70 percent to 50 percent in 1983, as well as a reduction in the marriage penalty. The House bill, though, included a more generous reduction in estate and gift taxes. All told, the individual income tax cuts approved by the House committee were estimated to cost $419 billion in lost revenue between 1982 and 1986, as compared with the $500 billion price tag of the Senate package.

The administration responded quickly to the Ways and Means Committee bill, reported out of committee on July 23. On the same day, the White House revised its bill, adding extra tax breaks for oil producers, annual indexing of tax rates to offset bracket creep due to inflation, increased relief from estate and gift taxation, additional charitable deductions, and a variety of other sweeteners. Both Republicans and Democrats admitted their bills were more products of political bidding battles than blueprints for economic recovery. Representative Jim Jones (D-Oklahoma) said, "We're in a bidding war. Any economic foundation for the tax bill has been abandoned."[39]

Both sides in the House conceded that the showdown between the

[38]Ibid.
[39]Quoted in Maitland, op. cit., 12.

administration and Rostenkowski was too close to call. Reagan called the administration tax cut "the most crucial item left on our agenda for prosperity."[40] Five days later, he made a nationally televised appeal for passage of the administration proposal and urged voters to write or call their representatives in support of the Republican bill. Voters responded in record numbers, swamping Capitol Hill switchboards in support of the president's plan. "We are experiencing a telephone blitz like this nation has never seen. It's had a devastating effect," said House Speaker Thomas P. O'Neill, Jr. (D-Massachusetts). Meanwhile, Reagan lobbied House Republicans and conservative Democratic members hard for passage of the administration bill. On July 29, the Democrat-controlled House bowed to a "tidal wave of public pressure" and administrative lobbying and adopted the president's package in place of a Ways and Means Committee version. "Forty-eight Democrats defected to Reagan in the crucial showdown as the House voted 238–195 to adopt provisions of the administration substitute."[41]

On the same day, the Republican-controlled Senate approved the Finance Committee bill, amended on the floor, by a vote of 89 to 11. Thirty-seven of the chamber's 47 Democrats voted for the bill and one Republican voted against it. As amended on the floor, the Finance Committee bill included a provision to index taxes, a proposal to extend the period during which all-savers certificates could be issued, and a reduction in corporate tax rates for small business.

The Senate and House bills now moved to a conference committee to reconcile the differences between the two proposals. Because both bills had been written with significant White House influence, there were few major disagreements, with the exception of tax benefits for oil producers. The Senate accepted the House provisions to give oil-royalty owners more generous exemptions from the windfall profits tax and to totally exempt "stripper" wells—those that produce 10 barrels a day or less—from the tax after 1982. Measures to reduce the windfall profits tax from 30 percent to 15 percent failed under pressure from liberal Democrats, upset by the $118 billion in tax breaks for oil producers that was included in the bill. A House plan to exempt professional commodity traders from the closing of a tax-straddle loophole failed in conference despite intense lobbying. The conferees approved a Senate-passed amendment for liberalized tax treatment of stock options. A number of miscellaneous special-interest provisions were dropped in conference, including tax breaks for "planting pecan trees and what Finance Committee Chairman Dole dubbed the 'Gong Show amendment'—a tax credit for investment in TV game shows."[42]

On August 4, Congress completed action on H.R. 4242, the Eco-

---

[40]Quoted in *Congressional Quarterly Almanac* (1981), 100.

[41]Ibid., 103.

[42]Ibid., 103.

nomic Recovery Tax Act of 1981. President Reagan signed the bill on
August 13 while vacationing in California. The main provisions of the
ERTA are summarized in Exhibit 1.

The business community, as represented in Washington, reacted
very favorably to passage of the tax bill. The Carlton group applauded
the core of the president's tax package—the individual rate cuts and ACRS,
both passed intact despite the bidding war. Though not all were exposed
to the same degree of temptation to seek specific tax benefits, most business representatives chose to consistently support the president's program, believing that a unified business position behind a clean bill would
avoid splintering and maximize the probabilities of ACRS (and the individual tax reductions) being passed. When it became clear that a clean
bill had no chance of surviving, most of the business community remained loyal to the president, adhering to the strategy of cohesion. Tip
O'Neill complained to the House that corporate giants such as "Philip
Morris, Paine Webber, Monsanto Chemical, Exxon, McDonnell-Douglas
. . . were so kind as to allow the use of their staff in flooding the switchboards of America."[43] Where business unity broke down and lobbyists
engaged in bidding battles, it involved narrow-based interests with relatively concrete legislative objectives. "The principal architects of the
business coalitions supporting the president were the major business organizations. These encompassing organizations played an indispensable
role by resolving intrabusiness conflicts and formulating a coherent stand
to which the administration and Congress could respond."[44]

- cummulative effect of all these provision for narrow-based interests is a tax plan not geared for economic recovery & efficiency, but instead of for the increased capture of profits by large corporations and the mid-size firms represented on the Hill by connected lobbyists

[43]Ellen Nehr, "White House's Lobbying Apparatus," *Congressional Quarterly Weekly Reports* (Aug. 1, 1981): 1372–1373.

[44]Maitland, op. cit., 20.

The Economic Recovery Tax Act of 1981

Exhibit 1   Provisions of the Economic Recovery Tax Act of 1981

Individual Income Taxes

Rates
Withholding taxes reduced by 5 percent on Oct. 1, 1981, 10 percent on July 1, 1982, and 10 percent on July 1, 1983. Top tax rate reduced to 50 percent next Jan. 1, from current 70 percent.

Marriage penalty relief
Five percent of income of lower-earning spouse, up to $1,500, is excluded in 1982; 10 percent exclusion, up to $3,000, in 1983 and beyond.

Indexing
Starting in 1985, annual adjustments will be made in personal exemption, zero-bracket amount, and income brackets to offset so-called "bracket creep" caused by wage inflation.

Child care
Maximum child-care credit for working couples raised from $400 to $720 for one child and $1,440 for two or more. Credits drop to $480 and $960, respectively, when income exceeds $30,000.

Capital gains
Maximum rate on long-term capital gains effectively set at 20 percent, down from 28 percent.

House sale
Homeowners who sell house at a profit permitted to forgo tax if they purchase another house of equal or greater value within 24 months, instead of present 18 months. For those 55 years and older, exclusion of profits on sale is raised from $100,000 to $125,000.

Charitable contributions
Taxpayers who do not itemize deductions are permitted to deduct one dollar for every four donated to churches, charities, colleges, and other tax-exempt institutions, up to $25 in 1982 and 1983 and up to $75 in 1984. In 1985 and 1986, they can deduct 50 percent and 100 percent, respectively, of unlimited contributions.

Dividend reinvestment
Taxpayers permitted to exclude up to $750 a year ($1,500 for a joint return) of dividends received from public utility corporations if dividends are reinvested in stock in the utility. Exclusion ends after 1985.

Business Tax Relief

Depreciation
Investment encouraged through faster write-off of capital expenditure over 3, 5, and 10 years for various kinds of equipment, rather than over so-called useful life of an asset. Most buildings could be written off over 15 years.

Investment credit
Investment tax credit of 6 percent allowed for equipment with life of up to 3 years; 10 percent for equipment with longer life.

Corporate tax rate
Tax rate on profits of up to $25,000 reduced from 17 to 16 percent in 1982 and to 15 percent in 1983; rate on profits of $25,000 to $50,000 reduced from 20 to 19 percent in 1982 and to 18 percent in 1983. No rate change for higher incomes.

Americans abroad
U.S. citizens working overseas tax-exempt on first $75,000 of income in 1982, with further $5,000 increments in subsequent years to a maximum of $95,000.

Exhibit 1 (Continued)

Savings Incentives

Savings certificates

Banks and savings institutions authorized to issue one-year savers certificates, yielding interest no greater than 70 percent of Treasury bill rate. Interest earned would be exempt from taxes up to $1,000 ($2,000 for joint return).

Retirement savings

Maximum deductions for contributions to individual retirement accounts increased from $1,500 a year to $2,000. Tax-qualified pension plans permitted to set up individual retirement accounts, to a limit of $2,000, which would not be subject to taxation until taken out of account.

Estate, Gift Taxes

Marital bequests

Estate and gift tax eliminated on all bequests and gifts between spouses.

Exclusion

Exclusion for gifts in a single year to one person is increased from $3,000 to $10,000. Unlimited exclusion for gifts to pay for medical expenses and school tuition.

Unified credit

The level of transfers at which estate and gift tax rates begin is raised from current $175,625 to $600,000, phased in over 6-year period.

Current use valuation

Limit by which fair market value of farm, woodland, and other business property can be reduced for estate tax purposes is increased from $500,000 in current tax year to $700,000 in 1982, $750,000 thereafter.

Oil Taxes

Newly discovered oil

"Windfall" profits tax on newly discovered oil reduced to 15 percent, from 30 percent, over stages by 1986.

Royalty owners

$2,500 tax credit provided in 1981 for about 2 million owners of mineral rights to property where oil is produced. In 1982, 1983, and 1984, exemption would amount to the value of 2 barrels a day, in 1985 and thereafter, 3 barrels a day.

Stripper oil

Oil from "stripper" wells that yield less than 10 barrels a day exempted from windfall profits tax.

Source: *New York Times*, Aug. 2, 1981, Sec. 4, 2.

The Economic Recovery Tax Act of 1981

Exhibit 2   Summary of Estimated Revenue Effects of the Economic Recovery Act of 1981 (Millions of Dollars; Calendar Years 1981–1986)

Provision	1981	1982	1983	1984	1985	1986
Title I—Individual income tax provisions, of which	−4,070	−41,879	−85,340	−120,150	−164,482	−215,434
Rate cuts	−3,642	−37,354	−75,820	−108,580	−127,868	−149,756
Deduction for two-income married couples	—	−3,541	−8,477	−10,189	−12,137	−14,332
Indexing	—	—			−21,022	−45,106
Deduction of non-itemizers' charitable contributions	—	−189	−188	−421	−2,344	−4,957
Title II—Business incentive provisions, of which	−5,926	−13,883	−24,425	−33,113	−46,636	−63,791
ACRS	−5,674	−12,043	−22,220	−30,938	−44,483	−62,172
Extended ITC	−85	−273	−303	−355	−554	−692
R & D Tax Credit	−154	−591	−847	−878	−817	−161
Title III—Savings provisions	−20	−869	−3,943	−3,791	−8,101	−8,964
Title IV—Estate and gift tax provisions	−18	−2,133	−3,231	−4,271	−5,589	−6,839
Title V—Tax straddles	1,421	722	112	60	36	16
Title VI—Energy provisions	−529	−1,043	−1,977	−2,348	−3,010	−3,877
Title VII—Administrative provisions	122	705	473	823	426	951
Title VIII—Miscellaneous provisions	—	−24	667	727	−64	−64
Total Revenue Effect	−9,020	−58,404	−117,664	−162,063	−227,420	−298,002

Source: Joint Committee on Taxation, *General Explanation of the Economic Recovery Tax Act of 1981* (Washington, DC: U.S. Government Printing Office, 1981), 381, 392–393.

Exhibit 3   Distribution of Personal Income Tax Cuts by Income Class (Millions of Dollars; 1981 Income Levels)

Expanded Income Class[a]	Prior Law Tax Liability[c]		1982 Total Reductions		1983 Total Reductions		1984 Reductions						Total as Percent of Prior Law Liability
							Rate Reductions		Deduction for Two-Earner Couples		Total		
	Amount	Percent	Amount	Percent	Amount	Percent	Amount	Percent	Amount	Percent	Amount	Percent	
	1	2	3	4	5	6	7	8	9	10	11	12	13
Under $5,000	-157	(-0.1)[b]	-69	(0.2)	-109	(0.2)	-114	(0.2)	0	(0.0)	-114	(0.2)	(d)
$5,000-$10,000	6,381	(2.2)	-937	(2.7)	-1,479	(2.5)	-1,718	(2.6)	-13	(0.2)	-1,731	(2.4)	27.1
$10,000-$15,000	16,317	(5.7)	-1,925	(5.6)	-3,287	(5.4)	-3,812	(5.8)	-88	(1.5)	-3,900	(5.4)	23.9
$15,000-$20,000	22,987	(8.0)	-2,651	(7.7)	-4,675	(7.7)	-5,407	(8.2)	-218	(3.7)	-5,625	(7.8)	24.5
$20,000-$30,000	58,558	(20.4)	-6,715	(19.4)	-12,349	(20.5)	-13,744	(20.8)	-1,149	(19.5)	-14,893	(20.7)	25.4
$30,000-$50,000	85,706	(29.9)	-10,183	(29.4)	-18,923	(31.4)	-19,695	(29.9)	-2,825	(48.0)	-22,520	(31.3)	26.3
$50,000-$100,000	51,631	(18.0)	-5,900	(17.1)	-11,002	(18.2)	-12,033	(18.2)	-1,222	(20.8)	-13,255	(18.4)	25.7
$100,000-$200,000	24,125	(8.4)	-2,639	(7.6)	-4,437	(7.4)	-5,116	(7.8)	-280	(4.8)	-5,396	(7.5)	22.4
Over $200,000	21,110	(7.4)	-3,583	(10.4)	-4,080	(6.8)	-4,328	(6.6)	-85	(1.4)	-4,413	(6.1)	20.9
Total	286,659	(100.0)	-34,603	(100.0)	-60,341	(100.0)	-65,966	(100.0)	-5,881	(100.0)	-71,847	(100.0)	25.1

[a]Expanded income equals adjusted gross income plus excluded capital gains and various tax preference items, less investment interest to the extent of investment income.

[b]Percentage distribution of revenue loss in parentheses.

[c]Net of outlay portion of the earned income credit.

[d]Not meaningful because this income class does not have positive tax liability.

Source: Joint Committee on Taxation, *General Explanation of the Economic Recovery Tax Act of 1981* (Washington, DC: U.S. Government Printing Office, 1981), 23.

The Economic Recovery Tax Act of 1981

Exhibit 4   Corporate Tax Rates in the United States: 1953–1981

Year	Average Corporate Rate[a]	Statutory Corporate Rate	Effective Tax Rates General Industrial Equipment	Industrial Structures	All Assets
1953	55.9%	52.0%	64.1%	55.6%	58.8%
1954	50.0	52.0	61.0	52.3	55.5
1955	48.4	52.0	58.2	50.6	53.5
1956	50.3	52.0	59.3	51.3	54.3
1957	49.4	52.0	60.2	51.9	55.0
1958	49.4	52.0	60.9	52.3	55.6
1959	47.6	52.0	59.7	51.5	54.6
1960	47.7	52.0	60.4	52.0	55.1
1961	46.9	52.0	58.8	51.0	53.9
1962	42.4	52.0	40.3	49.1	43.3
1963	42.2	52.0	41.5	49.6	44.0
1964	40.5	50.0	27.4	47.1	37.2
1965	38.6	48.0	26.1	45.5	35.7
1966	39.6	48.0	27.4	45.8	36.5
1967	39.4	48.0	49.4	46.6	45.5
1968	44.0	52.8	37.0	51.5	43.5
1969	46.4	52.8	41.0	52.7	45.8
1970	47.9	49.2	53.5	52.0	49.7
1971	45.1	48.0	53.2	51.2	49.1
1972	43.1	48.0	16.4	51.2	32.9
1973	45.2	48.0	14.4	50.9	31.8
1974	54.4	48.0	18.3	51.5	33.9
1975	45.8	48.0	24.1	52.6	37.0
1976	46.2	48.0	26.4	53.1	35.1
1977	43.5	48.0	21.2	52.1	32.0
1978	43.2	48.0	23.2	52.4	33.2
1979	45.0	46.0	19.0	50.3	30.1
1980	46.6	46.0	22.0	50.8	31.9
1981	42.6	46.0	−6.8	41.7	17.7

[a]Corporate tax liability as a percentage of corporate profits with inventory valuation and capital consumption adjustments.

Source: Alan Auerbach, "Corporate Taxation in the U.S.," *Brookings Papers on Economic Activity*, vol. 2 (1983): 456, 467.

The Economic Recovery Tax Act of 1981

Exhibit 5   Effective Tax Rates on New Depreciable Assets for Selected Industries[a]

Industry	Pre-ACRS	ACRS
Agriculture	32.7	16.6
Mining	28.4	−3.4
Primary metals	34.0	7.5
Machinery and instruments	38.2	18.6
Motor vehicles	25.8	−11.3
Food	44.1	20.8
Pulp and paper	28.5	.9
Chemicals	28.8	8.6
Petroleum refining	35.0	1.1
Transportation services	31.0	−2.9
Utilities	43.2	30.6
Communications	39.8	14.1
Services and trade	53.2	37.1

[a]Industries chosen had at least $5 billion in new investment in 1981.

Note: Assumes a 4 percent real after-tax rate of return and 8 percent inflation.

Source: *Economic Report of the President, 1982* (Washington, DC: U.S. Government Printing Office, 1982), 124.

The Economic Recovery Tax Act of 1981

Exhibit 6   Effective Tax Rates by Asset Type

Asset Type[a]	Law in Effect before 1981	Law Enacted in 1981[b]
Equipment		
Automobiles	17.0%	−32.8%
Office, computing, and accounting equipment	2.3	−49.4
Trucks, buses, and trailers	10.1	−45.2
Aircraft	17.7	−31.4
Construction machinery	7.6	−29.7
Mining and oil field machinery	16.7	−28.5
Service industry machinery	20.3	−28.5
Tractors	8.9	−28.2
Instruments	20.7	−17.5
Other equipment	13.4	−25.6
General industrial equipment	20.6	−14.0
Metal-working machinery	13.2	−20.2
Electric transmission and distribution equipment	29.2	3.2
Communications equipment	22.6	−21.1
Other electrical equipment	12.6	−21.1
Furniture and fixtures	7.1	−20.0
Special industrial equipment	12.6	−19.0
Agricultural equipment	6.6	−18.1
Fabricated metal products	26.8	−1.4
Engines and turbines	31.8	16.3
Ships and boats	27.9	−15.1
Railroad equipment	24.8	11.1
Plant		
Mining exploration, shafts, and wells	8.5	8.5
Other mining	51.7	41.6
Industrial structures	49.6	38.4
Public utility structures	27.3	15.5
Commercial structures	46.8	35.6
Farm structures	41.1	35.8

[a]Assets are approximately ordered from fastest to slowest economic depreciation rates.

[b]These rates would have been effective in 1986 had they not been overridden by 1982 tax law changes.

Source: Jane G. Gravelle, "Capital Income Taxation and Efficiency in the Allocation of Investment," *National Tax Journal*, vol. 36 (September 1983): 299.

Discussion Questions for Case

1. Evaluate President Reagan's strategy for implementing his tax plan.
2. What role might business have played in altering the legislative outcome?
3. What institutional changes could you suggest that would improve the legislative process?

Bibliography

Collender, Stanley E., *The Guide to the Federal Budget*, Fiscal 1986 Edition (Washington, DC: Urban Institute, 1985). Part I of this book (pages 13–60) illustrates the congressional budget process by leading the reader through the stages of the annual budget cycle.

Fox, J. Ronald, *Managing Business-Government Relations: Cases and Notes on Business-Government Problems* (Homewood, IL: Irwin, 1982). The notes on the roles of the executive branch and Congress in the U.S. government decision-making process (pp. 481–540) provide useful background information on these institutions.

Hulten, Charles R., and June A. O'Neill, "Tax Policy," in John L. Palmer and Isabel V. Sawhill, eds., *The Reagan Experiment: An Examination of Economic and Social Policies under the Reagan Administration* (Washington, DC: Urban Institute, 1982), 97–128. This chapter critically evaluates the economic consequences of ERTA, but it does not discuss the politics of implementing the legislation.

Pechman, Joseph, *Federal Tax Policy*, 4th ed. (Washington, DC: Brookings Institution, 1983). Chapter 3 describes the tax legislation process in detail.

Redman, Eric, *The Dance of Legislation* (New York: Simon & Schuster, 1973). This book describes how congressional staff members designed a strategy and tactics to guide a bill through Congress.

Reese, Thomas J., *The Politics of Taxation* (Westport, CT: Quorum, 1980). This book concentrates on the participants, rather than the process, of tax legislation politics.

CHAPTER 11
The Dangers of Fiscal Policy

The primary purpose of this chapter is to show the relationship of the budget deficits to the total savings and investment in the economy. The note, "Investment and Savings," presents the accounting framework that relates these items. The case, "The Reagan Deficits," describes the trends in the budget and the dispute on its effect on the economy in the 1980s. The secondary purpose of the chapter is to analyze the particular deficit reduction strategies for FY 1986. Repeated attempts to reduce the deficit during Reagan's first term in the presidency had failed to change significantly the deficits relative to the size of the economy. The issues in political economy posed by large deficits are not specific to any particular year, but will remain unchanged until the deficits return to their historical norms.

The first major issue is the economic consequences of the large budget deficits. The abundant data in the exhibits at the end of the case allow one to speculate on how the deficits may affect business investment, U.S. competitiveness, or the conduct of monetary policy. (In all exhibits where applicable, figures are presented both in dollars and as percentages of GNP for ease of comparison.) The second issue is how a society determines the trade-offs among its competing objectives. This case gives us some insights into the implied priorities of the Reagan administration and the Congress. How important is deficit reduction in that list of priorities? By going through the exercise of trying to reduce the deficit, one must ask whether more political harm will be done by deficit reduction or by continued deficits.

Case
The Reagan Deficits

Controlling the massive federal budget deficits was the major economic issue facing President Ronald Reagan as he started his second term in office in January 1985. The Reagan administration, with the Congress as an accomplice, had presided over approximately $700 billion in cumulative deficits during the first four fiscal years under its control.[1] The cumulative four-year deficit was greater than the total expenditures during fiscal year 1982 (FY 1982). The size of the nation's outstanding public debt almost doubled in those four years to a level of $1.5 trillion in FY 1985.

The deficit problem appeared to some participants to be almost intractable. The administration and Congress had already made the "easy" spending cuts and tax increases during the first term in an attempt to reduce the deficit. It was widely acknowledged that almost 75 percent of the budget was considered "uncontrollable" for current-year expenditures. Thirty-five percent of those expenditures were for interest on the national debt and for prior-year contracts and obligations that had to be paid. An additional 40 percent of the budget, covering the entitlements programs, farm price supports, and revenue sharing, were controllable only if the eligibility rules specified in the enabling legislation were changed. That left only 25 percent of the outlays that could be affected by current-year appropriations. The problem was further complicated by the lack of understanding on the fundamental issues: the cause of the existing deficits was in dispute, the consequences of continued deficits were uncertain and diffuse, and all options appeared politically unpalatable.

There was hope by some administration officials, however, that President Reagan would use the political mandate granted him in the 1984 reelection landslide to provide the leadership necessary to solve the deficit problem. Reagan demonstrated such leadership during his first year in office when he enacted legislation reversing most of the entrenched budgetary trends of the postwar years. The trends had been toward more taxes, less defense spending, more social spending, and persistent deficits. His budgetary objectives were to cut taxes, bolster defense, reduce social spending, and balance the budget.[2]

This case was prepared by Associate Professor Michael G. Rukstad.
Copyright © 1985 by the President and Fellows of Harvard College
Harvard Business School case 9-386-042

[1]Fiscal year 1982, the first year under the control of the Reagan administration, runs from October 1, 1981, to September 30, 1982. This cycle applies to all fiscal years since fiscal year 1977. The third quarter of 1976 is known as a transition quarter, since the fiscal years prior to and including 1976 ran from July 1 to June 30.

[2]See the Chapter 9 case, "The Reagan Plan."

Historical Trends in Taxes, Spending, and the Deficit

The total personal tax burden due to the individual income tax and the social insurance tax increased steadily during the two decades before Reagan's presidency. (See Exhibits 4 and 5 at the end of this case for data on the tax revenue trends.) Inflation was the primary culprit since inflated incomes pushed taxpayers into higher marginal tax brackets. It was estimated that this bracket creep was responsible for three quarters of the increased tax revenues in the late 1970s.[3] Some tax legislation, primarily increases in social security taxes since 1976, also contributed to the increased personal tax burden, though periodic reductions in the individual income tax helped to moderate the burden. At the same time that the share of personal taxes was rising, reliance on the corporate income tax and excise taxes was declining.

Defense spending had declined as a percentage of GNP from 9.6 percent in FY 1962 to 5.5 percent in FY 1981. The composition of the expenditures changed significantly over the same period, with a decrease in the share for military procurement and R&D from a half to a third and an increase in the share for salaries, pensions, and current operations from a half to two thirds. In the late 1970s, widely publicized estimates by the CIA showed that the Soviet Union's defense expenditures as a percentage of GNP were about twice that of the United States, giving the Soviet Union an estimated spending advantage of about 45 percent over the United States.[4] President Carter, recognizing the decline in U.S. military strength, pledged to the NATO allies a 3 percent real rate of growth in defense spending from FY 1979 to FY 1981—a pledge that became a reality. Nonetheless, the seizure of the American Embassy in Iran and the Soviet invasion of Afghanistan in late 1979 fostered doubts about U.S. military strength.

During the same 20-year period, nondefense spending increased by more than half as a percentage of GNP—rising from 10 percent in FY 1962 to 16.3 percent in FY 1981—though nearly all of this growth was achieved during the decade from 1966 to 1976, when the entitlements and other mandatory spending doubled as a percentage of GNP. The entitlement programs were not under the control of the congressional authorization committees, since participation in the program was automatically granted to anyone meeting the legislated criteria. Social security and Medicare made up over half of the entitlements and mandatory

---

[3]Frank de Leeuw and Thomas M. Holloway, "The High-Employment Budget: Revised Estimates and Automatic Inflation Effects," *Survey of Current Business* (April 1982): 21–33.

[4]Critics were quick to note that if their allies' defense spending were included on both sides, then the United States and its allies would have had a 10 percent spending advantage over the Soviet Bloc. In addition, an estimated 10 to 15 percent of Soviet spending was directed toward China. See Richard Stubbing, "The Defense Budget," in Gregory Mills and John Palmer, eds., *Federal Budget Policy in the 1980s* (Washington, DC: Urban Institute, 1984), 93.

spending component of federal outlays. Among the reasons often cited for the increase in transfer payments were the addition of new programs during the Great Society campaign of the late 1960s, liberalized eligibility and increased participation in the programs, economic and demographic shifts in the population, and generous funding under joint federal-state programs.[5]

The actual budget deficits generally remained less than 2 percent of GNP over this period, with the exception of the huge recession-induced deficits of 4.6 percent of GNP in 1975 and 3.1 percent of GNP in 1976. The last recorded surplus, measuring 0.9 percent of GNP, was the result of President Nixon's contractionary fiscal program in 1969. Some of the upward trend in the size of budget deficits was accounted for by the slower growth of the 1970s, but the cyclically adjusted budgets had also been trending upward since 1960. Generally, the cyclically adjusted deficits (see Exhibit 6) had been about 2 percent or less of GNP, with the exception of the peak military spending for Vietnam in 1967 (2.9 percent of GNP) and the post-OPEC recession in 1975 (2.6 percent of GNP). President Carter pledged a balanced budget by 1980, but the second oil shock and the military buildup prevented him from achieving that objective. As a candidate for president in 1980, Ronald Reagan criticized the president, saying that "Mr. Carter is acting as if he hadn't been in charge for the past 3½ years; as if someone else ran up nearly $200 billion in red ink; as if someone else was responsible for the largest deficit in American history; and as if someone else was predicting a budget deficit for this fiscal year of $30 billion."[6]

The Rise of Big Deficits under Reagan

The new administration of Ronald Reagan achieved a legislative triumph in 1981 with the enactment of its budget proposal. Within the first month of the new presidency, Reagan established a budgetary agenda for Washington that he would dominate throughout that first year. Eight months later, he had accomplished three of his budgetary objectives—tax cuts, defense-spending increases, and nondefense-spending cuts—by sacrificing his fourth objective, a balanced budget. Reagan and Congress would spend the next three years searching for a means to that end.

Reagan's strategy for the legislative triumph was to keep a focused agenda centered on the budget, to centralize the decision-making process, to pay close attention to the selection of administrative appointees, and to mobilize political support in Congress and the public. The budget decisions originated in the triumvirate of presidential advisers in the

[5]Gregory Mills and John Palmer, *The Deficit Dilemma* (Washington, DC: Urban Institute, 1983), 13.

[6]*Time*, Apr. 23, 1983, 15.

White House—James Baker, Michael Deaver, and Edwin Meese—and were primarily influenced by the new budget director at the Office of Management and Budget (OMB), David Stockman, who instituted "top-down" management of budget decisions that had relatively little input from the executive agencies. As he argued in his "Economic Dunkirk" memorandum to the president, the initial administration economic program should be "so bold, sweeping and sustained that it . . . totally dominates the Washington agenda in 1981."[7] It did dominate the Washington agenda, and it was Stockman's responsibility to keep the budget in the forefront of congressional attention. The cabinet was filled with loyal appointees whose attachments, according to Ed Meese, were closer to the president than to their spending agencies. Given the speed with which the budget policies were formulated, the new cabinet appointees had little time to study the consequences on their agencies. Their role was to implement the president's agenda through administrative, rather than legislative, actions whenever possible. The White House would actively court Congress, on the one hand, and attempt to monitor and mobilize public opinion on the other. Reagan's unique skills as a "great communicator" were a prominent instrument of this strategy.

In March 1981, Reagan announced his FY 1982 budget, which included (1) a 30 percent across-the-board cut in personal taxes and a significant acceleration of business depreciation tax write-offs; (2) real defense-spending increases of 9 percent for the next five years; (3) cuts in nondefense spending of $50 billion in 1982, growing to $100 billion in 1986; and (4) additional unspecified cuts of $30 billion in 1983, followed by cuts of $40 billion in the next three years. A key requirement for the success of this package, according to administration officials, was a favorable response in the money and capital markets, which would cause lower interest rates and thereby precipitate an economic boom. Because Stockman rejected the original OMB deficit projections as too pessimistic, he went searching for a supply-side forecasting model that would give him the desired results. The projected deficits from this model, given the administration's optimistic assumptions, would be eliminated by 1984.[8] There was reason to be skeptical of the projected results in March 1981, when the nonpartisan Congressional Budget Office (CBO) released its finding that modifying a few economic assumptions to accord with private forecasts would give an estimated deficit of $50 billion in 1984.[9] Congress, which was reluctant to cast doubt on the efficacy of the popular president's program, chose to adopt the president's assumptions in its subsequent budget debates for that year.

[7]See the Chapter 9 case, "The Reagan Plan," for excerpts of the Economic Dunkirk memorandum.

[8]See Exhibits 1 and 3 of the Chapter 9 case, "The Reagan Plan."

[9]Congressional Budget Office, *An Analysis of President Reagan's Budget Revisions for Fiscal Year 1982* (Washington, DC: U.S. Government Printing Office, 1981), xxiii.

The first part of Reagan's victory came in June with the passage of the Omnibus Budget Reconciliation Act. This was a masterful display of presidential control over a legislative agenda. By using a provision of the congressional budget process known as reconciliation,[10] the president was able to bundle his entire program into one bill that would be voted on as a package in highly publicized congressional action rather than being split up among 13 authorization committees. Congress approved the $8 billion requested for increased defense expenditures for FY 1982, but it could agree on only $33 billion of the specified nondefense-spending cuts.[11] No action was taken on the additional unspecified spending cuts.

Concern over the deficit was mounting as congressional and private estimates began to dispute the expected outcomes of the president's program. The House Budget Committee, chaired by Congressman James Jones (D-Oklahoma), estimated during the summer that if the president's economic assumptions were replaced by more conservative ones, the deficit would jump from zero in 1984 to $60 billion instead. Then if the committee also eliminated the assumption of the additional unspecified domestic spending cuts—the "magic asterisk" in the words of Senator Howard Baker (R-Tennessee)—the deficit estimate for 1984 would double to a level of $120 billion.[12]

The second part of the victory came in August with the cuts in personal and corporate taxes in the Economic Recovery Tax Act (ERTA).[13] The final bill contained a 25 percent reduction in marginal tax rates rather than the 30 percent Reagan had requested. The liberalized corporate depreciation plan was enacted with only a few changes in its initial provisions. In the legislative bidding for support of the tax bill, numerous baubles were attached to the bill, the most costly being the indexing of personal tax exemptions and brackets starting in 1985 and the elimination of the marriage penalty in the taxes of two-income households. These provisions were favored by the president but not initially included in his "clean" tax cut proposals.

The administration eagerly awaited the economic turnaround it had predicted from the enactment of its program. Instead, rising interest rates and slow economic growth had sobered the administration in its eval-

---

[10]Reconciliation was established by the Congressional Budget Act of 1974 to force Congress to conform tax and spending legislation to the levels voted by Congress in a budget resolution. This had been used in the second budget resolution passed each year in September, but since 1980 it has been used for the first budget resolution near May as well.

[11]All spending changes are measured relative to a baseline or current-services budget. This benchmark indicates what expenditures would be, given assumptions about the economy, if spending were sufficient to maintain the current level of services and to account for inflation whether or not the inflation adjustment is required by law. If the adjustment for inflation were not made in the current-services budget, the nondefense-spending cuts would have been $12 billion to $15 billion.

[12]The Wall Street Journal, Sept. 4, 1981.

[13]See the Chapter 10 case, "The Economic Recovery Tax Act of 1981," for a detailed account of the legislative process leading up to the enactment of ERTA.

uation of the deficit estimates. So, in September, the president announced another round of deficit-reducing measures that called for an additional $13 billion in spending cuts, most of which Congress granted. Under pressure to show large cuts in nondefense spending, Congress made some specious accounting changes in the reported budget for FY 1982 by moving $3.7 billion of the strategic petroleum reserve expenditures to off-budget status and by shifting $0.7 billion in Medicare expenditures from the first month of FY 1982 to the last month of FY 1981.[14] The total cut in nondefense spending was about 6 percent of the baseline expenditures for the 1982 fiscal year, increasing somewhat in future years.

Debate over the Economic Consequences of the Deficit

The economy continued to perform miserably during 1981 and 1982, largely in response to the tight monetary policies of the Federal Reserve.[15] Starting in early 1982, the Reagan administration became less sanguine about the prospects of reducing the deficit, though it argued that the effect of the deficits on the economy was negligible. In his economic report to Congress in February 1982, Reagan said: "We face high, continuing, and troublesome deficits. Although these deficits are undesirably high, they will not jeopardize the economic recovery. We must understand the reasons behind the deficits now facing us: recession, lower inflation, and higher interest rates than anticipated. Although my original timetable for a balanced budget is no longer achievable, the factors which have postponed it do not mean we are abandoning the goal of living within our means."[16]

Even when the new chairman of the Council of Economic Advisers, Professor Martin Feldstein of Harvard, repeatedly and publicly warned the president that the significant structural deficits caused by the administration's policies would hinder future capital formation, key members of the administration would not recant. Treasury Secretary Donald Regan explained to Congress that sufficient savings would be forthcoming from the tax cuts to finance the added deficits. He predicted that gross private savings as a percentage of GNP would rise from 16.7 to 19.1 percent by 1984 as all of the business tax cut and half of the personal tax cut would go into savings. Under the administration's tax plan, the personal savings rate would rise, Regan said, from 5 to 7 percent.[17] He also claimed that

[14]John Palmer and Gregory Mills, "Budget Policy," in John Palmer and Isabel Sawhill, eds., *The Reagan Experiment* (Washington, DC: Urban Institute, 1982), 78.

[15]These events are described in detail in the Chapter 3 case, "Paul Volcker and the Federal Reserve: 1979–1982."

[16]*Economic Report of the President, 1982* (Washington, DC: U.S. Government Printing Office, 1982), 6.

[17]Statement of Treasury Secretary Donald Regan before the House Appropriations Committee, Feb. 9, 1982.

"deficits don't cause high interest rates. The historical record shows no direct association of deficits and interest rates."[18]

While the administration was explaining that deficits do not matter, the CBO was predicting even larger deficits for the future. In February 1982, the CBO estimated that the baseline deficit with the president's program in place would be $200 billion in 1984 and $300 billion in 1986.[19] In an affront to the administration's credibility, Congress rejected the administration's more optimistic economic assumptions and estimates, opting instead for the CBO's baseline projections for the FY 1983 budget deliberations.

Repeated Attempts to Reduce the Deficit

From 1982 to 1984, "the country drifted into what Senator Robert Dole (R-Kansas) called an 'aimless stupor' on economic policy," as Congress and the administration tried to reduce the deficit by using a variety of gambits.[20] Congress, though implementing some additional spending cuts, relied more heavily on increased taxes to reduce the deficits. It forced the president to accept a major multiyear tax increase in 1982 and relatively minor tax increases in 1983 and 1984. The Tax Equity and Fiscal Responsibility Act (TEFRA) of 1982 reversed many of the special corporate tax provisions granted the previous year in the Economic Recovery Tax Act. This bill was politically disturbing to the president since it was initiated by Senate Republicans. The 1983 tax changes included an increase in excise taxes to finance highway reconstruction and an acceleration of the previously scheduled social security tax rate increase with partial taxation of social security benefits. The tax increase in 1984, called the Deficit Reduction Act (DRA), froze, delayed, or modified some of the smaller personal and corporate income tax provisions granted by ERTA. The effects on the deficit of the legislative changes enacted under Reagan before January 1, 1985, are shown in Exhibit 10.

On the basis of all of the policies enacted by President Reagan during his first term in office, the CBO projected a baseline budget for the fiscal years 1985 to 1990, shown in Table 1. The baseline budget is not a forecast; it is simply a benchmark for comparing alternative budget actions. Sometimes known as a current-services budget, it is calculated by extrapolating current spending and taxing policies so that they keep up with inflation.

On February 4, 1985, President Reagan announced the first budget of his second term in office. Since the president's options were limited

[18]*The Wall Street Journal*, Mar. 10, 1982, 33.

[19]Palmer and Mills, "Budget Policy," op. cit., 84.

[20]Lester Salamon and Alan Abrahamson, "Governance," in John Palmer and Isabel Sawhill, eds., *The Reagan Record* (Washington, DC: Urban Institute, 1984), 53.

Table 1   CBO Baseline Budget: Fiscal Years 1985–1990

	1985	1986	1987	1988	1989	1990
Billions of Dollars						
Revenues	735	788	855	934	1,005	1,088
Outlays[a]	950	1,008	1,095	1,191	1,284	1,390
Deficit[a]	215	220	240	257	280	302
Debt held by public	1,526	1,745	1,984	2,240	2,519	2,820
Percent of GNP						
Revenues	19.1	19.0	19.1	19.3	19.3	19.4
Outlays[a]	24.6	24.2	24.4	24.7	24.7	24.8
Deficit[a]	5.6	5.3	5.4	5.3	5.4	5.4
Debt held by public	39.6	42.0	44.3	46.4	48.4	50.3

[a]Includes programs that are off-budget under current law.

Source: Congressional Budget Office, *An Analysis of the President's Budgetary Proposals for Fiscal Year 1986* (Washington, DC: U.S. Government Printing Office, February 27, 1985), xvi.

by his pledge, repeated in the 1984 campaign, that he would neither raise taxes nor alter the "social safety net" and that he would continue to increase military spending, the administration could only continue to push for spending reductions. The budget proposed a one-year freeze in total spending other than debt service. The freeze would be achieved by cutbacks in selective programs rather than by a line-by-line procedure. The president also proposed a major tax simplification and reform package that would significantly broaden the tax base and further reduce the marginal tax rates without changing the total tax revenues. Over the next five years (FY 1986 to FY 1990), the proposals would increase defense spending by $43 billion, cut entitlements and other mandatory spending by $144 billion, cut nondefense discretionary spending by $187 billion, generate offsetting receipts of $32 billion, and save $43 billion in net interest expenses. In total, the president's budget would reduce by $368 billion the cumulative five-year deficits totaling $1.3 trillion, still leaving almost a trillion dollars in new public debt to be financed during that period.

The estimates of the size of the deficits remaining even if the president's new proposals were implemented depended on the economic assumptions used in making the forecast. The future trends in the deficits under the assumptions of the CBO and the administration are shown in Table 2. The major difference between the CBO and the administration was in the assumption on interest rates. The administration assumed that by 1990 Treasury bill rates would be over 3 percentage points lower than the CBO's estimate of 8.2 percent. In addition, the administration assumed higher real growth, lower inflation, and lower unemployment. The specific assumptions are shown in Exhibit 11.

Table 2   Estimates of the Deficits after Implementing the President's
          Proposals for FY 1986
          (In Billions of Dollars)

	1985	1986	1987	1988	1989	1990	Cumulative 5 Years
CBO economic assumptions[a]	215	186	185	186	187	187	931
Administration assumptions[a]	222	180	165	144	107	82	678

[a]President's FY 1986 proposal should be compared to CBO baseline budget in Table 1.

Source: Congressional Budget Office, *An Analysis of the President's Budgetary Proposals for Fiscal Year 1986* (Washington, DC: U.S. Government Printing Office, February 27, 1985), xxiii.

The sensitivity of the deficit estimates to the economic assumptions had been a critical factor in all previous budget debates under Reagan. Rules of thumb had been devised to help legislators determine the consequences of deficit-forecasting errors. For example, an underestimate by 1 percent in the annual Treasury bill rate from 1985 to 1990 would add about $100 billion to the cumulative deficit over that period. Alternatively, $100 billion might be added to the cumulative deficit by a real growth rate or an unemployment rate about a third of a percentage point lower, or by inflation that was about 2 percentage points higher if discretionary expenditures were allowed to be eroded by inflation. The sensitivity of the baseline deficits to economic assumptions is summarized in Exhibit 12. The limitations of these budgetary rules of thumb had to be recognized, however. The CBO warned:

First, they are not alternative forecasts. Sustained changes in one economic variable do not generally occur without changes in other economic variables as well. Second, adding up rules of thumb for two or more variables can produce misleading results. Third, one-percentage-point changes in variables were assumed as a convenience and not to reflect typical forecasting errors. For example, a one-percentage-point error in forecasting and projecting interest rates is more probable than a one-percentage-point error in projecting real growth rates over a five-year horizon.[21]

The Reagan administration had insisted that the United States could grow its way out of the deficits. To aid in that discussion, the CBO projected alternative budget paths given a consistent set of assumptions about high and low economic growth compared to the baseline. The high-growth path assumed a 5 percent annual rate of real growth, which would equal the boom of the 1960s, compared to the 4 percent growth rate assumed in the baseline projection. The low-growth path assumed a 3 percent growth rate. The assumptions on the other variables were set to be consistent with the high- or low-growth scenario. Under the high-

[21]Congressional Budget Office, *The Economic and Budget Outlook: Fiscal Years 1986–1990* (Washington, DC: U.S. Government Printing Office, February 1985), 76.

growth alternative, the cumulative five-year deficit would fall about $450 billion to a 1990 deficit of approximately 2 percent of GNP. Under the low-growth alternative, the cumulative deficit would rise about $490 billion to a 1990 level of 8.7 percent of GNP.[22]

Alternative Deficit Reduction Strategies

A strategy for reducing the deficit must first specify an acceptable target size for the deficit and then determine how fast that target ought to be reached. The strategy is largely predicated on the perceived economic consequences of the current and projected deficits. Next, a determination must be made as to how the deficit will be reduced. This is largely a question of the political feasibility of the mixture of the two broad options of spending cuts and tax increases. The CBO provided Congress with a menu of deficit reduction options for the fiscal years 1986 to 1990. The major spending and revenue proposals are listed in Exhibit 13. The spending cuts are grouped into four major categories: defense, nondefense discretionary, entitlements, and federal operations. Each spending option is then divided into subcategories; for example, defense spending is composed of procurement, military investment, military forces, and pay and benefits expenditures. The revenue options are grouped into seven major categories: income taxes, consumption taxes, investment tax preferences, industrial tax preferences, savings tax preferences, noninvestment/savings tax preferences, and general revenue measures.

[22]Ibid., 71.

The Reagan Deficits

Exhibit 1   Gross Savings and Investment: 1970–1984

A. Billions of Dollars

	National Savings								
		Gross Private Savings			Government Surplus			Gross Private Domestic Investment[c]	Net Foreign Investment[d]
Year	Total	Total	Personal Savings	Gross Business Savings[a]	Total	Federal Surplus[b]	State & Local Surplus		
	1	2	3	4	5	6	7	8	9
1970	148.9	158.6	55.8	102.8	−10.6	−12.4	1.9	144.2	3.2
1971	161.6	180.3	60.7	119.7	−19.4	−22.0	2.6	166.4	−0.7
1972	186.6	189.2	52.6	136.6	−3.3	−16.8	13.5	195.0	−5.1
1973	235.5	227.7	79.0	148.7	7.8	−5.6	13.4	229.8	6.5
1974	227.8	234.5	85.1	149.4	−4.7	−11.5	6.8	228.7	2.9
1975	218.9	282.7	94.3	188.4	−63.8	−69.3	5.5	206.1	18.3
1976	257.9	294.4	82.5	211.9	−36.5	−53.1	16.6	257.9	5.1
1977	309.1	326.9	78.0	248.9	−17.8	−45.9	28.0	324.1	−13.6
1978	374.8	374.0	89.4	284.6	0.8	−29.5	30.3	386.6	−14.3
1979	422.7	407.3	96.7	310.6	14.3	−16.1	30.4	423.0	−1.8
1980	405.9	435.4	110.2	325.2	−30.7	−61.2	30.6	401.9	6.3
1981	484.3	509.9	137.4	372.6	−26.7	−64.3	37.6	484.2	5.8
1982	408.8	524.0	136.0	388.0	−115.3	−148.2	32.9	414.9	−6.6
1983	437.2	571.7	118.1	453.6	−134.5	−178.6	44.1	471.6	−33.9
1984	551.0	675.3	156.9	518.4	−124.4	−176.4	52.0	637.3	−94.5

Exhibit 1 (Continued)

B. Percent of GNP

	National Savings					Government Surplus			
	Gross Private Savings								
Year	Total	National Savings	Personal Savings	Gross Business Savings[a]	National Savings	Federal Surplus[b]	State & Local Surplus	Gross Private Domestic Investment[c]	Net Foreign Investment[d]
	10	11	12	13	14	15	16	17	18
1970	15.0%	16.0%	5.6%	10.4%	-1.1%	-1.2%	0.2%	14.5%	0.3%
1971	15.0	16.7	5.6	11.1	-1.8	-2.0	0.2	15.4	-0.1
1972	15.7	16.0	4.4	11.5	-0.3	-1.4	1.1	16.4	-0.4
1973	17.8	17.2	6.0	11.2	0.6	-0.4	1.0	17.3	0.5
1974	15.9	16.4	5.9	10.4	-0.3	-0.8	0.5	15.9	0.2
1975	14.1	18.2	6.1	12.2	-4.1	-4.5	0.4	13.3	1.2
1976	15.0	17.1	4.8	12.3	-2.1	-3.1	1.0	15.0	0.3
1977	16.1	17.0	4.1	13.0	-0.9	-2.4	1.5	16.9	-0.7
1978	17.3	17.3	4.1	13.2	.0	-1.4	1.4	17.9	-0.7
1979	17.5	16.8	4.0	12.8	0.6	-0.7	1.3	17.5	-0.1
1980	15.4	16.5	4.2	12.4	-1.2	-2.3	1.2	15.3	0.2
1981	16.4	17.2	4.6	12.6	-0.9	-2.2	1.3	16.4	0.2
1982	13.3	17.1	4.4	12.6	-3.8	-4.8	1.1	13.5	-0.2
1983	13.2	17.3	3.6	13.7	-4.1	-5.4	1.3	14.3	-1.0
1984	15.0	18.4	4.3	14.2	-3.4	-4.8	1.4	17.4	-2.6

[a]See Exhibit 3 for the components of gross business savings.

[b]See Exhibit 4 for the components of the federal surplus.

[c]See Exhibit 2 for the components of gross private domestic investment.

[d]This equals the current account surplus (+) or deficit (−), after adjustments.

Source: *Economic Report of the President, 1985* (Washington, DC: U.S. Government Printing Office, 1985), 262.

The Reagan Deficits

Exhibit 2   Components of Gross Investment: 1970–1984

A. Billions of Dollars

Year	Total	Capital Consumption Allowance	Gross Private Domestic Investment Total	Net Private Domestic Investment Total	Net Fixed Investment Total	Nonresidential Investment Structures	Producers' Durable Equipment	Residential Investment	Change in Business Inventories
	1	2	3	4	5	6	7	8	9
1970	144.2	88.1	56.1	52.9	33.9	16.3	17.6	19.0	3.2
1971	166.4	96.5	69.9	62.3	31.1	15.6	15.5	31.2	7.7
1972	195.0	106.4	88.6	78.3	37.0	16.6	20.4	41.3	10.2
1973	229.8	116.5	113.3	94.8	51.9	20.7	31.2	42.9	18.5
1974	228.7	136.0	92.7	78.5	49.2	18.9	30.3	29.3	14.1
1975	206.1	159.3	46.8	53.8	30.4	13.1	17.3	23.4	-6.9
1976	257.9	175.0	82.9	71.1	34.3	14.1	20.2	36.8	11.8
1977	324.1	195.2	128.9	105.9	50.7	16.0	34.7	55.2	23.0
1978	386.6	222.5	164.1	137.7	73.7	23.3	50.4	64.0	26.5
1979	423.0	256.0	167.0	152.7	89.0	33.7	55.3	63.7	14.3
1980	401.9	293.2	108.7	118.6	77.1	36.2	40.9	41.5	-9.8
1981	484.2	330.3	153.9	127.9	90.6	50.9	39.7	37.3	26.0
1982	414.9	358.8	56.1	82.2	61.3	49.9	11.4	20.9	-26.1
1983	471.6	377.1	94.5	107.9	49.7	35.4	14.3	58.2	-13.5
1984	637.3	402.9	234.4	177.6	107.2	52.9	54.3	70.4	56.8

Exhibit 2 (Continued)

B. Percent of GNP

			Gross Private Domestic Investment						
				Net Private Domestic Investment					
					Net Fixed Investment				
					Nonresidential Investment				
Year	Total	Capital Consumption Allowance	Total	Total	Total	Structures	Producers' Durable Equipment	Residential Investment	Change in Business Inventories
	10	11	12	13	14	15	16	17	18
1970	14.5%	8.9%	5.7%	5.3%	3.4%	1.6%	1.8%	1.9%	0.3%
1971	15.4	9.0	6.5	5.8	2.9	1.4	1.4	2.9	0.7
1972	16.4	9.0	7.5	6.6	3.1	1.4	1.7	3.5	0.9
1973	17.3	8.8	8.5	7.1	3.9	1.6	2.4	3.2	1.4
1974	15.9	9.5	6.5	5.5	3.4	1.3	2.1	2.0	1.0
1975	13.3	10.3	3.0	3.5	2.0	0.8	1.1	1.5	-0.4
1976	15.0	10.2	4.8	4.1	2.0	0.8	1.2	2.1	0.7
1977	16.9	10.2	6.7	5.5	2.6	0.8	1.8	2.9	1.2
1978	17.9	10.3	7.6	6.4	3.4	1.1	2.3	3.0	1.2
1979	17.5	10.6	6.9	6.3	3.7	1.4	2.3	2.6	0.6
1980	15.3	11.1	4.1	4.5	2.9	1.4	1.6	1.6	-0.4
1981	16.4	11.2	5.2	4.3	3.1	1.7	1.3	1.3	0.9
1982	13.5	11.7	1.8	2.7	2.0	1.6	0.4	0.7	-0.9
1983	14.3	11.4	2.9	3.3	1.5	1.1	0.4	1.8	-0.4
1984	17.4	11.0	6.4	4.9	2.9	1.4	1.5	1.9	1.6

Source: *Economic Report of the President, 1985* (Washington, DC: U.S. Government Printing Office, 1985), 250.

The Reagan Deficits

Exhibit 3   Components of Gross Business Savings: 1970–1984

A. Billions of Dollars

Year	Total	Gross Business Savings			
		Undistributed Profits	Inventory Valuation Adjustment	Capital Consumption Adjustment	Capital Consumption Allowance
	1	2	3	4	5
1970	102.8	18.8	−6.6	2.5	88.1
1971	119.7	26.1	−4.6	1.3	96.9
1972	136.6	34.5	−6.6	2.7	106.0
1973	148.7	49.6	−20.0	2.7	116.4
1974	149.4	55.2	−40.0	−1.8	136.0
1975	188.4	50.7	−11.6	−10.1	159.4
1976	211.9	65.1	−14.7	−13.5	175.0
1977	248.9	81.2	−16.2	−11.3	195.2
1978	284.6	98.9	−24.0	−12.7	222.4
1979	310.6	112.4	−43.1	−14.8	256.1
1980	325.2	91.2	−42.9	−16.3	293.2
1981	372.6	73.5	−23.6	−7.6	330.3
1982	388.0	35.6	−9.5	3.1	358.8
1983	453.6	54.5	−11.2	33.2	377.1
1984	518.4	65.3	−5.7	55.9	402.9

Exhibit 3 (Continued)

B. Percent of GNP

Year	Total	Undistributed Profits	Inventory Valuation Adjustment	Capital Consumption Adjustment	Capital Consumption Allowance
	6	7	8	9	10
1970	10.4%	1.9%	−0.7%	0.3%	8.9%
1971	11.1	2.4	−0.4	0.1	9.0
1972	11.5	2.9	−0.6	0.2	8.9
1973	11.2	3.7	−1.5	0.2	8.8
1974	10.4	3.8	−2.8	−0.1	9.5
1975	12.2	3.3	−0.7	−0.7	10.3
1976	12.3	3.8	−0.9	−0.8	10.2
1977	13.0	4.2	−0.8	−0.6	10.2
1978	13.2	4.6	−1.1	−0.6	10.3
1979	12.8	4.6	−1.8	−0.6	10.6
1980	12.4	3.5	−1.6	−0.6	11.1
1981	12.6	2.5	−0.8	−0.3	11.2
1982	12.6	1.2	−0.3	0.1	11.7
1983	13.7	1.6	−0.3	1.0	11.4
1984	14.2	1.8	−0.2	1.5	11.0

Gross Business Savings (column group heading over Total, Undistributed Profits, Inventory Valuation Adjustment, Capital Consumption Adjustment, Capital Consumption Allowance)

Source: *Economic Report of the President, 1985* (Washington, DC: U.S. Government Printing Office, 1985), 257.

The Reagan Deficits

Exhibit 4   Components of the Federal Government Surplus: 1970–1984

A. Billions of Dollars

	Deficit	Receipts					Expenditures								
								Purchases of Goods and Services			Transfer Payments				
Year	Federal Government Surplus	Total	Personal Tax and Nontax Receipts	Corporate Profits Tax Accruals	Indirect Business Tax and Nontax Accruals	Contributions for Social Insurance	Total	Total	National Defense	Non-defense	To Persons	To Foreigners	Grants-in-aid to State and Local Governments	Net Interest Paid	Subsidies Less Current Surplus of Government Enterprises
	1	2	3	4	5	6	7	8	9	10	11	12	13	14	15
1970	−12.4	191.9	92.6	30.6	19.3	49.4	204.3	95.7	73.6	22.1	61.3	2.2	24.4	14.1	6.5
1971	−22.0	198.6	90.3	33.5	20.4	54.4	220.6	96.2	70.2	26.0	72.7	2.6	29.0	13.8	6.3
1972	−16.8	227.5	108.2	36.6	20.0	62.7	244.3	101.7	73.1	28.6	80.5	2.7	37.5	14.4	7.9
1973	−5.6	258.6	114.7	43.3	21.2	79.4	264.2	102.0	72.8	29.2	93.3	2.6	40.6	18.0	7.8
1974	−11.5	287.8	131.3	45.1	21.7	89.7	299.3	111.0	77.0	34.0	114.5	3.2	43.9	20.7	5.5
1975	−69.3	287.3	125.8	43.6	23.9	94.0	356.6	122.7	83.0	39.7	146.3	3.1	54.6	23.1	6.9
1976	−53.1	331.8	147.3	54.6	23.4	106.5	384.8	129.2	86.0	43.2	158.8	3.2	61.1	26.8	5.8
1977	−45.9	375.2	170.1	61.6	25.0	118.5	421.1	143.4	92.8	50.6	169.6	3.3	67.5	29.1	8.2
1978	−29.5	431.6	194.9	71.3	28.1	137.3	461.0	153.6	100.3	53.3	181.8	3.8	77.3	35.2	9.5
1979	−16.1	493.6	230.6	74.2	29.4	159.4	509.7	168.3	111.8	56.5	205.0	4.2	80.5	42.4	9.2
1980	−61.2	540.9	257.7	70.3	39.0	173.9	602.1	197.0	131.2	65.8	246.2	5.3	88.7	53.4	11.5
1981	−64.3	624.8	298.7	65.7	56.4	204.0	689.1	228.9	153.7	75.2	281.2	5.6	87.9	73.3	12.3
1982	−148.2	616.7	306.2	46.6	48.4	215.5	764.9	258.9	179.5	79.4	315.3	6.3	83.0	84.4	16.1
1983	−178.6	641.1	295.2	59.8	52.4	233.7	819.7	269.7	200.5	69.2	338.7	7.0	86.3	94.2	23.4
1984	−176.4	703.5	314.8	69.7	55.7	263.3	879.9	295.5	221.5	74.0	344.7	7.6	92.9	116.8	22.5

Exhibit 4 (Continued)

B. Percent of GNP

Year	Deficit: Federal Government Surplus (16)	Receipts: Total (17)	Personal Tax and Nontax Receipts (18)	Corporate Profits Tax Accruals (19)	Indirect Business Tax and Nontax Accruals (20)	Contributions for Social Insurance (21)	Expenditures: Total (22)	Purchases of Goods and Services: Total (23)	National Defense (24)	Non-defense (25)	Transfer Payments: To Persons (26)	To Foreigners (27)	Grants-in-aid to State and Local Governments (28)	Net Interest Paid (29)	Subsidies Less Current Surplus of Government Enterprises (30)
1970	-1.2%	19.3%	9.3%	3.1%	1.9%	5.0%	20.6%	9.6%	7.4%	2.2%	6.2%	0.2%	2.5%	1.4%	0.7%
1971	-2.0	18.4	8.4	3.1	1.9	5.0	20.5	8.9	6.5	2.4	6.7	0.2	2.7	1.3	0.6
1972	-1.4	19.2	9.1	3.1	1.7	5.3	20.6	8.6	6.2	2.4	6.8	0.2	3.2	1.2	0.7
1973	-0.4	19.5	8.6	3.3	1.6	6.0	19.9	7.7	5.5	2.2	7.0	0.2	3.1	1.4	0.6
1974	-0.8	20.1	9.2	3.1	1.5	6.3	20.9	7.7	5.4	2.4	8.0	0.2	3.1	1.4	0.4
1975	-4.5	18.5	8.1	2.8	1.5	6.1	23.0	7.9	5.4	2.6	9.4	0.2	3.5	1.5	0.4
1976	-3.1	19.3	8.6	3.2	1.4	6.2	22.4	7.5	5.0	2.5	9.2	0.2	3.6	1.6	0.3
1977	-2.4	19.6	8.9	3.2	1.3	6.2	22.0	7.5	4.8	2.6	8.8	0.2	3.5	1.5	0.4
1978	-1.4	19.9	9.0	3.3	1.3	6.3	21.3	7.1	4.6	2.5	8.4	0.2	3.6	1.6	0.4
1979	-0.7	20.4	9.5	3.1	1.2	6.6	21.1	7.0	4.6	2.3	8.5	0.2	3.3	1.8	0.4
1980	-2.3	20.6	9.8	2.7	1.5	6.6	22.9	7.5	5.0	2.5	9.4	0.2	3.4	2.0	0.4
1981	-2.2	21.1	10.1	2.2	1.9	6.9	23.3	7.7	5.2	2.5	9.5	0.2	3.0	2.5	0.4
1982	-4.8	20.1	10.0	1.5	1.6	7.0	24.9	8.4	5.8	2.6	10.3	0.2	2.7	2.7	0.5
1983	-5.4	19.4	8.9	1.8	1.6	7.1	24.8	8.2	6.1	2.1	10.2	0.2	2.6	2.9	0.7
1984	-4.8	19.2	8.6	1.9	1.5	7.2	24.0	8.1	6.0	2.0	9.4	0.2	2.5	3.2	0.6

Source: *Economic Report of the President, 1985* (Washington, DC: U.S. Government Printing Office, 1985), 322.

The Reagan Deficits

Exhibit 5   Federal Budget Deficit, Debt, Receipts, Outlays, and Deficit: Fiscal Years 1976–1984

(Including Outlays Off-Budget under Current Law; Millions of Dollars)

Description		1976	1977	1978	1979
Total Deficit (−)	1	**−73,719**	**−53,644**	**−58,989**	**−40,161**
(Percent of GNP)	2	(−4.5)	(−2.9)	(−2.8)	(−1.7)
Outstanding Debt Held by the Public[a]	3	**480,300**	**551,843**	**610,948**	**644,589**
(Percent of GNP)	4	(29.2)	(29.6)	(29.2)	(27.3)
Budget Receipts	5	**298,060**	**355,559**	**399,740**	**463,302**
(Percent of GNP)	6	(18.1)	(19.1)	(19.1)	(19.6)
Individual income taxes	7	131,603	157,626	180,988	217,841
Corporation income taxes	8	41,409	54,892	59,952	65,677
Social insurance taxes/contributions	9	90,769	106,485	120,967	138,939
Excise taxes	10	16,963	17,548	18,376	18,745
Estate and gift taxes	11	5,216	7,327	5,285	5,411
Customs duties	12	4,074	5,150	6,753	7,439
Deposits of earnings by Federal Reserve System	13	5,451	5,908	6,641	8,327
All other miscellaneous receipts	14	2,576	623	778	925
Budget Outlays	15	**371,779**	**409,203**	**458,729**	**503,464**
(Percent of GNP)	16	(22.6)	(22.0)	(21.9)	(21.3)
National defense	17	89,619	97,241	104,495	116,342
International affairs	18	6,433	6,353	7,482	7,459
General science, space, and technology	19	4,373	4,736	4,926	5,235
Energy	20	4,204	5,770	7,992	9,180
Natural resources and environment	21	8,184	10,032	10,983	12,135
Agriculture	22	3,170	6,787	11,357	11,236
Commerce and housing credit	23	7,619	3,093	6,254	4,686
Transportation	24	13,739	14,829	15,521	17,532
Community/regional development	25	5,442	7,021	11,841	10,480
Education, employment, social services	26	18,910	21,104	26,710	30,223
Health	27	15,734	17,302	18,524	20,494
Social security and medicare	28	89,736	104,414	116,629	130,567
Social security	29	73,903	85,068	93,861	104,073
Medicare	30	15,834	19,345	22,768	26,495
Income security	31	60,784	61,044	61,488	66,359
Veterans benefits and services	32	18,433	18,038	18,978	19,931
Administration of justice	33	3,324	3,602	3,810	4,169
General government	34	2,519	3,267	3,576	3,928
General purpose fiscal assistance	35	7,232	9,569	8,442	8,369
Net interest	36	26,711	29,878	35,441	42,615
Undistributed offsetting receipts	37	−14,386	−14,879	−15,720	−17,476

Through fiscal year 1976, the fiscal year was on a July 1-June 30 basis. Beginning October 1976 (fiscal year 1977), the fiscal year is on an October 1-September 30 basis. The three-month period from July 1, 1976, through September 30, 1976, is a separate fiscal period known as the transition quarter, not shown here.

[a]At end of period.

Exhibit 5 (Continued)

1980	1981	1982	1983	1984	
−73,808	−78,936	−127,940	−207,764	−185,324	1
(−2.9)	(−2.7)	(−4.2)	(−6.4)	(−5.2)	2
715,105	794,434	929,427	1,141,770	1,312,589	3
(27.8)	(27.5)	(30.5)	(35.4)	(36.7)	4
517,112	599,272	617,766	600,562	666,457	5
(20.1)	(20.8)	(20.3)	(18.6)	(18.6)	6
244,069	285,917	297,744	288,938	296,206	7
64,600	61,137	49,207	37,022	56,893	8
157,803	182,720	201,498	208,994	241,651	9
24,329	40,839	36,311	35,300	37,361	10
6,389	6,787	7,991	6,053	6,010	11
7,174	8,083	8,854	8,655	11,370	12
11,767	12,834	15,186	14,492	15,684	13
981	956	976	1,109	1,281	14
590,920	678,209	745,706	808,327	851,781	15
(23.0)	(23.5)	(24.5)	(25.1)	(23.8)	16
133,995	157,513	185,309	209,903	227,413	17
12,714	13,104	12,300	11,848	15,876	18
5,832	6,469	7,200	7,935	8,317	19
10,156	15,166	13,527	9,353	7,086	20
13,858	13,568	12,998	12,672	12,591	21
8,839	11,323	15,944	22,901	13,613	22
9,390	8,206	6,256	6,681	6,917	23
21,329	23,379	20,625	21,334	23,669	24
11,252	10,568	8,347	7,560	7,673	25
31,843	33,709	27,029	26,606	27,579	26
23,169	26,866	27,445	28,641	30,417	27
150,638	178,733	202,532	223,311	235,764	28
118,548	139,585	155,964	170,724	178,223	29
32,090	39,149	46,567	52,588	57,540	30
86,539	99,723	107,717	122,598	112,668	31
21,185	22,991	23,958	24,846	25,614	32
4,582	4,762	4,703	5,099	5,660	33
4,448	4,582	4,532	4,789	5,053	34
8,582	6,854	6,390	6,452	6,770	35
52,512	68,734	84,995	89,774	111,058	36
−19,942	−28,041	−26,099	−33,976	−31,957	37

The Reagan Deficits

**Exhibit 6   Cyclically Adjusted Budget:[a] 1970–1985
(Billions of Dollars, unless Otherwise Specified)**

| Year | Surplus or Deficit (−) | | Receipts | | Expenditures | |
| | Level | Percent of Trend GNP[b] | Level | Percent of Trend GNP[b] | Level | Percent of Trend GNP[b] |
	1	2	3	4	5	6
1970	−8.6	−0.9	196.2	19.6	204.8	20.4
1971	−15.9	−1.5	204.4	18.7	220.4	20.1
1972	−16.1	−1.4	228.3	19.3	244.4	20.6
1973	−15.0	−1.2	250.0	19.4	265.0	20.5
1974	−8.1	−0.6	291.8	20.2	300.0	20.7
1975	−42.8	−2.6	308.6	19.0	351.3	21.6
1976	−37.9	−2.2	344.6	19.6	382.4	21.7
1977	−45.7	−2.4	375.5	19.6	421.1	22.0
1978	−46.4	−2.2	417.5	19.8	463.9	22.0
1979	−37.1	−1.6	476.7	20.2	513.8	21.8
1980	−58.5	−2.2	544.7	20.6	603.2	22.8
1981	−57.3	−1.9	631.9	21.3	689.2	23.2
1982	−92.5	−3.0	665.0	20.5	757.5	23.5
1983	−129.2	−3.7	685.6	19.6	814.8	23.3
1984	−174.1	−4.8	710.4	19.6	884.5	24.4
1985 (est.)	−197.9	−5.3	769.3	20.6	967.1	25.9

[a]A cyclically adjusted budget is an estimate of what the budget would be if the economy were moving along some trend GNP path rather than along its actual path. Essentially, it eliminates the effects of economic fluctuations on the budget.

[b]Trend GNP is constructed to connect real GNP averages in middle periods of economic expansions.

Source: Frank deLeeuw and Thomas Holloway, "Cyclical Adjustment of the Federal Budget and Federal Debt," *Survey of Current Business* (Dec. 1983), 32, and Federal Reserve Bank of St. Louis, *Monetary Trends* (May 1985), 14.

Exhibit 7 Flow of Funds—Debt Outstanding and Net Credit Raised: 1970–1984

Stocks: Credit Market Debt Owed by Nonfinancial Sectors (Year-End Outstandings): 1970–1984

A. Credit Market Debt Outstanding (Billions of Dollars)

		1970	1971	1972	1973	1974	1975	1976	1977	1978	1979	1980	1981	1982	1983	1984
1	Domestic nonfinancial debt	1432	1570	1731	1919	2094	2289	2533	2854	3218	3604	3948	4328	4729	5255	5971
2	U.S. government debt	301	326	341	349	361	446	516	573	626	664	743	830	991	1178	1377
3	Private domestic nonfinancial	1131	1244	1390	1571	1733	1843	2017	2282	2592	2942	3206	3498	3737	4078	4594
4	State and local government	149	167	181	194	209	223	238	254	262	280	297	303	334	371	404
5	Households	481	526	591	671	724	775	867	1004	1183	1363	1487	1619	1712	1888	2134
6	Nonfinancial business	501	551	618	706	800	844	912	1024	1147	1299	1422	1576	1691	1819	2056
7	Foreign debt held in U.S.	51	55	61	67	80	91	111	124	162	183	210	237	226	245	248

B. Credit Market Debt Outstanding (Percentage of GNP)

		1970	1971	1972	1973	1974	1975	1976	1977	1978	1979	1980	1981	1982	1983	1984
8	Domestic nonfinancial debt	144%	146%	146%	145%	146%	148%	147%	149%	149%	149%	150%	146%	154%	159%	163%
9	U.S. government debt	30	30	29	26	25	29	30	30	29	27	28	28	32	36	38
10	Private domestic nonfinancial	114	115	117	118	121	119	117	119	120	122	122	118	122	123	125
11	State and local government	15	15	15	15	15	14	14	13	12	12	11	10	11	11	11
12	Households	48	49	50	51	50	50	50	52	55	56	56	55	56	57	58
13	Nonfinancial business	50	51	52	53	56	54	53	53	53	54	54	53	55	55	56
14	Foreign debt held in U.S.	5	5	5	5	6	6	6	6	7	8	8	8	7	7	7

Exhibit 7 (Continued)

Flows: Net Credit Raised by Nonfinancial Sectors: 1970–1984

C. Credit Raised (Billions of Dollars)

		1970	1971	1972	1973	1974	1975	1976	1977	1978	1979	1980	1981	1982	1983	1984
Domestic net borrowing	15	98.6	148.8	172.8	187.7	175.3	193.0	243.5	319.4	369.8	386.0	344.6	380.4	404.1	526.4	715.3
U.S. government	16	12.8	24.9	15.1	8.3	11.8	85.4	69.0	56.8	53.7	37.4	79.2	87.4	161.3	186.6	198.8
Private domestic nonfinancial	17	85.7	124.0	157.7	179.4	163.5	107.6	174.5	262.7	316.1	348.6	265.4	293.1	242.9	339.8	516.6
State and local government	18	13.9	17.7	14.5	12.8	14.6	12.3	13.2	12.0	16.5	17.6	17.2	6.2	31.3	36.7	33.0
Households	19	22.3	44.9	65.1	78.1	54.8	53.5	91.5	140.7	172.0	179.3	122.1	127.5	94.5	175.4	241.6
Nonfinancial business	20	49.5	61.4	78.1	88.5	94.1	41.8	69.8	110.0	127.6	151.7	126.1	159.4	117.1	127.7	242.0
Foreign net borrowing	21	3.0	5.1	4.0	6.3	15.0	11.3	19.3	13.5	33.8	20.2	27.2	27.2	15.7	18.9	1.7

D. Credit Raised (Percentage of GNP)

		1970	1971	1972	1973	1974	1975	1976	1977	1978	1979	1980	1981	1982	1983	1984
Domestic net borrowing	22	9.9%	13.8%	14.6%	14.2%	12.2%	12.5%	14.2%	16.7%	17.1%	16.0%	13.1%	12.9%	13.2%	15.9%	19.5%
U.S. government	23	1.3	2.3	1.3	0.6	0.8	5.5	4.0	3.0	2.5	1.5	3.0	3.0	5.3	5.6	5.4
Private domestic nonfinancial	24	8.6	11.5	13.3	13.5	11.4	6.9	10.2	13.7	14.6	14.4	10.1	9.9	7.9	10.3	14.1
State and local government	25	1.4	1.6	1.2	1.0	1.0	0.8	0.8	0.6	0.8	0.7	0.7	0.2	1.0	1.1	0.9
Households	26	2.2	4.2	5.5	5.9	3.8	3.5	5.3	7.3	7.9	7.4	4.6	4.3	3.1	5.3	6.6
Nonfinancial business	27	5.0	5.7	6.6	6.7	6.6	2.7	4.1	5.7	5.9	6.3	4.8	5.4	3.8	3.9	6.6
Foreign net borrowing	28	0.3	0.5	0.3	0.5	1.0	0.7	1.1	0.7	1.6	0.8	1.0	0.9	0.5	0.6	.0

Note: Since Exhibits 7A and 7B show the "stock" of debt outstanding at year-end, the difference between two consecutive years should be the "flow" of net credit raised in that year shown in Exhibits 7C and 7D. These calculations are approximations since the table was constructed from different sources.

Source: Board of Governors of the Federal Reserve System, *Flow of Funds Accounts*, Statistical Release Z.1 and Z.7, August 1983 and February 1985, *Economic Report of the President, 1979*, and *Economic Report of the President, 1985* (Washington, DC: U.S. Government Printing Office, 1979 and 1985).

The Reagan Deficits

Exhibit 8   Interest Rates and Exchange Rates (Nominal and Real): 1977—1984
(In Percent)

	1977	1978	1979	1980	1981	1982	1983	1984
Nominal Interest Rates								
United States	5.6	8.2	11.2	13.2	15.9	12.3	9.1	10.4
Average, 7 major industrial countries[a]	6.7	7.4	9.8	12.7	14.1	11.7	9.2	9.7
Real Interest Rates[b]								
United States	−1.0	−0.4	1.3	3.7	8.9	8.1	5.8	6.9
Average, 7 major industrial countries[a]	−0.2	−0.4	0.7	3.4	6.3	6.8	5.2	6.0
Nominal Effective Exchange Rate[c]	103.3	92.4	88.1	87.4	102.9	116.6	125.3	138.2
Real[d] Effective Exchange Rate[d]	93.1	84.2	83.2	84.8	100.8	111.7	117.3	128.7

[a]These composites are averages of individual country average rates, weighted for each year in proportion to the U.S. dollar values of the respective GNPs in the preceding three years. The seven countries are Canada, France, Germany, Italy, Japan, the United Kingdom, and the United States.

[b]Excess of nominal rate over expected inflation. Expected inflation is proxied by a weighted average of the rate of inflation in the current quarter and the next two quarters, with the deflator of private final domestic demand being used as the price variable.

[c]Multilateral trade-weighted value of U.S. dollar (March 1973 = 100).

[d]Adjusted by changes in consumer prices.

Source: International Monetary Fund, *World Economic Outlook* (April 1985), 120, and *Economic Report of the President, 1985* (Washington, DC: U.S. Government Printing Office, 1985), 351.

The Reagan Deficits

Exhibit 9 Gross National Product: 1970–1984

A. Nominal (Billions of Dollars, Except as Noted)

		Personal Consumption Expenditures				Gross Private Domestic Investment										Net Exports of Goods and Services			Government Purchases of Goods and Services						Percent Change from Preceding Period	
							Fixed Investment								Change in Business Inventories					Federal						
								Nonresidential		Residential																
Year	Gross National Product	Total	Durable Goods	Non-durable Goods	Services	Total	Total	Total	Structures	Producers' Durable Equipment	Total	Nonfarm Structures	Farm Structures	Producers' Durable Equipment	Change in Business Inventories	Net Exports	Exports	Imports	Total	Total	National Defense	Non-defense	State and Local	Final Sales	Gross National Product	Final Sales
	1	2	3	4	5	6	7	8	9	10	11	12	13	14	15	16	17	18	19	20	21	22	23	24	25	26
1970	992.7	621.7	85.2	265.7	270.8	144.2	141.0	103.9	38.7	65.2	37.1	35.4	.6	1.1	3.2	6.7	65.7	59.0	220.1	95.7	73.6	22.2	124.4	989.5	5.2	5.9
1971	1,077.6	672.2	97.2	278.8	296.2	166.4	158.8	107.9	40.5	67.4	50.9	48.9	.7	1.3	7.7	4.1	68.8	64.7	234.4	96.2	70.2	26.0	138.7	1,070.0	8.6	8.1
1972	1,185.9	737.1	111.1	300.6	325.3	195.0	184.8	121.0	44.1	76.9	63.8	61.5	.7	1.5	10.2	.7	77.5	76.7	253.1	101.7	73.1	28.5	151.4	1,175.7	10.1	9.9
1973	1,326.4	812.0	123.3	333.4	355.2	229.8	211.3	143.3	51.0	92.3	68.0	65.6	.7	1.7	18.5	14.2	109.6	95.4	270.4	102.0	72.8	29.1	168.5	1,307.9	11.8	11.2
1974	1,434.2	888.1	121.5	373.4	393.2	228.7	214.5	156.6	55.9	100.7	57.9	54.8	1.3	1.8	14.1	13.4	146.2	132.8	304.1	111.0	77.0	33.9	193.1	1,420.1	8.1	8.6
1975	1,549.2	976.4	132.2	407.3	437.0	206.1	213.0	157.7	55.4	102.3	55.3	52.4	1.0	1.9	-6.9	26.8	154.9	128.1	339.9	122.7	83.0	39.7	217.2	1,556.1	8.0	9.6
1976	1,718.0	1,084.3	156.8	441.7	485.7	257.9	246.0	174.1	58.8	115.3	72.0	68.8	1.1	2.1	11.8	13.8	170.9	157.1	362.1	129.2	86.0	43.2	232.9	1,706.2	10.9	9.6
1977	1,918.3	1,204.4	178.2	478.8	547.4	324.1	301.0	205.2	64.4	140.8	95.8	92.0	1.5	2.3	23.0	-4.0	182.7	186.7	393.8	143.4	92.8	50.6	250.4	1,895.3	11.7	11.1
1978	2,163.9	1,346.5	200.2	528.2	618.0	386.6	360.1	248.9	78.7	170.2	111.2	107.0	1.7	2.5	26.5	-1.1	218.7	219.8	431.9	153.6	100.3	53.3	278.3	2,137.4	12.8	12.8
1979	2,417.8	1,507.2	213.4	600.0	693.7	423.0	408.8	290.2	98.3	191.9	118.6	114.0	1.7	2.9	14.3	13.2	281.4	268.1	474.4	168.3	111.8	56.5	306.0	2,403.5	11.7	12.4
1980	2,631.7	1,668.1	214.7	668.8	784.5	401.9	411.7	308.8	110.9	197.9	102.9	98.1	1.8	3.0	-9.8	23.9	338.8	314.8	537.8	197.0	131.2	65.9	340.8	2,641.5	8.8	9.9
1981	2,957.8	1,849.1	235.4	730.7	883.0	484.2	458.1	353.9	135.3	218.6	104.3	99.8	1.3	3.2	26.0	28.0	369.9	341.9	596.5	228.9	153.7	75.2	367.6	2,931.7	12.4	11.0
1982	3,069.3	1,984.9	245.1	757.5	982.2	414.9	441.0	349.6	142.1	207.5	91.4	86.6	1.5	3.3	-26.1	19.0	348.4	329.4	650.5	258.9	179.5	79.4	391.5	3,095.4	3.8	5.6
1983	3,304.8	2,155.9	279.8	801.7	1,074.4	471.6	485.1	352.9	129.7	223.2	132.2	127.6	1.0	3.6	-13.5	-8.3	336.2	344.4	685.5	269.7	200.5	69.3	415.8	3,318.3	7.7	7.2
1984	3,661.3	2,342.3	318.4	858.3	1,165.7	637.3	580.4	426.0	150.3	275.7	154.4	149.3	1.1	4.0	56.8	-66.3	363.7	429.9	748.0	295.5	221.5	74.0	452.4	3,604.4	10.8	8.6

Exhibit 9 (Continued)

B. Real (Billions of 1972 Dollars, Except as Noted)

Year	Gross National Product	Personal Consumption Expenditures — Total	Durable Goods	Nondurable Goods	Services	Gross Private Domestic Investment — Total	Fixed Investment — Total	Nonresidential — Total	Structures	Producers' Durable Equipment	Residential — Total	Nonfarm Structures	Farm Structures	Producers' Durable Equipment	Change in Business Inventories	Net Exports	Exports	Imports	Government Purchases — Total	Federal — Total	National Defense	Nondefense	State and Local	Final Sales	% Change GNP	% Change Final Sales
	27	28	29	30	31	32	33	34	35	36	37	38	39	40	41	42	43	44	45	46	47	48	49	50	51	52
1970	1,085.6	672.1	89.1	283.7	299.3	158.5	154.8	113.8	43.9	69.9	41.0	39.2	.6	1.1	3.8	3.9	70.5	66.6	251.1	110.6	—	—	140.5	1,081.8	-.2	.5
1971	1,122.4	696.8	98.2	288.7	309.9	173.9	165.8	112.2	42.8	69.3	53.7	51.6	.7	1.3	8.1	1.6	71.0	69.3	250.1	103.7	—	—	146.4	1,114.3	3.4	3.0
1972	1,185.9	737.1	111.1	300.6	325.3	195.0	184.8	121.0	44.1	76.9	63.8	61.5	.7	1.5	10.2	.7	77.5	76.7	253.1	101.7	73.1	28.5	151.4	1,175.7	5.7	5.5
1973	1,254.3	767.9	121.3	307.4	339.2	217.5	200.4	138.1	47.4	90.7	62.3	59.9	.6	1.7	17.2	15.5	97.3	81.8	253.3	95.9	68.3	27.6	157.4	1,237.1	5.8	5.2
1974	1,246.3	762.8	112.3	302.5	348.0	195.5	183.9	135.7	43.6	92.1	48.2	45.3	1.1	1.7	11.6	27.8	108.5	80.7	260.3	96.6	66.9	29.7	163.6	1,234.7	-.6	-.2
1975	1,231.6	779.4	112.7	307.5	359.3	154.8	161.5	119.3	38.3	81.1	42.2	39.8	.8	1.6	-6.7	32.2	103.5	71.4	265.2	97.4	66.4	31.0	167.8	1,238.4	-1.2	.3
1976	1,298.2	823.1	126.6	321.9	374.7	184.5	176.7	125.6	39.5	86.1	51.2	48.7	.8	1.7	7.8	25.4	110.1	84.7	265.2	96.3	64.9	31.8	168.4	1,290.4	5.4	4.2
1977	1,369.7	864.3	138.0	333.4	393.0	214.2	200.9	140.3	40.4	99.9	60.7	57.9	1.0	1.8	13.3	22.0	112.9	90.9	269.2	100.4	65.4	35.0	168.8	1,356.4	5.5	5.1
1978	1,438.6	903.2	146.8	344.4	412.0	236.7	220.7	158.3	44.6	113.7	62.4	59.5	1.0	1.9	16.0	24.0	126.7	103.7	274.6	100.3	65.7	34.7	174.3	1,422.6	5.0	4.9
1979	1,479.4	927.6	147.2	353.1	427.3	236.3	229.1	169.9	49.1	120.8	59.1	56.3	.8	2.0	7.3	37.2	146.2	109.0	278.3	102.1	67.4	34.8	176.2	1,472.2	2.8	3.5
1980	1,475.0	931.8	137.5	355.6	438.8	208.5	212.9	165.8	48.8	117.0	47.1	44.2	.8	2.0	-4.4	50.3	159.1	108.8	284.3	106.4	70.0	36.4	177.9	1,479.4	-.3	.5
1981	1,512.2	950.5	140.9	360.8	448.8	230.9	219.6	175.0	53.2	121.8	44.5	42.0	.5	2.0	11.3	43.8	160.2	116.4	287.0	110.3	73.5	36.7	176.8	1,500.9	2.5	1.5
1982	1,480.0	963.3	140.5	363.1	459.8	194.3	204.7	166.9	53.3	113.5	37.9	35.3	.6	1.9	-10.4	25.7	147.6	118.0	292.7	117.0	79.1	37.9	175.7	1,490.4	-2.1	-.7
1983	1,534.7	1,009.2	157.5	376.3	475.4	221.0	224.6	171.0	49.2	121.8	53.7	51.2	.4	2.1	-3.6	12.6	139.5	126.9	291.9	116.2	84.7	31.5	175.7	1,538.3	3.7	3.2
1984	1,639.0	1,062.6	177.9	394.2	490.6	289.7	265.5	205.2	56.9	148.3	60.3	57.6	.4	2.3	24.2	-15.5	145.8	161.3	302.2	122.4	89.5	32.9	179.8	1,614.8	6.8	5.0

Source: *Economic Report of the President, 1985* (Washington, DC: U.S. Government Printing Office, 1985), 232–235.

The Reagan Deficits

Exhibit 10   Effect of Policy Changes Since 1981 on Budget Deficits (By Fiscal Year, in Billions of Dollars)

		1982	1983	1984	1985	1986	1987	1988	1989	1990
Deficit (−) or surplus under policies in effect Jan. 1, 1981	1	−106	−151	−95	−74	−64	−42	−17	11	68
Legislative changes—total	2	−5	−45	−81	−129	−143	−183	−223	−276	−359
Tax reductions	3	−41	−75	−99	−111	−130	−149	−162	−186	−228
ERTA of 1981[b]	4	−42	−93	−141	−169	−208	−244	−270	−299	−335
TEFRA of 1982[c]	5	a	16	34	37	48	58	58	54	53
Tax changes of 1983[d]	6	—	1	7	11	12	14	26	32	24
DRA of 1984[e]	7	—	—	1	9	16	22	24	26	30
Defense-spending increases	8	−3	−16	−23	−35	−41	−53	−65	−79	−95
Nondefense-spending cuts	9	40	48	50	38	63	69	73	82	88
Discretionary spending	10	29	28	23	16	23	24	25	26	27
Entitlements and other mandatory spending[f]	11	11	18	24	18	37	41	47	52	56
Net interest	12	—	1	2	2	1	1	−2	a	1
Offsetting receipts	13	—	1	2	2	2	3	3	3	3
Effect of legislative action on interest costs	14	a	−3	−10	−21	−35	−50	−69	−92	−123
Deficit under policies in effect Jan. 1, 1985	15	−111	−195	−175	−203	−206	−225	−240	−266	−290

Relationship among the rows: 1 + 2 = 15; 2 = 3 + 8 + 9 + 14; 3 = 4 + 5 + 6 + 7; 9 = 10 + 11 + 12 + 13.

[a]Less than $500 million.

[b]Economic Recovery Tax Act (ERTA) of 1981.

[c]Tax Equity and Fiscal Responsibility Act (TEFRA) of 1982.

[d]The Surface Transportation Assistance Act, Social Security amendments, repeal of the withholding of tax from interest and dividends.

[e]Deficit Reduction Act (DRA) of 1984.

[f]Includes one-time purchase of low-income housing notes in 1984 and 1985.

Source: Congressional Budget Office, The Economic and Budget Outlook: Fiscal Years 1986–1990 (Washington, DC: U.S. Government Printing Office, Feb. 6, 1985), 153–155.

The Reagan Deficits

Exhibit 11   Comparison of Administration and CBO Economic Assumptions: 1985–1990 (By Calendar Year)

	Actual 1984	1985	1986	1987	1988	1989	1990
Nominal GNP (in billions of dollars)	3661						
Administration		3948	4285	4642	5017	5399	5780
CBO		3927	4238	4567	4921	5301	5711
Real GNP (percent change)[a]	6.8						
Administration		3.9	4.0	4.0	4.0	3.9	3.6
CBO		3.5	3.2	3.3	3.4	3.4	3.4
Consumer Price Index (percent change)[b]	3.4						
Administration		4.1	4.3	4.2	3.9	3.6	3.3
CBO		3.8	4.5	4.2	4.2	4.2	4.2
91-day Treasury bill rate (percent)	9.5						
Administration		8.1	7.9	7.2	5.9	5.1	5.0
CBO		8.3	8.7	8.2	8.2	8.2	8.2
Civilian unemployment rate (percent)	7.5						
Administration[b]		7.0	6.9	6.6	6.3	6.1	5.8
CBO		7.1	6.9	6.7	6.6	6.4	6.2

[a]Year over year.

[b]Urban wage and clerical workers.

[c]The administration's projection is for the total labor force including armed forces residing in the United States, while CBO's is for the civilian labor force excluding armed forces. In recent years, the former has tended to be 0.1 to 0.2 percentage point below the rate for the civilian labor force.

Source: *An Analysis of the President's Budgetary Proposals for Fiscal Year 1986*, February 27, 1985, 4.

The Reagan Deficits

Exhibit 12   Effects on CBO Baseline Budget Projections of Selected Changes in Economic Assumptions (By Fiscal Year, in Billions of Dollars)

Economic Variables	1985	1986	1987	1988	1989	1990
Real Growth:						
Effect of one-percentage-point higher annual rate beginning January 1985						
Change in revenues	5	16	32	50	70	92
Change in budget outlays	−1	−3	−8	−14	−23	−35
Change in total deficit	−5	−19	−40	−64	−93	−128
Unemployment:						
Effect of one-percentage-point lower annual rate beginning January 1985						
Change in revenues	20	32	34	35	37	39
Change in budget outlays	−4	−7	−12	−17	−22	−28
Change in total deficit	−24	−40	−46	−52	−59	−68
Interest Rates:						
Effect of one-percentage-point higher annual rates beginning January 1985						
Change in revenues	a	1	1	1	1	1
Change in budget outlays	3	10	15	22	26	33
Change in total deficit	3	9	14	21	25	31
Inflation:						
Effect of one-percentage-point higher annual rate beginning January 1985						
Assuming inflation adjustments in discretionary appropriations						
Change in revenues	5	13	24	36	49	64
Change in budget outlays	3	13	25	40	54	71
Change in total deficit	−2	a	a	4	5	7
Assuming no change in discretionary appropriations						
Change in revenues	5	13	24	36	49	64
Change in budget outlays	3	12	19	29	35	43
Change in total deficit	−2	−1	−5	−8	−14	−21

aLess than $500 million.

Source: Congressional Budget Office, *The Economic and Budget Outlook: Fiscal Years 1986–1990* (Washington, DC: U.S. Government Printing Office, Feb. 6, 1985), 75.

The Reagan Deficits

Exhibit 13   Selected Spending and Revenue Options for Reducing the Deficit (Reductions from CBO Baseline Budget in Millions of Dollars)

	FY 1986 Savings	Cumulative 5-Year Savings (FY 1986 to FY 1990)
I. Defense-Spending Options[a]		
A. Procurement[a]		
1. Cancel the MX missile program	1,170	10,150
2. Amend the administration's airlift plan	270	6,180
3. Reduce construction of new submarines and LSDs	60	2,110
4. Cancel the F-15 fighter pilot program	430	9,220
5. Cancel the LANTIRN (an infrared navigation system for pilots) program	80	2,380
6. Cancel the Army Helicopter Improvement Program	30	1,210
7. Limit production of the M2 Bradley Fighting Vehicle	5	1,375
8. Cancel the Division Air Defense Gun	50	1,800
B. Military Investment[a]		
9. Limit spending growth for supporting Procurement		
a. Reduce real growth by 50 percent	230	4,080
b. Limit 1986 spending to real 1985 level	440	22,530
10. Limit growth in research and development		
a. Reduce spending by 8 percent	1,600	16,530
b. Limit 1986 spending to real 1985 level	3,230	45,320
11. Slow or limit growth in the Strategic Defense Initiative ("Star Wars" program)		
a. Spread spending over six years	430	6,240
b. Reinstate former spending level	960	15,420
12. Limit spending growth for military construction		
a. Limit growth to 6 percent	100	4,200
b. Limit 1986 spending to real 1985 level	200	10,400
C. Military Forces[a]		
13. Slow increases in the Tactical Air Force	0	2,040
14. Limit operation and maintenance spending		
a. Reduce spending by 3 percent	2,000	15,200
b. Limit spending to 1985 levels	2,900	74,700
D. Pay and Benefits[a]		
15. Eliminate the annual military pay raise	1,300	7,200
II. Nondefense Discretionary Spending Options[a]		
A. International Affairs and Space Programs[a]		
1. End the Export-Import Bank Direct Loan Program	320	7,110
2. Decrease funding for the Space Shuttle	200	1,260
B. Natural Resources Programs[a]		
3. Eliminate commercially oriented energy development	340	3,510
4. Eliminate federal maintenance assistance for deep-draft ports	430	2,320

(Continued)

Exhibit 13 (Continued)

C. Commercial, Regional, and Business Development[a]

5. End direct and indirect subsidies to the postal service		
a. End direct subsidies	790	4,310
b. End indirect subsidies	220	2,440
6. Eliminate new lending under Rural Housing Loan Program	1,950	12,750

D. Transportation Programs[a]

7. Reduce federal mass transit aid	700	6,790
8. Reduce and refocus highway spending	990	21,940
9. Raise aviation user fees to cover air traffic control costs	360	2,630
10. Establish user fees for certain Coast Guard services	870	4,750

E. Human Resources[a]

11. Terminate the elementary and secondary education block grant	40	2,320
12. Limit eligibility for VA hospital care to service-disabled and poor veterans	490	7,440

III. Entitlements and Other Mandatory Spending[a]

A. Health Care Programs[a]

1. Tax some employer-paid health insurance		
a. Income tax	3,500	35,300
b. Payroll tax	1,400	14,100
2. Reduce hospital reimbursements under Medicare	2,060	16,500
3. Extend freeze on physicians' fees paid by Medicare for one more year	490	3,180
4. Adopt a fee schedule for reimbursing physicians under Medicare	490	4,630
5. Increase Medicare's premium for physicians' services	1,650	17,200
6. Tax a portion of Medicare benefits	500	9,300
7. Increase Medicare's deductible for physicians' services	610	5,960
8. Increase cost sharing for Medicare and add catastrophy protection	1,710	15,690
9. Tax premiums for "Medigap" policies	3,150	23,950
10. Increase the hospital insurance payroll tax by half a percentage point	13,900	15,690
11. Limit payments for long-term care services through a block grant	850	7,300

B. Social Security and Other Retirement and Disability Programs[a]

12. Restrict cost-of-living adjustments in non-means-tested benefits		
a. Eliminate COLAs for one year	6,200	42,950
b. Limit COLAs to CPI increase minus 2 percentage points for five years.	3,600	70,750
13. Cover all newly hired state and local government workers under Social Security	210	7,050
14. Eliminate veterans' compensation payments for those with low-rated disabilities	1,500	7,400

C. Other Entitlements and Grants to State and Local Governments[a]

15. Require a two-week waiting period for unemployment insurance	—	3,590
16. Index the unemployment insurance taxable wage base	—	4,250
17. Reduce guaranteed student loan subsidies	−55	2,870
18. Reduce subsidy for nonpoor children in child nutrition programs	—	4,250

Exhibit 13 (Continued)

19. Terminate or restrict eligibility for general revenue sharing
    (GRS)
        a. Terminate GRS   3,450   23,800
        b. Restrict eligibility for GRS   1,050   7,150
20. Reduce and retarget aid for dependent care   55   2,605

D. Agriculture Policy Supports[a]

21. Strengthen crop prices with mandatory production controls   820   20,800
22. Limit income assistance to large-scale crop farms   0   4,000
23. Reduce the price-increasing features of major crop programs
        a. Eliminate deficiency payments   730   28,900
        b. Phase the elimination of deficiency payments   730   17,400
24. Reduce price supports in dairy industry   250   3,000

IV. Federal Operations[a]

A. Cut Federal Pay and Benefits[a]

1. Reduce middle-management jobs   430   5,140
2. Freeze annual pay adjustment for civilian employees in 1986   1,500   9,300
3. Modify civil service retirement provisions   110   2,730

V. Revenue Options[a]

A. Individual and Corporate Income Taxes[a]

1. Raise marginal tax rates for individuals
       a. Raise marginal tax rates 10%   21,100 151,600
       b. Raise marginal rates 10% on income in excess of
           $100,000 for joint filers, $70,000 for single filers   2,200   30,100
2. Amend or repeal indexing of income tax rates
       a. Repeal indexing   5,300 149,300
       b. Delay further indexing until Jan. 1, 1987   5,300   44,400
       c. Index for inflation in excess of 3 percent   4,300 107,500
3. Impose a corporate surtax
       a. Surtax on tax before credits—10%   6,600   58,500
       b. Surtax on tax before credits—5%   3,300   29,300
4. Reduced rates on the first $100,000 of corporate income
       a. Repeal lower rates   5,100   41,700
       b. Phase out above $100,000   600   5,200

B. Consumption Taxes[a]

5. Impose a value-added or national sales tax
       a. 5 percent tax, comprehensive base, effective Jan. 1,
          1987   — 395,500
       b. 5 percent tax, narrower base exemptions for food,
          housing, and medical care, effective Jan. 1, 1987   — 252,900
       c. 5 percent tax, narrower base, no exemptions for food,
          drugs, and medical care; low-income relief under
          food stamps and Medicaid, effective Jan. 1, 1987   — 331,000
6. Increase energy taxes
       a. Impose tax on domestic and imported oil   14,800 103,000
       b. Impose oil import fee ($5 per barrel)   6,600   44,400
       c. Impose excise tax on natural gas ($1 per 1,000 cubic ft.) 9,200   62,500
       d. Increase motor fuel excise tax (12¢ per gallon)   7,400   48,500
       e. Impose broad-based tax on domestic energy con-
          sumption   9,800   75,800

(Continued)

Exhibit 13 (Continued)

7. Increase excise taxes		
a. Extend TEFRA increase of telephone excise tax	—	6,600
b. Extend TEFRA increase of cigarette excise tax	1,500	8,300
c. Double excise taxes on beer and wine	800	5,500
d. Increase excise taxes on distilled spirits	1,100	7,500
e. Index current cigarette and alcohol excise tax rates and inflation	200	4,100
C. Investment Tax Preferences[a]		
8. Revise depreciation rules to reflect economic depreciation		
a. Revise depreciation rules	600	35,500
b. Revise depreciation rules and repeal ITC	15,500	196,000
9. Eliminate investment tax credit ITC or require full basis adjustment		
a. Eliminate credit	14,500	150,200
b. Require full basis adjustment	500	16,400
D. Industrial Tax Preferences[a]		
10. Reduce incentives for building rehabilitation		
a. Repeal rehabilitation tax credits	100	6,600
b. Limit credits to historic renovations	100	3,700
11. Repeal preferences for foreign sales corporations (DISC)	600	5,400
12. Repeal percentage depletion allowance and expensing of intangible drilling, exploration, and development costs		
a. Repeal percentage depletion allowance	1,300	10,900
b. Repeal percentage depletion allowance and expensing of intangible drilling, exploration, and development costs	2,900	18,300
13. Eliminate private-purpose tax-exempt bonds		
a. Mortgage revenue bonds	200	4,600
b. Industrial development bonds	100	5,700
c. Student loan bonds	—	1,100
d. Hospital bonds	100	4,400
14. Eliminate special capital gains treatment for timber and for coal and iron ore royalties	500	4,900
15. Eliminate preferences for all financial institutions	2,200	23,000
16. Restrict use of cash method of accounting	400	3,500
17. Tax limited partnerships with more than 35 limited partners as corporations	300	2,100
18. Extend the at-risk limitation	300	2,400
19. Repeal the tax credit for employee stock ownership plans (ESOP)	1,100	5,400
E. Savings Tax Preferences[a]		
20. Tax accrued interest on life insurance reserves	1,300	18,100
21. Reduce exclusion for long-term capital gains	—	13,800
22. Tax capital gains at death	—	19,300
23. Repeal the capital gains exclusion for home sales by persons aged 55 and over	100	3,900
24. Decrease maximum limits on pension contributions by one third	600	8,900

Exhibit 13 (Continued)

F. Noninvestment/Savings Tax Preferences[a]

25. Tax nonretirement fringe benefits		
a. Tax health insurance premiums—income tax	17,000	146,100
b. Tax health insurance premiums—payroll tax	6,600	57,900
c. Tax life insurance premiums—income tax	1,600	12,400
d. Tax life insurance premiums—payroll tax	600	4,000
e. Disallow "cafeteria" plans—income tax	200	8,500
26. Restrict deductions for business entertainment and meals	600	7,500
27. Eliminate or reduce itemized deductions		
a. Allow medical expense deduction only for costs over 10% adjusted gross income (AGI)	400	12,300
b. Eliminate deductibility of state and local taxes		
1. Income taxes	2,900	98,800
2. State taxes	700	23,400
3. Property taxes	1,600	54,000
c. Limit itemized interest deduction to $10,000 for joint returns ($7,500 for others)	600	19,900
d. Repeal charitable deduction for nonitemizers	400	3,200
e. Limit itemized charitable deduction to contributions over 2% of adjusted gross income (AGI)	800	25,400
28. Increase taxation of non-means-tested entitlement benefits		
a. Social Security	2,100	35,200
b. Unemployment compensation	300	3,900
c. Workers' compensation	1,500	13,800
29. Eliminate extra tax exemption for elderly and blind	1,000	13,300
G. General Revenue Measures		
30. Increase audit coverage and expand withholding		
a. Increase audit coverage from 1.5% to 2.3% of taxpayers	400	10,800
b. Extend coverage of withholding	1,600	19,800
31. Reduce tax preferences across the board (10% cut in deductions, 20% cut in credits, and lengthen depreciation lines by 20%)	8,000	178,000
32. Expand the existing corporate minimum tax or replace it with an alternative minimum tax		
a. Expand base of present add-on minimum tax on preferences	2,200	31,300
b. Impose 15% alternative minimum tax on comparable base	3,300	31,200
33. Place a per-country limit on foreign tax credit	900	13,300

[a]Options listed under this heading are not necessarily available at the same time, since overlap or interdependence may exist among the choices. For example, pay cuts assume the baseline number of employees; reductions in workforce assume the baseline pay. If both are implemented together, the total reduction will be less than the sum of individual options. Most options of less than $2 billion in cumulative savings have not been reported in this listing. In addition, the estimates do not account for the secondary effects of the spending cuts or revenue increases on the economy and hence on the deficit. Spending and revenue options should be compared to the CBO baseline budget in Table 1.

Source: Congressional Budget Office, *Reducing the Deficit: Spending and Revenue Options* (Washington, DC: U.S. Government Printing Office, Feb. 20, 1985), 307–350.

Note
Investment and Savings

President Reagan, fulfilling his campaign promise, restructured the tax system in 1981 in order to stimulate the "supply side" of the economy. After his first year in office, he prophesied that his tax policies "will have a powerful impact on the incentives for all Americans to work, save, and invest."[1] Critics charged that the Reagan program would fail since private savings would be inadequate to finance the large expected government deficits caused by the tax cuts. "We are confident," said Treasury Secretary Donald Regan, "that personal and business savings over the next few years will be adequate to finance both the projected deficits of the total government sector and a very rapid increase in real capital formation."[2] This note will provide background information on the definitions and determinants of investment and savings. These concepts are related to the government deficit and the current account balance by the accounting framework of the National Income Accounts first described in the Chapter 1 note, "An Introduction to Economics."

Investment

Investment is the addition to the capital stock in a given period. A broad interpretation of capital is long-lived assets enhancing the future capacity to produce output and hence income. This is consistent with the role of capital, mentioned in Chapter 1, as one of the four factors of production—the other three were labor, land, and managerial skills. Recall that when economists speak of capital and investment, they mean "real capital," which is the physical asset itself, and not the "financial capital," which is the paper claim to that physical asset.

If we measured total additions to the capital stock in a given period of time, we would call that *gross investment*. However, some of the total investment will be used to replace the capital stock which has depreciated through use, i.e., *replacement investment*. The amount of economic depreciation through use of the capital is not necessarily equal to accounting depreciation used for income reporting or tax purposes. The difference between gross investment and replacement investment is *net investment*,

This note was prepared by Associate Professor Michael G. Rukstad.
Copyright © 1983 by the President and Fellows of Harvard College
Harvard Business School note 9-383-086.

[1] *Economic Report of the President, 1982* (Washington, DC: U.S. Government Printing Office, 1982), 7.

[2] *Business Week*, Mar. 8, 1982, 60.

which may be either a net addition to or net subtraction from the total capital stock. These relationships are summarized as follows:

$$\text{Gross I} - \text{Replacement I} = \text{Net I.}$$
$$\text{(Depreciation)}$$

You will recall that the definition of GNP includes gross investment:

$$\text{GNP} = \text{C} + \text{Gross I} + \text{G} + (\text{X} - \text{M}).$$

In the note "An Introduction to Economics," we said that another broad measure of output for the economy is Net National Product (NNP). As the name suggests, the definition is:

$$\text{NNP} = \text{C} + \text{Net I} + \text{G} + (\text{X} - \text{M}).$$

The difference between the two measures of output is economic depreciation of the capital stock—a value which is not observed but is imputed. The National Income Accounts refer to this depreciation as Capital Consumption Allowance (CCA):

$$\text{GNP} - \text{CCA} = \text{NNP.}$$

The percentage of GNP accounted for by CCA varies with the business cycle, but, on average, CCA is roughly 10 percent of GNP for the United States.

The U.S. National Income Accounts record gross investment in an account called "Gross Private Domestic Investment." Each word is descriptive of what is and is not included in this component of GNP. Foreign investment and government or public investment are not included. However, the System of National Accounts (SNA) used by the United Nations and the 26 largest noncommunist developed countries forming the Organization of Economic Cooperation and Development (OECD) records data differently from the National Income Accounts (NIA) used by the United States. One difference of concern to us here is the treatment of government or public investment—in the SNA, government investment is included as part of gross investment.

The U.S. investment account is often disaggregated to identify three categories of investment: business plant and equipment, residential, and business inventory investment.[3] Part of the rationale for this distinction is the belief that there are different determinants for each of the categories. We will be focusing on the determinants of the investment in business plant and equipment, but before we move on to that topic, it is useful to clarify residential investment.

Although residential housing is clearly a long-lived asset, it is an investment decision made by households and it usually does not produce income in the future (since most people do not rent out their homes but live there themselves). The rationale for including homes in investment is that households are producing "housing services" for themselves or

---

[3]For an example of these categories of investment, see Exhibits 2 and 9 of the previous case.

for others for which they receive an "implicit rental income." It may be stretching the usual conception of the capital stock, but it is the convention nonetheless. Moreover, one may argue that other long-lived assets such as refrigerators or automobiles should also be included as investment, but they are not. These items are called "consumer durables" and are included in the consumption account, despite the fact that they often behave more like investments.

Economists had been discussing the determinants of investment spending long before Keynes and the Great Depression, but since that time there has been a synthesis of the early explanations of investment. The basic premise is that there is a desired level of the aggregate capital stock, which may or may not be the same as the present level. If the desired capital stock is larger than the current stock, positive net investment will be undertaken in order to close the gap, and vice versa.

The desired capital stock depends on business expectations of future sales and on the cost of capital. We will examine each of these factors in turn. The relationship between the desired capital stock and the expected sales or output is called the accelerator hypothesis which was first introduced by J. M. Clark in 1917. The hypothesis states that firms will increase their desired capital stock (i.e., increase net investment) if they expect sales will increase in the future. Thus the level of net investment depends on the change in expected sales. When there is an acceleration in expected sales, net investment increases (hence the name "accelerator"). If expected sales then level off at that higher level, net investment falls. If expected sales were ever to decline from that higher level, net investment would become negative.

This can be illustrated with a simple example. Suppose that firms need a capital stock twice as large as expected sales. Then $200 of capital will produce $100 of sales every year as long as there is enough replacement investment to cover the economic depreciation due to wear and tear on the capital. The top half of Figure 1 shows an acceleration of expected sales—a 10 percent increase from $100 to $110. Thus the firms will want to increase their capital stock 10 percent from $200 to $220. As a consequence, net investment rises in Period 1 by $20. Now, to maintain that 10 percent rise in net investment each year, expected sales must also rise 10 percent each year, because if expected sales are unchanged, as shown for Period 2 in the top graph of Figure 1, then net investment will fall, in this case, from $20 to zero. In fact, if expected sales decline to their original level of $100 as in Period 3, net investment becomes negative—in other words, replacement investment does not even cover all of the depreciated capital stock, causing it to decline by $20. Expectations of future sales must keep growing just to keep the level of net investment unchanged.

The other major determinant of the level of investment is the cost of capital. The cost of capital to a firm (also called the "user cost of capital" or "hurdle rate") is the cost of obtaining and using the piece of capital for a certain period of time expressed as a percentage of its pur-

Figure 1

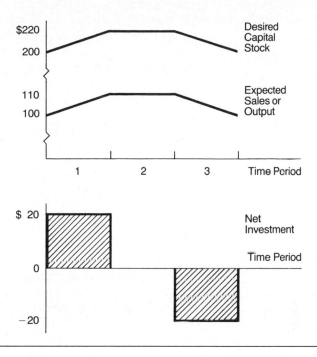

chase price. For our purposes, the cost of capital consists of two components—the real interest rate for borrowing funds[4] and the percentage depreciation rate. Even if the firm uses its own profits and does not borrow, those internally generated funds have an opportunity cost since the firm could lend them out to another borrower and earn the real rate of interest. Once the cost of capital is determined, a firm will compare this cost to the benefits received by adding an additional piece of capital. Only if the benefits exceed the cost will the investment be made. The typical method of comparing costs and benefits is to discount the expected future stream of earnings at the cost of capital; if the net present value is positive, the investment should be made.

It will be useful now to examine how investment can depend on both expected sales and the rate of interest at the same time. Even if expected sales remain unchanged, it is conceivable that a reduction in the cost of capital will encourage firms to rely more heavily on capital in the production process and less heavily on some other factor such as labor. Of course, this depends on the particular production process and

[4]The concept of the real rate of interest as a primary determinant of investment had been expounded before Keynes wrote the *General Theory* in 1936. Both Knut Wicksell and Irving Fisher had offered analogous arguments to that effect many years before. We will not examine the difficulties of Keynes' Marginal Efficiency of Capital theory of investment or its differences from the theories of Wicksell and Fisher.

the degree of substitutability between capital and labor. Returning to the previous example in Figure 1, imagine that the real interest rate and hence the cost of capital falls lower than the (unspecified) level used in that illustration. Some firms will have the incentive to invest in more efficient machines, which means that they will supply the $100 of output with, say, $250 of capital, instead of $200 as before. Of course, the firms will want reduced labor costs, since a smaller labor force using the more efficient machines will be able to supply the $100 of output.[5] Now we have a flexible accelerator where the capital/output ratio depends on the cost of capital. If the cost of capital falls, the desired capital/output ratio rises (from 2 to 2.5 in our example) as firms switch to more capital-intensive production processes. By definition, investment rises.

To understand the dynamics of the investment process, it is important to remember that a permanent increase in expected output or a permanent reduction in the cost of capital will only lead to a temporary increase in investment, as we can see in Periods 1 and 2 of Figure 1. Once firms have achieved the desired level for the stock of capital, the only investment that takes place will be for replacement. This is a very simple explanation that neither explicitly accounts for the broad strategic considerations in making an investment nor for uncertainty, information, and imperfect capital markets. A great deal of research in business policy, economics, and finance has been devoted to the analysis of these three crucial factors, but the general observations on the preceding pages remain valid.

Savings

Savings is the accumulation of wealth during a given period of time. Wealth is anything that has value because it is capable of producing future income, so it includes land (and other nonrenewable resources), labor, and capital.[6] Usually we think of savings in the form of money or financial capital (claims to the physical capital stock), but sometimes individuals invest their savings in land in hopes of finding oil, or in works of art (and other nonrenewable resources) in the expectation that they will appreciate in price. Some economists even go so far as to rationalize that investing one's savings in children is a useful concept since those children will produce future income. Though this example seems extreme, the definition of what constitutes savings is a major problem for economists

---

[5]Alternatively, we could have the same labor force supplying more than $100 of output.

[6]There are problems and disputes over whether money should be included in wealth. Money is useful in facilitating transactions; thus it aids in the production of future income. On the other hand, government could conceivably increase wealth by printing huge quantities of money. The inflation generated by such actions would reduce the real value of the remaining stock of wealth. Since money is such an insignificant fraction of the total wealth of a nation, little harm is done by excluding it here.

attempting to measure this variable. Is an economy better off if it invests a given fixed amount of savings in the education and training of the future work force or if it invests in the latest technology for plant and equipment? Which would produce the larger future income stream? Should the former be called savings that is invested in education, or should it be called consumption? This will prove important later when we compare savings rates of various countries. One needs to ask what is being measured and what should be included or excluded from that definition.

Much confusion is generated by the failure to distinguish between a variable that records a "flow" between two points in time and a variable that records a "stock" at a particular point in time. Savings, like income and investment, is an example of a flow, which must have a time dimension such as $100 of investment per year. If, for example, one views investment as a stock instead of a flow, then one might erroneously reason that if an increase in national income from $100 to $110, as in Figure 1, generated an added "stock of investment" of $20, then that $20 would be a constant "stock" available in successive periods, which is not true if it is viewed correctly as a flow. Wealth, like capital, labor, and land, is an example of a "stock."

Production takes place when stocks of resources are made available to firms. A flow of income is generated in payment for those resources. Households dispose of the income remaining after depreciation either as a flow of expenditures or as a flow of savings, the latter further increasing the stock of wealth. We can summarize these relationships in the simple circular flow diagram with only households and firms shown in Figure 2. One should recall the convention used in Chapter 1 that dotted lines indicate the physical flows of goods, services, and financial assets, and solid lines indicate money flows. Notice that the money inflows from depreciation and savings into the stock of wealth will remain as idle cash unless they are funneled back into productive investment, as shown in the outer ring of the circular flow diagram.

Indeed, all four sectors of the economy—households, business, government, and foreign—can accumulate wealth if they postpone current expenditure. That total pool of savings will then be available for capital investment by any sector. We will speak of four types of savings which are associated with the four sectors:

1. Personal savings ⎫
2. Business savings ⎬ Private savings ⎫
3. Government savings   ⎬ National savings
4. Foreign savings ⎭

In addition, one often hears the terms *private savings* and *national savings*, which are the sums of the savings categories indicated above. It is important that one be clear on which term is being used. Typically, the common usage of the word *savings* refers to the very narrow category of personal savings.

Figure 2

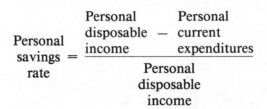

Personal Savings

Personal savings is defined as personal disposable income minus current personal consumption expenditures. The personal savings rate is:

$$\text{Personal savings rate} = \frac{\text{Personal disposable income} - \text{Personal current expenditures}}{\text{Personal disposable income}}$$

Disposable income is the income remaining after all taxes have been subtracted. Differences between countries in measured personal savings and the personal savings rate must be accounted for by three factors:

1.   Different accounting definitions of savings and disposable income.

2.   Different relative importance of various institutions to be described below.

3.   Different cultural, social, economic, and historical factors affecting the propensity to save.

The first factor is easily corrected by using uniform accounting procedures. The System of National Accounts (SNA) will produce a personal savings measure (and rate) which is slightly larger than that of the National Income Accounts (NIA) used by the United States, but most of the differences between countries stem from other causes.

The second factor highlights the problem of what savings is and how we should measure it. Differing institutional considerations, which will be illustrated below, may affect the definition either of current (as opposed to capital) expenditure or of disposable income. In order to illustrate how different institutional structures may affect savings, consider two countries with different relative sizes of their small business sector. Country A generates very little income from the small business sector, whereas Country B generates a large proportion of its income from that sector. Should this income be included in personal income or in business income? This answer is not clear-cut since there are elements of both personal and business income in the return the proprietors receive. But even if we can agree on some consistent accounting rule (say that we excluded small business income entirely from personal income), the relative difference in the size of this sector between the two countries will affect the amount of personal savings measured because disposable income will be affected. The exclusion would reduce the personal savings rate in each country, but it would be reduced more in Country B which has a larger proportion of small business income excluded. Other institutional arrangements affecting the measured savings rate are the relative importance of social security, government health and education services, and consumption taxes.

Even after adjustments are made for both accounting definitions and institutional arrangements, there are still economic, cultural, social, and historical factors that account for an individual's propensity to save. In terms of Figure 2, the question can be asked: For each additional dollar received by the household, what determines the proportion that an individual household will spend on consumption and the proportion that will be saved? People consume, presumably, for the satisfaction they receive from it. People save for a variety of motives, including:

1. Retirement.

2. Large anticipated purchases.

3. Large unanticipated expenses.

4. Bequests.

All of these motives may be thought of as ways that the individual "smooths out" future consumption. If one has savings, consumption will not have to fall drastically when one retires or when one faces a large purchase or expense in the future. Even bequests smooth consumption for one's heirs when one dies. The strength of these motives depends on how strongly one feels the need to smooth out the fluctuations in future consumption by saving more now. The strength of this desire depends on social, cultural, and historical factors that are difficult to quantify, but significant nonetheless. Savings will increase if an individual is more risk averse, since there will be a stronger desire to insure oneself against the possibility of a huge fluctuation in consumption in the future. Also, the desire to smooth consumption depends on how much one values the future. Savings will increase if the value one places on future consumption is high.

The proportion saved will also depend on economic variables such as the income and wealth that the individual already has. One would expect poorer people to save less because of the necessity to spend most of their income on consumption. In terms used in the Keynes reading in Chapter 6, the marginal propensity to consume declines (and hence the marginal propensity to save increases) as income and wealth increase.

Finally, the proportion saved might depend on another economic variable: the incentive to save that one is offered. The relevant incentive for savings should be the after-tax real rate of return that one can earn by forgoing consumption. It is a real return that is important, since inflation erodes the future value of nominal returns. For example, if one saved $100 at a 5 percent nominal interest rate, one would have $105 at the end of the year. If there were also a 5 percent inflation rate that year, $105 one year later would purchase only what $100 does today. Thus the $100 of savings will purchase only $100 worth of goods next year instead of the $105 worth of goods that was anticipated, so there was no real incentive for saving instead of consuming. The real rate of return is defined as:[7]

$$\text{Real return} = \text{Nominal return} - \text{Expected inflation}$$

$$r \quad = \quad i \quad - \quad \frac{\Delta p^e}{p}.$$

Therefore, if a 5 percent real return was desired and 5 percent inflation was expected, the individual should ask for a 10 percent nominal return. Then one should consider any tax that might be levied on the income earned from savings. Since the tax is levied on the nominal return one receives and not on the real return, the after-tax real rate of return is the real return we defined above adjusted for the tax that must be paid on the nominal return:

$$\text{After-tax real return} = \text{Real return} - (\text{Tax rate} \times \text{Nominal return})$$

$$\text{ATRR} \quad = \quad r \quad - \quad (t \quad \times \quad i).$$

Continuing our example in which the individual wants a 5 percent real return and expects 5 percent inflation, the after-tax real return for someone in the 50 percent tax bracket is zero since the nominal return must

---

[7] Notice that this is the same relationship discussed as the "Fisher effect on nominal interest rates" in the note in Chapter 3.

be 10 percent.[8] If the individual in our example can demand to be compensated for inflation, it is also possible that he or she can demand to be compensated for taxes as well in order to receive an after-tax real return of 5 percent. Under the same assumptions, the nominal rate would be 20 percent.

To summarize, the proportion of each additional dollar that an individual saves depends on a number of factors: the strength of the desire to smooth future consumption, which in turn depends on social, cultural, and historical values; the current level of one's income and wealth; and the after-tax real return to savings. Before moving on, one should note that the responsiveness of savings to the after-tax real return has been estimated to be very low (i.e., savings is "interest inelastic"). Of course, this does not mean that it is actually the case—all it means is that nobody has been able to demonstrate a high elasticity, statistically. Therefore, the explanations for the proportion which one saves have tended to focus on the other factors.

After this discussion of the proportion of any additional disposable income that an individual desires to save, we now return to the question of what determines the total quantity of personal savings generated by the household sector. The major determinants of personal savings for all households include:

1.   Growth and level of income.

2.   The level of wealth.

3.   The distribution of income.

4.   Demographic factors, such as age distribution, retirement age, and life expectancy.

Notice that all of these factors may move the distribution of the population such that more individuals are accumulating assets (saving) than are decumulating assets (dissaving). For example, as a cohort of "baby boom" workers reaches mid-career, one would expect to see a larger rate of total household personal savings, even though all individuals in the society who are saving may have the same individual savings rate; there is just a larger portion of the population who are in the saving phase of their lives.

Business Savings

Gross business savings in the United States has been about three times as large as personal savings in recent years. Business savings is adjusted undistributed business income. We have already touched on some of the

---

[8] Notice what happens as the inflation rate changes: if inflation is 15 percent, then the ATRR is 5 percent; if inflation is zero, then the ATRR is 2.5 percent.

problems of measuring business income with the small business sector problem. But there are other adjustments that must be made to rearrange business income before it reflects savings. These adjustments significantly alter recorded business income.

If we start with total corporate profits and then apply the appropriate tax rate, we obtain after-tax corporate profits. From this, firms must decide what portion will be paid out in dividends and what portion will be retained. The dividends are paid to the household sector which, in the United States, must treat them as taxable income. The tax treatment of corporate income varies significantly among countries, ranging from the "classical system" of double taxation of dividend income like that in the United States (i.e., taxed once at the corporate level and once at the personal level) to an integrated system of corporate and personal income taxation which relieves (at least partially) double taxation at either the corporate level (Japan and West Germany) or at the shareholder level (United Kingdom, France, and Canada). Finally, a number of significant adjustments to undistributed after-tax profits are made, including inventory and depreciation adjustments, the addition of corporate and non-corporate capital consumption allowances, and noncorporate after-tax business income, as well as other smaller adjustments. The first two adjustments reflect the fact that, in inflationary times, typical accounting practices overstate the value of profits since many firms use the FIFO method[9] of inventory valuation and historical cost depreciation methods. These are not trivial adjustments—in 1980 U.S. figures, they amounted to approximately a 50 percent reduction in measured after-tax profits.

There is one adjustment that is not made in the National Income Accounts but should be considered in measuring true business savings. Business as a whole is a net debtor, and the size of this debt has increased substantially in recent years. In times of inflation, there is a gain to a debtor that results from inflation reducing the real value of debts. The inflation gain on net debt in recent years has more than offset the loss due to inventory and depreciation adjustments. What should one conclude regarding the various measurements of business savings? Certainly the definition of business savings is sensitive to the accounting definition used and particularly sensitive to the level of inflation. Also, business savings is sometimes more difficult to detect than personal savings because it is often directly invested in capital by the firm and is not first made available to some financial intermediary that later relends it for investment.

---

[9]FIFO, which stands for "first in, first out," describes the assumption used in the valuation of inventory—the oldest inventory valued at its historical cost is sold first. This is often contrasted with LIFO, "last in, first out," in which the newest inventory valued at its current cost is sold first.

Government Savings

The third category of savings is government savings, more commonly known as government budget surplus. It is defined as total government receipts minus total government outlays. If outlays exceed receipts, then it is called a deficit. A government surplus is an addition to the pool of savings in the sense that it frees resources that could be transferred to other assets, just as a government deficit draws on resources that could be used for business investment or to purchase other assets.

There are four technical caveats regarding this relatively simple definition that will be helpful in interpreting the statistics on the budget and savings:

1. All levels of government are aggregated together in the government surplus, although separate balances can be calculated for the federal, state, and local levels.

2. Government transfer payments are included in outlays, along with government expenditures on goods and services, which is the G in the national income accounting identity defined on page 18.

3. Government investment expenditures are included in outlays in the National Income Accounts (NIA) used by the United States, but they are not included in the System of National Accounts (SNA) definition used by many other countries.

4. In the United States, there are two commonly used definitions of the government budget surplus or deficit: the unified budget,[10] which is the government's official budget statement, and the National Income Accounts budget,[11] which is used in the definition of government savings. For our purposes, we can think of them as interchangeable since the size of the outlays or receipts of one is within a few percentage points of the size of the other. The difference is largely one of timing and coverage.

The budget reflects as well as influences the economy. If the country is in a recession, tax collections will be smaller and unemployment insurance payments will be greater, thereby causing the budget deficit to increase. It is difficult to determine how much of a given deficit is caused

[10]The unified budget, first introduced in 1968, consolidates nondesignated federal funds and trust funds which are earmarked for special purposes such as social security, unemployment insurance, and highway grants-in-aid. Off-budget expenditures are excluded from the unified budget, but this budget does include net lending of government-owned enterprises. It was a substantial accounting improvement over its predecessors, the consolidated cash budget and the earlier administrative budget.

[11]The National Income Accounts budget is a better measure of the budget's impact on current income and output of the economy. It differs from the unified budget in that it records receipts and expenditures on an accrual basis and excludes net lending and certain other business transactions.

by the slow economic growth and how much is caused by government policies initiated to increase spending or to lower taxes. A policy-induced deficit would be more expansionary than the same deficit induced by economic weakness, since the former is an injection of new spending into the economy with subsequent income repercussions, whereas the latter is a reflection of income repercussions already experienced.[12]

To deal with this problem, the concept of a structural deficit was introduced in the early 1960s.[13] A structural deficit holds constant the effects of fluctuating income from year to year by comparing deficits at the same, usually high-employment, level of income. Thus a structural deficit answers the question: What would the deficit be if we were at a particular high-employment level of GNP rather than at the current level of GNP, whatever that may be? The high-employment level could be defined to be any level as long as it is consistent over all years.

Foreign Savings

Foreign savings, the fourth category, will not be discussed in detail here since we do so in the Chapter 14 note, "An Introduction to the Balance of Payments." The important point for our present purposes is that a current-account surplus is equivalent to net foreign investment and a current-account deficit is equivalent to net foreign savings. The current-account balance is defined as the exports of goods and services minus the imports of the same (plus net transfers, which are gifts). This is roughly equal to the term $(X - M)$ in the national income accounting identity after appropriate adjustments have been made.

If the United States has, for example, a deficit on the current account caused by importing more than it is exporting, then foreign capital must flow into this country in order to finance the deficit.[14] The United States is thus acquiring net foreign savings, and foreigners are acquiring net foreign investments.[15] These are two aspects of the same phenomenon: foreign capital flowing into the United States.

In the next section we will integrate all of the above forms of savings with our previous discussion of investment.

---

[12]See the discussion of the multiplier and its implications for the budget in the Chapter 6 case, "A Keynesian Cure for the Depression."

[13]The structural deficit, usually contrasted with the cyclical deficit, is also known as the "high-employment deficit," the "full-employment deficit," or the "cyclically adjusted budget." Note that these terms can also be applied to a surplus.

[14]Foreigners will not be willing to export the goods and services comprising the current-account deficit unless the United States is willing to send financial assets in exchange. Thus a current account deficit always implies a capital account surplus and vice versa.

[15]This fits with the common notion of savings and investment. For example, when money is deposited in a bank, the depositor receives an asset—an investment—such as a savings account, and the banker receives the depositor's savings. Similarly, when foreign capital flows into the same U.S. bank and the bank, in return, sends the foreigner a savings account, the foreigner has a foreign investment and the banker has foreign savings.

The Relationship between Investment and Savings

To visualize the relationship between investment and all forms of savings, we can return to the national income accounting identity:

$$GNP = C + I + G + (X - M).$$

Recall that GNP is a broad measure of income. Also recall from algebra that one may add or subtract any value one desires from both sides of an equation. Since we are interested in disposable income, we will add R, total transfers, and subtract T, total taxes, from both sides of the equation to get disposable income (earned income plus transferred income minus taxes) on the left-hand side:

$$GNP + R - T = C + I + G + R - T + (X - M).$$

Finally, we will subtract C from both sides of the equation and substitute S on the left-hand side since private savings (S) was defined to be disposable income (GNP + R − T) minus consumption (C):

$$S = I + G + R - T + (X - M).$$

This can be rearranged in a form that ties together gross private domestic investment with all categories of savings, as we discussed previously:

I	=	S	+	(T − G − R)	+	(M − X)
Gross	=	Private	+	Government	+	Net foreign
investment		savings		savings		savings.

This says that gross (domestic) investment must be financed by the total savings available from all four sectors. Alternatively, since a positive net foreign savings is identical to a negative net foreign investment, as we discussed in the previous section, one will sometimes see data recorded as follows:

S	+	(T − G − R)	=	I	+	(X − M)
Private	+	Government	=	Gross	+	Net foreign
savings		savings		investment		investment.

Exhibit 1 of the previous case, "The Reagan Deficits," records the sources and uses of gross savings in this manner.

This relationship can be a very useful guide in organizing a discussion of investment and savings. There cannot be a change in one variable without an offsetting change elsewhere. Other variables that are not included in this equation but are related nonetheless (such as income, interest rates, exchange rates, and prices) will also change as the savings and investment variables adjust to new levels. In short, this is simply an accounting identity that says nothing about causality. The analyst must make that judgment.

Discussion Questions for Case and Note

1. What were the primary causes of the deficit in 1985?
2. What were the economic and political consequences of the deficits occurring during President Reagan's administration?
3. What strategy regarding the deficit would you have suggested to President Reagan at the beginning of his second term?
4. Imagine you were chairperson of the House Ways and Means Committee in 1985. What strategy for reducing the deficit would you propose? How fast would you reduce the deficit? To what level by 1990? How much would you reduce spending? How much would you increase taxes? Choose from among the options presented in Exhibit 13 at the end of the case. How would you attempt to gain political support for your proposal?

Bibliography

Collender, Stanley E., *The Guide to the Federal Budget*, Fiscal 1986 Edition (Washington, DC: Urban Institute, 1985). For those confused by the terminology and reporting on the budget, Part II of this book (pages 61–102) describes the key elements in a readable, concise outline. Also included is a glossary of terms on the budget.

Dornbusch, Rudiger, and Stanley Fischer, *Macroeconomics*, 3rd ed. (New York: McGraw-Hill, 1984). Chapter 5, "Fiscal Policy, Crowding Out, and the Policy Mix," describes the way in which the financial and nonfinancial markets interact to crowd out private investment. Chapter 15, "Budget Deficits, Inflation, and the Public Debt," is a comprehensive treatment of these subjects and is directly applicable to the economic consequences of the deficit mentioned in our Chapter 11 case.

Friedman, Benjamin M., "Implications of the Government Deficit for U.S. Capital Formation," in the Federal Reserve Bank of Boston, *The Economics of Large Government Deficits*, Proceedings of a Conference Held in October 1983, Conference Series No. 27, 73–95. This paper and the other scholarly papers collected in this volume are an attempt to measure the impact of the deficits on economic performance. Professor Friedman concludes that the deficits will crowd out private investment in the latter half of the 1980s.

Gordon, Robert J., *Macroeconomics*, 3rd ed. (Boston: Little, Brown, 1984). In Chapter 17 (pages 528–547) there is a long discussion of the natural employment budget (full employment budget) and its applications as well as a brief comment on deficits and supply-side economics.

Greider, William, "The Education of David Stockman," *The Atlantic* (December 1981), 27–40. This is an insider's account of the legislative successes and failures in Reagan's first year in office as seen through the eyes of a journalist. Greider describes the transformation of Stockman's initial optimism to pessimism as he realized that the deficits were becoming uncon-

trollable and the expected boom in the financial markets failed to materialize.

Volcker, Paul A., "Facing Up to the Twin Deficits," *Challenge* (March/April
1984), 4–9. The chairman of the Federal Reserve describes how the
budget deficit and the trade deficit are interrelated and the problems
thereby posed for monetary policy.

CHAPTER 12
Selling Government Assets to Reduce Fiscal Deficits

Large fiscal deficits were widespread among industrial countries in the early 1980s. The two oil shocks not only ignited inflation but also slowed economic growth and consequently reduced tax revenues. At the same time, governments attempted to boost expenditures in order to stimulate their sluggish economies. As we saw in the case for Chapter 4, which recounted the achievements of Mrs. Thatcher's first term in office, reducing fiscal deficits was an important policy target in her economic campaign against inflation. Despite her strong intentions, however, she had only modest success in this effort in her first term.

Privatization was an issue that appealed to Mrs. Thatcher for a number of reasons. First, it offered a solution to the persistent fiscal deficit problem. Because of the size of the privatization proceeds and its effect on the fiscal budget, privatization was fundamentally a fiscal issue. Second, it promised to increase the efficiency of noncompetitive firms that were in the government's care. Third, it could extend stock ownership to a wider population. And, finally, it would reduce the size of government and its involvement in the private sector.

Mrs. Thatcher's success with the early privatizations has caused repercussions in finance ministries around the world. The United Kingdom has become a model for many countries of how to manage fiscal and competitive problems simultaneously. Given the cameo role of U.K. privatization in the world community, this case allows us to examine the validity of arguments for and against privatization in general and Mrs. Thatcher's management of the U.K. privatizations in particular.

Case
Privatization in the United Kingdom

The privatization of state industry and services has been the most visible achievement of the Thatcher era, save only the containment of inflation. Prime Minister Margaret Thatcher reduced inflation from over 10 percent to less than 4 percent during her first term in office, from 1979 to 1983. The key to her anti-inflation program was "sound money," embodied in the Medium-Term Financial Strategy that set explicit multiyear targets for monetary and fiscal policies.[1] From the beginning, privatization had been part of the overall plan to restore Britain's industrial competitiveness, but it had moved to center stage during Mrs. Thatcher's second and third terms of office. Along with monetary control and fiscal restraint, it represented a major vehicle for the broad Thatcherite political-economic agenda—the reduction of the state's role in the economy in favor of market mechanisms.

History of Nationalization and Privatization in the United Kingdom

The state-owned sector of the British economy was largely a creation of the postwar Labour government of Prime Minister Clement Atlee (1945–1951). However, some of the holdings of Her Majesty's government, including such companies (or their antecedents) as British Petroleum, British Telecom, the Central Electricity Generating Board, the British Broadcasting Corporation, the Bank of England, and British Airways, were taken over by various Conservative and Labour governments before World War II. The Atlee Labour government, which won an overwhelming mandate in the 1945 election, comparable only to Mrs. Thatcher's victories in 1979 and 1983, entered office committed to nationalizing the "commanding heights of the economy"—the heavy industrial sectors such as coal, steel, rail, gas, and electricity. This ideological justification differed fundamentally from the justifications for earlier nationalizations, which were rationalized as natural monopolies or as critical national interests in the traditional sense of defense.

This case was prepared by Associate Professor Michael G. Rukstad with the assistance of Andrew Regan, MBA 1988. Copyright 1988 by the President and Fellows of Harvard College Harvard Business School case 9–389–036.

[1]See the case in Chapter 4, "The United Kingdom under Thatcher," for a detailed discussion of Thatcher's monetary and fiscal policies during her first term in office.

The opposition, both Conservative and Liberal, vigorously contested the program at each step along the way. Winston Churchill branded the socialistic agenda as "abhorrent," claiming it was "reeking of totalitarianism." Nevertheless, the Atlee government pressed intrepidly ahead with its program. It nationalized the remaining portions of the Bank of England and of civil aviation in 1946. In the following year the coal and overseas telecommunications (Cable and Wireless) industries were nationalized. In 1948 transport (railway, canal, and road haulage companies) and electricity distribution sectors fell under government control. The gas industry was taken over in 1949 and iron and steel in 1951.

As the nationalizations were completed, Churchill gathered his arguments and evidence for shrinking the public sector:

Socialism, with its vast network of regulations and restrictions and its incompetent planning and purchasing by Whitehall officials, is proving itself every day to be a dangerous and costly folly. . . . Every major industry which the socialists have nationalized, without exception, has passed from the profitable or self-supporting side of the balance sheet to the loss-making, debit side. . . .[2]

Although Churchill was unable to distinguish a balance sheet from an income statement (as is clear from the above comment), he was certain of the proper demarcation between the public and private sectors. During his postwar administration (1951–1955), Churchill got his chance to reverse a portion of the socialist program. The iron and steel and road haulage industries were denationalized by Churchill in 1953, only to be renationalized by subsequent Labour governments.

Intermittent nationalizations by both Labour and Conservative governments followed in the years between 1955 and 1979, including the consolidated auto giant British Leyland, high-technology companies such as Rolls-Royce, Ferranti, ICL, and Fairey, shipbuilders such as Upper Clyde Shipbuilders and Harland & Wolff, and the British National Oil Corporation. During the Callaghan years (1976–1979), the shipbuilding and aerospace industries were regrouped under state ownership. Thus by 1979 the industrial holdings of Her Majesty's government were substantial. The state industrial sector employed 2 million people and accounted for approximately 10 percent of GDP.

Mrs. Thatcher's Economic Approach: Monetary and Fiscal Targets

Mrs. Thatcher's victory in 1979 signified a rejection of the "postwar consensus" said to have arisen between the Labour and the Conservative parties on most policy concerns, including the economy. That consensus was firmly Keynesian and interventionist. The two parties moderated

---

[2]Alan Sked and Chris Cook, *Postwar Britain,* 2nd ed. (London: Penguin, 1984), 329.

their views and converged at the political center. This centrist convergence—labeled "Butskellism" by *The Economist* after Churchill's Chancellor of the Exchequer, R. A. Butler, and Labour's Shadow Chancellor, Hugh Gaitskell—reached its full flowering during the two decades of the Macmillan-Wilson-Heath-Wilson prime ministerships (1957–1976). The electorate, however, became discontented with the poor performance of the British economy and the consensus policies during the stagflationary 1970s.

Mrs. Thatcher, for her part, found the postwar policy convergence insipid, once answering her own query "What is consensus?" with the contemptuous rejoinder "It is the politics of the lowest common denominator." The Thatcherite policy approach was reducible to a fundamental principle: The reduction of state agency in the economy and the wider society in favor of private, market-based initiative. During her first term (1979–1983), Thatcher's blueprint for implementing this principle was a macroeconomic remedy—"sound" money to reduce inflation by strict monetary targeting. Her chosen method for achieving the monetary targets, outlined in the Medium-Term Financial Strategy (MTFS), necessitated fiscal discipline, particularly the reduction of the Public Sector Borrowing Requirement (PSBR), often called (with some license) "the government deficit."

The combined effect of Thatcher's strict policies, not long in materializing, was nothing less than the worst economic downturn since the depression of the 1930s (see Exhibit 1). Tight money sent interest rates and the exchange rate soaring, thus crippling British exporters. In just two years (1981–1982) a tenth of Britain's manufacturing output disappeared. An explosion of unemployment—with joblessness more than doubling May 1979 levels by the end of 1981—seriously weakened the government's popular standing. Because of the serious economic downturn, the government was unable to meet its monetary and fiscal targets (see Exhibit 2). As the electorate became increasingly discouraged and skeptical, Mrs. Thatcher's standings in the polls fell almost 20 percentage points during her first two years as prime minister.

Mrs. Thatcher had entered office with the oft-repeated intention of cutting government expenditure in nominal terms. In her first months in office, Mrs. Thatcher was hampered in her efforts by commitments of her Labour predecessors. Moreover, the government was constrained by promises to increase defense spending. The much-decried assault on the "welfare state" never materialized. The only significant cuts in social-services spending came in higher education and housing. On the revenue side, Thatcher had promised tax cuts during the election campaign, undoubtedly aware that she stood to gain from the appreciable tax collections related to North Sea oil. After her election in 1979, she cut the personal income tax and had hoped for additional cuts in subsequent years. However, both the expenditure and revenue situations were exacerbated by the depth, severity, and duration of the recession of the early 1980s. As a consequence, the original goal of reducing nominal expenditure was subsequently restated as holding spending constant in real terms, and major cuts in personal income taxes were deferred until 1986.

The reality was that in no year was Mrs. Thatcher able to reduce spending in real terms, much less in nominal terms (see Exhibit 3). By 1986 real spending was 10 percent higher than in 1979. Through 1983 spending as a percentage of GDP climbed, reaching a high of 46 percent in 1983—a full 8 percent ahead of the 38 percent consumed by the Labour government in 1978. The level of spending as a percentage of GDP did not return to the levels prevailing at the end of the supposedly profligate Callaghan government until 1985–1986. In fact, the Labour government of James Callaghan retrenched much more than that of Thatcher: In the wake of the IMF loan to Britain, real expenditure was cut 8 percent in the two years after 1975 and then kept below the 1975 level throughout the balance of Mr. Callaghan's time in office.

Only with the publication of the budget for the 1988–1989 fiscal year in March 1988 was the government able to make any real claim as to having mastered expenditure. For in the budget not only were central government surpluses and a balanced budget for the 1988–1989 and 1989–1990 financial years projected, but the Chancellor of the Exchequer made a commitment in his budget speech to a balanced budget as a future "norm":

A balanced budget is a valuable discipline for the medium term. It represents security for the present and an investment for the future. Having achieved it, I intend to stick to it. In other words, henceforth a zero PSBR will be the norm. This provides a clear and simple rule, with a good historic pedigree.[3]

This promise was made despite the simultaneous announcement of dramatic cuts in personal taxation by an additional 20 percent "as soon as we prudently can."

All told, the government gathered through year-end 1988 upwards of £25 billion in privatization proceeds.[4] The chancellor's budgets in 1989 and 1990 included an additional £10 billion of negative expenditures represented by expected privatization proceeds, without which his "surpluses" would have been questionable.[5] Exhibit 6 shows the PSBR excluding the privatization proceeds from 1979 to 1992. The contribution

---

[3]*Financial Times*, March 16, 1988, 12.

[4]In addition, the Thatcher government gathered over £65 billion in oil-related taxes and royalties from 1979 to 1988.

[5]Mrs. Thatcher treated privatization proceeds not as additional receipts to be matched by any incremental spending financed by those proceeds, but as negative expenditures (see line 25 of Exhibit 3). Consequently, overall spending was reduced for reporting purposes by the amount of privatization proceeds. Moreover, this accounting treatment did not include the very substantial proceeds derived from other kinds of asset sales by local government—council housing, surplus land, and the like—which if not accruing directly to the Treasury could be substituted for other central government aid.

of public corporation accounts to the public sector borrowing requirement is detailed in Exhibit 5. Since the announcement in late 1985, the government had achieved its goal of annual asset sales of £5 billion.

The Ascendency of Privatization in Mrs. Thatcher's Agenda

Against the background of this early monetarist policy framework, privatization had only the most circumscribed of roles. The 1979 Election Manifesto of Thatcher's Conservative Party had included very little on the topic. Indeed, the word *privatization* was not even used in the Manifesto, which stated just these intentions under the heading "Nationalization":

> The British people strongly oppose Labour's plans to nationalize yet more firms and industries such as the building, banking, insurance, pharmaceuticals, and road haulage sectors. More nationalization would further impoverish us and further undermine our freedom. We will offer to sell back to private ownership the recently nationalized aerospace and shipbuilding concerns, giving their employees a chance to purchase shares.[6]

A determination to manage more effectively those concerns remaining in the public sector was also emphasized.[7] The Manifesto noted: "We want to see those industries that remain nationalized running more successfully and we will therefore interfere less with their management and set them a clearer financial discipline in which to work." But at this early juncture, privatization largely meant the sale of council housing (public rented housing) on easy terms to sitting tenants, to which the Manifesto devoted significantly more space.

By the end of 1983 and Mrs. Thatcher's first term in office, only £3 billion of the state's industrial holdings and £4.5 billion of council housing had been sold. The industrial holdings were a mishmash of partial and full sales of state shares in energy companies, Cable and Wireless, some high-technology companies held by the National Enterprise Board, the National Freight Corporation, British Aerospace, Associated British Ports, and some British Rail Hotels (see Exhibit 4 for a list of the major privatizations from 1979 to 1987). In early 1984, a British securities house, using conservative assumptions to determine valuation, estimated that there remained in the state larder readily disposable assets worth an estimated total of £28.5 billion, with another £55 billion of less marketable but still tradable property.[8]

---

[6]Conservative Party, *The Conservative Manifesto, 1979* (London: Conservative Central Office, 1979), 3.

[7]Evidence of the government's success in improving productivity is presented in Exhibits 8 and 9.

[8]Grieveson Grant Research, *Privatization* (London: Grieveson Grant, 1984), 10.

The 1983 Election Manifesto offered these intentions for Thatcher's second term as prime minister:

We shall transfer more state-owned businesses to independent owner-ship. Our aim is that British Telecom . . . Rolls-Royce, British Airways and substantial parts of British Steel, of British Shipbuilders, and of British Ley-land, and as many possible of Britain's airports, shall become private sector companies. We also aim to introduce substantial private capital into the Na-tional Bus Company. . . . We shall also transfer to the private sector the re-maining state-owned oil business—the British Gas Corporation's offshore oil interests.[9]

In addition, the 1983 Manifesto included broader commitments "to con-tinue our program to expose state-owned firms to real competition" through regulatory change, and "seek other means of increasing com-petition in and attracting private capital into the gas and electricity in-dustries."

By the end of 1987, the total proceeds (including council house sales of approximately £10 billion) amounted to between £25 billion and £30 billion, with the largest sales—the remainder of British Telecom, British Gas, the electricity industry, and the water authorities—still to come.

Mrs. Thatcher's Rationale for Privatization: Competition and Efficiency

A primary claim, both in the theory and political justification of priva-tization, was that it would enhance economic efficiency by subjecting the formerly cosseted state-owned companies to the cold shower of compe-tition. Nigel Lawson, Chancellor of the Exchequer, cast his argument in such terms: "The transfer of state-owned businesses to the free enterprise sector of the economy brings enormous long-term benefits to the nation as a whole, in terms of greater concern for the consumer and greater efficiency."[10] Through the sale of Jaguar in July 1984, the privatization docket had been principally comprised of formerly private industrial and commercial companies that had become wards of the state upon hitting hard times. These difficulties had generally been the result of the actions of other private competing firms, both in Britain and abroad. Without breaking stride, the government applied the same competition-based jus-tifications to entities facing little or no existing competition in the private sector.

Nevertheless, as the government progressed through the second stage of privatization—centered on the flotation of public monopolies like gas, telecommunications, water, and electricity—its faith in the overriding

---

[9]Conservative Party, *The Conservative Manifesto, 1983* (London: Conservative Central Of-fice, 1983), 4.

[10]*Financial Times*, November 13, 1985, 18.

beneficence of market discipline remained. John Moore, the first Minister of State for Privatization at the Treasury, embarked on a strenuous campaign to dispel any notion that the best place for a natural or seminatural monopoly might be in the public sector: "Privatization policies have now been developed to such an extent that regulated private ownership of natural monopolies is preferable to nationalization."

British Telecom

Concerns about the incompatibility of effective competition or regulation and the sale of a publicly owned monopoly had, however, come to worry many observers with the sale of 50.2 percent of British Telecom (BT) in November 1984. Critics of the BT sale had argued that, though international competitors were formidable, it was unwise to privatize the company before the post-1981 liberalization of the U.K. telecommunications market could produce any effective domestic competition. Others charged that the regulatory body, the Office of Telecommunications (Oftel), would have to choose continually between the conflicting interests of BT's customers and the company's private shareholders.

British Gas Corporation

Criticism intensified with the sale of the British Gas Corporation (BGC) in December 1986, a monopoly that clearly had no international competitors. Backing down from its 1983 Manifesto position, the government indicated its intention to sell BGC as a single unit rather than divide the company into competing units with less market power. Once again, the regulatory body—the Office of Gas (Ofgas)—was responsible for maintaining a competitive environment. The BGC offering was followed by the announcement of the British Airports Authority (BAA) privatization, which re-ignited the same debates.

British Airways

The proposal to denationalize British Airways (BA) had been one of the first floated by the Thatcher government following its installation in 1979. BA's sale was initially penciled in for early 1985 as the follow-up to the BT offering. Like BT and BGC, BA had been and would be subject to significant government regulation, but unlike the other two, it was not a utility and thus not vulnerable to the "natural monopoly" criticism. Critics argued that the success of the nearly £1 billion offering, delayed until 1987, stemmed from the market power it gained as a result of Thatcher's sponsorship. Regulations were instituted to protect BA's routes from competition and the government tacitly allowed BA to acquire its last major British competitor, British Caledonia, despite alternate bids from Scandinavian Air Systems.

Britoil

Britoil, one of the largest Scottish companies, had been created out of the North Sea oil properties of the former British National Oil Company and sold off in two chunks in 1982 and 1985. Britoil's fiercely coveted independence seemed to be guaranteed by the "golden share" held by Her Majesty's government. This share, which had no stated value, was created at the time of Britoil's privatization to enable the government to block any unwanted predation on the company. Such "golden shares" were employed in the privatization of ten other companies—including British Aerospace, British Telecom, Cable and Wireless—thought to be crucial to Britain's national interest. But in the last weeks of 1987 and early weeks of 1988, British Petroleum launched a takeover bid for Britoil, which attempted to resist. The Thatcher government approved the takeover.

Utility Companies on the Auction Block

Similar objections about the abuse of monopoly power have been widely voiced with regard to the two large remaining planned privatizations, water and electricity. Indeed, these two offerings alone promise to raise an amount equal to that raised by all the previous denationalizations combined. The ten water authorities slated for sale, all located in England and Wales, have an aggregate asset base of £27 billion. The electricity industry in England and Wales is even larger, with assets of £37 billion. This figure does not include the very sizable operations of the two Scottish electricity boards, which will also be sold. Estimates for the proceeds of the sale of the electricity industry in England and Wales alone fall between £19 billion and £27 billion, with one "optimistic" estimate at £40 billion.[11]

The sale of these operations will be more complex than anything previously achieved. In order for the equity market to meet this unprecedented call on its capital at a price high enough to preempt accusations of a "giveaway of the family silver," the government will have to provide inducements to potential shareholders beyond those historically associated with utility stocks in capital-intensive industries. This will be even more likely because of the projected pattern and timing of the offerings. In the case of the electricity industry, the government is contemplating two "jumbo" issues for the two successor entities envisaged; for the water industry, a series of offerings for a larger number of successory enterprises is to be made simultaneously.

The potential proceeds from the sale of the water industry are expected to be gigantic. City analysts estimate that the market value of the

[11]*Financial Times*, February 22, 1988, 8.

most attractive of the ten regional authorities—Thames—is at least £1 billion to £1.5 billion. The average water bill had been increased 43 percent during the 1981–1985 period in an effort to reduce the industry's borrowings from the Treasury. The water authorities were in a position as of 1985 to start making a substantial net positive contribution to the government's finances.

In late February 1988 the government announced its final plans for the privatization of the electricity industry. The enterprise responsible for the generation of electricity in England and Wales is the Central Electricity Generating Board (CEGB), which sells to 12 distribution and marketing boards with specific geographic regions. Similar structures exist in Scotland and Northern Ireland. The original proposal for the post-privatization structure had the following features: The CEGB would be sold as from four to six competing companies and the area boards would be grouped into four or five companies and sold off as entities that could compete to sell electricity. But by the end of 1987 the proposal had been modified so that the government would sell off the CEGB as is and sell the area boards as separate noncompeting companies. Earlier in 1987 the government had announced it would increase electricity prices 15 percent over the subsequent two years, despite the excess generating capacity in the system. Electricity had already been contributing significantly to the government's coffers since 1984 (see Exhibit 7).

Commercial Companies in Mrs. Thatcher's Cupboard

To some observers, perhaps even more puzzling than the utilities remaining under state ownership were the more conventional industrial companies that were still stewards of the state. Given Mrs. Thatcher's free-market stance, observers expected that these commercial entities would have long ago been freed from the government's industrial portfolio. Certainly companies such as the Rover Group (formerly known as British Leyland), British Steel, Harland & Wolff, Short Brothers, and British Coal all faced more potentially galvanizing competition—both at home and abroad—than British Telecom, or the gas, water, and electricity companies.

Rover Group

The Rover Group—the new moniker applied with great hopes to the old British Leyland (BL) in 1987—had long been a favorite Thatcherite whipping boy. Not that such abuse was undeserved: In the decade after 1976 the company had consumed almost £3 billion of taxpayers' money in grants, cash infusions, loans, and guarantees. As Mrs. Thatcher herself put it, this sum was "equivalent to every family in the U.K. contributing £200 to BL."

The government's involvement in the motor industry started in

1968 when the government sponsored the merger of Britain's remaining volume automakers into a single company, British Leyland. By 1975 BL was insolvent and the Labour government elected to take a 99.8 percent ownership stake in the company. From that time on, the performance of the company continued to deteriorate. But by the beginning of 1988 Rover was still in the state ward despite firm bids by Ford and General Motors in 1985–1986 for all significant parts of the company.

Vocal opposition, wrapping itself in the Union Jack, claimed that it was critical to Britain's national security that a distinctly British automaking capability be maintained. Publicly, the prime minister stressed that she was "fed up" with persons who were protesting that BL should remain British but who were slow to part with the cash needed to do so—they should "put up or shut up." But behind the scenes "the Government ha[d] in effect been trying to renegotiate the deal with GM to provide what one critic ha[d] called a Union Jack figleaf."[12] In a surprise bid in early 1988, British Aerospace (BAe) came to the rescue of BL—but not without conditions.

The actual agreement between BAe and the government was announced at the end of March 1988: In return for £150 million, the government would transfer its 99.8 per cent stake to BAe, but only after injecting an *additional* £800 million into the automaker. Also, £500 million in tax-loss carryforwards were included to set against any future profits. The government would in the future have no obligation to cover additional Rover debts or losses, and BAe would suffer financial penalties if it sold any of Rover's principal operations before 1993.[13] One analyst called the terms "a gift horse" for BAe, a sentiment echoed in the market after the announcement, as BAe's shares shot up 17 percent in one day.[14]

British Steel

British Steel Corporation (BSC) has long been a drain on government resources (see Exhibit 7) and a likely prospect for competitive revitalization through the market. During Mrs. Thatcher's first eight years in office, however, BSC was not actively promoted as a privatization candidate. In the Conservative Manifesto in early 1987, the sale of BSC was still not included in the proposed legislative program for the next session of parliament. Indeed, in an election press conference, Norman Tebbit, then Conservative Party chairman, stated that because BSC was operating in an industry troubled by "considerable problems" it was "not a very early candidate" for sale.[15] But at the end of 1987 the government an-

[12]*Financial Times*, March 26, 1986, 21.
[13]*The Wall Street Journal*, March 30, 1988, 15.
[14]*Financial Times*, March 3, 1988, 18.
[15]*Financial Times*, February 29, 1988, 18.

nounced that it intended to sell BSC by the end of 1988 since the company's prospects had finally improved. Thatcher's efforts to rationalize the company had yielded higher worker productivity (see Exhibit 9). In the mid-1970s a ton of steel required 15 worker-hours in its production; by 1987 capital investment had reduced that figure to 5.5 worker-hours.[16] Of course, this improvement did not come without pain: £7 billion of cumulative losses during the late 1970s and early 1980s, and a 75 percent reduction in BSC's labor force, to 50,000.[17]

Harland & Wolff and Short Brothers

Harland & Wolff and Short Brothers are Ulster-based companies that play pivotal roles in the deeply troubled economy of Northern Ireland. Unemployment in Northern Ireland has hovered stubbornly in the 18 percent to 20 percent range throughout the 1980s. Harland & Wolff (H&W) is a Belfast shipyard that, like many other European and American shipbuilders, fell on extremely hard times during the 1980s. In the 15 years prior to 1987, the company had gobbled up over £1 billion in government subsidies. Despite shedding 22 percent of its work force in 1987, the company's losses equaled fully 74 percent of its sales. Government subsidies in 1988 were projected at £60 million despite the expected layoff of an additional 18 percent of the work force.[18] H&W is the second largest employer in Belfast, employing 4,000 workers or 5 percent of the provincial manufacturing work force; related employment extends its economic impact even further. One recent study found that between 33 and 44 jobs in Ulster depend directly or indirectly on every 100 H&W jobs.[19] A similar story could be told for Short Brothers, the Ulster-based, loss-plagued aircraft manufacturer, which is one of the province's five largest employers.

British Coal

The British coal industry had been in the public sector since the 1940s and was considered by many to be inviolate despite the downsizing over the years and the steady drain on government funds (see Exhibit 7). From a peak annual production of almost 250 million tons and total employment of over 700,000 in the late 1940s, the coal industry had by 1979 declined to an annual output of around 100 million tons and employment of under 200,000. But time and again the industry's interests, especially its miners—and their union, the National Union of Mineworkers (NUM),

---

[16]*Ibid.*
[17]*The Economist,* March 26, 1988, 54.
[18]*Ibid.*
[19]*Financial Times,* March 15, 1988, 18.

the traditional standard-bearer of the British trade union movement—
had proved their strength in tests with the government of the day. The
last Tory prime minister before Mrs. Thatcher, Edward Heath, had found
his government toppled by a 1973–1974 struggle with the NUM, ending
in a nationwide strike. Indeed, Mrs. Thatcher herself, after a flirtation
with brinksmanship, refrained from provoking a NUM strike in 1981.
But three years later, in 1984–1985, Mrs. Thatcher accepted and weath-
ered a coal strike that became the bitterest industrial dispute in Britain
since the General Strike of 1926. She pressed on with the industry's
downsizing, so that by 1988 only 160,000 miners remained, producing
well under 100 million tons.

Another Rationale for Privatization: "Popular Capitalism"

As the "competition" and "efficiency" justifications increasingly came
under attack during the second Thatcher term, the government adopted
a new battle cry—"popular capitalism"—the ever-broadening spread of
the ownership of property (especially housing and corporate shares)
throughout society. By May 1987 Mrs. Thatcher was able to claim the
vision was well on its way to full realization. In her speech opening the
campaign for the June general election, she boasted: "Popular capitalism
is on the march—more families owning more property, more homes, more
shares, more second pensions, and more savings."[20] The extension of
home ownership in Britain, where rented public housing had long provided more than half of the country's dwellings and where private rental
accommodation had become almost insignificant, had been a constant
Thatcherite theme since 1979. But the public emphasis on broader share
ownership has a more recent pedigree, dating only from March 1986,
when Mrs. Thatcher announced with great fanfare the Personal Equity
Plans (PEP).

The distinctive populist achievement of the first two Thatcher terms—
and the truly distinctive commitment of the 1979 and 1983 Election
Manifestos—was the spread of home ownership through the sale of council housing. The results under Mrs. Thatcher were impressive: Owner-
occupied housing as a percentage of all housing in England and Wales
rose from 54 percent in 1979 to approximately 66 percent by the end of
1987, with upwards of 1 million council units sold by 1987.

These efforts were also good politics: Almost 60 percent of Labour
voters who purchased their council homes voted Conservative in 1983,
and of all the new home buyers 56 percent voted Tory and only 18 percent
voted Labour.[21] Labour Party pollsters concluded in 1987 that home-

[20]Sked and Cook, *Postwar Britain*, 349.
[21]*New York Times Sunday Magazine*, May 31, 1987, 82.

owners were twice as likely to vote Conservative as council house tenants.[22] The polls indicated that this tendency also applied to share ownership. In 1987 pollsters found that 57 percent of the people who bought stock in one of the privatized companies—including factory laborers, the hardcore of Labour's historic base—planned to vote Conservative in the June 1987 election. Exit polls in that election indicated that, indeed, 6 of 10 people who owned shares voted Tory.

The focus on share ownership specifically was new for the Thatcher government. Just as privatization had found little mention in the 1979 and 1983 manifestos, the concept of popular capitalism received only the most cursory treatment. Nonetheless, the government undertook indirect and direct actions to encourage broader share ownership vis-à-vis other investment alternatives. Share ownership grew as a result of indirect actions, such as the promotion of the Unlisted Stock Market and Third Market, the employee share ownership schemes (ESOPs), and changes in the tax treatment of some investments.

However, the direct actions to promote the sale of the large public offerings of nationalized firms, particularly after 1984, increased share ownership the most. For all but the smallest state holdings, the government employed public equity offerings rather than private sales to other companies. The large offerings all utilized some form of partial payment, whereby the nominal issuance price for the shares would actually be paid in installments over a set period. Moreover, the issues were always structured so that the actual price per share was low; therefore, the number of shares to be sold was large, permitting wide participation. Several offerings employed allotment or even maximum purchase provisions, ensuring that large institutions would not crowd out the small-lot buyers.

Inducements offered to potential investors, and particularly to employees, were perhaps even more inventive. Most of the offerings permitted employees of the nationalized companies either to purchase shares at highly concessionary prices or to receive them for free following an easy application process. Similarly, option- and warrant-like instruments were attached in several instances to the new shares, being either convertible into or assigning concessionary purchase rights for additional shares in the future. The BT offering was perhaps the greatest bonanza of them all, with, among other features, free shares, warrant-like devices, and £37.1 million worth of phone vouchers either applicable against future phone bills or directly convertible into additional shares.

Most visibly, the government indulged in an unprecedented media extravaganza. Advertising expenditures reached almost incredible levels: £50 million for BT and a similar amount for BGC. The blitz exploited all the various media, including prime-time television—going far beyond the conventional printed "tombstone" approach. The advertising firm

[22]*The Economist*, December 9, 1987, 86.

Saatchi and Saatchi—a Conservative favorite in the general election campaigns—was employed to spread the message.

Mrs. Thatcher's public commitment to popular capitalism surfaced in March 1986 when she announced the Personal Equity Plans (PEP). PEP received unprecedented coverage—front-page-center headlines on all newspapers, even the notorious tabloids. PEP would allow Britons to invest an annual maximum of £2,400 in British companies trading on the London Stock Exchange (but not in mutual funds). Existing equity investments were not transferable to the new PEP accounts. The tax benefit for the account was two-fold: tax exemption on the capital gains from the sale of PEP holdings (following the 12–23-month holding period) and income tax exemption for all dividends reinvested in the PEP account.[23] However, by year-end 1987, only 165,000 investors had subscribed to the scheme.

Despite the lukewarm reception for PEP, the results of popular capitalism were gratifying for Mrs. Thatcher. As of February 1987, some 8.5 million Britons owned shares—20 percent of the adult population—compared with 3 million in 1979.[24] But in a study published in the summer of 1987 the Labour Party claimed to have quantified the extent of small-holder withdrawals from earlier privatization offerings. The study found that more than one-third of the 1.2 million individuals who bought BA stock at the time of its February 1987 sale had sold their positions by mid-1987.[25] Only two-fifths of the over 2 million individuals who bought BT in November 1984 remained by June 1987. Looking back to the Amersham International sale of February 1982, after five years only one-tenth of the original individual holding group remained—despite a 330 percent price appreciation in that period. (Stock performance of privatized companies is presented in Exhibit 10.)

The Unfinished Agenda

Mrs. Thatcher's privatization crusade was far from finished in 1988. Indeed, the largest battles lay ahead with the gigantic utilities and problematic industrials in the government's portfolio. Given a third term as prime minister and strong popular standing, Mrs. Thatcher had the opportunity to reshape Britain's industrial landscape and to redefine the state's role in the economy through the creative use of fiscal policy.

[23]The annual tax exemption on capital gains profits under the existing tax law was £6,300; PEP would allow investors an additional £2,400. The average yield on equities in the Financial Times Ordinary Share Index at that time was under 4 percent.

[24]*The Economist*, December 9, 1987, 86.

[25]*Ibid.*

Privatization in the United Kingdom

Exhibit 1   U.K. Economic Data, 1976–1987

Year	Real GDP (Annual Percentage Rate)	Unemployed (Percent of Working Population)	Retail Prices (Percentage Increase)	Treasury Bill Yield (Last Day of Period)	Sterling Exchange Rate (1975 = 100)	Financial Times Index Industrial Ordinary Shares	
						Price Index	Earning Yield
	1	2	3	4	5	6	7
1976	3.5%	4.8%	15.0%	14.0%	85.6	368.0	17.6
1977	2.0	5.2	13.0	6.4	81.2	452.3	16.5
1978	1.3	5.2	8.1	11.9	81.5	479.4	16.5
1979	1.0	4.9	17.3	16.5	87.3	475.5	16.6
1980	−3.7	6.2	15.3	13.6	96.1	464.5	18.1
1981	0.6	8.5	11.9	15.4	94.9	518.5	12.1
1982	1.8	9.9	6.2	10.0	90.5	574.7	10.8
1983	3.3	10.8	5.0	9.0	83.2	692.6	9.6
1984	2.3	11.1	4.8	9.3	78.6	854.9	10.8
1985	2.5	11.3	5.5	11.5	78.3	1004.6	11.5
1986	4.3	11.5	3.7	10.9	72.9	1287.1	10.2
1987	5.1	10.4	4.1	8.4	71.8	1600.0	9.0

Source: U.K. Central Statistical Office, *Economic Trends,* various issues.

Privatization in the United Kingdom

Exhibit 2   Policy Targets and Actual Performance, 1979–1988

Fiscal Year	M3 Target	M3 Actual	PSBR Target	PSBR Actual
1979/80	7–11%	16.2%	4.50%	4.8%
1980/81	7–11	19.4	3.75	5.6
1981/82	6–11	12.8	4.25	3.4[a]
1982/83	8–12	11.2[a]	3.50	3.2[a]
1983/84	7–11	9.4[a]	2.75	3.2
1984/85	6–10	11.9	2.25	3.1
1985/86	5– 9[b]	16.5	2.00	1.6[a]
1986/87	11–15	NA	1.80	1.1[a]
1987/88	1– 5[c]	NA	1.80	0.8[a]

Note: Data are percentage annual growth rates for M3 and percent of GDP for PSBR.

[a]Actual performance is equal to or better than targeted levels.

[b]Abandoned on October 17, 1985.

[c]Target for M0 (the monetary base) rather than M3.

Source: *Financial Statement and Budget Reports,* various years, and U.K. Central Statistical Office, *Financial Statistics,* various issues.

Privatization in the United Kingdom

Exhibit 3   General Government^a Accounts and the PSBR

	Millions of Pounds			Composition (%)		
	1979	1983	1986	1979	1983	1986
General Government^a Expenditures						
1 General public services	4,781	5,946	6,762	5.6%	4.3%	4.2%
2 Defense	9,006	15,872	18,628	10.5	11.5	11.5
3 Public order and safety	2,893	5,312	6,692	3.4	3.8	4.1
4 Education	10,310	16,340	19,521	12.1	11.8	12.0
5 Health	9,082	15,924	19,446	10.6	11.5	12.0
6 Social security	20,944	39,142	50,195	24.5	28.3	30.9
7 Housing and community	7,250	7,384	8,033	8.5	5.3	5.0
8 Recreational and cultural	1,138	1,950	2,247	1.3	1.4	1.4
9 Fuel and energy	1,195	857	−857	1.4	0.6	−0.5
10 Agriculture, forestry, and fisheries	1,163	2,472	2,397	1.4	1.8	1.5
11 Mining, manufacturing, and construction	2,487	2,662	1,856	2.9	1.9	1.1
12 Transport and communications	3,241	4,850	3,681	3.8	3.5	2.3
13 Economic affairs and services	1,666	3,290	3,847	1.9	2.4	2.4
14 Other expenditures	10,349	16,508	19,743	12.1	11.9	12.2
15 Total expenditures (central + local governments)	85,505	138,509	162,191	100.0	100.0	100.0
16 (Total expenditures as % of GDP)	(43.3%)	(45.9%)	(42.8%)			

Exhibit 3 (Continued)

General Government [a] Revenues

17 Income taxes	25,238	43,486	52,348	31.9%	33.9%	34.4%
18 Expenditure taxes	29,737	49,384	62,535	37.6	38.5	41.1
19 Social security contributions	11,526	20,780	26,033	14.6	16.2	17.1
20 Other current receipts	11,640	13,059	8,505	14.7	10.2	5.6
21 Capital taxes	1,014	1,574	2,673	1.3	1.2	1.8
22 Total taxes (central + local governments)	79,155	128,283	152,094	100.0	100.0	100.0
23 (Total taxes as % of GDP)	(40.1%)	(42.5%)	(40.1%)			

Derivation of PSBR

24 Financial surplus/deficit	−6,350	−10,226	−10,097			
25 Net lending (asset acquisition)[b]	5,886	1,780	−6,828			
26 General gov't (central + local) borrowing requirement	12,236	12,006	3,269	96.5	103.2	143.7
27 Public corporation direct borrowing from central gov't	3,281	1,446	80	25.9	12.4	3.5
28 Public corporation borrowing requirement	3,726	1,076	−914	29.4	9.2	−40.2
29 PSBR	12,681	11,636	2,275	100.0	100.0	100.0
30 (PSBR as % of GDP)	(6.4%)	(3.9%)	(0.6%)			
31 Public corporation borrowing as % of PSBR = (27 + 28)/29	55.3%	21.7%	−36.7%			

Note: Relationship among rows: 24 = 22 − 15; 26 = 25 − 24; 29 = 26 − 27 + 28.

[a] General government is the combination of the central and local governments.

[b] Sales of government assets, including privatized industries, are recorded as a negative transaction.

Sources: Central Statistical Office, *National Income & Expenditure* (Tables 9.1–9.4) and *Financial Statistics* (Tables 2.1–2.3, 3.1–3.2), various issues.

Privatization in the United Kingdom

Exhibit 4   Privatizations of U.K. Public Corporations 1979–1987 (Representative Sample)

Company	Business	Date of Sale	What Was Sold	Means of Sale	Remaining Government Holdings	Net Proceeds (£ Millions)
(1)	(2)	(3)	(4)	(5)	(6)	(7)
British Petroleum	Oil	Oct. 79	5%	Public offering[a]	39%	276
ICL	Computers	Dec. 79	25%	Public offering	Nil	38
Ferranti	Industrial equipment	Jul. 80	50%	Public offering	50%	54
British Aerospace	Aerospace	Feb. 81	51.6%	Public offering	49.4%[d]	43
British Petroleum	Oil	Jun. 81	<1%	Rights sale[b]	39%	8
British Sugar	Sugar refiner	Jul. 81	24%	Public offering	Nil	44
Cable and Wireless	Telecommunications	Oct. 81	49.4%	Public offering	50.6%[d]	182
Amersham International	Radiochemicals	Feb. 82	100%	Public offering	Nil	64
National Freight	Road haulage	Feb. 82	100%	Management buyout	Nil	5
Britoil	Oil	Nov. 82	51%	Tender offer[c]	48.9%[d]	627
Associated British Ports	Seaports	Feb. 83	51.5%	Public offering	48.5%[d]	46
British Rail Hotels	Hotels	Mar. 83	10 hotels	Private sale	Nil	51
British Petroleum	Oil	Sep. 83	7%	Tender offer	31.7%	543
Cable and Wireless	Telecommunications	Dec. 83	27.9%	Tender offer	23.1%[d]	263
Associated British Ports	Seaports	Apr. 84	48.5%	Tender offer	Nil	52
British Gas-Wytch Farm	Oil	May 84	100%	Private sale	Nil	82
Enterprise Oil	Oil	Jun. 84	100%	Tender offer	Nil	380
British Rail/Sealink	Harbor and ferry	Jul. 84	51%	Private sale	Nil	66

Exhibit 4 (Continued)

Company (1)	Business (2)	Date of Sale (3)	What Was Sold (4)	Means of Sale (5)	Remaining Government Holdings (6)	Net Proceeds (£ Millions) (7)
Jaguar	Cars	Jul. 84	100%	Public offering	Nil	297
Inmos	Semiconductors	Jul. 84	76%	Private sale	Nil	95
British Telecom	Telecommunications	Nov. 84	50.2%	Public offering	49.8%	3,916
British Aerospace	Aerospace	May 85	48.4%	Public offering	Nil	346
Britoil	Oil	Aug. 85	49%	Public offering	Nil	450
Cable and Wireless	Telecommunications	Dec. 85	23.1%	Public offering	Nil	602
National Bus Company	Buses	Aug. 86	Piecemeal disposal	Private sale		7
Trustee Savings Banks	Banks	Oct. 86	100%	Public offering	Nil	1,500[e]
British Gas	Natural Gas	Dec. 86	100%	Public offering	Nil	5,500[e]
British Airways	Airline	Jan. 87	100%	Public offering	Nil	900[e]
Rolls-Royce	Aerospace, cars	May 87	100%	Public offering	Nil	1,360[e]

[a] A public offering is an issue of securities by the company that is offered to all investors.

[b] A rights issue is an issue of securities by the company that is offered to current stockholders.

[c] A tender offer is a general offer by a group of investors made directly to the company's stockholders in order to buy their stock.

[d] Subsequent privatizations shown in this exhibit reduced government holdings to nil.

[e] Represents gross proceeds from the sale.

Sources: *The Times*, April 23, 1986, 14; *The Economist*, June 21, 1986, 54; and *Financial Times*, various issues.

Privatization in the United Kingdom

Exhibit 5A   A Schematic Version of the Public Corporations' Accounts

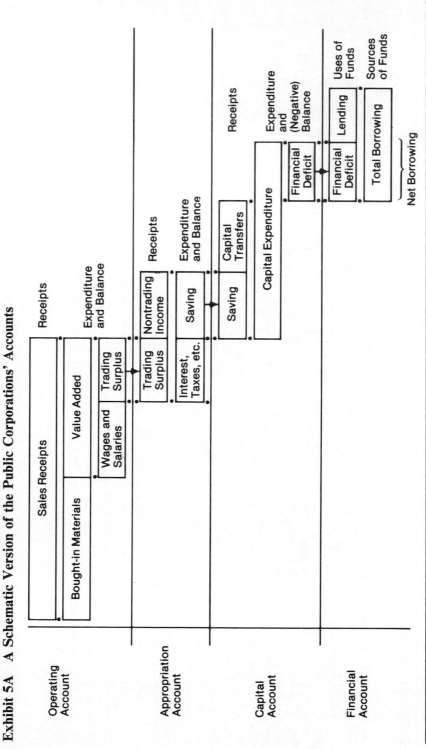

Source: D. Jackson, *Introduction to Economic Theory and Data* (New York: Macmillan, 1982), 457.

Exhibit 5B Financial Accounts of Public Corporations, 1978–1987 (Millions of Pounds)

Year	Gross Trading Surplus Total	Capital Receipts Total	Corporate Savings Total	Capital Transfers Total	Capital Expenditure Total	Financial Surplus (+) or Deficit (−)	Net Lending (Trade Credit, etc.)	Public Corporation Borrowing Requirement[a]
	1	2	3	4	5	6	7	8
1978	5,391	4,288	3,759	529	5,255	−967	192	1,159
1979	5,543	4,160	3,641	519	6,285	−2,125	1,601	3,726
1980	6,222	4,874	4,278	596	7,290	−2,416	184	2,600
1981	7,551	5,904	5,211	693	7,479	−1,575	−1,268	307
1982	9,019	6,303	5,683	620	8,453	−2,150	−387	1,763
1983	9,949	8,280	7,659	711	8,341	−61	1,105	1,076
1984	8,231	6,378	6,045	693	7,232	−494	781	1,275
1985	7,077	6,085	5,319	766	6,035	50	−249	−299
1986	8,086	6,820	6,182	638	5,562	1,258	344	−914
1987	6,715	5,723	4,979	744	4,717	1,006	−277	−1,283

Notes: Data for 1978–1982 are not completely compatible with data for 1983–1987 because of data revisions.

Relationships among columns: 3 + 4 = 2; 2 − 5 = 6, 6 − 7 = 8.

[a]This is the same number that can be found in Line 28 of Exhibit 3. Minus indicates a reduction in borrowing.

Source: U.K. Central Statistical Office, *Financial Statistics*, Tables 2.5 and 5.1–5.3, various issues.

Privatization in the United Kingdom

Exhibit 6   PSBR and Privatization Proceeds, 1979–1992

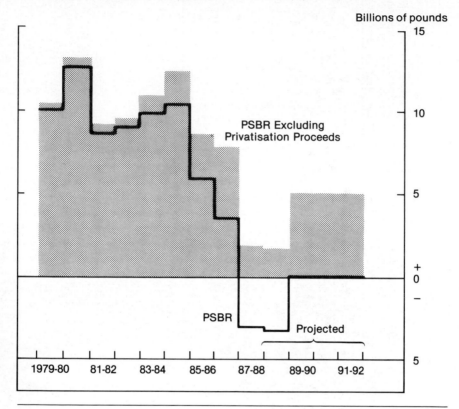

Source: *The Economist,* March 19, 1988, 60. © 1988 *The Economist,* distributed by Special
Features.

Privatization in the United Kingdom

Exhibit 7   Nationalized Industries'[a] External Finance

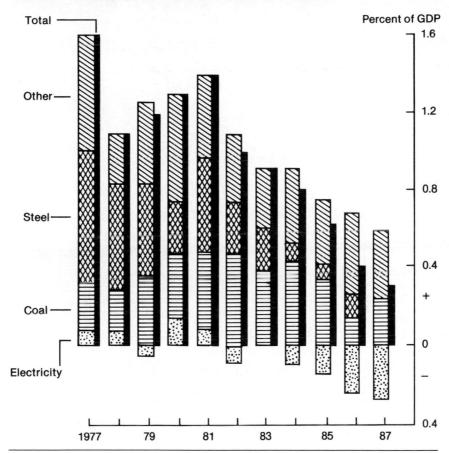

[a]Industries in the public sector at the end of 1987–1988, excluding British Shipbuilders and Girobank.

Source: *The Economist,* December 19, 1987, 49. © 1987 *The Economist,* distributed by Special Features.

Privatization in the United Kingdom

Exhibit 8   Productivity and Employment, 1975–1987

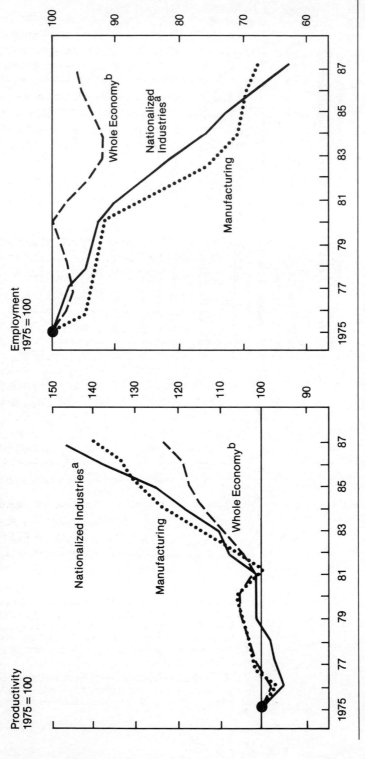

[a]Industries in the public sector at end of 1987–1988, excluding British Shipbuilders and Girobank.
[b]Excluding North Sea oil and nontrading public sector.
Source: Treasury and *The Economist*, December 29, 1987, 49. © 1987 *The Economist*, distributed by Special Features.

Privatization in the United Kingdom

Exhibit 9   Annual Changes in Public-Sector Total Factor Productivity

	Percentage Change	
	1968–1978	**1978–1985**
British Rail	(0.8)	2.8
British Steel	−2.5	12.9
Post Office	(−1.3)	1.9
British Telecom	5.2	0.5
British Coal	−1.4	0.0
Electricity	0.7	1.4
British Gas	(8.5)	1.2
National Bus	−1.4	0.1
British Airways	5.5	4.8
All manufacturing	1.7	n.a.

Note: Figures in parentheses are for labor productivity where total factor productivity is not available.

Sources: Molyneux and Thompson, "Nationalised Industry Performance," *Fiscal Studies,* February 1987; cited in *The Economist,* December 19, 1987, 49.

Privatization in the United Kingdom

Exhibit 10   Stock Price Performance for Selected Privatizations

Company	Date of Sale	Offer Price (Pence)	Opening Price (Pence)	Undervaluation (Millions of Pounds)	Price as of June 30, 1987 (Pence)	Percent Gain in Stock from Offering Date	Percent Gain in Financial Times Index over Same Period	Excess Gain or Loss of Stock over Financial Times Index
1	2	3	4	5	6	7	8	9
British Aerospace	Feb. 81	150	171	20.9	529	252.7	261.4	−8.7
Cable and Wireless	Oct. 81	168	203	46.6	389	131.6	271.0	−139.4
Amersham International	Feb. 82	142	190	21.3	598	321.1	211.1	110.0
Britoil	Nov. 82	100	81	−48.4	316	216.0	184.4	31.6
Associated British Ports	Feb. 83	112	130	3.5	604	439.3	172.2	267.1
British Telecom	Nov. 84	50	95	1,337.2	291	482.0	92.7	389.3
Enterprise Oil	Jun. 84	100	100	0	305	205.0	113.4	91.6
Jaguar	Jul. 84	165	179	25.0	554	235.8	123.4	112.4
British Airways	Jan. 87	125	227	73.4	146	16.8	26.4	−9.6
Rolls-Royce	May 87	170	294	99.3	124	−27.1	6.8	−33.9

Source: George Yarrow, "Privatizations in Theory and Practice," *Economic Policy* (April 1986): 36.

Discussion Questions for Case

1. Evaluate Mrs. Thatcher's management of macroeconomic policy during her three terms in office. What role did privatization play in any success or failure?
2. Based on the British experience, does privatization improve economic efficiency? Is this Mrs. Thatcher's strongest rationale for privatization?
3. Evaluate Mrs. Thatcher's implementation of her privatization policy. Are there other policies that might have been more effective in meeting her objectives?

Bibliography

Curwen, Peter J., *Public Enterprise* (New York: St. Martin's Press, 1986). This book contains institutional detail on the early U.K. privatizations.

Kay, John, Colin Mayer, and David Thompson, eds., *Privatization and Regulation: the U.K. Experience* (Oxford: Clarendon Press, 1986). This book is a compendium of essays on various issues regarding privatization. The essays are balanced in their support and criticism of Thatcher's policies.

MacAvoy, Paul W., W.T. Stanbury, George Yarrow, and Richard Zeckhauser, editors, *Privatization and State Owned Enterprises: Lessons from the United States, Great Britain, and Canada* (Norwell, MA: Kluwer Academic Publishers, 1988). This collection of conference papers discusses both the theoretical aspects of privatization and comparative lessons from three countries.

"Privatization: Everybody's Doing It, Differently," *The Economist,* Dec. 21, 1985, 69–84. This survey examines the British lead in privatizations and compares them to other privatizations around the world.

Vickers, John, and George Yarrow, *Privatization* (Cambridge, MA: MIT Press, 1988). The authors provide a thorough, up-to-date account of privatization in the United Kingdom and evaluate its economic rationales.

Yarrow, George, "Privatization in Theory and Practice," *Economic Policy,* April 1986, 324–377. This article covers some of the issues examined in the Vickers and Yarrow book above, such as the effect of privatization on firm performance.

PART IV
MANAGING IN THE INTERNATIONAL ECONOMY

The primary focus of this section is on exchange rates and how macroeconomic policies interact with the exchange rate regime. Of course, there is much more to the international economy than exchange rates; trade and protectionism, commodity shocks, credit defaults, and capital controls and liberalization are among the more important issues. These topics, usually considered in books on sectoral or industrial policy, are important to the discussion in this book only to the extent that they impinge on the conduct of macroeconomic policy.

There are two types of international regimes that determine how international transactions are conducted. The fixed exchange rate system offers a high degree of certainty for private market participants, but it places constraints on the actions of the government by forcing it to maintain its agreement to buy and sell its currency at a fixed price. The flexible exchange rate system places the risk of fluctuating exchange rates on private participants in international transactions, and it absolves the government from any active role in the functioning of the foreign exchange market. As we shall see in the following cases, the reality is that the international economy is managed whether it is operating under the fixed rate or flexible rate regime.

Fixed exchange rates have long been the dominant institutional regime, associated with periods of economic growth and increasing interdependence in trade and capital transactions. The functioning of a fixed rate system is illustrated by the Chapter 13 case, "The United Kingdom and the Gold Standard: 1925." The case contrasts the theory and the practice of the gold standard, a type of fixed rate system, and indicates the burden of maintaining this international institution.

The Chapter 14 case, "Kennedy and the Balance of Payments," continues with the theme of the burdens of maintaining fixed rates. By 1961, the size of the U.S. payments imbalances was destroying world confidence in the ability of the United States to keep its commitment to maintain the fixed rates of the Bretton Woods system, a modified gold standard. The cause of President Kennedy's problems and the potential solutions are the focus of this case.

Despite the attempts by all the major industrial countries to avoid persistent payments imbalances, the situation culminated in a series of crises at the end of the 1960s and in the early 1970s. The Chapter 15 case, "Nixon's New Economic Policy," describes how the United States responded in 1971 to the difficulties of maintaining the Bretton Woods system. Over the next two years, repeated attempts to realign the fixed rates failed.

The solution was the adoption of a system of flexible exchange rates, a system that is still in effect today. Exchange rates have proven to be more volatile than had been imagined in 1973. Countries have had long periods of currency appreciation or depreciation. The Chapter 16 case, "The Decline of the Dollar: 1978," examines the determinants and consequences of exchange rate fluctuations and the options for central bank intervention.

Finally, we will examine an issue that is not directly related to exchange rates—the third world debt crisis. The Chapter 17 case, "Mexico: Crisis of Confidence," traces the origins of the debt problems in Mexico and the events preceding the August 1982 crisis.

CHAPTER 13

The Fixed Exchange Rate System

The fixed exchange rate system was the predominant international monetary institution of the nineteenth and twentieth centuries. The United Kingdom had a long association with the gold standard, a particular type of fixed exchange rate system. The period spanned by the gold standard was one of rapid industrialization and growth in commerce and trade. Many believed that the economic benefits of this period were attributable to the gold standard.

In 1925, Chancellor of the Exchequer Winston Churchill had to decide whether Britain should or should not return to the gold standard that it had abandoned during World War I. The question involved economic issues of the consequences of returning to the gold standard. There was also the political question of who would benefit by the action and who would be hurt. If Churchill decided to return to gold, then at what level should the exchange rate be set? If he decided not to return, then what would be the consequences of this alternative? This chapter's case, "The United Kingdom and the Gold Standard: 1925," allows the reader to evaluate the investigation by which Churchill sought answers to these questions. Moreover, the issues raised by this case are the same as those raised by today's calls for a return to gold.

Case
The United Kingdom and the Gold Standard: 1925

A Question of Returning to the Gold Standard

On March 17, 1925, Winston Churchill, Chancellor of the Exchequer in the Conservative Party government of Prime Minister Stanley Baldwin, held an unusual dinner party. The topic under discussion was whether Great Britain should return to a gold standard for its currency, the pound sterling.[1] Present at the dinner were the famous economist John Maynard Keynes and Reginald McKenna, a banker who had formerly been Chancellor of the Exchequer himself; these were the most prominent opponents of a return to the gold standard. Also attending were Sir John Bradbury and Sir Otto Niemeyer—the leading supporters of the gold standard within the British Treasury's top ranks.

Churchill's private secretary reports that the discussion continued past midnight. Keynes and McKenna argued that returning to gold would require deliberate contraction of the British economy, accompanied by unemployment, class conflict, and prolonged strikes. Bradbury replied that returning to gold would make the British economy "knave-proof," free of manipulation for "political or even more unworthy reasons." Without the gold standard, the nation could fall into "a fool's paradise of false prosperity." After listening to both sides, Churchill turned to Reginald McKenna:

But this isn't entirely an economic matter; it is a political decision. . . . You have been a politician; indeed, you have been Chancellor of the Exchequer. Given the situation as it is, what decision would you take?[2]

Returning to a gold standard would require Britain to do two things. First, the Bank of England would have to agree to sell gold to anyone at a constant price fixed in terms of pounds sterling. Second, the government would have to allow gold to be exported from Great Britain as a means of payment for international transactions. These measures would set the value of the pound in terms of gold. Other major currencies—notably the U.S. dollar—either were already on the gold standard or were expected to return to it shortly. Since each gold standard currency had a constant

This case was prepared by Research Associate Daniel Pope under the supervision of Professor Thomas K. McCraw.
Copyright © 1982 by the President and Fellows of Harvard College
Harvard Business School case 9-383-081

[1]The term "sterling" apparently derives from a star that was printed on certain medieval English coins.

[2]Martin Gilbert, *Winston S. Churchill*, Vol. 5 (Boston: Houghton Mifflin, 1977), 92–100.

gold value, the exchange rates of these countries would also be fixed. It was universally understood that if Britain did restore the gold standard, the Bank of England would sell an ounce of gold for £3 17s 10½d. At this price, one pound sterling would buy gold worth $4.86 American. The ratio of £1 = $4.86 had been the exchange rate for decades before World War I.

Memories of the 40 or so years before the war, the heyday of the international gold standard, shaped British policymakers' thinking in the 1920s. The recollections were happy ones. From the 1870s to World War I, most of the major trading nations of the world had given their money a fixed value in gold and hence fixed exchange rates with other gold standard nations.

A nation on a gold standard never had to maintain a supply of gold equal to its total money supply. In Britain, some gold coins (known as gold sovereigns) were in circulation, but most of the money supply consisted of checking account deposits and paper bank notes issued by the Bank of England. Under the gold standard, it was taken for granted that most people would be happy to use notes and checking accounts instead of actually demanding gold. Thus the Bank of England in the late nineteenth century kept gold in reserve equal to only 2-3 percent of the money supply. In other words, the gold standard was a *fractional* reserve system.

To generations of British businessmen and bankers, the most appealing features of the international gold standard were its stability and predictability and its apparently self-regulating nature. National moneys, interchangeable at known rates, looked like the best way to facilitate the free flow of international trade and investment. A British merchant selling steel to an American railroad or buying wheat from farmers in Kansas knew that each pound was worth almost exactly $4.86, irrespective of the time of delivery.

How the Gold Standard Worked in Theory

Imbalances in international payments seemed to correct themselves automatically under the international gold standard. David Hume, the Scottish philosopher and political economist, had first described this process in the eighteenth century. Hume called it the specie-flow adjustment mechanism.[3] In principle, the mechanism worked like this: Suppose Great Britain began to pay more to the United States (in the form of imports from the United States, investments in the United States, and other payments) than it received from American payments to Britain (for British exports, dividends and interest on investments, etc.). To finance the def-

---

[3]"Specie" is gold, silver, or other precious metal used as money.

Figure 1   Specie-Flow Response to a Hypothetical British Payments Deficit to the United States

Given an initial condition of a British deficit and U.S. surplus:

Sequence	U.K.		U.S.
a	↓	Gold supply	↑
b	↓	Money supply	↑
c	↓	Price level	↑
d	↑	Exports	↓
		and	
e	↓	Imports	↑

This response continues until balance of payments equilibrium is restored.*

Assumptions:
1. Both nations are on gold standard and permit free export of gold.
2. Monetary authorities allow money supply to expand or contract as gold reserves rise or fall.
3. Prices adjust to changes in money supply.
4. Import and export demand responds to price changes.

*Notice how this story is a special case of the quantity theory of money discussed in the Chapter 2 note "Money and the Determination of Income." An increase in gold is assumed to increase the monetary base, which then, in turn, increases the money supply. An increase in the money supply will increase nominal income—in this case, nominal income rises because prices rise.

icit, the British would have to send some of their gold reserve to the United States. But a decline in the domestic (British) gold supply would reduce the British money supply and therefore reduce prices. (The connection between gold and the money supply was closer in Hume's day, before the advent of the fractional reserve system.) When British prices went down, her goods would become more saleable in foreign countries. Her exports would rise. Over in the United States, the opposite process would be taking place. The gold inflow would raise American money supply and prices and make American exports less competitive abroad. With British exports rising and American exports falling, the payments imbalance would correct itself: (see Figure 1).

A second process would also be at work to correct payment imbalances. As the British money supply went down (because of the gold outflow), British incomes would decline. The British would have less income to spend on imported goods. The opposite phenomenon would occur in the United States. Therefore the specie-flow mechanism worked through its impact on incomes and import demand as well as through prices and exports. This income effect might be particularly important where a nation's imports were luxury items. The demand for imported luxuries might be highly income elastic, so that a small change in income would have a relatively large effect on import demand.

Two aspects of the international gold standard made it particularly appealing to the financial establishment and advocates of laissez-faire conservatism. First, the process was thought to work quite automatically through market forces. It provided no opening for meddlesome restrictions on international trade and investments. It was knave-proof. Second, the gold standard soothed fears of inflation. It kept politicians from printing paper money at will and pushing prices up. Bankers and bondholders lived in terror of "fiat money" backed by nothing more solid than a government's insistence that it was legal tender.[4] The bankers' fear was that without a gold standard, politicians who catered to interest group pressures might yield to inflationary temptations. Bondholders had similar nightmares. Since most nineteenth-century financial investments took the form of long-term bonds, repayment in depreciating paper money would diminish the value of bondholders' assets. In other words, the gold standard in the late nineteenth century was a way for conservative economic forces to curb the redistributive zeal of the masses in democratic societies.

How the Gold Standard Worked in Practice

In practice, adjustments to payments imbalances in the pre-World War I era were not so simple as the specie-flow mechanism would suggest. For Great Britain, the "automatic" adjustment was usually managed by the Bank of England. Although a private institution until 1946, the Bank of England was already by the late nineteenth century playing the role of a central bank. This meant that it handled the British Treasury's banking needs and that it served as the banker for other British banks. By varying the terms on which it offered credit to other financial institutions, the Bank of England could control (although not completely) the nation's money supply. Its main weapon was known as "Bank Rate," the interest rate it would charge other banks and financial houses.[5] If it appeared that British payments were in deficit and an outflow of gold seemed imminent, the Bank Rate would be raised. London financiers, with their source of credit now more expensive, would have to raise their own interest rates. This would have two effects. First, higher interest rates in London would attract short-term capital investments from abroad and funds that otherwise might go overseas. This would increase the flow of payments into Great Britain and help to correct the prior payments deficit. As with the specie-flow mechanism, there was an income effect that complemented the price effect. Higher interest rates at home would probably reduce

---

[4]Legal tender is anything which the law requires to be accepted as payment for debts.

[5]The Bank Rate is also referred to as the "Minimum Lending Rate (MLR)" in the Chapter 4 case, "The United Kingdom under Thatcher." It is equivalent to the discount rate in the United States.

Figure 2   Impact of Bank Rate Change in Response to Hypothetical British Payments Deficit

Given an initial condition of U.K. payments in deficit:

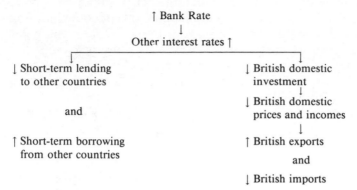

This response continues until balance of payments equilibrium is restored.

domestic investment and total output and incomes. Once again, these lower incomes would mean reduced spending on imports and a corrective to the payments deficit (see Figure 2).

Bank Rate was changed 195 times between 1880 and 1913, or about once every two months on average. But most changes were small; more than 90 percent of the time, Bank Rate stayed below 5 percent. These minor adjustments were potent enough to correct payments surpluses or deficits largely because London was the world's preeminent financial center. Even a minor increase in London interest rates would bring in funds from around the world. It was said that a 7 percent Bank Rate would draw money from the North Pole. To those in trade and finance who benefited from it, the operations of Bank Rate seemed almost as automatic and natural as the specie-flow mechanism itself.

Behind the smooth operation of the international gold standard was Great Britain's predominant position in world trade and finance. In the 1870s, about 38 percent of the world's manufactured exports were British. This share declined gradually, but was still about 30 percent on the eve of World War I. Conversely, Great Britain was the leading importer of raw materials and foodstuffs such as cotton and wheat. The London money market was itself a major pillar of British strength during this golden age. Businessmen around the world habitually used the London market to finance their transactions. They (or their banks) would often maintain accounts with London banks in order to make payments there. Moreover, London often served as a way station for trade between other nations. For example, a Japanese businessman importing a machine from the United States might buy sterling with yen and have the pounds credited to the American firm's London account. The American firm might use the sterling to pay for its international purchases or might convert the pounds into dollars. Governments, too, often kept large sterling balances in English banks. For some nations, these assets served as reserves for their own money supply. Between 1910 and 1913, financial institutions in the City of London earned an average of £78 million annually on foreign transactions. Income on foreign investments averaged £183 million and revenues from shipping averaged £99 million. These "invisible" credits on the balance of payments account equaled more than half the value of British imports during these years.

In retrospect, we can see more clearly what some contemporaries dimly perceived: the economic predominance enjoyed by Great Britain during the era of the international gold standard was not to be permanent. Britain's manufacturers faced increasingly stiff competition from Germany and the United States. Her strengths in older industries—textiles, iron and steel, shipbuilding—were not matched in newer branches such as chemicals and electrical machinery. Great Britain's percentage share of world trade was decreasing, even though it rose steadily in absolute terms. Some argued that the enormous volume of British investments overseas (one third of all net British investment between 1870 and 1914 went to foreign areas) hindered domestic firms' efforts to adapt to new competitive conditions. Despite these ominous signs, the world of the international gold standard was a comfortable one for well-to-do Britons. The gold standard symbolized and buttressed a world economy that seemed to offer many blessings. There had been no full-fledged European war since the Napoleonic era. Economic growth was, if not constant, at least fairly regular. The peaceful expansion of trade and investment seemed to be spreading the civilization of Victorian and Edwardian England around the globe. Even John Maynard Keynes recognized the charms of the gold-standard world:

What an extraordinary episode in the economic progress of man that age was which came to an end in August 1914! The greater part of the population, it is true, worked hard and lived at a low standard of comfort, yet were, to all appearances, reasonably contented with this lot. But escape was possible, for any man of capacity or character at all exceeding the average, into the middle and upper classes, for whom life offered, at a low cost and with the least trouble, conveniences, comforts and amenities beyond the compass of the richest and most powerful monarchs of other ages. The inhabitant of London could order by telephone, sipping his morning tea in bed, the various products of the whole earth, in such quantity as he might see fit, and reasonably expect their early delivery upon his doorstep; he could at the same moment and by the same means, adventure his wealth in the natural resources and new enterprises of any quarter of the world, and share without exertion or even trouble in their prospective fruits and advantages; or he could decide to couple the security of his fortunes with the good faith of the townspeople of any substantial municipality in any continent that fancy or information might recommend. He could secure forthwith, if he wished it, cheap and comfortable means of transit to any country or climate without passport or other formality, could dispatch his servant to the neighboring office of a bank for such supply of the precious metals as might seem convenient, and could then proceed abroad to foreign quarters, without knowledge of their religion, language or customs, bearing coined wealth upon his person, and would consider himself greatly aggrieved and much surprised at the least interference. But most important of all, he regarded this state of affairs as permanent, except in the direction of further improvement, and any deviation from it as aberrant, scandalous, and avoidable.[6]

Abandoning the Gold Standard during World War I

The gold-standard world was shattered when war broke out in Europe in the summer of 1914. Although the legal obligation of the Bank of England to sell gold at £3 17s 10½d was still on the books, regulations and appeals to patriotism soon stopped such conversions from taking place. Equally important, precious metals dealers refused to export gold. Gold could no longer be used to settle foreign accounts. Despite this, the exchange rates between the pound sterling, the French franc, and the U.S. dollar were not allowed to fluctuate. From January 1916 on, the sterling-dollar exchange rate was "pegged" at £1 = $4.76. If the rate dipped below this figure, the British government used dollars to buy sterling and thereby push the value of the pound back up. Because the war effort required heavy imports from the United States (which was not a belligerent until April 1917), Great Britain soon ran out of dollar holdings to use for stabilization. Beginning in the fall of 1916, the pegging efforts depended upon large loans from the United States. Official borrowings amounted to over $2 billion.

An even more crucial change was the decline of British predominance in international finance. The British continued to lend money to their European allies on a large scale, but in order to pay for American products and to support the $4.76 peg, British public and private loans from the United States totaled some $5 billion. Meanwhile, British investors in American enterprises were selling off many of their holdings during the war. New York was becoming a new center for the world's financial transactions. An active market for short-term loans was developing there, and nations and businesses were beginning to hold deposits of dollars in New York instead of pounds sterling in London.

World War I lasted more than four years, but that was not long enough to eradicate memories of pre-1914 Britain and the international gold standard. Few policymakers were prepared to admit that the conditions of the world economy had fundamentally changed. The period immediately following the Armistice (November 11, 1918) was conducive

[6]John Maynard Keynes, *Economic Consequences of the Peace* (New York: Harper & Row, 1920, 1971), 10-12.

to optimism. There was a boom, as men and equipment rapidly returned to peacetime activities. Businesses and consumers restocked their supplies of capital and consumer goods which had become scarce during the war. In some industries, notably shipbuilding, a frantic pace of investment based on speculative hopes brought about severe overcapacity by 1920. This was to have a damaging impact for more than another decade.

In the middle of 1920, the boom gave way to a sharp downturn. British output fell in real terms by about 6 percent between 1920 and 1922, and unemployment averaged 12.6 percent in 1922. In part, this slump was an inevitable aftermath of the restocking boom with its unsound investments and rapid buildup of inventories. A comparable reaction occurred in the United States, France, and most other developed nations. On the other hand, British decline was no doubt exacerbated by the tight money policies; Bank Rate remained above 7 percent for a full year. Rather than run a large deficit, the national budget also swung into surplus, which reduced aggregate spending as well.

Recovery between 1922 and 1925 was sluggish. Unemployment remained high in the so-called old industries, notably textiles, coal, iron and steel, and shipbuilding, which had been the mainstays of Britain's industrial development in the nineteenth century. Firms in these industries were losing out to competitors in international markets and were facing a long-term decline in total demand as well. At the same time, newer industries were more internationally competitive but did not grow fast enough to pick up all the slack. As a result, Great Britain's merchandise balance of trade showed a deficit of £337 million in 1924; in 1913 the gap had been only £134 million. Although income from services put the current account into surplus, the 1924 surplus was only about 35 percent as large as it had been in 1913. Postwar economic woes heightened nostalgia for the prewar decades, but Britain could not wish away the impact of war and economic transformation.

The Cunliffe Committee's Report on Restoration of the Gold Standard

At the end of the war, bankers and government officials shared an understanding that the prewar gold standard could not be restored immediately. Only by heavy borrowing had the pound been pegged at £1 = $4.76 during wartime. To return to gold at the prewar parity level, the Bank of England would have to sell $4.86 worth of gold for one pound sterling. Since the pound at the end of the war was worth considerably less than $4.86 (in terms of commodities it could purchase), buyers would purchase huge quantities of gold at this bargain rate and thereby drain away the bank's gold reserve. On the other hand, these leaders also agreed that as soon as possible the convertibility should be restored at the prewar $4.86 level. In 1918, the Chancellor of the Exchequer appointed a committee, chaired by Lord Walter Cunliffe, governor of the Bank of England, "to consider the various problems which will arise in connection with currency and the foreign exchanges during the period of reconstruction and report upon the steps required to bring about the restoration of normal conditions in due course."[7]

Issued on August 15, 1918, the Cunliffe Committee's First Interim Report was a manifesto of faith in the prewar gold standard. The gold standard had been, the report concluded, "complete and effective" and "operated automatically to correct unfavorable exchanges and to check undue expansions of credit." It was "imperative that after the war the conditions necessary to the maintenance of an effective gold standard should be restored without delay," for it was the "only effective remedy for an adverse balance of trade and an undue growth of credit."[8]

There were, however, prerequisites to restoration. First, the government had to cease borrowing and begin to retire its debt. Second, the Bank of England must raise the Bank Rate in order to curb the growth of credit and the outflow of gold. It was also important to consolidate the issue of notes (paper promises to pay) in the hands of the Bank of England. Unsecured (fiduciary) notes issued by the Treasury should be limited and eventually abolished. Although the Cunliffe Committee's members disagreed on some of the means of accomplishing restoration of the gold standard, they were united on the need to do so; implicitly they assumed that it would take about ten years to return fully. In the meantime, the Bank of England would not offer gold in exchange for bank notes.

How Floating Rates Worked after World War I

In March of 1919, the government ended its pegging of the dollar-sterling exchange rate at $4.76. A few days later, it issued Orders in Council forbidding the export of gold. In effect, therefore, and although her leaders venerated the gold standard, Great Britain, from 1919 on, had an inconvertible paper money supply and a floating exchange rate.

Under floating rates, if a nation began to run a trade deficit with another country, the demand for the deficit nation's money would go down. Since the price of money was no longer fixed in terms of gold or any other commodity, declining demand for (say) pounds sterling would lower its price in terms of the other currency (say dollars). An American importing goods from Great Britain and buying sterling in order to pay for them would find that his dollars bought more sterling. In other words, British goods would become cheaper for Americans. Each dollar, on the other hand, would cost more sterling, and American goods would become

---

[7]R. S. Sayers, *The Bank of England 1861-1944* (Cambridge: Cambridge University Press, 1976), III, 57.

[8]Ibid., 58.

Figure 3   Adjustments to Hypothetical British Payments Deficit with United States under Floating Exchange Rates

Given an initial British payments deficit and U.S. payments surplus:

Deficit: United Kingdom	Surplus: United States
Excess demand for dollars	*Excess supply of sterling*
↑ Price of dollars (in terms of sterling)	↓ Price of sterling (in terms of of dollars)
↑ Price of U.S. products (in terms of sterling)	↓ Price of U.K. products (in terms of dollars)
↓ Demand for imports from United States	↑ Demand for imports from United Kingdom
↓ Demand for dollars	↑ Demand for sterling

This response continues until balance of payments equilibrium is restored.

---

more expensive for the British. Under normal conditions, these price movements would correct payments imbalances: America's exports would fall and her imports rise; Britain's exports would rise and her imports decline. If the initial conditions had been a British payments surplus vis-à-vis the United States, it would be reflected in a rising price of the pound in terms of dollars and a consequent decline in British exports and rise in imports to eliminate the surplus. Thus, under floating exchange rates, the adjustment process occurs in the international sphere, with only an indirect effect on domestic prices and incomes (see Figure 3).

Most economists today would probably endorse the principle of floating exchange rates. The touted virtue of floating is that payments imbalances can be rectified without altering the level of domestic economic activity. In other words, under a floating rate system, it should not be necessary to impose a recession in order to alleviate a trade deficit. However, in 1919 and the early 1920s, few observers considered the floating pound anything better than an unfortunate temporary expedient.

After the spring of 1919 and the gold embargo, the price of the pound sterling was free to fluctuate on foreign exchange markets in response to supply and demand. In the boom of 1919-1920, the pound fell to as low as $3.40, but it rose in relation to the dollar during the 1920–1922 slump and reached $4.635 at the end of 1922. Tight money policies in Great Britain had pulled prices (in terms of pounds) down and induced short-term investments to come into London. This step had tended to raise the exchange rate of the pound. After 1922, however, the Bank of England chose to make money more freely available. Interest rates went down, and the pound slipped somewhat in relationship to the dollar. The victory of the first Labour Party government in January 1924 produced fears of socialism, which pushed the pound further down. But Labourites soon showed that they were also firmly committed to financial orthodoxy, including a timely return to the prewar gold standard. Through the spring and summer of 1924, the pound began to rise again.

Conditions Favoring the Restoration of the Gold Standard

International developments were making the prospect of a return to gold more attractive. In 1922, European powers at the Genoa Conference resolved in favor of an international gold-exchange standard, to be attained as soon as practicable. Under a gold-exchange system, one or more key countries would fix the value of their currencies in terms of gold and maintain their reserves in holdings of gold. Other nations would then fix their own currency values in terms of those key currencies, and could hold such gold-backed currency as part of reserves. The gold-exchange system would, it was hoped, maintain fixed rates while economizing on the amount of gold to be held as reserves. In 1923, the year after the Genoa gathering, the evils of a fiat money system were vividly demonstrated in Germany's hyperinflation, which was not checked until a new currency was issued in strictly limited amounts.

By 1924, returning to the gold standard was becoming a practical issue instead of an abstract ideal. Legislation which forbade the export of gold was scheduled to expire at the end of 1925. To call for extension of the ban would be tantamount to admitting that Britain was not yet capable of returning. Supporters of the gold standard saw national pride at stake.

Among those who spoke for this orthodoxy, the most important was Montagu Norman, governor of the Bank of England, the man who exercised the most influence over monetary policy. Norman himself personified nineteenth-century banking's allegiance to gold: both of his grandfathers had been directors of the Bank of England and pillars of financial conservatism. In April 1924, Norman wrote to Sir Otto Niemeyer, controller of finance at the British Treasury, suggesting that the Treasury appoint a committee to study a technical but significant question concerning currency issues. The committee, appointed the next month, was chaired first by Sir Austen Chamberlain and then by Sir John Bradbury. It soon agreed that the technical matter it had been appointed to consider could not be properly decided without reaching a judgment on the much broader issue of returning to the gold standard. Since all but two of the Chamberlain-Bradbury Committee's members had also served on the Cunliffe Committee of 1918, it was not surprising that the Chamberlain-Bradbury Committee did not seriously contemplate alternatives to reestablishing gold at its prewar par value. Members disagreed only on matters of timing and technique. Their February 1925 report stressed the "undoubted advantages of an immediate return to parity" and played down any "danger or inconvenience" that might result.

While the committee worked, the value of the pound was rising on international exchange markets. Norman collaborated with Benjamin Strong, the powerful governor of the Federal Reserve Bank of New York, to keep British interest rates higher than those in the United States. This had the effect of making the pound more valuable in terms of dollars.

On October 1, 1924, the pound was worth $4.46. Later that month, a political shift offered additional incentive for a rising pound. The Labour Party lost badly in a general election, and the Conservatives, with Stanley Baldwin as prime minister and Winston Churchill as Chancellor of the Exchequer, returned to power. Although Churchill had no set views on the gold standard or most other economic issues either, the election of the new Conservative government gladdened business and financial interests around the world. The pound sterling began to rise steadily. By the beginning of 1925, it was worth $4.70. This was only about 2 percent lower than the $4.86 prewar parity rate.

In addition to keeping a tight rein on the money supply and speaking out for an early return to the gold standard, Montagu Norman took steps to ensure that Great Britain would be able to preserve a $4.86 pound once restoration had taken place. At the end of 1924, Norman sailed to New York. His main task there was to acquire a "cushion." This was a standby line of credit which the Bank of England and the British Treasury could draw upon after restoration in case of crisis. When he sailed back, Norman had agreements from the Federal Reserve Banks and the Morgan Bank for $500 million. If, after reestablishing gold, Britain began to run a serious payments deficit which threatened her ability to maintain parity, she could use these funds to buy sterling and keep the exchange rate at $4.86.

By early 1925, then, pressure for an early restoration of the gold standard was intensifying. Support for the move seemed widespread among political and economic interests. Both Conservatives and Labourites were committed to return. Bankers in other countries awaited Britain's return to gold as a key element in the restoration of internationally fixed exchange rates that had been mandated at the Genoa Conference of 1922. London bankers, in their annual speeches to their stockholders in early 1924, spoke out almost unanimously in favor of restoration, although they did warn against undue haste. For the leaders of the financial community, there was really no question about the principle. Mr. J. W. Beaumont-Pease, chairman of the Lloyds Bank, stated:

There is, in fact, really no controversy. The whole world, though guilty of infidelity in varying degrees and divers phases, and in spite of some coquetting in other directions, is returning to its old love. There is no effective rival of any standing or consequence.[9]

Few openly opposed returning to gold. The most vocal and best respected critic was the economist John Maynard Keynes. Since the Versailles Peace Conference, Keynes had been warning anyone willing to listen that the prewar international economic system was shattered beyond repair. Attempts to restore it were hopeless. By 1923, Keynes had focused his attack on the gold standard, calling it a "barbarous relic." Reginald McKenna, chairman of the Midland Bank and a former Chan-

[9]*Bankers' Magazine*, CXIX (March 1925): 333–334.

cellor of the Exchequer, shared some of Keynes' opinions about the gold standard. As a banker, however, McKenna was less consistent and outspoken in his opposition than was Keynes. No organized interest group rallied to Keynes' position. Industrialists, who tended to favor low interest rates and expansionist policies, were divided on gold. By March 1925, the Federation of British Industries had adopted the position that restoration "would be greatly to the benefit of British industry" in the long run.

Mr. Churchill's Exercise

In one significant respect, the debate was not entirely unbalanced. Winston Churchill, the man who ultimately had to choose, seemed genuinely undecided. In order to provoke discussion, and apparently to clarify his own views, he submitted a memorandum to his economic advisers on January 29, 1925. Playing devil's advocate, Churchill began with a challenge:

> If we are to take the very important step of removing the embargo on gold export, it is essential that we should be prepared to answer any criticism which may be subsequently made upon our policy. I should like to have set out in writing, the counter case to the following argument.[10]

Churchill then presented the antigold standard position. The replies Churchill received dealt harshly with the arguments he had set forth. Lord Bradbury, writing to Sir Otto Niemeyer, complained that the memo itself had a demagogic tone. "Mr. Churchill's Exercise" and the officials' replies can be summarized by contrasting how proponents and opponents of the gold standard would answer the following six questions about restoration.

1. *What were the lessons of the prewar gold standard?*

For advocates of resumption, the prewar epoch showed that free trade with fixed exchange was the path to growth and prosperity. The whole world benefited, but Great Britain thrived most impressively. For opponents of resumption, however, the prewar system had been an anomaly, "intensely unusual, unstable, complicated, unreliable . . .," as Keynes wrote in 1919.[11] The international gold standard had depended upon steady increases in the world's gold supply, based on fortunate discoveries in Alaska, the Canadian Yukon, and South Africa. Also, during the prewar decades, there had been a rough equality in the balance of payments among major trading nations, so that chronic shortages of foreign exchange did not develop. For Britain, the blessings of the prewar system were heightened by her leadership in manufacturing, shipping, and fi-

---

[10]Donald Moggridge, *British Monetary Policy 1924–1931* (Cambridge: Cambridge University Press, 1972), 260.

[11]Keynes, op. cit., 1.

nance. As these advantages diminished, so did some of the benefits of the international gold standard.

2. *What were the key economic problems facing Great Britain in 1925?*

Supporters of the gold standard, though aware of unemployment, the woes of declining industries and regions, and the loss of foreign markets, were inclined to worry about price stability. The gold standard, with its automatic corrective mechanisms that worked through the money supply, was the best guarantee against inflation because market forces, not political considerations, would determine the money supply. Fresh in the minds of gold standard advocates was the experience of Germany in 1923. There, the old paper mark, not convertible into gold or silver, had become virtually worthless, depreciating to one trillionth of its prewar value before a new currency was introduced.

On the other hand, by 1923, Keynes was convinced that unemployment and idle capacity were more immediate evils than inflation. The gold standard required nations to "deflate"; that is, to sacrifice full employment and real output in order to adjust to external payments deficits. Admittedly, floating exchange rates might prove inflationary, but one could not have it both ways: "thus inflation is unjust and deflation is inexpedient," wrote Keynes. "Of the two, perhaps deflation is, if we rule out exaggerated inflations such as that of Germany, the worse; because it is worse, in an impoverished world, to provoke unemployment than to disappoint the *rentier*."[12]

3. *How much was the pound sterling worth?*

For backers of the gold standard, the rising price of the pound on international markets proved that the time for restoring the prewar $4.86 par was ripe. By the time of the Chamberlain-Bradbury Committee report, the pound was only 1.5 percent below $4.86. All it would take, the committee maintained, was a 1.5 percent increase in the prices of American exports or an equal decline in the prices of British exports for the pound and the dollar to have equivalent purchasing power when £1 = $4.86. The rising value of the pound reflected fundamental improvements in the U.K.'s international position and its commitment to noninflationary policies.

True, replied Keynes, the sterling-dollar exchange had improved (i.e., the pound sterling cost more dollars than it previously had), but the rise was misleading. Some of it resulted from speculation by those who anticipated that Britain would soon reestablish a $4.86 par. The speculators might then sell their pounds for gold at the par rate and cause a British balance of payments crisis. A second reason for the rise in the pound was that investors saw slightly higher interest rates in London than in New York and anticipated that British prices would increase more

---

[12]Ibid. *Rentier:* one who lives on the payments from fixed-income securities (such as bonds) and is therefore vulnerable to inflation.

slowly than American prices. In Keynes' view, these investors in the pound were thoroughly fickle. A minute change in relative interest rates or prices could cause the outflow of as much as £100 million. Keynes calculated that the pound sterling could actually purchase only about $4.40 worth of internationally traded goods and services. Thus to restore the par value of $4.86 would be to overvalue the pound by about 10 percent, and in so doing, overprice British exports.

4. *What was the status of the London money market?*

Financial interests in the City of London had thrived under the prewar gold standard. As we have seen, because the pound had been "as good as gold," international traders and foreign banks had held deposits in sterling in order to conduct international transactions. They had also borrowed extensively on the London money market to finance international trade. The financial institutions of "the City" (of London) were, themselves, major contributors to Great Britain's prewar balance of payments and national income. Moreover, under the gold standard, London had been the major source of long-term investment capital in almost every corner of the world. British investors had bought bonds to finance railroads, mines, factories, and public works overseas because they knew that these enterprises were obligated to pay interest and principal in a currency of fixed gold value. Hurt by the war and by the rise of the New York financial institutions, London's preeminence, according to gold advocates, could be restored only if the pound sterling were put back at its prewar level.

The counterargument held that London's financial predominance could not be easily reestablished because the economic strength of the United States and her postwar role as exporter of capital had changed the international context. If gold were restored, Churchill contended in his "Exercise," Great Britain might need to restrict the money supply and drive up interest rates. If so, London would be an unattractive market for foreign borrowers and the City would lose even more business to New York.

5. *What would be the impact of the gold standard on the domestic economy?*

The financial orthodoxy asserted that almost all interests would gain from a well-timed restoration. Even if a slight contraction of the money supply were required to maintain a $4.86 pound, the impact would be on prices, not output and employment. A stable, predictable, international monetary system would benefit all traders. A pound that was able to "look the dollar in the face" at $4.86 would actually help the working class, because it would mean lower prices for imported goods. These were mostly foodstuffs and other necessities for the working class. An expensive pound meant cheap bread. Even industrialists, traditionally borrowers who welcomed low interest rates and a touch of inflation, could recognize the benefits of low raw materials import prices, cheap food for the work force, and stable exchange rates for export sales. A brief adjustment period of tight money and high interest rates might cause a little pain, but it would not stifle businesses which could look forward to such a hospitable business climate.

Keynes disagreed with almost all of these points. Tight money, he argued, would be neither short-lived nor painless if the pound were indeed worth 10 percent less than $4.86. The gold standard would press down not only prices, but wages and employment. Workers would resist lower money wages with strikes. Class conflict would increase. Industrialists would lose confidence and cut back on output and investment plans. With the majority of the world's gold now in the United States, Americans could afford to maintain a fixed gold price and could tolerate minor fluctuations in their money and credit conditions. The United States, Keynes wrote, "lives in a vast and unceasing crescendo." But Britain's "rate of progress is slow at best." A fluctuation under the gold standard "which is only a ripple for them [the United States], will be an Atlantic roller for us."[13]

6. *What would happen if gold were not restored?*

According to restoration advocates, remaining off gold would cause a continuation of the perils of inflation and instability that Britain had experienced since 1919. But the problem went beyond that. A decision to continue the embargo on gold exports and the refusal to sell gold for pounds sterling would say to the world that Great Britain was not yet willing to keep its promises. Restoration of the gold standard was, therefore, a matter of national responsibility, pride, and honor. Failure to go back soon would also alarm investors and traders and might wipe out the progress of the preceding year. The year 1925 was a good time to do what had to be done sooner or later.

Opponents were perhaps less able to answer this question satisfactorily than any other. Even Keynes spent little time trying to rebut the point. He was willing to state that Britain should keep an inconvertible currency for the indefinite future. He believed that governments and central bankers had the wisdom needed to manage a nonconvertible money supply without creating a German-style hyperinflation. Yet, in his 1925 polemics, he concentrated his fire on the practical issues of timing and the alleged overvaluation of the pound; he kept his theoretical arguments in the background. Others were even less willing to make a case for a managed currency. They worried about restoring the gold standard prematurely, before Britain had the resources necessary to preserve it.

These were the main issues involved in the debates that culminated in Winston Churchill's dinner party. The scope of the controversy suggests that restoration of the gold standard was far more than a technical question. The French economist Alfred Sauvy did not exaggerate greatly when he said that, for Great Britain, reestablishing the pound at $4.86

[13]John Maynard Keynes, *Essays in Persuasion* (New York: Harcourt Brace, 1932), 234.

was "a question of prestige, a question of dogma . . . almost a question of religion."[14]

[14]Quoted in Charles P. Kindleberger, *The World in Depression* (London: Penguin, 1973), 44.

The United Kingdom and the Gold Standard: 1925

Exhibit 1   Percentage Distribution of World Manufacturing Production

	1870	1896–1900	1913	1926–1929
United Kingdom	31.8%	19.5%	14.0%	9.4%
United States	23.3	30.1	35.8	42.2
Germany	13.2	16.6	15.7	11.6
France	10.3	7.1	6.4	6.6
Russia	3.7	5.0	5.5	4.3

Source: Derek H. Aldcroft, *The Inter-War Economy: Britain 1919–1939* (New York: Columbia University Press, 1970), 22.

The United Kingdom and the Gold Standard: 1925

Exhibit 2   Percentage Distribution of World Exports of Manufactured Goods

	1880	1899	1913	1929
United Kingdom	41.4%	32.5%	29.9%	23.6%
United States	2.8	11.2	12.6	20.7
Germany	19.3	22.2	26.4	21.0
France	22.2	15.8	12.9	11.2
Japan	—	1.5	2.4	3.9
Belgium	5.0	5.6	4.9	5.5

Source: Derek H. Aldcroft, *The Inter-War Economy: Britain 1919–1939* (New York: Columbia University Press, 1970), 22.

The United Kingdom and the Gold Standard: 1925

Exhibit 3   Annual World Gold Production, 1805–1980

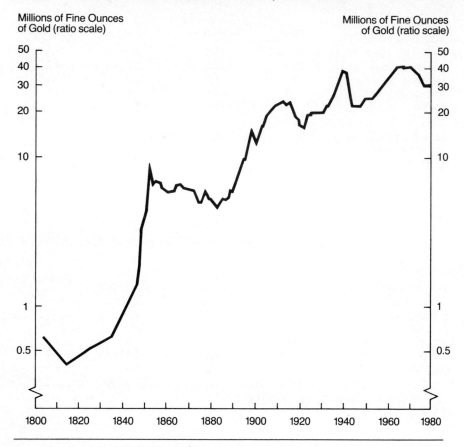

Millions of Fine Ounces
of Gold (ratio scale)

Note: the stock of gold in 1800 was 39 million fine ounces.

Source: R. N. Cooper, *Brookings Papers on Economic Activity*, 1 (1982), 15.

The United Kingdom and the Gold Standard: 1925

Exhibit 4   Wholesale Price Indices for Selected Years in Four Countries

Years and Period	U.K.	U.S.	France	Germany
	Indices (1913 = 100)			
1816	147	150	143	94
1849	86	82	94	67
1873	130	137	122	114
1896	72	64	69	69
1913	100	100	100	100
	Changes (in percent)			
1816–1849	−41	−45	−33	−29
1849–1873	51	67	30	70
1873–1896	−45	−53	−45	−40
1896–1913	39	56	45	45

Source: R. N. Cooper, *Brookings Papers on Economic Activity*, 1 (1982), 9.

Discussion Questions for Case

1. Evaluate the arguments for and against a return to the gold standard. Were the assumptions behind these arguments valid in 1925 for the United Kingdom? Are these assumptions valid for the United States today?
2. Why did the United Kingdom find it necessary to manage the gold standard with the Bank Rate?
3. What would be the outcome of a return to the gold standard in 1925 for the United Kingdom? Would the outcome be different for the United States today?

Bibliography

Bergsten, C. Fred, *The Dilemmas of the Dollar, The Economics and Politics of U.S. International Monetary Policy* (New York: New York University Press, 1975). Chapter 3 describes the evolution of the international monetary system from the gold standard, to the gold-exchange standard, to Bretton Woods and Bergsten's conception of a "tripartite system" based on dollar, sterling, and gold.

Eltis, W. A., and P. J. N. Sinclair, eds., *The Money Supply and the Exchange Rate* (London: Oxford University Press, 1981). This volume contains two scholarly papers that discuss the British return to the gold standard and the economic consequences of this action. See J. F. Wright, "Britain's Inter-War Experience," on pages 283–305, and N. H. Dimsdale, "British Monetary Policy and the Exchange Rate 1920-1938," on pages 306–349.

Fink, Richard H., ed., *Supply-Side Economics: A Critical Appraisal* (Frederick, MD: University Publications, 1982). Two articles are relevant for those interested in current proposals to return to the gold standard. The first article, "The Case for a Return to the Gold Standard: An Interview with Lewis Lehrman," on pages 431–453, is by James Roberts. The second article, "The 100 Percent Gold Standard: A Proposal for Monetary Reform," on pages 454–488, is by Joseph Salerno.

Keynes, John Maynard, *Essays in Persuasion* (New York: Norton, 1963). Part III contains essays written by Keynes between 1923 and 1931. In particular, see his famous essay, "The Economic Consequences of Mr. Churchill" (1925), on pages 244–270, for an argument against the return to the gold standard.

Ritter, Lawrence S., and William L. Silber, *Money*, 5th and rev. ed. (New York: Basic Books, 1985). Chapters 19, 20, and 21 (pages 249–280) are a lively, simple introduction to exchange rate systems and the gold standard.

CHAPTER 14
International Payments Imbalance

The objectives for this chapter's case, "Kennedy and the Balance of Payments," are to acquire another tool, balance of payments account-ing, and to consider a basic political economy problem, the constraints of international payments imbalances on national policies. Conventions regarding balance of payments accounting are described in the note to this chapter, "An Introduction to the Balance of Payments." A careful reading of the note and time spent on the worksheet exercise will facili-tate understanding of the key issues of the case. More than in most cases, the story is told in the detailed exhibits at the end of this chapter.

 Kennedy's problems stemmed from the imbalances in transactions on various accounts. The suspects were numerous in 1961, including declining trade competitiveness, foreign transfer payments, foreign di-rect investment, and short-term capital flows. Since the balance of all accounts must always be zero, a larger surplus on one account must be reflected by a larger deficit on another account. This makes it difficult to say that the problem is the surplus or the problem is the deficit, since they are two aspects of the same problem. The relevant questions are: Which accounts are most sensitive to changes in economic factors (and which accounts accommodate those changes)? Which accounts are most controllable by governmental policy? What trade-offs must be made among the accounts and, more broadly, among domestic and interna-tional policies?

Case
Kennedy and the Balance of Payments

In 1960 the United States had a balance of payments problem. American gold reserves were being drained, American products seemed to be losing some of their competitiveness, and the American dollar was under attack on international money markets. While the Eisenhower administration had taken a relatively passive approach to these difficulties, President-elect Kennedy committed his administration to a solution. As Arthur M. Schlesinger recounted: "Kennedy ... used to tell his advisers that the two things which scared him the most were nuclear war and the balance of payments deficit. Once he half-humorously derided the notion that nuclear weapons were essential to international strength. 'What really matters,' he said, 'is the strength of the currency.'"[1]

Three Traditional Approaches to Balance of Payments Deficits

Kennedy's dilemma was that most of the traditional means for correcting balance of payments deficits were inconsistent with his other economic goals. For example, deflation is a frequently recommended strategy for reducing the outflow of a nation's currency. If Kennedy had employed restrictive fiscal and monetary policies, American firms and consumers would have had less disposable income to buy imports; and higher interest rates in the United States would have attracted investment from foreign capital. But if Kennedy had wanted to keep his pledge to "get the country moving again," a deflationary strategy would not have been acceptable (see Table 1).

Another traditional way to deal with balance of payments problems was to change the exchange rate. A devaluation of the dollar would make American exports relatively cheaper and foreign imports relatively more expensive. All other things being equal, cheaper exports should cause the demand for American exports to rise. In the meantime, a devaluation should lead Americans to substitute cheaper domestic products for more costly foreign products.[2] Devaluation, however, was not an easy option

This case was prepared by Assistant Professor David B. Yoffie with the assistance of Research Associate Jane Kenney Austin.
Copyright © 1982 by the President and Fellows of Harvard College
Harvard Business School case 9-383-073

[1]Martin Mayer, *The Fate of the Dollar* (New York: Truman Talley Books, 1980), 85.

[2]The "all other things being equal" is related to the concept of price elasticity—the degree to which supply or demand for a good responds to changes in price. Cheaper exports, for example, may not stimulate greater foreign demand if the exports are of poor quality; similarly, domestic consumers may not cut back expensive imports if the imported goods are essentials such as oil or food.

462

Table 1 U.S. Gross National Product
(Billion of U.S. dollars)

	Current	1960 Prices	Real Growth (Per Annum)
1950	$284.6	$362.3	8.4%
1951	329.0	392.0	8.2
1952	347.0	406.8	3.8
1953	365.4	425.5	4.6
1954	363.1	416.8	(2.0)
1955	397.5	449.7	7.9
1956	419.2	459.2	2.1
1957	442.8	467.8	1.9
1958	444.2	459.7	(1.7)
1959	482.1	490.6	6.7
1960	503.2	503.2	2.6

Source: *Economic Report of the President, 1961* (Washington DC: U.S. Government Printing Office).

for the United States in 1960–1961. Under the rules of the international monetary system established at Bretton Woods, New Hampshire, in 1944, the U.S. dollar was pegged at $35 per ounce of gold. In addition, all other currencies were pegged to the U.S. dollar. Any hint that the Kennedy administration might change the value of the dollar would lead to a collapse in confidence in the American currency and would undermine the Bretton Woods system.

A third option for correcting balance of payments deficits was to reduce international commitments and place controls on the outflow of capital or the inflow of foreign goods. By raising import barriers, restricting American investment abroad, and bringing home American troops stationed overseas, Kennedy might have been able to reverse the trends toward growing deficits. Yet here again, all of these policies were contrary to existing U.S. goals. During the postwar period, American foreign policy promoted global security. The United States was making large military expenditures and maintaining substantial forces abroad to counter Soviet assertiveness. Reducing those expenditures might have been viewed as capitulation to the U.S.S.R. The United States was also fostering European cooperation and integration in the interest of political stability and economic growth. Since rapid economic development was viewed as the best defense against the spread of communism, it was not desirable to restrict capital outflow to American allies or to erect trade barriers.

All of these obligations presented Kennedy with a dilemma. If the United States sustained an active foreign policy with a worldwide political, economic, and military role, the balance of payments might continue to deteriorate. But a weak U.S. balance of payments could jeopardize America's ability to pursue postwar objectives. Hence each of Kennedy's standard options appeared to be constrained: adopting deflation, deval-

uation, retrenchment, capital controls, or trade controls implied sacrificing important objectives. Kennedy therefore charged his advisers with
the responsibility of finding a satisfactory solution. To understand Kennedy's dilemma, it is helpful to understand the origins of the American
participation in international trade and the background to the monetary
and trade institutions of the post-World War II period from a historical
perspective.

The Rationale for International Trade

The modern debate over trade policy has its roots in the 1600s and 1700s
when international trade operated on the principles of mercantilism. Based
on the assumption that economic power and welfare would be enhanced
by positive balances of trade and the accumulation of precious metals,
countries commonly used export subsidies and high import duties to
build trade surpluses. A positive balance of payments could fund a country's military, provide state treasuries with money for emergencies, and
build the most visible forms of wealth and prestige. An eighteenth-century
English scholar recounted: "The general measures of the trade . . . at
present are gold and silver, which are . . . the ultimate objects of trade.
. . . If the exports of Britain exceed its imports, foreigners must pay us
the balance in treasure, and the nation grows rich. But if the imports of
Britain exceed its exports, we must pay foreigners the balance in treasure,
and the nation grows poor."[3] The world trading system was viewed by
the major actors as a zero-sum competition in which one country's gain
was necessarily another's loss.

Adam Smith's *Wealth of Nations* (1776), however, attacked mercantilism as an economic doctrine. For the first time, countries were told
that national real income could be maximized by specializing in the
export sector and importing goods that others could make for less. David
Ricardo took this argument one step further with his exposition of the
theory of comparative advantage in *The Principles of Political Economy
and Taxation* (1821). By demonstrating that open trade was mutually
beneficial to two countries, even if one nation was more productive in
all commodities, Ricardo articulated an extraordinarily powerful theory
that has provided the foundation for international trade analysis.

The theory of comparative advantage is best explained through an
illustration. Picture two economies, the United States and the continental
Europe, for example, which are identical in most ways. Assume that both
economies have similar endowments of land, labor, and capital. Imagine
that they each produce only two crops—cotton and wheat. The single

[3]Matthew Decker, *An Essay on the Causes of the Decline of the Foreign Trade*, 1756, 1–2,
cited by Jacob Viner, *Studies in the Theory of International Trade* (New York: Harper &
Brothers, 1937), 18–19.

difference between the two is that the United States has a better climate than Europe. Therefore a production unit in the United States can produce more wheat and more cotton than an equivalent production unit in Europe. The question then arises: Does the United States need Europe as a trading partner, or would it be better off relying exclusively on its own resources?

It is tempting to say that the United States should go it alone. Such an analysis, however, would miss the Ricardian logic of comparative advantage. Take, for example, the case of a successful business consultant who is also the world's best typist. Should that consultant do his own typing since he can do it better and more efficiently than someone hired to do the job? In the same way the consultant can make more money consulting by paying a typist, the United States can have more wheat and more cotton if it trades with Europe. (A numerical illustration of this conclusion is presented in Exhibit 5 at the end of this case.)

The theory of comparative advantage suggested a powerful proposition for international economics: When countries lower trade barriers and exchange goods on the basis of comparative advantage, everyone is better off. When prices and relative productivity levels are introduced into the model, the same conclusion holds. Thus we should find that even the most inefficient poor countries in the world have some comparative advantage that they can exploit. And, theoretically, all countries should favor free trade policies.

When this theory is applied to the real world, however, the results are no longer so clear-cut. Ricardian comparative advantage is a static concept that assumes constant returns to scale. It helps to identify the gains from trade that are available through international specialization, but government policy makers have never been totally committed to free trade, and countries continue to use a variety of tools to protect their domestic economies.

Background of the Modern Trading System

The first movement toward global free trade began in the 1840s in Great Britain. In an effort to end the political dominance of the landed gentry and redistribute wealth more equitably, the Tory government of Sir Robert Peel repealed the high tariffs on grain known as the Corn Laws. While most countries in the world were using tariffs to generate revenue and protect their domestic markets, Britain took the bold step of unilaterally lowering its trade barriers (see Figure 1).

There was great trepidation at first, but instant success vindicated the British policy. The rapidly growing population of Europe, coupled with the expansion of the money supply,[4] created a worldwide demand

---

[4] The discovery of new gold fields after 1849 almost doubled the stock of the world's basic monetary unit during the following 25 years. See Exhibit 3 of the Chapter 13 case, "The United Kingdom and the Gold Standard: 1925."

Kennedy and the Balance of Payments

Figure 1   Average Import Duties, United Kingdom: 1796–1960

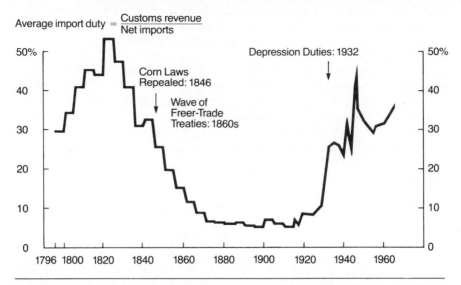

Average import duty $= \dfrac{\text{Customs revenue}}{\text{Net imports}}$

Source: Charles P. Kindleberger and Richard H. Lindert, *International Economics,* 6th ed. (Homewood, IL: Irwin, 1978), 221–222. Reprinted by permission.

for British goods. On the supply side, the reduced cost of imports re-strained pressures on wages, and the new technologies of the industrial revolution lowered transportation costs and spurred increased productivity. The result was prosperity throughout the British economy. Export trade in particular boomed as Britain became the "workshop of the world."

Three factors can account for British behavior: First, British elite were swayed by the power of Smith and Ricardo's arguments. The intellectual appeal of laissez-faire was growing at the time. Second, export interests were well organized to influence the course of politics. Export-minded industrialists banded together to offset the political power of protectionist groups. Third, Britain's position in the world was rising. With the defeat of Napoleon in 1815, there was no rival to Britain's political, military, or economic power in the world. Free trade for Britain was a way to exercise further leadership. In fact, hegemonic states generally favor free trade. Low trade barriers and open borders reinforce the most advanced country's supremacy, maintain political and social stability in the system, and increase aggregate income in the international system.

By the 1860s the British momentum toward free trade had become contagious. Britain negotiated tariff reductions with France, France negotiated tariff cuts with German custom unions, and so on. Furthermore, countries agreed to generalize trade concessions by employing an unconditional most-favored-nation policy (MFN). MFN provided that countries would treat all signator nations equally in trade relations, without requiring compensation. If, for example, France made a separate agreement with Italy to lower a tariff, then the French would be obliged under the MFN clause in other treaties to lower its tariff on that good to all its other trading partners. The net impact of these generalized reductions in tariff barriers was a dramatic growth in world trade and capital flows.

Free trade, however, can be difficult to sustain. The advantages of low cost imports are usually widely diffused across the economy, while those hurt by import competition are often concentrated groups. If growth slows, if large unemployment in particular sectors occurs, if strategic industries begin to go out of business, protectionist coalitions tend to form. Unless export and free trade interests can counterbalance these coalitions in the domestic political arena, or unless a hegemonic state can compel countries to maintain low trade barriers, protectionism will frequently result.

During a depression in the 1870s and 1880s, for example, protectionist interests were able to gain prominence in Europe. The British remained committed to low trade barriers, but they no longer possessed the power to offset a resurgence in tariffs. In the 1890s trade wars broke out on the Continent. Free trade declined as military goals, colonialism, and economic nationalism became the order of the day at the end of the nineteenth century.

The Twentieth Century

World War I marked the end of British dominance in the international economy. The war bankrupted Europe in general and Britain in particular. After the end of the hostilities, the Allies were heavily in debt to the United States, the Axis nations were burdened by reparations to the Allies, and the United Kingdom had sold off many of its foreign investments to finance the war. No country was then both willing and able to reestablish order. Britain was willing but not able; the United States was able but not willing.

The United States was the only country which had survived the war with its industry intact. Moreover, the outside world owed billions in war debts to the United States and could pay Americans back only if the United States maintained low trade barriers. With free trade, foreigners could earn the dollars necessary to service their debts. Yet, instead of trying to stabilize international trade, as the British had done in the past, the U.S. Congress reacted to the first downturn in the 1920s by raising tariffs (see Figure 2). The only positive move made by the United States at this time was to adopt an unconditional most-favored-nation policy. The Americans hoped that by reducing their own discrimination, others would stop discriminating against U.S. exports.[5]

[5]John Jackson, *International Economic Relations* (St. Paul: West Publishing, 1972), 517.

Kennedy and the Balance of Payments

Figure 2   Average Import Duties, United States: 1792–1960

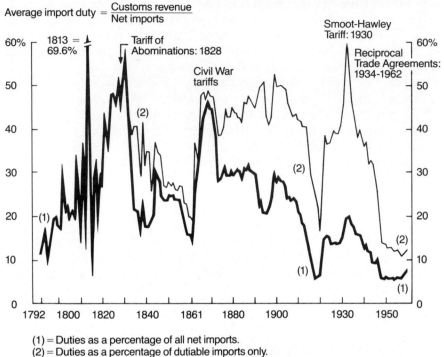

(1) = Duties as a percentage of all net imports.
(2) = Duties as a percentage of dutiable imports only.

Source: Charles P. Kindleberger and Richard H. Lindert, *International Economics,* 6th ed. (Homewood, IL: Irwin, 1978), 221–222. Reprinted by permission.

Amid signs of a general economic crisis, the slide toward global protectionism accelerated in the late 1920s. The League of Nations did its best to prevent a trade war, but all hope collapsed after the U.S. stock market crash in 1929. Industry after industry pleaded with the Congress for import restrictions to maintain employment. With no organized export interests, and no global leader, there was nothing to brake the protectionist drive. In what has been called an "orgy of log-rolling,"[6] Congress erected some of the highest tariff barriers in American history. The Smoot-Hawley tariff of 1930 raised the average import levy to almost 60 percent.

The new American tariffs set off a wave of global retaliation. Countries ranging from Australia to Cuba to France responded with their own increased duties, boycotts, and quotas. A number of countries devalued their currencies to stimulate exports, while others imposed exchange con-

[6]Peter Kenen and Raymond Lubitz, *International Economics,* 3rd ed. (Englewood Cliffs, NJ: Prentice-Hall, 1971), 28.

Kennedy and the Balance of Payments

Figure 3   Contracting Spiral of World Trade, January 1929 to March 1933: Total Imports of 75 Countries

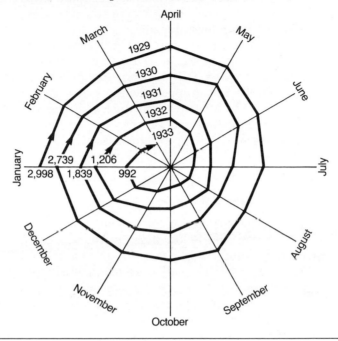

Monthly values in terms of old U.S. gold dollars, millions.

Source: Charles Kindleberger, *The World in Depression* (Berkeley: University of California Press, 1973), 172. Reprinted by permission.

trols to defend their foreign reserves. The combination of economic depression, high trade barriers, exchange restrictions, and competitive devaluations led to a severe contraction in world trade (see Figure 3). Between 1928 and 1938 global imports dropped from $60 billion to $25 billion.

It did not take long for the new Roosevelt administration in the early 1930s to realize that the Smoot-Hawley tariff was self-defeating. Therefore FDR asked Congress to give the executive branch the authority to negotiate tariff reductions on a reciprocal basis. If other countries would lower their trade barriers, the president told Congress, then there would be "a resumption of international trade (which) cannot but improve the general situation of other countries, and thus increase their purchasing power. Let us well remember that this in turn spells increased opportunity for American sales."[7]

When Congress passed the Reciprocal Trade Act of 1934, it marked

[7]Ibid., 39.

a turning point in U.S. trade policy and the history of world trade. For the first time in the United States, the leading role for setting tariffs passed from the Congress to the executive branch. This not only reduced the influence of protectionist groups over American trade policy, it also arrested the worldwide trend toward increasing protection.

Using its new authority to negotiate tariff cuts by as much as 50 percent, the U.S. government signed 31 bilateral treaties between 1934 and the outbreak of World War II. The most-favored-nation clause was reintroduced and tariff levels dropped slightly below their 1930 levels.[8] Free trade, however, was never realized during this period. Roosevelt was still more interested in lowering others' trade barriers than allowing foreigners to compete with American industries.

The Early Postwar System

It was widely recognized that "beggar-thy-neighbor" policies partly caused the economic disaster of the 1930s. If the world was going to avoid a return to depression in the 1940s, American officials believed that trade barriers would have to be eliminated, anticompetitive policies would have to be stopped, and a whole new international order created. And unlike the 1920s, the United States realized that this time it would have to take the lead. As the Department of State put it in 1945, "The only nation capable of taking the initiative in promoting a worldwide movement toward the relaxation of trade barriers is the United States."[9]

The United States' objective was an era of Pax Americana. The goal would be the "establishment of a liberal trading system," said the American secretary of state, "and the attainment of an expanding world economy."[10] The American strategy to achieve these goals was to promote long-range political objectives, even if it required the sacrifice of specific American economic interests.

The first policy stemming from this strategy was for the United States to commit itself to free trade—no matter what the consequences. To aid the reconstruction of the postwar trading system, the United States had already allowed its average tariff levels to decline significantly before 1945: Since many U.S. duties were *specific*, wartime inflation had eroded the *ad valorem* tariff values to 1919 levels. The United States planned to leave its borders open to create greater trading opportunities for the

---

[8]Part of the decline of U.S. tariffs can be explained by the rise in prices of imports during the slow recovery from the depression. The majority of U.S. tariffs were *specific*, i.e., they levied a fixed tax on imports, regardless of the import prices. As prices rose, the percentage tariff, or *ad valorem* rate, fell.

[9]Quoted in Joan Spero, *The Politics of International Economic Relations*, 2d ed. (New York: St. Martin's Press, 1981), 76.

[10]Quoted in Joyce and Gabriel Kolko, *The Limits of Power* (New York: Harper & Row, 1972), 12.

capitalist world, even though most other industrial and nonindustrial countries were using tariffs and quotas to exclude American exports.

The second component of the U.S. strategy was to find some way to liberalize world trade. Liberalizing trade, however, could not be done in isolation from an international monetary system. Unless nations could agree on a system of payments, it would be difficult for the world to progress beyond the barter of the 1930s. Therefore the next order on the American agenda was to create a set of rules that would provide monetary stability and worldwide liquidity.

The outcome of this effort was a series of agreements in 1944 at Bretton Woods, New Hampshire. These agreements, which later became known as the Bretton Woods system, included the creation of two international organizations—the International Monetary Fund (IMF) and the International Bank for Reconstruction and Development (World Bank), and the establishment of guidelines for managing the world's money. The central principle of the Bretton Woods system was that countries would fix their exchange rates. Convinced that the collapse of international economic activity during the Great Depression was aggravated by the instability of floating exchange rates, public officials believed that fixed rates would be most conducive to expanded trade. Hence the signatories at Bretton Woods agreed to fix their currencies in terms of gold and to defend that parity rate within plus or minus 1 percent.

Once the outline of the monetary system was in place, the United States proceeded to sponsor an international organization that would regulate a world trade system based on the principles of comparative advantage, competitive markets, and nondiscrimination. Beggar-thy-neighbor policies would be gone—international negotiations would take their place. But unlike America's apparent success in the monetary realm, the United States was unable to convince countries to give up substantial control of national trade prerogatives. It took several years of agonizing negotiations before an agreement on an International Trade Organization (ITO) could be reached, and when it was finally signed, it turned out to be complicated and filled with exceptions. To some it went too far in the direction of free trade; to others, it did not go far enough. When the Truman administration realized that its own Congress would not ratify the agreement, the ITO died.

Fortunately, major trading nations had agreed to an interim arrangement in 1947 that would provide a set of trading rules until the ITO could be implemented. Known as the General Agreement on Tariffs and Trade (GATT), this agreement incorporated many of the principles of the ITO, without some of its complexity and thoroughness. Once the United States pulled out of the ITO, the GATT became the guiding document.

The core of this agreement centered on three principles: (1) all signatories would extend unconditional most-favored-nation treatment to all member nations; (2) nontariff barriers, particularly quantitative restrictions, were to be abandoned; and (3) countries should consult on a multilateral basis to avoid trade disputes. Other features included commercial codes on dumping and subsidies, remedies for noncompliance, the granting of waivers from GATT commitments if there were international consensus, and the principle of reciprocity. Since the GATT was originally designed as a temporary arrangement, however, it did not include provisions for commodity agreements, regulations of state trading or restrictive business practices, and codes for such nontariff barriers as bilateral quotas. Nor was the GATT a formal international organization. As an institution, the General Agreement was more analogous to the Chicago Board of Trade than the IMF or the World Bank. The GATT, with offices and a small staff located in Geneva, Switzerland, merely provided a forum and a set of procedures for member nations to negotiate agreements. Although the GATT was a giant leap forward, it had little power of its own and numerous loopholes.

Sources of U.S. Balance of Payments Difficulties

If U.S. postwar efforts had created a truly Ricardian world complete with monetary stability, the United States might never have had a balance of payments problem when John Kennedy came into office. But the theory of monetary stability and trade liberalization did not operate as smoothly as Roosevelt and Truman had hoped. The dislocations of the war made it difficult for the Europeans and the Japanese to lower their trade barriers and accept responsibility for their currencies. Moreover, the United States preferred to manage the international system unilaterally: If the United States accepted the economic costs of managing the world economy, it gained political and economic influence over its allies. By 1960, however, the costs of America's hegemony seemed to be getting out of control. Three things in particular worried Kennedy: the creation of the European Community in 1957, the structure of the Bretton Woods system, and the slow progress toward liberalizing trade barriers under the GATT.

The European Economic Community (EEC)

In the aftermath of the Great Depression and World War II, the world was plagued with extensive trade barriers. Through the late 1950s, however, this was not a great concern of the United States. In fact, the United States took an active role in encouraging certain types of protectionism in Japan and Europe. During the American occupation of Japan, for example, the United States made no effort to dismantle trade barriers that restricted American imports. The Occupation's first economic priority was to help Japan recover. Therefore the United States left its borders open to the Japanese exports while it urged other nations to take more goods from Japan.

In addition, the idea behind the European Economic Community

(EEC) originated in the United States, even though customs unions of the EEC variety were traditionally considered discriminatory and at odds with the principle of free trade. When Secretary of State George Marshall put forth the offer of U.S. aid to Europe in 1947, he recommended that the Europeans reduce their internal barriers to trade to stimulate long-term competitiveness. The underlying economic logic behind this suggestion was that a customs union would create a large internal market in Europe, thus permitting greater specialization according to each nation's comparative advantage. It would also allow European industries to realize greater economies of scale. This was consistent with America's strategy because American officials believed that European recovery was essential to the freedom and prosperity of the capitalist world. And since the Europeans urgently needed aid and were critically dependent on the United States for military and economic assistance, the United States had powerful leverage to get its way.

The creation of a European community, however, could create long-term problems for American exports and balance of payments. When the Treaty of Rome establishing the EEC was signed on March 25, 1957, there were six signatories—Belgium, the Federal Republic of Germany, France, Italy, Luxembourg, and the Netherlands. The purpose of the treaty was to facilitate the free movement of goods, a common agricultural policy, free movement of persons, services, and capital, and a European transportation network. The free movement of goods was to be attained by reducing and eventually eliminating tariffs among the members and by creating a common external tariff wall. (Technically, the external tariffs were accepted under GATT because they were the arithmetical average of the duties applied by the countries prior to the treaty.) The free movement of goods was also to be attained by the removal of any quantitative import restrictions between member states.

If the EEC achieved this objective, the nations within the community would inevitably trade more among themselves and less with the United States. Furthermore, if the Treaty of Rome successfully eliminated capital controls and exchange restrictions, it could encourage capital outflows from the United States by causing American firms to invest in Europe rather than export from the United States.

The Bretton Woods System

The emergence of the European Community was not the only problem on Kennedy's mind concerning the deteriorating balance of payments. Of equal importance was the U.S. position on the Bretton Woods system. Under the rules of Bretton Woods, European nations had a great deal of latitude: they did not have to convert their currencies into gold until the early 1960s, and they were allowed to devalue their currencies to correct a fundamental disequilibrium in their balance of payments. These countries took advantage of their positions by maintaining capital controls and inconvertible currencies through 1958 and by devaluing their currencies whenever they had balance of payments problems. The United States, however, held special obligations under the conventions of Bretton Woods: it was the only nation obliged to defend the par value of its currency, which was $35 per ounce; it was the only nation committed to convert its currency freely into gold; and it was the only nation allowing unrestricted capital flows.

Fulfillment of these unique obligations posed no problem for the United States in the years immediately after the war. The prospect of American balance of payments deficits was dismissed lightly because the United States held the great bulk of the world's monetary gold (see Exhibit 3), and it had a strong economy with a big technological lead. During the years 1946 to 1949, the U.S. balance of trade totaled $32 billion; even after the Marshall Plan and other aid disbursements, the United States enjoyed a favorable balance of payments position. In fact, the United States in 1949 forced devaluations of the European and Japanese currencies against the dollar, ranging from 30 percent for British sterling to 98 percent for the Japanese yen, to make these countries more competitive. Although the U.S. current account balance shifted into deficit in 1950, the greatest concern among governmental officials was that there would be a sustained dollar shortage lasting well into the 1960s. Economies in war-ravaged Europe needed liquidity to rebuild and to trade. Until the late 1950s, foreign monetary authorities were far more anxious to obtain dollars than exchange dollars for gold.

America's commitment to unrestricted capital flows further enhanced the dollar's international role. Since the United States was the world's largest and freest capital market, and American interest rates were generally favorable (see Exhibit 4), foreign governments found it attractive to issue bonds in the United States. America's political stability and economic strength also led many foreigners to deposit their dollars in U.S. banks or buy T-bills. In addition, American multinationals and to some extent banks were an important source of funds for Europe and the developing world. The outflow of private capital from the United States rose steadily after World War II, with a sharp jump in 1956 and 1957 due to the acquisition of Venezuelan oil concessions.

As long as foreigners were content to hold and use dollars, and as long as the United States had adequate gold stocks to back its foreign liabilities, a net outflow of U.S. dollars was viewed positively by foreign governments. Since dollars were being used to finance world trade, U.S. deficits were critical for maintaining international liquidity. But as the 1950s wore to a close, the outflow of dollars and gold from the United States began to reach crisis proportions (see Exhibits 1, 2, and 3).

The American government first became sensitive to this problem around 1958. Concerned with domestic inflation, President Eisenhower introduced austerity measures that caused a recession. But for the first time in the postwar period, a recession in the United States did not produce a strong reduction in imports of foreign goods and services. The increasing quality of imports and the growing competitiveness of America's trading partners kept the demand for imports high. The result was that the U.S. current account surplus, which had been strongly positive in 1956 and 1957, all but disappeared (see Exhibits 1 and 2).[11] When U.S. growth picked up again in 1959, demand for imports rose even further and a major steel strike in the United States made matters worse.

The balance of payments situation was further aggravated by a declining demand for dollars. An increase in U.S. foreign investment in Europe and growing dollar reserves overseas reduced the incentive for foreign governments to hold U.S. currency. With the formation of the EEC and the restoration of convertibility among the Europeans, their need for dollars to finance internal trade declined. The dollar shortage was turning into a dollar glut. As a result, foreign central banks began to exchange dollars for gold; in 1958, $2.3 billion in gold flowed out of the United States, an amount equivalent to one tenth of all U.S. holdings. Ad hoc measures were taken to ease the pressure on U.S. reserves, including a 1958 arrangement for the Germans to prepay a half-billion dollar loan. By 1960, however, it was clear that foreign dollar holdings would soon exceed U.S. gold reserves (see Exhibit 3).

This reversal in the American balance of payments position threatened to topple the entire Bretton Woods system. Foreign governments needed dollars to finance international trade but the persistent U.S. deficits were lowering their confidence in America's ability to redeem their dollars for gold. Even though the dollar was pegged at $35 per ounce, speculators believed that under these conditions it was preferable to hold gold over dollars. Hence foreign monetary authorities increased their conversions of dollars into gold, while private investors began to acquire more of the metal on the London Gold Exchange—a small, private commodity market that the British government supported with its own reserves. For one day, on October 20, 1960, the British stopped supporting the price of gold on the London Exchange, causing the price to shoot up to $40 per ounce. The price was quickly reduced to official levels when the United States provided Britain with new gold reserves. Yet the psychological impact of breaking the official price, even for one day, was dramatic.

As he entered office in January 1961, President Kennedy's options were severely limited. If he wanted to keep the Bretton Woods system intact, the United States could not easily devalue its currency—a measure open to other countries. Since all currencies were valued in terms of the dollar, any effort to reduce the dollar's value would undermine all confidence in the American currency and destroy the supposed stability of

[11]In summer 1956, Egypt nationalized the Suez Canal, a step which provoked a military response by England, France, and Israel. In the aftermath of the conflict, the canal remained closed and oil supplies from the Middle East to Europe were disrupted. Therefore the United States shipped oil to its European allies, which led to a temporary surge in American exports.

the fixed-rate system. Furthermore, any effort to reverse America's balance of payments deficits could lead to a liquidity problem. If fewer dollars were available to finance world trade, there could be a stifling effect on world economic growth.

Slow Progress toward Free Trade

The final problem that concerned the Kennedy administration was the lack of progress toward freer world trade. The GATT had sponsored five rounds of tariff-cutting negotiations between 1947 and 1960, but none of these efforts realized much success. Part of the problem was that these negotiations were built around the rule of the principal supplier. Under this rule, a country would request a tariff concession only if it were the principal supplier (or largest exporter) of that specific good. Since an importer would have to generalize the tariff reduction under the most-favored-nation clause in the GATT, it would be reluctant to negotiate concessions with any country other than the principal supplier. The effect of this rule was to exclude a large number of countries from meaningful tariff bargaining during this period. Countries that were not the principal supplier of any product, such as many developing nations, were completely left out of the process.

In addition, the negotiations were being conducted on a product-by-product, country-by-country basis. The negotiations were exceedingly laborious, as participants would bargain for reciprocal tariff cuts on every individual item that they imported and exported. With the advent of the EEC, this process became even harder. After 1957 each proposal considered by EEC nations had to proceed through lengthy internal discussions to insure that tariff cuts did not weigh disproportionately on specific members.

Yet here again, President Kennedy's options to foster world trade appeared limited. The president's authority to negotiate tariff reductions was circumscribed by the Congress. No Congress in the past 25 years had allowed a president to go beyond the powers provided in the 1934 Reciprocal Trade Act, i.e., item-by-item reductions on a reciprocal, bilateral basis. If Kennedy wanted to find some way to correct the United States' deteriorating balance of trade, he would find no easy answer in the GATT procedures or at home.

Kennedy and the Balance of Payments

Exhibit 1 U.S. Balance of Payments—Systematic Presentation, 1950-1960
(Millions of U.S. Dollars)

		1950	1951	1952	1953	1954	1955	1956	1957	1958	1959	1960
A. GOODS AND SERVICES, NET	1	**2,090**	**4,285**	**3,045**	**1,078**	**2,396**	**2,812**	**5,008**	**6,988**	**3,046**	**1,047**	**4,964**
1. Merchandise, f.o.b., net	2	**1,009**	**2,921**	**2,481**	**1,291**	**2,445**	**2,763**	**4,575**	**6,099**	**3,312**	**972**	**4,736**
a. Imports	3	9,108	11,202	10,838	10,990	10,354	11,527	12,804	13,291	12,952	15,310	14,723
b. Exports	4	10,117	14,123	13,319	12,281	12,799	14,280	17,379	19,390	16,264	16,282	19,459
2. Transport, net	5	**215**	**582**	**373**	**117**	**145**	**202**	**209**	**398**	**2**	**−113**	**−283**
a. Debit	6	818	974	1,115	1,081	1,026	1,204	1,408	1,569	1,636	1,759	1,988
i. Shipping	7	643	787	911	864	805	946	1,125	1,226	1,255	1,309	1,416
ii. Other	8	175	187	204	217	221	258	283	343	381	450	572
b. Credit	9	1,033	1,536	1,488	1,198	1,171	1,406	1,617	1,967	1,638	1,646	1,705
i. Shipping	10	859	1,331	1,242	972	942	1,137	1,323	1,639	1,291	1,238	1,284
ii. Other	11	174	225	246	226	229	269	294	328	347	408	421
3. Foreign travel, net	12	**−335**	**−284**	**−290**	**−355**	**−414**	**−499**	**−570**	**−587**	**−635**	**−708**	**−776**
a. Debit	13	754	757	840	929	1,009	1,153	1,275	1,372	1,460	1,610	1,744
b. Credit	14	419	473	550	574	595	654	705	785	825	902	968
4. Investment income, net	15	**1,509**	**2,050**	**2,196**	**2,112**	**2,347**	**2,730**	**3,102**	**3,384**	**2,965**	**3,071**	**3,363**
a. Debit	16	559	583	555	624	582	676	735	796	825	1,061	1,113
i. Official	17	31	47	64	86	59	94	154	201	139	281	332
ii. Private direct investment[a]	18	359	355	315	358	338	367	344	344	369	451	423
iii. Other private	19	169	181	176	180	185	215	237	251	317	329	358
b. Credit	20	2,068	2,633	2,751	2,736	2,929	3,406	3,837	4,180	3,790	4,132	4,476
i. Official	21	109	198	204	252	272	274	194	205	307	349	349
ii. Private direct investment[a]	22	1,769	2,243	2,342	2,268	2,427	2,874	3,346	3,612	3,066	3,317	3,609
iii. Other private	23	190	192	205	216	230	258	297	363	417	466	518

(*Continued*)

Exhibit 1 (Continued)

		1950	1951	1952	1953	1954	1955	1956	1957	1958	1959	1960
5. Government transactions, n.e.s., net	24	−542	−1,213	−1,988	−2,329	−2,376	−2,640	−2,741	−2,800	−3,094	−2,698	−2,609
a. Debit	25	800	1,492	2,301	2,826	2,836	3,090	3,151	3,444	3,666	3,351	3,302
i. Military	26	576	1,270	2,054	2,615	2,642	2,901	2,949	3,216	3,435	3,107	3,048
ii. Other	27	224	222	247	211	194	189	202	228	231	244	254
b. Credit	28	258	279	313	497	460	450	410	644	572	653	693
i. Military	29	—	—	—	192	182	200	161	375	300	302	335
ii. Other	30	258	279	313	305	278	250	249	269	272	351	358
6. Other services, net	31	234	229	273	242	249	266	433	494	496	523	533
a. Debit	32	153	202	221	245	258	304	389	384	427	427	433
b. Credit	33	387	431	494	487	507	570	822	878	923	950	966
B. UNILATERAL TRANSFERS, NET	34	−4,033	−3,524	−2,535	−2,483	−2,290	−2,514	−2,431	−2,371	−2,389	−2,481	−2,565
7. Private, net	35	−444	−386	−417	−476	−486	−444	−530	−543	−540	−575	−628
a. Debit	36	474	416	449	516	527	473	562	577	573	609	660
b. Credit	37	30	30	32	40	41	29	32	34	33	34	32
8. Official, net	38	−3,589	−3,138	−2,118	−2,007	−1,804	−2,070	−1,901	−1,828	−1,849	−1,906	−1,937
a. Debit	39	3,742	3,261	2,203	2,110	1,869	2,112	1,956	1,900	1,888	1,940	1,971
b. Credit	40	153	123	85	103	65	42	55	72	39	34	34
C. CAPITAL AND MONETARY GOLD, NET	41	1,964	−1,238	−1,111	1,066	−279	−801	−3,120	−5,774	−1,145	1,022	−1,807
NONMONETARY SECTOR, NET	42	−1,333	−1,483	−2,025	−1,357	−1,241	−1,558	−3,501	−4,697	−4,122	−2,482	−4,589
9. Private direct investment, net[a]	43	−826	−1,000	−1,509	−1,240	−1,083	−1,401	−2,727	−3,493	−1,872	−1,990	−2,633
a. Liabilities	44	270	259	266	321	286	384	399	312	254	471	315
b. Assets	45	−1,096	−1,259	−1,775	−1,561	−1,369	−1,785	−3,126	−3,805	−2,126	−2,461	−2,948
10. Other private long-term, net	46	−336	−309	−142	140	−70	178	−74	−314	−1,268	−273	−413
a. Liabilities	47	−19	114	35	71	149	193	363	235	−17	472	282
b. Assets	48	−317	−423	−177	69	−219	−15	−437	−549	−1,251	−745	−695
11. Private short-term, net	49	−15	−18	46	−39	−181	−25	−71	68	−11	134	−438
12. Official long-term, net	50	−156	−156	−420	−218	93	−310	−629	−958	−971	−353	−1,105
a. Repayment of debt: liabilities	51	—	—	—	—	—	—	—	—	—	—	—
b. Repayment of debt: assets	52	295	305	429	475	497	407	467	627	530	1,028	613
c. Other liabilities	53	—	—	—	—	—	—	—	—	—	—	—
d. Other assets	54	−451	−461	−849	−693	−404	−717	−1,096	−1,585	−1,501	−1,381	−1,718
13. Official short-term, net	55	—	—	—	—	—	—	—	—	—	—	—

Exhibit 1 (Continued)

	MONETARY SECTOR, NET											
56		3,297	245	914	2,423	962	757	381	−1,077	2,977	3,504	2,782
57	**14. Private institutions, net**	**38**	**422**	**382**	**905**	**84**	**−363**	**506**	**−246**	**700**	**−629**	**298**
58	a. Long-term liabilities	7	1	−1	−1	1	—	−2	9	−8	−1	7
59	b. Long-term assets	−178	−14	−37	116	−101	−226	−166	−310	−193	−181	−155
60	c. Short-term liabilities	321	482	514	634	672	25	1,060	311	1,252	−390	1,441
61	d. Foreign exchange assets	−112	−47	−94	156	−488	−162	−386	−256	−351	−57	−995
62	**15. Central institutions, net[b]**	**3,259**	**−177**	**532**	**1,513**	**378**	**1,120**	**−125**	**−831**	**2,277**	**4,133**	**2,484**
63	a. Long-term liabilities	—	—	—	—	—	—	—	—	—	—	—
64	b. Long-term assets	—	—	—	—	—	—	—	—	—	—	—
65	c. EPU short-term balance, net	—	—	—	—	—	—	—	—	—	—	—
66	d. IMF position, net	16	19	−36	95	182	141	−363	−367	17	260	741
67	e. Other short-term liabilities	1,500	−143	947	262	398	938	544	334	−15	2,798	41
68	f. Gold and foreign exchange reserves	1,743	−53	−379	1,161	298	41	−306	−798	2,275	1,075	1,702
69	**D. ERRORS AND OMISSIONS, NET**	**−21**	**477**	**601**	**339**	**173**	**503**	**543**	**1,157**	**488**	**412**	**−592**
	Memorandum item: Short-term liabilities of the monetary sector to foreign official institutions											
70		—	—	—	—	—	—	930	20	735	948	1,240

OECD balance of payments statistics for the United States are based on U.S. Department of Commerce data. Due to differences in definitions and presentation, however, the statistics may differ from those issued by the Department of Commerce.

[a]Included reinvested earnings of subsidiaries.

[b]Included the Federal Reserve banks.

Source: OECD, *Statistics of Balance of Payments, 1950-1961* (Paris: 1964).

Kennedy and the Balance of Payments

Exhibit 2   U.S. Balance of Payments—Analytical Summary (Millions of U.S. Dollars)

	1950	1951	1952	1953	1954	1955	1956	1957	1958	1959
1. Trade balance (f.o.b.)	1,009	2,921	2,481	1,291	2,445	2,753	4,575	6,099	3,312	972
2. Services, net	1,081	1,364	564	−213	−49	59	433	889	−266	75
3. Balance on goods and services	2,090	4,285	3,045	1,078	2,396	2,812	5,008	6,988	3,046	1,047
4. Private transfers, net	−444	−386	−417	−476	−486	−444	−530	−543	−540	−575
5. Official transfers, net	−3,589	−3,138	−2,118	−2,007	−1,804	−2,070	−1,901	−1,828	−1,849	−1,906
6. Current balance	−1,943	761	510	−1,405	106	298	2,577	4,617	657	−1,434
7. Nonmonetary sector's long-term capital, net	−1,318	−1,465	−2,071	−1,318	−1,060	−1,533	−3,430	−4,765	−4,111	−2,616
8. Monetary sector's long-term capital, net	−171	−13	−38	115	−100	−226	−168	−301	−201	−182
9. Basic balance on current and long-term capital transactions	−3,432	−717	−1,599	−2,608	−1,054	−1,461	−1,021	−449	−3,655	−4,232

Exhibit 2 (Continued)

10. Nonmonetary sector's short-term capital, net	−15	−18	46	−39	−181	−25	−71	68	−11	134
11. Errors and omissions, net	−21	477	601	359	173	503	543	1,157	488	412
12. Overall balance[a]	**−3,468**	**−258**	**−952**	**−2,308**	**−1,062**	**−983**	**−549**	**776**	**−3,178**	**−3,686**
13. Private monetary institutions' short-term liabilities	321	482	514	634	672	25	1,060	311	1,252	−390
14. Private monetary institutions' short-term assets	−112	−47	−94	156	488	−162	−386	−256	−351	−57
15. IMF position, net	16	19	−36	95	182	141	−363	−367	17	260
16. Official gold and foreign exchange reserves	1,743	53	−379	1,161	298	41	−306	−798	2,275	1,075
17. Central monetary institutions' other liabilities and assets, net	1,500	−143	947	262	398	938	544	334	−15	2,798

Note: OECD balance of payments statistics for the United States are based on U.S. Department of Commerce data. Due to differences in definitions and presentation, however, the statistics may differ from those issued by the Department of Commerce.

[a]This calculation of the overall balance differed from the more commonly encountered overall balance. The OECD excluded from the overall balance private monetary institutions' short-term assets and liabilities, and central monetary institutions' other liabilities and assets (Lines 13, 14, and 17). Most other presentations included Lines 13, 14, and 17 in their calculations of the overall balance.

Source: OECD, *Statistics of Balance of Payments, 1950-1961* (Paris: 1964).

Kennedy and the Balance of Payments

Exhibit 3   U.S. Gold and Foreign Exchange Position, 1952–1960 (Billions of U.S. Dollars)

		1952	1953	1954	1955	1956	1957	1958	1959	1960
Gold	1	23.25	22.09	21.79	21.75	22.06	22.86	20.58	19.51	17.81
Short-term foreign assets	2	1.05	.90	1.38	1.55	1.95	2.20	2.54	2.62	3.55
Short-term foreign liabilities	3	8.96	10.02	11.15	11.72	13.49	13.64	14.62	16.23	17.42
By class of holder:										
Official	4	4.91	5.85	6.98	7.29	8.27	7.92	8.66	9.14	10.37
Banks	5	2.37	2.39	2.36	2.65	3.19	3.47	3.52	4.69	4.83
Other	6	1.68	1.78	1.80	1.78	2.08	2.25	2.43	2.40	2.21
By form of liability:										
Deposits with Federal Reserve banks	7	.55	.42	.49	.40	.32	.36	.27	.34	.22
Deposits with other banks	8	5.19	5.61	6.42	6.49	7.23	7.21	8.21	7.69	8.87
Government securities	9	2.69	3.32	3.53	4.08	4.88	4.68	4.83	6.55	6.59
Other	10	.54	.67	.71	.74	1.07	1.40	1.31	1.64	1.75
By area:										
Latin America	11	1.61	1.77	1.91	2.00	2.35	2.58	2.40	2.41	2.41
Continental Europe	12	2.71	3.63	4.61	5.39	5.57	5.52	6.18	6.90	7.06
United Kingdom	13	.82	.71	.64	.55	1.01	1.28	.85	.97	1.67
Other countries	14	3.82	3.91	4.00	3.78	4.56	4.27	5.19	5.95	6.27
Foreign-owned government bonds and notes	15	.90	.81	.75	1.31	1.10	1.22	.98	1.50	—
Canada	16	.31	.23	.09	.44	.37	.46	.34	.45	—
Latin America	17	.05	.06	.15	.20	.19	.18	.11	.10	—
Continental Europe	18	.30	.25	.26	.34	.29	.31	.27	.49	—
United Kingdom	19	.20	.23	.22	.28	.20	.20	.19	.32	—
Other countries	20	.04	.04	.03	.06	.06	.08	.07	.13	—
Net IMF position	21	1.46	1.37	1.19	1.04	1.61	1.98	1.96	2.00	1.56

Source: IMF, *International Financial Statistics*.

Kennedy and the Balance of Payments

**Exhibit 4   Short- and Long-Term Interest Rates:
An International Comparison**

	1955	1956	1957	1958	1959	1960
A. Selected Treasury Bill or Call Money Rates (Percent per Annum)						
United States	1.74%	2.66%	3.26%	1.84%	3.42%	2.94%
France	—	—	5.35	6.49	4.07	4.08
Germany	3.13	4.70	4.08	2.93	2.67	4.55
United Kingdom	3.73	4.93	4.80	4.56	3.37	4.88
B. Selected Yields on Long-Term Government Bonds[a] (Percent per Annum)						
	1955	**1956**	**1957**	**1958**	**1959**	**1960**
United States	2.80%	3.06%	3.47%	3.43%	4.07%	4.02%
France	5.21	5.28	5.92	5.68	5.27	5.15
Germany	—	6.23	6.64	6.28	5.86	6.40
United Kingdom	4.17	4.73	4.98	4.98	4.82	5.43

[a]Average yields on issues with at least 12 years to maturity.

Source: IMF, *International Financial Statistics.*

Kennedy and the Balance of Payments

Exhibit 5   Illustration of Comparative Advantage

Consider the hypothetical situation in which both the United States and Europe have similar endowments of land, labor, and capital, with the sole difference being that the United States has a better climate. The table below shows how much cotton and wheat the United States and Europe can produce without trade, and the asterisks indicate which bundle of goods each chooses to consume.

Production Possibilities of the United States and Europe (Each Country Contains 10,000 Production Units)

	United States		Europe	
Use of Production Units	Cotton (000 Bales)	Wheat (000 Bushels)	Cotton (000 Bales)	Wheat (000 Bushels)
10,000 in cotton; 0 in wheat	100	0	80	0
7,500 in cotton; 2,500 in wheat	75	15	60	5
5,000 in cotton; 5,000 in wheat	50	30	40*	10*
2,500 in cotton; 7,500 in wheat	25*	45*	20	15
0 in cotton; 10,000 in wheat	0	60	0	20

The above table demonstrates that the United States is more efficient in wheat compared to Europe. For every 10,000 uses of production units, the United States produces 100,000 bales of cotton vs. Europe's 80,000 (a ratio of 5:4), and 60,000 bushels of wheat to Europe's 20,000 (a ratio of 3:1). Therefore America's *comparative advantage* is greater in wheat than in cotton, while Europe is *relatively* more productive in cotton than wheat.

If both countries specialized fully in the products they make best, the two countries would both have more cotton and more wheat to consume. As one can see in the table above, total specialization would produce 80,000 bales of cotton and 60,000 bushels of wheat. Assuming that a pattern of trade and barter developed as represented in the table below, the United States would be able to consume 30,000 bales of cotton and 48,000 bushels of wheat with free trade compared to 25,000 bales and 45,000 bushels that were available with no trade. At the same time, Europe ends up with 50,000 bales and 12,000 bushels against the 40,000 bales and 10,000 bushels it would have produced in isolation.

The United States and Europe in Specialization and Trade

	United States Trades			Europe Trades		
	Produces	(Imports +, Exports −)	Consumes	Produces	(Imports +, Exports −)	Consumes
Cotton (000 bales)	0	+30	30	80	−30	50
Wheat (000 bushels)	60	−12	48	0	+12	12

Source: Adapted from Raymond Vernon. Louis T. Wells, Jr., *Manager in the International Economy*, 4th ed., © 1981, 87–88. Reprinted by permission of Prentice-Hall, Inc., Englewood Cliffs, New Jersey.

Note
An Introduction to the Balance of Payments

Few countries in the world run their economies in autarky. Most nations export and import goods and services, borrow and lend capital, and engage in government-to-government transactions. To record this activity, countries compile a balance of payments statement. When countries are heavily engaged in international commerce, an informed reading of a nation's balance of payments can be critical for evaluating a nation's ability to realize its objectives and for forecasting political, social, and economic developments.

The balance of payments statement of a country is simply a listing of the transactions taking place between the domestic economy and the rest of the world. The construction of a balance of payments statement is governed by a double-entry system, similar to corporate accounting with its own rules, conventions, and chart of accounts. Balance of payments statements are presented in a variety of formats that reflect the differing patterns of individual countries' international economic relationships and emphasize the aspects that are of particular interest to the user of the statement. This introductory note will briefly describe the accounting system behind a balance of payments statement and the most widely used format for presenting balance of payments data.

Balance of Payments Accounting

A balance of payments can be broadly described as the record of an economy's international economic transactions, that is, of the goods and services that an economy has received from and provided to the rest of the world and of the changes in the economy's claims on and liabilities to the rest of the world.[1]

For balance of payments purposes, a nation's economy consists of its government, the enterprises which operate within its territory, and its individual residents. The government includes not only the departments located in its territory but also those located abroad, such as embassies and military establishments. Embassy personnel, armed forces, and dependents are considered residents of their home country. Regardless of the legal status of a company's foreign branches and subsidiaries, they are considered part of the economy of the country in which they operate.

This note was prepared by Assistant Professor David B. Yoffie, with the assistance of Jane Kenney Austin, Research Associate.

Harvard Business School note 9-384-005

[1]IMF, *Balance of Payments Manual*, 4th ed. (Washington, DC, 1976).

Table 1 Standard Components of a Balance of Payments Statement

I. Current Account	*II. Capital Account*
A. *Goods and Services*	A. *Capital, excluding reserves*
Merchandise	Direct investment
Shipment	Portfolio investment
Other transportation	Other long-term capital
Travel	Short-term capital
Investment income	
Other	
B. *Transfers*	B. *Reserves*
Private	Monetary gold
Official	Special Drawing Rights (SDR)
	Reserve position in IMF
	Foreign exchange assets
	Other, including use of IMF credit

Most international transactions consist of an *exchange* of goods, services, or financial assets which are reflected in pairs of equal credit and debit entries. Credit entries are positive and made for the export of goods, services, or financial assets, while debit entries are negative and made for the import of goods, services, or financial assets. The balance of payments statement can be thought of as analogous to a sources and uses statement for a firm, with funds in this case defined as external purchasing power or foreign exchange. Credits are considered sources of funds and debits are considered uses of funds. The balance of payments statement is not analogous to either the income statement or balance sheet of a firm. Unlike an income statement, the balance of payments does not provide any information regarding the profitability of the underlying transactions. Unlike a balance sheet which shows stocks of assets and liabilities at a specific point in time, the balance of payments measures flows of goods, services, and capital occurring over a period of time.

The standard accounts which make up a balance of payments statement fall into two major groups: the current account which includes goods, services, and transfers, and the capital account which consists of financial assets. The major components of the two groups are listed in Table 1.

Application of the debit and credit rules and the analogy to the sources and uses statement is fairly straightforward when dealing with the goods and services accounts. An export of merchandise or the provision of services (such as transportation) to foreigners is a source of foreign exchange and a credit (+) entry. An import of goods or the use of foreign services (such as hotel accommodations) is a use of foreign exchange and treated as a debit (−).

The investment income account is somewhat different from the other goods and services accounts. Although financial in nature, income from foreign investments is treated as payment for the services of capital. This income includes dividends, interest, and earnings of foreign subsidiaries. Those received from foreigners are a source of foreign exchange and treated as credits $(+)$. Those paid to foreigners represent a use of foreign exchange and are treated as debits $(-)$. Reinvested earnings in foreign subsidiaries are credited to the investment income account and a matching debit made to the capital accounts under direct investment.

While most transactions involve an exchange and automatically give rise to both a credit and a debit entry, some goods, services, and financial resources, such as gifts from individuals or grants from governments, are exported or imported without a quid pro quo. In such cases, offsetting debits or credits are made to one of the transfer accounts, insuring that debits and credits are equal for the statement as a whole.

The capital accounts tend to be confusing from both an accounting and a conceptual standpoint. The accounting difficulties arise because the financial transactions are divided along several dimensions. Distinctions are made between assets and liabilities; the term of the securities based on original contractual maturity; and the type of capital (direct investment, portfolio investment, and other capital). Short-term capital consists of currency and financial obligations with original maturity of less than one year. Portfolio investment and direct investments are long term by definition but direct investments include only those equities and debt instruments which give the holder significant managerial control over the foreign firm. Some detailed statements provide additional information specifying whether the domestic debtor or creditor is a government body or banking (monetary) institution and identifying those liabilities that appear as reserves on the balance of payments statements of other countries. The components of the capital accounts are usually presented on a net basis, which may result in either a debit or a credit entry.

The conceptual problem arises because discussions about the capital accounts are conducted in terms of the underlying flows of *capital*, which will be opposite in direction to the movement of the *financial asset* involved. For example, when a resident purchases a bond from a foreigner, he imports a financial asset, giving rise to a debit $(-)$ entry in the balance of payments accounts; however, his action is called an export of capital.[2]

The assets that make up a country's foreign reserves are singled out within the capital account because these assets are available to the government to finance payments imbalances directly or to intervene in the foreign exchange markets. The accounting conventions are the same for reserve assets as for other financial assets, but the results tend to be counterintuitive. The import of foreign exchange or gold by the govern-

---

[2]Note that it makes no difference whether the bond purchased from the foreigner was originally issued by a foreign or domestic firm. Either way the transaction is assigned a debit since it is a use of funds. Because the bond represents a liability for its issuer and an asset for its holder, the purchase of a foreign-issued bond results in an increase in domestic assets (a use of funds), and the purchase of a domestic-issued bond (held by a foreigner) results in a decrease in liabilities to foreigners (again a use of funds).

ment gives rise to a debit ($-$) just like any other import of a good, service, or financial asset. In fact, the decision to import foreign exchange or gold can be considered a use of foreign purchasing power if only in the sense that the government could have acquired alternative assets.

Reserves are held in a variety of forms, including gold, foreign currencies, interest-bearing deposits, and foreign government securities. A significant subset of the reserve assets are related to the IMF and the workings of the international monetary system. SDRs are "money" created by the IMF whose value is based on a weighted basket of currencies and are used only in transactions among governments or between governments and the IMF. A country's reserve position in the Fund, which is based on its contributions to the IMF, and Fund Credit are available under various conditions to countries facing balance of payments difficulties.

The examples that follow illustrate how to interpret various transactions in U.S. balance of payments accounts in 1950.[3] In these examples we look at the international money flows generated to finance these transactions. When thinking about these examples, it may be helpful to keep the following identities in mind:

$$\text{Export} = \text{credit} = \text{source} = (+)$$
$$\text{Import} = \text{debit} = \text{use} = (-).$$

	1950 (In Millions)
Example 1:	
Merchandise, f.o.b. exports	$10,117 (Line 1b)[4]

The United States exports $10.117 billion in goods. F.o.b. stand for "free on board" and means that costs of insurance and freight (c.i.f.) are excluded.

Example 2:	
Foreign travel, debit	$754 (Line 3a)

American citizens spent $754 million in tourism and travel expenses.

Example 3:	
Unilateral transfers, official credit	$153 (Line 8b)

The U.S. government received $153 million in gifts from foreign sources.

---

[3]The terminology used in these examples is derived from OECD statements, which can be found in Exhibit 1 of the previous case, "Kennedy and the Balance of Payments."

[4]Line numbers refer to Exhibit 1 on pages 477–479 of the previous case, "Kennedy and the Balance of Payments."

Example 4:

Nonmonetary sector, private direct investment, assets $-1,096 (Line 9b)

Private U.S. firms invested a net of $1.096 billion in overseas companies. These investments were long term and entailed substantial control of the overseas company.

Example 5:

Monetary sector, central institutions, other short-term liabilities $1,500 (Line 15e)

Monetary sector means that a bank is involved; central institutions refer to the U.S. Treasury and the Federal Reserve; and short-term liabilities are usually T-bills. In other words, this line means that foreign holders of U.S. dollars purchased a net of $1.5 billion in U.S. Treasury bills in 1950.

In theory, every transaction in the balance of payments statement should be recorded separately, and, like all double-entry bookkeeping systems, there should always be a debit entry for every credit entry. In practice, however, this is impossible. Each side of a transaction is often obtained from different data sources, such as customs declarations and bank records, and in some cases entries have to be estimated. Furthermore, the debits and the credits do not always balance. For this reason an errors and omissions account is included to balance the statement. Errors and omissions, which can fluctuate widely from year to year, are believed to contain significant unrecorded short-term capital movements. The errors and omissions account and the variety of methods used to collect balance of payments data point to a need for caution in interpreting the data. A number of other issues also complicate the compilation of balance of payments data, including the recording of transactions at market value, timing differences, and the selection of a stable unit of account. Hence accuracy and consistency in collecting data cannot always be assumed for a given country, and care must be taken when comparing the statements of two countries.

Presentation of Balance of Payments Data

The reader may well ask at this point how these mechanical records of international transactions are transformed into weighty "balance" of payments statements full of deficits that worry presidents and finance ministers, and surpluses that aggravate trading partners. The "balances" rise from different analytical presentations of the data in which component accounts are grouped together and subtotals or partial balances struck.

Total debits and credits on a balance of payments statement are equal as a result of the double-entry system (with the aid of the errors and omissions account) and automatically net to zero. While true for the statement as a whole, debits and credits are not necessarily equal within

Table 2   Standard Payments Balances: A Hypothetical Example

Merchandise	
Exports	+6,000
Imports	−4,500
Balance of trade	+1,500
Services	+ 100
Balance on goods and services	+1,600
Transfers	− 150
Current account balance	+1,450
Long-term capital	−2,300
Basic balance	− 850
Short-term capital	+ 200
Errors and omissions	− 300
Overall balance	− 950
Official settlements balance	+ 950
Reserves	+ 950

individual accounts or for groups of accounts. A country's merchandise imports (debits) do not necessarily equal its merchandise exports (credits) during a given period, nor do its total imports of goods and services necessarily equal total exports. The net sum of the debits and credits of any particular account or group of accounts is called a *balance* and it may be a net credit or a net debit balance. A net credit balance is called a *surplus*. A net debit balance is called a *deficit*.

A surplus in any particular balance is not necessarily good for a country, nor a deficit necessarily bad, despite the connotation. Judgments about the appropriate sign or level for any balance depend on many factors, including the country's level of development and its national goals and strategy. For example, a developing country that must import capital goods to build an infrastructure is likely to show a net deficit in its merchandise accounts as well as rely heavily on foreign sources for capital to finance its development. On the other hand, a developed country may depend on a large and positive balance in its merchandise accounts to sustain the desired levels of foreign investment and aid. The balances used most frequently to evaluate a nation's balance of payments position can be obtained by a simple rearranging of the accounts presented earlier. Each of the balances highlights different aspects of a country's performance, policies, and international competitiveness. The groupings and their overlapping relationships can be seen in Table 2.

The balances range from the narrow balance of trade to the comprehensive overall balance. The *trade* balance focuses on exports and imports of goods, which tend to be the largest components in the balance of payments statement, and provides a measure of the country's international competitiveness. Examining the makeup of exports and imports, noting, for example, whether imports consist of consumer goods or capital goods, reveals information about a country's economic strategy and the key determinants of its trade performance. A country heavily reliant upon the export of a single raw material may be vulnerable to changes in world demand and commodity prices, while the fortunes of a country competing in world markets for manufactured goods may rest on domestic wage levels, productivity, and the value of its currency.

The *balance on goods and services* is the point at which the balance of payments ties in with the national income accounts. The balance on goods and services is roughly equivalent to the exports-minus-imports term of the GNP equation: $GNP = C + I + G + (X - M)$. The balance on goods and services measures the extent to which a country is supplying resources to the rest of the world or drawing in resources to satisfy its consumption and investment needs.

The *current account balance* is obtained by adding transfers to the balance on goods and services. The current account balance excludes all capital items and is made up of largely stable components. Therefore it is often used when measuring the effects of economic policies or setting economic goals.

The *basic balance* is designed to give a clearer picture of long-term trends in a country's competitive position. It incorporates long-term capital flows, which usually respond to higher anticipated returns over the long run. Since short-term capital is highly sensitive to relative interest rates, this measure attempts to reduce distortions caused by volatile or speculative capital movements.

The *overall balance* is the one most frequently referred to as "the" balance of payments. The overall balance includes goods, services, transfers, errors and omissions, and the capital accounts except for reserves.[5] In fact, the same total can be obtained simply by totaling the official reserve accounts (obtaining what is called the *official settlements balance*) and changing the sign. Because information about reserve changes is more precise and readily available, the balance is often calculated this way. The overall balance measures the imbalance between sources and uses of foreign exchange, which is financed through the loss or accumulation of reserves. Because the overall balance focuses on the use of reserves, it tends to be more relevant under a fixed exchange rate system in which reserve changes play a critical role. Under a system of freely floating exchange rates, a nation's foreign exchange rate (the value of its currency in terms of foreign purchasing power) theoretically changes to bring sources and uses into balance, and in theory there is no need for reserves. In practice, however, floating rate regimes are rarely pure. Some monetary authorities use reserves to intervene in foreign exchange markets as a way to alter the relative value of their currencies. Moreover, a developing country may not allow its currency to float in a floating rate system, but

---

[5]The overall balance is not always calculated on a consistent basis. In some cases, particular foreign assets may be included in reserves, while in other cases these assets are placed in the capital account. The OECD, for example, includes short-term foreign assets and liabilities of the private monetary sector in its definition of reserves, and excludes them from the overall balance.

will instead tie its currency to that of a major trading partner. As a consequence, most developing countries are in need of reserves in both fixed and floating rate regimes.

Reflecting the fact that no particular balance, positive or negative, tells the whole story of a country's balance of payments situation, the trend has been to deemphasize the standard balances. The intent is to force the user to examine the individual accounts, to identify the factors affecting each account, and to look at the patterns as well as the levels of international flows of real resources and capital. With practice and with attention to a country's context, goals, and domestic economic performance, a careful reading of the balance of payments is an important element of country analysis.

An Introduction to the Balance of Payments

Exhibit 1 Balance of Payments Worksheet ($ M)

	1959	1960
1. Trade balance	972	4,736
2. Services, net	75	228
3. Balance on goods and services	1,047	4,964
4. Unilateral transfers, net	−2,481	−2,565
5. Current balance	−1,434	2,399
6. Long-term capital, net	−2,798	−4,299
7. Basic balance	−4,232	−1,900
8. Short-term capital, net	2,485	49
9. Errors and omissions	412	−592
10. Overall balance[a]	−1,335	−2,443
11. Balance on official settlements	1,335	2,443
12. IMF position, net	260	741
13. Official gold and foreign exchange reserves	1,075	1,702

[a]This overall balance calculation differs from the OECD calculation found in Exhibit 2 of the "Kennedy and the Balance of Payments" case. Reserves in the above presentation (Lines 12 and 13) are narrowly defined to include only the IMF position and official gold and foreign exchange reserves. The OECD definition of reserves is broader. It also includes private monetary institutions' short-term assets and liabilities and central monetary institutions' other liabilities and assets.

Discussion Questions for Case and Note

1. Calculate and analyze the U.S. payment balances for 1960 using the worksheet in Exhibit 1 of the note and Exhibits 1 and 2 of the case.
2. What were President Kennedy's balance of payments problems and how are they reflected in the statistics?
3. What policy options were available to President Kennedy?

Bibliography

Kenen, Peter B., *The International Economy* (Englewood Cliffs, NJ: Prentice-Hall, 1985). Chapters 10 and 18 describe the political economy of international trade and money in the years following World War II.

Rodriguez, Rita M., and E. Eugene Carter, *International Financial Management*, 2nd ed. (Englewood Cliffs, NJ: Prentice-Hall, 1979). Chapters 2, 3, and 4 describe the balance of payments accounts, their determinants, and the options available to policymakers. The accounting detail is comparable to the case in this chapter, but the economic analysis is slightly more advanced than that expected for this case.

Solomon, Robert, *The International Monetary System, 1945–1981* (New York: Harper & Row, 1982). A more detailed account of the international events during the late 1950s can be found in this excellent history. See Chapter II for an account of the European and Japanese actions under the Bretton Woods system at the time of this chapter's case.

Vernon, Raymond, and Louis T. Wells, Jr., *Manager in the International Economy*, 4th ed. (Englewood Cliffs, NJ: Prentice-Hall, 1981). Chapters 4 and 5 discuss the balance of payments flows of goods and money. A comparison of corporate accounts and balance of payments accounts can be found on pages 181–185.

CHAPTER 15
The Collapse of Fixed Exchange Rates

The body of this chapter's case, "Nixon's New Economic Policy: 1971," is a speech by President Nixon delivered on August 15, 1971, to announce a dramatic change in his economic game plan. To address the domestic problem of inflation, he instituted a wage and price freeze followed by controls on any subsequent increases. The package was supplemented by various fiscal measures designed to increase employment. To address the international problem, which he said was "speculation," his primary move was to suspend the convertibility of the dollar into gold or other reserve assets, although exchange rates were to remain "fixed."

Though the class discussion could turn to the efficacy of wage and price controls, the primary objective of the case is to study the factors contributing to the eventual breakdown of the fixed exchange rate system as institutionalized by the Bretton Woods agreement. The domestic portion of Nixon's new economic policy is relevant for this objective to the extent that the domestic and international problems were interrelated. It is interesting to speculate why Nixon linked the domestic and international problems as he did in this speech.

A study of the events leading up to the speech are useful as an illustration of the process of institutional change. Establishing or terminating an international monetary system is a momentous undertaking. Consider the motivations for this speech and the alternatives available.

Case
Nixon's New Economic Policy: 1971

Soon after he won his narrow victory for the presidency in 1968, Richard
Nixon announced his economic program to deal with the inflation and balance of payments problems. It was an appeal to "fundamental economics"—
a strong budget surplus and monetary restraint coupled with a dismantling of
a network of direct capital controls.[1] The program resulted in the recession
of 1970, but it was not successful in breaking inflationary expectations entrenched through years of rapid expansion in the late 1960s.

The response of U.S. corporations and banks to the monetary tightening in 1969 was to abstain from depositing funds in the U.S. markets at interest rates limited by the Regulation Q ceiling and to abstain from borrowing
funds in the U.S. markets at high market interest rates; instead they would
deposit or borrow dollars in the Eurodollar market.[2] Because American
banks were able to circumvent the credit constraints of the Federal Reserve
by borrowing "unregulated" dollars from overseas and then continuing their
lending unchecked, the Fed imposed a reserve requirement on such borrowings in September 1969 in order to regain monetary control. In 1969, $15 bil-
lion came into the United States through the Eurodollar markets. During the
recession of 1970, interest rates fell as a result of the Fed's stimulative attempt to revive economic activity and to offset the consequences of the collapse in June of Penn Central, one of America's largest corporations. As a
result of the reserve requirement and the higher relative interest rates
abroad, the Eurodollar inflow was down to $8 billion in 1970 and to only $2
billion by mid-1971.[3]

In February 1971, President Nixon appointed John Connally, the refined, articulate, self-confident former lawyer and Democratic governor of
Texas, as Treasury Secretary. Connally soon became the administration's
chief economic spokesperson, presenting a strong viewpoint of economic
nationalism. This was evident when he spoke to an international conference
of central bankers assembled at Munich in late May. His message was that
foreign leaders must do their share in solving the problems of the Bretton
Woods system by removing trade restrictions and accepting greater defense
burdens; the United States would not devalue. The United States saw this

This case was prepared by Associate Professor Michael G. Rukstad.
Copyright © 1985 by the President and Fellows of Harvard College
Harvard Business School case 9-386-063

[1]For details, see John Rosenblum, "Nixon Economic Strategy—1969," Harvard Business
School case 8-378-258.

[2]A Eurodollar deposit or a Eurodollar loan is a dollar-denominated deposit or a dollar-
denominated loan held by a bank outside the United States. Eurodollar deposits are not
subject to Regulation Q ceilings.

[3]Martin Mayer, *The Fate of the Dollar* (New York: Times Books, 1980), 173.

not as a problem with the dollar but as a problem with other currencies. Earlier in the month the Bretton Woods system had nearly collapsed when Germany and the Netherlands allowed their currencies to float upward temporarily because of their unwillingness to continue massive purchases "in defense of the dollar." The United States did not want to appear enthusiastic about this move, with its minor effect on U.S. balance of payments, for fear it would encourage speculation against the dollar.[4] After a minor realignment of European currencies in the next few weeks, a fragile balance was regained.

But it was not until problems arose with the trade balance in mid-1971 that the administration changed its attitude from complacency to concern.[5] A major automobile strike at the end of 1970 hurt the trade balance, which then continually deteriorated until, by the spring of 1971, it became a deficit for the first time since 1893. The administration received many analyses of the trade problem. Some presidential advisers, such as Commerce Secretary Maury Stans and Pete Peterson, formally of Bell & Howell, assigned blame to decreased U.S. competitiveness, particularly vis-à-vis the Japanese.[6] Others, like Congressman Henry Reuss of the Joint Economic Committee, called for a realignment of the currencies, including a dollar devaluation if necessary. Finally, there was a pitch for wage and price controls, with only indirect reference to trade problems, from such diverse sources as the AFL-CIO, the Business Council, Chairman Arthur Burns of the Fed, and 50 percent of the American public, according to the Gallop poll of July 15, 1971.

In late June, Secretary Connally presented the administration's "four no's": no wage and price controls, no wage and price review board, no tax cut, and no spending increases. It was a reaffirmation of fundamental economics. But in a press conference on August 5, Nixon said he would keep an "open mind" on wage and price controls. A few days earlier, after steel companies announced an 8 percent price increase, a decision to abandon his anti-inflation policy, known as "gradualism," was reached privately with Connally and George Shultz of the Office of Management and Budget.

On the weekend of August 13, Nixon and his advisers met at Camp David in Maryland to discuss the details of his New Economic Policy.[7] President Nixon mused in his memoirs, "As I worked with Bill Safire on my speech that weekend, I wondered how the headlines would read: Would it be 'Nixon Acts Boldly'? Or would it be "Nixon Changes Mind'?" On Sunday night, August 15, 1971, President Nixon delivered the following address on television.

---

[4]Robert Solomon, *The International Monetary System, 1945-1981* (New York: Harper & Row, 1982), 179.

[5]Ibid., 176.

[6]The Japanese already feared a crumbling of their "special relationship" with the United States. Without even informing the Sato government, President Nixon announced in May that he would go to China the following year, a major shift in American foreign policy.

[7]Nixon and his advisers apparently did not notice the similarity, though in name only, with Lenin's New Economic Policy (NEP) of 1921.

Presidential Message—August 15, 1971[8]

Good evening,

I have addressed the Nation a number of times over the past two years on the problems of ending a war. Because of the progress we have made toward achieving that goal, this Sunday evening is an appropriate time for us to turn our attention to the challenges of peace.

America today has the best opportunity in this century to achieve two of its greatest ideals: to bring about a full generation of peace, and to create a new prosperity without war.

This not only requires bold leadership ready to take bold action— it calls forth the greatness in a great people.

Prosperity without war requires action on three fronts: We must create more and better jobs; we must stop the rise in the cost of living; we must protect the dollar from the attacks of international money speculators.

We are going to take that action—not timidly, not half-heartedly, and not in piecemeal fashion. We are going to move forward to the new prosperity without war as befits a great people—all together, and along a broad front.

The time has come for a new economic policy for the United States. Its targets are unemployment, inflation, and international speculation. This is how we are going to attack them.

Unemployment

First, on the subject of jobs. We all know why we have an unemployment problem. Two million workers have been eased from the Armed Forces and defense plants because of the success in winding down the war in Vietnam. Putting those people back to work is one of the challenges of peace, and we have begun to make progress. Our unemployment rate today is below the average of the four peacetime years of the 1960s.

But we can and must do better than that.

The time has come for American industry, which has produced more jobs at higher real wages than any other industrial system in history, to embark on a bold program of new investment in production for peace.

To give that system a powerful new stimulus, I shall ask the Congress, when it reconvenes after its summer recess, to consider as its first priority the enactment of the Job Development Act of 1971.

I will propose to provide the strongest short-term incentive in our history to invest in new machinery and equipment that will create new jobs for Americans: A 10 percent Job Development Credit for one year, effective as of today, with a 5 percent credit after August 15, 1972. This

[8]Text of President Richard M. Nixon's August 15, 1971, announcement of changes in economic policy as made available by the White House.

tax credit for investment in new equipment will not only generate new jobs; it will raise productivity and it will make our goods more competitive in the years ahead.

Repeal of Automobile Tax

Second, I will propose to repeal the 7 percent excise tax on automobiles, effective today. This will mean a reduction in price of about $200 per car. I shall insist that the American auto industry pass this tax reduction on to the nearly 8 million customers who are buying automobiles this year. Lower prices will mean that more people will be able to afford new cars, and every additional 100,000 cars sold means 25,000 new jobs.

Income Tax Exemption

Third, I propose to speed up the personal income tax exemptions scheduled for January 1, 1973, to January 1, 1972—so that taxpayers can deduct an extra $50 for each exemption one year earlier than planned. This increase in consumer spending power will provide a strong boost to the economy in general and to employment in particular.

The tax reductions I am recommending, together with the broad upturn of the economy which has taken place in the first half of this year, will move us strongly forward toward a goal this nation has not reached since 1956, 15 years ago—prosperity with full employment in peacetime.

Looking to the future, I have directed the Secretary of the Treasury to recommend to the Congress in January new tax proposals for stimulating research and development of new industries and new technologies to help provide the 20 million new jobs that America needs for the young people who will be coming into the job market in the next decade.

Reductions in Federal Spending

To offset the loss of revenue from these tax cuts which directly stimulate new jobs, I have ordered today a $4.7 billion cut in Federal spending.

Tax cuts to stimulate employment must be matched by spending cuts to restrain inflation. To check the rise in the cost of government, I have ordered a postponement of pay raises and a 5 percent cut in government personnel.

I have ordered a 10 percent cut in foreign economic aid.

In addition, since the Congress has already delayed action on two of the great initiatives of this Administration, I will ask Congress to amend my proposals to postpone the implementation of Revenue Sharing for three months and Welfare Reform for one year.

In this way, I am reordering our budget priorities to concentrate more on achieving full employment.

Cost of Living

The second indispensable element of the new prosperity is to stop the rise in the cost of living.

One of the cruelest legacies of the artificial prosperity produced by war is inflation. Inflation robs every American. The 20 million who are retired and living on fixed incomes are particularly hard hit. Homemakers find it harder than ever to balance the family budget. And 80 million wage-earners have been on a treadmill. In the four war years between 1965 and 1969 your wage increases were completely eaten up by price increases. Your paychecks were higher, but you were no better off.

We have made progress against the rise in the cost of living. From the high point of 6 percent a year in 1969, the rise in consumer prices has been cut to 4 percent in the first half of 1971. But just as is the case in our fight against unemployment, we can and we must do better than that.

The time has come for decisive action—action that will break the vicious circle of spiraling prices and costs.

Wage-Price Freeze

I am today ordering a freeze on all prices and wages throughout the United States for a period of 90 days. In addition, I call upon corporations to extend the wage-price freeze to all dividends.

I have today appointed a Cost of Living Council within the Government. I have directed this Council to work with leaders of labor and business to set up the proper mechanism for achieving continued price and wage stability after the 90-day freeze is over.

Let me emphasize two characteristics of this action: First, it is temporary. To put the strong, vigorous American economy into a permanent straitjacket would lock in unfairness; it would stifle the expansion of our free enterprise system. And second, while the wage-price freeze will be backed by Government sanctions, if necessary, it will not be accompanied by the establishment of a huge price control bureaucracy. I am relying on the voluntary cooperation of all Americans—each one of you—workers, employers, consumers—to make this freeze work.

Working together, we will break the back of inflation, and we will do it without the mandatory wage and price controls that crush economic and personal freedom.

Freeing the Dollar

The third indispensable element in building the new prosperity is closely related to creating new jobs and halting inflation. We must protect the position of the American dollar as a pillar of monetary stability around the world.

In the past seven years, there has been an average of one international monetary crisis every year. Who gains from these crises? Not the workingman; not the investors; and not the real producers of wealth. The gainers are international money speculators. Because they thrive on crises, they help to create them.

In recent weeks, the speculators have been waging an all-out war on the American dollar. The strength of a nation's currency is based on the strength of that nation's economy—and the American economy is by far the strongest in the world. Accordingly, I have directed the Secretary of the Treasury to take the action necessary to defend the dollar against the speculators.

I have directed Secretary Connally to suspend temporarily the convertibility of the dollar into gold or other reserve assets, except in amounts and conditions determined to be in the interest of monetary stability and in the best interests of the United States.

Now what is this action, which is very technical? What does it mean for you?

Let me lay to rest the bugaboo of what is called devaluation.

If you want to buy a foreign car or take a trip abroad, market conditions may cause your dollar to buy slightly less. But if you are among the overwhelming majority of Americans who buy American-made products in America, your dollar will be worth just as much tomorrow as it is today.

The effect of this action, in other words, will be to stabilize the dollar.

Now this action will not win us any friends among the international money traders. But our primary concern is with the American workers, and with fair competition around the world.

To our friends abroad, including the many responsible members of the international banking community who are dedicated to stability and the flow of trade, I give this assurance: The United States has always been, and will continue to be, a forward-looking and trustworthy trading partner. In full cooperation with the International Monetary Fund and those who trade with us, we will press for the necessary reforms to set up an urgently needed new international monetary system. Stability and equal treatment is in everybody's best interest. I am determined that the American dollar must never again be hostage in the hands of the international speculators.

Import Tax

I am taking one further step to protect the dollar, to improve our balance of payments, and to increase sales for Americans. As a temporary measure, I am today imposing an additional tax of 10 percent on goods imported into the United States. This is a better solution for international trade than direct controls on the amount of imports.

This import tax is a temporary action. It isn't directed against any other country. It is an action to make certain that American products will not be at a disadvantage because of unfair exchange rates. When the unfair treatment is ended, the import tax will end as well.

As a result of these actions, the product of American labor will be more competitive, and the unfair edge that some of our foreign competition has had will be removed. That is a major reason why our trade balance has eroded over the past fifteen years.

At the end of World War II the economies of the major industrial nations of Europe and Asia were shattered. To help them get on their feet and to protect their freedom, the United States has provided over the past 25 years $143 billion in foreign aid. This was the right thing for us to do.

Today, largely with our help, they have regained their vitality. They have become our strong competitors, and we welcome their success. But now that other nations are economically strong, the time has come for them to bear their fair share of the burden of defending freedom around the world. The time has come for exchange rates to be set straight and for the major nations to compete as equals. There is no longer any need for the United States to compete with one hand tied behind her back.

New Economic Policy

The range of actions I have taken and proposed tonight—on the job front, on the inflation front, on the monetary front—is the most comprehensive New Economic Policy to be undertaken by this nation in four decades.

We are fortunate to live in a nation with an economic system capable of producing for its people the highest standard of living in the world; a system flexible enough to change its ways dramatically when circumstances call for change; and most important—a system resourceful enough to produce prosperity with freedom and opportunity unmatched in the history of nations.

The purposes of the government actions I have announced tonight are to lay the basis for renewed confidence, to make it possible for us to compete fairly with the rest of the world, to open the door to a new prosperity.

But government, with all its powers, does not hold the key to the success of a people. That key, my fellow Americans, is in your hands.

A nation, like a person, has to have a certain inner drive in order to succeed. In economic affairs, that inner drive is called the competitive spirit.

Every action I have taken tonight is designed to nurture and stimulate that competitive spirit; to help us snap out of that self-doubt and self-disparagement that saps our energy and erodes our confidence in ourselves.

Whether this nation stays number one in the world's economy or resigns itself to second, third, or fourth place; whether we as a people have faith in ourselves, or lose that faith; whether we hold fast to the strength that makes peace and freedom possible in this world, or lose our grip—all that depends on you, on your competitive spirit, your sense of personal destiny, your pride in your country and in yourself.

We can be certain of this: As the threat of war recedes, the challenge of peaceful competition in the world will greatly increase.

We welcome competition, because America is at her greatest when she is called on to compete.

As there always have been in our history, there will be voices urging us to shrink from that challenge of competition, to build a protective wall around ourselves, to crawl into a shell as the rest of the world moves ahead.

Two hundred years ago a man wrote in his diary these words: "Many thinking people believe America has seen its best days." That was written in 1775, just before the American Revolution, at the dawn of the most exciting era in the history of man. Today we hear the echoes of those voices, preaching a gospel of gloom and defeat, saying the same thing: "We have seen our best days."

I say, let Americans reply: "Our best days lie ahead."

As we move into a generation of peace, as we blaze the trail toward the new prosperity, I say to every American: Let us raise our spirits. Let us raise our sights. Let all of us contribute all we can to the great and good country that has contributed so much to the progress of mankind.

Let us invest in our nation's future; and let us revitalize that faith in ourselves that built a great nation in the past, and will shape the world of the future.

Thank you, and good evening.

Nixon's New Economic Policy: 1971

Exhibit 1 Gross National Product and Prices—Percent Change from Preceding Period: 1969–1971 (III)

	Annual Percent Change		Quarterly Percent Change, Seasonally Adjusted at Annual Rates										
	1969	1970	1969				1970				1971		
			I	II	III	IV	I	II	III	IV	I	II	III
Gross national product:													
Current dollars	7.6	5.0	7.7	7.5	8.2	3.1	4.1	5.1	7.1	1.8	15.0	7.9	6.5
Constant dollars	2.7	−0.4	3.4	1.9	1.9	−2.3	−2.1	0.5	2.9	−4.3	9.1	2.9	3.6
Implicit price deflator	4.8	5.5	4.2	5.5	6.1	5.5	6.4	4.6	4.1	6.4	5.5	4.9	2.8
Chain price index	4.9	5.3	4.5	4.9	6.6	5.3	6.0	5.0	3.8	5.5	6.8	5.2	3.6

Source: *Economic Report of the President, 1972* (Washington, DC: U.S. Government Printing Office, 1972).

Nixon's New Economic Policy: 1971

Exhibit 2 Unemployment as Percent of Civilian Labor Force: 1967–1971
(Seasonally Adjusted)

Year or Month	Percent
1967	3.8
1968	3.6
1969	3.5
1970	4.9
1970 Jan.	3.9
Apr.	4.7
July	5.0
Oct.	5.5
1971 Jan.	6.0
Apr.	6.0
July	5.9

Source: *Economic Report of the President, 1972, 1973* (Washington, DC: U.S. Government Printing Office, 1972, 1973).

Nixon's New Economic Policy: 1971

Exhibit 3 Labor Productivity, Wages, and Unit Labor Costs: 1968–1971 (III)

Year or Quarter	Output per Man-Hour[a]		Compensation per Man-Hour[b]		Unit Labor Costs[c]	
	Total Private	Private Nonfarm	Total Private	Private Nonfarm	Total Private	Private Nonfarm
1968	2.9	2.9	7.6	7.3	4.6	4.3
1969	0.4	−0.1	7.6	7.0	7.1	7.2
1970	1.0	0.6	7.6	7.2	6.5	6.6
Seasonally Adjusted Annual Rates						
1970: I	−1.3	−1.8	6.9	6.5	8.3	8.4
II	4.3	4.7	5.9	7.2	1.6	2.4
III	6.9	6.9	9.4	9.0	2.4	2.0
IV	−1.9	−3.1	5.4	4.6	7.4	8.0
1971: I	7.5	7.4	9.2	9.1	1.7	1.5
II	2.2	3.2	6.2	7.5	3.9	4.2
III	3.2	2.5	5.8	5.2	2.6	2.5

[a]Output per man-hour is a measure of labor productivity.

[b]Wages and salaries of employees plus employers' contribution for social insurance and private benefit plans; also includes an estimate of wages, salaries, and supplemental payments for the self-employed.

[c]Unit labor costs are approximately equal to the compensation per man-hour in excess of output per man-hour or wages in excess of productivity gains.

Source: *Economic Report of the President, 1973* (Washington, DC: U.S. Government Printing Office, 1973).

Nixon's New Economic Policy: 1971

Exhibit 4   U.S. Balance of Payments: 1965–1971 (III)
(Millions of dollars)

Year or Quarter	Merchandise[a,b]			Military Transactions			Net Investment Income		Net Travel and Transportation Expenditures	Other Services, Net	Balance on Goods and Services[a]	Remittances, Pensions, and Other Unilateral Transfers[a]	Balance on Current account
	Exports	Imports	Net Balance	Direct Expenditures	Sales	Net Balance	Private[c]	U.S. Gov.-ernment					
	1	2	3	4	5	6	7	8	9	10	11	12	13
1965	26,438	−21,496	4,942	−2,952	830	−2,122	5,274	21	−1,318	301	7,038	−2,835	4,263
1966	29,287	−25,463	3,824	−3,764	829	−2,935	5,331	44	−1,380	286	5,170	−2,890	2,280
1967	30,638	−25,821	3,817	−4,378	1,240	−3,138	5,847	40	−1,763	334	5,136	−3,084	2,055
1968	33,576	−32,964	612	−4,535	1,392	−3,143	6,157	63	−1,565	302	2,425	−2,909	−484
1969	36,417	−35,796	621	−4,856	1,512	−3,344	5,820	155	−1,784	442	1,911	−2,946	−1,035
1970	41,963	−39,799	2,164	−4,852	1,478	−3,374	6,376	−115	−2,051	574	3,563	−3,209	356
Seasonally Adjusted													
1970: I	10,231	−9,731	500	−1,180	273	−907	1,559	33	−428	141	898	−765	133
II	10,565	−9,831	734	−1,259	441	−818	1,458	−1	−533	127	967	−773	194
III	10,705	−9,968	737	−1,210	329	−881	1,645	−66	−599	153	989	−821	168
IV	10,462	−10,269	193	−1,203	436	−767	1,714	−81	−501	154	712	−849	−137
1971: I	11,017	−10,728	289	−1,175	510	−665	1,899	−101	−498	212	1,136	−791	345
II	10,710	−11,722	−1,012	−1,214	516	−698	2,352	−161	−625	180	36	−846	−810
III	11,479	−11,951	−472	−1,198	474	−724	2,033	−327	−606	182	91	−946	−855

[a]Excludes military grants.

[b]Adjusted from census data for differences in timing and coverage.

[c]Includes fees and royalties from U.S. direct investments abroad or from foreign direct investments in the United States.

Source: *Economic Report of the President, 1973* (Washington, DC: U.S. Government Printing Office, 1973).

Exhibit 4 (Continued)

Year or Quarter	Long-term Capital Flows, Net U.S. Government[d]	Private[e]	Balance on Current Account and Long-Term Capital	Non-liquid Short-Term Private Capital Flows, Net[e]	Allocations of Special Drawing Rights	Errors and Omissions, Net	Net Liquidity Balance	Liquid Private Capital Flows, Net[e]	Official Reserve Transactions Balance	Changes in Liabilities to Foreign Official Agencies, Net[f]	Changes in U.S. Official Reserve Assets, Net[g]	U.S. Official Reserve Assets, Net (End of Period)
	14	15	16	17	18	19	20	21	22	23	24	25
1965	−1,532	−4,577	−1,846	−154	–	−476	−2,477	1,188	−1,289	67	1,222	15,450
1966	−1,469	−2,555	−1,744	−104	–	−302	−2,151	2,370	219	−787	563	14,882
1967	−2,424	−2,912	−3,280	−522	–	−881	−4,683	1,265	−3,418	3,366	52	14,830
1968	−2,159	1,198	−1,444	230	–	−399	−1,610	3,251	1,641	−761	−880	15,710
1969	−1,926	50	−3,011	−640	–	−2,470	−6,122	8,824	2,702	−1,515	−1,187	16,964[i]
1970	−2,018	−1,398	−3,059	−482	867	−1,174	−3,851	−5,988	−9,839	7,362	2,477	14,487
					Seasonally Adjusted							Unadjusted
1970: I	−462	−922	−1,251	−247	217	−51	−1,332	−1,461	−2,793	2,529	264	17,350
II	−563	−236	−605	−56	217	−410	−854	−1,211	−2,065	1,260	805	16,328
III	−324	−191	−347	42	717	−677	−765	−1,104	1,869	1,285	384	15,527
IV	−670	−49	−856	−221	216	−37	−898	−2,212	−3,110	2,286	824	14,487
1971: I	−702	−922	−1,279	−534	180	−944	−2,577	−2,848	5,425	4,743	682	14,342
II	−584	−1,605	−2,999	−315	179	−2,586	−5,721	−745	−6,466	5,807	659	13,504
III	−558	−1,883	−3,296	−883	179	5,380	−9,380	−2,551	−11,931	10,737	1,194	12,131

[d]Excludes liabilities to foreign official reserve agencies.

[e]Private foreigners exclude the International Monetary Fund (IMF) but include other international and regional organizations.

[f]Includes liabilities to foreign official agencies reported by U.S. government and U.S. banks, plus U.S. liabilities to the IMF arising from reversible gold sales to, and gold deposits with, the United States.

[g]Official reserve assets include gold, special drawing rights, convertible currencies, and the U.S. gold tranche position in the IMF.

[h]Not available separately.

[i]Includes gain of $67 million resulting from revaluation of the German mark in October 1969.

Discussion Questions for Case

1. Evaluate the situation facing President Nixon at the beginning of August 1971. How had the situation changed since 1969?
2. Evaluate President Nixon's actions of August 15, 1971. Were they appropriate to the situation? What were the likely outcomes?

Bibliography

Bergsten, C. Fred, *The Dilemmas of the Dollar, The Economics and Politics of U.S. International Monetary Policy* (New York: New York University Press, 1975). This is a scholarly book on the political economy of international monetary issues. A detailed understanding of the international role of the dollar can be gained from reading Chapters 4, 5, and 6.

Kenen, Peter B., *The International Economy* (Englewood Cliffs, NJ: Prentice-Hall, 1985). Chapters 10 and 18 describe the political economy of international trade and money since the beginning of the Bretton Woods system. These chapters provide continuity between the case studies in this volume.

Odell, John S., *U.S. International Monetary Policy: Markets, Power, and Ideas as Sources of Change* (Princeton, NJ: Princeton University Press, 1982). Chapter 4 describes the reasons for the change in policy under Nixon in 1971.

Okun, Arthur M., "Political Economy: Some Lessons of Recent Experience," *Journal of Money, Credit, & Banking* (February 1972), Part I, 23–34. Okun presents his views of the Nixon game plan from 1969 to 1971 and the change in policy on August 15, 1971. He presents an argument for policy activism.

Solomon, Robert, *The International Monetary System, 1945–1981* (New York: Harper & Row, 1982). The history of the events prior and subsequent to Nixon's August 15, 1971, announcement are recounted in detail in Chapters XI and XII.

Weber, Arnold R., *In Pursuit of Price Stability: The Wage-Price Freeze of 1971* (Washington, DC: Brookings Institution, 1973). For a more detailed account of the events leading to the decision to announce the freeze, see Chapter 1 of this book.

CHAPTER 16

Management of Flexible Exchange Rates

In March 1973, all major industrial countries allowed their exchange rates to float. Flexible exchange rates have been extremely volatile since that time, with prolonged periods of depreciation or appreciation. This has presented both government and corporate decision makers with a new set of problems. The purpose of this chapter's case, "The Decline of the Dollar: 1978," is to illustrate the factors that determine exchange rate movements and the role of government intervention in the foreign exchange market.

This case study surveys the depreciation of the dollar in 1977 and 1978 during the Carter administration. The events of this period are dramatic and unencumbered by major policy changes or external shocks. The case of the appreciation of the dollar or the pound during different periods in the early 1980s (described in Chapters 3 and 4), though dramatic, is less suitable for introducing exchange rate determination or government intervention, because the second oil shock, financial deregulation and liberalization, and drastic changes in monetary policy have had effects without historical precedent.

Part of the difficulty in determining the changes in exchange rates is keeping track of the numerous fundamental economic forces acting on exchange rates. The note in this chapter, "Exchange Rate Determination," suggests that one consider those transactions on the balance of payments that supply foreign exchange and those transactions for which foreign exchange is demanded. Changes in the international economic environment, expectations of future policies, and government intervention also interact with the fundamental economic determinants of exchange rates.

Case
The Decline of the Dollar: 1978

In 1976, after almost four years of experience with floating rates of exchange among the major industrial nations, the International Monetary Fund sounded an optimistic note about the functioning of the world monetary system:

> [T]he floating among major currencies has been characterized by some reduction in the amplitude of exchange-rate movements. . . . [This reflects] in part the fact that the disturbances in the global pattern of payments have been less severe than during the early period of floating rates; in part, however, they may represent an improvement in the ability of the market mechanism and official policies to cope with the realities of a more flexible exchange rate system.[1]

By early 1978, however, a depreciating dollar seemed to threaten that stability. From early 1977 until October 1978, the effective exchange rate (a weighted average of the exchange rates between the dollar and other currencies) declined by almost 13 percent (see Exhibit 6). Although news of the dollar's decline initially could be found only on the financial pages, not in the headlines, it was, in the words of one Carter administration official, "a very grim business."[2] Policymakers were keenly aware of their limited experience with floating exchange rates. There were two questions they needed to answer if they were going to make the system work. First, why had the U.S. exchange rate declined? And second, what should the government do about it? The answers to these questions depended on the interpretation of the world's experience since the fixed rate system had first been established at the Bretton Woods, New Hampshire, conference of 1945.

Bretton Woods and Its Demise: 1945–1973

Under the Bretton Woods system of fixed exchange rates, which prevailed from 1945 through March 1973, crises had mounted from the early 1960s onward. The provisions of the Bretton Woods system allowed countries to devalue or revalue their currencies in order to correct "fundamental imbalances" in their external payments. Great Britain, for example, after

---

This case was prepared by Research Associate Daniel Pope under the supervision of Associate Professor Michael G. Rukstad.
Copyright © 1984 by the President and Fellows of Harvard College
Harvard Business School case 9-384-116

[1]IMF, *Annual Report, 1976,* 32.

[2]*The Wall Street Journal,* Nov. 1, 1978, 1.

several years of emergency measures to defend the pound sterling at $2.80 in the face of serious payments deficits, devalued sterling by 14.3 percent to $2.40 on November 18, 1967. In the next two years, speculators and investors sold French francs and bought German marks in large quantities, forcing France to devalue the franc in August 1969 by 11.1 percent and the Germans to follow suit with an upward revaluation of the mark by 9.2 percent two months later. (All devaluations and revaluations under Bretton Woods were relative to the dollar.)

The United States also took an active role in controlling the exchange rate of its currency. Faced with accelerating inflation, a balance of payments deficit which was to reach $30 billion in 1971, and outstanding dollar liabilities to foreign governments and central banks of more than $50 billion, President Richard Nixon took decisive action on August 15, 1971. Fearing that foreign holders of dollars would demand gold at the fixed price of $35 an ounce, he announced that the United States would no longer allow foreign central banks and treasuries to trade their dollars for gold. This action directly undermined one of the basic principles of the Bretton Woods system. At the same time, Nixon also imposed a 10 percent surcharge on dutiable American imports (approximately half of total imports). This was akin to a partial devaluation of the dollar, because it raised the price of American purchases from abroad by 10 percent. Finally, the president instituted a 90-day wage and price freeze and subsequent controls aimed at slowing domestic inflation and improving international competitiveness of U.S. goods and services.

In the early seventies, world economic leaders recognized the need for new international monetary arrangements; but they did not, for the most part, wish to abolish fixed exchange rates. In 1969, Undersecretary of the Treasury for Monetary Affairs Paul Volcker had described floating rates as popular "in academic circles, and that's where they can stay."[3] Even the crisis of 1971 had not altered this opinion. Memories of the 1930s, when the fixed rates of the gold-exchange standard had fallen apart, haunted central bankers, finance ministers, and International Monetary Fund officials. In the 1930s, nations had competed in devaluing their currencies in order to take export markets from their competitors. At the same time, they had raised tariffs and other trade barriers, and these steps had stifled international trade and damaged the world economy. Between 1929 and 1933, the gold-exchange standard had been abandoned by 35 nations, including the United Kingdom and Japan in 1931 and the United States in 1933. Many other countries had imposed severe restraints on convertibility of their currencies.

The Nixon announcement of August 15, 1971, provoked fears that some of the travails of the 1930s might be repeated. Within days of Nixon's speech, Pierre-Paul Schweitzer, managing director of the IMF,

---

[3]Cited in Gerald M. Meier, *Problems of a World Monetary Order*, 2d ed. (New York: Oxford University Press, 1982), 129.

warned, "Unless prompt action is taken, the prospect before us is one of disorder and discrimination in currency and trade relationships which will seriously disrupt trade and undermine the system which served the world well . . . for a quarter of a century."[4]

Thus, in December 1971, finance ministers and central bank officials of the major industrial nations (the so-called Group of Ten) convened at the old Smithsonian Institution building in Washington, DC, to work out the new exchange rate parities that almost all believed were needed. The conferees agreed that the United States would raise the dollar price of gold from $35 to $38 an ounce, which effectively devalued the dollar in terms of gold. Since a dollar would now purchase less gold, the existing gold reserves would cover more dollar liabilities. Japan, Germany, and Switzerland consented to revalue their currencies significantly upward (which meant lowering the price of the dollar, and hence gold, in terms of their monies), while the British pound sterling and the French franc remained unchanged. Temporarily, the nations agreed to let currencies trade on financial markets at rates as much as 2.25 percent above and below the newly established parities. Fluctuations beyond that band would require government intervention. This would take the form of the central bank's selling a currency which had appreciated too much or buying one which had fallen too far in value. President Nixon told the television cameras that the Smithsonian accord was "the most significant monetary agreement in the history of the world."[5]

Despite the president's hopes, the Smithsonian agreements lasted little more than a year. In January 1973, Nixon relaxed wage and price controls, and international monetary traders, fearing more rapid inflation in the United States, sold dollars and put their funds into nations with "strong" currencies—Japan, Germany, Switzerland, and the Netherlands. During early February, in the space of less than one week, the German Bundesbank purchased over $5 billion to keep the dollar-mark relationship within the Smithsonian limits. Other nations' currency parities were also threatened by speculative flows. Recognizing that the Smithsonian parities were coming unglued, the Nixon administration sent Paul Volcker around the world to consult with finance ministers. Upon Volcker's return on February 12, 1973, Treasury Secretary George Shultz announced a 10 percent devaluation of the dollar. Meanwhile, most other members of the Group of Ten, led by Switzerland and Germany, gave up their efforts to maintain fixed exchange rates. They allowed their currencies to float, as Canada and the United Kingdom had already done during the previous year.

During this crisis, exchange markets became disorderly and were closed from March 1 through March 18, 1973. When they reopened on

[4]Ibid., 126.

[5]Cited in Robert Solomon, *The International Monetary System: 1945–1981* (New York: Harper & Row, 1981), 208.

March 19, the non-Communist world's major currencies were all floating. Although most smaller nations continued to peg their currency either to the currency of their largest trading partner or to a weighted average of leading currencies, the majority of the world's trade was now carried on among nations with floating exchange rates. (See Exhibit 1 for exchange rate practices.)

Economists in both the Keynesian and monetarist camps looked on floating rates as intrinsically healthy for the world's economy. Under a fixed rate system, they contended, nations had to subordinate domestic monetary policies to the maintenance of the pegged rates. Countries with payments deficits would find their monetary reserves shrinking, and surplus nations would face an influx of funds which might prove inflationary. A payments deficit might also require higher real interest rates at home to attract capital inflows, to cut back on demand for imports, and to lower the price of exports.[6] With flexible rates, the academics said, the price of a nation's currency would adjust to eliminate surpluses and deficits on the international accounts, so that nations could, as they saw fit, employ discretionary monetary and fiscal policy to deal primarily with domestic concerns. Thus it was believed that flexible rates could help to insulate a country from foreign economic shocks.

Academics might like floating rates. But for most policymakers in the early 1970s, such rates were "an inevitable evil for the time being," in the words of the French finance minister. They were necessary because national governments and central banks were unable to preserve fixed rates in the face of massive flows of speculative capital from one currency to another. From the 1950s onward, European nations had removed barriers to capital mobility. Meanwhile, the growth of the Eurocurrency market (which may have reached as much as $150 billion by 1971) and of multinational corporations meant that large amounts of "hot money" were available to seek the currency of the nation where the highest real interest rate was available.

Policymakers viewed floating not as a permanent solution but rather as a temporary expedient. From 1972 through 1974, foreign ministers, central bank officials, and their deputies met in the IMF Committee of Twenty to reconstitute the world's monetary system. Even as floating rates became the norm in the industrial world, the Committee of Twenty continued to assume that fixed rates were the goal of reform. Although "floating rates could provide a useful technique in particular situations," the "Committee recognized that exchange rates must be a matter for international concern and consultation and that in the reformed system, the exchange rate regime should remain based on stable but adjustable par values."[7]

---

[6]See the case in Chapter 13, "The United Kingdom and the Gold Standard: 1925."
[7]Solomon, op. cit., 248.

1973–1976: The Initial Performance of Floating Rates

The economic experience of the mid-1970s was paradoxical. On the one hand, forces quite independent of the world monetary system made these years a stormy era. On the other, the experience of floating rates persuaded even some of the most steadfast proponents of fixed rates that the float was the best way to handle the shocks the world was undergoing. Summarizing the experience, Thomas D. Willett, director of international monetary research at the Treasury Department, concluded: "Under extremely trying circumstances, generalized floating has proven itself to be a sound foundation on which to base the future evolution of the international monetary system."[8]

The shocks to the world economy during these years were many and disparate. Clearly, the single most important blow was the impact of petroleum shortages and the OPEC cartel. The fourfold rise in petroleum prices in late 1973 boosted consumer prices in oil-importing countries and functioned as a "tax" that reduced aggregate demand in these nations. If the industrialized world were to escape recession in the years following the OPEC price hikes of 1973, some means of restoring aggregate demand would have to be found. At the same time, the economies of the industrialized nations suffered a rapid rise in agricultural and raw material prices, which could be blamed on causes as varied as the disappearance of the anchovy from the Pacific Coast of South America (since these fish were used in high-protein animal feed) and the sale of large quantities of American wheat to the Soviet Union at below-market prices.

These "supply shocks" meant simultaneous pressures toward inflation and stagnation. With inflation in the final quarter of 1973 raging at 12 percent in the capitalist industrialized nations, few leaders were eager to pursue expansionary fiscal and monetary policies. By early 1974, real GNP in these nations had begun to slip, and by the spring of 1975 the world was experiencing the worst economic slump since the 1930s.

Despite these woes, the floating exchange rate system seemed to be performing reasonably well. Earlier fears of competitive depreciation of currencies and the imposition of protectionist measures proved largely unfounded. The OPEC financial surplus was recycled into investments in the oil-importing nations, especially the developing nations. However, the trend in the mid-1970s seemed to be toward exchange rate stability. In particular, the dollar's behavior appeared reasonably satisfactory. The dollar did dip sharply in the summer of 1973, a time of rapid American inflation, uncertainty about the Watergate affair, and fears that the dollar was still overvalued. The United States and other nations intervened to support the dollar by purchasing it with other currencies, and its foreign exchange value rose markedly during the last half of 1973. It dipped and

[8]Thomas D. Willett, *Floating Exchange Rates and International Monetary Reform*, American Enterprise Institute Studies, No. 172 (1977), 67.

rose again in 1974 and 1975, but from late 1975 through the autumn of 1977, its effective exchange rate remained in a narrow range, within a few percentage points of the level that had been set at the 1971 Smithsonian accord (see Exhibit 6). When corrected for relative price changes, to give "real" effective exchange rates (a measure of the competitiveness of American goods and services in export markets), the dollar appeared to be even more stable. According to some calculations, the real effective exchange rate at the end of 1977 was the same as it had been in March 1973.[9] (Compare this with the real exchange rates in Exhibit 4.) Major improvements in the U.S. balance of payments had accompanied exchange rate calm. Less reliant on imported energy than its industrialized competitors, the United States actually attaincd a current account surplus each year from 1973 through 1976 (see Exhibit 3).

Although the pound sterling had declined in value very rapidly in 1976, necessitating a large loan to the United Kingdom from the International Monetary Fund, the experience of most industrialized nations had been reasonably favorable. Fluctuations in exchange rates were becoming more moderate and were apparently fulfilling their prescribed function. When a nation's currency depreciated, its international competitive position generally improved and its payments deficit shrank. Similarly, as strong currencies rose in value, their payments surpluses tended to diminish.

Nevertheless, some disquieting problems remained. The industrialized nations had plunged into the recession almost simultaneously, but they climbed out at different rates. The recovery in the United States was more vigorous than in Germany and Japan. American industrial production rose at a 6.9 percent annual rate between the fourth quarter of 1976 and the third quarter of 1977. Germany's industrial production increased at a rate of 1.2 percent during the same period. Japan's rate was also 1.2 percent. Indeed, the United States was the only major industrial nation to achieve its forecast rate of real GNP growth during 1977 (see Exhibit 5). At the same time, American prices began to rise more rapidly (6.1 percent for the U.S. producer price index compared to 1.8 percent for German wholesale industrial prices and only 0.1 percent for Japan's wholesale price index).

Rapid American growth took its toll on the U.S. balance of payments. On the current account, imports increased faster than exports. The nation spent $45 billion on imported petroleum in 1977; combined with a declining surplus on trade in manufactured goods, the oil bill helped put the current account $15.3 billion in deficit. Almost equally important to the overall payments deficit was the negative flow of $13.4 billion on the capital account. Private investors and speculators had transferred over $13 billion of investments and deposits from dollars to other

[9]"Summary Measures of the Dollar's Foreign Exchange Value," *Federal Reserve Bulletin* (October 1978): 788.

currencies. In order to finance this deficit, German, Japanese, and OPEC official dollar holdings increased dramatically (see Exhibits 2 and 3).

1977–1978: The Decline of the Dollar

Onset: "Benign Neglect"

The depreciation of the dollar at the beginning of the new Carter administration in 1977 was at first rather gradual. Until late 1977, the effective exchange rate of the dollar remained near or even above the level it had reached when generalized floating began in March 1973. The decline was not equal against all currencies. For example, the dollar appreciated 9.4 percent against the Canadian dollar and 34.8 percent against the pound sterling between March 1973 and the end of 1977. The decline of the dollar was, properly speaking, its decline against several currencies, notably the German mark, the Japanese yen, and the Swiss franc. The dollar depreciated 25.5 percent against the mark, 10.5 percent against the yen, and 37.9 percent against the Swiss franc from March 1973 to December 1977 (see Exhibits 6 and 4).

To most American policymakers in 1977 and early 1978, this dollar decline was part of the solution, not the problem. Nevertheless, depreciation was not the administration's preferred response to sluggish world growth and the American payments imbalance. The favored method was known as the locomotive theory. First espoused by economists at the Brookings Institution and by the Organization for Economic Cooperation and Development (OECD), the doctrine held that the world's strong economies (notably the United States, Germany, and Japan) should adopt expansionary policies that would raise their growth rates and increase their demand for imports. This would, in turn, stimulate the weaker economies and accelerate world growth, pulling the world economy like a locomotive pulls a train. According to this account, the unwillingness of Japan and Germany to shoulder the burden of pulling the world economic train by stimulating their domestic spending was keeping their imports low, their current accounts in surplus, and their currencies strong. If they continued to refuse to pull, the next best solution was to be found in exchange rate readjustment. A depreciating dollar would at least make American products more competitive in the world market, and more expensive marks and yen would correct the German and Japanese payments surpluses.

The Carter administration feared that Japanese officials were hindering the adjustment process by engaging in a "dirty" float. They were said to be intervening in foreign exchange markets: selling yen and buying dollars in order to keep the yen's value from rising too far. They were doing this, said many critics, in order to protect Japanese export competitiveness (see Exhibit 3). Vice President Walter Mondale headed a trade delegation to Japan in January 1977 and allegedly complained about the dirty float. "We knew what the Japanese were doing, and we told them to knock it off," said C. Fred Bergsten, an economist who accompanied Mondale.[10] At a Paris meeting of the OECD in June 1977, Secretary of the Treasury Michael Blumenthal announced that exchange rate adjustments should "play their appropriate role" in restoring economic equilibrium.

Statements like these in 1977 persuaded foreign exchange dealers that Blumenthal, on behalf of the Carter administration, was "talking down the dollar." Europeans complained of the secretary's "open mouth policy." The top international money trader at the New York Federal Reserve Bank later put it pungently: "Every few days some . . . from Treasury would get up and say that the United States would not intervene to fix the value of the dollar, only to counter disorderly markets. When people heard that, the cry went up: 'Sell the bucks,' "[11] Was Secretary Blumenthal really trying to drive the dollar down? (After he left office, Blumenthal protested that his words had been misinterpreted. All he had meant to say was that the United States favored flexible rates and would not intervene in currency markets in order to peg the dollar at a given level. "I never said that I wanted the dollar to decline," he insisted.)[12]

As the dollar's decline commenced, Federal Reserve Chairman Arthur F. Burns pledged to a House banking subcommittee that the United States would protect the integrity of its currency, both domestically and internationally. A brief rally followed Chairman Burns' pronouncement in August 1977, but the dollar continued to decline. During the second half of 1977, the dollar lost 10.0 percent against the mark, 10.3 percent against the yen, and 18.7 percent against the Swiss franc. But some officials and economists responded that these figures were misleading, since they measured not only the decline of the dollar but also the general appreciation of these strong currencies. Looked at in another light, the dollar's decline was less alarming. The "effective exchange rate" (a weighted average) dropped by only about 5 percent in the second half of 1977 (see Exhibit 6).

In any case, the declining dollar did little to improve the U.S. balance of payments in the short term. The fourth quarter 1977 deficit on the current account was (seasonally adjusted) nearly $7 billion, or close to half the entire year's $15.3 billion deficit. To advocates of the locomotive doctrine, it was galling that German and Japanese current account surpluses in 1977 almost matched the U.S. deficit. In the first quarter of 1978, the American current account was again in deficit by $6.9 billion (see Exhibit 3).

Several reasons were offered to explain the failure of the current

[10]Quoted in Michael Moffitt, *The World's Money* (New York: Simon and Schuster, 1983), 134.

[11]Ibid., 114–115.

[12]Solomon, op. cit., 346.

account balance to respond well to depreciation. First, as William Nordhaus of the Council of Economic Advisers told a Senate committee in June 1978, "Unfortunately, things got worse before they got better. This is the well-known 'J-curve' effect." In the short run, import and export commitments are frequently unchangeable. With depreciation, it will take more dollars to pay for the same volume of imports while export revenues remain stable for the time being.[13] Second, many American exports, especially to Japan, were foodstuffs and raw materials. Demand for these goods, officials pointed out, was often inelastic, so that declining prices in strong currency countries did not greatly stimulate sales. At the same time, Americans who bought Japanese cars, cameras, or electronics equipment often had strong brand preferences. Even the rapid rise of the yen did not prevent Japanese auto sales in the United States from rising by 1 percent.[14]

Finally, as foreign bankers and officials repeatedly pointed out, the U.S. economy was overheated. U.S. growth rates outstripped those of its industrial trading partners, but so did inflation rates. For the United States, consumer prices increased 6.6 percent from March 1977 to March 1978; the corresponding figures for Japan and Germany were 4.3 percent and 3.2 percent.

A Move toward Activism

In its January 1978 report to President Carter, the Council of Economic Advisers restated the administration's belief that flexible rates had worked well: "In summary, while exchange rate fluctuations sometimes have been undesirably large and are often unpleasant reminders about unsatisfactory aspects of underlying economic conditions, the evolution of the system of market-determined exchange rates has been a major achievement of this decade."[15] Moreover, the council argued, official intervention to alter exchange rates was ineffective and undesirable. Private traders, including many of the world's largest commercial banks, have far more foreign exchange at their disposal than do official agencies. When central banks intervene to counteract market trends, they rarely can do more than slow down—at a high cost—the underlying movement. Moreover, intervention to eliminate trends would generally be unwise, because it would retard the process of restoring payments balances that result from exchange rate adjustments.[16] Intervention was proper to counteract short-run, "disorderly market conditions," not longer-term trends.

[13]U.S. Congress, Senate Foreign Relations Committee, *Hearings on the Decline of the Dollar,* 95th Cong., 2d sess., 1978.

[14]*Ward's Automotive Yearbook,* 1979. (Figures are for the five best-selling Japanese brands.)

[15]Council of Economic Advisers, *Economic Report of the President* (Washington, DC: U.S. Government Printing Office, 1978), 134.

[16]Ibid., 121–122.

Yet even before the Council of Economic Advisers' cautions appeared in print, the Carter administration moved to a more active defense of the dollar's value. On January 4, 1978, the Treasury Department announced that it had obtained a $2 billion "swap line" from the German Bundesbank. The new swap arrangement complemented over $20 billion of existing swap lines between the Federal Reserve and other central banks. Under swap arrangements, nations have standby lines of credit in their partners' currencies. They can support their own currency by borrowing foreign money on these lines of credit and then selling the foreign exchange to purchase their own money.

That very afternoon of January 4, the Treasury, the Fed, and foreign central banks jointly intervened to support the value of the dollar (see Exhibit 9). Even before the Fed could execute the intervention, the announcement itself had lowered the value of the mark by about 4 percent against the dollar. The dollar gained a full 6 percent against the Swiss franc. One American commercial bank official described the intervention as a "fundamental change in exchange policy," but a European official perceived it as merely a "bluff."[17]

Two days after the interventions began, the Federal Reserve raised its discount rate from 6 percent to 6.5 percent because "the recent disorder in foreign exchange markets constitutes a threat to orderly expansion of the domestic and international economy." The increase would, it was hoped, cool off domestic inflation and improve the capital account of the balance of payments by attracting funds from abroad. But some observers worried that the cure was worse than the disease and that tighter money might mean economic recession at home. Arthur Okun, a respected economic adviser to Democratic presidents, said he was "surprised, disappointed, and very concerned" by the Fed's step.[18]

In foreign exchange markets such statements and reports of discord within the administration heightened doubts that the dollar's fall was over. Despite frequent official support during January, the dollar fell back somewhat from the levels it had reached on January 5, directly after the initial intervention. The decline continued during February and the first part of March 1978.

As the spring of 1978 approached, however, there was a wave of optimism. President Carter and Chancellor Helmut Schmidt both asserted that their nations' economic policies were being harmonized. On March 13, the German Bundesbank placed another $2 billion worth of marks in the Fed's swap line, and the U.S. Treasury announced that it was prepared to acquire dollar support funds from the IMF as well. In April, President Carter announced that the United States would sell 300,000 ounces of gold each month for the next year. Putting this gold on the market was designed to raise the value of dollars in terms of gold

[17]*New York Times*, Jan. 5, 1978, D7.
[18]*New York Times*, Jan. 13, 1978, D1.

and, it was hoped, other currencies. The next month, the Fed tightened domestic credit another notch by raising the discount rate from 6.5 percent to 7 percent. In June, G. William Miller, who had recently been appointed chairman of the Fed's Board of Governors, addressed a businessmen's group in Zurich; he predicted that the worst of the dollar's troubles were past. Newspapers reported a generally favorable response from the audience. A few days later, the IMF issued an optimistic forecast of the American balance of payments. Figures later showed that the second quarter's current account deficit was already shrinking. It was $3.3 billion, less than half the first quarter's deficit (see Exhibit 3).

Nevertheless, in June 1978 the dollar slipped again from its springtime plateau. The weakening was particularly severe against the yen, whose price in dollars rose by more than 8 percent in June alone. The economic summit meeting in Bonn in July was no help. Shortly before it convened, the head of Japan's Economic Planning Agency told reporters that there was "great disappointment that President Carter seems to be going to Bonn empty-handed," unwilling to offer assurances that the United States would reduce energy imports and lower inflation rates.[19] Americans pointed to a forecast that the Japanese current account surplus for 1978 would be a whopping $18 billion, three times the official Japanese estimate. At the Bonn gatherings, the Germans pledged to introduce proposals in Parliament that would increase government spending to stimulate the economy. Japan promised to reduce its trade surplus within a year by increasing domestic demand and voluntarily restraining exports. But Prime Minister Fukuda, "stern-faced and tight-lipped," at a press conference, refused to say that these measures would really solve the surplus problem.[20] Carter, for his part, could offer little; from a peak of 8.8 million barrels a day in 1977, the United States vowed to reduce daily oil imports by 2.5 million barrels by 1985. Foreign exchange markets reacted to the Bonn summit with disdain, and the dollar continued to slide down.

By mid-August 1978, signs of distress were mounting. Congressman Henry Reuss, chairman of the Joint Economic Committee, was grimly warning, "We must not panic."[21] The influential Reuss, an unwavering supporter of floating rates since the early 1970s, was a voice who could not go unheeded. The next day, when President Carter expressed concern about the decline of the dollar during his news conference, one banker commented, "I thought he said nothing and he said it badly."[22] Accompanying the president's words, however, were actions to support the dollar. Official gold sales were tripled. The Fed raised the discount rate in July and boosted it again in August to 7.75 percent "in view of recent

[19]*New York Times*, July 9, 1978, A1.
[20]*New York Times*, July 18, 1978, D13.
[21]*New York Times*, Aug. 16, 1978, 145.
[22]Solomon, op. cit., 348.

disorderly conditions in foreign exchange markets."[23] Both the Bundesbank and the Fed intervened several times in August to support the dollar and hold down the value of the mark (see Exhibit 9). Nevertheless, throughout the second half of the month the mark cost more than 50¢, an important symbol of the weakening dollar.

American policymakers in the late summer found the situation frustrating. U.S. interest rates were up, forecasts of vigorous growth had been abandoned, and the real growth rate was predicted at a modest 3 to 3.5 percent. The Senate passed an energy program in September. Carter and Blumenthal were discussing ways to hold the federal budget deficit down. What else could they do? According to *The Wall Street Journal*, the solution was simple and obvious:

. . . [S]urely the price of the dollar depends on the supply and demand for the dollar. It declines because the Federal Reserve supplies more dollars than are demanded. For all the talk of swap networks, gold sales and so on, the *only* way the decline will be reversed is for the Fed to constrict the supply of dollars.[24] [Compare Exhibit 3.]

The Economist, however, saw things differently. Too much monetary tightening could bring on an American recession, "a remedy as primitive as chopping off a foot to deal with an ingrown toenail."[25]

When governors of the IMF and the World Bank convened in late September for their annual meeting in Washington, their anger and distress were visible. Administration spokesmen had leaked word of the components of a new anti-inflation program, to be announced the next month, but this news failed to move the IMF and World Bank officials. Nor did the Fed's increase of the discount rate to 8 percent on September 22 impress them. (The rate rose to 8.5 percent on October 10.)

President Carter had adamantly opposed compulsory wage-price controls and had often pledged not to fight inflation by increasing unemployment. Indeed, the administration had succeeded in reducing unemployment from its record post-Depression high of 9 percent in March 1975 to 6 percent in October 1978. This was particularly remarkable since the growth rate of the labor force during 1977 and 1978 had been 3.1 percent—far above the 2.4 percent rate of the previous decade—forcing the administration either to create an additional 1.4 million jobs or suffer an increase in the unemployment rate of 1.3 percentage points. The entry of the "baby boom" generation and the increased participation by women in the labor force accounted for the increased number of job seekers.

The IMF and World Bank governors doubted Carter's will or ability to control rising prices without drastic measures that would undoubtedly raise unemployment. "If you do only what we've read about," one banker

---

[23]*Federal Reserve Bulletin* (Sept. 1978): 777.
[24]*The Wall Street Journal*, Aug. 30, 1978.
[25]*The Economist*, August 26, 1978, 9.

reportedly told Secretary Blumenthal, "the dollar will explode"—that is, it would depreciate violently.[26]

October 1978: The Dollar Crisis

Soon after the IMF conference, Secretary Blumenthal instructed Anthony Solomon, Under Secretary for Monetary Affairs, to list all options for defending the dollar. Blumenthal wanted a "strong package to really turn this thing around."[27] Blumenthal then worked to pressure President Carter to include in his anti-inflation plan a pledge to limit the federal deficit in the fiscal year 1980 budget to $30 billion or less. Not until five hours before Carter went on television with his proposals on October 24 did the president accept this recommendation.

Faced with the unpalatable options of contractionary monetary and fiscal policies and mandatory controls, President Carter in his October 24 speech chose neither. The deficit-cutting pledge won mild applause from business circles, but other proposals—notably voluntary wage-price guidelines and regulatory reform—failed to impress the markets. The next day the stock market continued a steady downturn that saw it lose $110 billion on paper during the last twelve trading days in October. On the international currency market, the dollar started to fall in Tokyo trading even before the end of Carter's speech. The Fed and other central banks intervened with dollar purchases of $2 billion, but the mark rose 1.8 percent and the yen 1.7 percent against the dollar in one day (compare with past trends in Exhibit 9). The Carter administration was now facing an inescapable dilemma. Having tried a series of moderate measures and seen each fail one by one, the administration now had to decide which goal was more important: a strong dollar or a robust domestic economy. But it remained unclear just what were the *proportions* of this trade-off. How badly might the domestic economy be injured by measures taken to strengthen the dollar?

[26]*Fortune*, Dec. 4, 1978, 41.
[27]Ibid., 41.

The Decline of the Dollar: 1978

Exhibit 1   Exchange Rate Regimes of IMF Members

Industrialized Nations		Developing Nations	
Floating	16	Floating	36
Fixed	4	Fixed in terms of:	
		Dollars	38
		French Francs	14
		Other	36

The Decline of the Dollar: 1978

Exhibit 2   Measures of International Interdependence

A. Size of Exports in GNP (%)

	1958	1963	1968	1973	1978
United States	4.5	4.7	4.9	6.6	8.1
Germany	22.8	19.4	22.9	23.3	27.0
Japan	11.3	9.6	10.4	10.8	11.9
United Kingdom	20.3	19.1	20.4	22.9	29.0

B. Holdings of Financial Assets by Foreigners

	1958	1963	1968	1973	1978
Percent of U.S. Government Debt	3.0	5.0	4.5	16.1	22.3
$ Billions	6.9	12.6	12.5	54.7	137.8

C. Size of Eurocurrency Market

	1968	1973	1975	1976	1977	1978
Gross Eurocurrency Liabilities ($ Billions)	50	305	485	595	740	950
Eurodollars as Percent of Total Gross Liabilities in All Eurocurrencies	NA	NA	78	80	76	74

NA = not available.

Sources: Parts A and B are calculated by author from IMF, *International Financial Statistics*, 1982; Part C is from Board of Governors of the Federal Reserve System and Morgan Guaranty Trust Company.

The Decline of the Dollar: 1978

Exhibit 3   Selected Performance Statistics

Year/Quarter	Real GNPª	CPIª	M-1ª	Current Account Balance ($ Billions)	Change in Reservesᵇ ($ Billions)
	1	2	3	4	5
United States					
1974	−3.5%	12.1%	5.1%	$1.7	$−1.50
1975	2.4	7.2	4.6	18.4	−0.35
1976	4.6	5.0	5.8	4.3	−2.50
1977	5.5	6.7	7.9	−15.3	−0.24
1978:1	−0.1	8.0	6.3	−6.9	0.25
1978:2	8.7	10.6	10.3	−3.3	0.34
1978:3	2.6	8.3	7.9	−3.7	0.25
Germany					
1974	−1.7%	6.5%	10.6%	$9.8	$0.25
1975	1.5	5.6	15.1	4.0	1.22
1976	4.9	3.8	6.5	3.8	−3.93
1977	2.6	3.7	10.4	3.8	−4.40
1978:1	−0.6	2.9	25.3	1.4	−2.33
1978:2	8.8	1.8	6.5	1.8	1.69
1978:3	2.3	2.9	10.5	2.5	−3.31
Japan					
1974	−0.2%	24.4%	11.1%	$−4.7	$−1.26
1975	3.3	8.6	10.8	−0.7	0.66
1976	5.2	9.3	14.7	3.7	−3.80
1977	5.7	6.1	6.1	11.0	−6.53
1978:1	9.4	1.7	9.7	5.5	−6.31
1978:2	4.0	5.4	13.2	4.8	1.88
1978:3	3.9	7.1	17.2	4.5	−1.80
United Kingdom					
1974	−0.3%	18.2%	11.0%	$−8.3	$−0.45
1975	−2.0	25.3	19.0	−3.7	1.44
1976	4.9	15.0	10.3	−1.6	3.20
1977	−0.6	13.2	21.9	0.3	−14.80
1978:1	3.2	5.8	27.9	−0.6	0.09
1978:2	5.4	5.5	5.7	0.4	2.79
1978:3	4.6	12.5	20.4	−0.1	−0.15

ªAll quarterly percentages are compound annual rates of change from the previous quarter, seasonally adjusted.

ᵇNegative sign indicates an addition to reserves.

Sources: Columns 1, 2, and 3: Federal Reserve Bank of St. Louis, *International Economic Conditions*; Column 4: U.S. Dept. of Commerce, *International Economic Indicators*, Jan. 10, 1979; Column 5: IMF, *International Financial Statistics*.

The Decline of the Dollar: 1978

Exhibit 4   Derivation of Real Exchange Rates

Nominal Exchange Rates (End of Period Index)

	1972	1973	1974	1975	1976	1977	Nov. 1978
$/DM	100.0	118.6	133.0	122.1	135.6	152.2	159.6
$/yen	100.0	107.8	100.3	99.1	103.3	126.0	156.8
$/£	100.0	98.9	100.0	86.1	72.5	81.2	82.3

Ratio of Domestic Prices to Foreign Prices (End of Period Index)

	1972	1973	1974	1975	1976	1977	Nov. 1978
$P_\$/P_{DM}$	100.0	99.4	103.1	106.2	107.7	110.7	115.8
$P_\$/P_{yen}$	100.0	95.1	84.8	82.8	80.1	78.9	81.8
$P_\$/P_£$	100.0	97.4	93.1	81.9	74.3	68.3	67.8

Real Exchange Rates (End of Period Index)

	1972	1973	1974	1975	1976	1977	Nov. 1978
Real $/DM[a]	100.0	119.3	129.1	115.0	125.8	137.5	137.8
Real $/yen	100.0	113.4	118.2	119.7	128.9	159.6	191.7
Real $/£	100.0	101.5	93.1	105.2	97.5	118.9	121.3

[a]Real $/DM = ($/DM) $\times$ ($P_{DM}/P_\$$); i.e., the real exchange rate is the nominal exchange rate times the ratio of foreign prices over domestic prices.

Note: If the purchasing power parity condition holds, then the changes in the nominal exchange rate will be equal to the changes in the ratio of domestic prices to foreign prices.

Source: Indexes calculated by author from IMF, *International Financial Statistics*, 1982 Yearbook.

The Decline of the Dollar: 1978

Exhibit 5   National Forecasts and Realized Real GNP Growth for 1977

Country	Change from:	Early 1977 Forecast	Realized
United States	Fourth quarter to fourth quarter	5.75–6.0	5.75
Canada	Year to year	3.0–4.0	2.25
France	Year to year	4.6	2.75
West Germany	Year to year	4.5–5.0	2.5
Italy	Year to year	2.6	2.0
Japan	Fiscal year to fiscal year	6.7	5.0
United Kingdom	Year to year	1.2	0.5

Source: Council of Economic Advisers, *Economic Report of the President* (Washington, DC: U.S. Government Printing Office, 1978), 107.

The Decline of the Dollar: 1978

Exhibit 6   Movements in Exchange Rates: 1971-1978

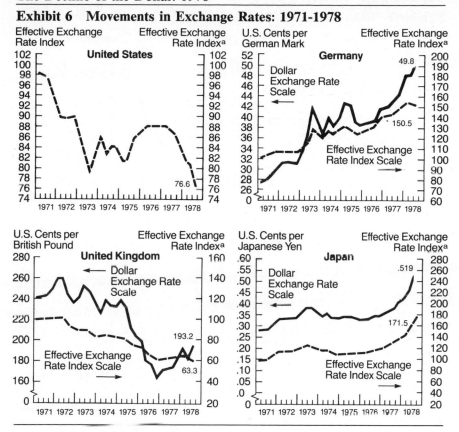

Note: An upward movement in all lines indicates an appreciation of the respective currency; a downward movement is a depreciation.

[a]Effective exchange rate changes are an indicator of the extent to which the external value of a country's currency has moved relative to other currencies. Effective exchange rate changes are computed as an index, combining the exchange rates between the currency in question and twenty other major currencies with weights derived from the International Monetary Fund's multilateral exchange rate model. Each weight represents the model's estimate of the effect on the trade balance of the country in question of a change of 1 percent in the domestic currency price of one of the other currencies. The weights, therefore, take account of the size of trade flows as well as of the relevant price elasticities and the feedback effects of exchange rate changes on domestic costs and prices. The measure is expressed as an index based on the par values in May 1970.

Source: Federal Reserve Bank of St. Louis.

The Decline of the Dollar: 1978

Exhibit 7   Relative Rates of Inflation: 1971-1978[a]

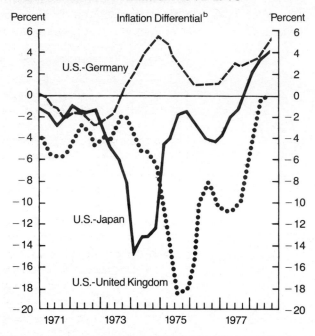

[a]Comparison of rates of change in consumer price index over corresponding four-quarter periods. Example: the United States-Germany inflation differential for January 1977 is computed by subtracting the percentage change in the German CPI over the January 1976– January 1977 period from the percentage change in the U.S. CPI over the same four-quarter period. Data are seasonally adjusted.

[b]If the line is above zero, then the United States has more inflation than the other countries and vice versa for the lines below zero.

Source: Federal Reserve Bank of St. Louis.

The Decline of the Dollar: 1978

**Exhibit 8   Short-Term Interest Rates—International Comparison:
1974–1978**

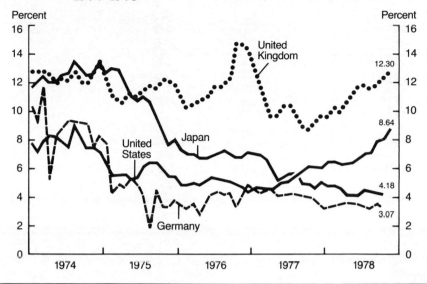

Source: International Monetary Fund.

The Decline of the Dollar: 1978

Exhibit 9   Federal Reserve and Treasury Department Intervention in Foreign Exchange Markets

Period	Sales of Foreign Currencies[a]	Purchases of Foreign Currencies[b]	Net Support for Dollar[c]
Feb. 1974–July 1974	$527.0	$317.1	$209.9
Aug. 1974–Jan. 1975	742.3	208.4	533.9
Feb. 1975–July 1975	1,045.0	1,260.5	−215.5
Aug. 1975–Jan. 1976	106.5	240.4	−133.9
Feb. 1976–July 1976	270.4	288.6	−18.2
Aug. 1976–Jan. 1977	175.6	205.0	−29.4
Feb. 1977–July 1977	212.4	150.7	61.7
Aug. 1977–Jan. 1978	1,736.8	35.4	1,701.4
Feb. 1978–July 1978	NA	NA	1,511.0

Note: Figures do not include purchases of Swiss francs and Belgian francs to repay debts incurred before August 1971.

NA = not available.

[a]Support for dollar through intervention sales of foreign currencies. Figures equal millions of dollar equivalents.

[b]Purchases of foreign currencies either to support foreign currency values or to repay obligations from previous dollar support interventions. Figures equal millions of dollar equivalents.

[c]Sales − Purchases. Positive values imply net support for dollar during period.

Source: Calculated by author from "Treasury and Federal Reserve Foreign Exchange Operations," *Federal Reserve Bulletin*, September 1974–1978 and March 1975–1979.

Note
Exchange Rate Determination

After the breakdown of the Bretton Woods system in the early 1970s, flexible exchange rates dominated in international monetary relations. As a result, much attention was given to understanding the determination of exchange rates.

A country's exchange rate, typically defined as the number of units of home currency per unit of foreign currency, is the price of foreign money. Like most other prices, it is determined by supply and demand. Sellers and buyers of currencies look for each other in the foreign exchange market and exchange one currency for the other at a mutually satisfying price. This price is the exchange rate.[1]

Supply and Demand in the Foreign Exchange Market

Suppose that the United Kingdom and Germany were the only two countries, that the United Kingdom is the "home" country, and that all international transactions take place in Deutschmarks (DM). We can then represent the foreign exchange market as in Figure 1.

Figure 1 shows that at an exchange rate of p_0 (i.e., each DM costs p_0 pounds), the foreign exchange market is in equilibrium: both demand for DMs and supply of DMs is q_0. It is clear from the figure that in order to understand exchange rate determination, we should look at supply and demand in the international money market. Below we list four ways in which supply and demand are generated and provide examples:

1. *International goods transactions.* One of the most obvious causes for the demand for foreign money is imports. If U.K. residents want to buy German goods, they have to pay in DMs and therefore must acquire DMs in exchange for their pounds; hence they will *demand* DMs. Similarly, German residents who want to buy English goods have to sell DMs and buy pounds sterling; thus they will *supply* DMs.

This note was prepared by Assistant Professor David M. Meerschwam.
Copyright © 1984 by the President and Fellows of Harvard College
Harvard Business School note 9-384-171

[1]A concept closely related to the exchange rate is the "effective exchange rate." The effective exchange rate is not like the ordinary or bilateral exchange rate, concerned with only two countries; rather it is concerned with many countries and is calculated as a weighted (geometric) average of the bilateral rates of one country vis-à-vis a number of other countries. The German effective exchange rate for the Deutschmark (DM) is a weighted average of the DM-pound rate, the DM-dollar rate, the DM-franc rate, etc.

Figure 1

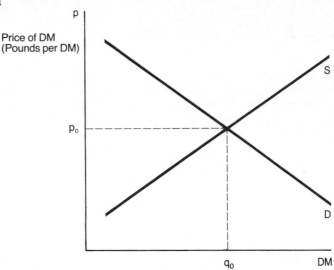

2. *International services and tourism.* English tourists in Germany have to buy DMs with their pounds to finance their stay. Hence they demand DMs. Conversely, Lloyd's of London, when it sells insurance to a German shipowner, has to be paid in pounds sterling.

3. *International trade in financial assets.* In a world without restrictions on international capital mobility, portfolio purchases for foreign assets generate supply of and demand for foreign money. If a German wants to buy British Treasury bills, pounds have to be bought first, and DMs will be supplied to buy the pounds. A Briton buying DM bills from the German Treasury must buy DMs first, and therefore will demand DMs.

4. *International investments.* Finally, the foreign direct investment behavior of firms generates foreign exchange transactions. For example, if the German electrical equipment firm Siemens decides to build a plant in the United Kingdom and wants to finance it with German funds, it has to sell DMs in the foreign exchange market in order to get the necessary pounds to pay for construction.

Exchange Rate Volatility

The four cases of supply and demand in the foreign exchange market just mentioned underlie Figure 1. In a world of flexible (or "floating") rates, these four causes determine exchange rates. It is clear from the

Figure 2

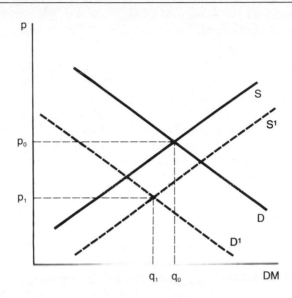

figure that once an exchange rate is determined at p_0, it should stay there. At any level above p_0 in Figure 1, more DMs are supplied than demanded; at any level below p_0, more are demanded than supplied.

Yet in a world of flexible exchange rates, as the name indicates, the exchange rate moves in response to shifting supply and demand. Corresponding to the four cases discussed above, we can list four examples that will cause such shifts:

1. The United Kingdom experiences a recession. As a result, people in the United Kingdom have less income and will spend less on imports. The demand for DMs is reduced and the demand curve shifts inward. In Figure 2, D moves to D^1.

2. Hotels in the United Kingdom improve their service. More Germans will take vacations in Britain, and the supply of DMs rises. Now the supply curve shifts outward (S to S^1 in Figure 2).

3. Interest rates in Germany fall. German investors respond by purchasing more U.K. Treasury bills, whose interest rate, even though unchanged, seems now more attractive. The supply of DMs increases and the supply curve shifts outward. In this case, however, another effect must also be considered. U.K. investors consider German bills less attractive and demand fewer such bills in their international portfolio. The demand for DMs then falls, and the demand curve shifts inward. Figure 2 illustrates this as D to D^1 and S to S^1.

4. The United Kingdom offers tax credits for investments in plant and equipment. More German firms will build plants in the United

Kingdom and the supply of DMs in the foreign exchange market goes up. S shifts to S^1.

It is seen that exchange rate volatility is caused by shifting supply of and demand for foreign currency. In our third example above, the exchange rate fell after the shifts, from p_0 to p_1, as in Figure 2. We then would say that the home country's (U.K.) currency "appreciated": it became more valuable in terms of the other currency.[2] If $p_0 = 1/2$ and $p_1 = 1/4$, it means that whereas one pound first bought two DMs it now buys four DMs. At the same time, the DM obviously lost value; it "depreciated."

What Matters When

In the framework developed above, goods transactions, services and tourism, financial asset transactions, and international investments interact to determine the total supply and demand of currencies, and hence the exchange rate. We should say more, however, about the relative importance of these four factors for the short, the intermediate, and the long run.

The Short Run

Most economists and other students of finance believe that in a world without restrictions on capital mobility across borders, short-run fluctuations in exchange rates are caused by international portfolio adjustments. Money chasing high interest rates across the world leads to international asset transactions. (This caused the demand and supply shifts discussed in the third example of the previous section.) Since portfolio adjustments are frequently made, these effects dominate short-run exchange rate determination. Hence higher interest rates at home will typically cause a nation's exchange rate to appreciate in the very near future, and lower interest rates will cause a depreciation.

Intermediate Run

In the intermediate run, nonfinancial transactions (i.e., transactions in goods, services and tourism, investment in real plant and equipment) become more important. Since all the "real" transactions depend on the level of economic activity of the country, changes therein will cause shifts in the demand and supply of foreign currency.

Suppose a country experiences a recession. In contrast to a quick

---

[2]Conversely, we could also say that the foreign country's (Germany's) currency "depreciated," since it became less valuable in terms of the other currency.

change in the interest rate, it takes some time for a recession to occur. But when it does occur, the volume of imports will start to fall, since people can spend less. As a result, the exchange rate for a nation in recession will appreciate. The reverse occurs, of course, once an economy starts to expand. Hence for the intermediate run the level of economic activity is very important, since it determines the level of real transactions, as opposed to financial ones.

The Long Run

In the long run, "goods arbitrage" becomes important. Suppose, for example, a product costs £10 in the United Kingdom and a similar product DM50 in Germany. If the exchange rate is 1/4 (i.e., DM4 per pound), Germans will start importing the goods from the United Kingdom, since at that exchange rate the imported good costs only DM40 against DM50 for the same local good. This causes more demand for pounds and more supply of DMs, and the DM will start to depreciate against the pound. Eventually, the exchange rate will fall to 1/5, all other things being equal. At that rate, goods arbitrage is no longer profitable.

This last mechanism leads to what is called "purchasing power parity": if enough time is available for goods arbitrage to do its job (i.e., "in the long run") and a bundle of goods costs £10 in the United Kingdom and DM50 in Germany, then the exchange rate is 1/5. Under purchasing power parity, inflation rates in the two countries become important. Suppose, for example, that all U.K. prices double. To buy the goods previously bought for £10, one now needs £20. If, in Germany, meanwhile, one can still buy the bundle of goods for DM50 (we assume there was no inflation there), then the new exchange rate has to be 1/2.5. In other words, a country that experiences inflation will see its exchange rate tend to depreciate.

Expectations

While the forces described in the above are important in determining the exchange rate, they are not sufficient to tell what the exchange rate "will be doing." Expectations of the market participants matter too. As in the stock market, expectations about future prices will cause people to buy and sell foreign currencies. As a result, the exchange rate can move simply because expectations change.

Fixed Exchange Rates

Suppose now that a government wants to stabilize the exchange rate for its currency. At present, the exchange rate is at p_0 in Figure 3, as we continue our U.K.-Germany illustration. Suppose we now move forward

Figure 3

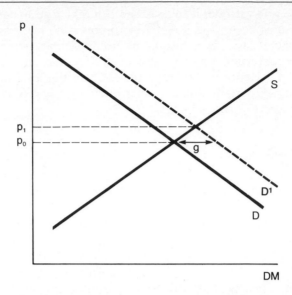

one year in time. The United Kingdom has experienced a major boom in its economy. As a result, more imports are demanded and D shifts to D^1, while the exchange rate depreciates from p_0 to p_1. The U.K. government, however, wants to keep the exchange rate at p_0, and it is willing to take steps to accomplish that goal. The most obvious action would be for the British government to sell, from its reserves, a quantity of DM (say, g amount). With new demand curve D^1 and the old supply curve S, and with the government selling g DM, the exchange rate is retained at P_0. This is called "government intervention in the foreign exchange markets."

A less direct policy used in fixing the exchange rate is for the government to take steps that induce shifts in either the supply or demand curve, or both, to get back to point p_0.

Both methods are sometimes used, even under the flexible rate system. In that case, however, the government does not try to fix the exchange rate, but rather to smooth or steer its path. This is called "dirty floating," and most governments engage in the practice—some in only small degree, some much more.

Discussion Questions for Case and Note

1. Why was President Carter worried about the decline of the dollar in 1978? Should he have been worried?
2. What were the primary forces accounting for the decline of the dollar during 1977 and 1978?
3. Was the dollar undervalued? Why or why not?
4. How would you evaluate President Carter's exchange rate policy?
5. What should President Carter have done in October 1978? What would you have done if you were the treasurer of a large multinational corporation?

Bibliography

Dornbusch, Rudiger, and Stanley Fischer, *Macroeconomics*, 3rd ed. (New York: McGraw-Hill, 1984). Chapter 19 is an excellent treatment of the determinants of exchange rates, the coordination of domestic policy with external policy, and government intervention in the foreign exchange market. Parts of this chapter assume some knowledge of the interaction of the financial and nonfinancial markets referenced in the bibliography of Chapter 5.

Gordon, Robert J., *Macroeconomics*, 3rd ed. (Boston: Little, Brown, 1984). Chapter 19 starts with a brief treatment of the balance of payments accounts. There is a good discussion of the determinants of exchange rates in terms of the supply of and the demand for foreign exchange (pages 603–615). The last part of the chapter concentrates on the coordination of domestic and external policies under fixed and flexible exchange rates.

Kenen, Peter B., *The International Economy* (Englewood Cliffs, NJ: Prentice-Hall, 1985). The basic concepts of exchange rate determination are developed in Chapters 11-14. More advanced concepts described in simple terminology are presented in Chapters 15-17.

Reynolds, Lloyd G., *Macroeconomics: Analysis and Policy*, 5th ed. (Homewood, IL: Irwin, 1985). A short, elementary description of the supply and demand for currency and a discussion of the advantages and disadvantages of the fixed and floating rate systems are given in Chapter 16.

Solomon, Robert, *The International Monetary System, 1945–1981* (New York: Harper & Row, 1982). Solomon, a top-ranking government official for international economic affairs, relates his observations of the floating exchange rate system in Chapter XVIII.

CHAPTER 17

The Origins of the Third-World Debt Crisis

In the decade following the first oil shock in 1973, the total amount of third-world debt increased fivefold. Third-world countries borrowed money to pay for the imports of oil and industrial products needed to sustain their rapid economic growth. For most countries the alternative to borrowing was fewer imports, slower growth, and the painful political and economic adjustment that these entailed. But even those developing countries that were net oil exporters, such as Mexico, were also vulnerable to rising external debt, as we shall see in this chapter.

The leading debtor nations in June 1982 were Mexico ($64.4 billion in debt owed to industrial-country banks), Brazil ($55.3 billion), Venezuela ($27.2 billion), Argentina ($25.3 billion), and South Korea ($20.0 billion). Approximately 40 percent of the debt in these countries was owed to U.S. banks. Despite the large amounts of debt outstanding, the major debtor countries had been able to met their interest payments—that is, until Mexico's problems in August 1982. Mexico's inability to meet its interest obligations in that month marked the beginning of the debt crisis. Since that time, more than 40 countries have been forced to reschedule their debts.

The focus in this chapter is on a borrowing country's management of its debt, its economy, and its development strategy. The implications of the borrowing country's economic management extend to a host of other issues critical to the developed world: the evolution of trade policy and protectionism, the conduct of monetary policy, the stability of the world financial system, and the regulation of banks' lending practices. Much of the attention in the press has been devoted to the lending banks' exposure in the major debtor countries. Indeed, their exposure has been high—often far exceeding 100 percent of a bank's capital base. Though this is an important issue, it is necessary first to understand the forces driving the borrowing country to accumulate the debt. Once these forces are identified, one can examine the appropriate public and private responses to the debtor nation's behavior.

Case
Mexico: Crisis of Confidence

"*Ahora trabajamos* (now we work)," declared Miguel de la Madrid Hurtado in reaction to his overwhelming presidential election victory on July 4, 1982. The campaign had gone smoothly, and despite the fact that de la Madrid's party, Partido Revolucionario Institucional (PRI), had won every election by similarly large margins since its rise to power in 1929, he had nonetheless campaigned vigorously throughout the nation.

At age 47 this was de la Madrid's first elected position. He had served as the secretary of planning and budgeting, and had worked in the Treasury, the Central Bank, and the national oil company. During the campaign, de la Madrid had called for a "moral renovation of society." He also discussed the economic challenges Mexico faced. Citing poor productivity, a lack of international competitiveness in manufactured goods, and high foreign borrowing requirements, he said the state would have to alter some of the policies by which it managed the economy. In particular, de la Madrid declared that industrial policy must emphasize basic consumer goods and export sectors; the nation's infrastructure must be improved, subsidies and protectionism decreased, and small and medium businesses encouraged.

But all of that was before the summer's disastrous drift into debt crisis. By inauguration time in December 1982, de la Madrid would face overwhelming challenges to his leadership ability and to the domestic tranquility of Mexico.

Summer of Crisis, 1982

July. Inflation was up, with estimates ranging from 40 percent to 75 percent. Many attributed this latest increase to the government's announcement that retail gas and fuel prices were to be increased 5 percent per month for a year.

August. On August 5 Jose Lopez Portillo, the incumbent president, made international headlines by devaluing the currency for the second time in 1982. Two exchange rates were established. A preferential rate of 49.5 pesos to the dollar would apply to priority transactions: servicing

This case was prepared by Rafael Cohen and Kent Thiry under the direction of Associate Professor Richard Vietor. Copyright © 1983 by the President and Fellows of Harvard College. Harvard Business School case 0–383–148.

government debt, credit institution obligations, basic food and capital goods imports, and the interest on corporate debt. A floating rate (104 pesos per dollar) would exist for all other transactions.

Many Mexicans reacted to the government decree by removing their deposits from Mexican banks and depositing them in the United States. Approximately 1,600 applications for the preferential rate were received in the first week of controls—none were processed.

On August 12 the government established a second fixed rate. All foreign currency exchanges were closed for a week, and foreign currency deposits were to be paid out in pesos only. The government suspended all interest payments on foreign debt for 90 days, and all principal payments until the end of 1983. It was also announced that those companies hardest hit by events to date could defer their taxes for one year.

The government increased the prices of tortillas, bread, and other staples by 50 percent to 100 percent. The subsidy on electricity for domestic use was cut by 50 percent and by 30 percent for industrial use. And work on the new PEMEX (Petroleos Mexicanos) skyscraper in Mexico City was halted halfway through construction.

September.   On September 1 in his last State of the Union address, President Lopez Portillo declared that "a group of Mexicans has looted more money from the country than the imperialists who have exploited us since the beginning of our history. It is now or never. They will not return to loot us again." With that, he proclaimed the nationalization of all private domestic banks in Mexico. Armed guards were simultaneously dispatched to each bank and telephone power was cut off to all bank buildings, which were closed until further notice.

Later in the month the government raised interest rates from 4.5 percent to 20 percent on ordinary savings, and lowered them from 34 percent to 11 percent on mortgages for low-income individuals (24 percent for others). It also froze repatriation of profits.

By mid-fall, the spiral toward economic collapse had at least been arrested. This was due in part to quick actions taken by the Reagan administration. It guaranteed a $1 billion export credit from U.S. commercial banks; increased its purchases of Mexican oil for the Strategic Oil Reserve by 300 percent (reversing a policy of not relying on one major supplier); paid $1 billion in advance for that oil; and contributed $925 million of a $1.85 billion bridge loan from the Bank for International Settlements. In addition to these temporary measures, a team from the International Monetary Fund (IMF) arrived in Mexico City to begin negotiating a long-term loan package. After more than a month, however, negotiations over a potential $4.65 billion loan still seemed deadlocked in disagreements over the conditions of the loan. Even with these funds, Mexico would still need an estimated $5 billion in net new loans from foreign banks to continue servicing its foreign debt.

What Had Gone Wrong?

During the autumn two major viewpoints emerged on the causes of the crisis. One view shared by foreign bankers and Mexico's Ministry of Finance stressed that "the Mexican economy is fundamentally sound, although it is facing a temporary liquidity problem." It had been a financial crisis, not an economic one. The cash flow problems were due in large measure to transient international developments, namely the unfortunate coincidence of global recession, an oil glut, continued inflation, depressed commodity prices, and high interest rates. The government had taken measures to deal with all of these, but had found itself in much the same situation as a rapidly growing, leveraged multinational corporation in such an environment.

The second view of the crisis was more critical of both Mexico's economic strength and the government's management of its development. In this view, Mexico's dual economy (a few large, modern firms and many small, rudimentary ones) was structurally weak and noncompetitive, while the huge, centralized bureaucracy was ill equipped to alleviate the widespread inefficiencies. Although crude oil had made economic growth possible, its exploitation appeared to have exacerbated some of the nation's economic weaknesses. Under the circumstances, external funding for further growth would be difficult because the tumultuous summer had turned Mexico, in the words of a U.S. banker, "into the pariah of the world."

Mexico—Land of Pride and Petroleum

With 750,000 square miles of land, Mexico is the thirteenth largest nation in the world—48 percent of its land is suitable for livestock, 29 percent is forested, and 18 percent is cultivable. Mexico has abundant natural resources—it is among the world leaders in oil, silver, and copper deposits. A key physical characteristic is the 1,760-mile border it shares with the United States.

It could be said that modern Mexico began in 1910, when Porfirio Diaz was ousted after 30 years as dictator. His ouster marked the beginning of the 20-year Mexican Revolution, a revolution driven by the people's desire for democracy, the redistribution of land, and freedom from foreign influence. The founding of PRI in 1929 began the process of restoring stability to political and economic life, yet the rhetoric of revolution was sustained. The land distributions and nationalization of all foreign oil companies that followed in the 1930s were highly emotional affairs that the government characterized as fulfillments of the people's revolutionary mandate.

Mexicans from all segments of society continue to be strongly and vocally nationalistic. The government has long nurtured these sentiments through its strident criticism of other nations and international institutions and by repeated declarations of Mexico's intent to determine its own course. For example, a law that passed in 1982 made it illegal to use any non-Mexican words in the name of a place of business.

Mexico's economy has grown rapidly since World War II. The average annual growth rate of real GNP was 6.2 percent through 1980, compared with 3.2 percent for the United States. Mexico's GNP was then among the top 20 nations in the world. During the 1977–1981 period alone, 4.2 million new jobs were created. This growth had been attained with only limited help from foreign direct investment, since the government's Mexicanization strategy sought to minimize dependence on foreign countries and companies by generally limiting foreign equity to 49 percent in any venture. Furthermore, the licensing of foreign technologies was tightly controlled, and often not allowed unless the foreign entity agreed to provide Mexicans with the education required to understand and duplicate the technology.

Mexico's population also grew rapidly after the war. The 1981 population of 69.3 million people made it the eleventh most populous country in the world. Almost a quarter of the population lives in Mexico City. By 1980 overcrowding in Mexico City had become a serious problem. Despite the fact that subway fares are held at one peso, Mexico City still accounts for 50 percent of the nation's automobile traffic. That, together with heavy industry, has created a serious air pollution problem. During the 1970s the urban population grew 4.3 percent per year, with 67 percent of all Mexicans living in the cities by 1980. This continuing urban migration has put severe pressure on housing and public services.

Quality of Life

By a variety of yardsticks Mexico's growth has led to progress in many areas of life. The infant mortality rate fell from 125.7 to 56.0 per 1,000 people between 1940 and 1980, and average life expectancy rose from 40 to 63 years during that same period. Between 1930 and 1979 the literacy rate increased from 33 percent to 84 percent, and during the 1970s the absolute number of people receiving some education increased at a faster rate than the population. Because of urban overcrowding, however, additional progress in education may be more difficult.

Rapid population growth continues to be a problem, although some progress has been achieved. The crude birth rate dropped from 45 per thousand in 1960 to 37 per thousand in 1980 (while the death rate fell from 12 to 7 per thousand). In 1979, an estimated 40 percent of married women were using contraceptives.[1] Still, children have historically constituted a familial source of social security, a pragmatic precaution in a country where at most 50 percent of the population is covered by any

[1]World Bank, *World Development Report*, 1982.

sort of old-age insurance. Such limited coverage, combined with the agrarian lifestyle of half the population, explains why economists estimate that 35 percent of the over-65-year-old population remain economically active.

Income distribution is more skewed in Mexico than in most of the more developed countries, but it is not unusual for a developing country. As of 1977, 10 percent of the population received 38 percent of the income, while the bottom 20 percent received only 3.3 percent of the national income. This trend in income distribution became more pronounced through the 1970s.[2] Figures for food consumption roughly parallel those of income. It is estimated that 25 percent of the population goes without meat and 50 percent without milk.

Mexican Politics

The Presidency   Both the executive and legislative branches are elected by popular vote. In practice, the president dominates by being "part king, part pope." The president is elected for one six-year term and is not allowed to run for reelection. The president plays the key role, however, in selecting the PRI's candidate for succession.

Parties   Organizationally, the group that runs the government is the president's party (PRI). Actually, PRI is more a collection of interest groups than it is a unified party. Its legacy of power is based on an ability to continually appease all major groups in Mexican society, typically through assimilation of the groups' leaders. PRI has had to face few serious challenges to its control since 1929. In 1976, 72 percent of the electorate voted, with 95 percent casting their ballot for Lopez Portillo. In 1982, 75 percent of the electorate voted, 75 percent of them for de la Madrid. Opposition parties do exist, however, and in 1977 Lopez Portillo sponsored an electoral reform that made it easier for other parties to achieve official recognition. In 1979 he legalized the Communist party. These reforms were generally believed to have been introduced to quiet the Left's complaints of exclusion from the political process.

The largest and oldest of the opposition parties is Partide Accion Nacional (PAN). Its supporters, staunchly Catholic and middle class, are concentrated in northern Mexico. In 1982 they received 12 percent of the popular vote by official count. Their growing support is attributed to the alienation of some of the middle class from PRI policies and conduct.

The largest party on the left is Partido Socialista Unificado de Mexico (PSUM). It was formed in 1979 from five separate parties, including the Communist party. In the 1982 election it garnered 5 percent of the vote.

[2]*Comercio Exterior*, Vol. 29, No. 5, May 1979, p. 507.

There is no party on the extreme right. One of the reasons is that the military, a small force of 90,000, has always worked very closely with PRI. As long as PRI is able to defuse any significant social unrest, there is little likelihood that its relationship with the military will change.

Labor Unions   PRI is no longer as closely tied to organized labor as it is to the military. The major union, Confederacion de Trabajadores (CTM), holds a PRI-like position among unions. Although CTM has historically worked smoothly with PRI, some of the younger members of the union leadership are not content with the existing relationship. Fidel Velasquez, chief of the union and *ex officio* member of the upper echelons of PRI, is 83 years old and in ill health. After his death, many expect CTM to move to the left to avoid losing members to the smaller, more independent unions. Although the official unemployment rate stood at 4.5 percent through mid-1982, underemployment was estimated to be 50 percent. Organized labor, which accurately viewed itself as better off than much of the population, tempered its activities accordingly.

Church and Press   Church and state are constitutionally separated in Mexico. Except on issues such as birth control, the Church has displayed no inclination to get involved in the formulation of public policy. Mexico's constitution also guarantees freedom of the press and speech. The newspapers must, however, purchase their paper from the government, which they are able to do at subsidized prices—unless their commentary runs counter to national interests.

Corruption   "Politics is the easiest and most profitable profession in Mexico," is an oft-quoted observation. Although President Lopez Portillo, upon taking office in 1976, prosecuted four officials of the previous administration, that action was dismissed by many as merely symbolic. "The precise amount a cabinet member or state industry manager accumulates," wrote one observer, "largely depends on himself, although when graft becomes excessive and injurious to his rule, the president of Mexico may step in and close some sources of subordinate income."[3] The emergence of billions of dollars of oil revenue made possible new levels of corruption within the government. But since amounts so large risk seriously offending the public, the pressure on PRI to step in and do something has been increased. The selection of de la Madrid was heralded by some as a victory of the new technocrats over the old guard politicos, especially in light of his campaign promise to make anticorruption his top priority.

[3]Frank Brandenburg, *The Making of Modern Mexico* (Englewood Cliffs, N.J.: Prentice-Hall, 1964), p. 162.

International Relations

The most consistent theme in Mexico's international activities is its desire to determine its own course. In this spirit Mexico declined to sign GATT and is uninterested in joining OPEC. Still, the country has actively sought to promote closer ties among Latin and Central American nations and to position itself as regional leader. Mexico provided $700 million in foreign aid to these countries in 1980–1982, much of it in the form of special oil credits.

Relations between Mexico and the United States have never been warm, and Mexicans feel a great deal of resentment toward the United States. One of the reasons for this goes back more than a century, to the time when Mexico lost nearly half of its territory in the war with the United States. Yet the economic and social ties between the two countries are substantial. Mexico is the United States' third largest trading partner. Two-thirds of Mexico's imports and exports are transacted with its neighbor to the north. An estimated 7 million Mexicans live in the United States. Despite, or perhaps because of, the two countries' interdependencies, several areas of conflict exist.

Many Mexicans resented the U.S. government's handling of the proposed 1977 gas deal when PEMEX and six American companies signed an agreement for the sale of 2 billion cubic feet per day of natural gas. The U.S. Department of Energy (DOE) did not approve the deal, however, for several reasons. The actual rejection explains only part of the ill will. What bothered many Mexicans even more was the arrogance they felt Secretary Schlesinger displayed toward them throughout the process. In 1979 a new deal was signed, at a price well below what the United States would have been committed to pay according to the previous proposal. Foreign Minister Castaneda stated at the time of the signing, "The deal will have an important psychological and political effect, and that is very desirable."[4]

The illicit drug trade between Mexico and the United States represented an estimated $4 billion commerce in 1980. This makes Mexico the biggest channel of illegal drugs into the United States, since many drugs not grown or processed in Mexico arrive in the United States via a Mexican connection. This was one area where the governments had agreed to work together, an agreement made easier by the fact that little of the money stayed in Mexico. At the same time Mexico itself stood to benefit little from the effort. As a Mexican official who was involved in the fight against the illicit drug trade said, "It is the position of our government to destroy the drug trade and we are trying, but I feel it is a war we can't win. If you ask me, we don't come out too badly losing it."[5]

[4]*New York Times*, September 23, 1979.

[5]L. Maizel, "Mexico 1980" (Boston: HBS Case Services, 1980), p. 26.

Worker migration is certainly the most emotionally charged issue in Mexican-U.S. relations. Anywhere from 500,000 to 900,000 Mexican workers enter the United States each year, compared with the 20,000 of that number who could enter legally.

For Mexico, migration constitutes an escape valve for unemployment problems. Mexican officials point out that the bulk of the migrant workers obtain only the most menial jobs, ones that most American workers do not want. In addition, they cite ineffectiveness and expense of American border patrol efforts as practical obstacles preventing them from mounting their own enforcement campaign. But beyond these problems, the government feels that "we cannot politically or morally or constitutionally impose any restrictions on the movement of Mexicans. The United States has the right to deport those who are there illegally, but we feel that if they do work there, they have a right to a fair salary and a certain respect for human rights."[6]

There are two areas in which Mexico would like to have greater control over intercountry flows. The first is the smuggling of goods from the United States to Mexico to avoid import duties and the overhead of government bribery. The second is the outflow of capital. As of 1982 Mexican citizens owned approximately $30 billion worth of U.S. real estate and had deposited an additional $14 billion in American banks.

Mexico must also be concerned about the threat of trade restrictions. U.S. vegetable farmers have accused their Mexican counterparts of dumping subsidized tomatoes on the U.S. market. Since Mexico is not a GATT signer, the prosecution needed only to establish the existence of the unfair practice, as opposed to proving damage to the domestic industry. The U.S. government, however, absolved the Mexican growers of the allegations.

A final area of major importance in Mexican-U.S. relations is oil trade. As a DOE official observed, "The importance of Mexican oil in today's energy picture is enormous. The threat of vast reserves in a nonmember country will force OPEC to use restraint. . . . Mexico could supply almost 50 percent of the additional needs of the Western world between 1980 and 2000."[7]

In spite of the prospect of a large, accessible U.S. market, not all Mexican officials had a positive reaction to such strong U.S. interest. One explained, "It seems as though the Americans have just discovered Mexico. Suddenly we are the best friends, and years of being considered second-class citizens should be immediately forgotten."[8]

[6]*Boston Globe*, November 19, 1979.
[7]L. Maizel, "Mexico 1980," p. 23.
[8]Ibid.

The Lopez Portillo Plan

When Lopez Portillo assumed office in December 1976, the economy was in disarray. His predecessor, Luis Echeverria, had devalued the peso by 50 percent the previous August, and the devaluation had precipitated a financial crisis. Industrial growth appeared to be slowing, and the government's options were limited by the conditions of an outstanding IMF loan. Strikes occurred with greater frequency, and acts of violence were not uncommon. Massive land distribution schemes and antibusiness pronouncements by Echeverria, together with economic deterioration, had led to a disastrous flow of capital out of the country.

President Lopez Portillo described his plan in broad terms: two years of recovery, two years of consolidation (growth with inflation), and finally, two years of stable growth. The accelerated development of Mexico's oil resource was the key to his plan, together with government and business alliance to rebuild Mexico.

His plan was structured with four major goals. First and foremost was job creation. Enough jobs would be created to meet the employment needs of the growing population and to begin to address the underemployment problem. Official estimates were that 800,000 new jobs would be required annually just to maintain present levels of employment. The other three major goals were to promote a more equitable distribution of the wealth, establish Mexico as the leader of Latin America, and achieve self-sufficiency in food and energy.

The industries Lopez Portillo targeted for special attention were capital goods (especially those related to oil), electricity, mining, petrochemicals, and agriculture. Lopez Portillo intended to encourage regionally balanced growth through tax credits, in an attempt to redress the problem of urban concentration and industrial bottlenecks (34 percent of all industrial production was located in the Mexico City area).

Mexico's Economic Performance

Prior to the nationalization of the banks in 1982, the government controlled approximately 50 percent of the nation's economic activities. Nationalization probably increased this percentage to about 70 percent. By 1980 the Mexican labor force was distributed as follows: 36 percent in agriculture, 26 percent in industry, and 38 percent in services (the corresponding figures were 55 percent, 20 percent, and 25 percent, respectively, in 1960).

Petroleum

Crude oil is indeed Mexico's "national patrimony," the spark plug igniting its recent economic growth. Between 1976 and 1982, the government's official estimates of proved reserves rose from 11 to 72 billion barrels (including natural gas in Btu-equivalent barrels). In 1982 probable reserves were estimated at 18 billion barrels, and potential reserves were estimated at 160 billion barrels. Reserves of this magnitude would rank Mexico as the number four oil producing nation in the world, behind the USSR, Saudi Arabia, and Iran. By these estimates, Mexico also has the seventh largest reserves of natural gas.

Mexico held a position of similar prominence many years earlier. In 1921 it was the world's second largest oil producer (behind the United States). Shortly after that time, Mexico became a net importer, and despite its expropriation of foreign oil companies in 1938, it did not become a net exporter again until 1974. Now oil again constitutes a means to national health, prosperity, and international prominence. Not surprisingly, the subject of oil dominates economic and political discussion—and PEMEX dominates oil. PEMEX is the government-owned national oil company that controls Mexican oil from the exploration stage to exportation or domestic retail sale. "It's a law completely unto itself," a London banker once commented. The director is appointed by, and reports to, the president of Mexico.

In 1977 the Lopez Portillo administration considered four development options:

1.   Severely limit production and refrain from exporting. This option was advocated mainly by students and members of the intelligentsia who felt that to do otherwise would mean misuse of the national patrimony.

2.   Limit exports to a platform of 1.1 million barrels per day of crude oil, plus .2 million bbls/day of refined products. This represented a sharp increase over 1977 levels, but was still far below the physical capacity of Mexico's oil fields, estimated at nearly 6 million bbls/day.

3.   Export at the platform level indicated above, but build excess production and infrastructural capacity that could be used on a contingency basis.

4.   Pursue maximum development immediately. The political right and some industrialists championed this proposal, believing that current world oil prices would force consumer nations to develop alternate energy sources or reduce demand in the long term.

President Lopez Portillo favored the second option, and between 1977 and 1981 it was adopted as official policy. But an immense investment was necessary to achieve even the platform level. In 1978 and 1979 oil development consumed 19.6 percent and 19.2 percent of the government's capital budget. Oil-related investment by PEMEX amounted to an estimated $27 billion between 1977 and 1982, not including many of the infrastructural improvements such as transportation that were necessary to facilitate increased oil output. In 1982 other industries were

experiencing difficulties transporting their products because of the bottlenecks created by the volume of PEMEX business.

The prominence of oil in Mexico's economic picture made it a target
for critics of the development policy. For example, in 1981 PEMEX
Director Diaz Serrano cut Mexico's oil price by several dollars a barrel
to sustain export volume in the face of global excess supply. The public
outcry that ensued, which condemned him for "sacrificing the national
patrimony," led to his ouster within a week of the price cut. When his
successor restored the old price, however, export levels fell so precipi-
tously that the price was subsequently lowered anyway.

The weakening of international oil prices in 1981 and 1982 also
affected the government's policies on domestic oil prices. As international
prices softened, PEMEX sought to expand export sales above the platform
level. This expansion, however, was limited by domestic demand, which
in turn had increased rapidly since product prices were fixed by the government well below prevailing market levels (for instance, gasoline sold
at $.50 per gallon). Inadequate port facilities also imposed a short-term
ceiling on the amount that could be exported.

Agriculture

The performance of Mexico's agricultural sector was disappointing in the
1970s. Its production did not keep pace with the growing population and
income-driven demand. Infrastructure was one problem. Earlier land re-
distributions left hundreds of thousands of family farms on very small
plots called ejidos. These ejidos, which are worked by traditional farm
practices, comprise 70 percent of the farms, but produce only 33 percent
of the harvests.

The fact that staple crops, once produced in self-sufficient quantities,
were now imported was more than merely an economic issue. As Lopez
Portillo observed, "A case in point is corn. It is still a basic foodstuff, a
religion, a custom, a currency, a rite. . . . Current production would guarantee the food supply of Mexicans if it weren't used to fatten cattle and
poultry for consumption by the classes that no longer care for corn and
can afford to pay for its transformation."[9]

During the first two years of Lopez Portillo's administration, agricultural production of the country's basic foodstuffs (corn, beans, wheat,
and feed grains) began to recover from stagnation. However, a severe
drought in 1979 forced massive imports of grain in 1980, with corn and
sorghum imports tripling to over 6 million tons. This sudden burden
added to the strain on port, rail, and trucking facilities.

The 1980 import crisis proved a catalyst in a new food strategy that
had been under study for the previous two years. On March 10, 1980,

[9]President Jose Lopez Portillo, *Third State of the Country Address*, September 1, 1979.

the anniversary of the petroleum nationalization, President Lopez Portillo announced the new strategy, designated SAM (Sistema Alimentario Mexicano). SAM's three principal objectives were: (1) self-sufficiency in corn and bean production by 1982 and in other important grains by 1985, (2) a more equitable distribution of the nation's wealth, and (3) reduction of the malnutrition suffered by a significant portion of the population. In effect, Mexico would sow its petroleum wealth to gain its independence in the food arena.

To implement this strategy, the government raised price supports for basic crops and provided subsidized agrochemicals, seeds, farm financing, and crop insurance. Most of these inputs were provided by state-owned enterprises. On the consumption side, subsidies for tortillas and other staples were continued, and the government's food marketing enterprise, CONASUPO, expanded its network of retail stores to 12,000. The cost of SAM was approximately US$3.4 billion in 1980, and somewhat less in 1981.

Corn production jumped 46 percent in 1980, reaching record levels in 1981. Sorghum, wheat, and beans also experienced significant gains. The growth of imports slowed, although not as rapidly as production increased, and sizable reserves accumulated. Just as the bill for food imports declined in 1982, the SAM program suffered budgetary cuts, resulting in lower subsidies to farmers. These cuts, plus more adverse weather, resulted in a 17 percent decline in food production and the prospect of rising food imports again in 1983.

The SAM was not without controversy. Critics argued that good weather, not the program's incentives, had caused the production gains. They claimed that many of the benefits never reached the small, needy farmers, but were raked off by larger farmers, middlemen, and bureaucrats. Defenders argued that more land was planted in response to the incentives and that consumption of modern inputs had risen greatly. Small farmers were said to have improved their techniques, while foreign exchange savings were realized from reduced imports.

For President-elect de la Madrid, the country's agricultural development and food policy were of key importance. The countryside mirrored many of Mexico's structural problems. Of the 2.6 million farms, 7 percent are modern-chemical, 41 percent traditional semicommercial, and 52 percent subsistence (not to mention 1.2 million landless, rural families). Although the rural population's needs were great, and signs of unrest were visible, the recent debt crisis would probably lead to further cutbacks, and possibly a reevaluation of the self-sufficiency strategy.

Industrial Production

Mexico's industrial sector is highly concentrated; 1.7 percent of all industrial enterprises produce 53.7 percent of the industrial output and account for 42.3 percent of employment. The government has provided tax incentives for smaller businesses, especially those willing to locate away from major cities, but concentration of market demand and available infrastructure in those centers limited the success of these efforts. State-owned enterprises met the energy needs of Mexico's fast-growing economy, almost doubling electricity output between 1977 and 1982. To insure long-term energy needs, the government began building nuclear and coal power plants in the late 1970s.

Through import substitution and credit policies, the government has also worked to alter the mix of goods produced. The existing industrial base is largely dedicated to the production of final goods as opposed to capital goods, a situation the government would like to see reversed. One of the obstacles to achieving this has been an acute shortage of skilled workers. Trade and tax policies also contribute to the problem. Since importation of capital goods requires government permission, the government has tried to use import permits to encourage regionally balanced economic growth. In effect, the government chooses both competitors and the level of competition within each industry affected, resulting in a great many captive markets.

To date, foreign direct investment has been relatively limited. In 1973 the government passed a law that required foreign-owned corporations entering Mexico to arrange majority ownership by Mexicans for their prospective Mexican subsidiary. Foreign firms that entered earlier have difficulty expanding their operations without losing control, and thus are more inclined to repatriate all of their profits.

Mexico's automotive industry exemplifies the pattern of import substitution. Although domestic production rose 22 percent in 1981, it proved to be a mixed blessing. Exports actually fell by 15 percent, while the industry's imports were up 15 percent in the same period. Thus the net trade deficit in this industry was $1.25 billion. Although the government moved quickly to redress the imbalance by imposing production ceilings on individual auto manufacturers until their exports exceeded their imports, the effect of this measure, in conjunction with declining demand, was to severely hurt industry profitability and lead to extensive layoffs.

Tourism

Historically, tourism has been one of Mexico's principal sources of foreign currency. Between 1977 and 1981 tourism was the source of 160,000 new jobs. Not surprisingly, it has been the object of considerable governmental attention. In 1978 and 1979 the government standardized hotel classifications, increased security in tourist areas, and lent funds at subsidized rates to foster the development of new resorts in underdeveloped areas.

Management of Mexico's Economy
Government Budget

In the late 1970s Mexico's government had quickly adjusted to its new-found wealth. President Lopez Portillo greatly increased government spending on many fronts, in part through subsidies on a wide range of consumer goods and activities, which were said to constitute 30 percent of government expenditures by 1980. Actual expenditures often exceeded the authorized budgets. In 1981, for example, these overruns reached 30 percent of the originally budgeted levels.

Tax revenues also grew rapidly, with increases varying between 30 percent and 36 percent per annum. The revenues from export taxes grew especially fast after 1979. One reason for the rapid increase in revenues was that the government changed its primary taxation method in 1980, adopting the value-added tax (VAT) common in Europe. This was done to curb consumption and mitigate the tax evasion that was widely practiced by individuals and companies alike. Despite the increases in revenues, at each fiscal year-end the government had a greater deficit (see Exhibit 7).

In 1981 the government began to consider whether a shift in spending priorities might be appropriate. Its continued inability to balance the budget put pressure on government programs involving current expenditures and investment. Consequently, in April 1982 the Ministry of Finance announced an austerity plan which would be implemented immediately. Its four goals were: (1) reduce government spending by 4 percent from budgeted levels, (2) increase prices on government-controlled items, (3) increase tax rates, and (4) decrease government imports.

Income Policy

Mexico instituted many measures in an effort to achieve a better income distribution. Employers paid a 5 percent housing contribution, a 1 percent education tax, a 9 percent to 12 percent social security tax, and an 8 percent profit-sharing levy. Laid-off employees were entitled to three months' pay plus additional pay based on seniority. It was estimated that these benefits made wage costs as much as 45 percent higher than they might have been in a free labor market. In January 1982 the government made its annual adjustment to the minimum wage, which translated into a 30 percent increase for unskilled labor. In March emergency increases of 10 percent to 30 percent were granted due to labor pressure after the February devaluation.

Money

In the early 1980s the "dollarization" of Mexico's economy had recently become a difficult problem for the government's monetary authorities. Dollar-denominated bank accounts grew substantially during Lopez Portillo's tenure (growing by 85 percent in 1981 alone). These deposits, together with the accessibility of American banks across the border, posed a considerable obstacle to the Mexican government's ability to control the money supply. Events in the fourth quarter of 1978 exemplified these problems. The government had attempted to contract the money supply by a relatively small number of pesos. Instead, its actions stimulated an almost simultaneous shift to borrowing dollars that more than frustrated the intended effect. By August 1982 Mexican banks had an estimated $13.4 billion in foreign currency liabilities to domestic depositors, plus substantial additional dollar liabilities to foreign banks (see Exhibits 4 and 8).

In April 1982 the government announced it was going to decrease the rate of growth in the money supply and impose interest rates that would encourage saving. Businesspeople had mixed reactions to these moves. The less sanguine pointed to the current government imposed reserve requirements of 70 percent to 90 percent, and the high market-loan interest rates (see Exhibit 5).

Mexico's inflation rate increased steadily throughout the 1970s, as it did worldwide, though in Mexico measuring the rate became increasingly difficult because of the pervasiveness of subsidies and controls. Most estimates placed the 1981 inflation at about 30 percent, and it climbed as high as 70 percent by summer 1982.

Exchange Rate

In his speeches President Lopez Portillo had consistently dedicated himself to the defense of the peso exchange rate established in 1976. Pronouncements like "a president who devalues is a devalued president" were traditional. In the words of one Mexican banker, the government had "nailed their prestige to the currency. People see a devaluation as a failure, a disgrace."[10]

By the end of 1981, however, even Lopez Portillo acknowledged a growing "devaluation psychosis."[11] The drop in oil export revenues apparently undermined the confidence in Mexico's future revenue stream that had helped maintain the peso-dollar exchange rate at its 1976 level. Capital flight increased sharply, culminating in what the president claimed was a $39 billion outflow at the hands of speculators and bankers.[12]

Debt

During the 1970s Mexico financed its growth largely through foreign borrowing (together with domestic debt in the form of treasury bills and petrobonds). Oil had made Mexico a very popular customer among international bankers. Compared with most other lending opportunities, Mexico seemed nearly ideal.

Mexico's honeymoon with foreign banks began to sour during 1981. By that time its debt service requirements had become especially burdensome, since three-fourths of its debt was at floating interest rates.

[10]Lopez Portillo, *Wall Street Journal*, January 28, 1982.
[11]Jacques Levy, *Wall Street Journal*, January 28, 1982.
[12]Alan Robinson, "Portillo Pockets the Banks," *Euromoney*, October 1982, pp. 47–53.

Projections for Mexico's gross foreign borrowing in 1982 were $28 billion: $8 billion to roll over short-term debt, $9 billion to repay medium-term debt, and $11 billion in new money to cover interest payments, the trade deficit, and continuing development. U.S. banks, which held the largest portion of Mexico's debt, grew reluctant to lend more, demanding shorter maturities, higher rates, and sweeter management fees. By November Mexico's total foreign debt was estimated at $80 billion (three-fourths to banks), second only to Brazil's debt among developing countries. The Mexican government and its state enterprises owed nearly three-fourths of that amount. It was also believed that an additional $7 billion was owed by Mexican bank branches or agencies located in the United States that had relied on short-term credit lines and the U.S. money market. Billions more were thought to be outstanding in mortgages on U.S. real estate investments by Mexicans. In all, more than 1,100 foreign banks had outstanding loans to Mexico's public and private sector. The exposure of nine of America's largest banks was thought to be more than $13 billion.

The President-Elect

Early in November, with only three weeks left before his inauguration, Miguel de la Madrid Hurtado gathered his advisors, a number of whom were youthful technocrats with relatively little political experience. At the time of de la Madrid's nomination just a year earlier, Mexico's future looked brighter than it had in decades. The mood of the people was overwhelmingly positive.

The prospects for fulfilling his constituents' expectations for prosperity, however, were truly bleak, at least in the short run. Real GNP growth for 1982 would be about −0.2 percent; down sharply from 7.9 percent in 1981. Inflation would be about 58 percent for the year, with the CPI at nearly 98.8 percent. The public sector deficit was above 16 percent of GNP, and investment was falling sharply. Although the trade surplus was up to $6.6 billion, and the current account deficit was down to $2.7 billion, total reserves had fallen to an estimated $800 million.

President-elect de la Madrid Hurtado needed to formulate a program that would relieve his country's economic crisis, maintain the political consensus on which his administration depended, and satisfy the stiff demands of the International Monetary Fund.

Mexico: Crisis of Confidence

Exhibit 1 Mexico's Real GNP at 1970's Prices, 1978–1982 (in Billions of Pesos)

	1978	1979	1980	1981	1982	Percent Changes			
						1978–79	1979–80	1980–81	1981–82
Gross National Product	712.0	777.2	841.9	908.7	907.3	9.2	8.3	7.9	(0.2)
Personal Consumption	490.8	534.2	574.5	616.7	626.1	8.8	7.5	7.3	1.5
Durable goods	52.1	60.0	65.7	na	na				
Nondurable goods	285.8	309.0	332.3	na	na				
Services	152.9	165.2	176.6	na	na				
Government Expenditures	62.4	68.5	75.0	82.5	86.5	9.8	9.5	10.0	4.8
Education	15.1	16.6	18.2	19.9	20.7				
Health	14.6	15.7	17.0	18.1	19.0				
Administration and defense	32.9	36.2	39.8	44.5	46.8				
Gross Domestic Investment	164.4	193.4	236.0	272.8	196.5	17.6	22.0	15.6	(28.0)
Private investment	80.7	99.0	112.6	128.2	102.6	22.7	13.7	13.9	(20.0)
Public investment	62.1	72.7	84.8	98.3	85.8	17.1	16.6	15.9	(12.7)
Changes in inventories	21.6	21.7	38.6	46.3	8.1				
Exports	64.4	72.3	76.7	81.5	83.7	12.3	6.1	6.3	2.7
Nonpetroleum goods	25.4	26.5	26.0	25.4	26.3	4.3	(1.9)	(2.3)	3.5
Petroleum goods	4.1	6.0	10.2	13.4	17.9	46.3	70.0	31.4	33.6
Services and other	34.9	39.8	40.5	42.7	39.5	14.0	1.8	5.4	(7.5)

Exhibit 1 (Continued)

Imports	70.2	91.2	120.3	144.7	85.4	29.9	31.9	20.3	(41.0)
Intermediate consumption goods	33.2	40.1	53.9	60.4	42.1	20.8	34.4	12.1	(30.3)
Capital formation goods	11.8	19.4	25.1	31.5	15.4	64.4	29.4	25.5	(51.1)
Final consumption goods	3.8	5.3	9.6	10.2	5.1	39.5	81.1	6.2	(50.0)
Services and other	21.4	26.4	31.7	42.6	22.8	23.4	20.1	34.4	(46.5)
Nominal GNP	2,337.4	3,067.5	4,276.5	5,874.4	9,255.8	31.2	39.4	37.4	57.6
Real GNP per Capita (Pesos)	11,177	11,866	12,491	13,113	12,725	6.2	5.3	5.0	(3.0)
Nominal GNP per Capita (Dollars)[a]	1,612	2,054	2,736	3,259	865	27.4	33.2	19.1	(73.5)
Number of Jobs (Millions)[b]	15.8	17.7	18.8	20.1	19.9	5.4	6.2	6.9	(1.0)
GNP Deflator (%)	15.7	20.3	28.7	27.2	57.8				
Population (Millions)	63.7	65.5	67.4	69.3	71.3				

[a]Based on the exchange rate at the end of the year.

[b]Estimated number of available openings; however, one person could hold more than one opening.

Source: Secretaria de programacion y presupuesto y Banamex, S.A.

Mexico: Crisis of Confidence

Exhibit 2   Mexico's Balance of Payments, 1977–1982 (Millions of Dollars)

	1977	1978	1979	1980	1981	1982
Current Account	(1,596)	(2,693)	(4,876)	(6,761)	(12,544)	(2,685)
Revenues	9,177	11,653	16,283	25,021	30,810	30,717
Export of goods	4,650	6,063	8,818	15,308	19,420	21,006
Border trade[a]	2,076	2,364	2,919	3,722	4,770	4,149
Tourism	867	1,121	1,443	1,671	1,760	1,406
Gold and silver	199	249	488	936	531	386
Other	1,386	1,856	2,615	3,384	4,330	3,770
Expenditures	10,774	14,346	21,159	31,782	43,354	33,402
Imports of goods	5,705	7,918	11,980	18,486	23,930	14,422
Border trade[aa]	1,361	1,632	2,246	3,130	4,584	3,577
Tourism	396	519	693	1,045	1,571	788
Payments of direct foreign investment	189	214	335	496	551	526
Interest on public sector debt	1,542	2,023	2,888	3,958	5,476	7,791
Interest on private sector debt	432	549	849	1,479	2,907	3,088
Other	1,149	1,492	2,169	3,188	4,335	3,211

Exhibit 2 (Continued)

Capital Account	2,276	3,254	4,521	9,799	21,860	6,079
Long-term capital	4,271	4,689	4,594	6,476	11,696	8,198
Public sector borrowing	6,232	8,343	10,415	7,771	13,823	11,196
Amortization of public sector debt	(2,295)	(4,264)	(7,286)	(3,723)	(4,806)	(3,767)
Direct foreign investment	327	385	782	1,071	1,189	603
Private sector borrowing	104	260	756	1,488	1,861	590
Other	(97)	(35)	(73)	(131)	(370)	(424)
Short-term capital	(1,995)	(1,435)	(72)	3,323	10,163	(2,118)
Net public sector borrowing	(950)	(1,489)	206	68	9,267	(1,439)
Other	(1,046)	55	(278)	3,255	896	(679)
Special Drawing Rights	0	0	70	74	70	0
Errors and Omissions	(23)	(127)	703	(1,961)	(8,373)	(6,580)
Changes in Reserves	657	434	419	1,151	1,012	(3,185)
Total Reserves Minus Gold	1,649	1,842	2,072	2,960	4,074	834[b]
Debt Service Ratio[c]	92%	113%	125%	60%	68%	70%

[a]Purchases across the border by border residents.

[b]Actual reserves believed to be nearly zero.

[c]Interest from public and private sector and amortization of public debt divided by exports of goods.

Source: Banco de Mexico, S.A.

Mexico: Crisis of Confidence

Exhibit 3   Composition of Trade (Millions of Dollars)

	1973	% of Total	1975	% of Total	1977	% of Total	1979	% of Total	1981	% of Total
Exports	2,071.73	100.00	3,062.39	100.00	4,649.76	100.00	8,817.72	100.00	19,379.03	100.00
Petroleum goods	24.79	1.20	479.94	15.67	1,037.31	22.31	3,974.98	45.08	14,562.60	75.15
Oil and natural gas	0.34		437.79		993.35		3,765.37		13,827.50	
Oil derivatives	20.76		26.43		39.38		96.36		604.99	
Petrochemicals	3.69		15.72		4.58		113.25		130.11	
Nonpetroleum goods	2,046.94	98.80	2,582.45	84.33	3,612.45	77.69	4,842.74	54.92	4,816.43	24.85
Agribusiness	1,124.16	54.26	1,346.95	43.98	1,950.87	41.96	2,577.79	29.23	2,141.87	11.05
Shrimp	100.62		249.61		321.29		358.87		344.32	
Coffee	157.01		184.97		458.36		574.95		343.40	
Cotton	165.95		174.98		195.24		309.67		301.21	
Tomatoes	127.11		132.63		215.02		206.98		249.59	
Fresh vegetables	na		54.43		80.72		153.98		185.53	
Other	573.47		550.33		680.24		973.34		717.82	
Minerals	182.39	8.80	330.96	10.81	301.69	6.49	483.66	5.49	753.79	3.89
Copper	31.79		22.81		35.52		56.27		306.31	
Other	150.60		308.15		266.17		427.39		447.48	

Exhibit 3 (Continued)

Manufacturing	740.39	35.74	904.54	29.54	1,359.89	29.25	1,781.29	20.20	1,920.77	9.91
Chemical industry	152.32		205.14		240.70		355.59		454.30	
Auto industry	152.84		141.51		266.91		392.32		450.89	
General machinery and equipment	23.80		103.71		180.84		184.33		287.21	
Textile industry	168.23		168.39		180.25		209.15		180.50	
Steel industry	42.96		48.38		91.74		131.46		63.59	
Other	200.24		237.41		399.45		308.44		484.28	
Imports	3,814.67	100.00	6,582.26	100.00	5,569.73	100.00	11,979.72	100.00	23,104.40	100.00
Agribusiness	na	na	951.26	14.45	829.79	14.90	1,314.27	10.97	3,441.53	14.90
Beans			64.19		9.81		4.15		355.58	
Corn			404.63		186.97		101.63		447.50	
Wheat			17.41		43.63		185.32		213.56	
Intermediate consumption goods	na		3,488.20	52.99	3,041.08	54.60	6,385.05	53.30	11,086.69	47.99
Capital goods	na		1,870.42	28.42	1,461.62	26.24	3,538.06	29.53	7,129.85	30.86
Final consumption goods	na		272.38	4.14	237.24	4.26	742.34	6.20	1,446.33	6.26
Balance of Trade	(1,742.94)		(3,519.87)		(919.97)		(3,162.00)		(3,725.37)	

Source: *Balanza de Pagos 1970–1978*, Informe Anual, 1980, 1981, Banco de Mexico, S.A.

Mexico: Crisis of Confidence

Exhibit 4   Money Supply at End of Each Period, 1977–1982 (Billions of Pesos)

	M1	% Yearly Change from Previous Period	M2	% Yearly Change from Previous Period	M4	% Yearly Change from Previous Period	% of Deposits in Foreign Currency	
							Checking Accounts	Savings Accounts
1977	196	26.4	210	26.2	521	31.8	11.4	19.0
1978	260	33.0	276	31.6	700	34.3	9.6	16.9
1979	347	33.1	369	33.7	948	35.5	10.1	20.4
1980	461	33.1	491	33.3	1,312	38.3	10.2	19.9
1981	612	32.8	655	33.3	1,965	49.8	11.5	23.9
1982								
January	580	na	621	na	1,982		11.7	24.1
February[a]	587	14.5	650	56.4	2,294	188.9	16.9	35.7
March	617	61.1	671	38.4	2,323	15.3	13.8	27.5
April	610	(14.8)	673	3.8	2,350	13.7	16.6	28.0
May	620	20.1	678	9.1	2,376	13.3	15.3	30.0
June	625	10.3	682	6.9	2,440	32.3	14.9	30.8
July	633	14.6	688	9.5	2,511	35.2	14.7	31.0
August[a]	687	102.4	751	111.0	2,825	150.2	15.6[b]	37.0[b]

Note: M1 = currency + checking accounts

        M2 = M1 + checking accounts in foreign currency

        M4 = M2 + savings accounts (short-term and long-term) in pesos and foreign currency

In August all deposits in foreign currency (US$13.4 billion at the beginning of the month, $11.9 billion at the end of the month) were frozen and paid out in pesos at the exchange rate of 70 pesos per dollar.

[a] During these months the peso was devalued.

[b] Using the August 31 exchange rate of 104 pesos per dollar, the proportion of deposits in foreign currency would have been 21.5 percent and 46.6 percent for checking and savings accounts, respectively.

Source: *Indicadores economicos*, Banco de Mexico, S.A.

Mexico: Crisis of Confidence

Exhibit 5 Interest and Exchange Rates, 1978–1982

	Mexican T-Bill 90 Days	Mexican Prime Rate on Loans (Pesos)	Mexican Prime Rate on Loans (Dollars)	U.S. Prime Rate	Exchange Rate (Pesos/ Dollars)
1978	10.53	na	na	na	22.77
1979	15.03	21.73	16.68	13.78	22.80
1980 (quarters)					
First	19.80	24.07	21.00	16.57	22.84
Second	22.07	27.47	20.43	16.78	22.87
Third	21.90	28.37	17.07	11.70	23.03
Fourth	26.09	31.27	21.17	16.77	23.19
1981 (quarters)					
First	28.73	37.20	23.37	19.28	23.57
Second	28.26	39.03	23.80	19.16	24.20
Third	32.68	42.00	26.27	20.38	24.92
Fourth	33.41	45.90	20.30	17.03	25.85
1982					
January	34.16	48.00	19.50	15.75	26.62
February	36.07	48.70	21.00	16.68	44.64
March	35.16	50.40	21.50	16.63	45.53
April	38.48	50.00	21.40	16.50	46.36
May	43.52	56.60	22.30	16.50	47.13
June	51.30	64.70	21.60	16.50	48.04
July	53.01	69.00	21.90	16.40	48.92
August	55.88	75.70	20.60	15.30	104.00
September	49.72				50/70/115[a]
October	43.02				50/70/115

Note: The interest earned on Mexican T-bills is tax free for individuals.

[a]In September 1982, a two-tier exchange rate was instituted. The 50 peso rate was the preferential rate, 70 pesos was the ordinary rate, and 115 pesos was the black market rate (casewriter estimates).

Source: *Indicadores economicos,* Banco de Mexico, S.A.

Mexico: Crisis of Confidence

Exhibit 6   Inflation Indicators, 1977–1981
(Percent Change from Previous Year)

Year	Consumer Price Index	Wholesale Price Index	GNP Price Deflator	Gasoline Price Index	Tortilla Price Index	Electricity Price Index
1977	28.4	41.8	30.0	27.6	24.7	14.0
1978	17.4	15.6	16.7	1.2	0	2.0
1979	18.3	18.5	20.3	0	15.1	18.0
1980	26.6	24.1	28.8			
1981	27.9	24.8	26.6			

Source: *Indices de precios y estadisticas historicas,* Banco de Mexico, S.A.; *Indicadores economicos,* Banco de Mexico, S.A.

United States and Mexico: Consumer Price Index (CPI)

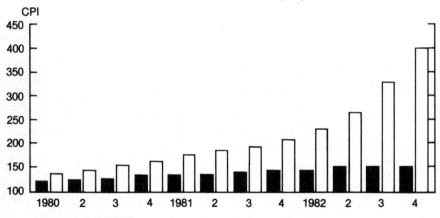

■ = United States' CPI.
□ = Mexico's CPI.
    1978 = 100

Mexico: Crisis of Confidence

Exhibit 7   Public Sector Finance, 1977–1982 (Billions of Pesos)

	1977	1978	1979	1980	1981	1982
Revenues	483.8	632.8	820.9	1,182.2	1,553.5	2,621.1
Central government revenues	231.8	309.2	418.7	575.5	752.4	1,395.4
Income tax	93.4	132.2	173.1	246.1	371.2	427.1
Value-added tax[a]	40.5	52.7	75.1	122.5	na	267.2
Production and commerce	48.1	57.2	68.1	59.9	92.8	170.5
Export tax[b]	15.5	20.7	35.7	59.8	78.2	235.5
Import tax	10.7	14.7	28.8	47.7	54.7	70.8
Other	23.6	31.7	37.9	39.5	na	224.3
Public sector revenues	252.0	323.6	402.2	606.7	801.1	1,225.7
Expenditures	730.2	937.4	1,199.1	1,744.1	2,430.7	4,462.2
Central government expenditures	354.7	442.0	635.3	802.5	1,302.7	2,748.2
Public sector expenditures	375.5	937.4	563.8	941.6	1,128.0	1,714.0
Deficit	(246.4)	(304.6)	(378.2)	(561.9)	(877.2)	(1,841.1)
Expenditures as percent of GNP	39.3	40.1	39.1	40.8	41.5	40.6
Deficit as percent of GNP	13.3	13.1	12.3	13.1	14.9	16.7

[a]Sales tax until 1980 when the value-added tax replaced the sales tax and the production and commerce tax on a few items. The production and commerce tax was primarily an excise tax on oil, tobacco, telephone, grain alcohol, electricity, soft drinks, and beer.

[b]The export tax is primarily a tax on petroleum and mineral goods exports. The data for 1982 are preliminary.

Sources: Compiled with data from S.H.C.P., S.P.P., C.E.E.S.P., and Analisis Economico.

Mexico: Crisis of Confidence

Exhibit 8   Mexico's External Public and Private Debt to Banks, 1976–1982

Date	External Debt ($ Billions)	% Debt to U.S. Banks	% Maturity Under One Year	% of Private Sector Debt to U.S. Banks	% of Public Sector Debt to U.S. Banks	% of Mexican Bank Debt to U.S. Banks	Mexican Loans as % of Total U.S. Bank Loans
December 1976	17.9	59.78	40.78	na	na	na	11.15
June 1977	19.1	59.16	41.88	44.25	52.21	3.54	10.12
December 1977	20.3	55.17	40.89	40.18	42.86	16.96	9.35
June 1978	20.9	51.67	37.32	40.74	42.59	16.67	8.32
December 1978	23.3	45.49	31.33	34.91	41.51	23.58	7.82
June 1979	25.8	40.31	34.11	37.50	41.35	21.15	8.05
December 1979	30.9	36.89	34.63	42.11	36.84	21.05	8.50
June 1980	34.7	36.60	38.33	45.67	36.22	18.11	8.98
December 1980	42.5	36.94	44.24	51.59	29.30	19.11	9.97
June 1981	46.6	38.84	47.21	53.59	29.28	17.13	10.64
December 1981	56.9	37.79	46.68	48.37	33.95	17.67	11.64
June 1982	64.4	38.66	50.00	46.99	35.34	17.67	12.72

Source: *Country Exposure Lending Survey*, Federal Reserve Bank, Bank for International Settlements.

Exhibit 8 (Continued)

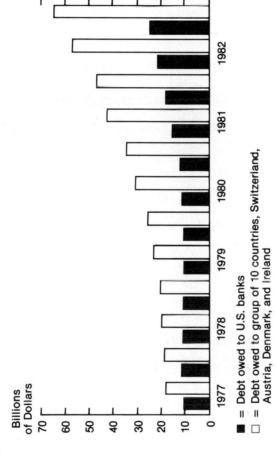

Billions
of Dollars

■ = Debt owed to U.S. banks

□ = Debt owed to group of 10 countries, Switzerland,
     Austria, Denmark, and Ireland

Mexico: Crisis of Confidence

Exhibit 9   Petroleum Products Data Summary
Oil Exports

	Volume (Thousands of Barrels per Day)	Average Price per Barrel (US$)	Revenue ($ Millions)
1977	204.5	13.23	987.7
1978	365.3	13.30	1,773.6
1979	531.9	19.39	3,765.4
1980	830.1	31.12	9,429.6
1981			
January	1,064.0	36.32	1,198.0
February	923.3	36.21	936.1
March	1,334.4	35.96	1,487.4
April	1,361.7	34.20	1,397.0
May	1,260.6	34.46	1,346.6
June	1,105.9	30.80	1,021.9
July	456.9	33.03	467.9
August	999.6	31.24	967.9
September	1,260.1[a]	31.21	1,179.8
October	1,054.1[a]	31.11	1,016.7
November	1,388.9[a]	31.90	1,329.1
December	972.8[a]	31.86	960.8
1982			
January	1,044.2[b]		
February	1,140.5[b]		
March	1,099.7[b]		
April	1,153.3[b]		
May	1,556.6[b]		
June	1,708.3[b]		
July	1,654.9[b]		
August	1,650.0[b]		
September	1,730.0[c]		

[a]Included sale of 200,000 barrels per day to the United States Government Strategic Oil Reserve.

[b]Included sale of 50,000 barrels per day to the United States Government Strategic Oil Reserve.

[c]Starting September U.S. Government purchases will increase to 190,000 barrels per day over the next year.

Exhibit 9 (Continued)
Oil Exports, Mid-1982

Market	
United States	44.3%
Spain	12.7
Japan	8.2
France	6.1
England	5.4
Italy	4.8
Israel	4.6
Brazil	3.6
Other	10.3
Total	100.0%

Petroleum Imports, 1970–1974

	Oil		Natural Gas		Gasoline	
	Thousands of Barrels	Millions of Dollars	Millions of Cubic Meters	Millions of Dollars	Millions of Gallons	Millions of Dollars
1970	0	0	1.3	24.8	100.3	9.1
1971	96.5	1.2	1.5	30.9	197.5	17.2
1972	9,308.9	27.7	1.9	40.8	214.6	22.0
1973	2,262.5	79.3	2.1	61.1	412.2	72.1
1974	9,445.5	92.6	1.6	96.1	263.4	121.0

Source: *Balanza de Pagos 1970–1978,* Informe Anual 1980, Banco de Mexico S.A., Petroleos Mexicanos, S.A.

Discussion Questions for Case

1. Evaluate Mexico's situation in November 1982. To what extent would you attribute Mexico's problems to its past policies and structural problems, or to transient financial and economic conditions in the world economy?
2. Reviewing Mexico's performance during the Lopez Portillo years, at what point might a bank analyst have raised a red flag, and on the basis of what criteria?
3. What are de la Madrid's policy options?
4. What sort of conditions is the International Monetary Fund likely to impose on Mexico?

Bibliography

Cardoso, Eliana A., "What Policy Makers Can Learn from Brazil and Mexico," *Challenge,* September–October, 1986, 19–28. This article, though analyzing events after the time of the case in this chapter, provides a sharp contrast between the Mexican-style IMF adjustment plan and the Brazilian-style wage–price freeze for managing the national economy. The author favors the Brazilian experience.

Cline, William R., *International Debt and the Stability of the World Economy,* Policy Analyses in International Economics, Institute for International Economics, Washington, DC (Cambridge, MA: MIT Press, September 1983). This monograph provides an overview of the conceptual issues in the debt crisis debate as well as the author's empirical estimates of the factors contributing to the crisis.

Dale, Richard S., and Richard P. Mattione, *Managing Global Debt* (Washington, DC: Brookings Institution, 1983). This study, which was published shortly after the events described in the Mexico case, focuses more on the solutions to the debt crisis than on its causes.

Enders, Thomas O., and Richard P. Mattione, *Latin America: The Crisis of Debt and Growth* (Washington, DC: Brookings Institution, 1984). This comparative study of Latin American debtor nations helps put the Mexican experience into a broader perspective.

"Mexico: A Survey," *The Economist,* Sept. 5, 1987, 1–22. This survey provides a balanced discussion of political, social, and economic events in Mexico. It is useful for updating the Mexican story after 1982.

Sachs, Jeffrey D., "External Debt and Macroeconomic Performance in Latin America and East Asia," *The Brookings Papers on Economic Activity,* 1985:2, 523–573. The author compares the poor performance of the Latin American debtors to the better performance of the East Asian debtors and offers explanations for the differences.

PART V

Appendix: Data on U.S. Economic Performance

APPENDIX A

Selected U.S. Statistics (through 1941)

Unless otherwise noted, the tables in this appendix are taken from U.S. Bureau of the Census, *Historical Statistics of the United States, Colonial Times to 1970, Bicentennial Edition* (Washington, DC: U.S. Government Printing Office, 1975).

Selected U.S. Statistics (through 1941)

Exhibit 1 Gross National Product in Current Dollars: 1919–1941

(All figures in "$" column are in billions of current dollars.[a] All figures in "%" columns are percentage annual compound growth rates.)

Year	Consumption Expenditures		Gross Private Domestic Investment		Net Exports of Goods and Services		Government Purchases of Goods and Services		Gross National Product	
	1	2	3	4	5	6	7	8	9	10
		%		%		%		%		%
1919	$53.8		$12.4		$4.9		$9.5		$80.0	
1920	62.8	16.7	17.5	41.1	3.5	−27.7	5.9	−37.6	89.7	12.1
1921	58.3	−7.2	7.8	−55.4	2.1	−40.0	6.3	6.8	74.5	−16.9
1922	57.4	−1.5	10.1	29.5	1.0	−52.8	5.9	−5.5	74.4	−0.1
1923	63.9	11.3	15.7	55.4	0.8	−15.0	6.2	4.0	86.6	16.4
1924	67.8	6.1	12.2	−22.3	1.3	60.7	6.7	8.2	88.0	1.6
1925	67.3	−0.7	16.2	32.8	1.1	−19.3	7.3	8.4	91.9	4.4
1926	73.1	8.6	17.0	4.9	0.8	−23.9	7.3	0.6	98.3	7.0
1927	72.7	−0.5	15.1	−11.2	1.1	28.9	7.9	7.8	96.7	−1.6
1928	75.0	3.2	14.1	−6.6	1.4	29.0	8.2	4.1	98.7	2.1
1929	78.8	5.0	16.2	12.5	1.1	−16.7	8.5	3.9	104.6	6.0
1930	70.8	−10.2	10.3	−36.4	1.0	−10.4	9.2	8.2	91.2	−12.8
1931	61.1	−13.7	5.6	−45.4	0.5	−49.5	9.2	0.2	78.5	−13.9
1932	49.1	−19.6	0.9	−82.9	0.4	−21.2	8.0	−12.3	58.6	−25.4
1933	46.2	−5.9	1.4	45.8	0.4	−12.2	8.0	−0.5	56.1	−4.3
1934	51.8	12.1	3.3	137.8	0.6	66.5	9.8	21.5	65.5	16.7
1935	56.2	8.5	6.4	92.5	0.1	−78.3	10.0	2.2	76.5	16.8
1936	62.6	11.4	8.4	32.4	0.1	−7.7	12.0	20.0	83.1	8.2
1937	67.2	7.3	11.8	39.0	0.3	150.0	11.9	−0.8	91.2	9.7
1938	64.6	−3.8	6.4	−45.0	1.3	330.0	13.0	9.2	85.4	−6.3
1939	67.6	4.6	9.2	42.9	1.1	−17.0	13.3	2.3	91.2	6.8
1940	71.7	6.1	13.1	41.5	1.7	70.8	14.0	5.3	100.5	10.2
1941	80.0	11.6	17.9	36.6	1.3	−25.0	24.8	77.1	124.7	24.1

[a]Some of the estimates in this exhibit will not correspond exactly with those of Exhibit 2 since different estimation methods were used here to make the figures compatible with the pre-1929 data.

Source: Joseph Swanson and Samuel Williamson, "Estimates of National Product and Income for the United States Economy, 1919–1941," *Explorations in Economic History*, X: 1 (Orlando, Florida: Academic Press, Fall 1972), 55.

Selected U.S. Statistics (through 1941)

Exhibit 2   Gross National Product, by Type of Expenditure, in Current and Constant (1958) Prices: 1929–1941 (Billions of Dollars)

	Personal Consumption Expenditures				Gross Private Domestic Investment							
						Fixed Investment						
							Nonresidential			Residential Structures		
Year	Gross National Product	Total	Durable Goods	Nondurable Goods	Services	Total	Total	Total	Structures	Producers' Durable Equipment	Total	Nonfarm	Farm
	1	2	3	4	5	6	7	8	9	10	11	12	13
					Current Prices								
1929	103.1	77.2	9.2	37.7	30.3	16.2	14.5	10.6	5.0	5.6	4.0	3.8	.2
1930	90.4	69.9	7.2	34.0	28.7	10.1	10.6	8.3	4.0	4.3	2.3	2.2	.1
1931	75.8	60.5	5.5	29.0	26.0	5.6	6.8	5.0	2.3	2.7	1.7	1.6	.1
1932	58.0	48.6	3.6	22.7	22.2	1.0	3.4	2.7	1.2	1.5	.7	.7	Z
1933	55.6	45.8	3.5	22.3	20.1	1.4	3.0	2.4	.9	1.5	.6	.5	Z
1934	65.1	51.3	4.2	26.7	20.4	3.3	4.1	3.2	1.1	2.2	.9	.8	.1
1935	72.2	55.7	5.1	29.3	21.3	6.4	5.3	4.1	1.2	2.9	1.2	1.1	.1
1936	82.5	61.9	6.3	32.9	22.8	8.5	7.2	5.6	1.6	4.0	1.6	1.5	.1
1937	90.4	66.5	6.9	35.2	24.4	11.8	9.2	7.3	2.4	4.9	1.9	1.8	.1
1938	84.7	63.9	5.7	34.0	24.3	6.5	7.4	5.4	1.9	3.5	2.0	1.9	.1
1939	90.5	66.8	6.7	35.1	25.0	9.3	8.9	5.9	2.0	4.0	2.9	2.8	.1
1940	99.7	70.8	7.8	37.0	26.0	13.1	11.0	7.5	2.3	5.3	3.4	3.2	.2
1941	124.5	80.6	9.6	42.9	28.1	17.9	13.4	9.5	2.9	6.6	3.9	3.7	.2

Exhibit 2 (Continued)

							Constant (1958) Prices[a]						
1929	203.6	139.5	16.3	69.3	54.0	40.4	36.9	26.5	13.9	12.6	10.4	9.9	.4
1930	183.5	130.4	12.9	65.9	51.5	27.4	28.0	21.7	11.3	9.9	6.3	6.0	.3
1931	169.3	126.1	11.2	65.6	49.4	16.8	19.2	14.1	7.5	6.6	5.1	4.9	.2
1932	144.2	114.8	8.4	60.4	45.9	4.7	10.9	8.2	4.4	3.8	2.7	2.5	.1
1933	141.5	112.8	8.3	58.6	46.0	5.3	9.7	7.6	3.3	4.3	2.1	1.9	.2
1934	154.3	118.1	9.4	62.5	46.1	9.4	12.1	9.2	3.6	5.6	2.9	2.7	.2
1935	169.5	125.5	11.7	65.9	47.9	18.0	15.6	11.5	4.0	7.5	4.0	3.8	.3
1936	193.0	138.4	14.5	73.4	50.5	24.0	20.9	15.8	5.4	10.3	5.1	4.8	.3
1937	203.2	143.1	15.1	76.0	52.0	29.9	24.5	18.8	7.1	11.8	5.6	5.3	.4
1938	192.9	140.2	12.2	77.1	50.9	17.0	19.4	13.7	5.6	8.1	5.7	5.4	.3
1939	209.4	148.2	14.5	81.2	52.5	24.7	23.5	15.3	5.9	9.4	8.2	7.8	.4
1940	227.2	155.7	16.7	84.6	54.4	33.0	28.1	18.9	6.8	12.1	9.2	8.6	.6
1941	263.7	165.4	19.1	89.9	56.3	41.6	32.0	22.2	3.1	14.2	9.8	9.1	.6

[a]The percentage change in these numbers is presented on pages 518 and 519.

(Continued)

Exhibit 2 (Continued)

| Year | Gross Private Domestic Investment—Cont. Net Change in Business Inventories | | | Net Exports of Goods and Services | | | Government Purchases of Goods and Services | | | | |
| | Total | Nonfarm | Farm | Total | Exports | Imports | Total | Total | Federal National Defense | Federal Other | State and Local |
	14	15	16	17	18	19	20	21	22	23	24
				Current Prices							
1929	1.7	1.8	-.1	1.1	7.0	5.9	8.5	1.3	—	—	7.2
1930	-.4	-.1	-.3	1.0	5.4	4.4	9.2	1.4	—	—	7.8
1931	-1.1	-1.6	.5	.5	3.6	3.1	9.2	1.5	—	—	7.7
1932	-2.5	-2.6	.1	.4	2.5	2.1	8.1	1.5	—	—	6.6
1933	-1.6	-1.4	-.2	.4	2.4	2.0	8.0	2.0	—	—	6.0
1934	-.7	.2	-.9	.6	3.0	2.4	9.8	3.0	—	—	6.8
1935	1.1	.4	.7	.1	3.3	3.1	10.0	2.9	—	—	7.1
1936	1.3	2.1	-.8	.1	3.5	3.4	12.0	4.9	—	—	7.0
1937	2.5	1.7	.8	.3	4.6	4.3	11.9	4.7	—	—	7.2
1938	-.9	-1.0	.1	1.3	4.3	3.0	13.0	5.4	—	—	7.6
1939	.4	.3	.1	1.1	4.4	3.4	13.3	5.1	1.2	3.9	8.2
1940	2.2	1.9	.3	1.7	5.4	3.6	14.0	6.0	2.2	3.8	8.0
1941	4.5	4.0	.4	1.3	5.9	4.6	24.8	16.9	13.8	3.1	7.9

Exhibit 2 (Continued)

					Constant (1958) Prices[a]						
1929	3.5	3.6	Z	1.5	11.8	10.3	22.0	3.5	—	—	18.5
1930	-.6	-.4	-.2	1.4	10.4	9.0	24.3	4.0	—	—	20.2
1931	-2.4	-3.9	1.5	.9	8.9	7.9	25.4	4.3	—	—	21.1
1932	-6.2	-7.0	.8	.6	7.1	6.6	24.2	4.6	—	—	19.6
1933	-4.3	-3.8	-.5	Z	7.1	7.1	23.3	6.0	—	—	17.3
1934	-2.7	.3	-3.0	.3	7.3	7.1	26.6	8.0	—	—	18.6
1935	2.4	1.0	1.4	-1.0	7.7	8.7	27.0	7.9	—	—	19.2
1936	3.1	4.7	-1.6	-1.2	3.2	9.3	31.8	12.2	—	—	19.6
1937	5.5	3.7	1.8	-.7	9.8	10.5	30.8	11.5	—	—	19.4
1938	-2.4	-2.6	.2	1.9	9.9	8.0	33.9	13.3	—	—	20.6
1939	1.2	.7	.5	1.3	10.0	8.7	35.2	12.5	—	—	22.7
1940	4.9	4.2	.7	2.1	11.0	8.9	36.4	15.0	—	—	21.4
1941	9.6	8.6	1.1	.4	11.2	10.8	56.3	36.2	—	—	20.1

[a]The percentage change in these numbers is presented on pages 518 and 519.

Z = Less than $50 million.

Source: *Historical Statistics*, Series F 47–70.

Selected U.S. Statistics (through 1941)

Exhibit 3   Average Annual Growth Rates of Real GNP: 1909–1940 (Percent)

Terminal Year	Initial Year														
	1909	1910	1911	1912	1913	1914	1915	1916	1917	1918	1919	1920	1921	1922	1923
1910	2.8	–	–	–	–	–	–	–	–	–	–	–	–	–	–
1911	2.7	2.6	–	–	–	–	–	–	–	–	–	–	–	–	–
1912	3.7	4.1	5.7	–	–	–	–	–	–	–	–	–	–	–	–
1913	3.0	3.0	3.3	.9	–	–	–	–	–	–	–	–	–	–	–
1914	1.5	1.1	.7	−1.7	−4.3	–	–	–	–	–	–	–	–	–	–
1915	1.1	.7	.3	−1.4	−2.6	−.8	–	–	–	–	–	–	–	–	–
1916	2.0	1.9	1.7	.8	.7	3.4	7.9	–	–	–	–	–	–	–	–
1917	1.9	1.7	1.6	.8	.7	2.5	4.2	.7	–	–	–	–	–	–	–
1918	3.0	3.0	3.0	2.6	2.9	4.9	6.8	6.3	12.3	–	–	–	–	–	–
1919	2.3	2.2	2.2	1.7	1.8	3.1	4.1	2.9	4.1	−3.5	–	–	–	–	–
1920	1.7	1.5	1.4	.9	.9	1.8	2.4	1.0	1.2	−3.9	−4.3	–	–	–	–
1921	.8	.6	.4	−.1	−.3	.3	.4	−.9	−1.3	−5.5	−6.5	−8.6	–	–	–
1922	1.8	1.8	1.7	1.3	1.3	2.1	2.5	1.6	1.8	−.5	.4	2.8	15.8	–	–
1923	2.5	2.5	2.5	2.2	2.4	3.1	3.7	3.1	3.5	1.8	3.2	5.8	13.9	12.1	–
1924	2.4	2.3	2.3	2.0	2.1	2.8	3.2	2.7	2.9	1.5	2.5	4.3	9.0	5.8	−.2
1925	2.7	2.7	2.7	2.5	2.6	3.3	3.7	3.3	3.6	2.4	3.5	5.1	8.9	6.6	4.0
1926	2.0	2.9	2.9	2.7	2.9	3.5	3.9	3.5	3.9	2.9	3.8	5.2	8.3	6.4	4.6
1927	2.7	2.7	2.7	2.5	2.7	3.2	3.6	3.2	3.5	2.5	3.3	4.4	6.8	5.1	3.4
1928	2.6	2.6	2.6	2.4	2.5	3.0	3.3	3.0	3.2	2.3	3.0	4.0	5.9	4.3	2.9
1929	2.8	2.8	2.8	2.7	2.8	3.3	3.6	3.3	3.5	2.7	3.4	4.3	6.0	4.7	3.5
1930	2.2	2.1	2.1	1.9	2.0	2.4	2.6	2.3	2.4	1.6	2.1	2.7	4.1	2.7	1.5
1931	1.7	1.7	1.6	1.4	1.4	1.8	1.9	1.6	1.6	.8	1.2	1.7	2.9	1.5	.3
1932	.9	.8	.8	.5	.5	.8	.9	.5	.4	−.3	−.0	.3	1.1	−.2	−1.5
1933	.8	.7	.6	.4	.4	.6	.7	.3	.3	−.4	−.1	.1	.9	−.3	−1.5
1934	1.1	1.1	1.0	.8	.8	1.0	1.1	.8	.8	.1	.4	.7	1.5	.4	−.6
1935	1.4	1.4	1.3	1.2	1.2	1.4	1.6	1.2	1.3	.7	.9	1.3	2.0	1.1	.2
1936	1.9	1.8	1.8	1.7	1.7	2.0	2.1	1.8	1.9	1.3	1.6	2.0	2.8	1.9	1.2
1937	2.0	2.0	1.9	1.8	1.8	2.1	2.3	2.0	2.1	1.6	1.8	2.2	2.9	2.1	1.5
1938	1.7	1.7	1.7	1.5	1.5	1.8	1.9	1.7	1.7	1.2	1.5	1.8	2.5	1.7	1.0
1939	2.0	1.9	1.9	1.8	1.8	2.1	2.2	2.0	2.0	1.5	1.8	2.1	2.8	2.1	1.5
1940	2.2	2.2	2.1	2.0	2.1	2.3	2.4	2.2	2.3	1.9	2.1	2.5	3.1	2.4	1.9

Note: To find the growth rate between any two years shown, locate the column for the initial year at the top of the table and read the figures in that column opposite the desired terminal year at the left.

Source: *Historical Statistics*, Series F−31.

						Initial Year									
1924	1925	1926	1927	1928	1929	1930	1931	1932	1933	1934	1935	1936	1937	1938	1939
—	—	—	—	—	—	—	—	—	—	—	—	—	—	—	—
—	—	—	—	—	—	—	—	—	—	—	—	—	—	—	—
—	—	—	—	—	—	—	—	—	—	—	—	—	—	—	—
—	—	—	—	—	—	—	—	—	—	—	—	—	—	—	—
—	—	—	—	—	—	—	—	—	—	—	—	—	—	—	—
—	—	—	—	—	—	—	—	—	—	—	—	—	—	—	—
—	—	—	—	—	—	—	—	—	—	—	—	—	—	—	—
—	—	—	—	—	—	—	—	—	—	—	—	—	—	—	—
—	—	—	—	—	—	—	—	—	—	—	—	—	—	—	—
—	—	—	—	—	—	—	—	—	—	—	—	—	—	—	—
—	—	—	—	—	—	—	—	—	—	—	—	—	—	—	—
—	—	—	—	—	—	—	—	—	—	—	—	—	—	—	—
—	—	—	—	—	—	—	—	—	—	—	—	—	—	—	—
—	—	—	—	—	—	—	—	—	—	—	—	—	—	—	—
8.4	—	—	—	—	—	—	—	—	—	—	—	—	—	—	—
7.2	5.9	—	—	—	—	—	—	—	—	—	—	—	—	—	—
4.7	2.9	.0	—	—	—	—	—	—	—	—	—	—	—	—	—
3.6	2.1	?	.6	—	—	—	—	—	—	—	—	—	—	—	—
4.2	3.2	2.3	3.6	6.7	—	—	—	—	—	—	—	—	—	—	—
1.7	.5	−.8	−1.0	−1.9	−9.8	—	—	—	—	—	—	—	—	—	—
.3	−.9	−2.2	−2.7	−3.8	−8.7	−7.6	—	—	—	—	—	—	—	—	—
−1.6	−3.0	−4.4	−5.3	−6.7	−10.8	−11.3	−14.7	—	—	—	—	—	—	—	—
−1.6	−2.8	−4.0	−4.7	−5.7	−8.6	−8.2	−8.5	−1.8	—	—	—	—	—	—	—
−.6	−1.6	−2.5	−2.8	−3.4	−5.3	−4.1	−3.0	3.4	9.1	—	—	—	—	—	—
.2	−.5	−1.2	−1.3	−1.6	−2.9	−1.5	.0	5.5	9.5	9.9	—	—	—	—	—
1.3	.7	.2	.2	.1	−.7	.8	2.7	7.6	10.0	11.8	13.9	—	—	—	—
1.6	1.0	.6	.7	.7	.0	1.5	3.1	7.1	9.5	9.6	9.5	5.3	—	—	—
1.1	.6	.1	.1	.1	−.5	.6	1.9	5.0	6.4	5.7	4.4	.0	−5.0	—	—
1.6	1.1	.8	.8	.8	.3	1.5	2.7	5.5	6.8	6.3	5.4	2.8	1.5	8.6	—
2.0	1.6	1.3	1.4	1.5	1.0	2.2	3.3	5.9	7.0	6.7	6.0	4.2	3.8	8.5	8.5

Selected U.S. Statistics (through 1941)

Exhibit 4   GNP, Total and Per Capita, in Current and 1958 Prices: 1919–1941
(Totals in Billions of Dollars; Per Capita in Dollars)

| Year | Current Prices | | 1958 Prices | | Implicit Price Index (1958 = 100) |
| | Total | Per Capita | Total | Per Capita | |
	1	2	3	4	5
1919	84.0	804	146.4	1,401	57.4
1920	91.5	860	140.0	1,315	65.4
1921	69.6	641	127.8	1,177	54.5
1922	74.1	673	148.0	1,345	50.1
1923	85.1	760	165.9	1,482	51.3
1924	84.7	742	165.5	1,450	51.2
1925	93.1	804	179.4	1,549	51.9
1926	97.0	826	190.0	1,619	51.1
1927	94.9	797	189.8	1,594	50.0
1928	97.0	805	190.9	1,584	50.8
1929	103.1	847	203.6	1,671	50.6
1930	90.4	734	183.5	1,490	49.3
1931	75.8	611	169.3	1,364	44.8
1932	58.0	465	144.2	1,154	40.2
1933	55.6	442	141.5	1,126	39.3
1934	65.1	514	154.3	1,220	42.2
1935	72.2	567	169.5	1,331	42.6
1936	82.5	643	193.0	1,506	42.7
1937	90.4	701	203.2	1,576	44.5
1938	84.7	651	192.9	1,484	43.9
1939	90.5	691	209.4	1,598	43.2
1940	99.7	754	227.2	1,720	43.9
1941	124.5	934	263.7	1,977	47.2

Source: *Historical Statistics*, Series F 1–5.

Selected U.S. Statistics (through 1941)

Exhibit 5   Sources and Uses of Gross Saving: 1929–1941 (In Billions of Current Dollars)

	Gross Saving and Statistical Discrepancy											Gross Investment		
	Private Saving						Government Surplus or Deficit (−)							
			Gross Business Saving							Capital Grants Received by the United States				
Year	Total	Personal Saving	Total	Undistributed Corporate Profits	Corporate Inventory Valuation Adjustment	Capital Consumption Allowances	Total	Federal[a]	State and Local		Statistical Discrepancy	Total	Gross Private Domestic Investment	Net Foreign Investment
	1	2	3	4	5	6	7	8	9	10	11	12	13	14
1929	15.3	4.2	11.2	2.8	.5	7.9	1.0	1.2	−.2	—	.7	17.0	16.2	.8
1930	12.1	3.4	8.6	−2.6	3.3	8.0	−.3	.3	−.6	—	−.8	11.0	10.3	.7
1931	8.0	2.6	5.3	−4.9	2.4	7.9	−2.9	−2.1	−.8	—	.7	5.8	5.6	.2
1932	2.5	−.6	3.2	−5.2	1.0	7.4	−1.8	−1.5	−.3	—	.3	1.1	1.0	.2
1933	2.3	−.9	3.2	−1.6	−2.1	7.0	−1.4	−1.3	−.1	—	.6	1.6	1.4	.2
1934	5.6	.4	5.2	−1.0	−.6	6.8	−2.4	−2.9	.5	—	.5	3.8	3.3	.4
1935	8.6	2.1	6.4	−.2	−.2	6.9	−2.0	−2.6	.6	—	−.2	6.4	6.4	−.1
1936	10.3	3.6	6.7	.4	−.7	7.0	−3.1	−3.6	.5	—	1.2	8.4	8.5	−.1
1937	11.5	3.8	7.7	.6	Z	7.2	.3	−.4	.7	—	Z	11.8	11.8	.1
1938	8.7	.7	8.0	−.2	1.0	7.3	−1.8	−2.1	.4	—	.6	7.6	6.5	1.1
1939	11.0	2.6	8.4	1.8	−.7	7.3	−2.2	−2.2	Z	—	1.3	10.2	9.3	.9
1940	14.3	3.8	10.5	3.2	−.2	7.5	−.7	−1.3	.6	—	1.0	14.6	13.1	1.5
1941	22.4	11.0	11.4	5.7	−2.5	8.2	−3.8	−5.1	1.3	—	.4	19.0	17.9	1.1

Z = Less than $50 million or −$50 million.

[a]The federal government surplus or deficit is measured on the basis of the National Income Accounts Budget and thus will not correspond to the surplus or deficit shown in Exhibit 22, which is calculated on the basis of an Administrative Budget.

Source: *Historical Statistics*, Series F, 552–565.

Selected U.S. Statistics (through 1941)

Exhibit 6 Value of New Private and Public Construction Put in Place: 1920–1940 (Millions of 1957–1959 Dollars)

| | | | | | Private Construction | | | | Public Utilities | | | |
| Year | Total New Construction | Total | Total Residential Buildings (Including Farm) | Total Nonresidential Buildings (Excluding Farm) | Farm Nonresidential | Total | Railroad | Petroleum Pipeline | Electric Light and Power | Gas | Telephone and Telegraph | All Other Private |
	1	2	3	4	5	6	7	8	9	10	11	12
1920	14,753	12,333	5,101	4,657	609	1,770	468	103	752	215	232	196
1921	16,167	12,745	6,208	4,441	346	1,525	523	90	520	200	192	225
1922	22,524	18,420	10,611	4,813	409	2,284	630	129	757	508	260	303
1923	25,011	21,415	12,386	5,040	459	3,222	961	157	1,358	443	303	308
1924	28,022	23,796	14,360	5,004	430	3,659	930	199	1,497	639	394	343
1925	31,323	26,366	15,793	6,246	435	3,552	1,013	160	1,365	550	464	340
1926	33,113	28,038	15,856	7,569	413	3,860	1,232	106	1,191	810	521	340
1927	33,238	27,528	14,908	7,712	505	4,025	1,239	238	1,220	860	468	378
1928	32,113	26,127	13,752	7,812	459	3,774	1,223	160	1,119	735	537	330
1929	29,213	23,157	10,096	8,144	417	4,194	1,398	289	1,105	631	771	306
1930	24,511	17,200	5,999	6,437	233	4,273	1,506	93	1,255	620	799	258
1931	19,559	11,998	4,856	4,001	119	2,826	951	253	769	420	433	196
1932	12,350	6,111	2,309	2,078	46	1,531	485	130	398	258	260	147
1933	9,232	4,570	1,763	1,725	71	847	342	24	208	137	136	164
1934	10,815	5,089	2,145	1,738	95	993	455	39	213	150	136	118
1935	12,780	6,764	3,555	1,809	206	1,102	449	64	277	166	146	92
1936	18,938	9,771	5,268	2,609	266	1,552	549	129	434	256	184	76
1937	19,051	11,504	5,690	3,443	318	1,963	633	196	620	243	271	90
1938	18,775	10,361	5,800	2,477	278	1,719	437	62	766	197	257	87
1939	22,379	12,600	7,676	2,567	324	1,946	534	103	861	188	260	87
1940	23,217	14,105	8,366	3,200	289	2,149	585	88	873	275	328	101

Exhibit 6 (Continued)

Year	Total[a]	Nonresidential Buildings					Public Construction					
		Total	Industrial	Educational	Hospital and Institutional	Other	Military Facilities	Highways, Roads, and Streets	Sewer and Water Systems	Conservation and Development	Public Service Enterprises	All Other Public
	13	14	15	16	17	18	19	20	21	22	23	24
1920	2,420	685	—	459	80	146	321	783	372	134	112	13
1921	3,422	1,223	—	866	126	231	122	1,228	544	159	133	13
1922	4,104	1,641	—	1,167	205	269	66	1,384	676	161	155	21
1923	3,596	1,464	—	1,053	167	244	38	1,141	594	190	148	21
1924	4,226	1,522	—	1,087	185	250	22	1,459	770	232	210	11
1925	4,957	1,801	—	1,258	192	351	20	1,681	836	219	389	11
1926	5,075	1,896	—	1,255	214	427	27	1,725	858	184	367	18
1927	5,710	1,874	—	1,154	251	469	30	2,004	935	188	644	35
1928	5,586	2,007	—	1,189	340	478	39	2,260	902	216	520	42
1929	6,056	2,072	—	1,223	318	531	50	2,296	751	341	478	68
1930	7,311	2,250	—	1,241	402	607	81	2,958	1,038	415	521	48
1931	7,561	2,346	—	1,093	421	832	124	2,951	869	502	714	55
1932	6,239	1,827	—	572	366	889	123	2,623	573	551	490	52
1933	4,662	1,028	9	228	218	573	122	1,819	330	1,101	225	37
1934	5,726	1,451	40	584	208	619	145	1,899	511	1,422	165	130
1935	6,016	1,342	7	628	155	552	115	1,681	540	1,932	213	164
1936	9,157	2,743	14	1,441	289	999	88	2,497	943	1,794	465	441
1937	7,547	1,843	6	853	246	738	104	2,396	798	1,513	330	295
1938	8,414	2,228	37	1,037	323	831	177	2,893	879	1,397	349	393
1939	9,779	3,220	76	1,555	434	1,155	354	2,877	946	1,441	353	414
1940	9,112	1,913	481	484	182	766	1,055	2,797	855	1,336	337	290

[a]The total of public construction includes a small amount of public residential construction after 1934 that is not itemized in the detail of the table.

Source: *Historical Statistics*, Series N 30–60.

Selected U.S. Statistics (through 1941)

Exhibit 7   Price Indexes: 1919–1941

Year	GNP Implicit Price Deflator[b]	Percent[c]	Consumer Price Index[a]	Percent[c]	Wholesale Price Indexes[a]					
					All Commodities	Percent[c]	Industrial Commodities	Percent[c]	Farm Commodities	Percent[c]
	1	2	3	4	5	6	7	8	9	10
1919	57.4	—	51.8	—	71.4	—	68.4	—	96.4	—
1920	65.4	13.9	60.0	15.8	79.6	11.5	85.7	25.3	92.2	−4.4
1921	54.5	−16.7	53.6	−10.6	50.3	−36.6	55.7	−35.0	54.1	−41.3
1922	50.1	−8.1	50.2	−6.3	49.9	−0.8	54.4	−2.3	57.4	6.1
1923	51.3	2.4	51.1	1.8	51.9	4.0	55.6	2.2	60.4	5.2
1924	51.2	−0.2	51.2	0.2	50.5	−2.7	53.1	−4.5	61.1	1.2
1925	51.9	1.4	52.5	2.5	53.3	5.5	54.6	2.8	67.1	9.8
1926	51.1	−1.5	53.0	0.9	51.6	−3.2	53.2	−2.6	61.3	−8.6
1927	50.0	−2.2	52.0	−1.9	49.3	−4.5	50.0	−6.0	60.8	−0.8
1928	50.8	1.6	51.3	−1.3	50.0	1.4	49.3	−1.4	64.8	6.6
1929	50.6	−0.4	51.3	0	49.1	−1.8	48.6	−1.4	64.1	−1.1
1930	49.3	−2.6	50.0	−2.5	44.6	−9.2	45.2	−7.0	54.2	−15.4
1931	44.8	−9.1	45.6	−8.8	37.6	−15.7	39.9	−11.7	39.7	−26.8
1932	40.2	−10.3	40.9	−10.3	33.6	−10.6	37.3	−6.5	29.5	−25.7
1933	39.3	−2.2	38.8	−5.1	34.0	1.2	37.8	1.3	31.4	6.4
1934	42.2	7.4	40.1	3.4	38.6	13.5	41.6	10.1	40.0	27.4
1935	42.6	0.9	41.1	2.5	41.3	7.0	41.4	−0.5	48.1	20.3
1936	42.7	0.2	41.5	1.0	41.7	1.0	42.2	1.9	49.5	2.9
1937	44.5	4.2	43.0	3.6	44.5	6.7	45.2	7.1	52.9	6.9
1938	43.9	−1.3	42.2	−1.9	40.5	−9.0	43.4	−4.0	42.0	−20.6
1939	43.2	−1.6	41.6	−1.4	39.8	−1.7	43.3	−0.2	40.0	−4.8
1940	43.9	1.6	42.0	1.0	40.5	1.7	44.0	1.6	41.4	3.5
1941	47.2	7.5	44.1	5.0	45.1	11.3	47.3	7.5	50.3	21.5

[a]1967 = 100.
[b]GNP Implicit Price Index: 1958 = 100.
[c]Percentage of annual compound growth rate.

Source: *Historical Statistics*, Series F 5 and E 1, Series E 135, and Series E 23–25.

Selected U.S. Statistics (through 1941)

Exhibit 8   Population, Income Distribution, and Unemployment: 1920–1941

Year	Population (in Thousands)	Share of Disposable Income Held by:		% Civilian Labor Force Unemployed
		Top 1 %	Top 5 %	
	1	2	3	4
1920	106,466	11.8	23.9	4.0
1921	108,541	14.2	29.3	11.9
1922	110,055	14.3	29.0	7.6
1923	111,950	13.0	27.0	3.2
1924	114,113	14.2	28.7	5.5
1925	115,832	16.5	31.0	4.0
1926	117,399	16.2	30.7	1.9
1927	119,038	17.2	31.9	4.1
1928	120,501	19.1	34.0	4.4
1929	121,770	18.9	33.4	3.2
1930	123,077	15.3	30.9	8.7
1931	124,040	14.5	31.2	15.9
1932	124,840	12.6	30.4	23.6
1933	125,579	13.0	30.2	24.9
1934	126,374	12.8	28.9	21.7
1935	127,250	12.7	27.8	20.1
1936	128,053	13.5	27.9	16.9
1937	128,825	12.8	27.0	14.3
1938	129,825	12.0	26.8	19.0
1939	130,880	12.1	26.8	17.2
1940	131,954	11.3	25.4	14.6
1941	133,121	9.8	22.9	9.9

Source: *Historical Statistics: Colonial Times to 1957,* Series A 1–3, Series D 46–47, Series G 337–352.

Selected U.S. Statistics (through 1941)

Exhibit 9   Earnings, Hours, and Production Index in Manufacturing: 1919–1941

Year	All Manufacturing						Federal Reserve Board Index of Manufacturing Production (1967 = 100)	
	Average Hourly Earnings		Average Weekly Hours		Average Weekly Earnings			
	1	2	3	4	5	6	7	8
1919	$0.47	—	46.3	—	$21.84	—	15	—
1920	.55	17.0%	47.4	2.4%	26.02	19.1%	15	0.0%
1921	.51	−7.3	43.1	−9.1	21.94	−15.7	12	−20.0
1922	.48	−5.9	44.2	2.6	21.28	−3.0	15	25.0
1923	.52	8.3	45.6	3.2	23.56	10.7	18	20.0
1924	.54	3.8	43.7	−4.2	23.67	0.5	17	− 5.6
1925	.54	0.0	44.5	1.8	24.11	1.9	19	11.8
1926	.54	0.0	45.0	1.1	24.38	1.1	20	5.3
1927	.54	0.0	45.0	0.0	24.47	0.4	20	0.0
1928	.56	3.7	44.4	−1.3	24.70	0.9	21	5.0
1929	.56	0.0	44.2	−0.5	24.76	0.2	23	9.5
1930	.55	−1.8	42.1	−4.8	23.00	−7.1	19	−17.4
1931	.51	−7.3	40.5	−3.8	20.64	−10.3	15	−21.0
1932	.44	−13.7	38.3	−5.4	16.89	−18.2	12	−20.0
1933	.44	0.0	38.1	−0.5	16.65	−1.4	14	16.7
1934	.53	20.5	34.6	−9.2	18.20	9.3	15	7.1
1935	.54	1.9	36.6	5.8	19.91	9.4	18	20.0
1936	.55	1.9	39.2	7.1	21.56	8.3	22	22.2
1937	.62	12.7	38.6	−1.5	23.82	10.5	23	4.5
1938	.62	0.0	35.6	−7.8	22.07	−7.3	18	−21.7
1939	.63	1.6	37.7	5.9	23.64	7.1	22	22.2
1940	.66	4.8	38.1	1.1	24.96	5.6	25	13.6
1941	.73	10.6	40.6	6.6	29.48	18.1	32	28.0

Source: *Historical Statistics,* Series D 802–804 and Series P 13.

Selected U.S. Statistics (through 1941)

Exhibit 10   Labor Union Membership and Work Stoppages: 1919–1941

Year	Membership— All Unions (Thousands)	Work Stoppages	Average Duration of Stoppages (Days)	Workers Involved (Thousands)
	1	2	3	4
1919	4,046	3,630	—	—
1920	5,034	3,411	—	—
1921	4,722	2,385	—	—
1922	3,950	1,112	—	—
1923	3,629	1,553	—	—
1924	3,549	1,249	—	—
1925	3,566	1,301	—	—
1926	3,592	1,035	—	—
1927	3,600	666	26.5	319
1928	3,567	620	27.6	323
1929	3,625	924	22.6	286
1930	3,632	651	22.3	182
1931	3,526	796	18.8	346
1932	3,226	852	19.6	325
1933	2,857	1,672	16.9	1,144
1934	3,728	1,817	19.5	1,480
1935	3,753	2,003	23.8	1,102
1936	4,107	2,156	23.3	710
1937	5,780	4,720	20.3	1,950
1938	6,081	2,772	23.6	688
1939	6,556	2,639	23.4	1,180
1940	7,282	2,493	20.9	573
1941	8,698	4,314	18.3	2,360

Source: *Historical Statistics,* Series D 935 and 940, D 977, D 981, and D 982. (U.S. Bureau of Labor Statistics compiled union membership data through 1934 and the National Bureau of Economic Research compiled data from 1935.)

Selected U.S. Statistics (through 1941)

Exhibit 11   **Money Stock—Currency, Deposits, Bank Vault Cash, and Gold: 1916–1941**
(Billions of Dollars; Annual Averages)

| Year | Currency Held by the Public | Deposits Adjusted, Commercial Banks | | | M₁ Money Supply (Currency plus Demand Deposits) | Percentage Annual Change in M₁ | M₂ Money Supply (M₁ plus Time Deposits) |
| | | Total | Demand | Time | | | |
	1	2	3	4	5	6	7
1916	2.17	18.68	12.53	6.15	14.70	—	20.85
1917	2.17	22.20	14.91	7.29	17.08	16.2	24.37
1918	2.76	23.97	16.20	7.77	18.96	11.0	26.73
1919	4.02	26.99	17.77	9.22	21.79	14.9	31.01
1920	4.48	30.32	19.25	11.07	23.73	8.9	34.80
1921	4.04	28.81	17.47	11.34	21.51	−9.4	32.85
1922	3.69	30.03	17.98	12.05	21.67	0.7	33.72
1923	3.96	32.64	18.97	13.67	22.93	5.8	36.60
1924	3.96	34.62	19.71	14.91	23.67	3.2	38.58
1925	3.96	38.09	21.70	16.39	25.66	8.4	42.05
1926	4.00	39.68	22.18	17.50	26.18	2.0	43.68
1927	3.98	40.75	22.12	18.63	26.10	−0.3	44.73
1928	3.89	42.53	22.49	20.04	26.38	1.1	46.42
1929	3.90	42.70	22.74	19.96	26.64	1.0	46.60
1930	3.73	42.00	22.03	19.97	25.76	−3.3	45.73
1931	4.16	38.53	19.98	18.55	24.14	−6.3	42.69
1932	4.92	31.13	16.19	14.94	21.11	−12.6	36.05
1933	5.09	27.13	14.82	12.31	19.91	−5.7	32.22
1934	4.63	29.73	17.23	12.50	21.86	9.8	34.36
1935	4.80	34.27	21.08	13.19	25.88	18.4	39.07
1936	5.23	38.25	24.32	13.93	29.55	14.2	43.48
1937	5.59	40.09	25.32	14.77	30.91	4.6	45.68
1938	5.55	39.96	24.97	14.99	30.52	−1.3	45.51
1939	6.04	43.23	28.11	15.12	34.15	11.9	49.27
1940	6.76	48.44	32.89	15.55	39.65	16.1	55.20
1941	3.40	54.11	38.12	15.99	46.52	17.3	62.51

Source: *Historical Statistics,* Series X 410–419.

Exhibit 11 (Continued)

Year	Percentage Annual Change in M_2	Bank Vault Cash	Monetary Gold Stock	Percentage Annual Change in Monetary Gold Stock	Deposits at Nonbank Thrift Institutions	
					Mutual Savings Banks	Savings and Loan Associations
	8	9	10	11	12	13
1916	—	1.55	2.48	—	4.13	1.06
1917	16.9	1.40	3.11	25.4	4.33	1.16
1918	9.7	1.01	3.16	1.6	4.39	−1.27
1919	16.0	1.01	3.13	−0.9	4.71	−1.39
1920	12.2	1.02	2.88	−8.0	5.15	−1.60
1921	−5.6	.90	3.29	14.2	5.48	1.85
1922	2.6	.87	3.80	15.5	5.72	2.09
1923	14.4	.90	4.06	6.8	6.18	2.42
1924	5.4	.92	4.44	9.4	6.59	2.89
1925	9.0	.93	4.38	−1.4	7.02	3.48
1926	3.9	.95	4.45	1.6	7.44	4.09
1927	2.4	.93	4.56	2.5	7.97	4.70
1928	3.8	.91	4.21	−7.8	8.53	5.39
1929	0.4	.90	4.28	1.6	8.83	6.00
1930	−1.9	.85	4.47	4.4	9.09	6.27
1931	−6.6	.83	4.70	5.1	9.81	6.11
1932	−15.6	.75	4.24	−9.8	9.89	5.62
1933	−10.6	.73	4.35	2.6	9.65	5.04
1934	6.6	.78	7.74	77.9	9.63	4.60
1935	13.7	.84	9.06	17.1	9.78	4.36
1936	11.3	.95	10.58	16.8	9.93	4.22
1937	5.1	.94	12.15	14.8	10.11	4.14
1938	−0.4	1.02	13.25	9.1	10.19	4.08
1939	8.3	1.10	16.08	21.4	10.39	4.10
1940	12.0	1.24	19.85	23.4	10.58	4.22
1941	13.2	1.37	22.54	13.6	10.58	4.50

Selected U.S. Statistics (through 1941)

Exhibit 12   Selected Federal Reserve Assets: 1919–1941[a,b]
(Annual Averages of Daily Figures; Millions of Dollars)

| Year | Federal Reserve Credit Outstanding | | | | Gold Stock[c] |
	Bills Discounted	Bills Bought	U.S. Government Securities	Total, Including All Others	
	1	2	3	4	5
1919	1,906	324	254	2,625	2,842
1920	2,523	385	324	3,390	2,582
1921	1,797	91	264	2,198	3,004
1922	571	159	455	1,226	3,515
1923	736	227	186	1,205	3,774
1924	373	172	402	996	4,152
1925	490	287	359	1,195	4,094
1926	572	281	350	1,258	4,165
1927	442	263	417	1,175	4,277
1928	840	328	297	1,505	3,919
1929	952	241	208	1,459	3,996
1930	272	213	564	1,087	4,173
1931	327	245	669	1,274	4,417
1932	521	71	1,461	2,077	3,952
1933	283	83	2,052	2,429	4,059
1934	36	25	2,432	2,502	7,512
1935	7	5	2,431	2,475	9,059
1936	6	4	2,431	2,481	10,578
1937	14	3	2,504	2,554	12,162
1938	9	1	2,565	2,600	13,250
1939	5	—	2,584	2,628	16,085
1940	4	—	2,417	2,487	19,865
1941	5	—	2,187	2,293	22,546

[a]Because these are only selected assets, they will not add to liabilities in Exhibit 13.
[b]These assets are analogous to the assets of an individual bank that has loans (Bill Discounted), investments (Bills Bought and U.S. Government Securities), and cash (gold). Compare columns 3, 4, 5 of Exhibit 14.
[c]Notice that these are the same numbers given in column 10 of Exhibit 11 for the monetary gold stock.

Source: U.S. Board of Governors, Federal Reserve System, *Banking and Monetary Statistics*, 1943, 368.

Selected U.S. Statistics (through 1941)

Exhibit 13   Selected Federal Reserve Liabilities: 1919–1941[a]
(Annual Averages of Daily Figures; Millions of Dollars)

	Money in Circulation[b]	Member Bank Reserves	
		Total[c]	Excess[d]
	1	2	3
1919	4,729	1,719	—
1920	5,191	1,835	—
1921	4,663	1,671	—
1922	4,248	1,781	—
1923	4,535	1,873	—
1924	4,592	2,023	—
1925	4,582	2,167	—
1926	4,645	2,209	—
1927	4,605	2,290	—
1928	4,496	2,355	—
1929	4,476	2,358	43
1930	4,245	2,379	55
1931	4,672	2,323	89
1932	5,328	2,114	256
1933	5,576	2,343	528
1934	5,403	3,676	1,564
1935	5,585	5,001	2,469
1936	6,101	5,989	2,512
1937	6,475	6,830	1,220
1938	6,510	7,935	2,522
1939	7,058	10,352	4,392
1940	7,879	13,249	6,326
1941	9,594	13,404	5,324

[a]Because these are only selected liabilities, they will not add to the assets in Exhibit 12.
[b]This is larger than the amount of Currency Held by the Public in Exhibit 11, since it also includes currency held by banks and the Treasury.
[c]Total reserves equals the sum of required and excess reserves.
[d]Figures for member bank excess reserves were not available prior to 1929.

Source: U.S. Board of Governors, Federal Reserve System, *Banking and Monetary Statistics*, 1943, 368.

Selected U.S. Statistics (through 1941)

Exhibit 14   All Banks—Number of Banks and Principal Assets and Liabilities: 1919–1941
(Millions of Dollars, except Number of Banks; as of June 30 or Nearest Available Date)

		Assets			Liabilities		
Year	Number of Banks	Total Assets or Liabilities	Total Loans	Total Investments	Total Cash	Total Deposits	Bank Notes	Capital Accounts
	1	2	3	4	5	6	7	8
1919	29,767	47,603	25,132	12,024	8,286	37,982	677	5,409
1920	30,909	53,094	31,189	11,043	8,489	41,838	688	6,019
1921	31,076	49,633	29,236	11,169	6,980	38,934	704	6,385
1922	30,736	50,368	28,000	12,328	7,830	41,227	725	6,599
1923	30,444	54,144	30,734	13,474	7,595	44,376	720	6,818
1924	29,601	57,420	32,030	13,843	9,034	47,961	729	7,073
1925	29,052	62,232	34,378	15,056	9,903	52,301	648	7,384
1926	28,350	65,079	36,658	15,562	9,806	54,416	651	7,841
1927	27,255	67,893	37,949	16,649	10,156	56,700	650	8,301
1928	26,401	71,121	39,946	18,146	9,454	58,138	649	8,954
1929	25,568	72,315	41,944	17,305	9,222	58,269	649	9,750
1930	24,273	74,290	40,990	18,090	11,201	60,365	649	10,372
1931	22,242	70,070	35,416	19,973	10,405	57,187	636	9,872
1932	19,317	57,295	28,071	18,406	7,407	45,569	649	8,525
1933	14,771	51,359	22,337	18,125	7,793	41,684	727	7,388
1934	15,913	55,915	21,309	21,262	10,158	46,480	695	7,865
1935	16,047	59,951	20,240	24,176	12,318	51,270	222	7,815
1936	15,884	66,854	20,640	27,857	15,038	58,068	—	8,016
1937	15,646	68,402	22,435	27,212	15,520	59,485	—	8,123
1938	15,419	67,730	21,033	26,267	17,374	59,000	—	8,107
1939	15,210	73,193	21,300	28,339	20,550	64,303	—	8,236
1940	15,076	79,729	22,311	29,040	25,603	70,854	—	8,252
1941	14,975	87,324	25,273	32,667	26,785	78,212	—	8,441

Source: *Historical Statistics*, Series X 580–587.

Selected U.S. Statistics (through 1941)

Exhibit 15 Bank Suspensions—Number and Deposits of Suspended Banks: 1921–1940

		Number of Suspensions						Deposits of Suspended Banks (Millions of Dollars)							
		State Commercial		Mutual Savings	Federal Reserve System				State Commercial		Mutual Savings	Federal Reserve System		Losses Borne by Depositors
Year	National	Incorporated	Private (Unincorporated)		Member	Non-member	Total	National	Incorporated	Private (Unincorporated)		Member	Non-member	
Total	National							National							
1	2	3	4	5	6	7	8	9	10	11	12	13	14	15
1921	505	52	409	44	—	71	434	172	21	143	9	—	38	134	60
1922	367	49	294	23	1	62	305	93	20	69	2	2	27	66	38
1923	646	90	533	23	—	122	524	150	34	114	2	—	47	103	62
1924	775	122	616	37	—	160	615	210	65	138	8	—	79	132	79
1925	618	118	461	39	—	146	472	168	56	104	8	—	65	102	61
1926	976	123	801	52	—	158	818	260	44	207	9	—	67	193	83
1927	669	91	545	33	—	122	547	199	46	149	4	—	63	136	61
1928	499	57	422	19	1	73	426	143	36	103	3	Z	47	96	44
1929	659	64	564	31	—	81	576	231	42	181	8	—	58	173	77
1930	1,352	161	1,181	58	2	188	1,164	869	170	668	15	16	373	496	237
1931	2,294	409	1,804	80	1	516	1,778	1,691	439	1,230	21	Z	733	958	391
1932	1,456	276	1,140	37	3	382	1,125	725	214	494	8	9	269	456	168
1933	4,004	1,101	2,790	109	4	1,275	3,729	2,601	1,611	1,975	13	2	2,394	1,207	540
1934–1940	448	45	383	19	2	61	388	477	59	412	2	4	232	245	9,173

Z = Less than $50 million.

Source: *Historical Statistics*, Series X 741–755.

Selected U.S. Statistics (through 1941)

Exhibit 16   Money Market Rates: 1916–1941
(Percent per Annum; Open Market Rates in New York City)

Year	Stock Exchange Time Loans 90 Days	Prime Commercial Paper, 4 to 6 Months	Stock Exchange Call Loans		Prime Bankers' Acceptances, 90 days	U.S. Government Securities 3-Month Bills[a]		Federal Reserve Bank of New York Discount Rate	
			New	Renewals		Rate on New Issues	Market Yield	Low	High
	1	2	3	4	5	6	7	8	9
1916	3.25	3.84	—	2.62	—	—	—	3.00	4.00
1917	4.62	5.07	—	3.43	—	—	—	3.00	3.50
1918	5.90	6.02	—	5.28	4.19	—	—	3.50	4.00
1919	5.83	5.37	6.70	6.32	4.37	—	—	4.00	4.75
1920	8.06	7.50	8.07	7.74	6.06	—	—	4.75	7.00
1921	6.15	6.62	5.97	5.97	5.28	—	—	4.50	7.00
1922	4.53	4.52	4.36	4.29	3.51	—	—	4.00	4.50
1923	5.14	5.07	4.87	4.86	4.09	—	—	4.00	4.50
1924	3.64	3.98	3.10	3.08	2.98	—	—	3.00	4.50
1925	4.23	4.02	4.20	4.18	3.29	—	—	3.00	3.50

Exhibit 16 (Continued)

1926	4.60	4.34	4.52	4.50	3.59	—	—	3.50	4.00
1927	4.35	4.11	4.05	4.06	3.45	—	—	3.50	4.00
1928	5.86	4.85	6.10	6.04	4.09	—	—	3.50	5.00
1929	7.75	5.85	7.74	7.61	5.03	—	—	4.50	6.00
1930	3.26	3.59	2.87	2.94	2.48	—	—	2.00	4.50
1931	2.15	2.64	1.74	1.74	1.57	1.402	1.40	1.50	3.50
1932	1.87	2.73	2.05	2.05	1.28	.879	.88	2.50	3.50
1933	1.11	1.73	1.14	1.16	.63	.515	.52	2.00	3.50
1934	.90	1.02	1.00	1.00	.25	.256	.26	1.50	2.00
1935	.55	.75	.56	.55	.13	.137	.14	1.50	1.50
1936	1.16	.75	.91	.91	.15	.143	.14	1.50	1.50
1937	1.25	.94	1.00	1.00	.43	.447	.45	1.00	1.50
1938	1.25	.81	1.00	1.00	.44	.053	.05	1.00	1.00
1939	1.25	.59	1.00	1.00	.44	.023	.02	1.00	1.00
1940	1.25	.56	1.00	1.00	.44	.014	.01	1.00	1.00
1941	1.25	.53	1.00	1.00	.44	.103	.13	1.00	1.00

[a]Treasury bills were first offered in 1929, but series begins in 1931.

**Exhibit 17   Basic Yields of Corporate Bonds, by Term to Maturity:
1916–1946
(Percent per Annum)**

	Years to Maturity				
Year	1 Year	5 Years	10 Years	20 Years	30 Years
	1	2	3	4	5
1916	3.48	4.03	4.05	4.05	4.05
1917	4.05	4.05	4.05	4.05	4.05
1918	5.48	5.25	5.05	4.82	4.75
1919	5.58	5.16	4.97	4.81	4.75
1920	6.11	5.72	5.43	5.17	5.10
1921	6.94	6.21	5.73	5.31	5.17
1922	5.31	5.19	5.06	4.85	4.71
1923	5.01	4.90	4.80	4.68	4.61
1924	5.02	4.90	4.80	4.69	4.66
1925	3.85	4.46	4.50	4.50	4.50
1926	4.40	4.40	4.40	4.40	4.40
1927	4.30	4.30	4.30	4.30	4.30
1928	4.05	4.05	4.05	4.05	4.05
1929	5.27	4.72	4.57	4.45	4.42
1930	4.40	4.40	4.40	4.40	4.40
1931	3.05	3.90	4.03	4.10	4.10
1932	3.99	4.58	4.70	4.70	4.70
1933	2.60	3.68	4.00	4.11	4.15
1934	2.62	3.48	3.70	3.91	3.99
1935	1.05	2.37	3.00	3.37	3.50
1936	.61	1.86	2.64	3.04	3.20
1937	.69	1.68	2.38	2.90	3.08
1938	.85	1.97	2.60	2.91	3.00
1939	.57	1.55	2.18	2.65	2.75
1940	.41	1.28	1.95	2.55	2.70
1941	.41	1.21	1.88	2.50	2.65
1942	.81	1.50	2.16	2.61	2.65
1943	1.17	1.71	2.16	2.61	2.65
1944	1.08	1.58	2.20	2.60	2.60
1945	1.02	1.53	2.14	2.55	2.55
1946	.86	1.32	1.88	2.35	2.43

Sources: *Historical Statistics,* Series X 487–491.

Selected U.S. Statistics (through 1941)

Exhibit 18   Bond and Stock Prices: 1916–1941

| Year | Bonds (Price per $100 Bond) | | | Standard and Poor's Index of Common Stocks (1941–1943 = 10) | | | |
	U.S. Government	Standard and Poor's State and Local Government	Corporate Aaa	Total	Industrial	Railroad	Utilities
	1	2	3	4	5	6	7
1916	—	100.9	90.7	9.47	6.62	28.35	20.26
1917	—	97.3	87.6	8.50	6.15	24.89	18.24
1918	—	93.5	82.3	7.54	5.57	22.40	14.70
1919	91.9	93.9	81.9	8.78	7.13	22.94	14.79
1920	85.9	87.7	75.2	7.98	6.50	20.86	18.36
1921	88.2	86.5	76.6	6.86	5.07	20.15	14.18
1922	96.6	96.9	85.5	8.41	6.35	23.71	17.39
1923	95.9	96.7	85.0	8.57	6.54	23.45	18.11
1924	99.3	97.4	86.6	9.05	6.83	25.02	19.34
1925	101.7	98.8	88.3	11.15	8.69	29.21	23.28
1926	103.8	99.0	90.1	12.59	10.04	32.72	24.11
1927	108.1	100.3	91.6	15.34	12.53	38.17	27.63
1928	108.3	99.3	91.8	19.95	16.92	40.40	36.86
1929	104.8	96.5	89.1	26.02	21.35	46.15	59.33
1930	108.8	99.0	90.9	21.03	16.42	39.82	53.24
1931	92.8	100.0	92.8	13.66	10.51	23.72	37.18
1932	88.9	91.7	84.4	6.93	5.37	8.75	20.65
1933	93.1	91.0	91.2	8.96	7.61	12.75	19.72
1934	95.4	99.7	98.2	9.84	9.00	14.05	15.79
1935	99.5	108.6	105.5	10.60	10.13	11.78	15.15
1936	100.8	113.8	109.6	15.47	14.69	17.71	22.47
1937	100.1	113.3	110.2	15.41	14.97	16.86	19.07
1938	101.8	116.6	111.7	11.49	11.39	9.15	14.17
1939	104.5	119.0	114.7	12.06	11.77	9.82	16.34
1940	106.6	123.6	116.3	11.02	10.69	9.41	15.05
1941	109.5	130.9	117.7	9.82	9.72	9.39	10.93

Source: *Historical Statistics,* Series X 492–498.

Selected U.S. Statistics (through 1941)

Exhibit 19 Balance of International Payments: 1919–1940 (Millions of Dollars; Calendar Years)

| | Exports of Goods and Services | | | | | | | Imports of Goods and Services | | | | | | |
| | | | | | Income on Investments Abroad | | | | | | | | | |
Year	Total	Merchandise, Adjusted	Transportation	Travel	Private	Government	Other Transactions	Total	Merchandise, Adjusted	Transportation	Travel	Direct Military Expenditures	Income on Foreign Investments in U.S.	Other Transactions
	1	2	3	4	5	6	7	8	9	10	11	12	13	14
1919	10,776	8,891	1,109	56	544	175	1	5,908	3,995	818	123	757	130	85
1920	10,264	8,481	1,119	67	588	8	1	6,741	5,384	848	190	123	120	76
1921	5,505	4,586	394	76	405	40	4	3,383	2,572	334	200	65	105	107
1922	4,954	3,929	286	61	544	126	8	3,957	3,184	341	243	42	105	42
1923	5,494	4,266	302	71	676	164	15	4,652	3,866	332	260	33	130	31
1924	5,911	4,741	315	77	602	160	16	4,560	3,684	361	303	36	140	36
1925	6,348	5,011	318	83	752	160	24	5,261	4,291	391	347	39	170	23
1926	6,381	4,922	370	110	793	160	26	5,555	4,500	415	372	43	200	25
1927	6,456	4,982	360	114	821	160	19	5,383	4,240	417	400	38	240	48
1928	6,842	5,249	372	121	922	158	20	5,465	4,159	460	448	44	275	79
1929	7,034	5,347	390	139	982	157	19	5,886	4,463	509	483	50	330	51
1930	5,448	3,929	325	129	876	164	25	4,416	3,104	477	463	49	295	28
1931	3,641	2,494	247	94	674	92	40	3,125	2,120	366	341	48	220	30
1932	2,474	1,667	171	65	460	67	44	2,067	1,343	255	259	47	135	28
1933	2,402	1,736	108	66	417	20	55	2,044	1,510	154	199	41	115	25
1934	2,975	2,238	133	81	437	86	86	2,374	1,763	196	218	34	135	28
1935	3,265	2,404	139	101	521	—	100	3,137	2,462	206	245	41	155	28
1936	3,539	2,590	158	117	567	2	105	3,424	2,546	247	297	38	270	26
1937	4,553	3,451	236	135	576	1	154	4,256	3,181	366	348	41	295	25
1938	4,336	3,243	267	130	583	2	111	3,045	2,173	303	303	41	200	25
1939	4,432	3,347	303	135	539	2	106	3,366	2,409	367	290	46	230	24
1940	5,355	4,124	402	95	561	3	170	3,636	2,698	334	190	61	210	143

Exhibit 19 (Continued)

| Year | Balance on Goods and Services | Unilateral Transfers, Net [to Foreign Countries (−)] | | U.S. Capital Flows, Net [Outflow of Funds (−)] | | | | | Foreign Capital Flows, Net [Outflow of Funds(−)] | | Transactions in U.S. Official Reserve Assets, Net [Increase (−)] | Errors and Omissions, Net |
| | | Private | Government | Government, Long- and Short-Term | Direct Long-Term | Private, Other Long-Term | Short-Term | | Long-Term | Short-Term | | |
	15	16	17	18	19	20	21		22	23	24	25
1919	4,868	−832	−212	−2,328	−94	−75	—		−215	—	166	−1,278
1920	3,523	−634	−45	−175	−154	−400	—		−278	—	68	−1,905
1921	2,122	−450	−59	30	−111	−477	—		−4	—	−735	−316
1922	997	−314	−38	31	−153	−669	—		7	—	−269	408
1923	842	−328	−37	91	−148	−235	−82		338	49	−315	−175
1924	1,351	−339	−25	28	−182	−703	−109		185	228	−256	−178
1925	1,087	−373	−30	27	−268	−603	−46		301	−60	100	−135
1926	826	−361	−20	30	−351	−470	−36		95	455	−93	−75
1927	1,073	−355	−2	46	−351	−635	−349		−50	934	113	−423
1928	1,377	−346	−19	49	−558	−752	−231		463	−117	238	−104
1929	1,148	−343	−34	38	−602	−34	−200		358	196	−143	−384
1930	1,032	−306	−36	77	−294	−70	−191		66	−288	−310	320
1931	516	−279	−40	14	−222	350	628		66	−1,265	133	99
1932	407	−217	−21	26	−16	267	227		−26	−673	−53	79
1933	358	−191	−17	−7	32	−80	42		125	−454	131	61
1934	601	−162	−10	−5	−17	202	104		15	126	−1,266	412
1935	128	−162	−20	1	34	82	−27		320	648	−1,822	364
1936	115	−176	−32	3	−12	189	52		600	376	−1,272	157
1937	297	−175	−60	2	35	241	43		245	311	−1,364	425
1938	1,291	−153	−29	−9	16	24	36		57	317	−1,799	249
1939	1,066	−151	−27	−14	9	104	226		−86	1,259	−3,174	788
1940	1,719	−178	−32	−51	32	36	177		−90	1,353	−4,243	1,277

Source: *Historical Statistics, Series U 1–25.*

Selected U.S. Statistics (through 1941)

Exhibit 20   Summary of Federal Government Finances—
Administrative Budget: 1916–1939
(Millions of Dollars; Fiscal Years Ending June 30)

Year	Budget Receipts[a]	Budget Expendi- tures[b]	Surplus or Deficit[c] (−)	Total Public Debt[d]
	1	2	3	4
1916	761	712	48	1,225
1917	1,100	1,953	−853	2,975
1918	3,645	12,677	−9,032	12,455
1919	5,130	18,492	−13,362	25,484
1920	6,648	6,357	291	24,299
1921	5,570	5,061	509	23,977
1922	4,025	3,289	736	22,963
1923	3,852	3,140	712	22,349
1924	3,871	2,907	963	21,250
1925	3,640	2,923	717	20,516
1926	3,795	2,929	865	19,643
1927	4,012	2,857	1,155	18,511
1928	3,900	2,961	939	17,604
1929	3,861	3,127	734	16,931
1930	4,057	3,320	737	16,185
1931	3,115	3,577	−461	16,801
1932	1,923	4,659	−2,735	19,487
1933	1,996	4,598	−2,601	22,538
1934	3,014	6,644	−3,629	27,053
1935	3,705	6,497	−2,791	28,700
1936	3,997	8,421	−4,424	33,778
1937	4,955	7,733	−2,777	36,424
1938	5,588	6,764	−1,176	37,164
1939	4,979	8,841	−3,862	40,439

[a]Excludes receipts from borrowing.
[b]Excludes debt repayment.
[c]Receipts compared with expenditures.
[d]As of end of period.

Source: *Historical Statistics,* Series Y 335–338.

Selected U.S. Statistics (through 1941)

Exhibit 21 **Outlays of the Federal Government, by Major Function: 1918–1939**
(Millions of Dollars; for Fiscal Years Ending June 30)

Year	Total	Major National Security	Inter- national Affairs and Finance	Veterans' Services and Benefits	Interest	All Other
	1	2	3	4	5	6
1918	12,662	7,110	4,748	235	198	371
1919	18,448	13,548	3,500	324	616	460
1920	6,357	3,997	435	332	1,024	569
1921	5,058	2,581	83	646	999	749
1922	3,285	929	10	686	991	669
1923	3,137	680	14	747	1,056	640
1924	2,890	647	15	676	941	611
1925	2,881	591	15	741	882	652
1926	2,888	586	17	772	832	681
1927	2,837	578	17	786	787	669
1928	2,933	656	12	806	731	728
1929	3,127	696	14	812	719	886
1930	3,320	734	14	821	697	1,054
1931	3,578	733	16	1,040	628	1,161
1932	4,659	703	19	985	619	2,333
1933	4,623	648	16	863	701	2,395
1934	6,694	540	12	557	770	4,815
1935	6,521	711	19	607	826	4,358
1936	8,494	914	18	2,350	756	4,456
1937	7,756	937	18	1,137	872	4,792
1938	6,792	1,030	19	581	933	4,229
1939	8,858	1,075	20	560	950	6,254

Source: *Historical Statistics*, Series Y 466–471.

Selected U.S. Statistics (through 1941)

Exhibit 22   Social Welfare Expenditures under Public Programs, by Source of Funds: 1890–1941 (Millions of Dollars)

| | From Federal Funds | | | | | | | | From State and Local Funds[a] | | | | | | | |
| Year | Total | Social Insurance | Public Aid | Health and Medical Programs | Veterans' Programs | Education | Housing | Other Social Welfare | Total | Social Insurance[b] | Public Aid | Health and Medical Programs | Veterans' Programs | Education | Housing | Other Social Welfare |
	1	2	3	4	5	6	7	8	9	10	11	12	13	14	15	16
1890	115	—	—	—	—	—	—	—	203	—	—	—	—	—	—	—
1913	196	—	—	—	—	—	—	—	804	—	—	—	—	—	—	—
1929	798	56	—	47	658	37	—	1	3,123	286	60	304	—	2,397	—	75
1930	817	60	—	47	668	40	—	2	3,268	301	78	331	—	2,483	—	76
1931	911	69	—	51	744	45	—	2	3,290	299	164	355	—	2,394	—	77
1932	1,022	75	—	55	825	46	—	2	3,301	281	256	379	—	2,306	—	79
1933	1,339	81	345	52	819	41	—	2	3,123	263	344	366	—	2,063	—	87
1934	2,771	95	2,004	48	530	93	Z	2	3,061	267	527	352	—	1,821	—	94
1935	3,207	119	2,374	50	598	53	13	2	3,341	287	624	378	—	1,955	—	97
1936	6,506	133	2,310	55	3,826	139	42	3	3,678	323	770	399	—	2,089	—	97
1937	3,788	193	2,494	70	880	143	3	4	4,070	352	942	430	12	2,232	—	101
1938	3,255	295	2,075	73	615	188	4	5	4,669	553	1,158	467	12	2,376	—	103
1939	3,987	358	2,871	79	596	73	3	7	5,226	823	1,359	496	10	2,431	—	107
1940	3,443	394	2,243	97	620	75	4	11	5,351	878	1,353	519	9	2,487	—	106
1941	3,660	470	2,188	232	605	136	9	22	5,293	860	1,336	493	8	2,482	—	114

Z = Less than $500,000.

[a] Includes expenditures from state accounts in unemployment trust fund; excludes federal grants-in-aid.

[b] Includes payments by private insurance carriers and self-insurers of benefits payable under state workmen's compensation and temporary disability insurance laws.

Source: *Historical Statistics*, Series Y32–47.

Selected U.S. Statistics (through 1941)

Exhibit 23   Demographic Statistics—Birth Rate, Death Rate, and Marriage Rate: 1919–1933

Year	Birth Rate[a]	Death Rate[b]	Marriage Rate[c]
	1	2	3
1919	26.1	12.9	NA
1920	27.7	13.0	12.0
1921	28.1	11.5	10.7
1922	26.2	11.7	10.3
1923	26.0	12.1	11.0
1924	26.1	11.6	10.4
1925	25.1	11.7	10.3
1926	24.2	12.1	10.2
1927	23.5	11.3	10.1
1928	22.2	12.0	9.8
1929	21.2	11.9	10.1
1930	21.3	11.3	9.2
1931	20.2	11.1	8.6
1932	19.5	10.9	7.9
1933	18.4	10.7	8.7

NA = Not available.
[a]Estimated total live births per 1,000 population.
[b]Number of deaths, excluding fetal deaths, per 1,000 population.
[c]Number of marriages per 1,000 population.

Selected U.S. Statistics (through 1941)

Exhibit 24   Electoral and Popular Vote Cast for President: 1920–1932

Year	Presidential Candidate[a]	Political Party	Electoral Vote	Popular Vote
	1	2	3	4
1920	Warren G. Harding	Republican	404	16,143,407
	James M. Cox	Democrat	127	9,130,328
	Eugene V. Debs	Socialist	—	919,799
1924	Calvin Coolidge	Republican	382	15,718,211
	John W. Davis	Democrat	136	8,385,283
	Robert M. LaFollette	Progressive	13	4,831,289
1928	Herbert C. Hoover	Republican	444	21,391,993
	Alfred E. Smith	Democrat	87	15,016,169
1932	Franklin D. Roosevelt	Democrat	472	22,809,638
	Herbert C. Hoover	Republican	59	15,758,901
	Norman Thomas	Socialist	—	881,951

[a]Minor party candidates receiving less than 500,000 votes not included.

Selected U.S. Statistics (through 1941)

Exhibit 25   Vote Cast for Representatives, by Political Party: 1920–1932 (Thousands)

Year	Total	Republican	Democrat	Other
	1	2	3	4
1920	25,214	14,773	9,038	1,403
1922	20,409	10,548	9,131	730
1924	26,884	14,932	10,854	1,098
1926	20,435	11,643	8,284	508
1928	33,906	19,163	14,361	382
1930	24,777	13,032	11,044	701
1932	37,657	15,575	20,540	1,542

Source: *Historical Statistics,* Series Y 211–214.

Selected U.S. Statistics
(through 1970s)

Selected U.S. Statistics (through 1970s)

Exhibit 1   Gross National Product or Expenditure: 1929–1970 (Billions of Dollars)

| | | | | | Government Purchases of Goods and Services[a] | | | | |
| | | | | | | Federal | | | |
Year	Total Gross National Product	Personal Consumption Expenditures	Gross Private Domestic Investment	Net Exports of Goods and Services	Total	Total	National Defense[b]	Other	State and Local
	1	2	3	4	5	6	7	8	9
1929	103.1	77.2	16.2	1.1	8.5	1.3	1.3		7.2
1930	90.4	69.9	10.3	1.0	9.2	1.4	1.4		7.8
1931	75.8	60.5	5.6	.5	9.2	1.5	1.5		7.7
1932	58.0	48.6	1.0	.4	8.1	1.5	1.5		6.6
1933	55.6	45.8	1.4	.4	8.0	2.0	2.0		6.0
1934	65.1	51.3	3.3	.6	9.8	3.0	3.0		6.8
1935	72.2	55.7	6.4	.1	10.0	2.9	2.9		7.1
1936	82.5	61.9	8.5	.1	12.0	4.9	4.9		7.0
1937	90.4	66.5	11.8	.3	11.9	4.7	4.7		7.2
1938	84.7	63.9	6.5	1.3	13.0	5.4	5.4		7.6
1939	90.5	66.8	9.3	1.1	13.3	5.1	1.2	3.9	8.2
1940	99.7	70.8	13.1	1.7	14.0	6.0	2.2	3.8	8.0
1941	124.5	80.6	17.9	1.3	24.8	16.9	13.8	3.1	7.9
1942	157.9	88.5	9.8	.0	59.6	51.9	49.4	2.5	7.7
1943	191.6	99.3	5.7	−2.0	88.6	81.1	79.7	1.4	7.4
1944	210.1	108.3	7.1	−1.8	96.5	89.0	87.4	1.6	7.5
1945	211.9	119.7	10.6	−.6	82.3	74.2	73.5	.7	8.1
1946	208.5	143.4	30.6	7.5	27.0	17.2	14.7	2.5	9.8
1947	231.3	160.7	34.0	11.5	25.1	12.5	9.1	3.5	12.6
1948	257.6	173.6	46.0	6.4	31.6	16.5	10.7	5.8	15.0
1949	256.5	176.8	35.7	6.1	37.8	20.1	13.3	6.8	17.7
1950	284.8	191.0	54.1	1.8	37.9	18.4	14.1	4.3	19.5

[a]Net of government sales.
[b]This category corresponds to the national defense classification in the "Budget of the United States Government for the Fiscal Year Ending June 30, 1972."

Source: Department of Commerce, Office of Business Economics.

Exhibit 1 (Continued)

Year	Total Gross National Product	Personal Consumption Expenditures	Gross Private Domestic Investment	Net Exports of Goods and Services	Government Purchases of Goods and Services[a]				
						Federal			State and Local
					Total	Total	National Defense[b]	Other	
	1	2	3	4	5	6	7	8	9
1951	328.4	206.3	59.3	3.7	59.1	37.7	33.6	4.1	21.5
1952	345.5	216.7	51.9	2.2	74.7	51.8	45.9	5.9	22.9
1953	364.6	230.0	52.6	.4	81.6	57.0	48.7	8.4	24.6
1954	364.8	236.5	51.7	1.8	74.8	47.4	41.2	6.2	27.4
1955	398.0	254.4	67.4	2.0	74.2	44.1	38.6	5.5	30.1
1956	419.2	266.7	70.0	4.0	78.6	45.6	40.3	5.3	33.0
1957	441.1	281.4	67.9	5.7	86.1	49.5	44.2	5.3	36.6
1958	447.3	290.1	60.9	2.2	94.2	53.6	45.9	7.7	40.6
1959	483.7	311.2	75.3	.1	97.0	53.7	46.0	7.6	43.3
1960	503.7	325.2	74.8	4.0	99.6	53.5	44.9	8.6	46.1
1961	520.1	335.2	71.7	5.6	107.6	57.4	47.8	9.6	50.2
1962	560.3	355.1	83.0	5.1	117.1	63.4	51.6	11.8	53.7
1963	590.5	375.0	87.1	5.9	122.5	64.2	50.8	13.5	58.2
1964	632.4	401.2	94.0	8.5	128.7	65.2	50.0	15.2	63.5
1965	684.9	432.8	108.1	6.9	137.0	65.9	50.1	16.8	70.1
1966	749.9	466.3	121.4	5.3	156.8	77.8	60.7	17.1	79.0
1967	793.9	492.1	116.6	5.2	180.1	90.7	72.4	18.4	89.4
1968	865.0	535.8	126.5	2.5	200.2	99.5	78.0	21.5	100.7
1969	931.4	577.5	139.8	1.9	212.2	101.3	78.8	22.6	110.8
1970[P]	976.8	616.8	135.8	3.6	220.5	99.7	76.6	23.1	120.8

[P]Preliminary data.

Selected U.S. Statistics (through 1970s)

Exhibit 2   Gross National Product or Expenditure, in 1958 Prices: 1929–1970
A. (Billions of Dollars; 1958 Prices)

		Personal Consumption Expenditures				Gross Private Domestic Investment						
							Fixed Investment					
								Nonresidential				
Year	Total Gross National Product	Total	Durable Goods	Non-durable Goods	Services	Total	Total	Total	Structures	Producers' Durable Equipment	Residential Structures	Change in Business Inventories
	1	2	3	4	5	6	7	8	9	10	11	12
1929	203.6	139.6	16.3	69.3	54.0	40.4	36.9	26.5	13.9	12.6	10.4	3.5
1930	183.5	130.4	12.9	65.9	51.5	27.4	28.0	21.7	11.8	9.9	6.3	−.6
1931	169.3	126.1	11.2	65.6	49.4	16.8	19.2	14.1	7.5	6.6	5.1	−2.4
1932	144.2	114.8	8.4	60.4	45.9	4.7	10.9	8.2	4.4	3.8	2.7	−6.2
1933	141.5	112.8	8.3	58.6	46.0	5.3	9.7	7.6	3.3	4.3	2.1	−4.3
1934	154.3	118.1	9.4	62.5	46.1	9.4	12.1	9.2	3.6	5.6	2.9	−2.7
1935	169.5	125.5	11.7	65.9	47.9	18.0	15.6	11.5	4.0	7.5	4.0	2.4
1936	193.0	138.4	14.5	73.4	50.5	24.0	20.9	15.8	5.4	10.3	5.1	3.1
1937	203.2	143.1	15.1	76.0	52.0	29.9	24.5	18.8	7.1	11.8	5.6	5.5
1938	192.9	140.2	12.2	77.1	50.9	17.0	19.4	13.7	5.6	8.1	5.7	−2.4
1939	209.4	148.2	14.5	81.2	52.5	24.7	23.5	15.3	5.9	9.4	8.2	1.2
1940	227.2	155.7	16.7	84.6	54.4	33.0	28.1	18.9	6.8	12.1	9.2	4.9
1941	263.7	165.4	19.1	89.9	56.3	41.6	32.0	22.2	8.1	14.2	9.8	9.6
1942	297.8	161.4	11.7	91.3	58.5	21.4	17.3	12.5	4.6	7.9	4.9	4.0
1943	337.1	165.8	10.2	93.7	61.8	12.7	12.9	10.0	2.9	7.2	2.9	−.2
1944	361.3	171.4	9.4	97.3	64.7	14.0	15.9	13.4	3.8	9.6	2.5	−1.9
1945	355.2	183.0	10.6	104.7	67.7	19.6	22.6	19.8	5.7	14.1	2.8	−2.9
1946	312.6	203.5	20.5	110.8	72.1	52.3	42.3	30.2	12.5	17.7	12.1	10.0
1947	309.9	206.3	24.7	108.3	73.4	51.5	51.7	36.2	11.6	24.6	15.4	−.2
1948	323.7	210.8	26.3	108.7	75.8	60.4	55.9	38.0	12.3	25.7	17.9	4.6
1949	324.1	216.5	28.4	110.5	77.6	48.0	51.9	34.5	11.9	22.6	17.4	−3.9
1950	355.3	230.5	34.7	114.0	81.8	69.3	61.0	37.5	12.7	24.8	23.5	8.3
1951	383.4	232.8	31.5	116.5	84.8	70.0	59.0	39.6	14.1	25.5	19.5	10.9
1952	395.1	239.4	30.8	120.8	87.8	60.5	57.2	38.3	13.7	24.6	18.9	3.3
1953	412.8	250.8	35.3	124.4	91.1	61.2	60.2	40.7	14.9	25.8	19.6	.9
1954	407.0	255.7	35.4	125.5	94.8	59.4	61.4	39.6	15.2	24.5	21.7	−2.0
1955	438.0	274.2	43.2	131.7	99.3	75.4	69.0	43.9	16.2	27.7	25.1	6.4
1956	446.1	281.4	41.0	136.2	104.1	74.3	69.5	47.3	18.5	28.8	22.2	4.8
1957	452.5	288.2	41.5	138.7	108.0	68.8	67.6	47.4	18.2	29.1	20.2	1.2
1958	447.3	290.1	37.9	140.2	112.0	60.9	62.4	41.6	16.6	25.0	20.8	−1.5
1959	475.9	307.3	43.7	146.8	116.8	73.6	68.3	44.1	16.2	27.9	24.7	4.8
1960	487.7	316.1	44.9	149.6	121.6	72.4	68.9	47.1	17.4	29.6	21.9	3.5
1961	497.2	322.5	43.9	153.0	125.6	69.0	67.0	45.5	17.4	28.1	21.6	2.0
1962	529.8	338.4	49.2	158.2	131.1	79.4	73.4	49.7	17.9	31.7	23.8	6.0
1963	551.0	353.3	53.7	162.2	137.4	82.5	76.7	51.9	17.9	34.0	24.8	5.8
1964	581.1	373.7	59.0	170.3	144.4	87.8	81.9	57.8	19.1	38.7	24.2	5.8
1965	617.8	397.7	66.6	178.6	152.5	99.2	90.1	66.3	22.3	44.0	23.8	9.0
1966	658.1	418.1	71.7	187.0	159.4	109.3	95.4	74.1	24.0	50.1	21.3	13.9
1967	675.2	430.1	72.9	190.2	167.0	101.2	93.5	73.2	22.6	50.6	20.4	7.7
1968	707.2	452.3	81.4	196.5	174.4	105.7	98.8	75.5	22.7	52.7	23.3	6.9
1969	727.1	467.7	84.9	201.2	181.6	111.3	104.1	80.8	24.0	56.9	23.3	7.2
1970[P]	724.3	477.2	82.1	207.9	187.3	103.0	99.9	79.3	23.1	56.2	20.6	3.1

[P]Preliminary data.

Exhibit 2A (Continued)

| Year | Net Exports of Goods and Services | | | Government Purchases of Goods and Services[a] | | |
	Net Exports	Exports	Imports	Total	Federal	State and Local
	13	14	15	16	17	18
1929	1.5	11.8	10.3	22.0	3.5	18.5
1930	1.4	10.4	9.0	24.3	4.0	20.2
1931	.9	8.9	7.9	25.4	4.3	21.1
1932	.6	7.1	6.6	24.2	4.6	19.6
1933	.0	7.1	7.1	23.3	6.0	17.3
1934	.3	7.3	7.1	26.6	8.0	18.6
1935	−1.0	7.7	8.7	27.0	7.9	19.2
1936	−1.2	8.2	9.3	31.8	12.2	19.6
1937	−.7	9.8	10.5	30.8	11.5	19.4
1938	1.9	9.9	8.0	33.9	13.3	20.6
1939	1.3	10.0	8.7	35.2	12.5	22.7
1940	2.1	11.0	8.9	36.4	15.0	21.4
1941	.4	11.2	10.8	56.3	36.2	20.1
1942	−2.1	7.8	9.9	117.1	98.9	18.3
1943	−5.9	6.8	12.6	164.4	147.8	16.6
1944	−5.8	7.6	13.4	181.7	165.4	16.3
1945	−3.8	10.2	13.9	156.4	139.7	16.7
1946	8.4	19.6	11.2	48.4	30.1	18.4
1947	12.3	22.6	10.3	39.9	19.1	20.8
1948	6.1	18.1	12.0	46.3	23.7	22.7
1949	6.4	18.1	11.7	53.3	27.6	25.7
1950	2.7	16.3	13.6	52.8	25.3	27.5
1951	5.3	19.3	14.1	75.4	47.4	27.9
1952	3.0	18.2	15.2	92.1	63.8	28.4
1953	1.1	17.8	16.7	99.8	70.0	29.7
1954	3.0	18.8	15.8	88.9	56.8	32.1
1955	3.2	20.9	17.7	85.2	50.7	34.4
1956	5.0	24.2	19.1	85.3	49.7	35.6
1957	6.2	26.2	19.9	89.3	51.7	37.6
1958	2.2	23.1	20.9	94.2	53.6	40.6
1959	.3	23.8	23.5	94.7	52.5	42.2
1960	4.3	27.3	23.0	94.9	51.4	43.5
1961	5.1	28.0	22.9	100.5	54.6	45.9
1962	4.5	30.0	25.5	107.5	60.0	47.5
1963	5.6	32.1	26.6	109.6	59.5	50.1
1964	8.3	36.5	28.2	111.2	58.1	53.2
1965	6.2	37.4	31.2	114.7	57.9	56.8
1966	4.2	40.2	36.1	126.5	65.4	61.1
1967	3.6	42.1	38.5	140.2	74.7	65.5
1968	.9	45.7	44.8	148.3	78.7	69.6
1969	.2	48.5	48.2	147.8	75.7	72.1
1970[p]	2.3	52.2	49.9	141.8	67.7	74.1

[a]Net of government sales.
[p]Preliminary data.

Source: Department of Commerce, Office of Business Economics.

Selected U.S. Statistics (through 1970s)

Exhibit 2   Gross National Product or Expenditure, in 1958 Prices, 1929–1970
B. (Percentage Change)

		Personal Consumption Expenditures				Gross Private Domestic Investment					
							Fixed Investment				
								Nonresidential			
Year	Total Gross National Product	Total	Durable Goods	Non-Durable Goods	Services	Total	Total	Total	Nonresidential Structures	Producers' Durable Equipment	Residential Structures	Change in Business Inventories
	19	20	21	22	23	24	25	26	27	28	29	30
1929	—	—	—	—	—	—	—	—	—	—	—	—
1930	−9.9%	−6.6%	−20.9%	−4.9%	−4.6%	−32.2%	−24.1%	−18.1%	−15.1%	−21.4%	−39.4%	−117.1%
1931	−7.7	−3.3	−13.2	−0.5	−4.1	−38.7	−31.4	−35.0	−36.4	−33.3	−19.0	300.0
1932	−14.8	−9.0	−25.0	−7.9	−7.1	−72.0	−43.2	−41.8	−41.3	−42.4	−47.1	158.3
1933	−1.9	−1.7	−1.2	−3.0	0.2	12.8	−11.0	−7.3	−25.0	13.2	−22.2	−30.6
1934	9.0	4.7	13.3	6.7	0.2	77.4	24.7	21.1	9.1	30.2	38.1	−37.2
1935	9.9	6.3	24.5	5.4	3.9	91.5	28.9	25.0	11.1	33.9	37.9	−188.9
1936	13.9	10.3	23.9	11.4	5.4	33.3	34.0	37.4	35.0	37.3	27.5	29.2
1937	5.3	3.4	4.1	3.5	3.0	24.6	17.2	19.0	31.5	14.6	9.8	77.4
1938	−5.1	−2.0	−19.2	1.4	−2.1	−43.1	−20.8	−27.1	−21.1	−31.4	1.8	−143.6
1939	8.6	5.7	18.9	5.3	3.1	45.3	21.1	11.7	5.4	16.0	43.9	−150.0
1940	8.5	5.1	15.2	4.2	3.6	33.6	19.6	23.5	15.3	28.7	12.2	308.3
1941	16.1	6.2	14.4	6.3	3.5	26.1	13.9	17.5	19.1	17.4	6.5	95.9
1942	12.9	−2.4	−38.7	1.6	3.9	−48.6	−45.9	−43.7	−43.2	−44.4	−50.0	−58.3
1943	13.2	2.7	−12.8	2.6	5.6	−40.7	−25.4	−20.0	−37.0	−8.9	−40.8	−105.0
1944	7.2	3.4	−7.8	3.8	4.7	10.2	23.3	34.0	31.0	33.3	−13.8	850.0
1945	−1.7	6.8	12.8	7.6	4.6	40.0	42.1	47.8	50.0	46.9	12.0	52.6
1946	−12.0	11.2	93.4	5.8	6.5	166.8	87.2	52.5	119.3	25.5	332.1	−444.8
1947	−0.9	1.4	20.5	−2.3	1.8	−1.5	22.2	19.9	−7.2	39.0	27.3	−102.0
1948	4.5	2.2	6.5	0.4	3.3	17.3	8.1	5.0	6.0	4.5	16.2	−2400.0
1949	0.1	2.7	8.0	1.7	2.4	−20.5	−7.2	−9.2	−3.3	−12.1	−2.8	−184.8
1950	9.6	6.5	22.2	3.2	5.4	44.4	17.5	8.7	6.7	9.7	35.1	−312.8
1951	7.9	1.0	−9.2	2.2	3.7	1.0	−3.3	5.6	11.0	2.8	−17.0	31.3
1952	3.1	2.8	−2.2	3.7	3.5	−13.6	−3.1	−3.3	−2.8	−3.5	−3.1	−69.7
1953	4.5	4.8	14.6	3.0	3.8	1.2	5.2	6.3	8.8	4.9	3.7	−72.7
1954	−1.4	2.0	0.3	0.9	4.1	−2.9	2.0	−2.7	2.0	−5.0	10.7	−322.2
1955	7.6	7.2	22.0	4.9	4.7	26.9	12.4	10.9	6.6	13.1	15.7	−420.0
1956	1.8	2.6	−5.1	3.4	4.8	−1.5	0.7	7.7	14.2	4.0	−11.6	−25.0
1957	1.4	2.4	1.2	1.8	3.7	−7.4	−2.7	0.2	−1.6	1.0	−9.0	−75.0
1958	−1.1	0.7	−8.7	1.1	3.7	−11.5	−7.7	−12.2	−8.8	−14.1	3.0	−225.0
1959	6.4	5.9	15.3	4.7	4.3	20.9	10.3	6.0	−2.4	11.6	18.7	−420.0
1960	2.5	2.9	2.7	1.9	4.1	−1.6	0.1	6.8	7.4	6.1	−11.3	−27.1
1961	1.9	2.0	−2.2	2.3	3.3	−4.7	−2.8	−3.4	0.0	−5.1	−1.4	−42.9
1962	6.6	4.9	12.1	3.4	4.4	15.1	9.6	9.2	2.9	12.8	10.2	200.0
1963	4.0	4.4	9.1	2.5	4.8	3.9	4.5	4.4	0.0	7.3	4.2	−3.3
1964	5.5	5.8	9.9	5.0	5.1	6.4	6.8	11.4	6.7	13.8	−2.4	0.0
1965	6.3	6.4	12.9	4.9	5.6	13.0	10.0	14.7	16.8	13.7	−1.7	55.2
1966	6.5	5.1	6.8	4.7	4.5	10.2	5.9	11.8	7.6	13.9	−10.5	54.4
1967	2.6	2.9	2.5	1.7	4.8	−7.4	3.2	−1.2	−5.8	1.0	−4.2	−44.6
1968	4.7	5.2	11.7	3.3	4.4	4.4	0.3	3.1	0.4	4.2	14.2	−10.4
1969	2.8	3.4	4.3	2.4	4.1	5.3	5.4	7.0	5.7	8.0	0.0	4.3
1970	−0.4	2.0	−3.3	3.3	3.1	−7.5	−4.0	−1.2	−3.7	−1.2	−11.6	−56.9

Exhibit 2B (Continued)

Year	Net Exports of Goods and Services			Government Purchases of Goods and Services		
	Net Exports	Exports	Imports	Total	Federal	State and Local
	31	32	33	34	35	36
1929	—	—	—	—	—	—
1930	−6.7%	−11.9%	−12.6%	10.5%	14.3%	9.7%
1931	−35.7	−14.4	−12.2	4.5	7.5	3.9
1932	−33.3	−20.2	−16.5	−4.7	7.0	−7.1
1933	−100.0	0.0	7.6	−3.7	30.4	−11.7
1934	—	2.8	0.0	14.2	33.3	7.5
1935	−433.3	5.5	22.5	1.5	−1.2	2.7
1936	20.0	6.5	6.9	17.8	54.4	2.6
1937	−41.7	19.5	12.9	−3.1	−5.7	−1.5
1938	−371.4	1.0	−23.8	10.1	15.7	6.7
1939	−31.6	1.0	8.7	3.8	−6.0	10.2
1940	61.5	10.0	2.3	3.4	20.0	−5.7
1941	−81.0	1.8	21.3	54.7	141.3	−6.1
1942	−625.0	−30.4	−8.3	108.0	173.2	−9.5
1943	181.0	−12.8	27.3	40.4	49.4	−8.8
1944	−1.7	11.8	6.3	10.5	11.9	−1.8
1945	−34.5	34.2	3.7	−13.9	−15.5	2.5
1946	−321.1	92.2	−19.4	−69.1	−78.5	9.6
1947	46.4	15.3	8.0	−17.6	−36.5	13.7
1948	−50.4	−19.9	16.5	16.0	24.1	8.7
1949	4.9	0.0	−2.5	15.1	16.5	13.7
1950	−57.8	−9.9	16.2	−0.9	−8.3	7.0
1951	96.3	18.4	3.7	42.8	87.4	1.8
1952	−43.4	−5.7	7.8	22.1	34.6	1.1
1953	−63.3	−2.2	9.9	8.4	9.7	5.3
1954	172.7	5.6	−5.4	10.9	−18.9	7.7
1955	6.7	11.2	12.0	−4.2	−10.7	7.5
1956	56.3	15.8	7.9	0.1	−2.0	3.2
1957	24.0	8.3	4.2	4.7	4.0	5.6
1958	−64.5	−11.8	5.0	5.5	3.7	8.0
1959	−86.4	3.0	12.4	0.5	−2.1	3.9
1960	1333.3	14.7	−2.1	0.2	−2.1	3.1
1961	18.6	2.6	−0.4	5.9	6.2	5.5
1962	−11.8	7.1	11.4	7.0	9.9	3.5
1963	24.4	7.0	4.3	2.0	−0.8	5.5
1964	48.2	13.7	6.0	1.5	−2.4	6.0
1965	−25.3	2.5	10.6	3.1	−0.3	7.0
1966	−32.3	7.5	15.7	10.3	13.0	7.6
1967	−14.3	4.7	6.6	10.8	14.2	7.2
1968	−75.0	8.6	16.4	5.8	5.4	6.3
1969	−77.8	6.1	7.6	−0.3	−3.8	3.6
1970	1050.0	7.6	3.5	−4.1	−10.6	2.8

Selected U.S. Statistics (through 1970s)

Exhibit 3   Implicit Price Deflators and Alternative Price Measures of Gross National Product and Gross Private Product: 1939–1972

Year	Gross National Product Price Measures, 1958 = 100				Percent Change from Preceding Period[a]			
	Total		Private		Total		Private	
	Implicit Price Deflator	Price Index, 1967 Weights	Implicit Price Deflator	Price Index, 1967 Weights	Implicit Price Deflator	Price Index, 1967 Weights	Implicit Price Deflator	Price Index, 1967 Weights
	1	2	3	4	5	6	7	8
1939	43.23	—	43.93	—	−1.5%	—	−1.6%	—
1940	43.87	—	44.69	—	1.5	—	1.7	—
1941	47.22	—	48.66	—	7.7	—	8.9	—
1942	53.03	—	55.51	—	12.3	—	14.1	—
1943	56.83	—	60.85	—	7.2	—	9.6	—
1944	58.16	—	62.02	—	2.3	—	1.9	—
1945	59.66	—	62.59	—	2.6	—	.9	—
1946	66.70	—	68.25	—	11.8	—	9.0	—
1947	74.64	—	76.27	—	11.9	—	11.8	—
1948	79.57	—	81.40	—	6.6	—	6.7	—
1949	79.12	—	80.60	—	−.6	—	−1.0	—
1950	80.16	—	81.41	—	1.3	—	1.0	—
1951	85.64	—	87.35	—	6.8	—	7.3	—
1952	87.45	—	88.99	—	2.1	—	1.9	—
1953	88.33	—	89.65	—	1.0	—	.7	—
1954	89.63	—	90.77	—	1.5	—	1.2	—
1955	90.86	—	91.57	—	1.4	—	.9	—
1956	93.99	—	94.53	—	3.4	—	3.2	—
1957	97.49	—	97.92	—	3.7	—	3.6	—
1958	100.00	—	100.00	—	2.5	—	2.1	—
1959	101.66	—	101.41	—	1.7	—	1.4	—
1960	103.29	—	102.76	—	1.6	—	1.3	—
1961	104.62	—	103.73	—	1.3	—	.9	—
1962	105.78	—	104.73	—	1.1	—	1.0	—
1963	107.17	—	105.80	—	1.3	—	1.0	—
1964	108.85	—	107.05	—	1.6	—	1.2	—
1965	110.86	110.75	108.83	108.65	1.8	—	1.7	—
1966	113.94	114.06	111.56	111.62	2.8	3.0%	2.5	2.7%
1967	117.59	117.58	114.79	114.78	3.2	3.1	2.9	2.8
1968	122.30	122.51	118.90	119.10	4.0	4.2	3.6	3.8
1969	128.20	128.61	124.30	124.67	4.8	5.0	4.5	4.7
1970	135.23	135.56	130.31	130.64	5.5	5.4	4.8	4.8
1971	141.61	142.40	135.91	136.53	4.7	5.1	4.3	4.5
1972[P]	145.88	147.97	139.49	140.92	3.0	3.9	2.6	3.2

[a]Changes are based on unrounded data and therefore may differ slightly from those obtained from published indexes.
[P]Preliminary data.

Source: Department of Commerce, Bureau of Economic Analysis, in *Economic Report of the President, 1973* (Washington, DC: U.S. Government Printing Office, 1973).

Selected U.S. Statistics (through 1970s)

Exhibit 4 Gross National Product by Industry, in 1958 Prices: 1947–1969
(Billions of Dollars; 1958 Prices)

Year	Total Gross National Product	Agriculture, Forestry, and Fisheries	Contract Construction	Manufacturing Total	Durable Goods Industries	Nondurable Goods Industries	Transportation, Communication, and Utilities	Wholesale and Retail Trade	Finance, Insurance, and Real Estate	Services	Government and Government Enterprises	All Other[a]
	1	2	3	4	5	6	7	8	9	10	11	12
1947	309.9	17.9	12.9	91.8	52.3	39.4	29.6	52.7	35.6	30.6	32.4	6.7
1948	323.7	20.0	14.1	96.3	55.0	41.3	30.4	54.2	36.5	31.9	33.2	7.1
1949	324.1	19.4	14.7	90.9	50.5	40.4	28.7	55.2	37.8	32.1	34.7	10.6
1950	355.3	20.4	16.2	105.5	60.8	44.7	30.8	60.4	41.0	33.1	35.9	12.1
1951	383.4	19.5	18.2	116.2	69.0	47.2	34.3	61.4	42.9	34.0	43.9	13.0
1952	395.1	20.2	18.3	118.7	71.5	47.3	34.6	62.9	44.7	34.5	47.2	14.0
1953	412.8	21.2	18.9	128.6	79.1	49.5	35.7	64.9	46.8	35.3	47.1	14.3
1954	407.0	21.6	19.3	119.5	71.2	48.3	36.4	65.5	49.8	35.4	46.1	13.5
1955	438.0	22.1	20.8	133.6	80.7	52.9	38.6	71.6	52.7	38.2	46.0	14.4
1956	446.1	22.0	21.8	134.1	79.4	54.6	40.5	73.8	54.8	40.2	46.2	12.7
1957	452.5	21.5	21.1	134.6	79.6	54.9	41.3	75.1	57.0	41.8	46.9	13.1
1958	447.3	22.0	20.7	123.7	69.6	54.0	40.6	75.1	59.2	42.9	47.3	16.0
1959	475.9	22.3	22.0	138.9	79.9	59.0	43.3	80.8	61.4	45.1	47.9	14.1
1960	487.7	23.1	21.7	140.9	81.0	59.9	44.9	82.3	64.1	46.7	49.2	14.7
1961	497.2	23.4	21.4	140.4	79.7	60.7	46.0	83.5	67.1	48.3	50.6	16.3
1962	529.8	23.3	21.7	154.6	90.0	64.7	48.9	88.9	71.2	50.8	52.6	17.9
1963	551.0	24.0	21.9	162.4	95.6	66.8	51.9	92.8	74.4	52.2	53.9	17.4
1964	581.1	23.6	23.3	173.7	102.4	71.3	54.7	98.9	78.3	54.7	56.1	17.8
1965	617.8	25.0	23.5	190.5	114.8	75.7	59.2	104.8	83.1	57.7	58.0	15.8
1966	658.1	23.7	24.7	205.7	125.1	80.7	64.0	111.6	86.8	60.6	61.8	19.4
1967	675.2	25.2	23.1	205.4	123.9	81.4	66.5	113.9	91.6	63.4	65.5	20.6
1968	707.2	25.1	23.6	219.0	132.0	87.1	70.9	120.7	95.2	65.7	68.6	18.5
1969	727.1	24.9	23.8	227.5	137.5	89.9	75.2	124.8	96.7	68.5	70.2	15.4

[a]Mining, rest of the world, and residual (the difference between gross national product measured as a sum of final products and gross national product measured as sum of gross product by industries).

Source: Department of Commerce, Office of Business Economics.

Selected U.S. Statistics (through 1970s)

Exhibit 5   Noninstitutional Population and the Labor Force: 1929–1970

Year	Nonin-stitu-tional Popu-lation	Total Labor Force (Includ-ing Armed Forces)	Armed Forces	Civilian Labor Force					Total Labor Force as Percent of Non-Institu-tional Popu-lation	Unem-ploy-ment as Per-cent of Civilian Labor Force
					Employment					
				Total	Total	Agri-cul-tural	Non-agri-cul-tural	Unem-ploy-ment		
	1	2	3	4	5	6	7	8	9	10
	Thousands of Persons 14 Years of Age and Over								Percent	
1929	—	49,440	260	49,180	47,630	10,450	37,180	1,550	—	3.2
1930	—	50,080	260	49,820	45,480	10,340	35,140	4,340	—	8.7
1931	—	50,680	260	50,420	42,400	10,290	32,110	8,020	—	15.9
1932	—	51,250	250	51,000	38,940	10,170	28,770	12,060	—	23.6
1933	—	51,840	250	51,590	38,760	10,090	28,670	12,830	—	24.9
1934	—	52,490	260	52,230	40,890	9,900	30,990	11,340	—	21.7
1935	—	53,140	270	52,870	42,260	10,110	32,150	10,610	—	20.1
1936	—	53,740	300	53,440	44,410	10,000	34,410	9,030	—	16.9
1937	—	54,320	320	54,000	46,300	9,820	36,480	7,700	—	14.3
1938	—	54,950	340	54,610	44,220	9,690	34,530	10,390	—	19.0
1939	—	55,600	370	55,230	45,750	9,610	36,140	9,480	—	17.2
1940	100,380	56,180	540	55,640	47,520	9,540	37,980	8,120	56.0	14.6
1941	101,520	57,530	1,620	55,910	50,350	9,100	41,250	5,560	56.7	9.9
1942	102,610	60,380	3,970	56,410	53,750	9,250	44,500	2,660	58.8	4.7
1943	103,660	64,560	9,020	55,540	54,470	9,080	45,390	1,070	62.3	1.9
1944	104,630	66,040	11,410	54,630	53,960	8,950	45,010	670	63.1	1.2
1945	105,530	65,300	11,440	53,860	52,820	8,580	44,240	1,040	61.9	1.9
1946	106,520	60,970	3,450	57,520	55,250	8,320	46,930	2,270	57.2	3.9
1947	107,608	61,758	1,590	60,168	57,812	8,256	49,557	2,356	57.4	3.9
	Thousands of Persons 16 Years of Age and Over								Percent	
1947	103,418	60,941	1,591	59,350	57,039	7,891	49,148	2,311	58.9	3.9
1948	104,527	62,080	1,459	60,621	58,344	7,629	50,713	2,276	59.4	3.8
1949	105,611	62,903	1,617	61,286	57,649	7,656	49,990	3,637	59.6	5.9
1950	106,645	63,858	1,650	62,208	58,920	7,160	51,760	3,288	59.9	5.3
1951	107,721	65,117	3,100	62,017	59,962	6,726	53,239	2,055	60.4	3.3
1952	108,823	65,730	3,592	62,138	60,254	6,501	53,753	1,883	60.4	3.0
1953	110,601	66,560	3,545	63,015	61,181	6,261	54,922	1,834	60.2	2.9
1954	111,671	66,993	3,350	63,643	60,110	6,206	53,903	3,532	60.0	5.5
1955	112,732	68,072	3,049	65,023	62,171	6,449	55,724	2,852	60.4	4.4
1956	113,811	69,409	2,857	66,552	63,802	6,283	57,517	2,750	61.0	4.1
1957	115,065	69,729	2,800	66,929	64,071	5,947	58,123	2,859	60.6	4.3
1958	116,363	70,275	2,636	67,639	63,036	5,586	57,450	4,602	60.4	6.8
1959	117,881	70,921	2,552	68,369	64,630	5,565	59,065	3,740	60.2	5.5
1960	119,759	72,142	2,514	69,628	65,778	5,458	60,318	3,852	60.2	5.5
1961	121,343	73,031	2,572	70,459	65,746	5,200	60,546	4,714	60.2	6.7
1962	122,981	73,442	2,828	70,614	66,702	4,944	61,759	3,911	59.7	5.5
1963	125,154	74,571	2,738	71,833	67,762	4,687	63,076	4,070	59.6	5.7
1964	127,224	75,830	2,739	73,091	69,305	4,523	64,782	3,786	59.6	5.2
1965	129,236	77,178	2,723	74,455	71,088	4,361	66,726	3,366	59.7	4.5
1966	131,180	78,893	3,123	75,770	72,895	3,979	68,915	2,875	60.1	3.8
1967	133,319	80,793	3,446	77,347	74,372	3,844	70,527	2,975	60.6	3.8
1968	135,562	82,272	3,535	78,737	75,920	3,817	72,103	2,817	60.7	3.6
1969	137,841	84,239	3,506	80,733	77,902	3,606	74,296	2,831	61.1	3.5
1970	140,182	85,903	3,188	82,715	78,627	3,462	75,165	4,088	61.3	4.9

Source: Department of Labor, Bureau of Labor Statistics.

Selected U.S. Statistics (through 1970s)

Exhibit 6 Sources and Uses of Gross Saving: 1942–1970
(In Billions of Dollars)

				Gross Saving and Statistical Discrepancy								Gross Investment		
		Private Saving					Government Surplus (+) or Deficit (−)							
				Gross Business Saving						Capital Grants Received by the United States	Statistical Discrepancy		Gross Private Domestic Investment	Net Foreign Investment
Year	Total	Personal Saving	Total	Undistributed Corporate Profits	Corporate Inventory Valuation Adjustment	Capital Consumption Allowances	Total	Federal	State and Local			Total		
	1	2	3	4	5	6	7	8	9	10	11	12	13	14
1942	42.0	27.6	14.5	5.9	−1.2	9.8	−31.4	−33.1	1.8	—	−1.1	9.6	9.8	−.2
1943	49.7	33.4	16.3	6.6	−.8	10.3	−44.1	−46.6	2.5	—	−2.0	3.5	5.7	−2.2
1944	54.3	37.3	17.1	6.5	−.3	11.0	−51.8	−54.5	2.7	—	2.5	5.0	7.1	−2.1
1945	44.7	29.6	15.1	4.4	−.6	11.3	−39.5	−42.1	2.6	—	3.9	9.1	10.6	−1.4
1946	29.7	15.2	14.5	9.9	−5.3	9.9	5.4	3.5	1.9	—	.1	35.2	30.6	4.6
1947	27.5	7.3	20.2	13.9	−5.9	12.2	14.4	13.4	1.0	—	.9	42.9	34.0	8.9
1948	41.4	13.4	28.0	15.6	−2.2	14.5	8.5	8.4	.1	—	−2.0	47.9	46.0	1.9
1949	39.0	9.4	29.7	11.3	1.9	16.6	−3.2	−2.4	−.7	—	.3	36.2	35.7	.5
1950	42.5	13.1	29.4	16.0	−5.0	18.3	7.9	9.1	−1.2	—	1.5	51.8	54.1	−2.2
1951	50.3	17.3	33.1	13.0	−1.2	21.2	5.8	6.2	−.4	—	3.3	59.5	59.3	.2
1952	53.3	18.1	35.1	11.0	1.0	23.2	−3.8	−3.8	Z	—	2.2	51.6	51.9	−.3
1953	54.4	18.3	36.1	11.5	−1.0	25.7	−6.9	−7.0	.1	—	3.0	50.5	52.6	−2.1
1954	55.6	16.4	39.2	11.3	−.3	28.2	−7.0	−5.9	−1.1	—	2.7	51.3	51.7	−.5
1955	62.1	15.8	46.3	16.5	−1.7	31.5	2.7	4.0	−1.3	—	2.1	66.9	67.4	−.5

Exhibit 6 (Continued)

	Gross Saving and Statistical Discrepancy											Gross Investment		
	Private Saving						Government Surplus (+) or Deficit (−)							
			Gross Business Saving											
Year	Total	Personal Saving	Total	Undistributed Corporate Profits	Corporate Inventory Valuation Adjustment	Capital Consumption Allowances	Total	Federal	State and Local	Capital Grants Received by the United States	Statistical Discrepancy	Total	Gross Private Domestic Investment	Net Foreign Investment
	1	2	3	4	5	6	7	8	9	10	11	12	13	14
1956	67.8	20.6	47.3	15.9	−2.7	34.1	4.9	5.7	−.9	—	−1.1	71.6	70.0	1.5
1957	70.5	20.7	49.8	14.2	−1.5	37.1	.7	2.1	−1.4	—	Z	71.2	67.9	3.4
1958	71.7	22.3	49.4	10.8	−.3	38.9	−12.5	−10.2	−2.3	—	1.6	60.7	60.9	−.2
1959	75.9	19.1	56.8	15.9	−.5	41.4	−2.1	−1.2	−.8	—	−.8	73.0	75.3	−2.3
1960	73.9	17.0	56.8	13.2	.2	43.4	3.7	3.5	.2	—	−1.0	76.5	74.8	1.7
1961	79.8	21.2	58.7	13.5	−.1	45.2	−4.3	−3.8	−.5	—	−.8	74.7	71.7	3.0
1962	87.9	21.6	66.3	16.0	.3	50.0	−2.9	−3.8	.9	—	.5	85.5	83.0	2.5
1963	88.7	19.9	68.8	16.6	−.5	52.6	1.8	.7	1.2	—	−.3	90.3	87.1	3.1
1964	102.4	26.2	76.2	20.6	−.5	56.1	−1.4	−3.0	1.7	—	−1.3	99.7	94.0	5.7
1965	113.1	28.4	84.7	26.7	−1.7	59.8	2.2	1.2	1.0	—	−3.1	112.2	108.1	4.1
1966	123.8	32.5	91.3	29.1	−1.8	63.9	1.1	−.2	1.3	—	−1.0	123.9	121.4	2.4
1967	133.4	40.4	93.0	25.3	−1.1	68.9	−13.9	−12.4	−1.6	—	−.7	118.8	116.6	2.2
1968	135.2	39.8	95.4	24.2	−3.3	74.5	−6.8	−6.5	−.3	—	−2.7	125.6	126.0	−.4
1969	135.2	38.2	97.0	20.5	−5.1	81.6	8.8	8.1	.7	—	−6.1	137.9	139.0	−1.0
1970	153.2	56.2	97.0	14.6	−4.8	87.3	−10.1	−11.9	1.8	0.9	−6.4	137.6	136.3	1.3

Z = Less than $50 million or −$50 million.

Source: *Historical Statistics of the United States, Colonial Times to 1970, Bicentennial Edition* (Washington, DC; U.S. Government Printing Office, 1975), Series F 552–565.

Selected U.S. Statistics (through 1970s)

Exhibit 7 Wage and Salary Workers in Nonagricultural Establishments: 1929–1970
(All Employees; Thousands of Persons)

Year	Total Wage and Salary Workers	Manufacturing Total	Durable Goods	Nondurable Goods	Mining	Contract Construction	Transportation and Public Utilities	Wholesale and Retail Trade	Finance, Insurance, and Real Estate	Services	Government Federal	Government State and Local
	1	2	3	4	5	6	7	8	9	10	11	12
1929	31,339	10,702	—	—	1,087	1,497	3,916	6,123	1,509	3,440	533	2,532
1930	29,424	9,562	—	—	1,009	1,372	3,685	5,797	1,475	3,376	526	2,622
1931	26,649	8,170	—	—	873	1,214	3,254	5,284	1,407	3,183	560	2,704
1932	23,628	6,931	—	—	731	970	2,816	4,683	1,341	2,931	559	2,666
1933	23,711	7,397	—	—	744	809	2,672	4,755	1,295	2,873	565	2,601
1934	25,953	8,501	—	—	883	862	2,750	5,281	1,319	3,058	652	2,647
1935	27,053	9,069	—	—	897	912	2,786	5,431	1,335	3,142	753	2,728
1936	29,082	9,827	—	—	946	1,145	2,973	5,809	1,388	3,326	826	2,842
1937	31,026	10,794	—	—	1,015	1,112	3,134	6,265	1,432	3,518	833	2,923
1938	29,209	9,440	—	—	891	1,055	2,863	6,179	1,425	3,473	829	3,054
1939	30,618	10,278	4,715	5,564	854	1,150	2,936	6,426	1,462	3,517	905	3,090
1940	32,376	10,985	5,363	5,622	925	1,294	3,038	6,750	1,502	3,681	996	3,206
1941	36,554	13,192	6,968	6,225	957	1,790	3,274	7,210	1,549	3,921	1,340	3,320
1942	40,125	15,280	8,823	6,458	992	2,170	3,460	7,118	1,538	4,084	2,213	3,270
1943	42,452	17,602	11,084	6,518	925	1,567	3,647	6,982	1,502	4,148	2,905	3,174
1944	41,883	17,328	10,856	6,472	892	1,094	3,829	7,058	1,476	4,163	2,928	3,116
1945	40,394	15,524	9,074	6,450	836	1,132	3,906	7,314	1,497	4,241	2,808	3,137
1946	41,674	14,703	7,742	6,962	862	1,661	4,061	8,376	1,697	4,719	2,254	3,341
1947	43,881	15,545	8,385	7,159	955	1,982	4,166	8,955	1,754	5,050	1,892	3,582
1948	44,891	15,582	8,326	7,256	994	2,169	4,189	9,272	1,829	5,206	1,863	3,787
1949	43,778	14,441	7,489	6,953	930	2,165	4,001	9,264	1,857	5,264	1,908	3,948
1950	45,222	15,241	8,094	7,147	901	2,333	4,034	9,386	1,919	5,382	1,928	4,098
1951	47,849	16,393	9,089	7,304	929	2,603	4,226	9,742	1,991	5,576	2,302	4,087
1952	48,825	16,632	9,349	7,284	898	2,634	4,248	10,004	2,069	5,730	2,420	4,188
1953	50,232	17,549	10,110	7,438	866	2,623	4,290	10,247	2,146	5,867	2,305	4,340
1954	49,022	16,314	9,129	7,185	791	2,612	4,084	10,235	2,234	6,002	2,188	4,563
1955	50,675	16,882	9,541	7,340	792	2,802	4,141	10,515	2,335	6,274	2,187	4,727
1956	52,408	17,243	9,834	7,409	822	2,999	4,244	10,858	2,429	6,536	2,209	5,069
1957	52,894	17,174	9,856	7,319	828	2,923	4,241	10,886	2,477	6,749	2,217	5,399
1958	51,363	15,945	8,830	7,116	751	2,778	3,976	10,750	2,519	6,806	2,191	5,648
1959	53,313	16,675	9,373	7,303	732	2,960	4,011	11,127	2,594	7,130	2,233	5,850
1960	54,234	16,796	9,459	7,336	712	2,885	4,004	11,391	2,669	7,423	2,270	6,083
1961	54,042	16,326	9,020	7,256	672	2,816	3,903	11,337	2,731	7,664	2,279	6,315
1962	55,596	16,853	9,480	7,373	650	2,902	3,906	11,566	2,800	8,028	2,340	6,550
1963	56,702	16,995	9,616	7,380	635	2,963	3,903	11,778	2,877	8,325	2,358	6,868
1964	58,331	17,274	9,816	7,458	634	3,050	3,951	12,160	2,957	8,709	2,348	7,248
1965	60,815	18,062	10,406	7,656	632	3,186	4,036	12,716	3,023	9,087	2,378	7,696
1966	63,955	19,214	11,284	7,930	627	3,275	4,151	13,245	3,100	9,551	2,564	8,227
1967	65,857	19,447	11,439	8,008	613	3,208	4,261	13,606	3,225	10,099	2,719	8,679
1968	67,915	19,781	11,626	8,155	606	3,285	4,310	14,084	3,382	10,623	2,737	9,109
1969	70,274	20,169	11,893	8,277	619	3,437	4,431	14,645	3,557	11,211	2,758	9,446
1970ᴾ	70,669	19,401	11,210	8,190	622	3,346	4,499	14,947	3,679	11,577	2,707	9,893

ᴾPreliminary data.

Selected U.S. Statistics (through 1970s)

Exhibit 8   Average Weekly Earnings, Gross and Spendable, in Manufacturing Industries, in Current and 1967 Prices: 1939–1970

Year	Average Gross Weekly Earnings		Average Spendable Weekly Earnings[b]			
			Worker with No Dependents		Worker with Three Dependents	
	Current Prices	1967 Prices[a]	Current Prices	1967 Prices[a]	Current Prices	1967 Prices[a]
	1	2	3	4	5	6
1939	$ 23.64	$ 56.83	$23.37	$56.18	$ 23.40	$56.25
1940	24.96	59.43	24.46	58.24	24.71	58.83
1941	29.48	66.85	27.96	63.40	29.19	66.19
1942	36.68	75.16	31.80	65.16	36.31	74.41
1943	43.07	83.15	35.95	69.40	41.33	79.79
1944	45.70	86.72	37.99	72.09	43.76	83.04
1945	44.20	82.00	36.82	68.31	42.59	79.02
1946	43.32	74.05	37.31	63.78	42.79	73.15
1947	49.17	73.50	42.10	62.93	47.58	71.12
1948	53.12	73.68	46.57	64.59	52.31	72.55
1949	53.88	75.46	47.21	66.12	52.95	74.16
1950	58.32	80.89	50.26	69.71	56.36	78.17
1951	63.34	81.41	52.97	68.08	60.18	77.35
1952	67.16	84.48	55.04	69.23	62.98	79.22
1953	70.47	87.98	57.59	71.90	65.60	81.90
1954	70.49	87.57	58.45	72.61	65.65	81.55
1955	75.70	94.39	62.51	77.94	69.79	87.02
1956	78.78	96.78	64.92	79.75	72.25	88.76
1957	81.59	96.79	66.93	79.40	74.31	88.15
1958	82.71	95.51	67.82	78.31	75.23	86.87
1959	88.26	101.10	71.89	82.35	79.40	90.95
1960	89.72	101.15	72.57	81.82	80.11	90.32
1961	92.34	103.06	74.60	83.26	82.18	91.72
1962	96.56	106.58	77.86	85.94	85.53	94.40
1963	99.63	108.65	79.82	87.04	87.58	95.51
1964	102.97	110.84	84.40	90.85	92.18	99.22
1965	107.53	113.79	89.08	94.26	96.78	102.41
1966	112.34	115.58	91.57	94.21	99.45	102.31
1967	114.90	114.90	93.28	93.28	101.26	101.26
1968	122.51	117.57	97.70	93.76	106.75	102.45
1969	129.51	117.95	101.90	92.81	111.44	101.49
1970[p]	133.73	115.19[c]	106.62	91.83[c]	115.90	99.83[c]

[a]Earnings in current prices divided by the consumer price index on a 1967 base.
[b]Average gross weekly earnings less social security and income taxes.
[c]Based on 11-month average for the consumer price index.
[p]Preliminary data.

Source: Department of Labor, Bureau of Labor Statistics.

Selected U.S. Statistics (through 1970s)

Exhibit 9 Indexes of Output per Man-Hour and Related Data, Private Economy, 1947–1970 (1967 = 100)

Year	Compensation per Man-hour				Output per Man-hour[a]				Unit Labor Cost				Implicit Price Deflator[d]			
	Total Private[b]	%	Manufac-turing	%	Total Private[b]	%	Manufac-turing	%	Total Private[b]	%	Manufac-turing	%	Total Private[e]	%	Manufac-turing	%
	1	2	3	4	5	6	7	8	9	10	11	12	13	14	15	16
1947	36.2	—	37.1	—	51.3	—	54.8	—	70.6	—	67.7	—	66.4	—	66.9	—
1948	39.5	9.1%	40.7	9.7%	53.6	4.5%	57.5	5.7%	73.7	4.4%	70.3	3.8%	70.9	6.8%	71.3	6.6%
1949	40.1	1.5	42.6	4.7	55.3	3.2	60.0	3.6	72.5	-1.6	71.0	1.0	70.2	-1.0	72.8	2.1
1950	42.8	6.7	44.7	4.9	59.7	3.0	64.4	7.3	71.7	-1.1	69.5	-2.1	70.9	1.0	73.0	0.3
1951	46.9	9.6	49.3	10.3	61.5	3.0	65.9	2.3	76.3	6.4	74.8	7.6	76.1	7.3	77.9	6.7
1952	49.8	6.2	52.4	6.3	62.7	2.0	66.2	0.5	79.4	4.1	79.1	5.7	77.5	1.8	79.6	2.2
1953	52.9	6.2	55.3	5.5	65.3	4.1	68.3	3.2	81.0	2.0	80.9	2.3	78.1	0.8	80.0	0.5
1954	54.5	3.0	57.8	4.5	66.9	2.5	69.5	1.8	81.5	0.6	83.2	2.8	79.1	1.3	81.6	2.0
1955	55.9	2.6	60.0	3.8	69.9	4.5	73.7	6.0	80.1	-1.7	81.4	-2.2	79.8	0.9	83.1	1.8
1956	59.5	6.4	63.9	6.5	70.0	0.1	72.9	-1.1	85.0	6.1	87.6	7.6	82.3	3.1	86.9	4.6
1957	63.3	6.4	67.7	5.9	72.0	2.9	74.4	2.1	87.9	3.4	91.1	4.0	85.3	3.6	89.7	3.2
1958	66.0	4.3	70.6	4.3	74.3	3.2	74.4	0.0	88.9	1.1	94.9	4.2	87.1	2.1	91.9	2.5
1959	69.0	4.5	73.5	4.1	76.9	3.5	78.5	5.5	89.8	1.0	93.7	-1.3	88.3	1.4	93.3	1.5
1960	71.7	3.9	76.6	4.2	78.2	1.7	79.9	1.8	91.8	2.2	95.9	2.3	89.5	1.4	94.1	0.9
1961	74.4	3.8	79.0	3.1	80.9	3.5	81.8	2.4	92.1	0.3	96.5	0.6	90.4	1.0	94.4	0.3
1962	77.7	4.4	82.3	4.2	84.7	4.7	86.6	5.9	91.8	-0.3	95.0	-1.6	91.2	0.9	94.4	0.0
1963	80.8	4.0	85.0	3.3	87.7	3.5	90.1	4.0	92.1	0.3	94.4	-0.6	92.2	1.1	94.5	0.1
1964	84.9	5.1	89.0	4.7	91.1	3.9	94.5	4.9	93.1	1.1	94.1	-0.3	93.2	1.1	95.4	1.0
1965	88.4	4.1	91.2	2.5	94.2	3.4	98.3	4.0	93.8	0.8	92.8	-1.4	94.8	1.7	95.7	0.3
1966	94.5	6.9	95.3	4.5	98.0	4.0	99.9	1.6	96.5	2.9	95.5	2.9	97.2	2.5	97.4	1.8
1967	100.0	5.8	100.0	4.9	100.0	2.0	100.0	0.1	100.0	3.6	100.0	4.7	100.0	2.9	100.0	2.7
1968	107.6	7.6	107.1	7.1	102.9	2.5	104.7	4.7	104.6	4.6	102.3	2.3	103.6	3.6	102.3	2.3
1969	115.4	7.2	113.9	6.3	103.7	0.8	106.9	2.1	111.3	6.4	106.6	4.2	108.2	4.4	104.5	2.2
1970[f]	123.6	7.1	121.6	6.8	104.6	0.9	108.1	1.1	118.1	6.1	112.5	5.5	113.4	4.8	—	—

Note: For more information on sources, methodology, trends, and underlying factors influencing the measures, see Bureau of Labor Statistics, Department of Labor, Bulletin No. 1249, Trends in Output per Man-Hour in the Private Economy, 1909–58, December 1959.

[a]Output refers to gross national product in 1958 prices.
[b]Hours of all persons in private industry engaged in production, including man-hours of proprietors and unpaid family workers. Man-hours estimates based primarily on establishment data.
[c]Wages and salaries of employees plus employers' contribution for social insurance and private benefits plans. Also includes an estimate of wages, salaries, and supplemental payments for the self-employed.
[d]Current dollar gross product divided by constant dollar product.
[e]Total Private includes both farm and nonfarm sectors. The nonfarm sector is divided into manufacturing and nonmanufacturing sectors.
[f]Preliminary data.

Source: Department of Labor, Bureau of Labor Statistics.

Selected U.S. Statistics (through 1970s)

Exhibit 10   Manufacturing Output, Capacity, and Utilization Rate: 1948–1970

| Period | Output | Capacity[a] | Utilization Rate (Percent)[b] | | |
			Total	Advanced Products	Primary Products
	1	2	3	4	5
			(1967 Output = 100)		
1948	43.1	48.1	89.7	87.9	92.2
1949	40.8	50.8	80.2	80.3	80.0
1950	47.5	52.8	90.4	87.3	94.8
1951	51.3	54.7	94.0	91.0	98.1
1952	53.4	58.0	91.3	91.9	90.4
1953	58.0	61.6	94.2	94.1	94.4
1954	54.0	64.7	83.5	83.8	83.0
1955	60.9	67.9	90.0	87.8	93.2
1956	62.7	71.6	87.7	86.0	90.1
1957	63.1	75.6	83.6	82.3	85.3
1958	58.4	78.8	74.0	73.6	74.6
1959	66.4	81.5	81.5	81.0	82.1
1960	68.2	84.5	80.6	81.1	80.0
1961	68.6	87.4	78.5	78.9	78.1
1962	74.3	90.4	82.1	82.5	81.6
1963	78.2	93.8	83.3	83.1	83.6
1964	83.3	97.4	85.7	84.4	87.4
1965	90.8	102.7	88.5	87.6	89.7
1966	99.3	109.6	90.5	90.5	90.5
1967	100.0	116.5	85.3	85.9	84.6
1968	104.5	123.2	84.6	83.8	85.8
1969	108.9	130.0	83.7	81.6	86.7
1970[p]	104.0	136.8	76.6	73.9	80.2

[a]For description and source of data see "A Revised Index of Manufacturing Capacity," Frank de Leeuw, Frank E. Hopkins, and Michael D. Sherman, *Federal Reserve Bulletin,* November 1966: 1605–1615. See also McGraw-Hill surveys on "Business Plans for New Plants and Equipment" for data on capacity and operating rates.
[b]Output as percent of capacity; based on unrounded data.

[p]Preliminary data.

Source: Board of Governors of the Federal Reserve System (output) and sources in Note a (capacity and utilization rate).

Selected U.S. Statistics (through 1970s)

Exhibit 11　Money Stock: 1947–1970
(Average of Daily Figures; Billions of Dollars)

Year	M_2	M_1 Total	Currency Component[a]	Demand Deposit Component[b]	Percentage Change in M_2	Percentage Change in M_1
	1	2	3	4	5	6
			Seasonally Adjusted			
1947: Dec.	148.5	113.1	26.4	86.7	—	—
1948: Dec.	147.6	111.5	25.8	85.8	−0.6%	−1.4%
1949: Dec.	147.6	111.2	25.1	86.0	0.0	−0.3
1950: Dec.	152.9	116.2	25.0	91.2	3.6	4.5
1951: Dec.	160.8	122.7	26.1	96.5	5.2	5.6
1952: Dec.	168.6	127.4	27.3	100.1	4.9	3.8
1953: Dec.	173.3	128.8	27.7	101.1	2.8	1.1
1954: Dec.	180.6	132.3	27.4	104.9	4.2	2.7
1955: Dec.	185.2	135.2	27.8	107.4	2.5	2.2
1956: Dec.	188.8	136.9	28.2	108.7	1.9	1.3
1957: Dec.	193.3	135.9	28.3	107.6	2.4	−0.7
1958: Dec.	206.6	141.1	28.6	112.6	6.9	3.8
1959: Dec.	210.0	142.6	28.9	113.7	1.6	1.1
1960: Dec.	214.6	141.7	28.9	112.8	2.2	−0.6
1961: Dec.	228.7	146.0	29.6	116.5	6.6	3.0
1962: Dec.	245.9	148.1	30.6	117.6	7.5	1.4
1963: Dec.	265.8	153.6	32.5	121.1	8.1	3.7
1964: Dec.	287.1	160.5	34.2	126.3	8.0	4.5
1965: Dec.	314.8	168.0	36.3	131.7	9.6	4.7
1966: Dec.	330.0	171.7	38.3	133.4	4.8	2.2
1967: Dec.	366.6	183.1	40.4	142.7	11.1	6.6
1968: Dec.	402.2	197.4	43.4	154.0	9.7	7.8
1969: Dec.	398.2	203.6	46.0	157.7	−1.0	3.1
1970: Dec.[P]	445.0	214.6	48.9	165.6	11.8	5.4

Note: M_1 is composed of currency and demand deposits of commercial banks. M_2 is M_1 plus time deposits at commercial banks.
[a]Currency outside the Treasury, the Federal Reserve System, and the vaults of all commercial banks.
[b]Demand deposits at all commercial banks, other than those due to domestic commercial banks and the U.S. Government, less cash items in process of collection and Federal Reserve float, plus foreign demand balances at Federal Reserve Banks.
[d]Deposits at all commercial banks.

[P]Preliminary data.

Source: Board of Governors of the Federal Reserve System.

Selected U.S. Statistics (through 1970s)

Exhibit 12   Total Funds Raised in Credit Markets by Nonfinancial Sectors: 1962–1970 (Billions of Dollars)

Nonfinancial Sector	Line Number	1962	1963	1964
Total funds raised	**1**	**54.1**	**57.7**	**66.9**
U.S. government	2	7.0	4.0	6.4
Public debt securities	3	6.2	4.1	5.4
Budget agency issues	4	.8	—.1	1.0
All other sectors	5	47.1	53.7	60.5
Capital market instruments	6	33.1	35.7	37.9
Corporate equity shares	7	.6	−.2	1.6
Debt capital instruments	8	32.6	35.9	36.3
State and local governments	9	5.3	5.9	5.7
Corporate and foreign bonds	10	5.5	4.9	4.5
Mortgages	11	21.7	25.1	26.1
Home	12	12.8	15.1	15.6
Other residential	13	2.8	3.2	4.5
Commercial	14	4.8	5.1	3.8
Farm	15	1.3	1.6	2.1
Other private credit	16	14.0	18.0	22.6
Bank loans n.e.c.[a]	17	5.2	6.0	8.3
Consumer credit	18	5.8	7.9	8.5
Open-market paper	19	.1	.0	.7
Other	20	2.8	4.1	5.1
Total funds supplied directly	**21**	**54.1**	**57.7**	**66.9**
U.S. government	22	2.0	1.5	2.8
U.S. government credit agencies, net	23	.1	.1	.4
Funds advanced	24	1.6	1.6	.7
Less funds raised	25	1.5	1.4	.4
Federal Reserve System	26	2.0	2.9	3.4
Commercial banks, net	27	19.5	19.1	21.8
Private nonbank finance	28	26.6	29.9	31.0
Savings institutions, net	29	12.9	15.5	16.0
Insurance	30	14.4	14.3	15.6
Finance n.e.c., net[a]	31	−.7	.1	−.5
Funds advanced	32	4.6	5.8	5.5
Less funds raised	33	5.3	5.8	6.1
Foreign	34	1.5	.9	.6
Private domestic nonfinancial	35	2.4	3.4	7.0
Business	36	1.8	2.9	2.0
State and local government	37	1.2	1.1	.9
Households	38	−.8	1.3	4.0
Less net security credit	39	−.2	2.0	−.2

[a]N.E.C. = not elsewhere classified.

Source: Board of Governors of the Federal Reserve System.

Exhibit 12 (Continued)

1965	1966	1967	1968	1969	1970 Seasonally Adjusted Annual Rates I	II	III	Line Number
70.4	**68.5**	**82.6**	**97.4**	**88.2**	**80.0**	**101.3**	**103.0**	**1**
1.7	3.5	13.0	13.4	−3.6	3.3	17.2	18.8	2
1.3	2.3	8.9	10.3	−1.3	5.6	17.8	18.4	3
.4	1.2	4.1	3.0	−2.4	−2.3	−.6	.4	4
68.7	64.9	69.6	84.1	91.9	76.7	84.1	84.2	5
39.1	39.9	48.0	50.5	53.6	52.7	63.1	64.1	6
.3	.9	2.4	−.7	4.5	6.3	6.2	5.6	7
38.8	39.0	45.7	51.2	49.1	46.4	56.9	58.6	8
7.3	5.7	7.7	9.9	8.5	9.2	11.0	11.7	9
5.9	11.0	15.9	14.0	13.3	14.7	22.3	19.7	10
25.6	22.3	22.0	27.3	27.4	22.5	23.6	27.2	11
15.4	11.4	11.6	15.2	15.7	11.4	11.8	15.2	12
3.6	3.1	3.6	3.5	4.4	6.0	5.5	5.5	13
4.4	5.7	4.7	6.6	5.2	5.0	4.8	4.9	14
2.2	2.1	2.1	2.1	2.0	.1	1.5	1.6	15
29.5	25.0	21.6	33.6	38.3	24.0	21.0	20.1	16
14.2	10.3	9.6	13.4	14.2	7.8	4.5	4.5	17
10.0	7.2	4.6	11.1	9.3	4.8	6.2	6.4	18
−.3	1.0	2.1	1.6	3.3	5.0	2.2	.5	19
5.7	6.4	5.2	7.5	11.3	6.4	8.1	8.8	20
70.4	**68.5**	**82.6**	**97.4**	**88.2**	**80.0**	**101.3**	**103.0**	**21**
2.8	4.9	4.6	5.2	2.6	2.7	2.8	2.7	22
.0	.3	.5	−.2	.1	−.6	1.9	−.6	23
2.2	5.1	−.1	3.2	8.9	14.2	6.6	8.6	24
2.3	4.8	−.6	3.5	8.8	14.7	4.7	9.1	25
3.8	3.5	4.8	3.7	4.2	1.3	5.9	7.5	26
28.3	16.7	36.8	39.0	9.4	3.8	23.9	60.5	27
30.1	25.9	36.1	33.5	30.9	25.9	36.7	44.5	28
13.7	7.8	16.9	14.5	10.3	5.3	15.6	20.6	29
17.9	19.3	20.4	21.5	22.3	22.7	21.0	25.2	30
−1.4	−1.3	−1.3	−2.4	−1.7	−2.1	.2	−1.3	31
6.9	5.8	4.3	9.8	10.0	−.8	−1.7	17.3	32
8.3	7.1	5.6	12.3	11.7	1.2	−1.9	18.6	33
−.3	−1.8	2.8	2.5	2.0	8.1	9.4	7.8	34
5.6	19.1	−2.9	13.7	39.0	38.8	20.7	−19.5	35
1.0	3.6	−.6	9.0	11.4	10.7	.9	−23.2	36
2.5	3.4	1.2	.7	7.2	1.4	2.0	−7.8	37
2.5	11.9	−1.3	5.4	18.8	21.5	15.2	11.3	38
.3	−.2	2.2	1.4	−1.6	−5.2	−2.7	−.2	39

Exhibit 13 Bond Yields and Interest Rates: 1929–1970 (Percent per Annum)

Year or Month	U.S. Government Securities				Corporate Bonds (Moody's)		High-Grade Municipal Bonds (Standard & Poor's)	Average Rate on Short-Term Bank Loans to Business—Selected Cities	Prime Commercial Paper, 4–6 Months	Federal Reserve Bank Discount Rate	FHA New Home Mortgage Yields [e]
	3-Month Treasury Bills [a]	9–12 Month Issues [b]	3–5 Year Issues [c]	Taxable Bonds [d]	Aaa	Baa					
	1	2	3	4	5	6	7	8	9	10	11
1929	f	—	—	—	4.73	5.90	4.27	g	5.85	5.17	—
1930	f	—	—	—	4.55	5.90	4.07	g	3.59	3.04	—
1931	1.402	—	—	—	4.58	7.62	4.01	g	2.64	2.12	—
1932	.879	—	—	—	5.01	9.30	4.65	g	2.73	2.82	—
1933	.515	—	2.66	—	4.49	7.76	4.71	g	1.73	2.56	—
1934	.256	—	2.12	—	4.00	6.32	4.03	g	1.02	1.54	—
1935	.137	—	1.29	—	3.60	5.75	3.40	g	.75	1.50	—
1936	.143	—	1.11	—	3.24	4.77	3.07	g	.75	1.50	—
1937	.447	—	1.40	—	3.26	5.03	3.10	g	.94	1.33	—
1938	.053	—	.83	—	3.19	5.80	2.91	g	.81	1.00	—
1939	.023	—	.59	—	3.01	4.96	2.76	2.1	.59	1.00	—
1940	.014	—	.50	—	2.84	4.75	2.50	2.1	.56	1.00	—
1941	.103	—	.73	—	2.77	4.33	2.10	2.0	.53	1.00	—
1942	.326	—	1.46	2.46	2.83	4.28	2.36	2.2	.66	1.00[h]	—
1943	.373	0.75	1.34	2.47	2.73	3.91	2.06	2.6	.69	1.00[h]	—
1944	.375	.79	1.33	2.48	2.72	3.61	1.86	2.4	.73	1.00[h]	—
1945	.375	.81	1.18	2.37	2.62	3.29	1.67	2.2	.75	1.00[h]	—
1946	.375	.82	1.16	2.19	2.53	3.05	1.64	2.1	.81	1.00[h]	—
1947	.594	.88	1.32	2.25	2.61	3.24	2.01	2.1	1.03	1.00	—
1948	1.040	1.14	1.62	2.44	2.82	3.47	2.40	2.5	1.44	1.34	—
1949	1.102	1.14	1.43	2.31	2.66	3.42	2.21	2.68	1.49	1.50	4.34
1950	1.218	1.26	1.50	2.32	2.62	3.24	1.98	2.69	1.45	1.59	4.17
1951	1.552	1.73	1.93	2.57	2.86	3.41	2.00	3.11	2.16	1.75	4.21
1952	1.766	1.81	2.13	2.68	2.96	3.52	2.19	3.49	2.33	1.75	4.29
1953	1.931	2.07	2.56	2.94	3.20	3.74	2.72	3.69	2.52	1.99	4.61
1954	.953	.92	1.82	2.55	2.90	3.51	2.37	3.61	1.58	1.60	4.62
1955	1.753	1.89	2.50	2.84	3.06	3.53	2.53	3.70	2.18	1.89	4.64

Note: Yields and rates computed for New York City except for short-term bank loans.

[a] Rate on new issues within period. Issues were tax exempt prior to March 1, 1941, and fully taxable thereafter. For the period 1934–1937, series includes issues with maturities of more than 3 months.

[b] Certificates of indebtedness and selected note and bond issues (fully taxable).

[c] Selected note and bond issues. Issues were partially tax exempt prior to 1941, and fully taxable thereafter.

[d] First issued in 1941. Series includes bonds which are neither due nor callable before a given number of years as follows: April 1953 to date, 10 years; April 1952-March 1953, 12 years; October 1941-March 1952, 15 years.

[e] Data for first of the month, based on the maximum permissible interest rate (8 percent beginning December 2, 1970). Through July 1961, computed on 25-year mortgages paid in 12 years and thereafter, 30-year mortgages prepaid in 15 years.

[f] Treasury bills were first issued in December 1929 and were issued irregularly in 1930.

[g] Not available on same basis as for 1939 and subsequent years.

[h] From October 30, 1942, to April 24, 1946, a preferential rate of 0.50 percent was in effect for advances secured by Government securities maturing in 1 year or less.

Exhibit 13 (Continued)

	1	2	3	4	5	6	7	8	9	10	11
1956	2.658	2.83	3.12	3.08	3.36	3.88	2.93	4.20	3.31	2.77	4.79
1957	3.267	3.53	3.62	3.47	3.89	4.71	3.60	4.62	3.81	3.12	5.42
1958	1.839	2.09	2.90	3.43	3.79	4.73	3.56	4.34	2.46	2.15	5.49
1959	3.405	4.11	4.33	4.08	4.38	5.05	3.95	5.00'	3.97	3.36	5.71
1960	2.928	3.55	3.99	4.02	4.41	5.19	3.73	5.16	3.85	3.53	6.18
1961	2.378	2.91	3.60	3.90	4.35	5.08	3.46	4.97	2.97	3.00	5.80
1962	2.778	3.02	3.57	3.95	4.33	5.02	3.18	5.00	3.26	3.00	5.61
1963	3.157	3.28	3.72	4.00	4.26	4.86	3.23	5.01	3.55	3.23	5.47
1964	3.549	3.76	4.06	4.15	4.40	4.83	3.22	4.99	3.97	3.55	5.45
1965	3.954	4.09	4.22	4.21	4.49	4.87	3.27	5.06	4.38	4.04	5.46
1966	4.881	5.17	5.16	4.65	5.13	5.67	3.82	6.00	5.55	4.50	6.29
1967	4.321	4.84	5.07	4.85	5.51	6.23	3.98	6.00ʰ	5.10	4.19	6.55
1968	5.339	5.62	5.59	5.26	6.18	6.94	4.51	6.68	5.90	5.17	7.13
1969	6.677	7.06	6.85	6.12	7.03	7.81	5.81	8.21	7.83	5.87	8.19
1970	6.458	6.90	7.37	6.58	8.04	9.11	6.51	8.48	7.72	5.95	9.05
1968:											
Jan.	5.081	5.39	5.53	5.18	6.17	6.84	4.34	—	5.60	4.50	6.81
Feb.	4.969	5.37	5.59	5.16	6.10	6.80	4.39	6.36	5.50	4.50	6.81
Mar.	5.144	5.55	5.77	5.39	6.11	6.85	4.56	—	5.64	4.66	6.78
Apr.	5.365	5.63	5.69	5.28	6.21	6.97	4.41	—	5.81	5.20	6.83
May	5.621	6.06	5.95	5.40	6.27	7.03	4.56	6.84	6.18	5.50	6.94
June	5.544	6.01	5.71	5.23	6.28	7.07	4.56	—	6.25	5.50	—
July	5.382	5.68	5.44	5.09	6.24	6.98	4.36	—	6.19	5.50	7.52
Aug.	5.095	5.41	5.32	5.04	6.02	6.82	4.31	6.89	5.88	5.48	7.42
Sept.	5.202	5.40	5.30	5.09	5.97	6.79	4.47	—	5.82	5.25	7.35
Oct.	5.334	5.44	5.42	5.24	6.09	6.84	4.56	—	5.80	5.25	7.28
Nov.	5.492	5.56	5.47	5.36	6.19	7.01	4.68	6.61	5.92	5.25	7.29
Dec.	5.916	6.00	5.99	5.66	6.45	7.23	4.91	—	6.17	5.36	7.36
1969:											
Jan.	6.177	6.26	6.04	5.74	6.59	7.32	4.95	—	6.53	5.50	7.50
Feb.	6.156	6.21	6.16	5.86	6.66	7.30	5.10	7.32	6.62	5.50	—
Mar.	6.080	6.22	6.33	6.05	6.85	7.51	5.34	—	6.82	5.50	7.99
Apr.	6.150	6.11	6.15	5.84	6.89	7.54	5.29	—	7.04	5.95	8.05
May	6.077	6.26	6.33	5.85	6.79	7.52	5.47	7.86	7.35	6.00	8.06
June	6.493	7.07	6.64	6.05	6.98	7.70	5.83	—	8.23	6.00	8.06
July	7.004	7.59	7.02	6.07	7.08	7.84	5.84	—	8.65	6.00	8.35
Aug.	7.007	7.51	7.08	6.02	6.97	7.86	6.07	8.82	8.33	6.00	8.36
Sept.	7.129	7.76	7.58	6.32	7.14	8.05	6.35	—	8.48	6.00	8.36
Oct.	7.040	7.63	7.47	6.27	7.33	8.22	6.21	—	8.56	6.00	8.40
Nov.	7.193	7.94	7.57	6.52	7.35	8.25	6.37	8.83	8.46	6.00	8.48
Dec.	7.720	8.34	7.98	6.81	7.72	8.65	6.91	—	8.84	6.00	8.48
1970:											
Jan.	7.914	8.22	8.14	6.86	7.91	8.86	6.80	—	8.78	6.00	8.62
Feb.	7.164	7.60	7.80	6.44	7.93	8.78	6.57	8.86	8.55	6.00	—
Mar.	6.710	6.88	7.20	6.39	7.84	8.63	6.14	—	8.33	6.00	9.29
Apr.	6.480	6.96	7.49	6.53	7.83	8.70	6.55	—	8.06	6.00	9.20
May	7.035	7.69	7.97	6.94	8.11	8.98	7.02	8.49	8.23	6.00	9.10
June	6.742	7.50	7.86	6.99	8.48	9.25	7.06	—	8.21	6.00	9.11
July	6.468	7.00	7.58	6.57	8.44	9.40	6.69	—	8.29	6.00	9.16
Aug.	6.412	6.92	7.56	6.75	8.13	9.44	6.33	8.50	7.90	6.00	9.11
Sept.	6.244	6.68	7.24	6.63	8.09	9.39	6.45	—	7.32	6.00	9.07
Oct.	5.927	6.34	7.06	6.59	8.03	9.33	6.55	—	6.85	6.00	9.01
Nov.	5.288	5.52	6.37	6.24	8.05	9.38	6.20	8.07	6.30	5.85	8.97
Dec.	4.860	4.94	5.86	5.97	7.64	9.12	5.71	—	5.73	5.52	8.90

'Beginning 1959, series revised to exclude loans to nonbank financial institutions.

ʲBeginning February 1967, series revised to incorporate changes in coverage, in the sample of reporting banks, and in the reporting period (shifted to the middle month of the quarter).

Sources: Treasury Department, Board of Governors of the Federal Reserve System, Moody's Investors Service, Standard & Poor's Corporation, and Federal Housing Administration.

Selected U.S. Statistics (through 1970s)

Exhibit 14   U.S. Money Supply

A. Compounded Annual Rates of Change: 1968–1973

Terminal Quarter	3–68	4–68	1–69	2–69	3–69	4–69	1–70	2–70	3–70	4–70	1–71	2–71	3–71	4–71	1–72	2–72	3–72	4–72	1–73	Billions of Dollars (Seasonally Adjusted)
4–68	8.2																			200.2
1–69	7.9	7.6																		203.9
2–69	6.9	6.3	5.0																	206.4
3–69	5.8	5.0	3.7	2.3																207.6
4–69	5.0	4.2	3.2	2.2	2.1															208.7
1–70	4.9	4.3	3.5	3.0	3.3	4.5														211.0
2–70	5.2	4.7	4.1	3.9	4.5	5.6	6.8													214.5
3–70	5.2	4.8	4.4	4.2	4.7	5.6	6.2	5.5												217.4
4–70	5.3	5.0	4.6	4.5	5.0	5.7	6.1	5.8	6.0											220.6
1–71	5.4	5.1	4.8	4.8	5.2	5.9	6.2	6.0	6.3	6.5										224.1
2–71	6.0	5.8	5.6	5.7	6.1	6.8	7.3	7.4	8.1	9.1	11.7									230.4
3–71	6.1	5.9	5.8	5.8	6.3	6.9	7.3	7.4	7.9	8.5	9.5	7.3								234.5
4–71	5.8	5.6	5.4	5.5	5.8	6.3	6.6	6.5	6.7	6.9	7.0	4.7	2.2							235.8
1–72	5.8	5.6	5.4	5.5	5.8	6.2	6.4	6.3	6.5	6.6	6.6	4.9	3.8	5.4						238.9
2–72	6.0	5.8	5.7	5.7	6.1	6.5	6.7	6.7	6.8	7.0	7.0	5.9	5.4	7.1	8.8					244.0
3–72	6.1	6.0	5.9	5.9	6.2	6.6	6.8	6.8	7.0	7.1	7.2	6.3	6.1	7.4	8.5	8.1				248.8
4–72	6.2	6.1	6.0	6.0	6.3	6.7	6.9	6.9	7.0	7.2	7.2	6.5	6.4	7.4	8.1	7.8	7.4			253.3
1–73	6.1	6.0	5.9	5.9	6.2	6.5	6.7	6.7	6.8	6.9	6.9	6.3	6.1	6.9	7.2	6.7	6.0	4.7		256.2
2–73	6.1	6.0	5.9	6.0	6.3	6.6	6.7	6.7	6.8	6.9	6.9	6.4	6.2	6.9	7.2	6.8	6.4	5.8	7.0	260.6

+3.5%   +6.1%   +6.9%

Source: Federal Reserve Bank of St. Louis, Sept. 20, 1973.

Exhibit 14 (Continued)

Ratio Scale
Billions of Dollars

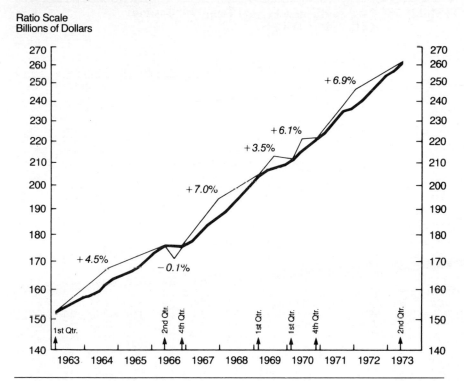

Percentages are annual rates of change for periods indicated.

Source: *Rate of Change in Economic Data for Ten Industrial Countries,* Federal Reserve Bank of St. Louis, September 27, 1973, J-1.

Selected U.S. Statistics (through 1970s)

Exhibit 15   Net Public and Private Debt: 1929–1969[a] (Billions of Dollars)

End of Year	Total	Public			Private		Individual and Noncorporate		Nonfarm		
		Fed-eral[b]	Federal Finan-cial Agen-cies[c]	State and Local	Total	Cor-porate	Total	Farm[d]	Total	Mort-gage	Com-mer-cial and Finan-cial[e]	Con-sumer
	1	2	3	4	5	6	7	8	9	10	11	12
1929	191.9	16.5	—	13.6	161.8	88.9	72.9	12.2	60.7	31.2	22.4	7.1
1930	192.3	16.5	—	14.7	161.1	89.3	71.8	11.8	60.0	32.0	21.6	6.4
1931	182.9	18.5	—	16.0	148.4	83.5	64.9	11.1	53.8	30.9	17.6	5.3
1932	175.0	21.3	—	16.6	137.1	80.0	57.1	10.1	47.0	29.0	14.0	4.0
1933	168.5	24.3	—	16.3	127.9	76.9	51.0	9.1	41.9	26.3	11.7	3.9
1934	171.6	30.4	—	15.9	125.3	75.5	49.8	8.9	40.9	25.5	11.2	4.2
1935	175.0	34.4	—	16.1	124.5	74.8	49.7	8.9	40.8	24.8	10.8	5.2
19_6	180.6	37.7	—	16.2	126.7	76.1	50.6	8.6	42.0	24.4	11.2	6.4
1937	182.2	39.2	—	16.1	126.9	75.8	51.1	8.6	42.5	24.3	11.3	6.9
1938	179.9	40.5	—	16.1	123.3	73.3	50.0	9.0	41.0	24.5	10.1	6.4
1939	183.3	42.6	—	16.4	124.3	73.5	50.8	8.8	42.0	25.0	9.8	7.2
1940	189.8	44.8	—	16.4	128.6	75.6	53.0	9.1	43.9	26.1	9.5	8.3
1941	211.4	56.3	—	16.1	139.0	83.4	55.6	9.3	46.3	27.1	10.0	9.2
1942	258.6	101.7	—	15.4	141.5	91.6	49.9	9.0	40.9	26.8	8.1	6.0
1943	313.2	154.4	—	14.5	144.3	95.5	48.8	8.2	40.5	26.1	9.5	4.9
1944	370.6	211.9	—	13.9	144.8	94.1	50.7	7.7	42.9	26.0	11.8	5.1
1945	405.9	252.5	—	13.4	140.0	85.3	54.7	7.3	47.4	27.0	14.7	5.7

[a]Net public and private debt is a comprehensive aggregate of the indebtedness of borrowers after eliminating certain types of duplicating governmental and corporate debt.

[b]Net federal government and agency debt is the outstanding debt held by the public, as defined in the "Budget of the United States Government, for the fiscal year ending June 30, 1972."

[c]This comprises the debt of federally sponsored agencies, in which there is no longer any federal proprietary interest. The obligations of the Federal Land Banks are included beginning with 1947, the debt of the Federal Home Loan Banks is included beginning with 1951, and the debts of the Federal National Mortgage Association, Federal Intermediate Credit Banks, and Banks for Cooperatives are included beginning with 1968.

[d]Farm mortgages and farm production loans. Farmers' financial and consumer debt is included in the nonfarm categories.

[e]Financial debt is debt owed to banks for purchasing or carrying securities, customers' debt to brokers, and debt owed to life insurance companies by policyholders.

Sources: Department of Commerce (Office of Business Economics), Treasury Department, Department of Agriculture, Board of Governors of the Federal Reserve System, Federal Home Loan Bank Board, Federal Land Banks, and Federal National Mortgage Association.

Exhibit 15 (Continued)

End of Year	Total	Fed-eral[b]	Public Fed-eral finan-cial agen-cies[c]	State and local	Total	Cor-porate	Private Individual and noncorporate Total	Farm[d]	Nonfarm Total	Mort-gage	Com-mer-cial and finan-cial[e]	Con-sumer
	1	2	3	4	5	6	7	8	9	10	11	12
1946	396.6	229.5	—	13.7	153.4	93.5	59.9	7.6	52.3	31.8	12.1	8.4
1947	415.7	221.7	0.7	15.0	178.3	108.9	69.4	8.6	60.7	37.2	11.9	11.6
1948	431.3	215.3	.6	17.0	198.4	117.8	80.6	10.8	69.7	42.4	12.9	14.4
1949	445.8	217.6	.7	19.1	208.4	118.0	90.4	12.0	78.4	47.1	13.9	17.4
1950	486.2	217.4	.7	21.7	246.4	142.1	104.3	12.3	92.0	54.8	15.8	21.5
1951	519.2	216.9	1.3	24.2	276.8	162.5	114.3	13.7	100.6	61.7	16.2	22.7
1952	550.2	221.5	1.3	27.0	300.4	171.0	129.4	15.2	114.2	68.9	17.8	27.5
1953	581.6	226.8	1.4	30.7	322.7	179.5	143.2	16.8	126.4	76.7	18.4	31.4
1954	605.9	229.1	1.3	35.5	340.0	182.8	157.2	17.5	139.7	86.4	20.8	32.5
1955	665.8	229.6	2.9	41.1	392.2	212.1	180.1	18.7	161.4	98.7	24.0	38.8
1956	698.4	224.3	2.4	44.5	427.2	231.7	195.5	19.4	176.1	109.4	24.4	42.3
1957	728.3	223.0	2.4	48.6	454.3	246.7	207.6	20.2	187.4	118.1	24.3	45.0
1958	769.6	231.0	2.5	53.7	482.4	259.5	222.9	23.2	199.7	128.1	26.5	45.1
1959	833.0	241.4	3.7	59.6	528.3	283.3	245.0	23.8	221.2	141.0	28.7	51.5
1960	874.2	239.8	3.5	64.9	566.1	302.8	263.3	25.1	238.2	151.3	30.8	56.1
1961	930.3	246.7	4.0	70.5	609.1	324.3	284.8	27.5	257.3	164.5	34.8	58.0
1962	996.0	253.6	5.3	77.0	660.1	348.2	311.9	30.2	281.7	180.3	37.6	63.8
1963	1,070.9	257.5	7.2	83.9	722.3	376.4	345.8	33.2	312.6	198.6	42.3	71.7
1964	1,151.6	264.0	7.5	90.4	789.7	409.6	380.1	36.0	344.1	218.9	45.0	80.3
1965	1,244.1	266.4	8.9	98.3	870.4	454.3	416.1	39.3	376.8	236.8	49.7	90.3
1966	1,341.4	271.8	11.2	104.8	953.5	506.6	446.9	42.4	404.5	251.6	55.4	97.5
1967	1,435.5	286.5	9.0	112.8	1,027.2	546.6	480.6	48.3	432.3	256.9	63.3	102.1
1968	1,567.8	291.9	21.4	123.2	1,131.4	610.9	520.5	52.3	468.2	285.3	69.7	113.2
1969	1,699.5	289.3	30.5	132.4	1,247.3	692.2	555.1	56.7	498.4	304.5	71.4	122.5

Selected U.S. Statistics (through 1970s)

Exhibit 16   Budget Receipts, Outlays, Financing, and Debt: 1959–1973 (Billions of Dollars; Fiscal Years Ending June 30)

Description	Row Number	1959	1960	1961	1962	1963	1964	1965	1966
Receipts and Outlays									
Budget receipts	1	79.2	92.5	94.4	99.7	106.6	112.7	116.8	130.9
Budget outlays	2	92.1	92.2	97.8	106.8	111.3	118.6	118.4	134.7
Surplus or deficit (−)	3	−12.9	.2	−3.4	−7.2	−4.7	−5.9	−1.6	−3.8
Budget Financing									
Net borrowing from the public or repayment of borrowing (−)	4	8.7	2.1	1.5	9.7	6.1	3.1	4.1	3.1
Other means of financing	5	4.3	−2.4	2.0	−2.6	−1.4	2.8	−2.5	.7
Total means of financing	6	12.9	−.2	3.4	7.2	4.7	5.9	1.6	3.8
Outstanding Debt, End of Year									
Gross federal debt	7	287.7	290.8	292.9	303.2	310.8	316.7	323.2	329.5
Held by:									
Government agencies	8	—	—	—	—	—	—	61.5	64.8
The public	9	235.0	237.1	238.6	248.3	254.4	257.5	261.6	264.7
Federal Reserve System	10	—	—	—	—	—	—	39.1	42.2
Other	11	—	—	—	—	—	—	222.5	222.5

Exhibit 16 (Continued)

Description	Row Number	1967	1968	1969	1970	1971	1972	1973
Receipts and Outlays								
Budget receipts	1	149.6	153.7	187.8	193.7	188.4	208.6	232.2
Budget outlays	2	158.3	178.8	184.5	196.6	211.4	231.9	246.5
Surplus or deficit (−)	3	−8.7	−25.2	3.2	−2.8	−23.00	−23.2	−14.3
Budget Financing								
Net borrowing from the public or repayment of borrowing (−)	4	2.8	23.1	−1.0	3.8	19.4	19.4	19.3
Other means of financing	5	5.9	2.1	−2.2	−1.0	3.6	3.8	−5.0
Total means of financing	6	8.7	25.2	−3.2	2.8	23.0	23.2	14.3
Outstanding Debt, End of Year								
Gross federal debt	7	341.3	369.8	367.1	382.6	409.5	437.3	468.4
Held by:								
Government agencies	8	73.8	79.1	87.7	97.7	105.1	113.6	125.4
The public	9	267.5	290.6	279.5	284.9	304.3	323.8	343.0
Federal Reserve System	10	46.7	52.2	54.1	57.7	65.5	71.4	75.2
Other	11	220.8	238.4	225.4	227.2	238.8	252.3	267.9

Source: *The United States Budget in Brief, Fiscal Year 1975* (Washington, DC: U.S. Government Printing Office), 46.

Selected U.S. Statistics (through 1970s)

Exhibit 17 Budget Receipts by Source and Outlays by Function: 1959–1973
(Billions of Dollars; Fiscal Years Ending June 30)

Description	Row Number	1959	1960	1961	1962	1963	1964	1965	1966
Receipts by Source									
Individual income taxes	1	36.7	40.7	41.3	45.6	47.6	48.7	48.8	55.4
Corporation income taxes	2	17.3	21.5	21.0	20.5	21.6	23.5	25.5	30.1
Social insurance taxes and contributions	3	11.7	14.7	16.5	17.0	19.8	22.0	22.3	25.6
Excise taxes	4	10.6	11.7	11.9	12.5	13.2	13.7	14.6	13.1
Estate and gift taxes	5	1.3	1.6	1.9	2.0	2.2	2.4	2.7	3.1
Customs duties	6	.9	1.1	1.0	1.1	1.2	1.3	1.4	1.8
Miscellaneous receipts	7	.6	1.2	.9	.8	1.0	1.1	1.6	1.9
Total receipts	8	79.2	92.5	94.4	99.7	106.6	112.7	116.8	130.9
Budget Outlays by Function									
National defense[a]	9	46.6	46.0	47.4	51.1	52.3	53.6	49.6	56.8
International affairs and finance	10	3.3	3.1	3.4	4.5	4.1	4.1	4.3	4.5
Space research and technology	11	.1	.4	.7	1.3	2.6	4.2	5.1	5.9
Agriculture and rural development	12	5.4	3.3	3.3	4.1	5.1	5.2	4.8	3.7
Natural resources and environment	13	1.2	1.0	1.6	1.7	1.5	2.0	2.1	2.0
Commerce and transportation	14	4.5	4.8	5.0	5.4	5.7	6.5	7.4	7.3
Community development and housing	15	.9	1.0	.2	.6	-.9	-.2	.3	2.6
Education and manpower	16	1.1	1.3	1.5	1.7	1.7	2.0	2.3	4.3
Health	17	–	–	–	–	–	–	–	2.5
Health and welfare	18	17.7	18.7	21.8	23.4	25.3	26.6	25.7	–
Income security	19	–	–	–	–	–	–	–	28.9
Veterans' benefits and services	20	5.4	5.4	5.7	5.6	5.5	5.7	5.7	5.9
Interest	21	7.0	8.3	8.1	8.3	9.2	9.8	10.4	11.3
General government	22	1.2	1.3	1.5	1.7	1.8	2.1	2.2	2.2
General revenue sharing	23	–	–	–	–	–	–	–	–
Undistributed intragovernmental transactions	24	-2.2	-2.3	-2.5	-2.6	-2.7	-2.9	-3.1	-3.4
Total outlays	25	92.1	92.2	97.8	106.8	111.3	118.6	118.4	134.7

Exhibit 17 (Continued)

Description	Row Number	1967	1968	1969	1970	1971	1972	1973
Receipts by Source								
Individual income taxes	1	61.5	68.7	87.2	90.4	86.2	94.7	103.2
Corporation income taxes	2	34.0	28.7	36.7	32.8	26.8	32.2	36.2
Social insurance taxes and contributions	3	33.3	34.6	39.9	45.3	48.6	53.9	64.5
Excise taxes	4	13.7	14.1	15.2	15.7	16.6	15.5	16.3
Estate and gift taxes	5	3.0	3.1	3.5	3.6	3.7	5.4	4.9
Customs duties	6	1.9	2.0	2.3	2.4	2.6	3.3	3.2
Miscellaneous receipts	7	2.1	2.5	2.9	3.4	3.9	3.6	3.9
Total receipts	8	149.6	153.7	187.8	193.7	188.4	208.6	232.2
Budget Outlays by Function								
National defense[a]	9	70.1	80.5	81.2	80.3	77.7	78.3	76.0
International affairs and finance	10	4.5	4.6	3.8	3.6	3.1	3.7	3.0
Space research and technology	11	5.4	4.7	4.2	3.7	3.4	3.4	3.3
Agriculture and rural development	12	4.4	5.9	6.2	6.2	5.1	7.1	6.2
Natural resources and environment	13	1.9	1.7	2.2	2.6	2.7	3.8	.6
Commerce and transportation	14	7.6	8.1	7.9	9.5	11.4	11.3	13.1
Community development and housing	15	2.6	4.1	2.0	3.0	3.4	4.3	4.1
Education and manpower	16	5.9	6.7	6.5	7.3	8.2	9.8	10.2
Health	17	6.7	9.6	11.6	12.9	14.5	17.1	18.4
Health and welfare	18	—	—	—	—	—	—	—
Income security	19	31.2	34.1	37.7	43.7	56.1	64.9	73.1
Veterans' benefits and services	20	6.9	5.9	7.6	8.7	9.8	10.7	12.0
Interest	21	12.6	13.7	15.8	18.3	19.6	20.6	22.8
General government	22	2.4	2.5	2.8	3.3	3.9	4.8	5.5
General revenue sharing	23	—	—	—	—	—	—	6.6
Undistributed intragovernmental transactions	24	-3.9	-4.5	-5.1	-6.4	-7.4	-7.9	-8.4
Total outlays	25	158.3	178.8	184.5	196.6	211.4	231.9	246.5

[a]Includes allowances for All-Volunteer Force, military retirement systems reform, and civilian and military pay raises for Department of Defense.

Source: *The United States Budget in Brief, Fiscal Year 1975* (Washington, DC: U.S. Government Printing Office), 47.

Exhibit 18   Maximum Interest Rates Payable on Time and Savings Deposits, 1966–1973, Set by Board of Governors under Regulation Q
(Percent per Annum)

Type of Deposit	July 20, 1966	Sept. 26, 1966	Apr. 19, 1968	Jan. 21, 1970	June 24, 1970	May 16, 1973	July 1, 1973
Savings deposits	4	4	4	4½	4½	4½	5
Other time deposits:[a]							
Multiple maturity[b]							
30–89 days	4	4	4	4½	4½	4½	5
90 days-1 year	5	5	5	5	5	5	5½
1 year to:							
2 years	5	5	5	5½	5½	5½	—
2½ years	—	—	—	—	—	—	6
2 years and over	5	5	5	5¾	5¾	5¾	—
2½ years and over	—	—	—	—	—	—	6½
4 years and over (minimum denom. of $1,000)	—	—	—	—	—	—	c
Single maturity:							
Less than $100,000:							
30–89 days	5½	5	5	5	5	5	5
90 days-1 year	5½	5	5	5	5	5	5½
1 year to:							
2 years	5½	5	5	5½	5½	5½	—
2½ years	—	—	—	—	—	—	6
2 years and over	5½	5	5	5¾	5¾	5¾	—
2½ years and over	—	—	—	—	—	—	6½
4 years and over (minimum denom. of $1,000)	—	—	—	—	—	—	c
$100,000 and over:							
30–59 days	5½	5½	5½	6¼	d	—	—
60–89 days	5½	5½	5¾	6½	d	—	—
90–179 days	5½	5½	6	6¾	6¾	d	—
180 days-1 year	5½	5½	6¼	7	7	d	—
1 year or more	5½	5½	6¼	7½	7½	d	—

Note: Maximum rates that may be paid by member banks are established by the Board of Governors under provisions of Regulation Q; however, a member bank may not pay a rate in excess of the maximum rate payable by state banks or trust companies on like deposits under the laws of the state in which the member bank is located. Beginning Feb. 1, 1936, maximum rates that may be paid by nonmember insured commercial banks, as established by the FDIC, have been the same as those in effect for member banks.

For previous changes, see earlier issues of the *Federal Reserve Bulletin*.

[a]For exceptions with respect to certain foreign time deposits, see *Federal Reserve Bulletin*, Feb. 1968, 167.

[b]Multiple-maturity time deposits include deposits that are automatically renewable at maturity without action by the depositor and deposits that are payable after written notice of withdrawal.

[c]Between July 1 and Oct. 31, 1973, there was no ceiling for 4-year certificates with minimum denomination of $1,000. The amount of such certificates that a bank could issue was limited to 5 percent of its total time and savings deposits. Sales in excess of that amount were subject to the 6½ percent ceiling that applies to time deposits maturing in 2½ years or more. Effective Nov. 1, 1973, a ceiling rate of 7¼ percent was imposed on certificates maturing in 4 years and over with minimum denomination of $1,000. There is no limitation on the amount of these certificates that banks may issue.

[d]Suspended as of this date.

Source: *Federal Reserve Bulletin*, November 1973, A-10.

Selected U.S. Statistics (through 1970s)

Exhibit 19   International Economic Comparisons: 1960–1973
A. Real GNP Trends (1960 = 100)

	United States	United Kingdom	Japan	West Germany	Italy	France
1960	100	100	100	100	100	100
1961	102	102	116	105	108	105
1962	109	105	123	110	115	112
1963	113	109	136	113	121	119
1964	119	115	154	121	125	127
1965	127	118	161	128	129	133
1966	135	120	177	132	137	140
1967	138	123	200	131	146	147
1968	145	126	229	141	155	154
1969	149	128	258	152	163	166
1970	148	130	287	159	173	175
1971	153	133	304	164	175	185
1972	162	138	331	170	181	195
1973[a]	172	146	367	179	190	208

[a]Estimated.

B. Industrial Production Trends (1960 = 100)

	United States	United Kingdom	Japan	West Germany	Italy	France
1960	100	100	100	100	100	100
1961	101	100	119	106	111	106
1962	109	101	129	110	121	111
1963	116	105	143	114	132	118
1964	124	114	166	123	133	127
1965	136	117	173	130	139	129
1966	149	119	194	132	155	139
1967	152	119	231	130	168	142
1968	160	125	279	144	179	148
1969	169	129	323	164	186	167
1970	162	132	367	174	197	176
1971	163	133	379	177	191	187
1972	174	144	404	183	191	200
1973[a]	190	160	474	197	202	219

[a]Estimated.

Exhibit 19 (Continued)
C. World Trade: Exports (Billions of U.S. Dollars)[a]

	1960	1965	1972
Total	129.6	188.5	416.5
United States	20.6	27.5	49.8
European community	42.3	64.7	154.9
Of which:			
United Kingdom	10.6	13.7	24.3
Japan	4.1	8.5	28.6
Other developed countries	19.5	29.0	66.9
Less-developed countries	26.9	35.7	71.7
Communist countries	16.2	23.1	44.6
China	2.0	2.0	3.1
U.S.S.R.	5.6	8.2	15.4
Other	8.6	12.9	26.1

[a]Data are f.o.b.

D. World Trade: Imports (Billions of U.S. Dollars)[a]

	1960	1965	1972
Total	135.8	198.7	431.2
United States	16.4	23.2	59.0
European community	45.1	69.2	154.5
Of which:			
United Kingdom	13.0	16.1	27.9
Japan	4.5	8.2	23.5
Other developed countries	23.8	37.4	76.9
Less-developed countries	29.6	37.6	71.4
Communist countries	16.4	23.1	43.9
China	2.0	1.8	2.8
U.S.S.R.	5.6	8.1	16.0
Other	8.8	13.2	27.1

[a]Data are c.i.f.

Exhibit 19 (Continued)
E. Export and Consumer Price Indexes (1960 = 100)

	1960	1961	1962	1963	1964	1965	1966	1967	1968	1969	1970	1971	1972	1973[a]
Export Prices[b]														
United States	100	102	101	101	102	105	108	111	112	116	122	126	131	151
Canada	100	96	94	94	95	97	101	102	105	108	114	118	124	149
United Kingdom	100	100	101	104	106	109	113	113	105	109	117	127	140	163
France	100	100	101	102	106	107	110	109	108	111	114	120	135	172
West Germany	100	106	106	106	106	105	109	108	107	111	121	128	142	184
Italy	100	97	98	99	102	100	98	98	98	101	107	113	115	124
Japan	100	96	93	95	96	96	96	96	97	99	104	107	119	143
Consumer Prices														
United States	100	101	102	104	105	107	109	113	118	124	132	138	142	151
Canada	100	100	102	105	107	111	114	118	122	128	132	136	142	153
United Kingdom	100	104	107	109	114	119	123	126	132	139	147	161	173	189
France	100	104	109	115	117	121	125	128	134	142	151	159	169	181
West Germany	100	103	106	109	112	115	119	121	123	127	131	138	146	156
Italy	100	102	107	115	122	127	130	134	136	140	146	154	162	179
Japan	100	109	113	121	127	134	142	147	155	164	176	187	196	219

[a]Estimated.
[b]Based on export prices in U.S. dollars.

Exhibit 19 (Continued)
F. Trends in Productivity and Wage Earnings in Manufacturing (1965 = 100)

	1960	1961	1962	1963	1964	1965	1966	1967	1968	1969	1970	1971	1972	1973[a]
Productivity Index[b]														
United States	81.5	83.5	88.3	91.8	96.2	100.0	101.3	101.2	106.1	108.6	109.3	117.1	123.3	129.9
Canada	80.3	84.8	89.2	92.5	96.5	100.0	102.8	105.9	113.5	119.8	121.7	128.7	134.3	141.3
United Kingdom	83.3	84.0	86.2	90.7	96.7	100.0	103.3	107.3	114.1	116.5	119.5	125.5	135.9	140.0
Japan	66.4	75.1	78.4	84.7	96.0	100.0	110.1	126.4	142.4	164.3	185.2	191.8	211.1	250.8
France	78.5	82.1	85.8	90.0	94.7	100.0	106.9	112.7	122.2	129.8	136.3	142.8	153.1	165.3
West Germany	73.5	77.8	82.4	86.8	93.6	100.0	104.1	110.6	119.0	125.9	129.3	135.4	144.5	155.5
Italy	71.1	73.6	80.9	83.5	89.0	100.0	104.8	109.2	118.3	122.5	128.6	134.2	142.5	N.A.
Earnings Index[c]														
United States	84.0	86.6	90.2	93.2	97.6	100.0	104.5	109.6	117.5	125.0	134.0	143.4	152.4	164.6
Canada	83.9	86.1	88.5	91.8	95.2	100.0	107.9	116.1	124.6	133.9	144.6	156.2	167.8	182.8
United Kingdom	72.0	77.6	81.7	85.3	91.4	100.0	110.1	110.5	120.0	129.8	148.7	167.2	187.8	213.4
Japan	53.2	62.0	70.7	79.0	86.6	100.0	110.2	123.5	143.5	169.8	201.7	233.3	271.0	327.3
France	65.2	71.8	79.0	86.4	93.1	100.0	107.2	115.6	129.8	141.6	160.8	180.8	203.4	229.9
West Germany	62.6	70.1	79.0	84.4	91.0	100.0	109.0	115.3	122.3	133.3	154.0	175.3	194.7	219.7
Italy	55.6	59.0	69.1	82.2	92.5	100.0	102.7	112.4	120.4	132.1	158.5	187.6	212.2	N.A.

[a]Estimated.
[b]Output per man-hour.
[c]Based on hourly compensation in national currencies.

Exhibit 19 (Continued)
G. Trends in Unit Labor Costs in Manufacturing (1965 = 100)[a]

	United States	United Kingdom	Japan	France	West Germany	Italy	Canada
1960	103.1	86.8	80.5	83.0	81.7	78.8	104.4
1961	103.8	92.3	82.3	87.4	89.8	80.7	101.5
1962	102.2	95.0	90.4	92.0	95.8	85.8	99.2
1963	101.5	94.0	93.3	96.0	97.5	99.0	99.2
1964	101.3	94.2	92.3	98.3	97.8	104.0	98.8
1965	100.0	100.0	100.0	100.0	100.0	100.0	100.0
1966	103.1	106.2	99.8	100.0	104.6	98.0	104.9
1967	108.3	101.1	97.5	102.1	104.5	103.0	109.8
1968	110.8	89.9	101.1	103.2	102.8	102.0	109.8
1969	115.2	95.0	104.2	103.3	107.7	107.4	111.9
1970	122.6	106.4	109.8	104.6	130.6	122.8	118.8
1971	122.4	116.2	126.6	112.6	149.0	141.2	121.4
1972	123.6	123.4	153.1	129.1	168.8	159.3	124.9
1973[b]	126.7	133.6	175.4	153.4	212.7	N.A.	129.4

[a]Based on unit labor costs in U.S. dollars.

[b]Estimated.

Source: *International Economic Report of the President, Feburary 1974* (Washington, DC: U.S. Government Printing Office, 1974).

Selected U.S. Statistics (through 1970s)

Exhibit 20   U.S. Foreign Trade
A. U.S. Foreign Trade
   (Billions of U.S. Dollars)[a]

	Exports[b]	Imports	Balance
1958	16.4	13.4	3.0
1959	16.4	15.7	0.7
1960	19.7	15.1	4.6
1961	20.2	14.8	5.4
1962	21.0	16.5	4.5
1963	22.5	17.2	5.3
1964	25.8	18.7	7.1
1965	26.7	21.4	5.3
1966	29.5	25.6	3.9
1967	31.0	26.9	4.1
1968	34.1	33.2	0.9
1969	37.3	36.0	1.3
1970	42.7	40.0	2.7
1971	43.5	45.6	−2.1
1972	49.2	55.6	−6.4
1973	70.8	69.1	1.7

[a]Exports and imports are f.o.b.
[b]Excluding Department of Defense shipments.

B. U.S. Foreign Trade Trends: Agricultural Products
(Billions of U.S. Dollars)[a]

	Exports	Imports	Balance
1958	3.9	3.9	0.0
1959	4.0	4.1	−0.1
1960	4.9	3.8	1.1
1961	5.0	3.7	1.3
1962	5.0	3.9	1.1
1963	5.6	4.0	1.6
1964	6.3	4.1	2.2
1965	6.2	4.1	2.1
1966	6.9	4.5	2.4
1967	6.4	4.5	1.9
1968	6.2	5.1	1.1
1969	5.9	5.1	0.8
1970	7.2	5.8	1.4
1971	7.7	5.8	1.9
1972	9.4	6.5	2.9
1973	17.7	8.4	9.3

[a]Exports and imports are f.o.b.

Exhibit 20 (Continued)
C. U.S. Foreign Trade Trends: Minerals and Fuels
   (Billions of U.S. Dollars)[a]

	Exports	Imports	Balance
1958	1.9	3.7	−1.8
1959	1.9	4.1	−2.2
1960	2.3	4.0	−1.7
1961	2.3	4.1	−1.8
1962	2.1	4.5	−2.4
1963	2.4	4.6	−2.2
1964	2.6	4.9	−2.3
1965	2.6	5.4	−2.8
1966	2.7	5.8	−3.1
1967	3.1	5.6	−2.5
1968	3.2	6.3	−3.1
1969	3.5	6.7	−3.2
1970	4.5	7.0	−2.5
1971	3.8	7.9	−4.1
1972	4.3	9.7	−5.4
1973	6.0	14.1	−8.1

[a]Exports and imports are f.o.b.

D. U.S. Foreign Trade Trends: Manufactured Products
(Billions of U.S. Dollars)[a]

	Exports	Imports	Balance
1958	11.2	5.3	5.9
1959	10.9	7.1	3.8
1960	12.7	6.8	5.9
1961	12.9	6.5	6.4
1962	13.8	7.6	6.2
1963	14.5	8.1	6.4
1964	16.7	9.1	7.6
1965	17.6	11.2	6.4
1966	19.5	14.4	5.1
1967	21.1	15.8	5.3
1968	24.1	20.6	3.5
1969	27.1	23.0	4.1
1970	29.7	25.9	3.8
1971	30.8	30.4	0.4
1972	34.3	37.8	−3.5
1973	44.7	44.8	−0.1

[a]Exports and imports are f.o.b.

Exhibit 20 (Continued)
E. U.S. Trade Balance in Selected Commodities (Millions of U.S. Dollars)ᵃ

	1960	1961	1962	1963	1964	1965	1966	1967	1968	1969	1970	1971	1972	1973ᵇ
Products with a rising trade surplus trend														
Nonelectric machineryᶜ	2,576	2,773	2,986	3,002	3,409	3,504	3,508	3,474	3,579	3,976	4,364	4,183	4,330	5,176
Aircraft and parts	970	766	857	726	791	989	823	1,270	2,016	2,139	2,382	3,049	2,508	3,359
Computers and parts	44	105	128	177	214	219	280	412	524	768	1,176	1,142	1,167	1,513
Basic chemicals and compounds	52	141	155	329	521	589	556	644	690	739	883	818	652	931
Products with a declining trade balance trend														
Motor vehicles and parts	643	803	850	955	1,063	934	537	237	−588	−1,104	−1,823	−2,897	−3,492	−3,820
Steel products	204	108	−2	−93	−51	−533	−646	−750	−1,380	−783	−764	−1,855	−1,945	−1,571
Textiles, clothing, and footwear	−396	−284	−540	−567	−548	−824	−978	−1,016	−1,498	−1,819	−2,220	−2,823	−3,294	−3,444
Consumer electronics	−53	−80	−109	−130	−164	−258	−374	−431	−632	−912	−1,123	−1,304	−1,736	−1,879

ᵃExports and imports are f.o.b.
ᵇEstimated. Based on January-September data.
ᶜExcluding aircraft and auto engines and parts, computers, and other office machinery.

Source: *International Economic Report of the President, February 1974* (Washington, DC: U.S. Government Printing Office, 1974).

Exhibit 20 (Continued)
F. U.S. Trade with Canada
  (Billions of U.S. Dollars)[a]

	Exports	Imports	Balance
1958	3.5	3.0	0.5
1959	3.8	3.4	0.4
1960	3.8	3.2	0.6
1961	3.8	3.3	0.5
1962	4.1	3.7	0.4
1963	4.3	3.9	0.4
1964	4.9	4.3	0.6
1965	5.7	4.9	0.8
1966	6.7	6.2	0.5
1967	7.2	7.1	.0
1968	8.1	9.0	−0.9
1969	9.1	10.4	−1.3
1970	9.1	11.1	−2.0
1971	10.4	12.7	−2.3
1972	12.4	14,9	−2.5

[a]Exports and imports are f.o.b.

G. U.S. Trade with the European Community
  (Billions of U.S. Dollars)[a]

	Exports	Imports	Balance
1958	3.9	2.6	1.3
1959	4.1	3.7	0.4
1960	5.7	3.4	2.3
1961	5.6	3.3	2.3
1962	5.9	3.6	2.3
1963	6.4	3.8	2.6
1964	7.2	4.1	3.1
1965	7.2	4.9	2.3
1966	7.6	6.2	1.4
1967	8.0	6,5	1.5
1968	8.7	8.3	0.4
1969	9.7	8.3	1.4
1970	11.3	9.2	2.1
1971	11.1	10.4	0.7
1972	11.9	12.5	−0.6

[a]Exports and imports are f.o.b.

Exhibit 20 (Continued)
H. U.S. Trade with Japan
  (Billions of U.S. Dollars)[a]

	Exports	Imports	Balance
1958	1.0	0.7	0.3
1959	1.1	1.0	0.1
1960	1.5	1.1	0.4
1961	1.8	1.1	0.7
1962	1.6	1.4	0.2
1963	1.8	1.5	0.3
1964	2.0	1.8	0.2
1965	2.1	2.4	−0.3
1966	2.4	3.0	−0.6
1967	2.7	3.0	−0.3
1968	3.0	4.1	−1.1
1969	3.5	4.9	−1.4
1970	4.7	5.9	−1.2
1971	4.1	7.3	−3.2
1972	4.9	9.1	−4.2

[a]Exports and imports are f.o.b.

I. U.S. Trade with the Less-Developed Countries
  (Billions of U.S. Dollars)[a]

	Exports	Imports	Balance
1958	8.1	6.1	2.0
1959	7.1	6.3	0.8
1960	7.7	6.2	1.5
1961	8.0	6.0	2.0
1962	8.3	6.3	2.0
1963	8.9	6.6	2.3
1964	9.9	7.0	2.9
1965	9.9	7.5	2.4
1966	11.1	8.2	3.0
1967	11.0	8.2	2.8
1968	11.8	9.4	2.4
1969	12.5	9.9	2.6
1970	14.4	11.0	3.3
1971	14.8	12.2	2.5
1972	16.3	15.3	1.0

[a]Exports and imports are f.o.b.

Exhibit 20 (Continued)
J. Origin of Imports for Selected Areas (Percent)ᵃ

Imported by	Exported by								
	1960			1965			1970		
	United States	European Community	Japan	United States	European Community	Japan	United States	European Community	Japan
United States	—	22	8	—	23	11	—	23	15
Canada	67	16	2	70	13	3	71	11	4
Japan	35	7	—	29	7	—	29	8	—
European Community	13	36	1	11	43	1	11	49	1
Other Western Europe	11	56	1	10	56	2	9	53	3
Other Asia	17	25	13	24	24	19	22	18	27
Western Hemisphere, other	39	28	2	38	28	4	38	25	6
New Zealand, Australia, and South Africa	17	46	5	20	43	8	21	40	11
Communist countries	1	11	1	1	12	1	1	18	3
Other	10	55	4	13	49	8	11	49	7

ᵃCalculated from data of importing country or area.

Source: *International Economic Report of the President, March 1973*, 88.

Exhibit 21   U.S. Balance of Payments: 1946–1970
(Millions of Dollars)

Year or Quarter	Exports of Goods and Services						Imports of Goods and Services				Balance on Goods and Services	Remittances and Pensions
	Total	Merchandise[a]	Military Sales	Income on Investments		Other Services	Total	Merchandise[a]	Military Expenditures	Other Services		
				Private	Government							
	1	2	3	4	5	6	7	8	9	10	11	12
1946	14,792	11,764	[b]	751	21	2,256	−6,985	−5,067	−493	−1,425	7,807	−648
1947	19,819	16,097	[b]	1,036	66	2,620	−8,202	−5,973	−455	−1,774	11,617	−728
1948	16,861	13,265	[b]	1,238	102	2,256	−10,343	−7,557	−799	−1,987	6,518	−631
1949	15,834	12,213	[b]	1,297	98	2,226	−9,616	−6,874	−621	−2,121	6,218	−641
1950	13,893	10,203	[b]	1,484	109	2,097	−12,001	−9,081	−576	−2,344	1,892	−533
1951	18,864	14,243	[b]	1,684	198	2,739	−15,047	−11,176	−1,270	−2,601	3,817	−480
1952	18,122	13,449	[b]	1,624	204	2,845	−15,766	−10,838	−2,054	−2,874	2,356	−571
1953	17,078	12,412	192	1,658	252	2,564	−16,546	−10,975	−2,615	−2,956	532	−644
1954	17,889	12,929	182	1,955	272	2,551	−15,930	−10,353	−2,642	−2,935	1,959	−633
1955	19,948	14,424	200	2,170	274	2,880	−17,795	−11,527	−2,901	−3,367	2,153	−597
1956	23,772	17,556	161	2,468	194	3,393	−19,627	−12,803	−2,949	−3,875	4,145	−690
1957	26,653	19,562	375	2,612	205	3,899	−20,752	−13,291	−3,216	−4,245	5,901	−729
1958	23,217	16,414	300	2,538	307	3,658	−20,861	−12,952	−3,435	−4,474	2,356	−745
1959	23,652	16,458	302	2,694	349	3,849	−23,342	−15,310	−3,107	−4,925	310	−815
1960	27,488	19,650	335	3,000	348	4,155	−23,355	−14,744	−3,087	−5,523	4,133	−596
1961	28,770	20,107	402	3,561	381	4,318	−23,148	−14,519	−2,998	−5,631	5,622	−632
1962	30,506	20,779	656	3,948	471	4,651	−25,357	−16,218	−3,105	−6,035	5,149	−695
1963	32,601	22,252	657	4,151	498	5,043	−26,617	−17,011	−2,961	−6,647	5,984	−798
1964	37,271	25,478	747	4,930	456	5,659	−28,691	−18,647	−2,880	−7,164	8,580	−809
1965	39,399	26,447	830	5,384	509	6,230	−32,278	−21,496	−2,952	−7,831	7,121	−950
1966	43,360	29,389	829	5,659	593	6,891	−38,060	−25,463	−3,764	−8,833	5,300	−898
1967	46,203	30,681	1,240	6,235	638	7,409	−40,990	−26,821	−4,378	−9,791	5,213	−1,167
1968	50,622	33,588	1,395	6,922	765	7,952	−48,129	−32,964	−4,535	−10,630	2,493	−1,121
1969	55,514	36,473	1,515	7,906	932	8,688	−53,564	−35,835	−4,850	−12,879	1,949	−1,190
1970[c]	62,907	42,148	1,375	8,656	955	9,773	−58,964	−39,409	−3,863	−14,692	4,943	−1,397
					Seasonally Adjusted Annual Rates							
1968: I	47,728	31,784	1,208	6,236	824	7,676	−45,908	−31,280	−4,412	−10,216	1,820	−1,068
II	50,740	33,544	1,376	7,136	824	7,860	−47,328	−32,528	−4,448	−10,352	3,412	−1,028
III	53,180	35,512	1,572	7,160	840	8,096	−49,776	−34,276	−4,588	−10,912	3,404	−1,288
IV	50,856	33,512	1,428	7,164	576	8,176	−49,496	−33,772	−4,692	−11,032	1,360	−1,104
1969: I	47,792	29,888	1,564	7,444	912	7,984	−46,472	−30,304	−4,792	−11,376	1,320	−1,080
II	57,164	38,340	1,252	7,676	924	8,972	−55,912	−38,424	−4,748	−12,740	1,252	−1,176
III	58,260	38,324	1,832	8,172	972	8,960	−55,636	−37,052	−4,880	−13,704	2,624	−1,272
IV	58,848	39,340	1,408	8,332	924	8,844	−56,244	−37,560	−4,980	−13,704	2,604	−1,236
1970: I	61,368	40,912	1,032	9,020	976	9,428	−58,040	−38,892	−4,712	−14,436	3,328	−1,312
II	63,656	42,820	1,728	8,232	976	9,900	−59,240	−39,504	−5,020	−14,716	4,416	−1,440
III[p]	63,696	42,712	1,364	8,716	912	9,992	−59,612	−39,832	−4,856	−14,924	4,084	−1,440

Note: Data exclude military grant-aid and U.S. subscriptions to International Monetary Fund. Relationship among columns: 11 = 1 − 7, 19 = −(21 + 23 + 24), 19 = 11 + 12 + 13 + 14 + 15 + 16 + 17 + 18, 20 = −(21 + 22 + 24), and 20 = 11 + 12 + 13 + 14 + 15 + 16 + 17 + 18 + 23 − 22)
[a]Adjusted from customs data for differences in timing and coverage.
[b]Not reported separately.
[c]Average of the first three quarters on a seasonally adjusted annual rates basis.
[d]Includes certain special government transactions.
[e]Equals changes in liquid liabilities to foreign official holders, changes in liabilities to other foreign holders, and changes in official reserve assets consisting of gold, Special Drawing Rights, convertible currencies, and the U.S. gold tranche position in the IMF.
[f]Equals changes in liquid and nonliquid liabilities to foreign official holders and changes in official reserve assets consisting of gold, Special Drawing Rights, convertible currencies, and the U.S. gold tranche position in the IMF.
[g]Includes short-term official and banking liabilities, foreign holdings of U.S. Government bonds and notes, and certain nonliquid liabilities to foreign official holders.

Exhibit 21 (Continued)

Year or Quarter	U.S. Government Grants and Capital, Net[d]	U.S. Private Capital, Net			Foreign Capital, Net[d]	Errors and Unrecorded Transactions	Balance		Changes in Selected Liabilities (Decrease (−))[g]			Changes in U.S. Official Reserve Assets [Increase (−)]
		Direct Investment	Other Long-Term	Short-Tem			Liquidity Basis[e]	Official Reserve Transactions Basis[f]	To Foreign Offical Holders[h]		To Other Foreign Holders[i]	
									Liquid	Non-liquid		
	13	14	15	16	17	18	19	20	21	22	23	24
1946	−5,293	−230	127	−310	−615	155	993	−	−	−	−	−623
1947	−6,121	−749	−49	−189	−432	861	4,210	−	−	−	−	−3,315
1948	−4,918	−721	−69	−116	−361	1,115	817	−	−	−	−	−1,736
1949	−5,649	−660	−80	187	44	717	136	−	−	−	−	−266
1950	−3,640	−621	−495	−149	181	−124	−3,489	−	−	−	−	1,758
1951	−3,191	−508	−437	−103	540	354	−8	−	−	−	−	−33
1952	−2,380	−852	−214	−94	52	497	−1,206	−	−	−	−	−415
1953	−2,055	−735	185	167	146	220	−2,184	−	−	−	−	1,256
1954	−1,554	−667	−320	−635	249	60	−1,541	−	−	−	−	480
1955	−2,211	−823	−241	−191	297	371	−1,242	−	−	−	−	182
1956	−2,362	−1,951	−603	−517	615	390	−973	−	−	−	−	−869
1957	−2,574	−2,442	−859	−276	545	1,012	578	−	−	−	−	−1,165
1958	−2,587	−1,181	−1,444	−311	186	361	−3,365	−	−	−	−	2,292
1959	−1,986	−1,372	−926	−77	736	260	−3,870	−	−	−	−	1,035
1960	−2,768	−1,674	−855	−1,349	364	−1,156	−3,901	−3,403	1,448	−	308	2,145[j]
1961	−2,779	−1,598	−1,025	−1,556	702	−1,103	−2,371	−1,347	681	−	1,084	606[j]
1962	−3,013	−1,654	−1,227	−546	1,026	−1,746	2,204	−2,702	457	250	214	1,533[j]
1963	−3,578	−1,976	−1,698	−785	690	−509	−2,670	−2,011	1,673	−39	620	377
1964	−3,564	−2,328	−2,103	−2,147	689	−1,118	−2,800	−1,564	1,075	318	1,554	171
1965	−3,406	−3,468	−1,079	753	270	−576	−1,335	−1,289	−18	85	131	1,222
1966	−3,444	−3,661	−256	−415	2,531	−514	−1,357	266	−1,595	761	2,384	568
1967	−4,223	−3,137	−1,292	−1,209	3,360	−1,088	−3,544	−3,418	2,020	1,346	1,472	52
1968	−3,975	−3,209	−1,116	−1,087	8,701	−514	171	1,641	−3,101	2,340	3,810	−880
1969	−3,828	−3,070	−1,588	−575	4,131	−2,841	−7,012	2,700	−517	−996	8,716	−1,187
1970[p]	−3,119	−4,805	−1,427	−297	3,859	−2,040	[k]−4,415	[k]−8,667	−	−	−	−
				Seasonally Adjusted Annual Rates					Quarterly Totals Unadjusted			
1968: I	−4,340	−1,804	−520	−412	6,672	−1,316	−976	−244	−1,358	363	721	904
II	−4,240	−3,512	−616	−1,588	10,124	−2,112	424	6,608	−2,190	777	2,222	−137
III	−3,852	−4,192	−876	−1,272	7,308	1,340	580	1,632	−38	537	1,031	−571
IV	−3,468	−3,324	−2,456	−1,076	10,696	32	656	−1,432	485	663	−164	−1,076
1969: I	−3,108	−3,608	−1,072	−172	7,096	−4,784	−5,408	5,812	−1,708	45	3,024	−48
II	−4,636	−4,060	−2,352	−2,192	1,652	−3,688	−15,204	5,260	−538	−367	4,653	−299
III	−4,088	−3,508	−1,796	1,384	1,244	−3,708	−9,116	−2,328	2,235	−509	1,423	−686
IV	−3,480	−1,104	−1,132	−1,320	6,540	816	1,680	2,056	−506	−165	−384	−154
1970: I	−3,420	−5,644	−1,936	828	2,254	−728	[k]−5,756	[k]−11,572	2,762	−413	−1,695	−386
II	−2,900	−5,736	460	−2,204	5,280	−3,680	[k]−4,936	[k]−7,108	526	513	−122	1,022
III[p]	−3,036	−3,036	−2,804	484	4,044	−1,712	[k]−2,552	[k]−7,320	2,046	−236	−1,186	801

[h]Central banks, governments, and U.S. liabilities to the IMF arising from reversible gold sales to, and gold deposits with, the United States.

[i]Private holders: Includes banks and international and regional organizations; excludes IMF.

[j]Includes change in Treasury liabilities to certain foreign military agencies; including these changes, data ($ millions) are 1,258 (1960), 741 (1961), 918 (1962).

[k]Includes allocation of Special Drawing Rights.

[p]Preliminary data.

Source: Department of Commerce, Office of Business Economics.

Bibliographic Essay

The two appendices in this section contain data on the United States from before the Great Depression to around 1970. These data are to be used with Chapters 1, 2, 6, 7, 14, and 15, which are the U.S. cases set before the 1980s.

More comprehensive data may be found in the following selected sources:

> International Monetary Fund, *International Monetary Statistics Year-book* (published annually). This reference contains detailed exchange rate, monetary, and national income account data for 110 countries, but the tables should be comprehensible to readers of this casebook.

> U.S. Board of Governors, Federal Reserve System, *Federal Reserve Bulletin* and *Federal Reserve Chart Book* (published monthly). The *Bulletin* is the primary document of the Board of Governors. See the list of other publications, many of them free, at the end of each issue. The *Chart Book* is a convenient source of graphical data.

> U.S. Bureau of the Census, Department of Commerce, *Historical Statistics of the United States: Colonial Times to 1970*, two volumes (Washington, DC: U.S. Government Printing Office, 1976). This is a very good source for consistent time-series data covering many years, and it is the most convenient source for data on the early years of American history.

> U.S. Council of Economic Advisers, *The Economic Report of the President* (published annually). The appendix of this document contains a compilation of economic data from many sources on all aspects of U.S. economic performance.

> U.S. Department of Commerce, *Survey of Current Business* (published monthly). This is the primary publication of the Department of Commerce reporting the national income and product accounts data.

> U.S. Federal Reserve Bank of St. Louis, *National Economic Trends, Monetary Trends*, and *International Economic Conditions* (published monthly). These three publications, which are free, contain excellent graphical presentations and detailed tables of compound growth rates for economic data.

Five publications that are useful for interpreting economic data are:

> Collender, Stanley E., *The Guide to the Federal Budget* (Washington, DC: Urban Institute Press, published annually). This volume, which contains many examples, explains both the budget process and the budget documents themselves.

> Hoel, Arline, Kenneth Clarkson, and Roger LeRoy Miller, *Economics Source Book of Government Statistics* (Lexington, MA: Lexington Books, 1983). This book provides a concise description and interpretation of a wide range of economic statistics and cross references to their original sources.

International Monetary Fund, *Balance of Payments Manual*, 4th ed. (Washington, DC: IMF, 1977). Although this book is more difficult than the others listed in this section, it is a useful reference for interpreting balance of payments statements.

Samansky, Arthur W., *Statfacts: Understanding Federal Reserve Statistical Reports* (New York: Federal Reserve Bank of New York, 1981). This volume, distributed without charge by the New York Fed, is an excellent guide to line-by-line interpretation of the Federal Reserve reports.

Sommers, Albert T., *The U.S. Economy Demystified: What the Major Economic Statistics Mean and Their Significance for Business* (Lexington, MA: Lexington Books, 1985). This book describes in simple terminology the national income accounts and includes a wide variety of data on the business cycle.

GLOSSARY

Note: Numbers in parentheses at the ends of items indicate the primary chapter case (C), chapter note (N), or appendix (A) in which the concepts are presented.

Accelerated Cost Recovery System (ACRS) The system of depreciation accounting required for income tax purposes that was established in the Economic Recovery Tax Act of 1981. ACRS was the centerpiece of the business tax cut included in this act. It is sometimes referred to as "10-5-3" to recall the three classes of depreciable assets initially included in the Act—structures depreciable in 10 years, machinery and equipment depreciable in 5 years, and vehicles and R&D equipment depreciable in 3 years. The final version of the bill added a fourth category for 15-year public utility property. (10C)

Accelerated depreciation A rate of accounting depreciation for fixed assets faster than that based on their economic depreciation. It is allowed for income tax purposes to enable companies to defer the payment of taxes by writing off larger depreciation expenses in the early life of an asset. (10C)

Accelerated Depreciation Range (ADR) The system of depreciation accounting acceptable for income tax purposes from 1971 to 1980. It included numerous asset categories and some flexibility in the choice of useful life for the asset. (10C)

Accelerator hypothesis of investment The hypothesis that firms will increase their desired capital stock and hence net investment if they expect sales to increase in the future. Thus the *level* of net investment depends on the *change* in expected sales. *Compare* Flexible accelerator. (11N)

Accommodative monetary policy A monetary policy that provides adequate growth in the money supply in order to accommodate the growth in the economy initiated by other sectors, such as fiscal policy. The usual indicator is that interest rates remain unchanged as the economy expands.

Add factors Adjustments made to the equations in the DRI econometric model in order to gain internal consistency, to correct statistical problems, or to introduce information not already incorporated in the model. (1ND)

Adjustment to factor cost All indirect taxes and subsidies. GNP (GDP) at factor cost means GNP (GDP) at market prices minus all indirect taxes and subsidies. (4C)

Administered interest rate An interest rate that is not set by market forces, but rather by administrative decision. The discount rate, the prime rate, and the Bank Rate in England are examples of administered interest rates. (2N)

Administrative budget The conventional budget presentation in use from 1923 until 1969, when the unified budget replaced it as the primary budget document. The administrative budget excludes trust funds, records the timing of receipts and payments on a cash rather than accrual basis, and includes net lending. *Compare*

Consolidated cash budget, Unified budget, and National income accounts budget. (A)

Ad valorem   A type of tax or tariff in which the levy is set as a percentage of the price of the product. *Compare* Excise tax and Specific tariff. (14C)

After-tax real return (ATRR)   The real return minus the tax on the nominal return. (11N)

Aggregate demand   The total expenditure on goods and services by all sectors of the economy. (1NA)

Aggregate supply   The total production of goods and services in the economy. (1NA)

Allocation of SDRs   The periodic allocation of SDRs by the IMF is treated as an inflow of capital on the balance of payments statement. The allocations are distributed to each IMF member in proportion to their IMF quota. (14N)

Appreciation   A rise in the value of a currency relative to another country's currency. (16C)

Arbitrage   Purchasing something from one market at a lower price and then selling it in another market at a higher price—buy low, sell high—in order to profit on the difference. Usually it is used to describe a process by which prices are equalized in security or foreign exchange markets. (16N)

Autarky   A policy of having a self-sufficient and independent economy. (14N)

Automatic stabilizers   Fiscal instruments built into the budget that automatically dampen fluctuations in the economy. The personal income tax, the corporate income tax, and unemployment insurance payments are examples of automatic stabilizers. As the economy slows down, personal and corporate income tax revenues fall while unemployment compensation increases. The result is a larger budget deficit.

Balance of payments (BOP)   A re-cord of an economy's international economic transactions, i.e., of the goods and services that an economy has received from and provided to the rest of the world and of the changes in the economy's claims on and liabilities to the rest of the world. "Balance of payments" is also used in some cases to indicate a particular (often unspecified) broad balance in the balance of payments statement, usually the overall balance. However, there is no generally accepted balance that is *the* balance of payments. (1NC, 14N)

Balance of trade (BOT)   A country's exports of goods minus its imports of goods. The balance of trade will vary depending on, among other factors, changes in domestic income, foreign income, the exchange rate, and the ratio of export prices to import prices (i.e., the terms of trade). It is also called "merchandise balance" or "visible balance." (14C, 14N)

Balance on goods and services   A country's exports of goods and services minus its imports of goods and services. It is approximately equal to the $(X - M)$ in the national income accounting identity. (14N)

Balance on official settlements   The total of the official reserve accounts. It will equal (usually, but it depends on the particular definition used) the negative of the overall balance. (14N)

Bank Rate   The interest rate at which the Bank of England would lend to the banking system. Though now obsolete, it was the British equivalent of the discount rate in the United States. Between October 1972 and August 1981, the Bank of England used the term "minimum lending rate," which was set by a formula that tied it to the market rate for Treasury bills. After August 20, 1981, the Bank no longer announced a minimum lending rate. (4C, 13C)

Banker's acceptances   Short-term credits that are "accepted" for guaranteed payment by a bank. Usually they are used for trade finance, though they may be used to finance any short-term, self-liquidating commercial transaction. (2C, 2N, 3N)

Base year The reference year for comparing economic and business data. In forming an index, the base year data are set equal to 100 and all other years' data are then compared to the base year. Generally, statisticians try to chose a "normal" year for the base year. (1NC)

Baseline budget A benchmark budget for comparing alternative budget actions. It is calculated by extrapolating current spending and taxing policies so that they keep up with inflation; thus it is not a forecast, only a projection. It is also known as a "current services budget." (11C, 11N)

Basic balance The sum of the current account balance and the balance on long-term capital transactions. (14C, 14N)

Beggar-thy-neighbor policies Policies that attempt to improve one country's trade balance at the expense of the trade balances of other countries. The imposition of tariffs and central bank intervention to promote currency depreciation are policies that are often classified as beggar-thy-neighbor policies.

Behavioral equation An equation based on economic theory that relates the behavior of one variable to movements in explanatory variables and, possibly, a random error variable. (1ND)

Bill of exchange A bill drawn to finance foreign trade transactions. (5C)

Borrowed reserves The part of total bank reserves borrowed from the Federal Reserve through the discount window. Borrowed reserves plus nonborrowed reserves equal total reserves. (3N)

Bretton Woods conference An international conference of 45 nations held at Bretton Woods, New Hampshire, between July 1 and July 20, 1944, to set up a comprehensive international arrangement to govern world trade and payments. The International

Monetary Fund and the International Bank for Reconstruction and Development (the World Bank) were established by the participants. The international monetary order instituted at this conference lasted until the collapse of the Smithsonian agreements in March 1973. (14C)

Brookings Institution A nonprofit research institution located in Washington, DC, devoted to the study of government economic and foreign policy. (16C)

Bundesbank The West German central bank. (16C)

Business cycle Fluctuations in the aggregate economic activity of nations. For the United States, the National Bureau of Economic Research makes that subjective determination based on multiple measures of economic activity, including real GNP growth and unemployment.

Call loan A commercial bank loan payable on demand by the lender and repayable at any time by the borrower. Most broker borrowing is on a call loan basis. This type of loan was more widely used before the stock market crash of 1929.

Call money rate The short-term interest rate charged by commercial banks to brokers. (14C)

Capacity *See* Potential GNP. (7N)

Capacity utilization rate An estimate of the proportion of total productive capacity that is currently being used to produce output. As a rough rule of thumb, utilization rates above 85 percent are considered high, and the higher the capacity utilization the more investment one would expect as firms attempt to increase capacity to avoid production bottlenecks and increased costs. (A)

Capital Long-lived assets enhancing the future capacity to produce output and hence income. This is the narrow definition, but "capital" more commonly refers to the financial liabilities (such as bonds, commercial paper, and other "financial capital") enabling one to purchase these tangible assets. (11N)

Capital account On the balance of payments statement, the account that records international transactions in financial claims or assets. It is conventionally divided into long-term (over one year) and short-term (less than one year) transactions. If official reserves are included in the broad definition of the capital account (as they sometimes are), then the balance of payments statement consists of two parts—the current account and the capital account—which must sum to zero. Therefore a current account deficit necessarily implies a capital account surplus, and vice versa. (14N)

Capital consumption adjustment (CCA) An adjustment to business profits in the national income accounts that is designed to correct the accounting definition of depreciation used on the books so that it reflects current replacement cost. In times of high inflation, the historical cost depreciation will be less than the replacement cost depreciation. The result is the overstatement of reported profits. This adjustment will reduce the reported profits to reflect more accurately the true economic profits. *See also* Inventory valuation adjustment. (11C, 11N)

Capital consumption allowance (CCA) An estimate of the economic depreciation of the nation's capital stock. This is not necessarily equal to the value of the accounting depreciation recorded by the nation's businesses; thus it is invariant to changes in accounting definitions. (11C, 11N)

Capital expenditure An expenditure for any long-lived (over one year) asset that will enhance the future ability to produce output and hence income. *Compare* Current expenditure. (11N)

Capital flight An undesirable capital outflow from a governnment's perspective. (17C)

Capital gain The increase in the price of a capital asset between the time of purchase and the time of sale. (8C)

Capital gains preferences *See* Tax expenditures. (8C)

Capital market The generic description for all markets for long-term financial instruments such as Treasury bonds, corporate bonds, mortgages, and municipal bonds. *Compare* Money market. (2N)

Carlton Group An informal group of about ten business tax lobbyists that derived its name from the Sheraton-Carlton Hotel in Washington, DC. Since 1975, they have sought tax legislation that is favorable to capital formation and have been instrumental in the passage of the capital gains tax reduction in 1978 and the Accelerated Cost Recovery System in 1981. (10C)

Central bank A banker's bank run by the government that serves as a lender of last resort and controls the money supply and credit. (2N, 3N)

Certificate of deposit (CD) A large-denomination (over $100,000), negotiable, unsecured time deposit issued by a commercial bank and generally sold to the nonbank public; it is similar to commercial paper for a nonfinancial corporation. CDs were first issued in 1961. (2N, 3C)

Chain price index A price index whose value at any point in time is related to the base in the immediately preceding period rather than to a fixed base in the more distant past. Its accuracy diminishes as the time periods become longer because it is recording both the change in price and changes in the base weights. (15C)

Charged in full (c.i.f.) *See* Cost, insurance, freight.

C.i.f. *See* Cost, insurance, freight.

Clegg Commission Commission initiated by John Callaghan's Labour government to recommend pay raises for several public sector unions. Margaret Thatcher, the newly elected prime minister in May 1979, promised during the election campaign to accept the findings of the Commission. The findings offering generous pay increases were announced in the summer of 1979. (4C)

Commercial paper A short-term unsecured financial instrument (a promissory note or IOU) issued by corporations. (2C, 2N)

Common market An agreement among member countries in which members allow free movement of labor and capital among themselves in addition to having a free trade area. The EEC is an example of a common market. *Compare* Free trade area and Customs union.

Comparative advantage If a country exports those goods that it produces *relatively* more efficiently and imports those goods that another country produces *relatively* more efficiently, then there will be gains to trade that could benefit both countries. Even if one country is absolutely more efficient (i.e., incurs the lowest cost) in producing all goods, it should specialize in those goods in which it has a "comparative advantage." (14C)

Compound growth rate The percentage growth rate on both the base amount and on any increments to the base amount owing to past growth. (1NC)

Congressional Budget Act of 1974 Act that established the congressional budget process (including the first and second budget resolutions and reconciliation process), the House and Senate Budget Committees, and the Congressional Budget Office. It also established a congressional review of presidential impoundments of funds. (11C)

Congressional Budget Office (CBO) A nonpartisan research arm of Congress that investigates the economic consequences of budget legislation. It was established by the Congressional Budget Act of 1974. (11C)

Consolidated cash budget Budget statement used from 1957 to 1969, when the current unified budget format was adopted. The cash budget was an improvement over the previous administrative budget in that it included trust funds, but it also recorded payments and receipts on a cash rather than accrual basis and included net lending of the federal government, thereby allowing no distinction between federal spending and federal lending. *Compare* Administrative budget, Unified budget, and National income accounts budget.

Constant returns to scale A condition such that a doubling of all of a firm's resource inputs results in a doubling of the firm's outputs. (14C)

Consumer price index (CPI) A general price index calculated as a ratio of the current value of a "market basket" of goods and services (using current prices) to the base-year value of that market basket. The number of items included in the basket were agreed upon in the base year and are held constant for all other years. (1NC)

Consumption (C) Household expenditures on final goods and services required for current use. Its typical components are durable goods, nondurable goods, and services. Consumption typically moves in the same direction as changes in disposable income. *See* also Durable goods. (1NA)

Convertible currency A currency that can be freely exchanged for another currency or for gold. The pound (and other European currencies) was inconvertible from the end of World War II until 1958. (14C)

Corn Laws A series of trade laws in England between 1400 and 1846 that intended to protect the domestic grain ("corn") industry by imposing import tariffs on grain to keep domestic grain prices high. A combination of the Irish potato famine and a poor British grain crop in 1845 led Prime Minister Robert Peel to repeal the Corn Laws in 1846 over the opposition of the Conservative party leader Benjamin Disraeli. (14C)

Corset A popular term for the "supplementary deposits requirement," a reserve requirement on various sources of bank funds that was used by the Bank of England to control banks' balance sheets and thus their lending capacity. It was introduced in

1973 and discontinued in June 1980. (4C)

Cost of capital The cost of obtaining and using funds for business investment. (3N, 11N)

Cost, insurance, freight (c.i.f.) A method of valuing foreign trade in which the cost of insurance and freight are included in the recorded value of the imports or exports; sometimes called "charged in full." *Compare* Free on board. (4C)

Council of Economic Advisers A three-person branch of the Executive Office of the President that was established by the Employment Act of 1946 to provide the president with economic advice and to write the annual Economic Report of the President. A small temporary staff of academic economists provides support for the three presidential advisers. (7C)

Credit The use or possession of goods, services, or assets in exchange for a promise to repay in the future, usually with interest. The person granting this is known as a "creditor" or "investor." *Compare* Debt. (3C)

Credit aggregate Any of the various measures of financial assets, including bank credit (bank loans), debt (private sector credit), and nonfinancial domestic credit (private and public sector credit). (3N)

Credit Control Act of 1969 Act that allows the president to authorize the Federal Reserve to regulate and control credit in order to control inflation. (3C)

Credit entry A positive balance of payments accounting entry that is used to record an export of goods, services, or financial assets. Credits are a source of foreign exchange. *Compare* Debit entry. (14N)

Crowding out The decrease in one component of spending when another component increases. Usually it refers to the decline in investment spending when government spending rises. (11C)

Cunliffe Committee A committee appointed by the Chancellor of the Exchequer in 1918 and chaired by Lord Walter Cunliffe, Governor of the Bank of England, to investigate the problems in a restoration of the gold standard by the United Kingdom. (13C)

Current account The net effect of exports and imports of goods and services plus net unilateral transfers. It shows the extent to which a country is sending its real resources to the rest of the world, or is drawing on real resources abroad, to supply its own current consumption and investment demands. (14N)

Current expenditure An expenditure for any good or service that yields short-term benefits such as consumption. *Compare* Capital expenditure. (11N)

Current services budget *See* Baseline budget. (11C, 11N)

Customs union An agreement among member countries to remove all barriers to trade among themselves and to adopt uniform external barriers for all nonmember countries. The EEC is a customs union. *Compare* Free trade area and Common market. (14C)

Cyclically adjusted budget An estimate of what the budget would be if the economy were moving along some trend GNP path rather than along its actual path. (Trend GNP is constructed to connect real GNP averages in the middle periods of economic expansions.) Essentially, it eliminates the effects of economic fluctuations on the budget. *Compare* Full-employment budget and High-employment budget. (11C, 11N)

Debit entry A negative balance of payments accounting entry that is used to record an import of goods, services, or financial assets. Debits are a use of foreign exchange. *Compare* Credit entry. (14N)

Debt Receiving the use or possession of goods, services, or assets in exchange for a promise to repay in the future, usually with interest. The person receiving this is known as a "debtor" or "borrower." Debt allows one to correct the mismatches in the timing of income and spending. It is usually classified into five classes of borrowers: federal government, state and local governments, households, nonfinancial business, and financial business. *Compare* Credit. (11C)

Debt service ratio A measure of a country's ability to service its foreign debt. Usually it is the ratio of interest payments and repayments of principal to the country's export earnings. This definition varies widely in the literature on the debt crisis. (17C)

Deficit The excess of government expenditures over revenues (fiscal deficit) or the excess of international payments over international receipts (balance of payments deficit). (11C)

Deficit Reduction Act of 1984 (DRA) The tax increase in 1984 that froze, delayed, or modified some of the smaller personal and corporate income tax provisions granted by the Economic Recovery Tax Act of 1981. (11C)

Deflation A slowing down of the growth rate of the economy in an attempt to lower prices (deflation) or, in its modern usage, a lowering of the rate of inflation. It is the opposite of "reflation." (13C)

Demand curve A schedule of prices and quantities such that for a given price buyers are willing and able to purchase a particular quantity of the good. Increased prices are associated with decreased quantities demanded. (1NA)

Demand deposit A checking account. The bank receiving the deposit must pay on demand. (2N)

Depository Institutions Deregulation and Monetary Control Act of 1980 (DIDMCA) The major financial legislation signed by President Carter on March 31, 1980, that improved monetary control, deregulated interest rates, and introduced competition in financial products across all depository institutions. (3C)

Depreciation A decline in the market value of a currency relative to the value of another country's currency. It is the opposite of "appreciation." *Compare* Devaluation. (16C)

Depression A prolonged period of very low economic activity associated with negative growth rates of real GNP and high unemployment. Two of the longest depressions in U.S. history were the depression of 1873, which lasted five and a half years, and the "Great Depression" of 1929, which lasted four years. (6C)

Devaluation A decline in the fixed value of a currency relative to gold or some hard currency to which it is tied. "Devaluation" is used in reference to a fixed exchange rate system and "depreciation" is used in reference to a flexible exchange rate system. "Devaluation" is the opposite of "revaluation." (14C)

Direct finance The user of funds obtains the funds directly from the supplier of funds. *Compare* Indirect finance. (5C)

Direct foreign investment (DFI) *See* Foreign direct investment.

Direct tax A tax whose burden cannot be easily shifted away from the person upon whom the tax is levied. Generally, the income tax is considered a direct tax. *Compare* Indirect tax. (4C)

Dirty float A pejorative term for "managed float." (16C)

Discount rate The interest rate the Federal Reserve charges on loans to member banks. It is one of the tools that the Fed uses to control the money supply. It is also known as the "rediscount rate." (2C, 2N)

Discount window The mechanism by which member banks of the Federal Reserve borrow reserves for which they are charged the discount rate.

Discretion The frequent changing of a policy instrument in response to new information. *Compare* Rule. (3N)

Disintermediation The withdrawal

of funds from financial intermediaries by savers in order to supply the funds directly to the ultimate investors. Five periods of disintermediation in the United States occurred in 1966–1967, 1969–1970, 1973–1974, 1979–1980, and 1982. The periods of disintermediation have been predominately caused by tight money and inflation pushing market interest rates above the Regulation Q ceilings. (3C)

Disposable income The income remaining after all taxes have been paid. (4C)

Dollar gap (shortage) During the years following World War II, Western Europe demanded huge quantities of imports from the United States but their gold and dollar reserves were inadequate to finance their balance of payments deficits. The shortage of dollars lasted until the mid-1950s. (14C)

Dollar overhang (glut) In the late 1950s the dollar liabilities held in the world's reserves were larger than needed to accommodate international liquidity. The continued U.S. balance of payments deficits threatened to force a devaluation of the dollar if the United States could not honor its dollar liabilities by converting them to gold. (14C)

Domestic credit expansion (DCE) A measure of internal credit availability that was introduced in 1968 by the IMF as an appropriate target for monetary control. For the United Kingdom, it is calculated as the public sector borrowing requirement that is not financed by the sale of bonds plus the increase in Sterling lending to the U.K. private sector. (4C)

Domestic nonfinancial debt The debt owed by the federal, state, and local governments, households, and nonfinancial businesses. *See* Debt. (11C)

Durable goods A type of consumption good that is assumed to last longer than three years, such as automobiles, appliances, books, and furniture. (A)

Easy money An expansionary mon-

etary policy associated with low interest rates and a faster growth of the money supply and credit. The economic consequences are usually faster economic growth and, eventually, higher inflation. It is the opposite of "tight money."

Econometric model A set of equations relating economic variables to each other, either behaviorally or by definition, so as to approximate the actual economic structure of the real world. (1ND)

Econometrics The application of statistics to economic problems. (1ND)

Economic depreciation The reduction in the value of an asset that is due to physical deterioration and obsolescence. (11N)

Economic growth Increased output of goods and services. (7N)

Economic Recovery Tax Act of 1981 The largest personal and corporate income tax cut in U.S. history, signed by President Reagan in August 1981. (10C)

Economics A social science that attempts to explain the behavior and interactions of economic actors in terms of the items of value that they exchange. (1NA)

Economies of scale As the scale of productive capacity increases for a firm or an industry, total production costs increase less than proportionately with output. (7N)

Effective exchange rate A weighted (geometric) average of all of the bilateral exchange rates for a country; for example, the dollar-Deutschmark rate, the dollar-yen rate, and the dollar-pound rate. The weights are often that country's share of total trade. (16C, 16N)

Effective tax rate The amount of taxes paid divided by the total income (or whatever is the relevant tax base) before deductions and exclusions. (8C)

Efficiency Getting the maximum

output from a given amount of resources used as inputs. (1NA)

Elasticity   Usually a shortened term for "price elasticity." The percentage change in quantity divided by the percentage change in price, or more intuitively, the "responsiveness" of a quantity to a change in price. (1NA)

Employee stock option plan (ESOP) A payroll deduction plan that permits employees to purchase stock in their company, often at a discount, and to defer delivery of the stock in order to defer taxes. (10C)

Employment Act of 1946   An act passed on February 20, 1946, that sought "high" levels of employment, production, and purchasing power. It ordered the president to make an annual economic report to Congress and established the Council of Economic Advisers in the White House staff. (7C)

Endogenous variable   A variable determined by the model. Once all exogenous and predetermined variables are given, the model will give an estimate of all endogenous variables. (1ND)

Equilibrium   That combination of price and quantity transacted such that nobody has an incentive to change. (1NA)

Errors and omissions   The residual account in the balance of payments. Since the line items that enter the balance of payments are derived from many different sources using different methods for collecting information—tax data, customs data, financial reports—errors and omissions are very likely. Some analysts interpret this account as measuring "hot money" that is seeking high interest rates, speculative capital gains, or safety from political or economic risks. (14C, 14N)

Eurocurrency   A currency held outside its own country. The most common type of Eurocurrency is the Eurodollar. (16C)

Eurodollar   A dollar held overseas (but not necessarily in Europe) in commercial banks. It is one type of Eurocurrency. Eurodollar borrowing and lending among international banks is done at an interest rate called "LIBOR" or the "London interbank offer rate." (3N)

European Economic Community (EEC)   Six countries in Western Europe—France, West Germany, Italy, Belgium, the Netherlands, and Luxembourg—signed the Treaty of Rome in 1957 to create a common market starting January 1, 1958. The EEC would remove all barriers to the flow of goods, services, capital, and labor between member countries and establish a common external trade policy, a common agricultural policy, and a common transport policy. Today, the members also include the United Kingdom (which joined in 1973), Ireland (1973), Denmark (1973), Greece (1981), Spain (1986), and Portugal (1986), and the name has been changed to the "European Community" (EC). (14C)

European Payments Union (EPU) The seventeen member countries of the OEEC established the EPU in 1950 as a clearing system for international payments with automatic credit for nations that are in deficit on their balance of payments. EPU was terminated in 1958. (14C)

Excess reserves   Reserves in excess of those required to support deposits. Excess reserves plus required reserves equal total reserves. Excess reserves are an indication of the ability of banks to expand the money supply by granting additional loans. Banks that do not make additional loans may lend their excess reserves to other banks overnight in the federal funds market. (2N, A)

Exchange rate   The price of a nation's currency. It is calculated as the number of units of the home currency per unit of foreign currency. Notice, for example, if the Deutschmark (DM) were \$0.25/DM and the exchange rate rose to \$0.50/DM, it is said that the DM has appreciated while the dollar has depreciated. (16C, 16N)

Excise tax   A sales tax on certain

commodities that is levied as either a fixed rate per unit or ad valorem. (11C)

Exogenous variable A variable determined outside of the model. It is treated as a "given" assumption by the decision maker. *Compare* Endogenous variable. (1ND)

Export-Import Bank A U.S. government agency established in 1934 to encourage U.S. trade by supplying credit and financial guarantees to foreign countries. Also known as the "Eximbank," it was involved in over 10 percent of nonagricultural exports during the 1970s. (9C)

Exports (X) An outflow of goods and services giving rise to a source of foreign exchange. Exports vary according to, among other factors, foreign income, exchange rates, and export prices relative to prices of foreign competing goods. In the balance of payments statements, exports generally mean only an outflow of goods and not of services. (1NA)

Externality An action of one actor that affects another actor either favorably or unfavorably, but it does not affect that actor directly by changing the prices paid. A common example is a polluter that unfavorably affects the air that we breathe, but the prices that we pay are not altered as a result of the pollution. (1NA)

Factor income Payments to the factors of production: labor receives wages, capital receives interest, land receives rent, and entrepreneurial and management skills receive profits. Also known as "factor costs" or "factor payments."

Factor inputs *See* Resources.

Factors of production *See* Resources.

Federal funds In the budget lexicon, funds received and spent by the federal government for general purposes, in contrast to the trust funds that are earmarked for specific purposes. In a different context, Federal funds can also mean the excess reserves of banks

that are borrowed and lent short term in the interbank market for which the federal funds rate is charged. *See also* Federal funds rate. (2N, 11C)

Federal funds rate The interest rate charged for very short-term (typically one-day) loans of excess reserves from one bank to another. (2N)

Federal Open Market Committee (FOMC) A twelve-member committee composed of the seven governors and five revolving positions for Reserve Bank presidents. It generally meets every six weeks to determine open market operations for the Federal Reserve System. (2C, 3C)

Federal Reserve The central bank of the United States, established by the Federal Reserve Act of 1913. Unlike the unitary central banks of most countries, the Federal Reserve is decentralized into twelve District Banks and controlled by the Federal Reserve Board of Governors in Washington, DC. (3C, 3N)

Federal Reserve Credit Outstanding Federal Reserve assets affecting total bank reserves. Over 90 percent of the credit outstanding consists of federal government securities, with the remaining amount consisting of discount window loans and float. (A)

Federal Reserve note Paper currency. (Look at the top line on the front of a bill of any denomination.) (2C, 2N)

Fiat money Money not backed by anything other than the promise of the government that it is legal tender. (13C)

FIFO "First in, first out." An inventory valuation method in which the price of the inventory is assumed to be the price of the "oldest" products in the inventory. *Compare* LIFO. (11N)

Final sales GNP or GDP minus the change in business inventories. The term indicates the amount of the year's final production (GNP or GDP) that was sold within that year. (11C)

Financial intermediation The role of

financial institutions as "intermediaries" between the initial savers and the ultimate investors in the economy. *Compare* Disintermediation. (3C)

Fiscal drag Situation in which the full-employment revenues automatically rise more rapidly than the full-employment expenditures as economic growth pushes taxable incomes into higher marginal tax brackets. Sometimes called "fiscal dividend" of economic growth, it may be used to finance additional expenditures or to cut taxes. (4C, 7C)

Fiscal policy The governmental policies regarding expenditures, taxes, and the financing of deficits or surpluses. (6C, 7C, 9C, 11C)

Fiscal year (FY) The twelve-month period used for the preparation of annual budgets. It does not necessarily coincide with the calendar year. FY 1986 for the U.S. federal government runs from October 1, 1985, to September 30, 1986; FY 1986 for the United Kingdom runs from April 6, 1985, to April 5, 1986. (4C, 11C)

Fisher effect on nominal interest rates The effect of inflation on nominal interest rates. The theory says that a nominal interest rate is composed of the real interest rate and an inflation premium. (3N)

Fixed exchange rate system An arrangement among countries in which the exchange rate for currencies is fixed or pegged at some preannounced level by the participating central banks in relation to the value of some commodity (gold) or some other currency (the dollar). The central banks must be ready and able to buy or sell as much currency as supplied or demanded by the foreign exchange market. (2N, 13C, 16C, 16N)

Fixed investment All investment except business inventory investment. It typically is divided into nonresidential investment (structures and producers' durable equipment) and residential investment. (A)

Flexible accelerator The theory of investment that says that the desired capital stock depends on the expected sales and the user cost of capital. *Compare* Accelerator hypothesis. (11N)

Float The total amount of checks outstanding at one time. It is effectively an unintentional loan of reserves to the banking system from the Federal Reserve that is caused by an inability to clear checks fast enough because of transportation delays. An increase in float causes an increase in the money supply. If, for example, a check for $100 drawn on New York Bank is deposited in California Bank, but the check has not had time to be returned to New York Bank, then both New York Bank and California Bank have demand deposits recorded on their books. The money supply, in this case, will increase by $100 until the New York Bank debits its demand deposit account and the double counting of the $100 is eliminated.

Floating exchange rate system An arrangement among countries in which the exchange rate for currencies is determined by the market forces of supply and demand, rather than by having the exchange rate fixed or pegged at some preannounced level by the central banks, as in a fixed exchange rate system. (2N, 13C, 16C, 16N)

Flow A type of economic variable that must be stated as a certain amount per unit of time. For example, GNP, income, investment, consumption, saving, credit raised, the fiscal deficit, the trade deficit are all flow variables, since it only makes sense to say that GNP is $X *per year*. (11N)

Flow of funds An economic accounting system recording the sources and uses of funds for financial transactions between sectors of the economy such as households, nonfinancial businesses, financial businesses, state and local governments, the federal government, and foreigners. (11C)

F.o.b. *See* Free on board.

Foreign direct investment (FDI) The

acquisition of physical assets overseas with substantial management control held by the parent corporation of the home country. "Substantial management control" is often defined as 10 percent or more of the ownership of a company. It is also called "direct foreign investment" (DFI). (1NB, 14N)

Foreign exchange   All monetary instruments that give residents of one country a financial claim on residents of another country. The most common forms are foreign currencies and gold, though it may also include interest-bearing securities. (14N)

Fractional reserve system   A banking system in which only a fraction of deposits must be held as reserves. A bank may safely make a loan equal to the size of those funds not held as reserves. Consequently, a 100 percent reserve system would mean that banks could not "create" money (demand deposits) by making loans, since all money is held in reserves (or cash). (2N, 13C)

Free on board (f.o.b.)   A method of valuing foreign merchandise trade such that the costs of insurance and freight are excluded from the recorded value of the merchandise exports or imports. *Compare* Cost, insurance, freight. (4C, A)

Free trade area   An agreement among member countries to remove trade barriers among themselves, but not to have common external barriers toward nonmember countries as in a customs union. *Compare* Customs union and Common market.

Full-employment budget   The estimated budget if income were at the "full-employment" level rather than at the actual level of income for that period. It is a useful concept for comparing the economic stimulus of budgets over many years because the full-employment budget will not be distorted by changes in income, which affect the level of receipts and to a lesser extent the level of expenditures. (11N)

General Agreement on Tariffs and Trade (GATT)   A small international organization, formed in 1948 and located in Geneva, to promote the expansion of multilateral trade by reducing trade barriers. (14C)

Gensaki market   A Japanese short-term money market in which bonds are sold conditional on their repurchase after an agreed period of time. (5C)

Gilt-edged securities   Fixed interest rate securities of the British government, excluding the short-term Treasury bills, that are publicly traded. They are the British equivalent of U.S. Treasury notes and bonds. (4C)

Glass-Steagall Act   The Banking Act of 1933, in which commercial banks and trust companies were prohibited from engaging in investment banking, and investment banks were not allowed to accept deposits. (5C)

GNP deflator   *See* Implicit GNP deflator.

Gold   A precious metal used at various times by many countries as domestic bank reserves "backing up" domestic currency and deposits, and as international reserves for making international payments between countries. Gold was nationalized in the United States in 1933. Between 1934 and 1968, gold reserves were required to cover 25 percent of notes and deposits outstanding. In 1968, the domestic gold cover was eliminated, and in 1971, the international convertibility of gold was also eliminated. (13C, 14C, 15C)

Gold exchange standard   A special form of the gold standard in which a country's central bank will not exchange its currency for gold on demand (as in the case of a gold standard), but will exchange its currency for another currency (such as the dollar during the 1950s and 1960s) that is on the gold standard. It is a type of fixed exchange rate system. (2N)

Gold standard   An international monetary arrangement in which the central bank must stand ready to exchange gold for its currency at a preannounced price. It is a type of fixed exchange rate system. (2C, 2N, 13C)

Government purchases of goods and services (G) This term, used in the national income accounting identity, is different from the government expenditures included in the federal budget. First, it does not include transfer payments of any kind, and second, it includes all levels of government, not just the federal government. Finally, this term includes government capital purchases in the U.S. national income accounts. In some countries, only government current expenditures on goods and services are included under "G" and government capital expenditures are included under "I," gross domestic investment. (1NA, A)

Gross business savings The adjusted undistributed business profits plus the capital consumption allowance. (11C, 11N)

Gross domestic product (GDP) A measure of a nation's output or income. It is the same as GNP except that it excludes factor income from abroad. (1NA)

Gross domestic product at factor cost *See* Adjustment to factor cost.

Gross national expenditure (GNE) Another name for gross national product. (1NA)

Gross national product (GNP) A measure of a nation's output or income; the market value of all final goods and services produced by nationals of a country within a given time period. (1NA)

Gross national product at factor cost *See* Adjustment to factor cost.

Gross private domestic investment *See* Investment. Notice that the inclusion of the word "private" indicates that public investment would be included in government expenditures, not the investment accounts. (11C, 11N)

Group of Ten Ten countries (also known as the "Paris Club"), including the United States, the United Kingdom, West Germany, France, Belgium, the Netherlands, Italy, Sweden, Canada, and Japan, that signed in 1962 the General Agreement to Borrow, under which credit would be made available to the International Monetary Fund if it should be necessary. Switzerland, though not a member of the IMF, occasionally participated. In December 1971, representatives of the Group of Ten met at the Smithsonian Institution in Washington, DC, to establish new par values for their countries' currencies in what became the Smithsonian Agreement. (16C)

Hard currency A currency that is freely convertible into gold or other currencies. It is acceptable as an international currency.

High-employment budget The budget if the economy were at a "high-employment" level of income instead of the actual level. *See also* Full-employment budget. (11N)

High-powered money *See* Monetary base.

Hot money Capital flight caused by speculation or fears of changes in the exchange rate, political unrest, a change in government or government policy, or inflation. Since much of this capital flight is difficult to trace, it often appears as the residual in the "errors and omissions" column of the balance of payments.

Hurdle rate The threshold rate used by corporations in evaluating the desirability of the returns from a capital investment. It is also known as the "cost of capital." (11N)

Ideology The conceptual links between individual and community values and the collected experiences, thoughts, and institutions of a society. (1NA)

Implicit GNP deflator A general price index. It is a weighted sum of the current prices of the current production of goods and services compared to the weighted sum of the base-year prices of that production. Effectively, this is equal to the nominal GNP divided by the real GNP. (1NC)

Implicit price deflator *See* Implicit GNP deflator.

Imports (M) An inflow of goods and services into a country requiring foreign exchange in the transaction. Imports vary with, among other factors, domestic income, the exchange rate, and import prices relative to domestic prices of competing products. Sometimes imports will refer only to an inflow of goods, and not services, as in most balance of payments statements. (1NA)

Import substitution A type of development strategy for a country, whereby the country would encourage the internal development of domestic industries protected by import barriers in order to produce products that could replace imports. (17C)

Income multiplier The respending of an initial expenditure in order to create more income; technically, the ratio of a change in income to a change in autonomous expenditure. (6C)

Income velocity The average number of times per year that the money supply is used for purchasing final goods and services. It is calculated as nominal GNP divided by the money supply. (2N)

Incomes policy Wage and price guidelines or controls. (4C)

Index A number without units such as dollars, pounds, tons, or feet that is used to make comparisons over time. Common examples are consumer price index, wholesale price index, productivity index, and capacity utilization index, though any data series can be converted into an index. It is calculated by dividing a data series by a chosen base year and then multiplying by 100. The base-year value for all indexes will, of course, be 100. (1NC)

Indirect finance The user of funds

obtains the funds from a financial intermediary that has received (and often repackaged) the funds from the initial supplier of funds. *Compare* Direct finance. (5C)

Indirect tax A tax whose burden can be easily shifted from the person upon whom the tax is levied. Generally, the excise tax is considered an indirect tax. (4C)

Inflation An increase in the general price level.

Instrument An economic variable that is directly affected and controlled by the central bank, such as a reserve aggregate or a short-term interest rate. (3N)

Interest equalization tax A U.S. tax on foreign securities purchased by U.S. citizens. It was used in the 1960s to prevent capital outflows and thereby strengthen the dollar. (7C)

Interest rate The rental price of money. (3N)

Intermediate target An economic variable that has a direct effect on the policy goal and is controllable by the use of the policy instruments. Also known as "monetary target." (3N)

International Bank for Reconstruction and Development (IBRD) The official name of the World Bank, established in 1944 by the Bretton Woods agreement. The World Bank was originally chartered to provide long-term, low-interest loans to developing countries. In the years since the oil shocks, it has reevaluated its mission. (14C)

International Monetary Fund (IMF) Established by the Bretton Woods agreement of 1944 and started operating in March 1947. It was designed to stabilize exchange rates, within ± 1 percent of the par value of the currency, with the dollar, which was tied to gold. Member countries with a balance of payments deficit could borrow foreign exchange short term from the IMF in exchange for their own currency. (14C)

International Trade Organization

(ITO) An international institution under the United Nations, proposed in 1947 but never ratified. It was supposed to devise the principles for the international trading system. The interim proposal, the General Agreement on Tariffs and Trade (GATT), became the effective international organization for meeting this goal. (14C)

International reserves The stock of foreign exchange, gold, and SDRs held by the government. (3N)

Intervention The purchase or sale of foreign exchange by the central bank to influence the country's exchange rate. (16C)

Inventory valuation adjustment (IVA) An adjustment to business profits in the national income accounts that is designed to reduce the reported profits that result from the inflation of inventories. *See also* Capital consumption adjustment. (11C, 11N)

Investment (I) Business expenditures to increase future output of final goods and services. In the national income accounts this is called "gross private domestic investment." Among other factors, investment tends to vary with changes in expected sales, capacity utilization, cash flow (after-tax profits plus depreciation), and the cost of capital. Investment has a more specific usage by economists than by the general public. Economists use it to refer only to expenditures on business capital stock, housing, and business inventories, not to expenditures by households on financial assets (the latter action would be called "saving" in the strict sense used by economists, though in common usage it too is referred to as "investment"). (1NA)

Investment tax credit A percentage of the value of an eligible investment is allowed to be deducted from taxes payable. In the United States, a 7 percent, nonrefundable investment tax credit was first allowed in 1962 for domestic equipment investment, but the rates and eligibility rules have been changed many times since then. (7C, 10C)

J-curve When a currency depreciates or is devalued, the trade balance will often worsen before it improves (when the trade balance is plotted against time in a graph, it traces out a "J" pattern). The volume of exports and imports will remain unchanged in the short run because of trade commitments and contracts. However, the import prices (and import revenue) will rise because more home currency must be used to purchase foreign currency, whereas export prices (and export revenue) will remain unchanged because the export prices measured in home currency will not change. (16C)

Kennedy Round of trade negotiations The sixth round of GATT-sanctioned multilateral trade negotiations to reduce tariffs. It started in 1964 and ended in 1967, during which time tariffs were reduced about 30 percent on average. (14C)

Keynesian economics The macroeconomic theory first expounded by John Maynard Keynes in *The General Theory of Employment, Interest, and Money* (1936). It is predominately an explanation of the determinants of total expenditures in the economy and the resulting level of income. Its revolutionary thesis was that the economy may be in an equilibrium at a very low level of income such as in the Great Depression. Classical economists believed that the economy would always return to a full-employment equilibrium. Keynes' diagnosis was that low levels of income were caused by insufficient spending by the private sector; his solution was that the public sector should spend to raise income. (6C)

Labor productivity The amount of output per unit of labor input (usually measured in man-hours). It is also called "output per man-hour." *Compare* Productivity. (7N)

Laffer curve The relationship between marginal tax rates and total tax revenue popularized by the University of Southern California economist

Arthur Laffer. It says that tax revenues will be zero if marginal tax rates are zero and if marginal tax rates are confiscatory (100 percent). At some marginal tax rate between these two extremes, tax revenues will be maximized. Laffer argued that if the United States cut marginal tax rates in 1981, total tax revenues would increase because rates were too close to the confiscatory extreme. (10C)

Laissez faire   From the French, meaning "allow (them) to do." It came to mean the nonintervention by government in economic affairs and is associated with the classical economists such as Adam Smith. (14C)

Law of comparative advantage   *See* Comparative advantage. (14C)

Leakage   The portion of income that leaks out of a spending stream and is unavailable for consumption spending; or the portion of demand deposits that leaks out of a lending stream and is unavailable for relending. Typical leakages from the spending stream are savings and taxes; typical leakages from the lending stream are reserves and cash. (2N, 6C)

Legal tender   Anything that the law requires to be accepted as payment for debts. (13C)

LIFO   "Last in, first out." An inventory valuation method in which the price of the inventory is set at the most recent price of items entering the inventory. *Compare* FIFO. (11N)

Locomotive theory   The theory, espoused in 1977 and early 1978 especially in the United States, that the world's strong economies such as Germany and Japan should adopt expansionary policies that would raise their demand for imports and pull world growth along like a locomotive pulling a train. (16C)

Lombard Street   A term for the money market in the City of London. Many financial firms in this market are located on or near this street. (2C)

M1   The narrow definition of the money supply: currency and all types of checking accounts. (2N, 3N)

M2   A broader definition of the money supply: M1 plus small-denomination time and savings deposits, overnight Eurodollar deposits, and money market mutual funds. (3N)

Macroeconomics   The branch of economics that studies relationships among economic aggregates such as output, the price level, interest rates, exchange rates, and unemployment.

Managed float   Central bank intervention in a system of flexible exchange rates to reduce currency fluctuations. (16C)

Man-hour   The product of the average number of employees in a year and the average number of hours worked. (A)

Marginal propensity to consume   The proportion of an additional dollar of income that is consumed. (6C)

Marginal propensity to save   The proportion of an additional dollar of income that is saved. (6C)

Marshall Plan   U.S. aid (over $15 billion) given to Europe between 1948 and 1952 to help its recovery from World War II. It was announced in a speech by U.S. Secretary of State George C. Marshall in 1947. It was also called the "European Recovery Program" and was administered by the OEEC.

Medium-Term Financial Strategy (MTFS)   A multiyear, integrated economic program of Prime Minister Thatcher that announced targets for monetary and fiscal policies starting in 1980. (4C)

Mercantilism   A political and economic doctrine, held predominately by merchants in the sixteenth and seventeenth centuries, that maintained that a country should try to maximize its wealth by regulating trade so that it would have a trade surplus and thus an inflow of specie. (14C)

Merchandise balance   *See* Balance of trade.

Microeconomics The branch of economics that studies the behavior of individual economic agents, such as consumers, investors, households, firms, or industries. It tries to determine how economic agents allocate resources and how markets operate. (1NA)

Minimum lending rate (MLR) *See* Bank rate. (4C, 13C)

Monetarism The school of economic thought, often associated with the views of Professor Milton Friedman of the University of Chicago, in which the primary determinant of national income and macroeconomic fluctuations is the growth of the money supply. (2N, 4C)

Monetary aggregate Any of the various measures of the money stock, including M1, M2, M3, and L (Liquidity) for the United States. (3N)

Monetary base Currency plus bank reserves. Because the monetary base is the liability of the central bank, it increases whenever the central bank adds assets such as Treasury bills from open market purchases, discount loans to financial institutions, or gold and foreign exchange from overseas. Through the money supply process, the monetary base is expanded by the private sector into the money supply. It is also known as "high-powered money" or "reserve money." (2N, 3N)

Monetary Control Act of 1980 (MCA) *See* Depository Institutions Deregulation and Monetary Control Act of 1980. (3C)

Monetary policy Control of the money supply and credit by manipulating short-term interest rates or bank reserves in order to affect the economy. (2N, 3N)

Monetary target *See* Intermediate target. (3C, 3N)

Monetizing the debt The central bank increases its holdings of government securities, thereby expanding reserves and hence increasing the money supply. The alternative action would be the sale of the government securities to the public (rather than the central bank), which would not change the money supply but would drive up interest rates. (3C, 11C)

Money market The generic description of all markets for short-term financial instruments, such as Treasury bills, federal funds, commercial paper, and banker's acceptances. *Compare* Capital market. (2N)

Money multiplier The amount by which a given quantity of reserves is expanded in the relending stage of the money supply process into the larger money supply. (2N)

Money supply process The process by which the money supply is created by the extension of bank loans and the resultant leakage of reserves and currency into the monetary base. (2N)

Moral suasion One of the "tools" of the Federal Reserve wherein the Fed uses its powers of persuasion to encourage financial institutions to behave differently. (3C)

Most favored nation (MFN) Policy in which a country would treat all signator nations equally in trade relations without requiring compensation. (14C)

National income (NI) A measure of a nation's output or income. It equals GNP less capital consumption allowances and indirect business taxes. (1NA)

National income accounts (NIA) The system of recording the output or income, and composition of that output or income, used by the United States. Also called the "national income and product accounts (NIPA)." (1NA)

National income accounts budget This budget format is the best measure of the impact of the federal budget on the economy. It differs from the unified budget in that it records most transactions on an accrual basis (with some exceptions for personal tax receipts and defense expenditures), excludes federal lending (except nonrecourse agricultural commodity loans), and includes those transactions recorded either off-budget or as a net of receipts in the unified budget. Despite the differences, it is approximately the same magnitude as the unified budget. (11C, 11N)

National income accounting identity The fundamental relationship in the national income accounts that relates total output or income to its components: GNP = C + I + G + (X − M). (1NA)

National income and product accounts (NIPA) *See* National income accounts.

National savings The total savings of the private and public sectors available for domestic and net foreign investment. National savings equals gross private savings and the government surplus. (11C, 11N)

Negotiable order of withdrawal (NOW) An interest-bearing checking account. Technically, it is a savings account in which withdrawal slips are negotiable. It was first introduced by Massachusetts savings banks in 1972. After the passage of the Monetary Control Act of 1980, interest-bearing checking accounts could be offered nationwide starting in 1981. (3C)

Net exports (NX) The narrow definition of this term is the balance of trade, but often it refers to the balance on goods and services, especially when used in conjunction with the national income accounts. (A)

Net foreign investment The amount of a home country's investments in foreign countries minus the amount of foreign investments in the home country. After allowing for unilateral international transfers, net foreign investment is equal to the current account surplus. *Compare* Net foreign savings and Net investment. (11C, 11N)

Net foreign savings The amount of foreigners' savings that is sent to a country minus the amount of domestic savings sent to foreign countries. After allowing for unilateral international transfers, net foreign savings is equal to the current account deficit. *Compare* Net foreign investment. (11C, 11N)

Net investment Gross investment minus depreciation. (11C, 11N)

Net national product (NNP) A measure of a nation's output or income. It equals GNP less capital consumption allowances. (1NA)

Net private savings The total savings of the private sector (households and businesses) after subtracting the savings allowed for replacing depreciated capital stock (capital consumption allowance). (11C, 11N)

Newly industrializing countries (NICs) The rapidly developing nations such as Brazil, Mexico, Hong Kong, Korea, Taiwan, Singapore, Spain, Portugal, Greece, and Yugoslavia. (1NB)

NIA budget or **NIPA budget** *See* National income accounts budget. (11N)

Nonborrowed reserves That portion of total reserves that is not borrowed from the Federal Reserve. Nonborrowed reserves plus borrowed reserves equal total bank reserves. (3C, 3N)

Off-budget expenditures Since 1973, the outlays of certain federal entities have been excluded from the unified budget expenditures. The major components of off-budget expenditures are the Strategic Petroleum Reserve, the Postal Service deficit or surplus, and net lending by the Federal Financing Bank. The amount peaked at $21 billion (0.7 percent of GNP) in fiscal year 1981 and is expected to decline further in the future. (11C, 11N)

Official settlements balance *See* Balance on official settlements.

Open market operations The purchase and sale of government securities by the Federal Open Market Committee (FOMC) of the Federal Reserve. An open market purchase increases the money supply and an open market sale decreases the money supply. (2N)

Opportunity cost That which must be given up in terms of the value of the alternative opportunities in order to gain something else, which may be more than cash outlays. For example, the cost of retained earnings is not zero because there are no cash outlays to using retained earnings (as there are with the interest costs that must be paid to receive borrowed funds). The opportunity cost of retained earnings would include the next best alternative for using those funds, such as investing them to earn the market rate of return on financial securities. (11N)

Organization for Economic Cooperation and Development (OECD) A Paris-based international organization of the 24 largest noncommunist industrial countries, designed to improve the economic policies of its signatories. It was established in 1961 and replaced the OEEC. (1NB)

Organization for European Economic Cooperation (OEEC) A Paris-based international organization established in 1948, after the announcement of the Marshall Plan the previous year, to propose and implement a recovery program for Europe. In 1961, it was replaced by the OECD and added the United States and Canada as members.

Organization of Petroleum Exporting Countries (OPEC) A group of 13 countries—Saudi Arabia, Iran, Iraq, Kuwait, Venezuela, Algeria, Ecuador, Gabon, Indonesia, Libya, Nigeria, Quatar, the United Arab Emirates—that are among the largest producers and exporters of crude petroleum. It was formed in September 1960 by the first five of the countries listed.

Output gap The difference between potential and real GNP. (7C, 7N)

Output per man-hour *See* Labor productivity. (A)

Overall balance Includes the balance on goods, services, transfers, errors and omissions, and all capital accounts except official reserves. Often

it is referred to as the "balance of payments," though no particular balance has officially been given that title. The OECD presentations exclude short-term foreign assets and liabilities of the private monetary sector in its definition of the overall balance (since they are included in reserves). (14C, 14N)

Overloan A condition in which the banking system as a whole is in debt to the central bank. It was a characteristic of the Japanese financial system through much of the postwar period. (5C)

Overvalued currency An exchange rate for the currency that is higher than the long-run, free market level of the exchange rate (a level often assumed to be equal to purchasing power parity). It is the opposite of "undervalued currency." (13C)

Participation rate The proportion of the working-age population that is part of the labor force. (16C)

PEMEX Petroleos Mexicanos, the huge, powerful, state-owned oil company in Mexico. (17C)

Personal savings The personal disposable income of the household sector that is not consumed. (11C, 11N)

Personal savings rate The ratio of personal savings to personal disposable income. (11N)

Phillips curve The inverse relationship between unemployment and inflation. In the 1960s and early 1970s, it was believed that policymakers had a menu of trade-offs between unemployment and inflation—if less inflation is wanted, low unemployment must be sacrificed. The current understanding is that this trade-off is, at best, a short-run relationship. In the long run, unemployment is independent of the rate of inflation.

Portfolio investments Long-term investments (both bonds and stocks) on the balance of payments statement wherein the investor does not hold substantial management control.

Compare Foreign direct investment. (12N)

Potential GNP   The level of GNP if all labor and capital resources were "fully employed." It is also known as "potential output." (7C, 7N)

Predetermined variable   A variable whose value at the current time has already been determined or must be set judgmentally. It includes both exogenous variables and lagged endogenous variables. (1ND)

Prime rate   The rate of interest charged by U.S. commercial banks for short-term loans to their best corporate borrowers. (3C)

Private savings   The disposable income of the private sector (households and businesses) that is not used for current expenditures. (11C, 11N)

Privatization   The sale of government assets (such as public housing or public firms) to private owners, or the provision of government services by private companies (such as garbage collection). Privatization includes denationalization, which is generally considered to be the transfer of at least 50 percent of the share ownership of a public firm to private owners. (12C)

Production gap   *See* Output gap.

Productivity   The efficiency with which an economy transforms inputs (resources) into useful outputs (goods and services). It is also called "total factor productivity" in more technical presentations. *Compare* Labor productivity. (7N)

Progressive tax   A tax whose tax rates increase with an increase in the tax base. (10C)

Proposition 13   A referendum to cut property taxes in California, passed June 6, 1978. (10C)

Protectionism   A movement by government to raise import barriers in order to protect home markets. (14C)

Public good   A good whose benefits can be consumed by one person without preventing others from also consuming the same benefits. Examples are national defense or public parks. (1NA)

Public sector borrowing rate (PSBR)   The amount by which the revenues of the U.K. public sector (government departments and agencies) and publicly owned corporations fall short of expenditures by the central and local governments and the nationalized industries. (4C)

Purchasing power parity (PPP)   The theory that the ratio of domestic to foreign price levels equals the equilibrium exchange rate between domestic and foreign currencies. (16C, 16N)

Quantity theory of income   The theory that money is the primary determinant of national income. It is usually expressed as $M \times V = P \times Q$, where M is money, V is velocity, and $P \times Q$ is income. (2N)

Ratio scale   A scale, often used on the vertical axis in plotting time series data, in which the logarithm of the data is plotted instead of the actual data. The usefulness of this scale is that the slope of the line indicates the rate of growth of the variable plotted. (7N)

Real   A qualifier added before some variable name, such as real GNP, real investment, real wages, real interest rates, or real exchange rates, to indicate that the variable has been adjusted for the effects of general price inflation. Thus a data series on real GNP gives the actual output of goods and services in each year assuming that prices were unchanged over all the years. Real GNP will increase only if the quantity (but not the price) of the output increases. (1NC)

Real bills doctrine   The doctrine holding that commercial banks should lend only for "productive" purposes, and not for "speculative" purposes. Productive loans were believed to be those for short-term, self-liquidating commercial transactions such as the financing of trade or inventory accumulation (i.e., "real bills"). In that case, it was believed that the money supply would adjust itself so as to be exactly adequate for business needs. (2C)

Real exchange rate The nominal exchange rate times the ratio of foreign prices over domestic prices. For example, the real exchange rate of the German Deutschmark (DM) equals the dollar price of the DM times the German price level over the U.S. price level. (16C, 16N)

Real interest rate The nominal interest rate minus the expected inflation over the term of the security. Since expected inflation is unknown, we can approximate it by using the actual inflation over that period when working with historical data. (11C, 16C)

Real wage A worker's earnings adjusted to take its purchasing power into account. It is calculated as the nominal wage divided by a general price level index.

Recession A downturn in business activity that does not depend on any one variable but is usually associated with slower real GNP growth and rising unemployment. *See also* Business cycle.

Reciprocal Trade Act of 1934 Trade legislation passed under President Franklin D. Roosevelt in which the president could negotiate tariff cuts by as much as 50 percent in bilateral treaties and the most-favored-nation clause was reintroduced. With this legislation, the executive branch, rather than the Congress, gained the leading role for setting trade policy. (14C)

Reconciliation A process established by the Congressional Budget Act of 1974 by which Congress conforms tax and spending legislation to the levels voted by Congress in an earlier budget resolution. (11C)

Reduced form An equation or set of equations that expresses the endogenous variable(s) only in terms of the predetermined variables. (1ND)

Reflation A macroeconomic policy that expands aggregate demand, such as expansionary monetary or fiscal policy. *Compare* Deflation.

Regressive tax A tax in which the tax rates decrease as the tax base increases. (10C)

Regulation Q The legal interest rate ceilings imposed by the Federal Reserve. (3C)

Repurchase agreement (RP) An agreement in which an investor purchases securities from a dealer who will buy them back at a higher price on a later date, thereby giving the investor an implicit yield. The investor is said to have a repurchase agreement or a "repo" and the dealer is said to have a "reverse repo." A repo is a way of investing funds; a reverse repo is a way of borrowing funds. (3C)

Required reserves Those assets that must be set aside as reserves to cover the required fixed percentage of deposits (liabilities). Required reserves are not available for covering the bank's need for currency in case of a run on the bank. Their primary purpose is to give the central bank control over the creation of demand deposits, and hence money. Required reserves plus excess reserves equal total bank reserves. (2N)

Reserve aggregate Any of the various measures of reserves, including the monetary base, total reserves, nonborrowed reserves, borrowed reserves, and international reserves. (3N)

Reserve currency A currency in which countries are willing to hold their foreign exchange reserves in addition to or instead of gold or SDRs. It must be stable, convertible, marketable, and used in a large share of world trade. (14C)

Reserve money *See* High-powered money. (This is a term often used by the IMF.)

Reserve requirement The proportion of demand and time deposits that must be kept as reserves. (2N)

Reserves Reserves consist of gold,

foreign exchange, SDRs, and a country's reserve position in the International Monetary Fund. Reserves are available to a government to finance payments imbalances directly and to intervene in foreign exchange markets to alter the relative value of its currency. *Do not confuse with* Total (bank) reserves. (14N)

Resources Those inputs to the production process that are needed in the production of outputs. The four classes of resources are labor, capital, land (including natural resources), and entrepreneurial skills. (1NA)

Retail price index (RPI) The British analog to the consumer price index. (4C)

Revaluation An increase in the fixed value of a currency relative to gold or some hard currency to which it is tied. "Revaluation" refers to a fixed exchange rate and "appreciation" refers to flexible exchange rate systems. "Devaluation" is the opposite of "revaluation." *Compare* Appreciation. (14C, 16C, 16N)

Rule Fixing (or pegging) a policy instrument for long periods of time without change. *Compare* Discretion. (3N)

Rule of principal supplier The operating rule in GATT negotiations from 1947 to 1960 wherein a country would request a tariff concession only if it were the principal supplier (or largest exporter) of that specific good. (14C)

Safe-harbor leasing provision A provision of the Economic Recovery Tax Act of 1981 that allowed companies to transfer tax benefits from those companies that cannot use them to those that can. Instead of buying needed equipment outright and wasting the tax benefits, a company owing no taxes agrees to lease the equipment from another company, which buys it and uses the investment tax credit and depreciation write-offs to reduce its own tax bill. (10C)

Savings The accumulation of wealth

during a given period of time. Any sector of the economy (households, businesses, governments, and foreigners) can save if its current expenditure is less than its income. (If its current expenditure is greater than its income, it is "dissaving," or borrowing.) (11C, 11N, A)

Secondary market A market for the sale and purchase of securities that have already been sold by their initial buyer. (2N)

Semilogarithmic scale *See* Ratio scale.

Smithsonian Accord (Agreement) An agreement reached in December 1971 by the Group of Ten at the Smithsonian Institution in Washington, DC, in which the major currencies would be restored to fixed parities to the dollar but with a wider margin of ± 2.25 percent of par values. The dollar was effectively devalued by about 8 percent by this agreement. It lasted until March 1973, when the major currencies of the world were forced to float freely. (16C)

Smoot-Hawley tariffs The tariff barriers erected in 1930 in which the U.S. Congress raised the average import levy to almost 60 percent, the highest level in American history. (14C)

Social contract The implicit agreement between the Labour government of Prime Minister Harold Wilson and the trade unions in 1974–1975 to hold down pay increases. (4C)

Soft currency A currency that is not freely convertible into gold or some hard currency. Often it is regulated by exchange controls, which prevents free convertibility. It is also used to indicate a currency with a depreciating exchange rate.

Special Credit Constraint Program The program authorized by President Carter and implemented by the Federal Reserve to restrain the growth of credit by asking financial institutions to comply voluntarily with regulatory limits. (3C)

Special Drawing Rights (SDRs) A

form of international currency issued by the International Monetary Fund and used only by governments in place of gold as a monetary reserve. It is sometimes called "paper gold." It was established in July 1969 by the Group of Ten, linked to gold, and set equal to $1/SDR. The Smithsonian system valued the SDR in terms of a basket of 16 currencies. Since July 1974, its value has floated.

Specie Gold, silver, or other precious metal used as money. (13C)

Specific tariff A fixed tax levied on imports regardless of the import prices. *Compare* Ad valorem and Excise tax. (14C)

Stagflation A term that describes the combination of *stag*nation and in*flation* occurring at the same time. (16C)

State-owned enterprise (SOE) A business in which the government owns a controlling share of the firm's equity. It is sometimes referred to as a "nationalized firm." (1NB)

Sterilization An action of the central bank in which it decreases some asset (such as Treasury securities through open market sales) in order to offset an increase in foreign assets (such as gold or foreign exchange). The result is that the money supply is left unchanged. If the foreign asset inflow were not sterilized, the liabilities of the central bank (high-powered money) would have to increase to match the increase in assets flowing into the central bank from abroad. Sterilization can be used to offset some decrease in other assets as well. (2N)

Sterling M3 Currency plus all Sterling demand and time deposits held by both the U.K. public and private sector. (4C)

Stochastic equation An equation that contains a random error variable to represent unexplained movements in the variable on the left-hand side of the equation. This is contrasted with a definitional equation that contains no random error variables. (1ND)

Stock A type of economic variable that relates a certain amount at a particular point in time. For example, the money supply, the capital stock, wealth, and debt are all stocks. (11N)

Structural deficit The budget deficit after the fluctuations in income have been eliminated. *See* Full-employment budget or Cyclically adjusted budget. (11C, 11N)

Structural unemployment A mismatching in location or skills of unemployed workers and job vacancies. (7C)

Supply curve A schedule of prices and quantities such that for a given price the producers would be willing and able to produce a given quantity of goods. Increased prices are associated with increased quantities supplied. (1NA)

Supply shock A reduction in the aggregate supply curve such that any given level of output will cost more to produce. The oil shocks of 1973 and 1979 and the world food shortages of 1972 and 1973 are examples. (16C)

6**Supply-side economics** A theory popularized in the early 1980s in which both short-run and long-run economic growth were largely attributed to more efficient allocation of capital and labor resources. The increased efficiency would result from removing the obstacles to economic growth, such as lowering marginal tax rates, improving the structure of the tax system, and reducing regulations. It was a return to the beliefs of the classical economists. (9C)

Swap agreement An official arrangement between central banks for short-term standby lines of credit to exchange holdings of each other's currency. The lines of credit are used for intervening in the foreign exchange market. (16C)

System of National Accounts (SNA) The national accounting framework used by the United Nations. It differs from conventions in the National Income and Product Accounts used by the United States. (11N)

Talking down the dollar The policy of the Carter administration in 1977 announced by Treasury Secretary W. Michael Blumenthal, which held that the decline of the dollar was the solution to the then-current account deficit problem, and not a problem in itself. (16C)

Tariff Taxes on merchandise imports that are usually levied on an ad valorem basis. (14C)

Tax Equity and Fiscal Responsibility Act of 1982 (TEFRA) A major tax increase in 1982 that was initiated by Senate Republicans and attempted to reduce the large expected fiscal deficits and the numerous tax expenditures associated with the Economic Recovery Tax Act of 1982. (11C)

Tax expenditures Losses of tax revenue attributable to provisions of the federal tax laws that allow a special exclusion, exemption, or deduction from gross income or that provide a special credit, preferential rate of tax, or deferral of tax liability. (8C, 10C)

Tax preference *See* Tax expenditure. (8C)

Term structure of interest rates The relationship between short-term and long-term interest rates. (3N)

Terms of trade The ratio of the index of export prices to the index of import prices. An increase in this ratio is termed "an improvement" in the terms of trade because fewer units of exports need to be exchanged in order to obtain a given unit of imports. A decrease in this ratio is termed "a worsening" of the terms of trade for the opposite reason.

Thrift institutions Savings institutions established to channel personal savings into mortgages. The two main types are savings and loan institutions and mutual savings banks. (3C)

Tight money A restrictive monetary policy associated with high interest rates and a slower growth of the money supply and credit. The economic consequences are usually slower economic growth and, eventually, lower

inflation. It is the opposite of "easy money." (3C)

Tokyo Round of trade negotiations The seventh round of GATT-sanctioned multilateral trade negotiations that started in September 1973 and ended in April 1979. It produced both tariff cuts and moved toward cutting nontariff barriers. The U.S. Trade Act of 1974 gave the United States the necessary authority to proceed with these negotiations.

Total factor productivity *See* Productivity.

Total (bank) reserves Those deposits at the Federal Reserve Bank (and vault cash earmarked as reserves) that are at least as large as the stipulated reserve requirement on bank deposits. They equal required reserves plus excess reserves, or equivalently, nonborrowed reserves plus borrowed reserves. (2N, 3N)

Transfers Goods, services, or financial assets provided without any quid pro quo are considered unilateral transfers. Because a transfer is a one-sided transaction and does not automatically give rise to a pair of debit and credit entries, offsetting entries are created and made to the transfer accounts. (14N)

Treasury bill (T-bill) Short-term instrument for borrowing by the government. T-bills do not have attached interest rates but are sold at a discount so the buyer receives an implicit yield from the price appreciation. They were first issued in the United Kingdom in 1877 and in the United States in 1929. (3C, A)

Treasury bond A long-term government security with maturity greater than five years.

Treasury note An intermediate-term government security with maturity between one and five years.

Treaty of Rome *See* European Economic Community. (14C)

Underemployment Workers who are employed at jobs requiring less skill than those jobs for which they were trained but who are unable to get a better job. (17C)

Undervalued currency A currency whose value is less than the long-run free-market level, which is usually approximated by the purchasing power parity level of the exchange rate. Also, if a country has a persistent current account surplus, it is sometimes said to have an overvalued currency, though this meaning is less precise. It is the opposite of "overvalued currency." (13C)

Unemployment rate Those workers without jobs or on temporary layoff who are actively looking for employment divided by the sum of those employed and unemployed.

Unified budget The official U. S. federal budget statement since 1968. It provides a comprehensive picture of the financial impact of federal programs that is more extensive than either of its predecessors, the administrative or consolidated cash budget. The distinguishing characteristics are: (1) both the federal funds and the trust funds, such as social security and unemployment insurance, are included (but interfund transfers are excluded), (2) net lending of the government-owned enterprises is included (but lending of wholly privately owned enterprises such as the Federal Home Loan Banks is excluded), (3) most receipts and payments are recorded on a collection basis (but interest is recorded on an accrual basis), and (4) some outlays since 1973 have been recorded off-budget (but these are scheduled to be re-included in the unified budget). *Compare* Administrative budget, Consolidated cash budget, and National income accounts budget. (11C, 11N)

Unilateral transfers *See* Transfers.

Unit labor costs Labor costs in excess of labor productivity gains. (4C)

User cost of capital The implicit rental value of capital services, which includes borrowing costs, depreciation, and taxes. (11N)

Value added The price of the product minus the cost of the purchased material inputs. (1NA)

Value-added taxes (VAT) A sales tax levied on the value added at each stage of processing. The VAT was introduced in the United Kingdom in 1973. Value-added tax was adopted in Mexico in 1980. (4C,17C)

Vault cash Currency and coins held in the bank. Required reserves can be held as either vault cash or deposits with the Federal Reserve (the vast majority is held in the latter form). The vault cash that is not held as required reserves can be used to satisfy customers' needs for cash withdrawals. (A)

Velocity *See* Income velocity. (2N)

Visible balance *See* Balance of trade.

Wealth Anything that has value because it is capable of producing future income. It includes land (and other nonrenewable resources), labor, and capital. (11N)

Window guidance The process by which a central bank directs the allocation of funds among the banking system and among its ultimate uses. This was an important tool of the Bank of Japan. (5C)

Winter of discontent The popular phrase describing the extensive public sector strikes that plagued the United Kingdom under the Labour government in the winter of 1978–1979. (4C)

World Bank *See* International Bank for Reconstruction and Development. (14C)

Index